Advanced Machine Learning with R

Tackle data analytics and machine learning challenges and build complex applications with R 3.5

Cory Lesmeister
Dr. Sunil Kumar Chinnamgari

BIRMINGHAM - MUMBAI

Advanced Machine Learning with R

First published: May 2019

Production reference: 2250719

Published by Packt Publishing Ltd.
Livery Place
35 Livery Street
Birmingham
B3 2PB, UK.

ISBN 978-1-83864-177-1

www.packtpub.com

`mapt.io`

Mapt is an online digital library that gives you full access to over 5,000 books and videos, as well as industry-leading tools to help you plan your personal development and advance your career. For more information, please visit our website.

Why subscribe?

- Spend less time learning and more time coding with practical eBooks and Videos from over 4,000 industry professionals

- Improve your learning with Skill Plans built especially for you

- Get a free eBook or video every month

- Mapt is fully searchable

- Copy and paste, print, and bookmark content

Packt.com

Did you know that Packt offers eBook versions of every book published, with PDF and ePub files available? You can upgrade to the eBook version at `www.packt.com` and as a print book customer, you are entitled to a discount on the eBook copy. Get in touch with us at `customercare@packtpub.com` for more details.

At `www.packt.com`, you can also read a collection of free technical articles, sign up for a range of free newsletters, and receive exclusive discounts and offers on Packt books and eBooks.

Contributors

About the authors

Cory Lesmeister has over fourteen years of quantitative experience and is currently a senior data scientist for the Advanced Analytics team at Cummins, Inc. in Columbus, Indiana. Cory spent 16 years at Eli Lilly and Company in sales, market research, Lean Six Sigma, marketing analytics, and new product forecasting. He also has several years of experience in the insurance and banking industries, both as a consultant and as a manager of marketing analytics. A former US Army active duty and reserve officer, Cory was stationed in Baghdad, Iraq, in 2009 serving as the strategic advisor to the 29,000-person Iraqi Oil Police, succeeding where others failed by acquiring and delivering promised equipment to help the country secure and protect its oil infrastructure. Cory has a BBA in Aviation Administration from the University of North Dakota and a commercial helicopter license.

Dr. Sunil Kumar Chinnamgari has a Ph.D. in computer science (specializing in machine learning and natural language processing). He is an AI researcher with more than 14 years of industry experience. Currently, he works in the capacity of a lead data scientist with a US financial giant. He has published several research papers in Scopus and IEEE journals and is a frequent speaker at various meet-ups. He is an avid coder and has won multiple hackathons. In his spare time, Sunil likes to teach, travel, and spend time with family.

Packt is searching for authors like you

If you're interested in becoming an author for Packt, please visit authors.packtpub.com and apply today. We have worked with thousands of developers and tech professionals, just like you, to help them share their insight with the global tech community. You can make a general application, apply for a specific hot topic that we are recruiting an author for, or submit your own idea.

Table of Contents

Preface   1

Chapter 1: Preparing and Understanding Data   9
   Overview   10
   Reading the data   11
   Handling duplicate observations   13
      Descriptive statistics   14
      Exploring categorical variables   15
   Handling missing values   17
   Zero and near-zero variance features   19
   Treating the data   21
      Correlation and linearity   23
   Summary   27

Chapter 2: Linear Regression   29
   Univariate linear regression   30
      Building a univariate model   33
      Reviewing model assumptions   36
   Multivariate linear regression   38
      Loading and preparing the data   39
      Modeling and evaluation – stepwise regression   46
      Modeling and evaluation – MARS   52
      Reverse transformation of natural log predictions   56
   Summary   59

Chapter 3: Logistic Regression   61
   Classification methods and linear regression   62
   Logistic regression   62
   Model training and evaluation   63
      Training a logistic regression algorithm   64
         Weight of evidence and information value   66
         Feature selection   68
         Cross-validation and logistic regression   71
      Multivariate adaptive regression splines   77
      Model comparison   81
   Summary   83

Chapter 4: Advanced Feature Selection in Linear Models   85
   Regularization overview   86
      Ridge regression   87
      LASSO   87

Elastic net — 88
Data creation — 88
Modeling and evaluation — 91
Ridge regression — 91
LASSO — 96
Elastic net — 99
Summary — 104

Chapter 5: K-Nearest Neighbors and Support Vector Machines — 105
K-nearest neighbors — 106
Support vector machines — 107
Manipulating data — 111
Dataset creation — 111
Data preparation — 114
Modeling and evaluation — 117
KNN modeling — 117
Support vector machine — 125
Summary — 131

Chapter 6: Tree-Based Classification — 133
An overview of the techniques — 134
Understanding a regression tree — 134
Classification trees — 135
Random forest — 136
Gradient boosting — 137
Datasets and modeling — 138
Classification tree — 138
Random forest — 144
Extreme gradient boosting – classification — 152
Feature selection with random forests — 157
Summary — 160

Chapter 7: Neural Networks and Deep Learning — 161
Introduction to neural networks — 162
Deep learning – a not-so-deep overview — 167
Deep learning resources and advanced methods — 169
Creating a simple neural network — 171
Data understanding and preparation — 171
Modeling and evaluation — 173
An example of deep learning — 176
Keras and TensorFlow background — 176
Loading the data — 177
Creating the model function — 178
Model training — 180
Summary — 182

Chapter 8: Creating Ensembles and Multiclass Methods 183
  Ensembles 184
  Data understanding 185
  Modeling and evaluation 187
    Random forest model 187
    Creating an ensemble 190
  Summary 191
Chapter 9: Cluster Analysis 193
  Hierarchical clustering 195
    Distance calculations 196
  K-means clustering 197
  Gower and PAM 197
    Gower 198
    PAM 199
  Random forest 200
  Dataset background 201
  Data understanding and preparation 201
  Modeling 204
    Hierarchical clustering 204
    K-means clustering 212
    Gower and PAM 215
    Random forest and PAM 216
  Summary 218
Chapter 10: Principal Component Analysis 219
  An overview of the principal components 220
    Rotation 223
  Data 225
    Data loading and review 226
    Training and testing datasets 229
  PCA modeling 231
    Component extraction 231
    Orthogonal rotation and interpretation 234
    Creating scores from the components 235
    Regression with MARS 236
    Test data evaluation 240
  Summary 242
Chapter 11: Association Analysis 243
  An overview of association analysis 243
    Creating transactional data 245
  Data understanding 246
  Data preparation 247
  Modeling and evaluation 249

Summary 254
Chapter 12: Time Series and Causality 255
  Univariate time series analysis 256
    Understanding Granger causality 264
  Time series data 265
    Data exploration 267
  Modeling and evaluation 272
    Univariate time series forecasting 272
    Examining the causality 282
      Linear regression 283
      Vector autoregression 284
  Summary 290
Chapter 13: Text Mining 291
  Text mining framework and methods 292
    Topic models 294
    Other quantitative analysis 295
  Data overview 297
    Data frame creation 297
  Word frequency 299
    Word frequency in all addresses 299
    Lincoln's word frequency 301
  Sentiment analysis 305
  N-grams 309
  Topic models 311
  Classifying text 316
    Data preparation 316
    LASSO model 318
  Additional quantitative analysis 320
  Summary 327
Chapter 14: Exploring the Machine Learning Landscape 329
  ML versus software engineering 329
  Types of ML methods 334
    Supervised learning 334
    Unsupervised learning 336
    Semi-supervised learning 338
    Reinforcement learning 339
    Transfer learning 341
  ML terminology – a quick review 344
    Deep learning 344
    Big data 345
    Natural language processing 345
    Computer vision 345
    Cost function 346

Model accuracy 346
Confusion matrix 346
Predictor variables 347
Response variable 347
Dimensionality reduction 347
Class imbalance problem 348
Model bias and variance 349
Underfitting and overfitting 349
Data preprocessing 350
Holdout sample 351
Hyperparameter tuning 351
Performance metrics 352
Feature engineering 352
Model interpretability 353
ML project pipeline 354
Business understanding 355
Understanding and sourcing the data 355
Preparing the data 356
Model building and evaluation 358
Model deployment 358
Learning paradigm 360
Datasets 361
Summary 361

Chapter 15: Predicting Employee Attrition Using Ensemble Models 363
Philosophy behind ensembling 364
Getting started 366
Understanding the attrition problem and the dataset 366
K-nearest neighbors model for benchmarking the performance 381
Bagging 384
Bagged classification and regression trees (treeBag) implementation 386
Support vector machine bagging (SVMBag) implementation 387
Naive Bayes (nbBag) bagging implementation 388
Randomization with random forests 389
Implementing an attrition prediction model with random forests 390
Boosting 391
The GBM implementation 392
Building attrition prediction model with XGBoost 394
Stacking 395
Building attrition prediction model with stacking 396
Summary 399

Chapter 16: Implementing a Jokes Recommendation Engine 401
Fundamental aspects of recommendation engines 402
Recommendation engine categories 404

Content-based filtering 404
Collaborative filtering 404
Hybrid filtering 405
Getting started 405
Understanding the Jokes recommendation problem and the dataset 405
Converting the DataFrame 409
Dividing the DataFrame 410
Building a recommendation system with an item-based collaborative filtering technique 411
Building a recommendation system with a user-based collaborative filtering technique 415
Building a recommendation system based on an association-rule mining technique 419
The Apriori algorithm 420
Content-based recommendation engine 427
Differentiating between ITCF and content-based recommendations 429
Building a hybrid recommendation system for Jokes recommendations 430
Summary 433
References 434

Chapter 17: Sentiment Analysis of Amazon Reviews with NLP 435
The sentiment analysis problem 437
Getting started 438
Understanding the Amazon reviews dataset 438
Building a text sentiment classifier with the BoW approach 443
Pros and cons of the BoW approach 449
Understanding word embedding 450
Building a text sentiment classifier with pretrained word2vec word embedding based on Reuters news corpus 453
Building a text sentiment classifier with GloVe word embedding 458
Building a text sentiment classifier with fastText 462
Summary 469

Chapter 18: Customer Segmentation Using Wholesale Data 471
Understanding customer segmentation 472
Understanding the wholesale customer dataset and the segmentation problem 474
Categories of clustering algorithms 478
Identifying the customer segments in wholesale customer data using k-means clustering 479
Working mechanics of the k-means algorithm 485
Identifying the customer segments in the wholesale customer data using DIANA 490

Identifying the customer segments in the wholesale customers data using AGNES 496
Summary 501

Chapter 19: Image Recognition Using Deep Neural Networks 503
Technical requirements 504
Understanding computer vision 504
Achieving computer vision with deep learning 505
Convolutional Neural Networks 506
Layers of CNNs 507
Introduction to the MXNet framework 510
Understanding the MNIST dataset 511
Implementing a deep learning network for handwritten digit recognition 515
Implementing dropout to avoid overfitting 522
Implementing the LeNet architecture with the MXNet library 527
Implementing computer vision with pretrained models 532
Summary 536

Chapter 20: Credit Card Fraud Detection Using Autoencoders 537
Machine learning in credit card fraud detection 538
Autoencoders explained 540
Types of AEs based on hidden layers 542
Types of AEs based on restrictions 543
Applications of AEs 545
The credit card fraud dataset 546
Building AEs with the H2O library in R 547
Autoencoder code implementation for credit card fraud detection 548
Summary 572

Chapter 21: Automatic Prose Generation with Recurrent Neural Networks 573
Understanding language models 574
Exploring recurrent neural networks 577
Comparison of feedforward neural networks and RNNs 581
Backpropagation through time 584
Problems and solutions to gradients in RNN 585
Exploding gradients 585
Vanishing gradients 586
Building an automated prose generator with an RNN 587
Implementing the project 593
Summary 603

Chapter 22: Winning the Casino Slot Machines with Reinforcement Learning 605

Understanding RL   606
  Comparison of RL with other ML algorithms   608
  Terminology of RL   609
  The multi-arm bandit problem   610
  Strategies for solving MABP   614
    The epsilon-greedy algorithm   615
    Boltzmann or softmax exploration   616
    Decayed epsilon greedy   616
    The upper confidence bound algorithm   616
    Thompson sampling   618
Multi-arm bandit – real-world use cases   618
Solving the MABP with UCB and Thompson sampling algorithms   619
Summary   628

Creating a Package   629

Other Books You May Enjoy   635

Index   639

Preface

R is one of the most popular languages when it comes to exploring the mathematical side of machine learning and easily performing computational statistics.

This Learning Path shows you how to leverage the R ecosystem to build efficient machine learning applications that carry out intelligent tasks within your organization. You'll tackle realistic projects such as building powerful machine learning models with ensembles to predict employee attrition. You'll explore different clustering techniques to segment customers using wholesale data and use TensorFlow and Keras-R for performing advanced computations. Each chapter will help you implement advanced machine learning algorithms using real-world examples. You'll also be introduced to reinforcement learning along with its various use cases and models. Additionally, this book provides you with a glimpse into how some of these black-box models can be diagnosed and understood.

By the end of this Learning Path, you'll be equipped with the skills you need to deploy machine learning techniques in your own projects.

Who this book is for

If you're a data analyst, data scientist, or machine learning developer who wants to master machine learning techniques using R, this is an ideal Learning Path for you. Each project will help you test your skills in implementing machine learning algorithms and techniques. A basic understanding of machine learning and working knowledge of R programming is necessary to get the most out of this Learning Path.

What this book covers

Chapter 1, *Preparing and Understanding Data*, covers the loading of data and demonstrates how to obtain an understanding of its structure and dimensions, as well as how to install the necessary packages.

Chapter 2, *Linear Regression*, provides you with a solid foundation before learning advanced methods such as Support Vector Machines and Gradient Boosting. No more solid foundation exists than the least squares linear regression.

Chapter 3, *Logistic Regression*, presents a discussion on how logistic regression and discriminant analysis is used in order to predict a categorical outcome. Multivariate adaptive regression splines have been added. This technique performs well, handles non-linearity, and is easy to explain.

Chapter 4, *Advanced Feature Selection in Linear Models*, shows regularization techniques to help improve the predictive ability and interpretability as feature selection is a critical and often extremely challenging component of machine learning. It also includes techniques not only for regression but also for a classification problem.

Chapter 5, *K-Nearest Neighbors and Support Vector Machines*, begins the exploration of the more advanced and nonlinear techniques. The real power of machine learning will be unveiled.

Chapter 6, *Tree-Based Classification*, offers some of the most powerful predictive abilities of all the machine learning techniques, especially for classification problems. Single decision trees will be discussed along with the more advanced random forests and boosted trees. It also contains very popular techniques provided by the XGBOOST package.

Chapter 7, *Neural Networks and Deep Learning*, shows some of the most exciting machine learning methods currently used. Inspired by how the brain works, neural networks and their more recent and advanced offshoot, Deep Learning, will be put to the test. It also includes code for the H2O package, including hyperparameter search.

Chapter 8, *Creating Ensembles and Multiclass Methods*, has completely new content, involving the utilization of several great packages.

Chapter 9, *Cluster Analysis*, covers unsupervised learning. Instead of trying to make a prediction, the goal will focus on uncovering the latent structure of observations. Three clustering methods will be discussed: hierarchical, k-means, and partitioning around medoids. It also includes the methodology for executing unsupervised learning with random forests.

Chapter 10, *Principal Component Analysis*, continues the examination of unsupervised learning with principal components analysis, which is used to uncover the latent structure of the features. Once this is done, the new features will be used in a supervised learning exercise.

Chapter 11, *Association Analysis*, explains association analysis and applies not only to making recommendations, product placement, and promotional pricing, but can also be used in manufacturing, web usage, and healthcare.

Chapter 12, *Time Series and Causality*, discusses univariate forecast models, bivariate regression, and Granger causality models, including an analysis of carbon emissions and climate change, along with a demonstration of different causality test methods.

Chapter 13, *Text Mining*, demonstrates a framework for quantitative text mining and the building of topic models. Along with time series, the world of data contains vast volumes of data in a textual format. With so much data as text, it is critically important to understand how to manipulate, code, and analyze the data in order to provide meaningful insights.

Chapter 14, *Exploring the Machine Learning Landscape*, will briefly review the various ML concepts that a practitioner must know. In this chapter, we will cover topics such as supervised learning, reinforcement learning, unsupervised learning, and real-world ML uses cases.

Chapter 15, *Predicting Employee Attrition Using Ensemble Models*, covers the creation of powerful ML models through ensemble learning. We will introduce the problem at hand and then attempt to explore the dataset with **exploratory data analysis** (**EDA**). Then in the preprocessing phase, we will create new features using prior domain experience. Once the dataset is fully prepared, models will be created using multiple ensemble techniques, such as bagging, boosting, stacking, and randomization. Lastly, we will deploy the finally selected model for production.

Chapter 16, *Implementing a Joke Recommendation Engine*, introduces recommendation engines. We start by understanding the concepts and types of collaborative filtering algorithms. We will then build a recommendation engine to provide personalized joke recommendations using collaborative filtering approaches such as user-based collaborative filters and item-based collaborative filters. Apart from this, we will be exploring various libraries available in R that can be used to build recommendation systems.

Chapter 17, *Sentiment Analysis of Amazon Reviews with NLP*, covers sentiment analysis, which entails finding the sentiment of a sentence and labeling it as positive, negative, or neutral and covers the various techniques that can be used to analyze text. We will understand text-mining concepts and the various ways that text is labeled based on the tone. Apart from using various popular R text-mining libraries to preprocess the reviews to be classified, we will also be leveraging a wide range of text representations, such as a bag of words, word2vec, fastText, and Glove.

Chapter 18, *Customer Segmentation Using Wholesale Data*, covers the segmentation, grouping, or clustering of customers, which can be achieved through unsupervised learning. In this chapter, we learn the various techniques of customer segmentation. We will be applying advanced clustering techniques, such as k-means, DIANA, and AGNES. We will explore the ML techniques for dealing with such ambiguity and have ML find out the number of groups possible based on the underlying characteristics of the input data. Evaluating the output of the clustering algorithms is an area that is often challenging to practitioners.

Chapter 19, *Image Recognition Using Deep Neural Networks*, covers **convolutional neural networks** (**CNNs**). We explore why CNNs work so well with computer vision problems such as object detection. We will learn about all of these concepts by applying a CNN in the building of a multi-class classification model on a popular open dataset called MNIST. We will learn about the various preprocessing techniques that can be applied to the image data in order to use the data with deep learning models.

Chapter 20, *Credit Card Fraud Detection Using Autoencoders*, covers autoencoders and how they are different from the other deep learning networks, such as **recurrent neural networks** (**RNNs**)and CNNs. We will learn about autoencoders by implementing a project that identifies credit card fraud. We will become familiar with dimensionality reduction and how it can be used to identify credit card fraud detection.

Chapter 21, *Automatic Prose Generation with Recurrent Neural Networks*, introduces some **deep neural networks** (**DNNs**). We will implement a neural network from scratch and will learn how to apply an RNN by doing a project. We will create an application based on **long short-term memory** (**LSTM**) network, a variant of RNNs that generates text automatically. To accomplish this task, we make use of the MXNet framework, which extends its support for the R language to perform deep learning.

Chapter 22, *Winning the Casino Slot Machines with Reinforcement Learning*, begins with an explanation of RL. We discuss the various concepts of RL, including strategies for solving what is called as the multi-arm bandit problem. We implement a project that uses UCB and Thompson sampling techniques in order to solve the multi-arm bandit problem.

Appendix, *Creating a Package*, includes additional data packages.

To get the most out of this book

Assuming the reader has a working knowledge of R and of basic statistics, this book will provide the skills and tools required to get the reader up and running with R and ML as quickly and painlessly as possible. There will probably always be detractors who complain that it does not offer enough math or does not do this, or that, or the other thing, but my answer to that is that these books already exist! Why duplicate what has already been done, and very well, for that matter? Again, I have sought to provide something different, something to hold the reader's attention and allow them to succeed in this competitive and rapidly changing field.

The projects covered in this book are intended to expose you to practical knowledge on the implementation of various ML techniques to real-world problems. It is expected that you have a good working knowledge of R and some basic understanding of ML. Basic knowledge of ML and R is a must prior to starting this project.

It should also be noted that the code for the projects is implemented using R version 3.5.2 (2018-12-20), nicknamed Eggshell Igloo. The project code has been successfully tested on Linux Mint 18.3 Sylvia. There is no reason to believe that the code does not work on other platforms, such as Windows; however, this is not something that has been tested by the author.

Download the example code files

You can download the example code files for this book from your account at `www.packt.com`. If you purchased this book elsewhere, you can visit `www.packt.com/support` and register to have the files emailed directly to you.

You can download the code files by following these steps:

1. Log in or register at `www.packt.com`.
2. Select the **SUPPORT** tab.
3. Click on **Code Downloads & Errata**.
4. Enter the name of the book in the **Search** box and follow the onscreen instructions.

Once the file is downloaded, please make sure that you unzip or extract the folder using the latest version of:

- WinRAR/7-Zip for Windows
- Zipeg/iZip/UnRarX for Mac
- 7-Zip/PeaZip for Linux

The code bundle for the book is also hosted on GitHub at `https://github.com/PacktPublishing/Advanced-Machine-Learning-with-R`. In case there's an update to the code, it will be updated on the existing GitHub repository.

We also have other code bundles from our rich catalog of books and videos available at `https://github.com/PacktPublishing/`. Check them out!

Conventions used

There are a number of text conventions used throughout this book.

`CodeInText`: Indicates code words in the text, database table names, folder names, filenames, file extensions, pathnames, dummy URLs, user input, and Twitter handles. Here is an example: "Mount the downloaded `WebStorm-10*.dmg` disk image file as another disk in your system."

A block of code is set as follows:

```
html, body, #map {
  height: 100%;
  margin: 0;
  padding: 0
}
```

When we wish to draw your attention to a particular part of a code block, the relevant lines or items are set in bold:

```
[default]
exten => s,1,Dial(Zap/1|30)
exten => s,2,Voicemail(u100)
exten => s,102,Voicemail(b100)
exten => i,1,Voicemail(s0)
```

Any command-line input or output is written as follows:

```
$ mkdir css
$ cd css
```

Bold: Indicates a new term, an important word, or words that you see onscreen. For example, words in menus or dialog boxes appear in the text like this. Here is an example: "Select **System info** from the **Administration** panel."

Warnings or important notes appear like this.

Tips and tricks appear like this.

Get in touch

Feedback from our readers is always welcome.

General feedback: If you have questions about any aspect of this book, mention the book title in the subject of your message and email us at customercare@packtpub.com.

Errata: Although we have taken every care to ensure the accuracy of our content, mistakes do happen. If you have found a mistake in this book, we would be grateful if you would report this to us. Please visit www.packt.com/submit-errata, selecting your book, clicking on the Errata Submission Form link, and entering the details.

Piracy: If you come across any illegal copies of our works in any form on the Internet, we would be grateful if you would provide us with the location address or website name. Please contact us at copyright@packt.com with a link to the material.

If you are interested in becoming an author: If there is a topic that you have expertise in and you are interested in either writing or contributing to a book, please visit authors.packtpub.com.

Reviews

Please leave a review. Once you have read and used this book, why not leave a review on the site that you purchased it from? Potential readers can then see and use your unbiased opinion to make purchase decisions, we at Packt can understand what you think about our products, and our authors can see your feedback on their book. Thank you!

For more information about Packt, please visit `packt.com`.

Preparing and Understanding Data

1

"We've got to use every piece of data and piece of information, and hopefully that will help us be accurate with our player evaluation. For us, that's our lifeblood."

– Billy Beane, General Manager Oakland Athletics, subject of the book Moneyball

Research consistently shows that machine learning and data science practitioners spend most of their time manipulating data and preparing it for analysis. Indeed, many find it the most tedious and least enjoyable part of their work. Numerous companies are offering solutions to the problem but, in my opinion, results at this point are varied. Therefore, in this first chapter, I shall endeavor to provide a way of tackling the problem that will ease the burden of getting your data ready for machine learning. The methodology introduced in this chapter will serve as the foundation for data preparation and for understanding many of the subsequent chapters. I propose that once you become comfortable with this tried and true process, it may very well become your favorite part of machine learning—as it is for me.

The following are the topics that we'll cover in this chapter:

- Overview
- Reading the data
- Handling duplicate observations
- Descriptive statistics
- Exploring categorical variables
- Handling missing values
- Zero and near-zero variance features
- Treating the data
- Correlation and linearity

Overview

If you haven't been exposed to large, messy datasets, then be patient, for it's only a matter of time. If you've encountered such data, has it been in a domain where you have little subject matter expertise? If not, then once again I proffer that it's only a matter of time. Some of the common problems that make up this term *messy* data include the following:

- Missing or invalid values
- Novel levels in a categorical feature that show up in algorithm production
- High cardinality in categorical features such as zip codes
- High dimensionality
- Duplicate observations

So this begs the question *what are we to do?* Well, first we need to look at what are the critical tasks that need to be performed during this phase of the process. The following tasks serve as the foundation for building a learning algorithm. They're from the paper by SPSS, *CRISP-DM 1.0*, a step-by-step data-mining guide available at `https://the-modeling-agency.com/crisp-dm.pdf`:

- Data understanding:
    1. Collect
    2. Describe
    3. Explore
    4. Verify
- Data preparation:
    1. Select
    2. Clean
    3. Construct
    4. Integrate
    5. Format

Certainly this is an excellent enumeration of the process, but what do we really need to do? I propose that, in practical terms we can all relate to, the following *must be done* once the data is joined and loaded into your machine, cloud, or whatever you use:

- Understand the data structure
- Dedupe observations
- Eliminate zero variance features and low variance features as desired
- Handle missing values

- Create dummy features (one-hot encoding)
- Examine and deal with highly correlated features and those with perfect linear relationships
- Scale as necessary
- Create other features as desired

Many feel that this is a daunting task. I don't and, in fact, I quite enjoy it. If done correctly and with a judicious application of judgment, it should reduce the amount of time spent at this first stage of a project and facilitate training your learning algorithm. None of the previous steps are challenging, but it can take quite a bit of time to write the code to perform each task.

Well, that's the benefit of this chapter. The example to follow will walk you through the tasks and the R code that accomplishes it. The code is flexible enough that you should be able to apply it to your projects. Additionally, it will help you gain an understanding of the data at a point you can intelligently discuss it with **Subject Matter Experts (SMEs)** if, in fact, they're available.

In the practical exercise that follows, we'll work with a small dataset. However, it suffers from all of the problems described earlier. Don't let the small size fool you, as we'll take what we learn here and use it for the more massive datasets to come in subsequent chapters.

As background, the data we'll use I put together painstakingly by hand. It's the Order of Battle for the opposing armies at the Battle of Gettysburg, fought during the American Civil War, July 1st-3rd, 1863, and the casualties reported by the end of the day on July 3rd. I purposely chose this data because I'm reasonably sure you know very little about it. Don't worry, I'm the SME on the battle here and will walk you through it every step of the way. The one thing that we won't cover in this chapter is dealing with large volumes of textual features, which we'll discuss later in this book. Enough said already; let's get started!

 The source used in the creation of the dataset is *The Gettysburg Campaign in Numbers and Losses: Synopses, Orders of Battle, Strengths, Casualties, and Maps, June 9-July 14, 1863*, by J. David Petruzzi and Steven A. Stanley.

Reading the data

This first task will load the data and show how to get a how level understanding of its structure and dimensions as well as install the necessary packages.

You have two ways to access the data, which resides on GitHub. You can download `gettysburg.csv` directly from the site at this link: `https://github.com/PacktPublishing/Advanced-Machine-Learning-with-R/blob/master/Data/gettysburg.csv`, or you can use the RCurl package. An example of how to use the package is available here: `https://github.com/opetchey/RREEBES/wiki/Reading-data-and-code-from-an-online-github-repository`.

Let's assume you have the file in your working directory, so let's begin by installing the necessary packages:

```
install.packages("caret")
install.packages("janitor")
install.packages("readr")
install.packages("sjmisc")
install.packages("skimr")
install.packages("tidyverse")
install.packages("vtreat")
```

Let me make a quick note about how I've learned (the hard way) about how to correctly write code. With the packages installed, we could now specifically call the libraries into the R environment. However, it's a best practice and necessary when putting code into production that a function that isn't in base R be specified. First, this helps you and unfortunate others to read your code with an understanding of which library is mapped to a specific function. It also eliminates potential errors because different packages call different functions the same thing. The example that comes to my mind is the `tsoutliers()` function. The function is available in the `forecast` package and was in the `tsoutliers` package during earlier versions. Now I know this extra typing might seem unwieldy and unnecessary, but once you discipline yourself to do it, you'll find that it's well worth the effort.

There's one library we'll call and that's `magrittr`, which allows the use of a pipe-operator, `%>%`, to chain code together:

```
library(magrittr)
```

We're now ready to load the `.csv` file. In doing so, let's utilize the `read_csv()` function from `readr` as it's faster than base R and creates a tibble dataframe. In most cases, using tibbles in a `tidyverse` style is easier to write and understand. If you want to learn all the benefits of `tidyverse`, check out their website: `tidyverse.org`.

The only thing we need to specify in the function is our filename:

```
gettysburg <- readr::read_csv("~/gettysburg.csv")
```

Here's a look at the column (feature) names:

```
colnames(gettysburg)
 [1]  "type"           "state"           "regiment_or_battery" "brigade"
 [5]  "division"       "corps"           "army"
"july1_Commander"
 [9]  "Cdr_casualty"   "men"             "killed"              "wounded"
[13]  "captured"       "missing"         "total_casualties"    "3inch_rifles"
[17]  "4.5inch_rifles" "10lb_parrots"    "12lb_howitzers"
"12lb_napoleons"
[21]  "6lb_howitzers"  "24lb_howitzers"  "20lb_parrots"
"12lb_whitworths"
[25]  "14lb_rifles"    "total_guns"
```

We have 26 features in this data, and some of you're asking yourself things like, *what the heck is a 20 pound parrot?* If you put it in a search engine, you'll probably end up with the bird and not the 20 pound Parrot rifled artillery gun. You can see the dimensions of the data in RStudio in your Global Environment view, or you can dig on your own to see there're 590 observations:

```
dim(gettysburg)
[1] 590 26
```

In RStudio, you can click on the tibble name in the Global Environment or run the View(tibblename) code and it'll open a spreadsheet of all of the data.

So we have 590 observations of 26 features, but this data suffers from the issues that permeate large and complex data. Next, we'll explore if there're any duplicate observations and how to deal with them efficiently.

Handling duplicate observations

The easiest way to get started is to use the base R duplicated() function to create a vector of logical values that match the data observations. These values will consist of either TRUE or FALSE where TRUE indicates a duplicate. Then, we'll create a table of those values and their counts and identify which of the rows are dupes:

```
dupes <- duplicated(gettysburg)

table(dupes)
dupes
FALSE TRUE
```

```
587     3
```

```
which(dupes == "TRUE")
[1] 588 589
```

 If you want to see the actual rows and even put them into a tibble dataframe, the janitor package has the `get_dupes()` function. The code for that would be simply: `df_dupes <- janitor::get_dupes(gettysburg)`.

To rid ourselves of these duplicate rows, we put the `distinct()` function for the `dplyr` package to good use, specifying `.keep_all = TRUE` to make sure we return all of the features into the new tibble. Note that `.keep_all` defaults to `FALSE`:

```
gettysburg <- dplyr::distinct(gettysburg, .keep_all = TRUE)
```

Notice that, in the Global Environment, the tibble is now a dimension of 587 observations of 26 variables/features.

With the duplicate observations out of the way, it's time to start drilling down into the data and understand its structure a little better by exploring the descriptive statistics of the quantitative features.

Descriptive statistics

Traditionally, we could use the base R `summary()` function to identify some basic statistics. Now, and recently I might add, I like to use the package `sjmisc` and its `descr()` function. It produces a more readable output, and you can assign that output to a dataframe. What works well is to create that dataframe, save it as a `.csv`, and explore it at your leisure. It automatically selects numeric features only. It also fits well with `tidyverse` so that you can incorporate `dplyr` functions such as `group_by()` and `filter()`. Here's an example in our case where we examine the descriptive stats for the infantry of the Confederate Army. The output will consist of the following:

- `var`: feature name
- `type`: integer
- `n`: number of observations
- `NA.prc`: percent of missing values
- `mean`
- `sd`: standard deviation
- `se`: standard error

- `md`: median

- `trimmed`: trimmed mean

- `range`

- `skew`

```
gettysburg %>%
  dplyr::filter(army == "Confederate" & type == "Infantry") %>%
  sjmisc::descr() -> descr_stats

readr::write_csv(descr_stats, 'descr_stats.csv')
```

The following is abbreviated output from the preceding code saved to a spreadsheet:

var	n	NA.prc	mean	sd	se	md	trimmed	range	skew
men	171	-	335.26	104.01	7.95	316.00	325.76	708 (135-843)	1.24
killed	171	-	26.27	22.79	1.74	19.00	23.07	172 (0-172)	2.35
wounded	171	-	69.53	52.86	4.04	61.00	62.80	440 (3-443)	2.62
captured	170	0.58	-	-	-	-	-	0 (0-0)	NaN
missing	160	6.43	34.16	30.25	2.39	26.00	29.77	158 (0-158)	1.46
total_casualties	170	0.58	127.34	88.30	6.77	106.50	117.82	680 (7-687)	2.05

In this one table, we can discern some rather interesting tidbits. In particular is the percent of missing values per feature. If you modify the precious code to examine the Union Army, you'll find that there're no missing values. The reason the usurpers from the South had missing values is based on a couple of factors; either shoddy staff work in compiling the numbers on July 3rd or the records were lost over the years. Note that, for the number of men captured, if you remove the missing value, all other values are zero, so we could just replace the missing value with it. The Rebels did not report troops as captured, but rather as missing, in contrast with the Union.

Once you feel comfortable with the descriptive statistics, move on to exploring the categorical features in the next section.

Exploring categorical variables

When it comes to an understanding of your categorical variables, there're many different ways to go about it. We can easily use the base R `table()` function on a feature. If you just want to see how many distinct levels are in a feature, then `dplyr` works well. In this example, we examine `type`, which has three unique levels:

```
dplyr::count(gettysburg, dplyr::n_distinct(type))
```

The output of the preceding code is as follows:

```
# A tibble: 1 x 2
   `dplyr::n_distinct(type)`               n
                                      <int> <int>
                                          3     587
```

Let's now look at a way to explore all of the categorical features utilizing `tidyverse` principles. Doing it this way always allows you to save the tibble and examine the results in depth as needed. Here is a way of putting all categorical features into a separate tibble:

```
gettysburg_cat <-
   gettysburg[, sapply(gettysburg, class) == 'character']
```

Using `dplyr`, you can now summarize all of the features and the number of distinct levels in each:

```
gettysburg_cat %>%
   dplyr::summarise_all(dplyr::funs(dplyr::n_distinct(.)))
```

The output of the preceding code is as follows:

```
# A tibble: 1 x 9
   type   state regiment_or_battery brigade division corps   army
july1_Commander   Cdr_casualty
  <int> <int>                                 <int>     <int>        <int>
  <int> <int>                       <int>               <int>
          3      30                                      275          124
38        14        2                            586
6
```

Notice that there're `586` distinct values to `july1_Commander`. This means that two of the unit Commanders have the same rank and last name. We can also surmise that this feature will be of no value to any further analysis, but we'll deal with that issue in a couple of sections ahead.

Suppose we're interested in the number of observations for each of the levels for the `Cdr_casualty` feature. Yes, we could use `table()`, but how about producing the output as a tibble as discussed before? Give this code a try:

```
gettysburg_cat %>%
   dplyr::group_by(Cdr_casualty) %>%
   dplyr::summarize(num_rows = n())
```

The output of the preceding code is as follows:

```
# A tibble: 6 x 2
  Cdr_casualty              num_rows
     <chr>                     <int>
1 captured                        6
2 killed                         29
3 mortally wounded               24
4 no                            405
5 wounded                       104
6 wounded-captured               19
```

Speaking of tables, let's look at a tibble-friendly way of producing one using two features. This code takes the idea of comparing commander casualties by army:

```
gettysburg_cat %>%
  janitor::tabyl(army, Cdr_casualty)
```

The output of the preceding code is as follows:

army	captured	killed	mortally wounded	no	wounded	wounded-captured
Confederate	2	15	13	165	44	17
Union	4	14	11	240	60	2

Explore the data on your own and, once you're comfortable with the categorical variables, let's tackle the issue of missing values.

Handling missing values

Dealing with missing values can be a little tricky as there's a number of ways to approach the task. We've already seen in the section on descriptive statistics that there're missing values. First of all, let's get a full accounting of the missing quantity by feature, then we shall discuss how to deal with them. What I'm going to demonstrate in the following is how to put the count by feature into a dataframe that we can explore within RStudio:

```
na_count <-
  sapply(gettysburg, function(y)
    sum(length(which(is.na(
      y
    )))))

na_df <- data.frame(na_count)

View(na_df)
```

The following is a screenshot produced by the preceding code, after sorting the dataframe by descending count:

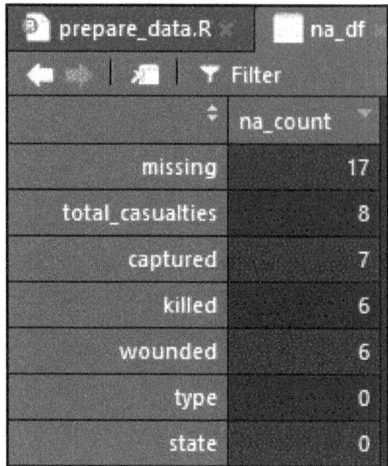

You can clearly see the count of missing by feature with the most missing is ironically named missing with a total of 17 observations.

So what should we do here or, more appropriately, what can we do here? There're several choices:

- **Do nothing**: However, some R functions will omit NAs and some functions will fail and produce an error.
- **Omit all observations with NAs**: In massive datasets, they may make sense, but we run the risk of losing information.
- **Impute values**: They could be something as simple as substituting the median value for the missing one or creating an algorithm to impute the values.
- **Dummy coding**: Turn the missing into a value such as 0 or -999, and code a dummy feature where if the feature for a specific observation is missing, the dummy is coded 1, otherwise, it's coded 0.

I could devote an entire chapter, indeed a whole book on the subject, delving into *missing at random* and others, but I was trained—and, in fact, shall insist—on the latter method. It's never failed me and the others can be a bit problematic. The benefit of dummy coding—or indicator coding, if you prefer—is that you don't lose information. In fact, missing-ness might be an essential feature in and of itself.

 For a full discussion on the handling of missing values, you can reference the following articles: `http://www.stat.columbia.edu/~gelman/arm/missing.pdf` and `https://pdfs.semanticscholar.org/4172/f558219b94f850c6567f93fa60dee7e65139.pdf`.

So, here's an example of how I manually code a dummy feature and turn the NAs into zeroes:

```
gettysburg$missing_isNA <-
   ifelse(is.na(gettysburg$missing), 1, 0)

gettysburg$missing[is.na(gettysburg$missing)] <- 0
```

The first iteration of code creates a dummy feature for the missing feature and the second changes any NAs in missing to zero. In the upcoming section, where the dataset is fully processed (treated), the other missing values will be imputed.

Zero and near-zero variance features

Before moving on to dataset treatment, it's an easy task to eliminate features that have either one unique value (zero variance) or a high ratio of the most common value to the next most common value such that there're few unique values (near-zero variance). To do this, we'll lean on the `caret` package and the `nearZeroVar()` function. We get started by creating a dataframe and using the function's defaults except for `saveMetrics = TRUE`. We need to make that specification to return the dataframe:

```
feature_variance <- caret::nearZeroVar(gettysburg, saveMetrics = TRUE)
```

 To understand the default settings of the `nearZeroVar()` function and determine how to customize it to your needs, just use the R help function by typing `?nearZeroVar` in the Console.

The output is quite interesting, so let's peek at the first six rows of what we produced:

```
head(feature_variance)
```

The output of the preceding code is as follows:

	freqRatio	percentUnique	zeroVar	nzv
type	3.186047	0.5110733	FALSE	FALSE
state	1.094118	5.1107325	FALSE	FALSE
regiment_or_battery	1.105263	46.8483816	FALSE	FALSE
brigade	1.111111	21.1243612	FALSE	FALSE
division	1.423077	6.4735945	FALSE	FALSE
corps	1.080000	2.3850085	FALSE	FALSE

The two key columns are `zeroVar` and `nzv`. They act as an indicator of whether or not that feature is zero variance or near-zero variance; `TRUE` indicates yes and `FALSE` not so surprisingly indicates no. The other columns must be defined:

- `freqRatio`: This is the ratio of the percentage frequency for the most common value over the second most common value.
- `percentUnique`: This is the number of unique values divided by the total number of samples multiplied by 100.

Let me explain that with the data we're using. For the `type` feature, the most common value is `Infantry`, which is roughly three times more common than `Artillery`. For `percentUnique`, the lower the percentage, the lower the number of unique values. You can explore this dataframe and adjust the function to determine your relevant cut points. For this example, we'll see whether we have any zero variance features by running this code:

```
which(feature_variance$zeroVar == 'TRUE')
```

The output of the preceding code is as follows:

```
[1] 17
```

Alas, we see that row `17` (feature `17`) has zero variance. Let's see what that could be:

```
row.names(feature_variance[17, ])
```

The output of the preceding code is as follows:

```
[1] "4.5inch_rifles"
```

This is quite strange to me. What it means is that I failed to record the number of the artillery piece in the one Confederate unit that brought them to the battle. An egregious error on my part discovered using an elegant function from the `caret` package. Oh well, let's create a new tibble with this filtered out for demonstration purposes:

```
gettysburg_fltrd <- gettysburg[, feature_variance$zeroVar == 'FALSE']
```

This code eliminates the zero variance feature. If we wanted also to eliminate near-zero variance as well, just run the code and substitute `feature_variance$zerVar` with `feature_variance$nzv`.

We're now ready to perform the real magic of this process and `treat` our data.

Treating the data

What do I mean when I say let's treat the data? I learned the term from the authors of the `vtreat` package, Nina Zumel, and John Mount. You can read their excellent paper on the subject at this link: `https://arxiv.org/pdf/1611.09477.pdf`.

The definition they provide is: *processor or conditioner that prepares real-world data for predictive modeling in a statistically sound manner*. In treating your data, you'll rid yourself of many of the data preparation headaches discussed earlier. The example with our current dataset will provide an excellent introduction into the benefits of this method and how you can tailor it to your needs. I kind of like to think that treating your data is a smarter version of one-hot encoding.

The package offers three different functions to treat data, but I only use one and that is `designTreatmentsZ()`, which treats the features without regard to an outcome or response. The functions `designTreatmentsC()` and `designTreatmentsN()` functions build dataframes based on categorical and numeric outcomes respectively. Those functions provide a method to prune features in a univariate fashion. I'll provide other ways of conducting feature selection, so that's why I use that specific function. I encourage you to experiment on your own.

The function we use in the following will produce an object that you can apply to training, validation, testing, and even production data. In later chapters, we'll focus on training and testing, but here let's treat the entire data without considerations of any splits for simplicity. There're a number of arguments in the function you can change, but the defaults are usually sufficient. We'll specify the input data, the feature names to include, and `minFraction`, which is defined by the package as the optional minimum frequency a categorical level must have to be converted into an indicator column. I've chosen 5% and the minimum frequency. In real-world data, I've seen this number altered many times to find the right level of occurrence:

```
my_treatment <- vtreat::designTreatmentsZ(
  dframe = gettysburg_fltrd,
  varlist = colnames(gettysburg_fltrd),
  minFraction = 0.05
)
```

We now have an object with a stored treatment plan. Now we just use the `prepare()` function to apply that treatment to a dataframe or tibble, and it'll give us a treated dataframe:

```
gettysburg_treated <- vtreat::prepare(my_treatment, gettysburg_fltrd)

dim(gettysburg_treated)
```

The output of the preceding code is as follows:

```
[1]    587      54
```

We now have 54 features. Let's take a look at their names:

```
colnames(gettysburg_treated)
```

The abbreviated output of the preceding code is as follows:

```
[1]      "type_catP"        "state_catP"     "regiment_or_battery_catP"
[4]   "brigade_catP"     "division_catP"                "corps_catP"
```

As you explore the names, you'll notice that we have features ending in `catP`, `clean`, and `isBAD` and others with `_lev_x_` in them. Let's cover each in detail. As for `catP` features, the function creates a feature that's the frequency for the categorical level in that observation. What does that mean? Let's see a table for `type_catP`:

```
table(gettysburg_treated$type_catP)
```

The output of the preceding code is as follows:

```
0.080068143100    0.21976149914    0.70017035775
            47              129              411
```

This tells us that `47` rows are of category level *x* (in this case, Cavalry), and this is 8% of the total observations. As such, 22% are Artillery and 70% Infantry. This can be helpful in further exploring your data and to help adjust the minimum frequency in your category levels. I've heard it discussed that these values could help in the creation of a distance or similarity matrix.

The next is `clean`. These are our numeric features that have had missing values imputed, which is the feature mean, and outliers winsorized or collared if you specified the argument in the `prepare()` function. We didn't, so only missing values were imputed.

 Here's an interesting blog post of the merits of winsorizing from SAS: `https://blogs.sas.com/content/iml/2017/02/08/winsorization-good-bad-and-ugly.html`.

Speaking of missing values, this brings us to `isBAD`. This feature is the 1 for missing and 0 if not missing we talked about where I manually coded it.

Finally, `lev_x` is the dummy feature coding for a specific categorical level. If you go through the levels that were hot-encoded for `states`, you'll find features for Georgia, New York, North Carolina, Pennsylvania, US (this is US Regular Army units), and Virginia.

My preference is to remove the `catP` features and remove the `clean` from the feature name, and change `isBAD` to `isNA`. This a simple task with these lines of code:

```
gettysburg_treated <-
  gettysburg_treated %>%
  dplyr::select(-dplyr::contains('_catP'))

colnames(gettysburg_treated) <-
  sub('_clean', "", colnames(gettysburg_treated))

colnames(gettysburg_treated) <-
  sub('_isBAD', "_isNA", colnames(gettysburg_treated))
```

Are we ready to start building learning algorithms? Well, not quite yet. In the next section, we'll deal with highly correlated and linearly related features.

Correlation and linearity

For this task, we return to our old friend the `caret` package. We'll start by creating a correlation matrix, using the Spearman Rank method, then apply the `findCorrelation()` function for all correlations above `0.9`:

```
df_corr <- cor(gettysburg_treated, method = "spearman")

high_corr <- caret::findCorrelation(df_corr, cutoff = 0.9)
```

 Why Spearman versus Pearson correlation? Spearman is free from any distribution assumptions and is robust enough for any task at hand: `http://www.statisticssolutions.com/correlation-pearson-kendall-spearman/`.

The `high_corr` object is a list of integers that correspond to feature column numbers. Let's dig deeper into this:

```
high_corr
```

The output of the preceding code is as follows:

```
[1]   9   4   22   43   3   5
```

The column indices refer to the following feature names:

```
colnames(gettysburg_treated)[c(9, 4, 22, 43, 3, 5)]
```

The output of the preceding code is as follows:

```
[1]                        "total_casualties"        "wounded"
"type_lev_x_Artillery"
 [4] "army_lev_x_Confederate" "killed_isNA"             "wounded_isNA"
```

We saw the features that're highly correlated to some other feature. For instance, `army_lev_x_Confederate` is perfectly and negatively correlation with `army_lev_x_Union`. After all, you can only two armies here, and Colonel Fremantle of the British Coldstream Guards was merely an observer. To delete these features, just filter your dataframe by the list we created:

```
gettysburg_noHighCorr <- gettysburg_treated[, -high_corr]
```

There you go, they're now gone. But wait! That seems a little too clinical, and maybe we should apply our judgment or the judgment of an SME to the problem? As before, let's create a tibble for further exploration:

```
df_corr <- data.frame(df_corr)

df_corr$feature1 <- row.names(df_corr)

gettysburg_corr <-
  tidyr::gather(data = df_corr,
                key = "feature2",
                value = "correlation",
                -feature1)

gettysburg_corr <-
  gettysburg_corr %>%
  dplyr::filter(feature1 != feature2)
```

What just happened? First of all, the correlation matrix was turned into a dataframe. Then, the row names became the values for the first feature. Using `tidyr`, the code created the second feature and placed the appropriate value with an observation, and we cleaned it up to get unique pairs. This screenshot shows the results. You can see that the Confederate and Union armies have a perfect negative correlation:

	feature1	feature2	correlation
1933	army_lev_x_Union	army_lev_x_Confederate	-1.0000000
1978	army_lev_x_Confederate	army_lev_x_Union	-1.0000000
968	type_lev_x_Infantry	type_lev_x_Artillery	-0.8110109
1057	type_lev_x_Artillery	type_lev_x_Infantry	-0.8110109
878	type_lev_x_Infantry	total_guns	-0.8006141
1055	total_guns	type_lev_x_Infantry	-0.8006141
2025	Cdr_casualty_lev_x_wounded	Cdr_casualty_lev_x_no	-0.6922053
2070	Cdr_casualty_lev_x_no	Cdr_casualty_lev_x_wounded	-0.6922053

You can see that it would be safe to dedupe on correlation as we did earlier. I like to save this to a spreadsheet and work with SMEs to understand what features we can drop or combine and so on.

After handling the correlations, I recommend exploring and removing as needed linear combinations. Dealing with these combinations is a similar methodology to high correlations:

```
linear_combos <- caret::findLinearCombos(gettysburg_noHighCorr)

linear_combos
```

The output of the preceding code is as follows:

```
$`linearCombos`
$`linearCombos`[[1]]
[1] 16 7 8 9 10 11 12 13 14 15

$remove
[1] 16
```

The output tells us that feature column `16` is linearly related to those others, and we can solve the problem by removing it. What are these feature names? Let's have a look:

```
colnames(gettysburg_noHighCorr)[c(16, 7, 8, 9, 10, 11, 12, 13, 14, 15)]
```

The output of the preceding code is as follows:

```
[1]              "total_guns"        "X3inch_rifles" "X10lb_parrots"
"X12lb_howitzers" "X12lb_napoleons"
 [6] "X6lb_howitzers" "X24lb_howitzers" "X20lb_parrots" "X12lb_whitworths"
"X14lb_rifles"
```

Removing the feature on the number of `"total_guns"` will solve the problem. This makes total sense since it's the number of guns in an artillery battery. Most batteries, especially in the Union, had only one type of gun. Even with multiple linear combinations, it's an easy task with this bit of code to get rid of the necessary features:

```
linear_remove <- colnames(gettysburg_noHighCorr[16])

df <- gettysburg_noHighCorr[, !(colnames(gettysburg_noHighCorr) %in%
linear_remove)]

dim(df)
```

The output of the preceding code is as follows:

```
[1] 587    39
```

There you have it, a nice clean dataframe of 587 observations and 39 features. Now depending on the modeling, you may have to scale this data or perform other transformations, but this data, in this format, makes all of that easier. Regardless of your prior knowledge or interest of one of the most important battles in history, and the bloodiest on American soil, you've developed a workable understanding of the Order of Battle, and the casualties at the regimental or battery level. Start treating your data, not next week or next month, but right now!

 If you desire, you can learn more about the battle here: `https://www.battlefields.org/learn/civil-war/battles/gettysburg`.

Summary

This chapter looked at the common problems in large, messy datasets common in machine learning projects. These include, but are not limited to the following:

- Missing or invalid values
- Novel levels in a categorical feature that show up in algorithm production
- High cardinality in categorical features such as zip code
- High dimensionality
- Duplicate observations

This chapter provided a disciplined approach to dealing with these problems by showing how to explore the data, treat it, and create a dataframe that you can use for developing your learning algorithm. It's also flexible enough that you can modify the code to suit your circumstances. This methodology should make what many feels is the most arduous, time-consuming, and least enjoyable part of the job an easy task.

With this task behind us, we can now get started on our first modeling task using linear regression in the following chapter.

Linear Regression

2

"An approximate answer to the right problem is worth a good deal more than an exact answer to an approximate problem."

– John Tukey

It's essential that we get started with a simple yet extremely effective technique that's been used for a long time: **linear regression**. Albert Einstein is believed to have remarked at one time or another that things should be made as simple as possible, but no simpler. This is sage advice and a good rule of thumb in the development of algorithms for machine learning. Considering the other techniques that we'll discuss later, there's no simpler model than tried and tested linear regression, which uses the **least squares approach** to predict a quantitative outcome. We can consider it to be the foundation of all the methods that we'll discuss later, many of which are mere extensions. If you can master the linear regression method, well then quite frankly I believe you can master the rest of this book. Therefore, let's consider this as a good starting point for our journey towards becoming a machine learning guru.

This chapter covers introductory material and an expert in this subject can skip ahead to the next topic. Otherwise, ensure that you thoroughly understand this topic before venturing to other, more complex learning methods. I believe you'll discover that many of your projects can be addressed by just applying what's discussed in the following sections. Linear regression is probably the most straightforward model to explain to your customers, most of whom will have at least a cursory understanding of **R-squared**. Many of them will have been exposed to it at great depth and hence will be comfortable with variable contribution, collinearity, and the like.

The following are the topics that we'll be covering in this chapter:

- Univariate linear regression
- Multivariate linear regression

Univariate linear regression

We begin by looking at a simple way to predict a quantitative response, Y, with one predictor variable, x, assuming that Y has a linear relationship with x. The model for this can be written as follows:

$$Y = B_o + B_{1X} + e$$

We can state it as the expected value of Y is a function of the parameters B_o (the intercept) plus B_1 (the slope) times x, plus an error term e. The least squares approach chooses the model parameters that minimize the **Residual Sum of Squares (RSS)** of the predicted y values versus the actual Y values. For a simple example, let's say we have the actual values of $Y1$ and $Y2$ equal to 10 and 20 respectively, along with the predictions of $y1$ and $y2$ as *12* and *18*. To calculate RSS, we add the squared differences:

$$RSS = (Y1 - y1)^2 + (Y2 - y2)^2$$

This, with simple substitution, yields the following:

$$(10 - 12)^2 + (20 - 18)^2 = 8$$

Before we begin with an application, I want to point out that if you read the headlines of various research breakthroughs, you should do so with a jaded eye and a skeptical mind as the conclusion put forth by the media may not be valid. As we shall see, R—and any other software, for that matter—will give us a solution regardless of the input. However, just because the math makes sense and a high correlation or R-squared statistic is reported doesn't mean that the conclusion is valid.

To drive this point home, let's have a look at the famous `Anscombe` dataset, which is available in R. The statistician Francis Anscombe produced this set to highlight the importance of data visualization and outliers when analyzing data. It consists of four pairs of X and Y variables that have the same statistical properties but when plotted show something very different. I've used the data to train colleagues and to educate business partners on the hazards of fixating on statistics without exploring the data and checking assumptions. I think this is an excellent place to start should you have a similar need. It's a brief digression before moving on to serious modeling:

```
> #call up and explore the data

> data(anscombe)

> attach(anscombe)
```

```
> anscombe
   x1 x2 x3 x4    y1   y2    y3    y4
1  10 10 10  8  8.04 9.14  7.46  6.58
2   8  8  8  8  6.95 8.14  6.77  5.76
3  13 13 13  8  7.58 8.74 12.74  7.71
4   9  9  9  8  8.81 8.77  7.11  8.84
5  11 11 11  8  8.33 9.26  7.81  8.47
6  14 14 14  8  9.96 8.10  8.84  7.04
7   6  6  6  8  7.24 6.13  6.08  5.25
8   4  4  4 19  4.26 3.10  5.39 12.50
9  12 12 12  8 10.84 9.13  8.15  5.56
10  7  7  7  8  4.82 7.26  6.42  7.91
11  5  5  5  8  5.68 4.74  5.73  6.89
```

As we shall see, each of the pairs has the same correlation coefficient: 0.816. The first two are as follows:

```
> cor(x1, y1) #correlation of x1 and y1
[1] 0.8164205

> cor(x2, y2) #correlation of x2 and y2

[1] 0.8164205
```

The real insight here, as Anscombe intended, is when we plot all four pairs together, as follows:

```
> par(mfrow = c(2,2)) #create a 2x2 grid for plotting

> plot(x1, y1, main = "Plot 1")

> plot(x2, y2, main = "Plot 2")

> plot(x3, y3, main = "Plot 3")

> plot(x4, y4, main = "Plot 4")
```

Downloading the example code

You can download the example code files for all Packt books you've purchased from your account at http://www.packtpub.com. If you bought this book elsewhere, you can visit http://www.packtpub.com/support and register to have the files emailed directly to you.

The output of the preceding code is as follows:

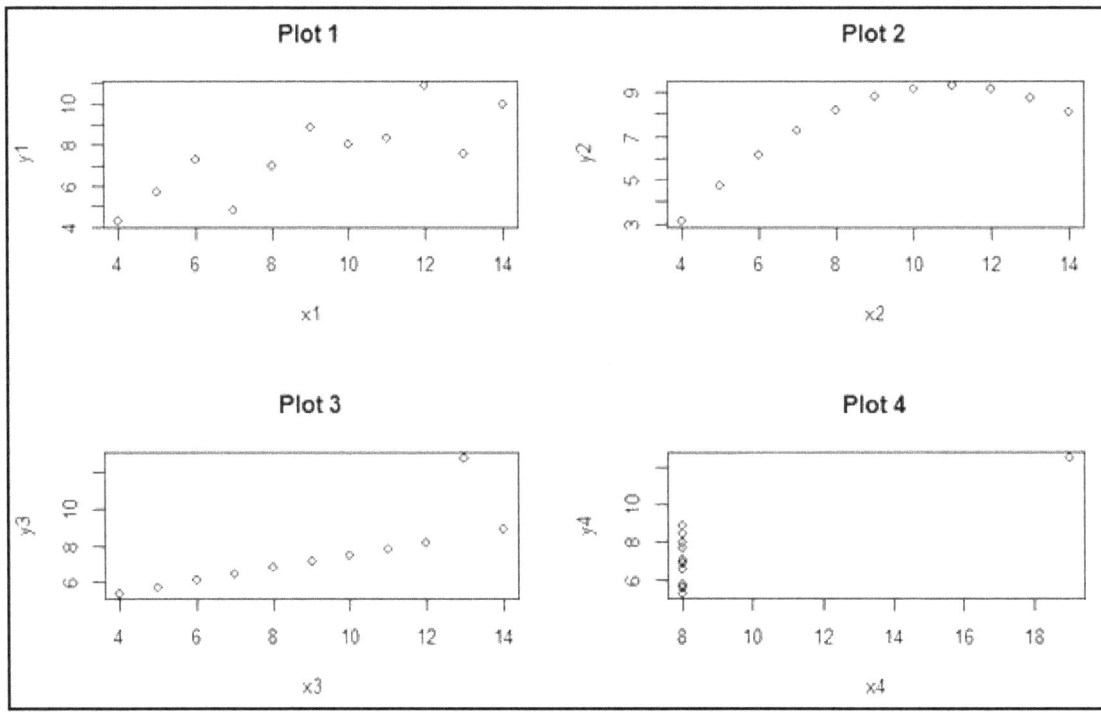

We can see the following:

- **Plot 1** appears to have a true linear relationship
- **Plot 2** is curvilinear, **Plot 3** has a dangerous outlier
- **Plot 4** is driven by one outlier

There you have it: a cautionary tale about the dangers of solely relying on correlation.

Building a univariate model

Our first case focuses on the goal of predicting the water yield (in inches) of the Snake River Watershed in Wyoming, USA, as a function of the water content of the year's snowfall. This forecast will be useful in managing the water flow and reservoir levels, as the Snake River provides much-needed irrigation water for the farms and ranches of several western states. The snake dataset is available in the alr3 package (note that alr stands for applied linear regression):

```
> install.packages("alr3")
> library(alr3)
> data(snake)
> dim(snake)
[1] 17  2
> head(snake)
     X    Y
1 23.1 10.5
2 32.8 16.7
3 31.8 18.2
4 32.0 17.0
5 30.4 16.3
6 24.0 10.5
```

Now that we have 17 observations, data exploration can begin. But first, let's change X and Y to meaningful variable names, as follows:

```
> names(snake) <- c("content", "yield")
> attach(snake) # attach data with new names
> head(snake)

  content yield
1    23.1  10.5
2    32.8  16.7
3    31.8  18.2
4    32.0  17.0
5    30.4  16.3
6    24.0  10.5

> plot(content,
       yield, main = "Scatterplot of Snow vs. Yield",
       xlab = "water content of snow",
       ylab = "water yield")
```

The output of the preceding code is as follows:

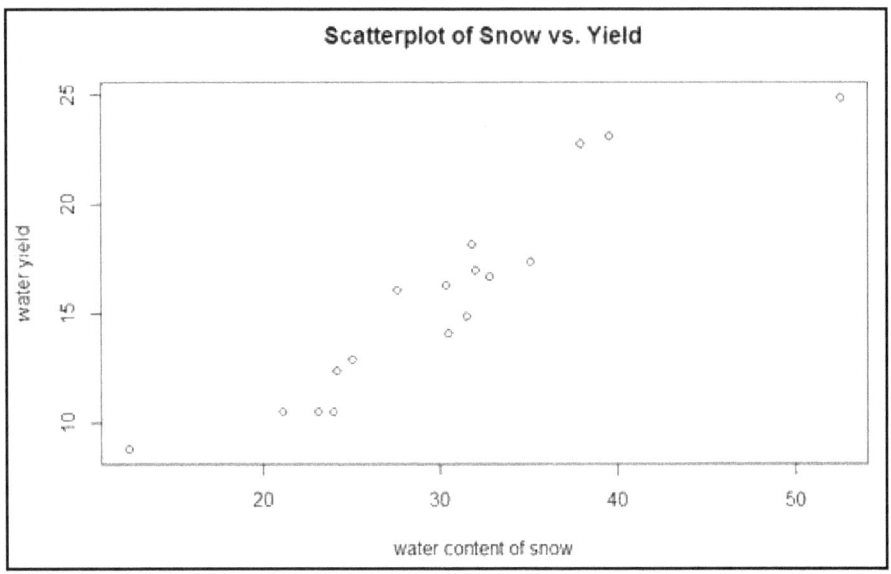

This is an intriguing plot as the data is linear and has a slight curvilinear shape driven by two potential outliers at both ends of the extreme.

To perform a linear regression in R, we use the `lm()` function to create a model in the standard form of *fit = lm(Y ~ X)*. You can then test your assumptions using various functions on your fitted model by using the following code:

```
> yield_fit <- lm(yield ~ content)

> summary(yield_fit)

Call:
lm(formula = yield ~ content)

Residuals:
        Min      1Q   Median      3Q      Max
-2.1793 -1.5149 -0.3624   1.6276   3.1973
```

```
Coefficients: Estimate Std. Error t value Pr(>|t|)
(Intercept)   0.72538    1.54882   0.468    0.646
content       0.49808    0.04952  10.058 4.63e-08
     ***
---
Signif. codes:  0 '***' 0.001 '**' 0.01 '*' 0.05
       '.' 0.1 ' ' 1

Residual standard error: 1.743 on 15 degrees of
       freedom
Multiple R-squared:  0.8709,    Adjusted R-squared:
       0.8623
F-statistic: 101.2 on 1 and 15 DF,  p-value:
       4.632e-08
```

With the `summary()` function, we can examine some items, including the model specification, descriptive statistics about the residuals, the coefficients, codes to model significance, and a summary of the model error and fit. Right now, let's focus on the parameter coefficient estimates, and see whether our predictor variable has a significant `p-value` and whether the overall model F-test has a significant `p-value`. Looking at the parameter estimates, the model tells us that `yield` is equal to `0.72538` plus `0.49808` times `content`. We can state that for every one unit change in the content, the yield will increase by `0.49808` units. `F-statistic` is used to test the null hypothesis that the model coefficients are all zero.

Since `p-value` is highly significant, we can reject the null and move on to the t-test for content, which tests the null hypothesis that it's zero. Again, we can reject the null. Additionally, we can see the `Multiple R-squared` and `Adjusted R-squared` values. `Adjusted R-squared` will be covered under the multivariate regression topic, so let's zero in on `Multiple R-squared`; here, we see that it's `0.8709`. In theory, it can range from zero to one and is a measure of the strength of the association between *X* and *Y*. The interpretation, in this case, is that the water content of snow can explain 87 percent of the variation in the water yield. On a side note, R-squared is nothing more than the correlation coefficient of [*X, Y*] squared.

We can recall our scatter plot and now add the best fit line produced by our model using the following code:

```
> plot(content, yield)

> abline(yield_fit, lwd = 3, col = "red")
```

The output of the preceding code is as follows:

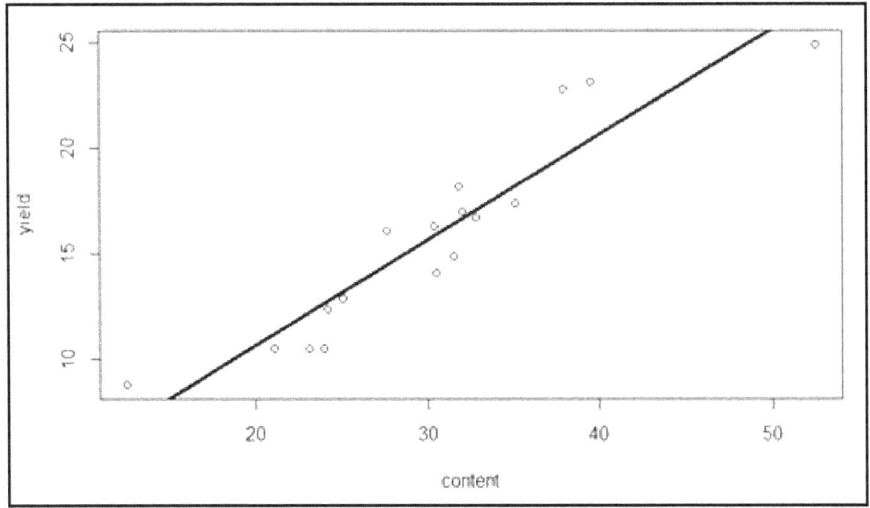

Reviewing model assumptions

A linear regression model is only as good as the validity of its assumptions, which can be summarized as follows:

- **Linearity**: This is a linear relationship between the predictor and the response variables. If this relationship is not explicitly present, transformations (log, polynomial, exponent, and so on) of X or Y may solve the problem.
- **Non-correlation of errors**: This is a common problem in time series and panel data where $e_n = beta_{n-1}$; if the errors are correlated, you run the risk of creating a poorly specified model.
- **Homoscedasticity**: This refers to normally distributed and constant variance of errors, which means that the variance of errors is constant across different input values. Violations of this assumption don't create biased coefficient estimates, but because of improper standard errors for the coefficients can lead to statistical tests for significance that can be either too high or too low, leading to wrong conclusions. This violation is also called **heteroscedasticity**.
- **No collinearity**: No linear relationship should exist between two predictor variables, which is to say that there should be no correlation between the features. This issue can lead to incorrect statistical tests for the coefficients.

- **Presence of outliers**: Outliers can severely skew the estimation, and they must be examined and handled via removal or transformation while fitting a model using linear regression; as we saw in the Anscombe example, outliers can lead to a biased estimate.

A simple way to initially check the assumptions is by producing plots. The `plot()` function, when combined with a linear model fit, will automatically generate four plots, allowing you to examine the assumptions. R produces the plots one at a time, and you advance through them by hitting the *Enter* key. It's best to explore all four simultaneously, and we can do so in the following manner:

```
> par(mfrow = c(2,2))

> plot(yield_fit)
```

The output of the preceding code is as follows:

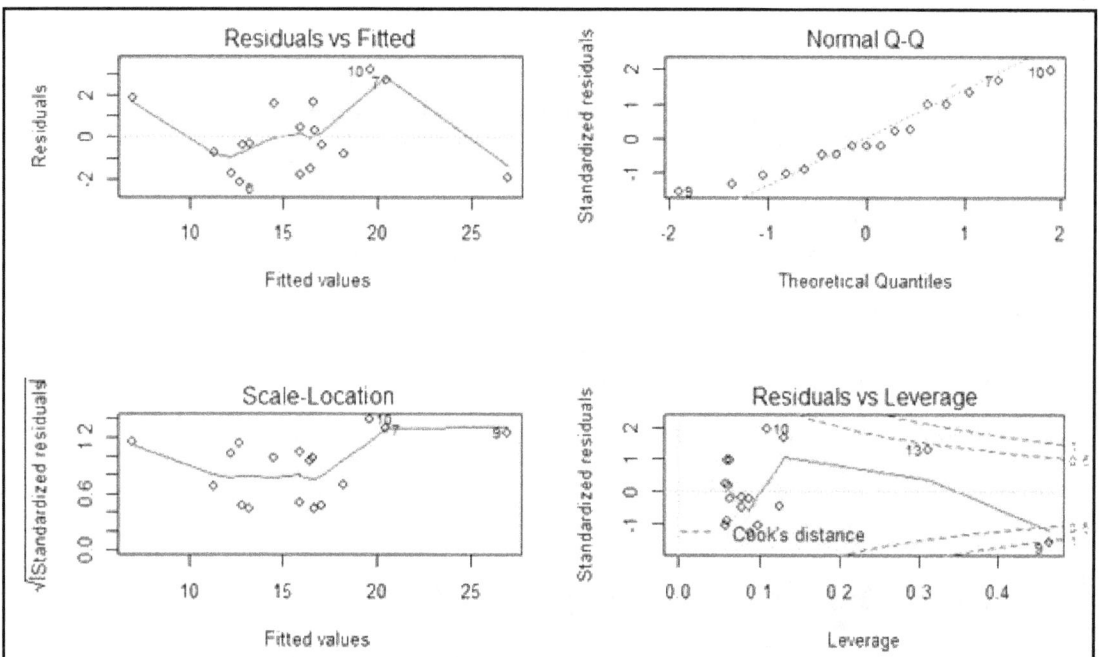

The two plots on the left allow us to examine the homoscedasticity of errors and non-linearity. What we're looking for is some pattern or, more importantly, that no pattern exists. Given the sample size of only 17 observations, nothing visible exists. Common heteroscedastic errors will appear to be u-shaped, inverted u-shaped, or clustered close together on the left of the plot. They'll become wider as the fitted values increase (a funnel shape). It's safe to conclude that no violation of homoscedasticity is apparent in our model.

The **Normal Q-Q** plot in the upper-right corner helps us to determine whether the residuals are normally distributed. The **Quantile-Quantile (Q-Q)** represents the quantile values of one variable plotted against the quantile values of another. It appears that the outliers (observations **7**, **9**, and **10**) may be causing a violation of the assumption. The **Residuals vs Leverage** plot can tell us what observations, if any, are unduly influencing the model; in other words, if there are any outliers we should be concerned about. The statistic is **Cook's distance** or **Cook's D**, and it's generally accepted that a value greater than one should be worthy of further inspection.

What exactly is further inspection? This is where art meets science. The easy way out would be to delete the observation, in this case number **9**, and redo the model. However, a better option may be to transform the predictor and/or the response variables. If we just delete observation **9**, then maybe observations **10** and **13** would fall outside the band for greater than one. In this simple example, I believe that this is where domain expertise can be critical. More times than I can count, I've found that exploring and understanding outliers can yield valuable insights. When we first examined the previous scatter plot, I pointed out the potential outliers and these happen to be observations number **9** and number **13**. It seems important to discuss with the appropriate subject matter experts to understand why this is the case. Is it a measurement error? Is there a logical explanation for these observations? I certainly don't know, but this is an opportunity to increase the value that you bring to an organization.

Let's leave this simple case behind us and move on to a supervised learning case involving multivariate linear regression.

Multivariate linear regression

In the case study that follows, we're going to look at the application of some exciting methods on an interesting dataset. Like in the previous chapter, once the data is loaded we'll *treat* it, but unlike the previous example, we'll split it into training and testing sets. Given the dimensionality of the data, feature reduction and selection are critical.

We'll explore the oft-maligned stepwise selection, then move on to one of my favorite methodologies, which is **Multivariate Adaptive Regression Splines** (**MARS**). If you're not using MARS, I highly recommend it. I've been told, but cannot verify it, that Max Kuhn stated in a conference that it's his starting procedure. I'm not surprised if it's true. I learned the technique from a former Senior Director of Analytics at one of the largest banks in the world and haven't looked back since.

Loading and preparing the data

To get the data into your working directory, you can find it on my GitHub at this link: `hhttps://github.com/PacktPublishing/Advanced-Machine-Learning-with-R/blob/master/Data/ames.csv`.

The file we're using is `ames.csv`. This data is from the sales of homes sold in Ames, Iowa, which is the location of Iowa State University, and I believe has a population of around 70,000. I downloaded the data from `Kaggle.com`, and the response we're trying to predict is the final sales price. It's a nice size to practice machine learning methods with 1,460 observations of 84 features, and many of the features are categorical.

Before we load the data, if not already done, load the necessary packages, call the `magrittr` library, and, if you so choose, update the options. I prefer not to have scientific number notation and want to round the values to four decimals:

```
library(magrittr)
options(scipen = 999)
options(digits = 4)
# install.packages("caret")
# install.packages("ggthemes")
# install.packages("janitor")
# install.packages("leaps")
# install.packages("plm")
# install.packages("readr")
# install.packages("sjmisc")
# install.packages("tidyverse")
# install.packages("vtreat")
```

Now, load the data and confirm the dimensions:

```
> ames <- readr::read_csv(~/ames.csv")

> dim(ames)

[1] 1460    84
```

I don't believe there are any duplicate observations, but let's confirm:

```
> dupes <- duplicated(ames)

> table(dupes)
dupes
FALSE
 1460
```

Excellent! There are no duplicates. Here, we create a tibble of the descriptive statistics. Open the data in RStudio and explore it by feature to get a feel for it:

```
> ames %>%
    sjmisc::descr() -> ames_descr

> View(ames_descr)
```

There are some thought-provoking features but focus first on `Id`. Notice that this has a unique value for all of the observations. Hence, we can remove it as it has no value in predictions:

```
> range(ames$Id)
[1] 1 1460

> ames <- ames[, -1]
```

Three other features are interesting as they are the year that an event happened. Instead of the year as the value of the feature, how about we create a feature of years since the event? This is easy to do by taking `YrSold` and subtracting in sequence `YearBuilt`, `YearRemodAdd`, and `GarageYrBuilt` just like this:

```
 > ames %>%
     dplyr::mutate(yearsOld = YrSold - YearBuilt) -> ames

> ames %>%
    dplyr::mutate(yearsRemodel = YrSold - YearRemodAdd) -> ames

> ames %>%
    dplyr::mutate(yearsGarage = YrSold - GarageYrBlt) -> ames
```

Another thing of interest when you look at the descriptive stats is the fact that `GarageYrBlt` has roughly 5.5% missing values. So, `yearsGarage` will have a corresponding amount of missing values. As is my standard procedure, I want us to code a dummy feature that indicates missing values and changes those missing values to zero.

I'm not sure that any imputation here would add value:

```
> ames$yearsGarage_isNA <-
    ifelse(is.na(ames$yearsGarage), 1, 0)

> ames$yearsGarage[is.na(ames$yearsGarage)] <- 0
```

Let's remove those unnecessary features given that we created a new feature of years since the event:

```
> ames <- ames[, c(-19, -20, -59)]
```

Another feature of interest is `MoSold`. This is a numeric that corresponds to the month it was sold, so 1 = January, 2 = February, and so on. This is probably better conditioned as a character feature and will end up as dummy features during one-hot encoding:

```
> ames$MoSold <- as.character(ames$MoSold)
```

The one plot we should look at is of the response, which is `SalesPrice`. I like to try out different plot themes, so I'll use different themes for different plots for illustration purposes, which should help you discover your favorite ones:

```
> ggplot2::ggplot(ames, ggplot2::aes(x = SalePrice)) +
    ggplot2::geom_histogram() +
    ggthemes::theme_few()
```

The output of the preceding code is as follows:

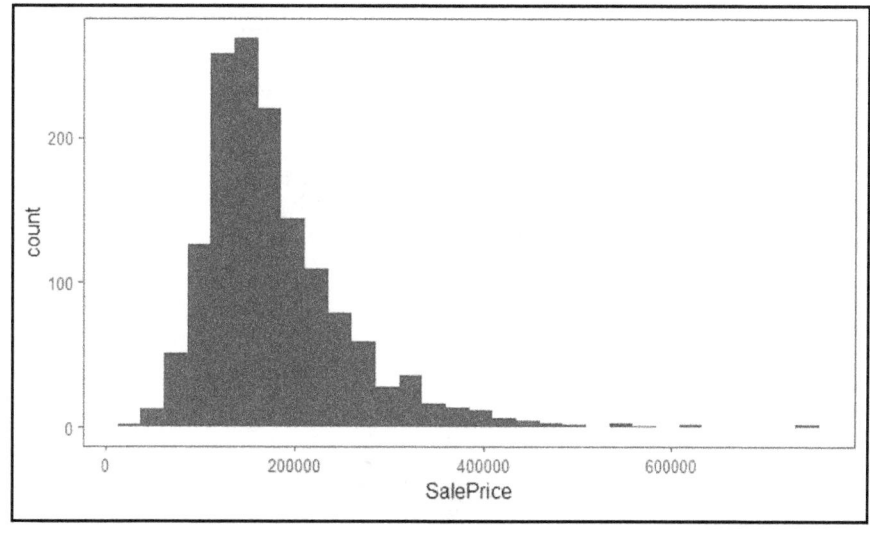

The histogram shows the data is skewed to the right. In non-linear methods, this may not be a problem, but in linear models, you can usually count on biased estimates and/or severe problems with outliers in your residuals. It seems like a good idea to transform this using the natural log:

```
> ames %>%
    dplyr::mutate(logSales = log(SalePrice)) -> ames

> ggplot2::ggplot(ames, ggplot2::aes(x = logSales)) +
    ggplot2::geom_histogram() +
    ggthemes::theme_economist_white()
```

The output of the preceding code is as follows:

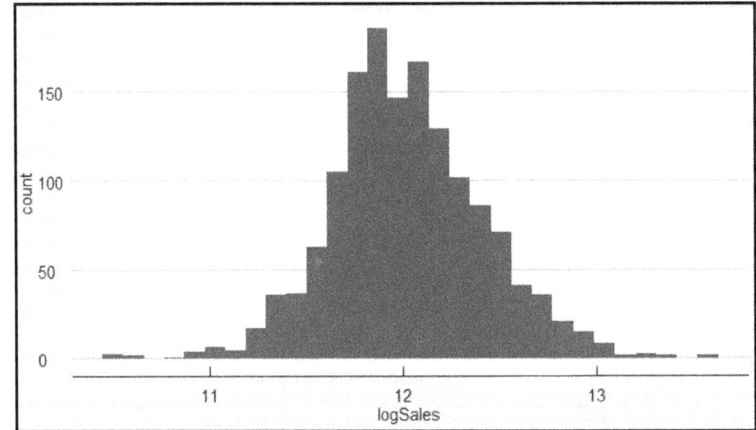

We now have a much more normal distribution but can see some potentially problematic outliers of homes selling at meager and very high prices.

My usual next step is to finalize any missing values in features of interest. Again, we code a dummy feature and turn the missing values into zero:

```
> ames$LotFrontage_isNA <-
    ifelse(is.na(ames$LotFrontage), 1, 0)

> ames$LotFrontage[is.na(ames$LotFrontage)] <- 0

> ames$MasVnrArea_isNA <-
    ifelse(is.na(ames$MasVnrArea), 1, 0)

> ames$MasVnrArea[is.na(ames$MasVnrArea)] <- 0
```

I don't believe we have any zero variance features (we removed Id) but let's double-check:

```
> feature_variance <- caret::nearZeroVar(ames, saveMetrics = TRUE)

> table(feature_variance$zeroVar)

FALSE
   84
```

All good! We now come to the point where we can safely split the data into training and testing sets. I guess you could call the training set a validation set, as the real test data is a separate file that you would submit to Kaggle for evaluation. That is out of scope here; hence, I call our holdout sample test.

In this example, let's use an 80/20 split:

```
> set.seed(1944)

> ames %>%
    dplyr::sample_frac(.8) -> train

> ames %>%
    dplyr::anti_join(train) -> test
```

If you look in the **Global Environment** tab of RStudio, you'll see that train has 1,168 observations and test 292 observations.

We now come to the point where we're almost ready to treat the training data. However, let's create an object called varlist, which we'll feed into the treat function, which is the predictor features, and generate response variables:

```
> varlist = colnames(ames[, !colnames(ames) %in% c('SalePrice',
'logSales')])

> train_y <- train$SalePrice
> train_logy <- train$logSales
> test_y <- test$SalePrice
> test_logy <- test$logSales
```

Now you can design a treatment scheme. Do this by only treating the training data, so you don't bias your model building. As you'll see, you can apply that treatment scheme to the test data or any currently unseen data for that matter. We'll just specify our training data, varlist, and set minFraction for coding character feature levels to 10%:

```
> df_treatment <- vtreat::designTreatmentsZ(
    dframe = train,
    varlist = varlist,
```

```
minFraction = 0.10
)
```

 For a further discussion on designing data treatment strategies, refer to `Chapter 1`, *Preparing and Understanding Data*.

Now, apply the treatment to both train and test datasets:

```
> trained <- vtreat::prepare(df_treatment, train)

> tested <- vtreat::prepare(df_treatment, test)
```

Notice that we now have 155 features in each of these treated datasets. Feel free to explore them, keeping in mind how the features are renamed as discussed in `Chapter 1`, *Preparing and Understanding Data*.

As I stated in the previous chapter, we can drop the _catP features and rename the others as in the following code:

```
> trained <-
    trained %>%
    dplyr::select(-dplyr::contains('_catP'))

> tested <-
    tested %>%
    dplyr::select(-dplyr::contains('_catP'))

> colnames(trained) <-
    sub('_clean', "", colnames(trained))

> colnames(tested) <-
    sub('_clean', "", colnames(tested))

> colnames(trained) <-
    sub('_isBAD', "_isNA", colnames(trained))

> colnames(tested) <-
    sub('_isBAD', "_isNA", colnames(tested))
```

Just removing the category percentage features reduced the number of them to 114. The final step before moving on to model creation is to remove highly correlated pairs of features and verify there are no linear dependencies. In linear models, this is critical to sort out. During one-hot encoding, if you create as many indicator/dummy features as levels in the parent categorical feature, you would fall into the dummy variable trap, which results in perfect multicollinearity. The classic example is a feature with levels of only male or female. One-hot would give us two features, whereas it should be encoded to one feature with, say, female = 1 and male = 0. Then, in the linear regression, the expectation for male would just be the intercept *B0*, while for female it would be *B0 + B1x*.

As for correlation, we could explore the various relationships in depth, as discussed in `Chapter 1`, *Preparing and Understanding Data*. Given the size of this data, let's identify and remove those pairs with correlation greater than `0.79`. I encourage you to experiment with this specification:

```
> df_corr <- cor(trained)

> high_corr <- caret::findCorrelation(df_corr, cutoff = 0.79)

> length(high_corr)
[1] 19
```

There are 19 features we can eliminate. As I stated, you can examine this problem in more depth, but let's proceed by merely removing them:

```
trained <- trained[, -high_corr]
```

For linear dependencies, the `caret` package comes in handy again. To be sure, I like to double check with the `detect_lin_dep()` function:

```
> caret::findLinearCombos(trained)
$`linearCombos`
list()

$`remove`
NULL

> # linear dependency
> plm::detect_lin_dep(trained)
[1] "No linear dependent column(s) detected."
```

The results from the `caret` package tell us there are no features to remove since no dependency exists, and the `plm` package confirms this.

We'll now move on to training our model. This should be interesting!

Modeling and evaluation – stepwise regression

The model we're looking to create will consist of the following form:

$$Y = B0 + B1x1 + \ldots Bnxn + e$$

In this formula, the predictor variables (features) can be from 1 to n.

One of the critical elements that we'll cover here is the vital task of feature selection. Later chapters will include more advanced techniques.

Forward selection starts with a model that has zero features; it then iteratively adds features one at a time until achieving the best fit based on say the reduction in residual sum of squares or overall model AIC. This iteration continues until a stopping rule is satisfied for example, setting maximum p-values for features in the model at 0.05.

Backward selection begins with all of the features in the model and removes the least useful, one at a time.

Stepwise selection is a hybrid approach where the features are added through forward stepwise regression, but the algorithm then examines whether any features that no longer improve the model fit can be removed.

It's important to add here that stepwise techniques can suffer from serious issues. You can perform a forward stepwise on a dataset then a backward stepwise and end up with two completely conflicting models. The bottom line is that stepwise can produce biased regression coefficients; in other words, they're too large and the confidence intervals are too narrow (Tibshirani, 1996).

Best subsets regression can be a satisfactory alternative to the stepwise methods for feature selection. In best subsets regression, the algorithm fits a model for all of the possible feature combinations; so, if you have three features, seven models are created. As you might've guessed, if your dataset has many features like the one we're analyzing here, this can be a heavy computational burden. A possible solution you can try is to use forward, backward, or stepwise selection to reduce your features to a point where best subset regression becomes practical. A key point to remember is that we still need to focus on our holdout sample performance as best subsets are no guarantee of producing the best results.

For both of the stepwise models, we'll use cross-validation k = 3 folds. We can specify this in an object using the caret package function, trainControl(), then pass that to our model for training:

```
> step_control <-
    caret::trainControl(method = "cv",
    number = 3,
    returnResamp = "final")
```

The method for training the model is based on forward feature selection from the leaps package.

This code gets us our results and, using trace = FALSE, we suppress messages on training progress. I'm also constraining the minimum and the maximum number of features to consider as 10 and 25. You can experiment with that parameter as you desire, but I am compelled to advise that you can end up with dozens of features and easily overfit the model:

```
> set.seed(1984)

> step_fit <-
    caret::train(trained, train_logy, method = "leapForward",
    tuneGrid = data.frame(nvmax = 10:25),
    trControl = step_control,
    trace = FALSE)
```

You can see all of the resulting metrics for each number of features using step_fit$results. However, let's just identify the best model:

```
> step_fit$bestTune
    nvmax
11    20
```

The output shows up that the model with the lowest **Root Mean Square Error** (**RMSE**) is with 20 features included, which corresponds to model number 11. To understand more about the specific model and its corresponding coefficients, it's quite helpful to put the features into a dataframe or, in this case, a tibble:

```
> broom::tidy(coef(step_fit$finalModel, 20)) -> step_coef

> View(step_coef)
```

The abbreviated output of the preceding code is as follows:

	names	x
1	(Intercept)	10.506606336
2	LotArea	0.000001535
3	OverallQual	0.097091379
4	OverallCond	0.051498387
5	X1stFlrSF	0.000238579
6	X2ndFlrSF	0.000171223
7	LowQualFinSF	0.000202540
8	BsmtFullBath	0.066315399

As you can see, it includes the intercept term. You can explore this data further and see if it makes sense.

We should build a separate model with these features, test out of sample performance, and explore the assumptions. An easy way to do this is to drop the intercept from the tibble then paste together a formula of the names:

```
> step_coef <- step_coef[-1, ]

> lm_formula <- as.formula(paste("y ~ ",paste(step_coef$names,
collapse="+"), sep = ""))
```

Now, build a linear model, incorporating the response in the dataframe:

```
> trained$y <- train_logy

> step_lm <- lm(lm_formula, data = trained)
```

You can examine the results the old fashioned way using `summary()`. However, let's stay in the `tidyverse` format, putting the coefficients into a tibble with `tidy()` and using `glance()` to see how the entire model performs:

```
> # summary(step_lm)

> # broom::tidy(step_lm)

> broom::glance(step_lm)
```

```
# A tibble: 1 x 11
  r.squared adj.r.squared sigma statistic p.value     df logLik    AIC
*     <dbl>         <dbl> <dbl>     <dbl>   <dbl>  <int>  <dbl>  <dbl>
1     0.862         0.860 0.151      359.       0     21   563. -1082.
# ... with 3 more variables: BIC <dbl>, deviance <dbl>, df.residual <int>
```

A quick *glance* shows us we have an adjusted R-squared value of 0.86 and a highly statistic p-value for the overall model. What about our assumptions? Let's take a look:

```
> par(mfrow = c(2,2))

> plot(step_lm)
```

The output of the preceding code snippet is as follows:

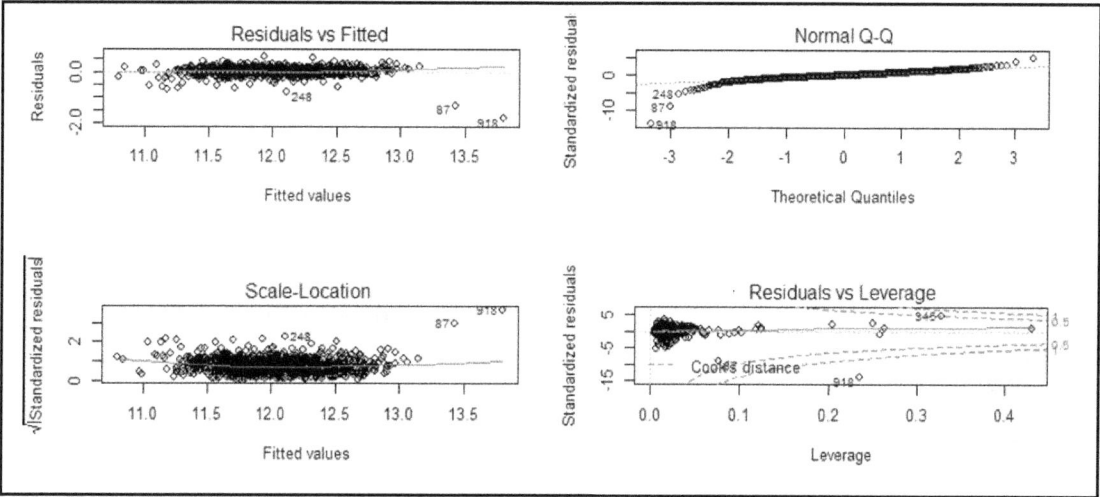

Even a brief examination shows we're having some issues with three observations: **87**, **248**, and **918**. If you look at the Q-Q plot, you can see a pattern known as heavy-tailed. What's happening is the model isn't doing very well at predicting extreme values.

Recall the histogram plot of the log response and how it showed outlier values at the high and low ends of the distribution. We could truncate the response, but that may not help in out of sample predictions. In this case, let's drop those three observations noted and re-run the model:

```
> train_reduced <- trained[c(-87, -248, -918), ]

> step_lm2 <- lm(lm_formula, data = train_reduced)
```

Here, we just look at the Q-Q plot:

```
> car::qqPlot(step_lm2$residuals)
```

The output of the preceding code is as follows:

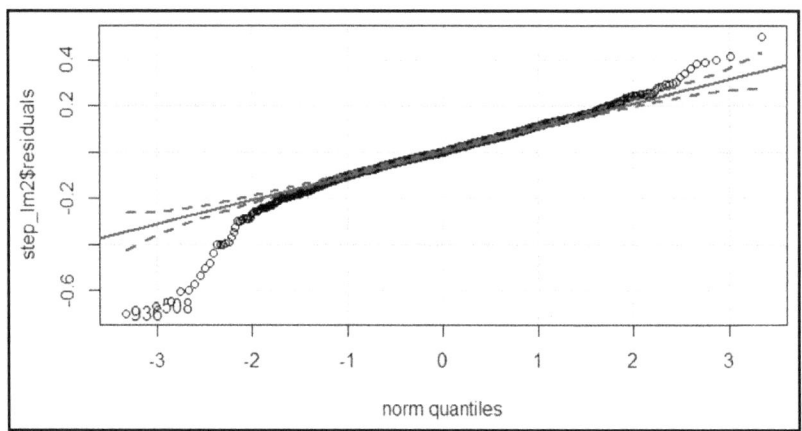

Clearly, we have some issues here where the residuals are negative (actual price-predicted price). What are the implications of our analysis? If we're producing *prediction intervals*, there could be problems since they're calculated on the assumption of normally distributed residuals. Also, with a dataset of this size, our other statistical tests are very robust to the problem of heteroscedasticity.

To investigate the issue of collinearity, one can call up the **Variance Inflation Factor (VIF)** statistic. VIF is the ratio of the variance of a feature's coefficient when fitting the full model, divided by the feature's coefficient variance when fitted by itself. The formula is as follows:

$$1/(1 - R_i^2)$$

In the preceding equation, R_i^2 is the R-squared for our feature of interest, *i*, being regressed by all the other features. The minimum value that the VIF can take is 1, which means no collinearity at all. There are no hard and fast rules, but in general, a VIF value that exceeds 5 (or some say 10) indicates a problematic amount of collinearity (James, p.101, 2013).

A precise value is difficult to select because there's no hard statistical cut-off point for when multi-collinearity makes your model unacceptable.

The `vif()` function in the `car` package is all that's needed to produce the values, as we can put them in a tibble and examine them:

```
> step_vif <- broom::tidy(car::vif(step_lm2))

> View(step_vif)
```

The abbreviated output of the preceding code is as follows:

	names	x
20	X2ndFlrSF	3.926
19	X1stFlrSF	3.917
18	yearsOld	3.850
17	TotRmsAbvGrd	3.574
16	OverallQual	2.755
15	yearsRemodel	2.172
14	GarageArea	1.891
13	GarageFinish_lev_x_Unf	1.550
12	OverallCond	1.540

I've sorted the view in descending order by VIF value. I believe we can conclude that there are no apparent problems with multicollinearity.

Finally, we have to see how we're doing out of sample, that is, on our test data. We make the model predictions and examine the results as follows:

```
> step_pred <- predict(step_lm2, tested)

> caret::postResample(pred = step_pred, obs = test_logy)
    RMSE Rsquared      MAE
 0.12978  0.89375 0.09492

> caret::postResample(step_lm2$fitted.values, train_reduced$y)
    RMSE Rsquared      MAE
 0.12688  0.90072 0.09241
```

We see the error increases only slightly: `0.12688` versus `0.12978` in the test data. I think we can do better with our MARS model. Let's not delay in finding out.

Modeling and evaluation – MARS

How would you like a modeling technique that provides all of the following:

- Offers the flexibility to build linear and nonlinear models for both regression and classification
- Can support variable interaction terms
- Is simple to understand and explain
- Requires little data processing
- Handles all types of data: numeric and categorical
- Performs well on unseen data, that is, it does well in a bias-variance trade-off

If that all sounds appealing, then I cannot recommend the use of MARS models enough. I've found them to perform exceptionally well. In fact, in a past classification problem of mine, they outperformed both a random forest and boosted trees on test/validation data.

To understand MARS is quite simple:

1. First, just start with a linear or generalized linear model like we discussed previously.
2. Then, to capture any nonlinear relationship, a hinge function is added. These hinges are simply points in the input feature that equate to a coefficient change. For example, say we have this:
   $Y = 12.5(our\ intercept) + 1.5(variable\ 1) + 3.3(variable\ 2)$
   Where variables 1 and 2 are on a scale of 1 to 10.
3. Now, let's see how a hinge function for variable 2 could come into play:
   $Y = 11(new\ intercept) + 1.5(variable\ 1) + 4.26734(max(0, variable\ 2 - 5.5))$

We read the `hinge` function as we take the maximum of either 0 or *variable 2-5.50*. So, whenever variable 2 has a value greater than 5.5, that value will be multiplied times the coefficient; otherwise, it will be zero. The method will accommodate multiple hinges for each variable and also interaction terms.

The other interesting thing about MARS is the automatic variable selection. This can be done with cross-validation, but the default is to build through a forward pass, much like forward selection, then a backward pass to prune the model, which after the forward pass is likely to overfit the data. This backward pass prunes input features and removes hinges based on **Generalized Cross Validation (GCV)**:

$GCV = RSS/(N * (1 - Effective\ Number\ of\ Parameters/N)2) Effective\ Number\ of\ Parameters = Number\ of\ Input\ Features + Penalty * (Number\ of\ Input\ Features - 1)/2$

In the `earth` package in R, `Penalty` = 2 for an additive model and 3 for a multiplicative model. A multiplicative model is one with interaction terms. In `earth`, there are quite a few parameters you can tune. I'll demonstrate, in the example, a practical and straightforward way to implement the methodology. If you so desire, you can learn more about its flexibility in the excellent vignette on the `earth` package by Stephen Milborrow, available at this link: `http://www.milbo.org/doc/earth-notes.pdf`.

I'll specify a model selection of a five-fold cross-validation (`pmethod` = *cv* and `nfold` = 5) as an additive model only with no interactions (`degree` = 1) and only one hinge per input feature (`minspan` = −1). I also want to have a maximum of 25 features (`nprune` = 25). The code is as follows:

```
> set.seed(1988)
> earth_fit <-
    earth::earth(
      x = train_reduced[, -96],
      y = train_reduced[, 96],
      pmethod = 'cv',
      nfold = 5,
      degree = 1,
      minspan = -1,
      nprune = 25
    )
```

`summary()` of `earth_fit` is quite lengthy, so here's the abbreviated version:

```
> summary(earth_fit)

Selected 20 of 26 terms, and 13 of 95 predictors using pmethod="cv"
Termination condition: RSq changed by less than 0.001 at 26 terms
Importance: OverallQual, X1stFlrSF, X2ndFlrSF, yearsOld, ...
Number of terms at each degree of interaction: 1 19 (additive model)
GRSq 0.9052 RSq 0.9113 mean.oof.RSq 0.8979 (sd 0.0115)
```

What we can discern is that only 13 features were selected with a total of 20 terms, including hinged features. `mean.oof.RSq` is the average of the out of fold R-squared values (`0.8979`), and the full-model R-squared is `0.9113`. You can call feature importance as well:

```
> earth::evimp(earth_fit)
               nsubsets    gcv    rss
OverallQual          19  100.0  100.0
X1stFlrSF            17   49.7   50.0
X2ndFlrSF            16   42.7   43.0
yearsOld             14   33.8   34.1
OverallCond          13   28.0   28.4
```

```
BsmtFinSF1                  11   22.6   23.1
LotArea                     10   19.1   19.7
Fireplaces                   7   12.7   13.4
yearsGarage_isNA             6   10.9   11.6
CentralAir_lev_x_Y           4    7.9    8.5
Functional_lev_x_Typ         3    6.3    6.9
Condition1_lev_x_Norm        2    5.1    5.6
ScreenPorch                  1    3.4    3.8
```

We see the feature name, *n* subsets, which is the number of model subsets that include the feature if we did the pruning pass instead of cross-validation, and the `gcv` and `rss` columns show the decrease in the respective value that the feature contributes (`gcv` and `rss` are scaled 0 to 100). Notice that the feature we created, `yearsGarage_isNA`, was selected by the model. You can ponder the hinge functions, but there's an excellent visual to see the various piecewise linear functions:

```
> plotmo::plotmo(earth_fit, nrug = TRUE, rug.col = "red")
```

The output of the preceding code is as follows:

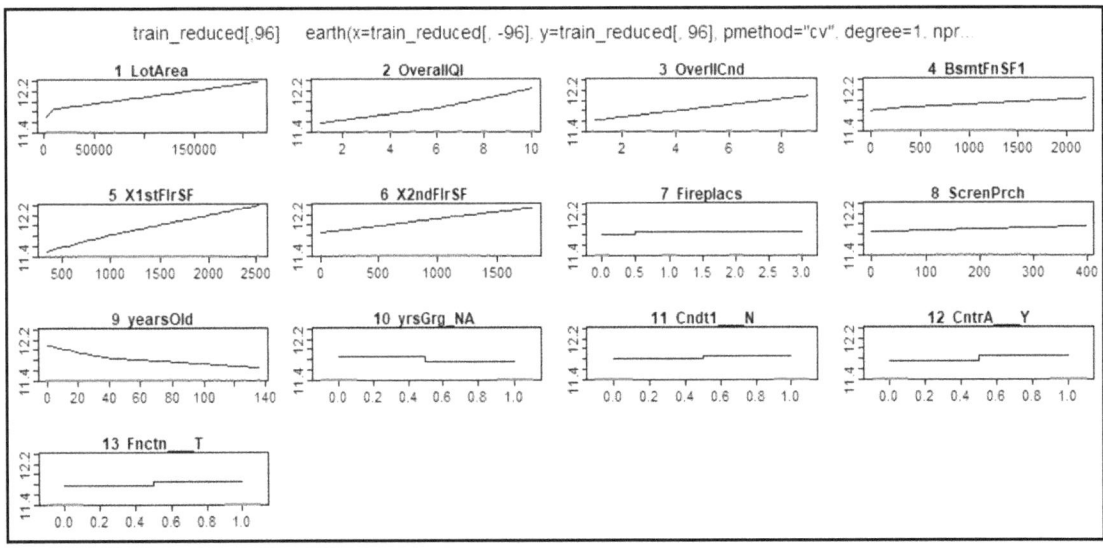

Notice in the plot that **LotArea** contains a hinge. Initially, as the size of the property increases, the increase is rather dramatic, then at a certain point, a new slope is applied from there to the maximum observed value. Contrast that with **OverallCond**, which has only one slope coefficient over all possible values. An excellent example of how MARS can capture linear and non-linear relationships in a piecewise fashion.

Now, we must see how it performs out of sample:

```
> earth_pred <- predict(earth_fit, tested)
```

```
> caret::postResample(earth_pred, test_logy)
    RMSE Rsquared      MAE
 0.12363  0.90120 0.08986
```

This is a superior RMSE than what we saw with simple linear regression! I'm curious how the residuals look on the test set:

```
> earth_residTest <- test_logy - earth_pred
```

```
> car::qqPlot(earth_residTest)
```

The output of the preceding code is as follows:

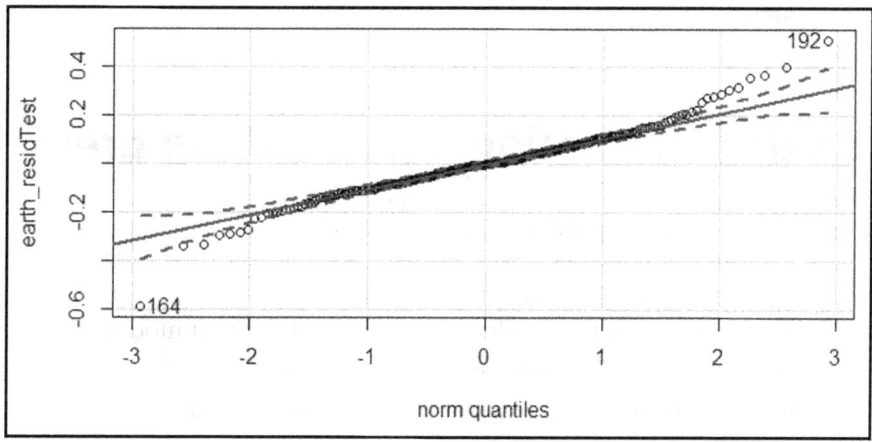

We still see a heavy-tailed distribution of the residuals. What this tells me is that we may have to resort to quantile regression (out-of-scope here) or create separate models for specific cuts of the response. Another option is to build an ensemble of models, but that's the subject of a later chapter.

Now, the issue I have here is that we predicted the natural log of sales price. How do we reverse transform to get actual sales price? I hear you saying, *just take the exponent*, correct? Well, maybe—or maybe not! I learned this painful lesson through experience, suffering the wrath of a PhD econometrician that just applying the exponent can lead to severe bias.

This is because the expected value of the response (sales price) is a function of the exponent of the predicted value plus an error term. If the error term isn't perfectly normal, then you have bias. The solution is **Duan's Smearing Estimator**. I shall address that with a custom function in the next section.

Should you desire to amuse yourself with the math behind all this, you can get started with Duan's paper:
Smearing Estimate: A Nonparametric Retransformation Method

Naihua Duan
Journal of the American Statistical Association
Vol. 78, No. 383 (Sep., 1983), pp. 605-610
Published by: Taylor & Francis, Ltd. on behalf of the American Statistical Association
DOI: 10.2307/2288126
`https://www.jstor.org/stable/2288126?seq=1/subjects`

Reverse transformation of natural log predictions

Now that you have read Duan's paper several times, here's how to apply to our work. I'm going to provide you with a user-defined function. It will do the following:

1. Exponentiate the residuals from the transformed model
2. Exponentiate the predicted values from the transformed model
3. Calculate the mean of the exponentiated residuals
4. Calculate the smeared predictions by multiplying the values in step 2 by the value in step 3
5. Return the results

Here's the function, which requires only two arguments:

```
> duan_smear <- function(pred, resid){
    expo_resid <- exp(resid)
    expo_pred <- exp(pred)
    avg_expo_resid <- mean(expo_resid)
    smear_predictions <- avg_expo_resid * expo_pred
    return(smear_predictions)
}
```

Next, we calculate the new predictions from the results of the MARS model:

```
> duan_pred <- duan_smear(pred = earth_pred, resid = earth_residTest)
```

We can now see how the model error plays out at the original sales price:

```
> caret::postResample(duan_pred, test_y)
      RMSE  Rsquared        MAE
 23483.5659    0.9356 16405.7395
```

We can say that the model is wrong, on average, by $16,406. How does that compare with not smearing? Let's see:

```
> exp_pred <- exp(earth_pred)
> caret::postResample(exp_pred, test_y)
      RMSE  Rsquared        MAE
 23106.1245    0.9356 16117.4235
```

The error is slightly less so, in this case, it just doesn't seem to be the wise choice to smear the estimate. I've seen examples where Duan's method, and others, are combined in an ensemble model. Again, more on ensembles later in this book.

Let's conclude the analysis by plotting the non-smeared predictions alongside the actual values. I'll show how to do this in ggplot fashion:

```
> results <- data.frame(exp_pred, test_y)

> colnames(results) <- c('predicted', 'actual')

> ggplot2::ggplot(results, ggplot2::aes(predicted, actual)) +
      ggplot2::geom_point(size=1) +
      ggplot2::geom_smooth() +
      ggthemes::theme_fivethirtyeight()
```

The output of the preceding code is as follows:

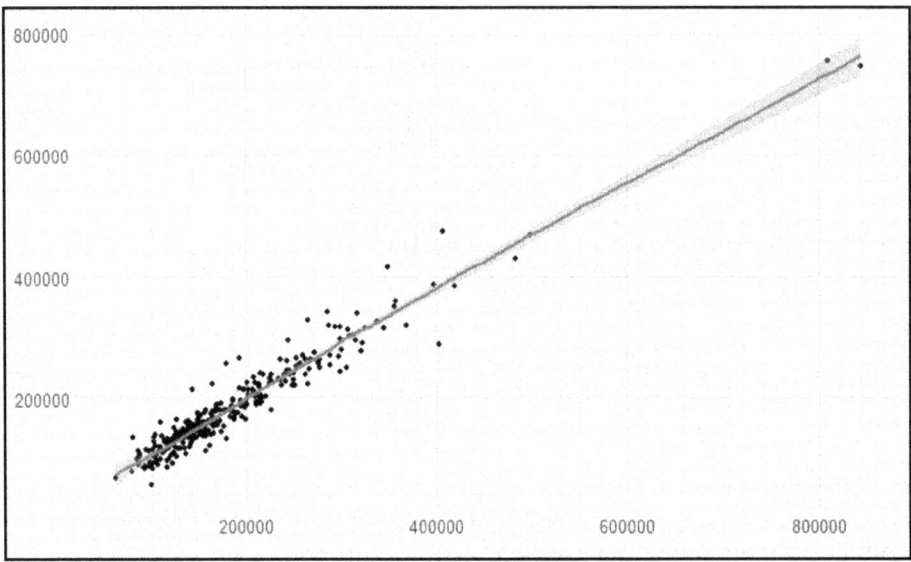

This is interesting as you can see that there's almost a subset of actual values that have higher sales prices than we predicted with their counterparts. There's some feature or interaction term that we could try and find to address that difference. We also see that, around the $400,000 sale price, there's considerable variation in the residuals—primarily, I would argue, because of the paucity of observations.

For starters, we have a pretty good model and serves as an excellent foundation for other modeling efforts as discussed. Additionally, we produced a model that's rather simple to interpret and explain, which in some cases may be more critical than some rather insignificant reduction in error. Hey, that's why you make big money. If it were easy, everyone would be doing it.

Summary

In the context of machine learning, we train a model and test it to predict an outcome. In this chapter, we had an in-depth look at the simple yet extremely effective methods of linear regression and MARS to predict a quantitative response. We also applied the data preparation paradigm put forth in Chapter 1, *Preparing and Understanding Data*, to quickly and efficiently get the data ready for modeling. We produced several simple plots to understand the response we were trying to predict, explore model assumptions, and model results.

Later chapters will cover more advanced techniques like Logistic regression, Support Vector Machines, Classification, Neural Networks, and Deep Learning but many of them are mere extensions of what we've learned in this chapter.

3
Logistic Regression

"The true logic of this world is the calculus of probabilities."

- James Clerk Maxwell, Scottish physicist

In the previous chapter, we took a look at using **Ordinary Least Squares** (**OLS**) to predict a quantitative outcome or, in other words, linear regression. It's now time to shift gears somewhat and examine how we can develop algorithms to predict qualitative outcomes. Such outcome variables could be binary (male versus female, purchase versus doesn't purchase, or a tumor is benign versus malignant) or multinomial categories (education level or eye color). Regardless of whether the outcome of interest is binary or multinomial, our task is to predict the probability of an observation belonging to a particular category of the outcome variable. In other words, we develop an algorithm to classify the observations.

To begin exploring classification problems, we'll discuss why applying the OLS linear regression isn't the correct technique and how the algorithms introduced in this chapter can solve these issues. We'll then look at the problem of predicting whether or not a banking customer is satisfied. To tackle this problem, we'll begin by building and interpreting a logistic regression model. We'll also start examining a univariate method to select features. Next, we'll turn to multivariate regression splines and discover ways to choose the best overall algorithm. This chapter will set the stage for more advanced machine learning methods in subsequent chapters.

We'll be covering the following topics in this chapter:

- Classification methods and linear regression
- Logistic regression
- Model training and evaluation

Classification methods and linear regression

So, why can't we use the least square regression method that we learned in the previous chapter for a qualitative outcome? Well, as it turns out, you can, but at your own risk. Let's assume for a second that you have an outcome that you're trying to predict and it has three different classes: mild, moderate, and severe. You and your colleagues also assume that the difference between mild and moderate and moderate and severe is an equivalent measure and a linear relationship. You can create a dummy variable where 0 is equal to mild, 1 is equal to moderate, and 2 is equal to severe. If you have reason to believe this, then linear regression might be an acceptable solution. However, qualitative labels such as the previous ones might lend themselves to a high level of measurement error that can bias the OLS. In most business problems, there's no scientifically acceptable way to convert a qualitative response into one that's quantitative. What if you have a response with two outcomes, say fail and pass? Again, using the dummy variable approach, we could code the fail outcome as 0 and the pass outcome as 1. Using linear regression, we could build a model where the predicted value is the probability of an observation of pass or fail. However, the estimates of Y in the model will most likely exceed the probability constraints of [0,1] and hence be a bit difficult to interpret.

Logistic regression

As previously discussed, our classification problem is best modeled with the probabilities that are bound by 0 and 1. We can do this for all of our observations with some different functions, but here we'll focus on the logistic function. The logistic function used in logistic regression is as follows:

$$Probability\ of\ Y = e^{B0+B1x}/1 + e^{B0+B1x}$$

If you've ever placed a friendly wager on horse races or the World Cup, you may understand the concept better as odds. The logistic function can be turned to odds with the formulation of *Probability (Y) / 1 - Probability (Y)*. For instance, if the probability of Brazil winning the World Cup is 20 percent, then the odds are *0.2 / 1 - 0.2*, which is equal to *0.25*, translating to odds of one in four.

To translate the odds back to probability, take the odds and divide by one plus the odds. The World Cup example is hence *0.25 / 1 + 0.25*, which is equal to 20 percent. Additionally, let's consider the odds ratio. Assume that the odds of Germany winning the Cup are *0.18*. We can compare the odds of Brazil and Germany with the odds ratio. In this example, the odds ratio would be the odds of Brazil divided by the odds of Germany. We'll end up with an odds ratio equal to *0.25/0.18*, which is equal to *1.39*. Here, we'll say that Brazil is *1.39* times more likely than Germany to win the World Cup.

One way to look at the relationship of logistic regression with linear regression is to show logistic regression as the log odds or *log (P(Y)/1 - P(Y))* is equal to *Bo + B1x*. The coefficients are estimated using a maximum likelihood instead of the OLS. The intuition behind the maximum likelihood is that we're calculating the estimates for *Bo* and *B1,* which will create a predicted probability for an observation that's as close as possible to the actual observed outcome of *Y*, a so-called likelihood. The R language does what other software packages do for the maximum likelihood, which is to find the optimal combination of beta values that maximize the likelihood.

With these facts in mind, logistic regression is a potent technique to predict the problems involving classification and is often the starting point for model creation in such problems. Therefore, in this chapter, we'll attack the future problem with logistic regression first.

Model training and evaluation

As mentioned previously, we'll be predicting customer satisfaction. The data is based on a former online competition. I've taken the training portion of the data and cleaned it up for our use.

 A full description of the contest and the data is available at the following link: `https://www.kaggle.com/c/santander-customer-satisfaction/data`.

This is an excellent dataset for a classification problem for many reasons. Like so much customer data, it's very messy— especially before I removed a bunch of useless features (there was something like four dozen zero variance features). As discussed in the prior two chapters, I addressed missing values, linear dependencies, and highly correlated pairs. I also found the feature names lengthy and useless, so I coded them V1 through V142. The resulting data deals with what's usually a difficult thing to measure: satisfaction. Because of proprietary methods, no description or definition of satisfaction is given.

Having worked previously in the world of banking, I can assure you that it's a somewhat challenging proposition and fraught with measurement error. As such, there's quite a bit of noise relative to the signal and you can expect model performance to be rather poor. Also, the outcome of interest, *customer dissatisfaction*, is relatively rare when compared to customers not dissatisfied. The classic problem is that you end up with quite a few false positives when trying to classify the minority labels.

As always, you can find the data on GitHub: `https://github.com/PacktPublishing/Advanced-Machine-Learning-with-R/blob/master/Data/santander_prepd.RData`.

So, let's start by first loading the data and training a logistic regression algorithm.

Training a logistic regression algorithm

Follow these simple steps to train a logistic regression algorithm:

1. The first step is to make sure we load our packages and call the `magrittr` library into our environment:

```
> library(magrittr)
> install.packages("caret")
> install.packages("classifierplots")
> install.packages("earth")
> install.packages("Information")
> install.packages("InformationValue")
> install.packages("Metrics")
> install.packages("tidyverse")
```

2. Here, we load the file then check the dimensions and examine a table of the customer labels:

```
> santander <- read.csv("~/santander_prepd.csv")

> dim(santander)
[1] 76020 143

> table(santander$y)

    0    1
73012 3008
```

We have 76,020 observations, but only 3,008 customers are labeled 1, which means dissatisfied. I'm going to use caret next to create training and test sets with an 80/20 split.

3. Within caret's `createDataPartition()` function, it automatically stratifies the sample based on the response, so we can rest assured about having a balanced percentage between the train and test sets:

```
> set.seed(1966)

> trainIndex <- caret::createDataPartition(santander$y, p = 0.8,
list = FALSE)

> train <- santander[trainIndex, ]

> test <- santander[-trainIndex, ]
```

4. Let's see how the response is balanced between the two datasets:

```
> table(train$y)

    0    1
58411 2405

> table(test$y)

    0    1
14601  603
```

There are roughly 4 percent in each set, so we can proceed. One interesting thing that can happen when you split the data is that you now end up with what was a near zero variance feature becoming a zero variance feature in your training set. When I treated this data, I only took out the zero variance features.

5. There were some low variance features, so let's see if we can eliminate some new zero variance ones:

```
> train_zero <- caret::nearZeroVar(train, saveMetrics = TRUE)

> table(train_zero$zeroVar)

FALSE TRUE
  142    1
```

6. OK, one feature is now zero variance because of the split, and we can remove it:

```
> train <- train[, train_zero$zeroVar == 'FALSE']
```

Our data frame now has 139 input features and the column of labeled customers. As we did with linear regression, for logistic regression to have meaningful results, which is to say not to overfit, you need to reduce the number of input features. We could press forward with stepwise selection or the like, as we did in the previous chapter. We could implement feature regularization methods as we'll discuss in the next chapter. However, I want to introduce a univariate feature reduction method using **Weight Of Evidence** (**WOE**) and **Information Value** (**IV**) and discuss how we can get an understanding of how to use it in a classification problem in conjunction with logistic regression.

Weight of evidence and information value

I stumbled into this method several years ago during consulting work. The team I was on was really into big datasets and constrained to using SAS statistical software. It was also a critical requirement that the customer teams could easily interpret the models.

Given the possibility of hundreds, even thousands, of possible features, I was privileged enough to learn the use of WOE and IV by a former rocket scientist. That's right: a person who actually worked on manned space flight. I became an eager pupil. Now, this method isn't a panacea. First of all, it's univariate, so features that are thrown out can become significant in a multivariate model and vice versa. I can say that it provides a nice complement to other methods, and you should keep it in your modeling toolbox. I believe it had its origins in the world of credit scoring, so if you work in the financial industry, you may already be familiar with it.

First, let's look at the formula for WOE:

$$WOE = ln(\frac{percentOfEvents}{percentOfNonEvents})$$

The WOE serves as a component in the IV. For numeric features, you would bin your data then calculate WOE separately for each bin. For categorical ones, or when one-hot encoded, bin for each level and calculate the WOE separately. Let's take an example and demonstrate in R.

Our data consists of one input feature coded as 0 or 1, so we'll have just two bins. For each bin, we calculate our WOE. In bin 1, or where values are equal to 0, there are four observations as events and 96 as non-events. Conversely, in bin 2, or where values are equal to 1, we have `12` observations as events and 88 as non-events. Let's see how to calculate the WOE for each bin:

```
> bin1events <- 4

> bin1nonEvents <- 96

> bin2events <- 12

> bin2nonEvents <- 88

> totalEvents <- bin1events + bin2events

> totalNonEvents <- bin1nonEvents + bin2nonEvents
# Now calculate the percentage per bin
> bin1percentE <- bin1events / totalEvents

> bin1percentNE <- bin1nonEvents / totalNonEvents

> bin2percentE <- bin2events / totalEvents

> bin2percentNE <- bin2nonEvents / totalNonEvents
# It's now possible to produce WOE
> bin1WOE <- log(bin1percentE / bin1percentNE)

> bin2WOE <- log(bin2percentE / bin2percentNE)
```

With completing this, you end up with the WOE for `bin1` and `bin2` of roughly -0.74 and 0.45 respectively. We now use that to calculate the IV per bin, then sum that up to arrive at an overall IV for the feature. The formula is as follows:

$$IV = \sum_{i=1}^{n}(Percent of Events - Percent of Non Events) * WOE$$

Taking our current example; this is our feature IV:

```
> bin1IV <- (bin1percentE - bin1percentNE) * bin1WOE

> bin2IV <- (bin2percentE - bin2percentNE) * bin2WOE

> bin1IV + bin2IV
[1] 0.3221803
```

The IV for the feature is `0.322`. Now, what does that mean? The short answer is that it depends. There's a heuristic provided to help decide what IV threshold makes sense for inclusion in model development:

- < 0.02 not predictive
- 0.02 to 0.1 weak
- 0.1 to 0.3 medium
- 0.3 to 0.5 strong
- > 0.5 suspicious

Our following example will provide us with interesting decisions to make regarding where to draw the line.

Feature selection

What we're going to do now is use the `Information` package to calculate the IVs for our features. Then, I'll show you how to evaluate those values and run some plots as well. Since there are no hard and fast rules about thresholds for feature inclusion, I'll provide my judgment about where to draw the line. Of course, you can reject that and apply your own.

In this example, the code will create a series of tables you can use to explore the results. To get started, you only need to specify the data and the response or "y" variable:

```
IV <- Information::create_infotables(data = train, y = "y", parallel =
FALSE)
```

This will give us an IV summary of the top 25 features:

```
> knitr::kable(head(IV$Summary, 25))
```

```
|     |Variable |      IV|
|:---|:--------|------:|
|2    |V2       | 0.7006|
|102  |V103     | 0.5296|
|124  |V125     | 0.5281|
|45   |V45      | 0.5273|
|31   |V31      | 0.5213|
|125  |V126     | 0.4507|
|55   |V55      | 0.3135|
|140  |V141     | 0.0982|
|108  |V109     | 0.0711|
|130  |V131     | 0.0681|
|33   |V33      | 0.0672|
```

```
|104  |V105   |  0.0640|
|66   |V66    |  0.0519|
|92   |V93    |  0.0519|
|128  |V129   |  0.0499|
|121  |V122   |  0.0461|
|24   |V24    |  0.0417|
|131  |V132   |  0.0365|
|34   |V34    |  0.0323|
|47   |V47    |  0.0323|
|123  |V124   |  0.0289|
|129  |V130   |  0.0194|
|83   |V84    |  0.0189|
|19   |V19    |  0.0181|
|35   |V35    |  0.0181|
```

The results show us the feature column number, the feature name, and the IV. Notice that we have five features that are possibly suspicious. I'm all for taking any feature with an IV above 0.02, which is the bottom of the weak predictors. That will give us 21 input features. The V2 feature is interesting. If you look at the values and think about the data, it seems clear that it's the customer's age. Let's see how the data is binned, the WOE values, and the IVs:

```
> knitr::kable(IV$Tables$V2)
```

```
|V2         |     N| Percent|     WOE|     IV|
|:----------|-----:|-------:|-------:|------:|
|[5,22]     |   951 | 0.0156 | 0.0000 | 0.0000|
|[23,23]    | 16222| 0.2667 | -1.6601| 0.3705|
|[24,24]    |  4953 | 0.0814 | -1.2811| 0.4481|
|[25,26]    |  6048 | 0.0994 | -0.7895| 0.4919|
|[27,31]    |  8088 | 0.1330 | 0.2261 | 0.4994|
|[32,36]    |  6037 | 0.0993 | 0.4923 | 0.5297|
|[37,42]    |  6302 | 0.1036 | 0.6876 | 0.5975|
|[43,51]    |  6095 | 0.1002 | 0.7328 | 0.6737|
|[52,105]   |  6120 | 0.1006 | 0.4636 | 0.7006|
```

OK, you've got to be kidding me. Look at bin number 2, which I believe is customer age of 23 years. It constitutes almost 27 percent of the total observations and contributes over half of the IV. Suspicious indeed! How is any algorithm we produce on this data going to help if this feature is genuine AGE as I suspect? However, that's outside the scope of this endeavor and not worth wasting any more time or effort. Here we can quickly bring up a bar plot of the WOEs by bin:

```
> Information::plot_infotables(IV, "V2", show_values = TRUE)
```

The output of the preceding code is as follows:

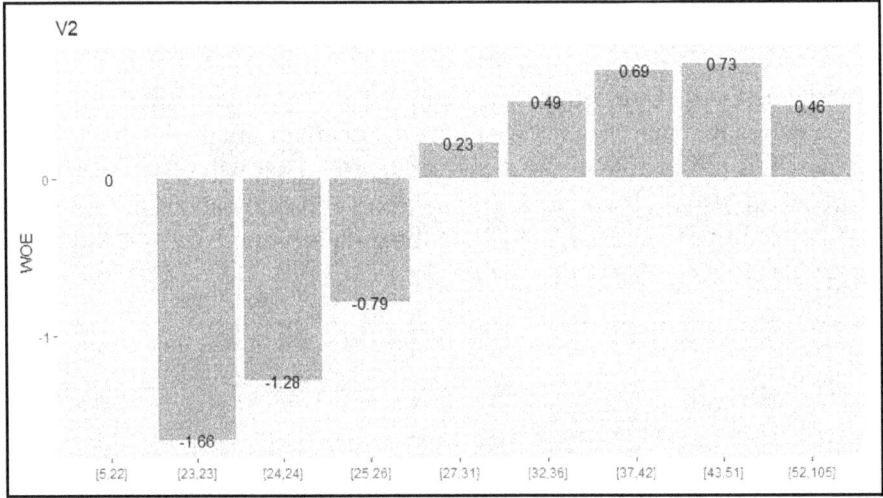

Interesting that there's a somewhat linear relationship between this feature and the response. What can be done is we can create features that turn the binned values into the WOE values. These new features would be linear and could be used in place of the original features. We shall forgo that because what method will do that for us? That's right, MARS in the next section can do that for us! Here is a grid plot of the top four features:

```
> Information::plot_infotables(IV, IV$Summary$Variable[1:4],
same_scales=TRUE)
```

The output of the preceding code is as follows:

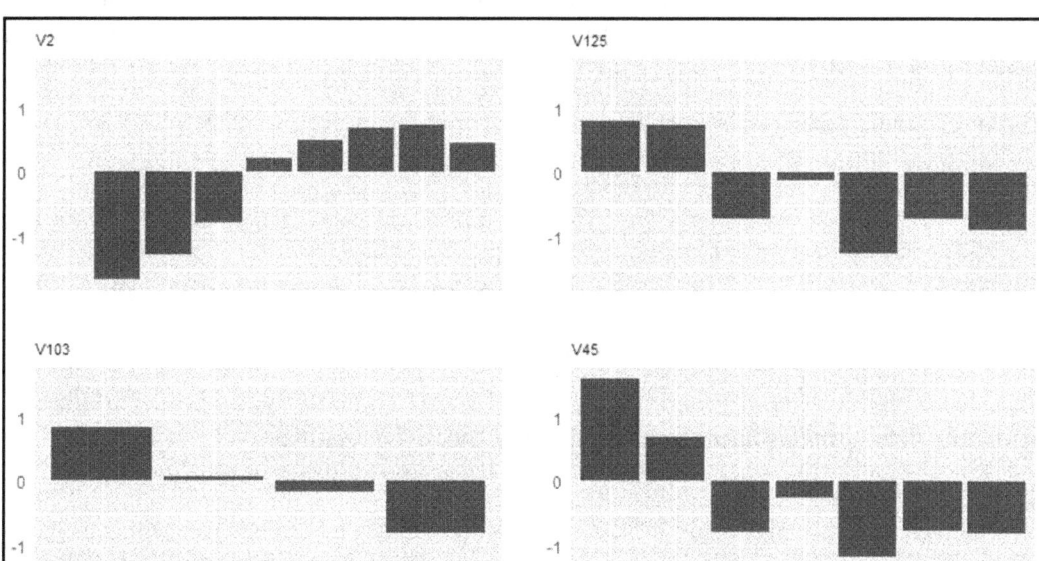

Now, given the cutoff point I picked previously, we can select those 21 features:

```
> features <- IV$Summary$Variable[1:21]

> train_reduced <- train[, colnames(train) %in% features]

> train_reduced$y <- train$y
```

There you go. We're now ready to begin training our algorithm.

Cross-validation and logistic regression

Our goal here is to build a model using 5-fold cross-validation. We'll utilize the `caret` package to establish our sampling scheme and to produce the final model. Start by building a separate `trainControl()` function:

```
> glm_control <-
    caret::trainControl(method = "cv",
    number = 5,
    returnResamp = "final")
```

This object is passed as an argument to train the algorithm. We now produce our input features, response variable (must be a factor for caret to train as logistic regression), set our random seed, and train the model. For the `train()` function, specify `glm` for **Generalized Linear Model** (**GLM**):

```
> x <- train_reduced[, -22]

> y <- as.factor(train_reduced$y)

> set.seed(1988)

> glm_fit <-
    caret::train(x, y, method = "glm",
                trControl = glm_control,
                trace = FALSE)
```

When that's done *grinding away*, you can quickly check the results:

```
> glm_fit$results
   parameter Accuracy     Kappa AccuracySD  KappaSD
1       none   0.9602 0.0002369  0.0001591 0.001743
```

Look at that, 96 percent accuracy! I know that's entirely meaningless because if we just guessed that all labels in the response were zero, we would achieve 96 percent. That may seem obvious, but I've interviewed people with *Data Science degrees* that missed that fact. `Kappa` refers to what's known as Cohen's Kappa statistic. The Kappa statistic provides an insight into this problem by adjusting the accuracy scores, which is done by accounting for the model being entirely correct by mere chance. The formula for the statistic is as follows:

$$Kappa = (percent\ of\ agreement\ -\ percent\ of\ chance\ agreement)/(1\ -\ percent\ of\ chance\ agreement)$$

The *percent of agreement* is the rate that the model agreed on for the class (accuracy) and *percent of chance agreement* is the rate that the model randomly agreed. The higher the statistic, the better the performance is with the maximum agreement being one. So, with this Kappa score, the model is pathetic.

Well, Kappa would be useful with more balanced labels. We're now left to find other ways to examine model results. It's always a good idea to compare the probability distributions of the different classes with a density or box plot.

Here we produce an elegant and colorful density plot on the training data:

```
> glm_train_pred <- predict(glm_fit, train, type = "prob")

> colnames(glm_train_pred) <- c("zero", "one")

> classifierplots::density_plot(train_reduced$y, glm_train_pred$one)
```

The output of the preceding code is as follows:

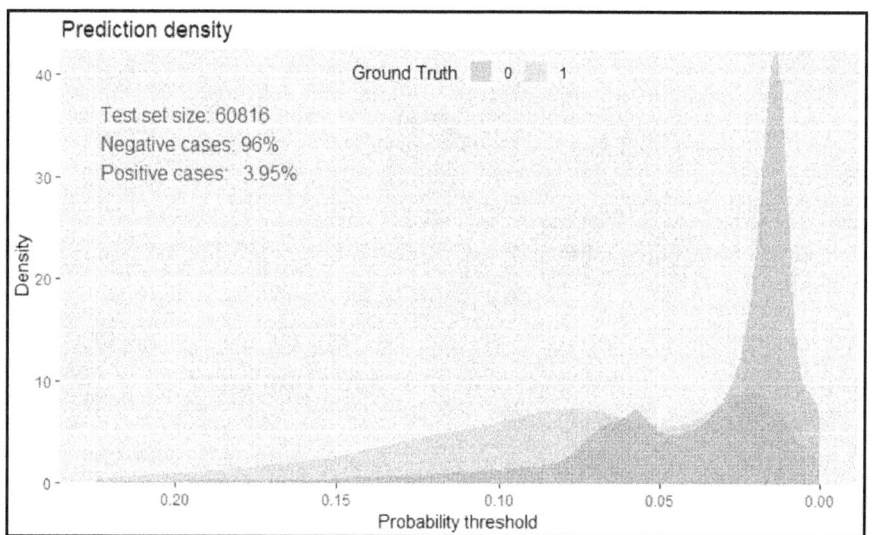

This gives us an interesting look at what the model's doing. We don't see any predictive power until we get around 7 percent. We can identify an optimal probability threshold to maximize our classification objective. There's an excellent function in the `InformationValue` package we'll apply later. It allows for the determination of four different thresholds:

- `misclasserror`: The default setting in the function, this identifies the threshold that minimizes a classification error
- `Ones`: This is the threshold that maximizes detection of 1s
- `Zeros`: This is the threshold that maximizes detection of 0s
- `Both`: This is the threshold that maximizes Youden's Index, which is *(sensitivity + specificity) - 1*

 *Sensitivity = True Positives / (True Positives + False Negatives)*: This is also called the True Positive Rate or Recall and is a measure of correctly identifying positive labels. *Specificity = True Negatives / (True Negatives + False Positives)*: Also called the True Negative Rate, this is a measure of correctly identifying negative labels.

In this case, we shall take a look at the threshold for `Both`. We'll also ask for all of the diagnostics:

```
> glm_cutoff <-
    InformationValue::optimalCutoff(
    train_reduced$y,
    glm_train_pred$one,
    optimiseFor = 'Both',
    returnDiagnostics = TRUE
    )
```

If you click on `glm_cutoff` in your global environment or run `View(glm_cutoff)`, you'll see a list of six different results:

- `optimalCutoff` = 0.0606
- A sensitivity table you can examine further on your own
- Misclassification error = 0.2006
- TPR = 0.6079
- FPR = 0.1927
- Specificity = 0.8073

If we select a cutoff of 0.0606, we'll achieve a **True Positive Rate** (**TPR**) of almost 61 percent. However, over 19 percent will be false positives.

Given the imbalance in the classes, that's a huge amount of customers. A confusion matrix can demonstrate that fact:

```
> InformationValue::confusionMatrix(train_reduced$y, glm_train_pred$one,
threshold = 0.0607)
        0     1
0 47164   944
1 11247 1461
```

Of the training data, customers that were dissatisfied, a total of 2,405; if we correctly classify 1,461 of them, we'll incorrectly classify 11,247. So where we decide to put an optimal threshold depends on the needs of the business. We'll see how to portray that differently during model comparison.

Let's now see how the algorithm ranked variable importance:

```
> caret::varImp(glm_fit)
glm variable importance

only 20 most important variables shown (out of 21)

        Overall
V2     100.0000
V103    70.2840
V141    33.2809
V105    18.0160
V24     13.1048
V129    12.4327
V55     10.7379
V34      8.7920
V45      8.5681
V124     7.1968
V122     5.9959
V109     5.8668
V33      4.8295
V125     3.6369
V131     1.5439
V126     0.8383
V47      0.7430
V132     0.4286
V66      0.3133
V31      0.0912
```

Our suspicious variable is number one in overall importance. I would recommend you to try other models dropping V2 from any consideration. But this is up to you as I'm of the mindset right now to see how performance is on the test data:

```
> glm_test_pred <- predict(glm_fit, test, type = "prob")

> colnames(glm_test_pred) <- c("zero", "one")

> classifierplots::density_plot(test$y, glm_test_pred$one)
```

The output of the preceding code is as follows:

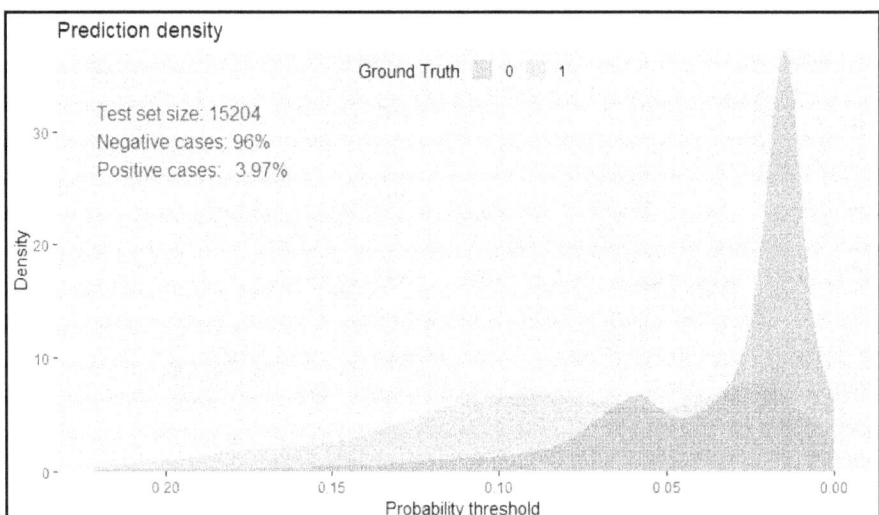

Very similar results on the test data. What about a confusion matrix given our threshold determined during training? Let's see:

```
> InformationValue::confusionMatrix(test$y, glm_test_pred$one, threshold =
0.0607)
       0    1
0  11710  227
1   2891  376
```

Consistent results! Now, let's examine this model's performance on the test data so that we can compare it to what the upcoming MARS model will produce. Two metrics should address the issue, **Area Under the Curve** (**AUC**), and log-loss. The AUC provides you with a useful indicator of performance, and it can be shown that the AUC is equal to the probability that the observer will correctly identify the positive case when presented with a randomly chosen pair of cases in which one case is positive and one case is negative (Hanley JA & McNeil BJ, 1982). In our case, we'll switch the observer with our algorithm and evaluate accordingly. Log-loss is an effective metric as it takes into account the predicted probability and how much it deviates from the correct label. The following formula produces it:

$$logloss = -\frac{1}{n}\sum_{i=1}^{n}[y_i \, log y_i + (1 - y_i)log(1 - y_i)]$$

Like golf, a lower value is better with values between 0 and 1. A perfect model would have a value of 0. We can produce these values easily with the `Metrics` package:

```
> Metrics::auc(test$y, glm_test_pred$one)
[1] 0.7794

> Metrics::logLoss(test$y, glm_test_pred$one)
[1] 0.1499
```

Our AUC isn't that great, I would say. If the model were no better than a random guess, then AUC would be equal to 0.5, and if perfect, it would be 1. Our log-loss is only essential when comparing it to the next model.

Multivariate adaptive regression splines

In the prior chapter, we went through a discussion on MARS, how it works, why use it, and so on, so I won't duplicate that here; other than that, it can be applied in a classification problem as a generalized linear model. One of the key benefits is its power to conduct feature selection, so there's no need to run stepwise or IV—or even regularization, for that matter.

We'll train it with 5-fold cross-validation and set `nprune = 15` to limit the maximum number of features at 15. Recall from the previous chapter that more than 15 terms are possible as it fits piecewise splines.

This code will give us our `model` object. Be advised that this may take some time to complete:

```
> set.seed(1972)

> earth_fit <-
    earth::earth(
    x = train[, -142],
    y = train[, 142],
    pmethod = 'cv',
    nfold = 5,
    degree = 1,
    minspan = -1,
    nprune = 15,
    glm = list(family = binomial)
    )
```

Here's the model summary:

```
> summary(earth_fit)
Call: earth(x=train[,-142], y=train[,142], pmethod="cv",
            glm=list(family=binomial), degree=1, nprune=15, nfold=5,
            minspan=-1)

GLM coefficients
                          y
(Intercept)        -3.4407
V23                -6.6750
V24                -1.3539
V105               -0.8200
h(28-V2)           -0.4769
h(V2-28)            0.0071
h(1-V31)            1.4876
h(V31-1)            0.0947
h(106449-V141)      0.0000
h(V141-106449)      0.0000

Earth selected 10 of 10 terms, and 6 of 141 predictors using pmethod="cv"
```

As you can see in the summary, the model ended up with six total predictive features and a total of ten terms, including a `hinge` function on V2. By standard protocol, the paired hinge terms can be read first predictor less than the hinge value, and then predictor greater than or equal to hinge. For instance, for V31, a value less than 1 has a coefficient of 1.4876, otherwise 0.0947.

We can plot the linear interactions with respect to predicted probability. Setting `ylim` to `NA` helps to show changes in *y* (predicted probability) versus changes in feature values:

```
> plotmo::plotmo(earth_fit, ylim = NA)
```

The output of the preceding code is as follows:

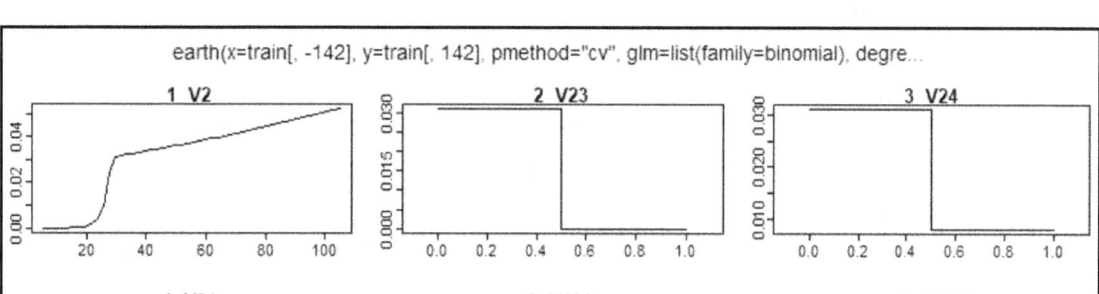

Notice how, for V31, values equal to zero have one coefficient else another one as described previously. Feature importance is trivial to produce:

```
> earth::evimp(earth_fit)
     nsubsets   gcv    rss
V31        9  100.0  100.0
V2         8   74.8   75.0
V141       7   40.2   41.1
V105       6   31.5   32.5
V23        5   26.8   27.8
V24        4   20.7   21.8
```

The nsubsets criterion counts the number of model subsets that include the feature. Features that included in more subsets are considered more important. These subsets are of the terms generated by earth's pruning pass.

Now, we specified cross-validation, but earth concurrently does forward and backward feature selection and elimination, using **Generalized Cross-Validation (GCV)** as discussed in the previous chapter. So, GCV and rss results for a feature are normalized from 0 to 100 for comparison purposes.

Like we did previously, a plot of the probability densities is useful, and `earth` comes with its own `plotd()` function:

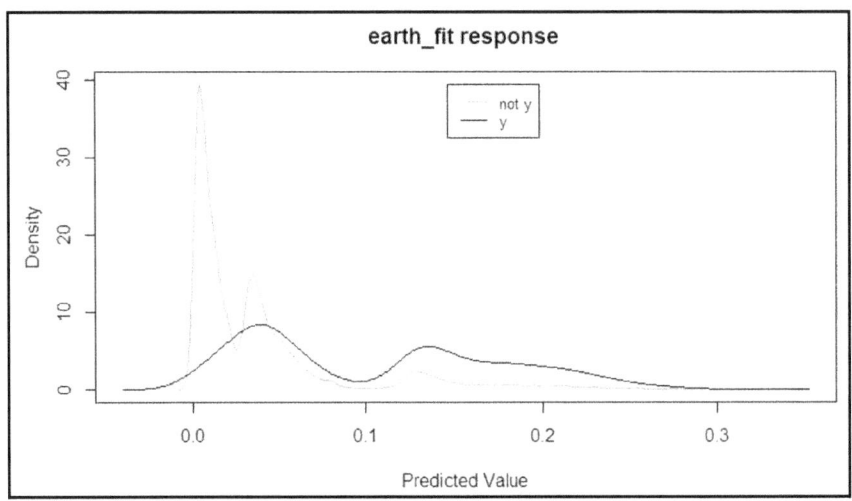

I like how the predicted values are reversed compared to the prior plots. Other than that, it's hard to discern anything meaningful with the exception that the densities are quite similar. Let's get the `cutoff` value:

```
> mars_cutoff <-
    InformationValue::optimalCutoff(
    train$y,
    pred,
    optimiseFor = 'Both',
    returnDiagnostics = TRUE
    )
```

Examination of the object provides the following:

- Optimal cutoff = 0.04976
- TPR = 0.6449
- FPR = 0.208

In comparison with logistic regression, we have a higher rate of finding true positives at the expense of a slightly higher rate of false positives.

Let's move on to evaluating performance on the test set:

```
> test_pred <- predict(earth_fit, test, type = 'response')

> Metrics::auc(test$y, test_pred)
[1] 0.8079

> Metrics::logLoss(test$y, test_pred)
[1] 0.1406
```

What do we see here? A slight improvement in AUC, and a lower (better) log-loss. While not dramatic, it may be of value. We can now turn to visually comparing the two models to confirm that MARS is indeed the preferred algorithm.

Model comparison

A useful tool for a classification model comparison is the **Receiver Operating Characteristic** (**ROC**) chart. ROC is a technique for visualizing, organizing, and selecting classifiers based on their performance (Fawcett, 2006). On the ROC chart, the y axis is the **True Positive Rate** (**TPR**), and the x axis is the **False Positive Rate** (**FPR**).

To create a ROC chart in R, you can use the ROCR package. I think this is a great package and allows you to build a chart in just three lines of code. The package also has an excellent companion website (with examples and a presentation) that can be found at the following link: http://rocr.bioinf.mpi-sb.mpg.de/.

For each model, you create a prediction object of the actual labels and the predicted probabilities, then create a performance object that embeds TPR and FPR, and finally plot it:

```
> pred.glm <- ROCR::prediction(glm_test_pred$one, test$y)

> perf.glm <- ROCR::performance(pred.glm, "tpr", "fpr")

> ROCR::plot(perf.glm, main = "ROC", col = 1)
```

That gives us the plot for the GLM (logistic regression). Now, we'll superimpose the MARS model on the same plot and create a legend:

```
> pred.earth <- ROCR::prediction(test_pred, test$y)

> perf.earth <- ROCR::performance(pred.earth, "tpr", "fpr")

> ROCR::plot(perf.earth, col = 2, add = TRUE)

> legend(0.6, 0.6, c("GLM", "MARS"), 1:2)
```

The output of the preceding code is as follows:

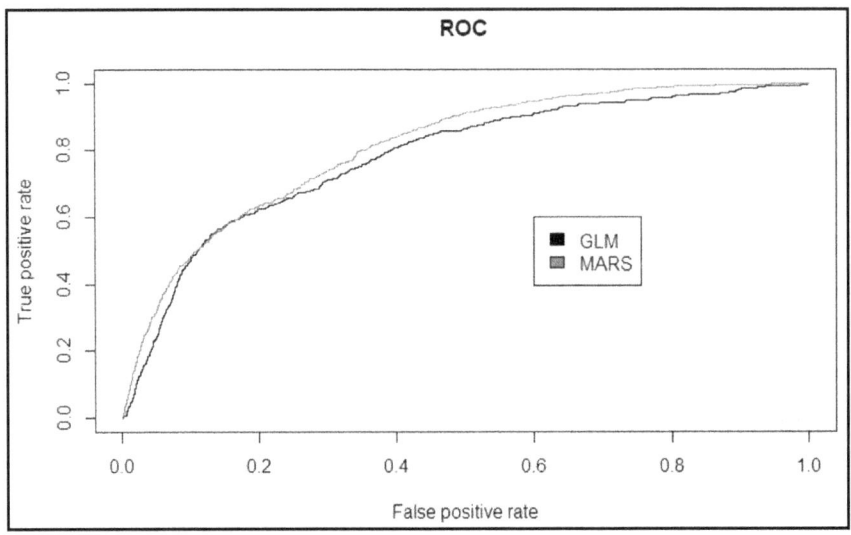

The area under the ROC curves corresponds to the prior calculated AUCs. The MARs model had a higher AUC; hence, its curve is slightly higher than the GLM model. It's noteworthy that around a TPR of 0.5, they have almost the same FPR. The bottom line though is the MARS model with fewer input features outperformed logistic regression albeit just slightly.

In a problem such as that which this data provides, there are quite a few things we could do to increase performance. You could further explore the data to try and add custom features. You could also use more advanced methods, creating more models for comparison, or even build several models and create an ensemble. As for advanced techniques and building ensembles, we'll cover those in subsequent chapters. Let your imaginations run wild!

Summary

In this chapter, we looked at using probabilistic linear models to predict a qualitative response with two generalized linear model methods: logistic regression, and multivariate adaptive regression splines. We explored using the weight of information and information value as a technique to do univariate feature selection. We covered the concept of finding the proper probability threshold to minimize classification error. Additionally, we began the process of using various performance metrics such as AUC, log-loss, and ROC charts to explore model selection visually and statistically. These metrics proved to be more informative than just pure accuracy, especially in a situation where class labels are highly imbalanced. In the next chapter, we'll cover regularization methods for feature selection, and how it can be used in training your algorithms. We'll see how we can create a dataset. We'll know about ridge regression and dive deeper in feature selection.

4
Advanced Feature Selection in Linear Models

"There is nothing permanent except change."

– Heraclitus

So far, we've examined the usage of linear models for both quantitative and qualitative outcomes with an eye on the techniques of feature selection, that is, the methods and techniques that exclude useless or unwanted predictor variables. We saw that linear models can be quite useful in machine learning problems, how piece-wise linear models can capture non-linear relationships as multivariate adaptive regression splines. Additional techniques have been developed and refined in the last couple of decades that can improve predictive ability and interpretability above and beyond the linear models that we discussed in the preceding chapters. In this day and age, many datasets, such as those in the two prior chapters, have numerous features. It isn't unreasonable to have datasets with thousands of potential features.

The methods in this chapter might prove to be a better way to approach feature reduction and selection. In this chapter, we'll look at the concept of regularization where the coefficients are constrained or shrunk towards zero. There're many methods and permutations to these methods of regularization, but we'll focus on ridge regression, **Least Absolute Shrinkage and Selection Operator** (LASSO), and, finally, elastic net, which combines the benefits of both techniques into one.

The following are the topics we'll cover in this chapter:

- Overview of regularization
- Dataset creation
- Ridge regression
- LASSO
- Elastic net

Regularization overview

You may recall that our linear model follows the form: $Y = B0 + B_1x_1 + ...B_nx_n + e$, and that the best fit tries to minimize the RSS, which is the sum of the squared errors of the actual minus the estimate, or $e_1^2 + e_2^2 + ... e_n^2$.

With regularization, we'll apply what is known as a **shrinkage penalty** in conjunction with RSS minimization. This penalty consists of a lambda (symbol λ), along with the normalization of the beta coefficients and weights. How these weights are normalized differs in terms of techniques, and we'll discuss them accordingly. Quite simply, in our model, we're minimizing *(RSS + λ (normalized coefficients))*. We'll select λ, which is known as the tuning parameter, in our model building process. Please note that if lambda is equal to 0, then our model is equivalent to OLS, as it cancels out the normalization term. As we work through this chapter, the methods can be applied to a classification problem.

So what does regularization do for us and why does it work? First of all, regularization methods are very computationally efficient. In a best subsets of features, we're searching **2^p models** and, in large datasets, it isn't feasible to attempt this. In the techniques that follow, we only fit one model to each value of lambda and, as you can imagine this, is far less computationally demanding. Another reason goes back to our bias-variance trade-off, discussed in the preface. In the linear model, where the relationship between the response and the predictors is close to linear, the least squares estimates will have low bias but may have high variance. This means that a small change in the training data can cause a significant change in the least squares coefficient estimates (James, 2013). Regularization through the proper selection of lambda and normalization may help you improve the model fit by optimizing the bias-variance trade-off. Finally, the regularization of coefficients may work to solve multicollinearity problems as we shall see.

Ridge regression

Let's begin by exploring what ridge regression is and what it can and can't do for you. With ridge regression, the normalization term is the sum of the squared weights, referred to as an **L2-norm**. Our model is trying to minimize $RSS + \lambda(sum\ Bj^2)$. As lambda increases, the coefficients shrinks toward zero but never become zero. The benefit may be an improved predictive accuracy but, as it doesn't zero out the weights for any of your features, it could lead to issues in the model's interpretation and communication. To help with this problem, we can turn to LASSO.

LASSO

LASSO applies the **L1-norm** instead of the L2-norm as in ridge regression, which is the sum of the absolute value of the feature weights and so minimizes $RSS + \lambda(sum\ |Bj|)$. This shrinkage penalty will indeed force a feature weight to zero. This is a clear advantage over ridge regression, as it may improve the model interpretability.

The mathematics behind the reason that the L1-norm allows the weights/coefficients to become zero is beyond the scope of this book (refer to Tibsharini, 1996 for further details).

If LASSO is so great, then ridge regression must be obsolete in machine learning. Not so fast! In a situation of high collinearity or high pairwise correlations, LASSO may force a predictive feature to zero, hence you can lose the predictive ability; that is, if both feature A and B should be in your model, LASSO may shrink one of their coefficients to zero. The following quote sums up this issue nicely:

"One might expect the lasso to perform better in a setting where a relatively small number of predictors have substantial coefficients, and the remaining predictors have coefficients that are very small or that equal zero. Ridge regression will perform better when the response is a function of many predictors, all with coefficients of roughly equal size."

– James, 2013

There is the possibility of achieving the best of both worlds and that leads us to the next topic, elastic net.

Elastic net

The power of elastic net is that it performs feature extraction, unlike ridge regression, and it'll group the features that LASSO fails to do. Again, LASSO will tend to select one feature from a group of correlated ones and ignore the rest. Elastic net does this by including a mixing parameter, alpha, in conjunction with lambda. Alpha will be between 0 and 1, and as before, lambda will regulate the size of the penalty. Please note that an alpha of zero is equal to ridge regression and an alpha of 1 is equivalent to LASSO. Essentially, we're blending the L1 and L2 penalties by including a second tuning parameter with a quadratic (squared) term of the beta coefficients. We'll end up with the goal of minimizing *(RSS + λ[(1-alpha) (sum | Bj|²)/2 + alpha (sum | Bj|)])/N)*.

Let's put these techniques to the test. We'll utilize a dataset I created to demonstrate the methods. In the next section, I'll discuss how I created the dataset with a few predictive features and some noise features, including those with high correlation. I recommend that, once you feel comfortable with this chapter's content, you go back and apply them to the data examined in the prior two chapters, comparing performance.

Data creation

In this section, I'll discuss how I created the dataset used for this chapter and provide insight into the features and the class labels we'll endeavor to predict. The data is available on GitHub at `https://github.com/PacktPublishing/Advanced-Machine-Learning-with-R/blob/master/Data/sim_df.csv`:

1. Let's get our libraries and data loaded:

```
> library(magrittr)

> install.packages("glmnet")

> install.packages("caret")

> install.packages("classifierplots")

> install.packages("DataExplorer")

> install.packages("InformationValue")
```

```
> install.packages("Metrics")

> install.packages("ROCR")

> install.packages("tidyverse")

> options(scipen=999)

> sim_df <- readr::read_csv('sim_df.csv')
```

The dataframe is 10,000 observations of 17 variables, consisting of 16 input features and 1 response. I created this dataset using the `twoClassSim()` function from the `caret` package. The full code with seeds is available in the online code, allowing you to make changes and create whatever data you would like to explore. A full explanation of your options in creating your own set is available in the function's help.

2. Now, let me go over the column names and tell you what this is all about:

```
> colnames(sim_df)
 [1] "TwoFactor1" "TwoFactor2" "Linear1" "Linear2" "Linear3"
"Linear4"
 [7] "Linear5" "Linear6" "Nonlinear1" "Nonlinear2" "Nonlinear3"
"Noise1"
[13] "Noise2" "Noise3" "Noise4" "Class" "random1"
```

First of all, the `TwoFactor` features are correlated with each other and slightly predictive of the response, *y*. Five of the six linear features, the three non-linear features, and the feature named `random1` might have some predictive power. The four noise features should have absolutely no predictive power unless by pure chance. Also, the `Linear5` and `Linear6` features are highly correlated. I created that relationship to help point out how the different methods will handle it.

3. The y labels are somewhat imbalanced, roughly 70/30:

```
> table(sim_df$y)

   0    1
7072 2928
```

4. The data isn't too wide to include all of it in a correlation plot:

```
> DataExplorer::plot_correlation(sim_df)
```

The output of the preceding code is as follows:

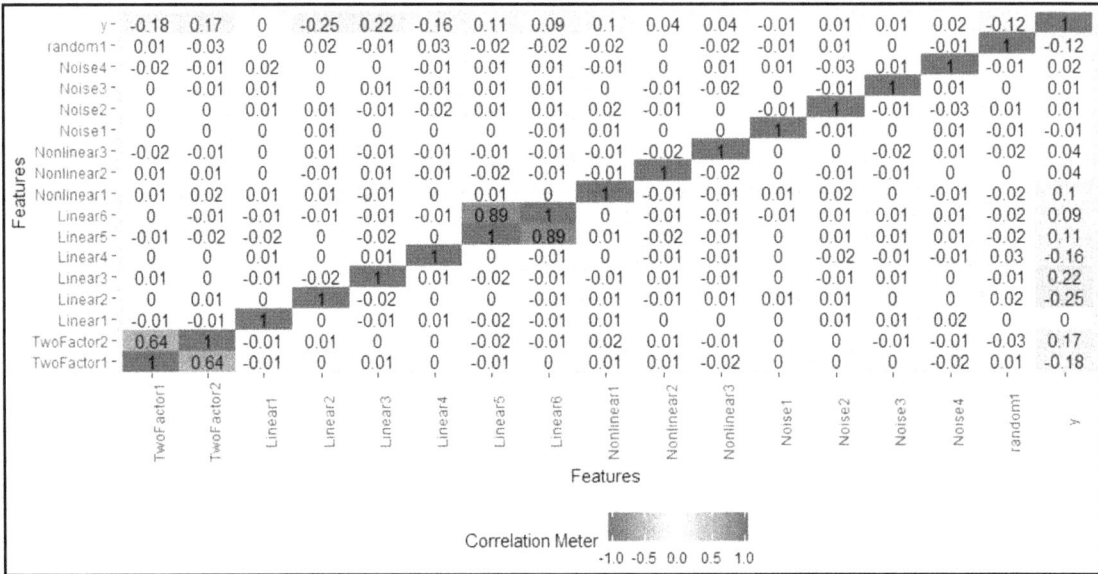

The plot confirms visually what I described previously. The highest correlation is between **Linear5** and **Linear6**. What we can do is eliminate one of the pairs of highly correlated features, which I did in `Chapter 2`, *Linear Regression*. In this instance, we'll keep both in and let the algorithms handle it.

This data is fully prepared for modeling in this chapter, so let's begin.

Modeling and evaluation

We'll begin the modeling process of developing a classification algorithm to predict *y*. We'll conduct, in sequence, ridge regression, LASSO, and elastic net models, evaluating their performance as we go using the area under the curve and log-loss.

Ridge regression

The package we're using will be `glmnet`. I like it because it has a built-in cross-validation function, standardizes the input features, and returns coefficients on their original scale, so it's quite easy to implement. If you standardize your features yourself, you can specify `standardize = FALSE` in the function. Either way, don't run features that aren't standardized as the results will be undesirable as the regularization won't be applied evenly. If you do standardize on your own, I recommend utilizing the `vtreat` package functions as we did in Chapter 2, *Linear Regression*, specifying `scale = TRUE` in the `prepare()` function. This will help us apply the centering and scaling values from your training data to the test/validation sets.

I'll let `glmnet` handle the standardizing, and we can begin with a 70/30 train/test split:

```
> set.seed(1066)

> index <- caret::createDataPartition(sim_df$y, p = 0.7, list = F)

> train <- sim_df[index, ]

> test <- sim_df[-index, ]
```

Now, `glmnet` requires that your features are input as a matrix, and if you're doing a classification problem, the response is a factor. This code handles the requirement:

```
> x <- as.matrix(train[, -17])

> y <- as.factor(train$y)
```

For the function to train the algorithm, there're a couple of things you can specify. Here, I'll execute five-fold cross-validation—the loss function for training, which in the case of classification can be `class` for misclassification errors or `auc` for the area under the curve. I'll go with `auc`, and leave it up to you to assess. Since this is ridge regression, our alpha will be equal to 0.

Accordingly, we'll set the `family` argument to `binomial`. This makes the function run a logistic regression instead of its standard linear regression. The following is the code to train the ridge regression algorithm:

```
> set.seed(1999)

> ridge <- glmnet::cv.glmnet(
    x,
    y,
    nfolds = 5,
    type.measure = "auc",
    alpha = 0,
    family = "binomial"
  )
```

To begin, `glmnet` offers a number of different plots. The default plot shows the relationship of the log of the lambda values searched and its relation to the loss function, in our case `auc`:

```
> plot(ridge)
```

The output of the preceding code is as follows:

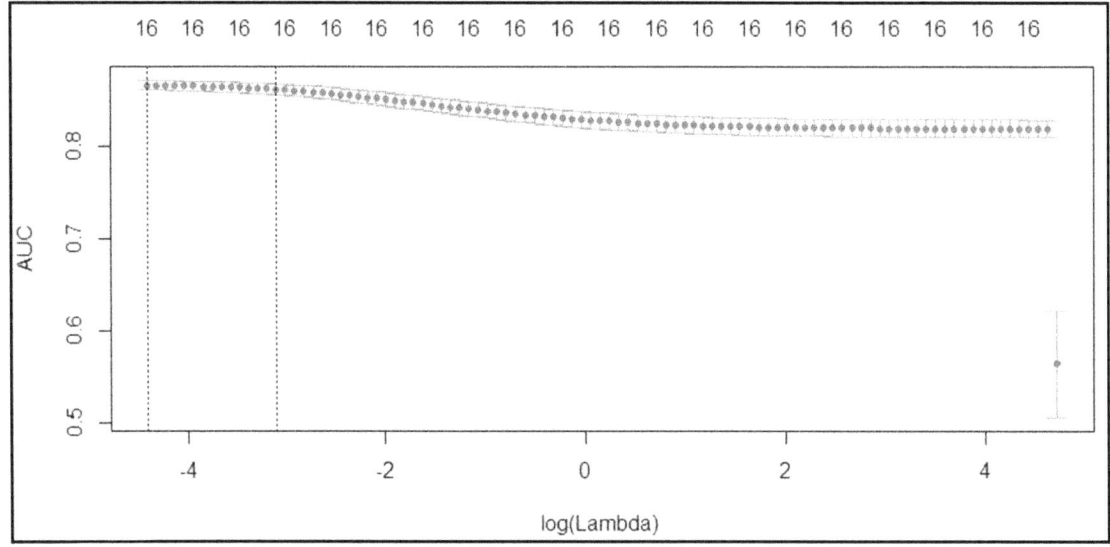

We see **log(Lambda)** on the *x* axis and **AUC** on the *y* axis. At the top of the plot is a series of the value 16. This tracks the number of non-zero coefficients corresponding to **log(Lamda)**. We'll see how that changes with LASSO. The two dotted vertical lines show the **log(Lambda)** value with the maximum **AUC** and the **log(Lamda)** value with the maximum **AUC** within one standard error of the maximum, for the left and right lines respectively.

Let's review what those actual lambda values are:

```
> ridge$lambda.min
[1] 0.01216653

> ridge$lambda.1se
[1] 0.04475312
```

Recall that, if lambda were equal to zero, there would be no regularization penalty at all.

To see the coefficients, run this code:

```
> coef(ridge, s = "lambda.1se")
17 x 1 sparse Matrix of class "dgCMatrix"
                         1
(Intercept)  0.535798579
TwoFactor1  -0.541881256
TwoFactor2   0.530637287
Linear1     -0.005472570
Linear2     -0.506143897
Linear3      0.454702486
Linear4     -0.316847306
Linear5      0.182733133
Linear6      0.070036471
Nonlinear1   0.354214422
Nonlinear2   0.238778841
Nonlinear3   0.322499067
Noise1      -0.028226796
Noise2       0.002973271
Noise3       0.014767631
Noise4       0.038038078
random1     -0.237527142
```

To convert the logistic regression coefficients, called **logits**, into a probability, do the following:

1. Calculate the odds by exponentiation, for example, `exp(coef)`
2. Calculate the probability with the formula, *probability = odds / 1+ odds*

Notice that the `noise` features and `Linear1`, which are irrelevant to making a prediction, are close, but not equal to, zero. The algorithm puts a larger coefficient on `Linear5` versus `Linear6`. By the way, those features are on the same scale, so a direct comparison is possible. To predict the probabilities with a `glmnet` model, be sure to specify `type = "response"` and which lambda value to use. I recommend starting with using the `lambda.1se` value to prevent overfitting. But you can experiment accordingly:

```
> ridge_pred <-
    data.frame(predict(ridge, newx = x, type = "response", s =
"lambda.1se"))
```

Like in the previous chapter on logistic regression, a plot of the probability distributions by class is in order:

```
> classifierplots::density_plot(y, ridge_pred$X1)
```

The output of the preceding code is as follows:

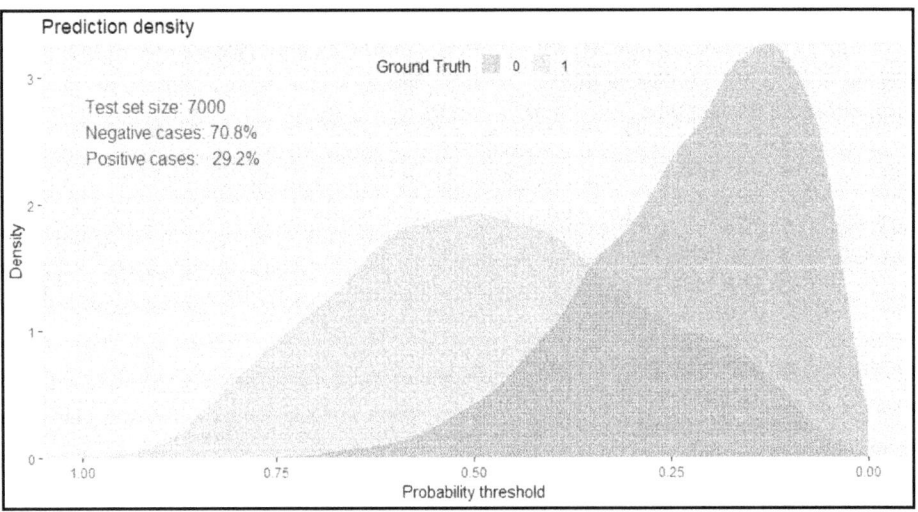

There seems to be an excellent separation in the probabilities above 50%.

Let's see the AUC:

```
> Metrics::auc(y, ridge_pred$X1)
[1] 0.8632982
```

The AUC is above `0.86`. This brings us to the question of whether or not this will remain consistent on the test data:

```
> ridge_test <-
    data.frame(predict(ridge, newx = as.matrix(test[, -17]),
    type = 'response'), s = "lambda.1se")

> Metrics::auc(test$y, ridge_test$X1)
[1] 0.8706708

> Metrics::logLoss(test$y, ridge_test$X1)
[1] 0.4307592

> classifierplots::density_plot(test$y, ridge_test$X1)
```

The output of the preceding code is as follows:

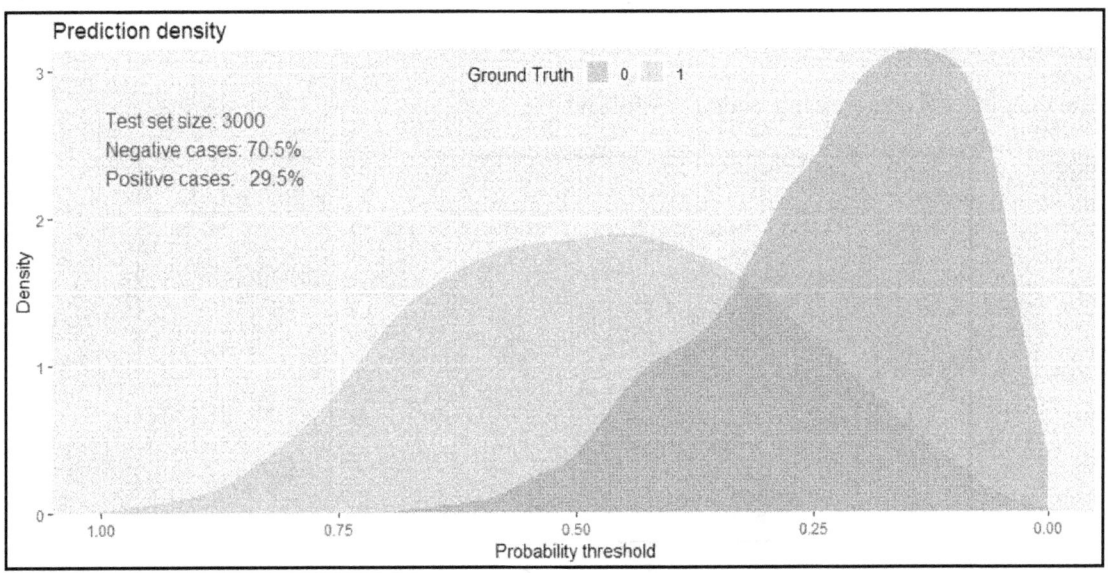

There's very consistent performance between the train and test data. The AUC is now above 0.87, and we have a benchmark log-loss of 0.4307592. You can try different k-folds, a different loss function, and even different random seeds to see how the model changes. For now, we need to move on to the next algorithm, LASSO.

LASSO

It's a simple matter to update the code we used for ridge regression to accommodate LASSO. I'm going to change just two things: the random `seed` and I'll set `alpha` to 1:

```
> set.seed(1876)

> lasso <- glmnet::cv.glmnet(
    x,
    y,
    nfolds = 5,
    type.measure = "auc",
    alpha = 1,
    family = "binomial"
  )
```

The plot of the model is quite interesting:

```
> plot(lasso)
```

The output of the preceding code is as follows:

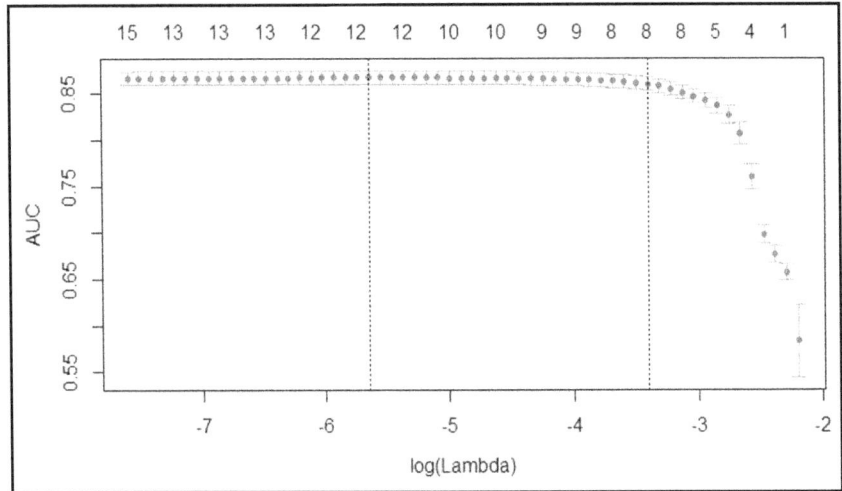

You can now see the number of non-zero features as the Lambda changes. The number of features included at one standard error is just eight!

Let's have a gander at those coefficients:

```
> coef(lasso, s = "lambda.1se")
17 x 1 sparse Matrix of class "dgCMatrix"
                           1
(Intercept) -0.30046007
TwoFactor1  -0.53307368
TwoFactor2   0.52110703
Linear1          .
Linear2     -0.42669146
Linear3      0.35514853
Linear4     -0.20726177
Linear5      0.10381320
Linear6          .
Nonlinear1   0.10478862
Nonlinear2       .
Nonlinear3       .
Noise1           .
Noise2           .
Noise3           .
Noise4           .
random1     -0.06581589
```

Now, this looks much better. LASSO threw out those nonsense noise features and `Linear1`. However, before we start congratulating ourselves, look at how `Linear6` was constrained to zero. Does it need to be in the model or not? We could undoubtedly adjust the lambda value and see where it enters and what effect it makes.

It's time to check how it does on the training data:

```
> lasso_pred <-
    data.frame(predict(
    lasso,
    newx = x,
    type = "response",
    s = "lambda.1se"
  ))

> Metrics::auc(y, lasso_pred$X1)
[1] 0.8621664

> classifierplots::density_plot(y, lasso_pred$X1)
```

The output of the preceding code is as follows:

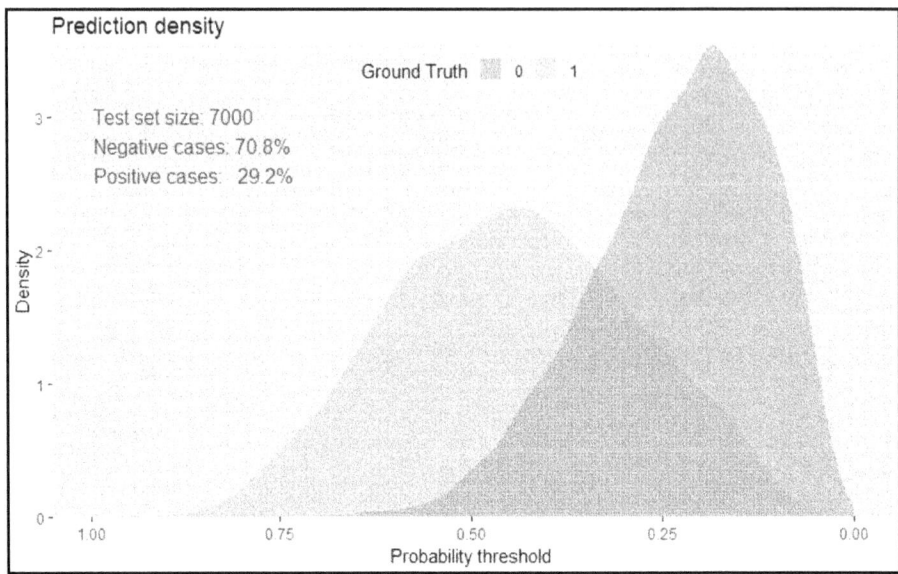

These are quite similar results to those with ridge regression. Correct evaluation, however, is done on the test data:

```
> lasso_test <-
    data.frame(predict(lasso, newx = as.matrix(test[, -17]), type =
'response'),
    s = "lambda.1se")

> Metrics::auc(test$y, lasso_test$X1)
[1] 0.8684276

> Metrics::logLoss(test$y, lasso_test$X1)
[1] 0.4512764

> classifierplots::density_plot(test$y, lasso_test$X1)
```

The output of the preceding code is as follows:

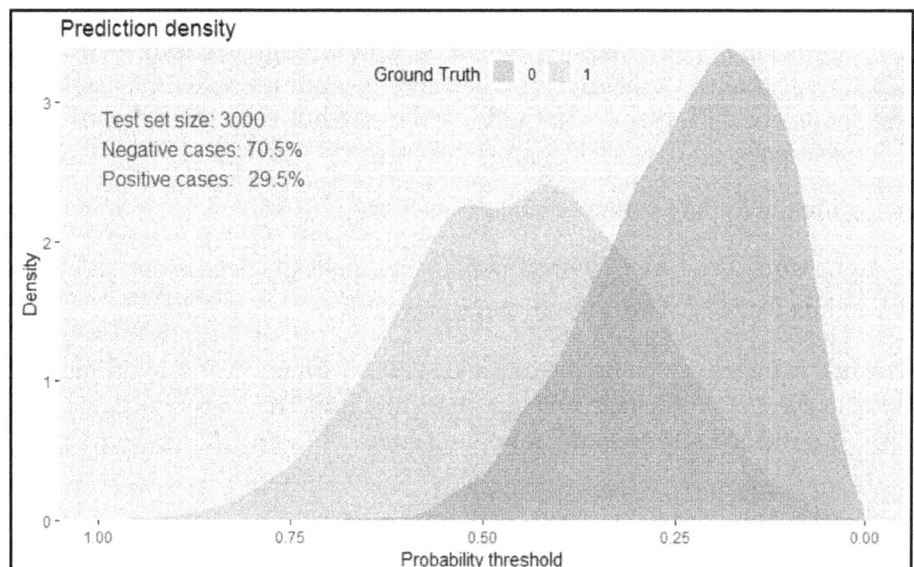

The LASSO model does have a slightly lower AUC and marginally higher log-loss (0.45 versus 0.43). In the real world, I'm not sure that would be meaningful given that we have a more parsimonious model with LASSO. I guess that's another dimension alongside bias-variance, *predictive power versus complexity*.

Speaking of complexity, let's move on to elastic net.

Elastic net

For our purposes here, we want to focus on finding the optimal mix of lambda and our elastic net mixing parameter, `alpha`. This is done using the following simple three-step process:

1. Use the `expand.grid()` function in base R to create a vector of all of the possible combinations of `alpha` and `lambda` that we want to investigate.
2. Use the `trainControl()` function from the `caret` package to determine the resampling method; we'll use 5-fold cross-validation again.
3. Train a model to select our `alpha` and `lambda` parameters using `glmnet()` in caret's `train()` function.

Once we've selected our parameters, we'll apply them to the `test` data in the same way as we did with ridge regression and LASSO.

 Our grid of combinations should be large enough to capture the best model but not so large that it becomes computationally unfeasible. That won't be a problem with this big a dataset, but keep this in mind for future reference.

The following are the hyperparameters values we'll try:

- Alpha from `0` to `1` by `0.2` increments; remember that this is bound by `0` and `1`
- Lambda from `0.01` to `0.03` in steps of `0.002`

You can create this matrix by using the `expand.grid()` function and building a sequence of numbers that the `caret` package will automatically use. The `caret` package will take the values for `alpha` and `lambda` with the following code:

```
> grid <-
    expand.grid(.alpha = seq(0, 1, by = .2),
    .lambda = seq(0.01, 0.03, by = 0.002))

> head(grid)
  .alpha .lambda
1   0.0    0.01
2   0.2    0.01
3   0.4    0.01
4   0.6    0.01
5   0.8    0.01
6   1.0    0.01
```

There are 66 different models to be built, compared, and selected. The preceding list shows the various combinations with all of the possible alpha parameters for a lambda of 0.01. Now, we set up an object to specify we want to do 5-fold cross-validation:

```
> control <- caret::trainControl(method = 'cv', number = 5)
```

Training the model with `caret` in this instance requires *y* to be a factor, which we've already done. It also requires the specification of train control or passing an object as we just did. There're a couple of different selection metrics you can choose from for a classification problem: accuracy or Kappa. Well, we covered this in the previous chapter, in a class imbalance situation; I think Kappa is preferred. Refer to the previous chapter if you need to refresh your understanding of Kappa. The following is the relevant code:

```
> set.seed(2222)
> enet <- caret::train(x,
                    y,
                    method = "glmnet",
                    trControl = control,
                    tuneGrid = grid,
                    metric = "Kappa")
```

To find the best overall model according to Kappa, we call the best-tuned version:

```
> enet$bestTune
    alpha lambda
23    0.4   0.01
```

The best model is alpha `0.4` and lambda `0.01`. To see how it affects the coefficients (logits), we will run them through `glmnet` without cross-validation:

```
> best_enet <- glmnet::glmnet(x,
      y,
      alpha = 0.4,
      lambda = 0.01,
      family = "binomial")

> coef(best_enet)
17 x 1 sparse Matrix of class "dgCMatrix"
                      s0
(Intercept)   1.310419410
TwoFactor1   -0.933300729
TwoFactor2    0.917877320
Linear1           .
Linear2      -0.689547039
Linear3       0.619432149
Linear4      -0.416603510
Linear5       0.315207408
Linear6       0.002005802
Nonlinear1    0.454620511
Nonlinear2    0.224564104
Nonlinear3    0.343687158
Noise1       -0.009290811
Noise2            .
```

```
Noise3          .
Noise4          0.014674805
random1        -0.261039240
```

With alpha at 0.4, three features are forced to zero. Examining the metrics on training data comes next:

```
> enet_pred <- predict(enet, train, type = "prob")

> Metrics::auc(y, enet_pred$`1`)
[1] 0.8684076

> classifierplots::density_plot(y, enet_pred$`1`)
```

The output of the preceding code is as follows:

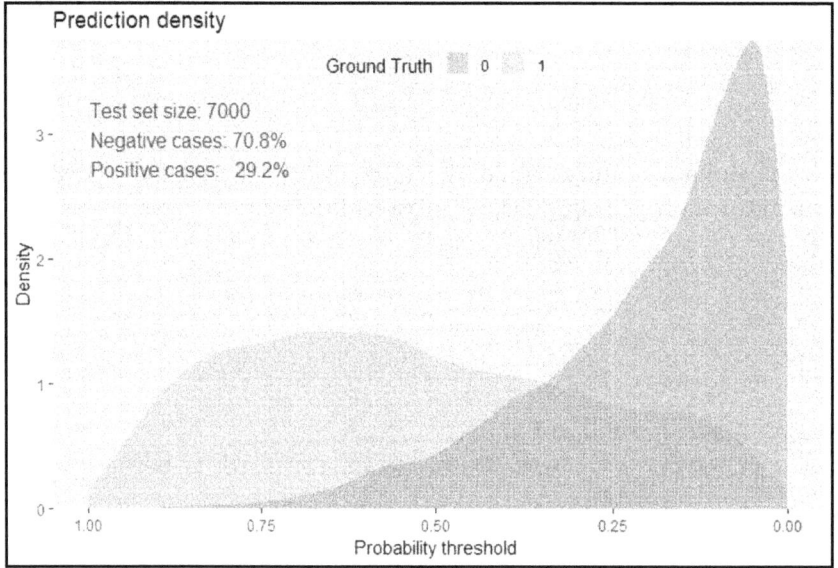

The probability skew for labels of 1 seems higher than the previous models as well as for labels of 0. The AUC is in line with the other models as well. The proof will lie in predicting the test data:

```
> enet_test <-
    predict(enet, test, type = "prob")

> Metrics::auc(test$y, enet_test$`1`)
[1] 0.8748963

> Metrics::logLoss(test$y, enet_test$`1`)
```

```
[1] 0.3977438

> classifierplots::density_plot(test$y, enet_test$`1`)
```

The output of the preceding code is as follows:

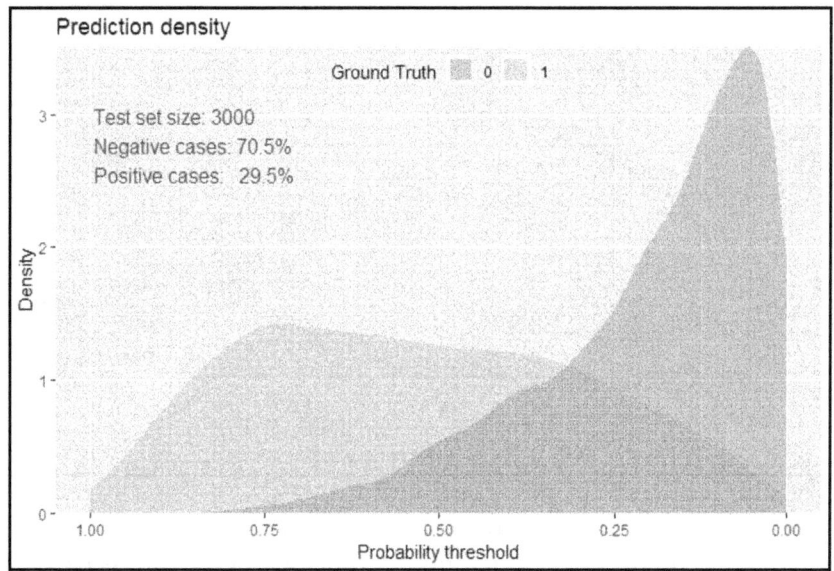

There's a consistent skew in the distributions and a superior AUC and log-loss versus the other two models, so it seems our elastic net version is the *best*. We can confirm this by looking at the ROC plots of all three models, using a similar technique to evaluate the classifiers visually, as in the previous chapter:

```
pred.ridge <- ROCR::prediction(ridge_test$X1, test$y)

perf.ridge <- ROCR::performance(pred.ridge, "tpr", "fpr")

ROCR::plot(perf.ridge, main = "ROC", col = 1)

pred.lasso <- ROCR::prediction(lasso_test$X1, test$y)

perf.lasso <- ROCR::performance(pred.lasso, "tpr", "fpr")

ROCR::plot(perf.lasso, col = 2, add = TRUE)

pred.enet <- ROCR::prediction(enet_test$'1', test$y)

perf.enet <- ROCR::performance(pred.enet, "tpr", "fpr")
```

```
ROCR::plot(perf.enet, col = 3, add = TRUE)

legend(0.6, 0.6, c("Ridge", "LASSO", "ENET"), 1:3)
```

The output of the preceding code is as follows:

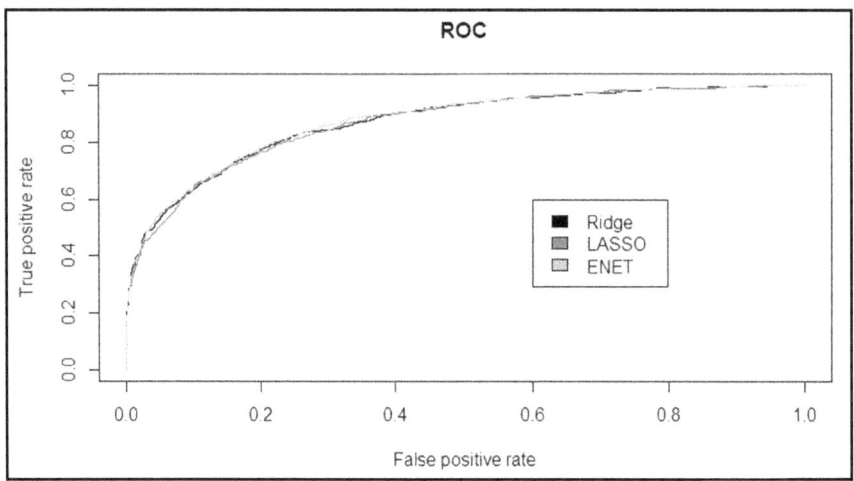

I think, as we would expect, the elastic net is just ever so slightly better than the other two. Which model goes into production is a matter for you and your business partners to decide as you balance complexity and performance.

Summary

In this chapter, the goal was to use a simulated dataset to provide an introduction to learning how to apply advanced feature selection for linear and generalized linear models. We used the `glmnet` package to predict class probabilities for a binary classification problem using logistic regression. These methods can be adapted to linear regression and multinomial classifications. An introduction to regularization and the three techniques that incorporate it was provided and utilized to build and compare models. Regularization is a powerful technique to improve computational efficiency and to possibly extract more meaningful features when compared to the other modeling techniques. We saw how to use various performance metrics to compare and select the most appropriate model.

Up to this point, we've been purely talking about linear and generalized linear models. In the next couple of chapters, we'll begin to use more complex nonlinear models for both classification and regression problems we'll encounter in further chapters.

5

K-Nearest Neighbors and Support Vector Machines

"Statistical thinking will one day be as necessary for efficient citizenship as the ability to read and write."

–H.G. Wells

In Chapter 3, *Logistic Regression*, we discussed using generalized linear models to determine the probability that a predicted observation belongs to a categorical response what we refer to as a classification problem. That was just the beginning of classification methods, with many techniques that we can use to try and improve our predictions.

In this chapter, we'll delve into two nonlinear techniques: **K-Nearest Neighbors** (**KNN**) and **Support Vector Machines** (**SVMs**). These techniques are more sophisticated than those we discussed earlier because the assumptions on linearity can be relaxed, which means a linear combination of the features to define the decision boundary isn't needed. Be forewarned, though, that this doesn't always equal superior predictive ability. Additionally, these models can be a bit problematic to interpret for business partners, and they can be computationally inefficient. When used wisely, they provide a powerful complement to the other tools and techniques discussed in this book. They can be used for continuous outcomes in addition to classification problems; however, for this chapter, we'll focus only on the latter.

After a high-level background on the techniques, we'll put both of them to the test, starting with KNN.

Following are the topics that we'll be covering in this chapter:

- K-nearest neighbors
- Support vector machines
- Manipulating data
- Modeling and evaluation

K-nearest neighbors

In our previous efforts, we built models that had coefficients or, to put it in another way, parameter estimates for each of our included features. With KNN, we have no parameters as the learning method is so-called instance-based learning. In short, *labeled examples (inputs and corresponding output labels) are stored, and no action is taken until a new input pattern demands an output value* (Battiti and Brunato, 2014, p. 11). This method is commonly called **lazy learning**, as no specific model parameters are produced. The `train` instances themselves represent the knowledge. For the prediction of any new instance (a new data point), the `training` data is searched for an instance that most resembles the new instance in question. KNN does this for a classification problem by looking at the closest points—the nearest neighbors—to determine the proper class. The *k* comes into play by deciding how many neighbors should be examined by the algorithm, so if *k=5*, it will consider the five nearest points. A weakness of this method is that all five points are given equal weight in the algorithm even if they're less relevant in learning. We'll look at methods using R and try to alleviate this issue.

The best way to understand how this works is with a simple visual example of a binary classification learning problem. In the following screenshot, we have a plot showing whether a tumor is **benign** or **malignant** based on two predictive features. The **X** in the plot indicates a new observation that we would like to predict. If our algorithm considers **K=3**, the circle encompasses the three observations that are nearest to the one that we want to score. As the most commonly occurring classifications are **malignant**, the **X** data point is classified as **malignant**, as shown in the following screenshot:

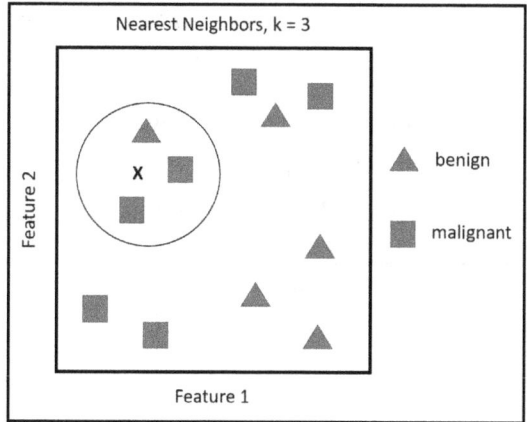

Even from this simple example, it's clear that the selection of *k* for the nearest neighbors is critical. If *k* is too small, you may have a high variance on the `test` set observations even though you have a low bias. On the other hand, as *k* grows, you may decrease your variance, but the bias may be unacceptable. Cross-validation is necessary to determine the proper *k*.

It's also important to point out the calculation of the distance or the nearness of the data points in our feature space. The default distance is **Euclidean distance**. This is merely the straight-line distance from point A to point B—as the crow flies—or you can utilize the formula that states it's equivalent to the square root of the sum of the squared differences between the corresponding points. The formula for Euclidean distance, given point A and B with coordinates p1, p2, ... pn and q1, q2, ... qn respectively, would be as follows:

$$\text{Euclidean Distance (A, B)} = \sqrt{\sum_{i=1}^{n}(pi - qi)^2}$$

This distance is highly dependent on the scale that the features were measured on, so it's critical to standardize them. Other distance calculations as well as weights can be used, depending on the distance. We'll explore this in the upcoming example.

Support vector machines

The first time I heard of support vector machines, I have to admit that I was scratching my head, thinking that this was some form of academic obfuscation or inside joke. However, my fair review of SVM has replaced this natural skepticism with a healthy respect for the technique.

SVMs have been shown to perform well in a variety of settings and are often considered one of the best out-of-the-box classifiers (James, G., 2013). To get a practical grasp of the subject, let's look at another simple visual example. In the following screenshot, you'll see that the classification task is linearly separable. However, the dotted line and solid line are just two among an infinite number of possible linear solutions.

You would have separating hyperplanes in a problem that has more than two dimensions:

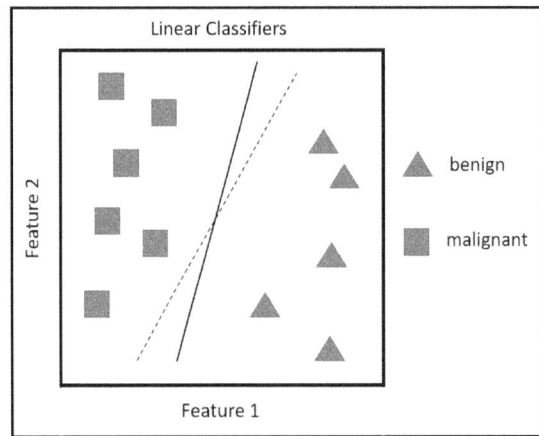

So many solutions can be problematic for generalization because, whatever solution you choose, any new observation to the right of the line will be classified as **benign**, and to the left of the line, it'll be classified as **malignant**. Therefore, either line has no bias on the train data but may have a widely divergent error on any data to test. This is where the support vectors come into play. The probability that a point falls on the wrong side of the linear separator is higher for the dotted line than the solid line, which means that the solid line has a higher margin of safety for classification. Therefore, as Battiti and Brunato say, *SVMs are linear separators with the largest possible margin and the support vectors the ones touching the safety margin region on both sides.*

The following screenshot illustrates this idea. The thin solid line is the optimal linear separator to create the aforementioned largest possible margin, hence increasing the probability that a new observation will fall on the correct side of the separator. The thicker black lines correspond to the safety margin, and the shaded data points constitute the support vectors. If the support vectors were to move, then the margin and, subsequently, the decision boundary would change. The distance between the separators is known as the **margin**:

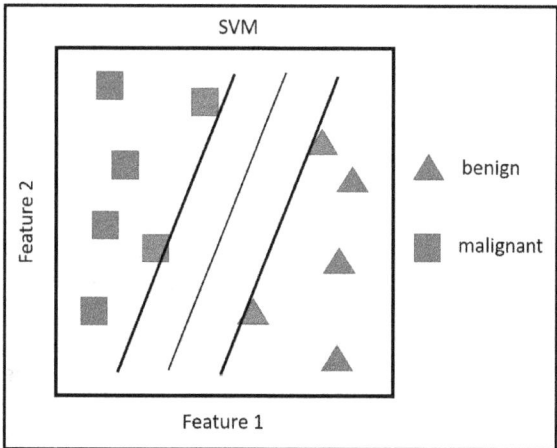

This is all fine and dandy, but real-world problems aren't so clear-cut.

In data that isn't linearly separable, many observations will fall on the wrong side of the margin (these are so-called slack variables), which is a misclassification. The key to building an SVM algorithm is to solve for the optimal number of support vectors via cross-validation. Any observation that lies directly on the wrong side of the margin for its class is known as a **support vector**.

If the tuning parameter for the number of errors is too large, which means that you have many support vectors, you'll suffer from a high bias and low variance. On the other hand, if the tuning parameter is too small, the opposite might occur. According to James et al., who refer to the tuning parameter as C, as C decreases, the tolerance for observations being on the wrong side of the margin decreases and the margin narrows. This C, or rather, the cost function, allows for observations to be on the wrong side of the margin. If C were set to zero, then we would prohibit a solution where any observation violates the margin. This is a hyperparameter you can tune to optimize bias/variance.

Another essential aspect of SVM is the ability to model nonlinearity with quadratic or higher order polynomials of the input features. In SVMs, this is known as the **kernel trick**. These can be estimated and selected with cross-validation. In the example, we'll look at the alternatives.

As with any model, you can expand the number of features using polynomials to various degrees, interaction terms, or other derivations. In large datasets, the possibilities can quickly get out of control. The kernel trick with SVMs allows us to efficiently expand the feature space, with the goal that you achieve an approximate linear separation.

To check out how this is done, let's first look at the SVM optimization problem and its constraints. We're trying to achieve the following:

- Creating weights that maximize the margin
- Subject to the constraints, no (or as few as possible) data points should lie within that margin

Now, unlike linear regression, where each observation is multiplied by a weight, in SVM, the weights are applied to the inner products of just the support vector observations.

What does this mean? Well, an inner product for two vectors is just the sum of the paired observations' product. For example, if vector one is 3, 4, and 2 and vector two is 1, 2, and 3, then you end up with *(3x1) + (4x2) + (2x3)* or *17*. With SVMs, if we take a possibility that an inner product of each observation has an inner product of every other observation, this amounts to the formula that there would be *n(n-1)/2* combinations, where *n* is the number of observations. With just *10* observations, we end up with *45* inner products. However, SVM only concerns itself with the support vectors' observations and their corresponding weights. For a linear SVM classifier, the formula is as follows:

$$f(x) = \beta o + \sum_{i=1}^{n} a(x, xi)$$

Here, (x, xi) are the inner products of the support vectors, as α is non-zero only when an observation is a support vector.

This leads to far fewer terms in the classification algorithm and allows the use of the `kernel` function, commonly referred to as the kernel trick.

The trick in this is that the `kernel` function mathematically summarizes the transformation of the features in higher dimensions instead of creating them explicitly. In a simplistic sense, a kernel function computes a dot product between two vectors. This has the benefit of creating the higher dimensional, nonlinear space, and decision boundary while keeping the optimization problem computationally efficient. The `kernel` functions compute the inner product in a higher dimensional space without transforming them into the higher dimensional space.

The notation for popular kernels is expressed as the inner (dot) product of the features, with x_i and x_j representing vectors, gamma, and c parameters, as follows:

- linear, no transformation, $K(x_i, x_j) = x_i \bullet x_j$

- polynomial, where d = degree of polynomial, $K(x_i, x_j) = (\gamma x_i \bullet x_j + c)^d$

- radial basis function, $K(x_i, x_j) = e(-\gamma |x_i - x_j|^2)$

- sigmoid function, $K(x_i, x_j) = \tanh(\gamma x_i \bullet x_j + c)$

As for the selection of the nonlinear techniques, they require some trial and error, but we'll walk through the various selection techniques.

Manipulating data

In the upcoming case study, we'll apply KNN and SVM to the same dataset. This will allow us to compare R code and learning methods on the same problem, starting with KNN. We'll also spend time drilling down into new ways of comparing different classifiers on the same data.

Dataset creation

The data we use in this chapter can be downloaded from any source on the internet or from GitHub at this link: `https://github.com/PacktPublishing/Advanced-Machine-Learning-with-R/tree/master/Chapter05`.

I found this data on a website dedicated to providing datasets for support vector machine analysis. You can follow the following link to find numerous sets to test your learning methods: `https://www.csie.ntu.edu.tw/~cjlin/libsvmtools/datasets/`.

The authors have asked to cite their work, which I will abide by:

Chih-Chung Chang and Chih-Jen Lin, LIBSVM: a library for support vector machines. ACM Transactions on Intelligent Systems and Technology, 2:27:1--27:27, 2011

The data we're using is named a5a, consisting of the training data with 6414 observations. This is a sufficient size dataset for the interest of facilitating learning, and not causing computational speed issues. Also, when doing KNN or SVM, you need to center/scale or normalize your data to 0/1 if the input features are of different scales. Well, this data's input features are of just two levels, 0 or 1, so we can forgo any normalization efforts.

I'll show you how to load this data into R, and you can replicate that process on any data you desire to use.

While we're at it, we may as well load all of the packages needed for this chapter:

```
> library(magrittr)

> install.packages("ggthemes")

> install.packages("caret")

> install.packages("classifierplots")

> install.packages("DataExplorer")

> install.packages("e1071")

> install.packages("InformationValue")

> install.packages("kknn")

> install.packages("Matrix")

> install.packages("Metrics")

> install.packages("plm")

> install.packages("ROCR")

> install.packages("tidyverse")

> options(scipen=999)
```

It's a simple matter to access this data using R's `download.file()` function. You need to provide the link and give the file a name:

```
>
download.file('https://www.csie.ntu.edu.tw/~cjlin/libsvmtools/datasets/bina
ry/
    a5a', 'chap5')
```

What's rather interesting now is that you can put this downloaded file into a usable format with a function created explicitly for this data from the `e1071` library:

```
> df <- e1071::read.matrix.csr("chap5")
```

The `df` object is now an extensive list of input features, and the response labels structured as a factor with two levels (-1 and +1). This list is what is saved on GitHub in an R data file like this:

```
> saveRDS(df, file = "chapter05")
```

Let's look at how to turn this list into something usable, assuming we need to start by loading it into your environment:

```
> df <- readRDS("chapter05")
```

We'll create the classification labels in an object called `y`, and turn -1 into 0, and +1 into 1:

```
> y <- df$y

> y <- ifelse(y == "+1", 1, 0)

> table(y)
y
   0    1
4845 1569
```

The table shows us that just under 25% of the labels are considered an `event`. What event? It doesn't matter for our purposes, so we can move on and produce a dataframe of the predictors called *x*. I tried a number of ways to put the sparse matrix into a dataframe, and it seems that the following code is the easiest, using a function from the `Matrix` package:

```
> x <- Matrix::as.matrix(df$x)

> x <- as.data.frame(x)

> dim(x)
[1] 6414 122
```

We now have our dataframe of 6,414 observations and 122 input features. Next, we'll create train/test sets and explore the features.

Data preparation

What we should do now is create our training and test data using a 70/30 split. Then, we should subject it to the standard feature exploration we started discussing in Chapter 1, *Preparing and Understanding Data*, with these tasks in mind:

- Eliminate low variance features
- Identify and remove linear dependencies
- Explore highly correlated features

The first thing then is for us to turn the numeric outcome into a factor to be used for creating a stratified data index, like so:

```
> y_factor <- as.factor(y)

> set.seed(1492)

> index <- caret::createDataPartition(y_factor, p = 0.7, list = F)
```

Using the index, we create train/test input features and labels:

```
> train <- x[index, ]

> train_y <- y_factor[index]

> test <- x[-index, ]

> test_y <- y_factor[-index]
```

With our training data in hand, let's find and eliminate the low variance features, which I can state in advance are quite a few:

```
> train_NZV <- caret::nearZeroVar(train, saveMetrics = TRUE)

> table(train_NZV$nzv)

FALSE  TRUE
   48    74

> table(train_NZV$zeroVar)

FALSE  TRUE
  121     1
```

We see that 74 features are low variance, and one of those is zero variance. Let's rid ourselves of these pesky features:

```
> train_r <- train[train_NZV$nzv == FALSE]
```

Given our new dataframe of reduced features, we now identify and eliminate linear dependency combinations:

```
> linear_combos <- caret::findLinearCombos(x = train_r)

> linear_combos
$`linearCombos`
$`linearCombos`[[1]]
 [1] 13 1 2 3 4 5 9 10 11 12

$`linearCombos`[[2]]
[1] 19 16

$`linearCombos`[[3]]
[1] 20 15

$`linearCombos`[[4]]
 [1] 22 1 2 3 4 5 15 16 18 21

$`linearCombos`[[5]]
[1] 40 1 2 3 4 5 39

$`linearCombos`[[6]]
[1] 42 1 2 3 4 5 41

$`linearCombos`[[7]]
 [1] 47 1 2 3 4 5 43 44 45 46

$remove
[1] 13 19 20 22 40 42 47
```

The output provides a list of 7 linear dependencies and recommends the removal of 7 features. The number in $remove corresponds to the column index number in the dataframe. For example, in combination number 2, the indices would be indicative of the column names, V36 and V22. Here's a table of these two features for demonstration purposes:

```
> table(train_r$V36, train_r$V22)
       0    1
  0 3032    0
  1    0 1459
```

It's clear these two features are measuring the same thing. We'll remove those recommended, but there's one more thing to discuss. When doing cross-validation during the modeling process, you may run into warnings that linear dependencies exist even though you ran this methodology. I found that to be the case with this dataset in the modeling exercises that follow. After some exploration of features V1 through V5, I found that, by dropping V5, this was no longer a problem. Let's proceed with that in mind:

```
> train_r <- train_r[, -linear_combos$remove]

> train_r <- train_r[, -5]

> plm::detect_lin_dep(train_r)
[1] "No linear dependent column(s) detected."
```

Here we can check if there're any correlations over 0.7, and remove a feature if it's highly correlated with another:

```
> high_corr <- caret::findCorrelation(my_data_cor, cutoff = 0.7)

> high_corr
[1] 29

> train_df <- train_r[, -high_corr]
```

The code found and removed the feature with a column index of 30 and 34. We now have a dataframe ready for modeling. If you want to look at a correlation heatmap, then run this handy function from the DataExplorer package:

```
> DataExplorer::plot_correlation(train_df)
```

The output of the preceding code is as follows:

Notice that features **V67** and **V71** are highly correlated. In a real-world setting, this would probably warrant further investigation, but we'll feed both into our learning algorithms, as no subject matter expert can tell us otherwise.

We can now proceed with our model training, starting with KNN, then SVM, and comparing their performance.

Modeling and evaluation

Now we'll discuss various aspects of modeling and assessment. In both the KNN and SVM cases, we'll do feature selection using a technique known as **Recursive Feature Elimination (RFE)** in conjunction with cross-validation. As with all feature reduction and selection, this will help to prevent overfitting the model.

KNN modeling

As stated previously, we'll begin with feature selection. The `caret` package helps out in this matter. In RFE, a model is built using all features, and a feature importance value is assigned. Then the features are recursively pruned and an optimal number of features selected based on a performance metric such as accuracy. In short, it's a type of backward feature elimination.

To do this, we'll need to set the random seed, specify the cross-validation method in caret's `rfeControl()` function, perform a recursive feature selection with the `rfe()` function, and then test how the model performs on the `test` set. In `rfeControl()`, you'll need to specify the function based on the model being used. There are several different functions that you can use. Here we'll need `lrFuncs`. To see a list of the available functions, your best bet is to explore the documentation with `?rfeControl` and `?caretFuncs`. The metric we'll use is **Cohen's Kappa statistic**, which we used and explained in a prior chapter.

To recap, the `Kappa` statistic is commonly used to provide a measure of how well two evaluators can classify an observation correctly. It gives an insight into this problem by adjusting the accuracy scores, which is done by accounting for the evaluators being entirely correct by mere chance. The formula for the statistic is: *Kappa = (percent of agreement - percent of chance agreement) / (1 - percent of chance agreement)*.

The *percent of agreement* is the rate that the evaluators agreed on for the class (accuracy), and *percent of chance agreement* is the rate that the evaluators randomly agreed on. The higher the statistic, the better they performed, with the maximum agreement being one.

Altman (1991) provides a heuristic to assist us in the interpretation of the statistic, which is shown in the following table:

Value of *K*	Strength of Agreement
<0.20	Poor
0.21-0.40	Fair
0.41-0.60	Moderate
0.61-0.80	Good
0.81-1.00	Very good

The following code gets our control function established:

```
> ctrl <- caret::rfeControl(
    functions = caret::lrFuncs,
    method = "cv",
    number = 10,
    verbose = TRUE
  )
```

I now specify the number of feature subsets for consideration between 25 and 35. After setting the random seed, we can run the RFE using a KNN algorithm. With `verbose = TRUE`, the status of training is displayed in the console. Of course, setting that to `FALSE` will hide it:

```
> subsets <- c(25:35)

> set.seed(1863)

> knnProfile <- caret::rfe(
    train_df,
    train_y,
    sizes = subsets,
    rfeControl = ctrl,
    method = "knn",
    metric = "Kappa"
  )
```

Calling the `knnProfile` object tells us what we need to know:

```
> knnProfile #33

Recursive feature selection
Outer resampling method: Cross-Validated (10 fold)
Resampling performance over subset size:

 Variables Accuracy  Kappa AccuracySD KappaSD Selected
```

```
25    0.8377 0.5265      0.01524 0.05107
26    0.8383 0.5276      0.01594 0.05359  *
27    0.8377 0.5271      0.01616 0.05462
28    0.8375 0.5257      0.01612 0.05416
29    0.8370 0.5247      0.01668 0.05503
30    0.8370 0.5241      0.01654 0.05464
31    0.8381 0.5272      0.01649 0.05465
32    0.8368 0.5233      0.01727 0.05623
33    0.8361 0.5212      0.01623 0.05393
34    0.8366 0.5231      0.01676 0.05525
35    0.8361 0.5218      0.01644 0.05487
39    0.8361 0.5217      0.01705 0.05660

The top 5 variables (out of 26):
   V74, V35, V22, V78, V20
```

The results state that 26 features provide the highest Kappa statistic of 0.5276 (moderate strength), and it offers the highest accuracy rate of 83.83%. The output also gives us the top 5 features based on importance score. If you want, you can plot the results by putting it into a dataframe and passing it to ggplot:

```
> knn_results <- knnProfile$results

> ggplot2::ggplot(knn_results, aes(Variables, Kappa)) +
    ggplot2::geom_line(color = 'darkred', size = 2) +
    ggthemes::theme_economist()
```

The output of the preceding code is as follows:

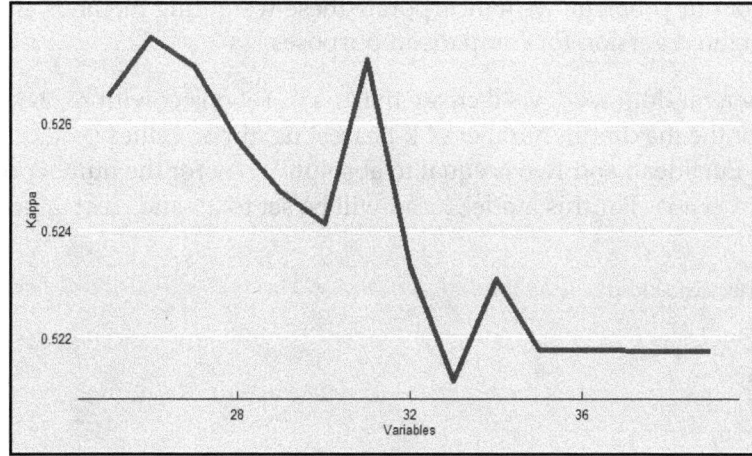

Let's select those 26 features in a new dataframe, then add to the dataframe the response, `train_y`. This will get our data ready for training the KNN model:

```
> vars <- knnProfile$optVariables

> x_selected <-
    train_df[, (colnames(train_df) %in% vars)]

> knn_df <- cbind(x_selected, train_y)
```

What I like to do is use the `train.kknn()` function from the `kknn` package. We use cross-validation again within the `train.kknn()` function to select the best parameters for the optimal `k` neighbors and a `kernel` function.

The kernel function allows you to specify an unweighted `k` neighbors algorithm using the Euclidian distance and weighted functions for distance.

For the weighting of the distances, many different methods are available. For our purpose, the package that we'll use has ten different weighting schemas, which includes unweighted. They're rectangular (unweighted), triangular, Epanechnikov, biweight, triweight, cosine, inversion, Gaussian, rank, and optimal. A full discussion of these weighting techniques is available in *Hechenbichler K.* and *Schliep K.P.* (2004).

For simplicity, let's focus on just two: `triangular` and `epanechnikov`. Before having the weights assigned, the algorithm standardizes all of the distances so that they're between zero and one. The triangular weighting method multiplies the observation distance by one minus the distance. With Epanechnikov, the distance is multiplied by ¾ times (one minus the distance). For our problem, we'll incorporate these weighting methods along with the standard unweighted version for comparison purposes.

After specifying a random seed, we'll create the `train` set object with `kknn()`. This function asks for the maximum number of k-nearest neighbor values (`kmax`), `distance` (one is equal to Euclidean and two is equal to absolute), `kcv` for the number of k-fold cross-validation, and `kernel`. For this model, `kmax` will be set to 25 and `distance` will be 1:

```
> knn_fit <-
    kknn::train.kknn(
    train_y ~ .,
    data = knn_df,
    distance = 1,
    kmax = 25,
    kcv = 10,
    kernel = c("rectangular", "triangular", "epanechnikov")
  )
```

A nice feature of the package is the ability to plot and compare the results, as follows:

```
> plot(knn_fit)
```

The following is the output of the preceding command:

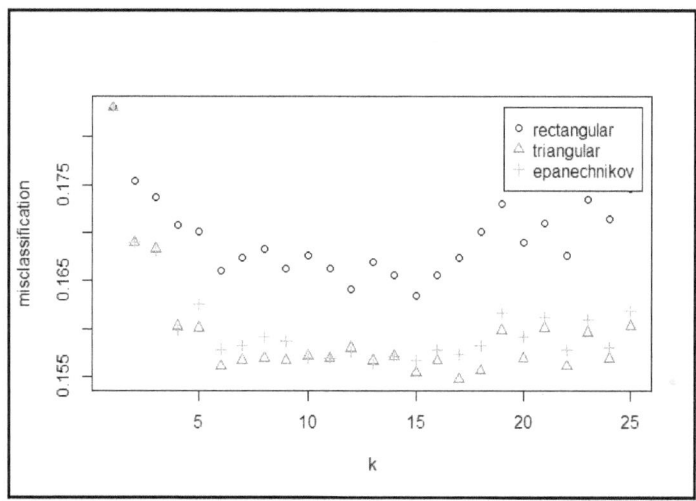

This plot shows **k** on the *x* axis and the percentage of misclassified observations by the `kernel` on the *y* axis. The weighted (triangular) version at `k: 17` performs the best. You can also call the object to see what the classification error and the best parameter are in the following way:

```
> knn_fit

Call:
kknn::train.kknn(formula = train_y ~ ., data = knn_df, kmax = 25, distance
= 1, kernel = c("rectangular", "triangular", "epanechnikov"), kcv = 10)

Type of response variable: nominal
Minimal misclassification: 0.154754
Best kernel: triangular
Best k: 17
```

With the model object created, it's time to see how it performs, starting with the predicted probabilities on the training data:

```
> knn_pred_train <-
    data.frame(predict(knn_fit, newdata = knn_df, type = "prob"))

> classifierplots::density_plot(train_y, knn_pred_train$X1)
```

The output of the preceding code is as follows:

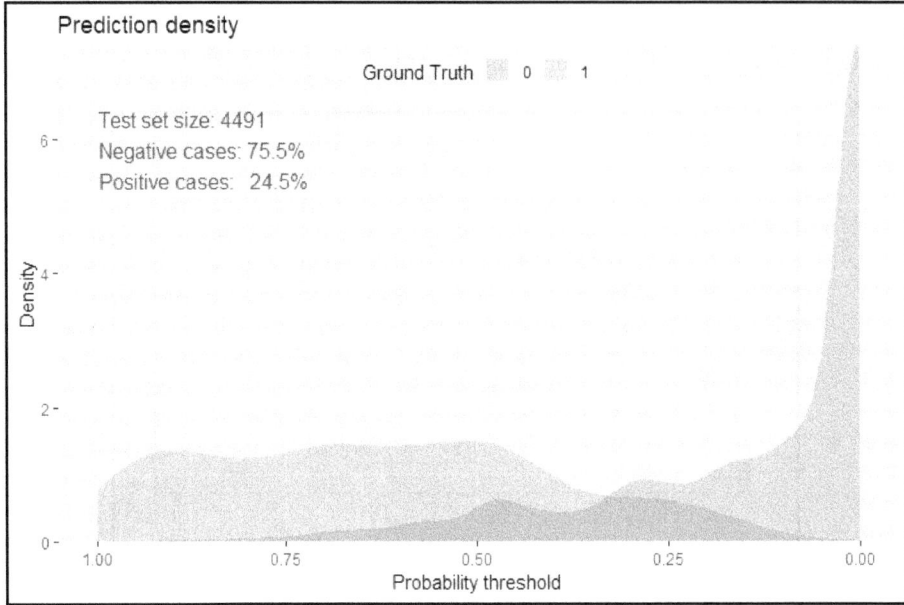

The plot shows quality separation between the probability densities for events versus non-events. This should have a high area under the curve value:

```
> Metrics::auc(train_y, knn_pred_train$X1)
[1] 0.9460519
```

Almost 0.95! Well, let me say that it's quite good, but I sense that we've overfitted and will see this low bias on train turn into a miss on the test set. Let's have a look, but also determine the probability cut point to minimize misclassification error:

```
> InformationValue::optimalCutoff(train_y, knn_pred_train$X1)
[1] 0.48
```

So, `0.48` minimizes error on the training data. This will help us produce a confusion matrix, but first, here's the density plot and AUC for test data:

```
> knn_pred_test <-
    data.frame(predict(knn_fit, newdata = test, type = "prob"))

> classifierplots::density_plot(test_y, knn_pred_test$X1)
```

The output of the preceding code is as follows:

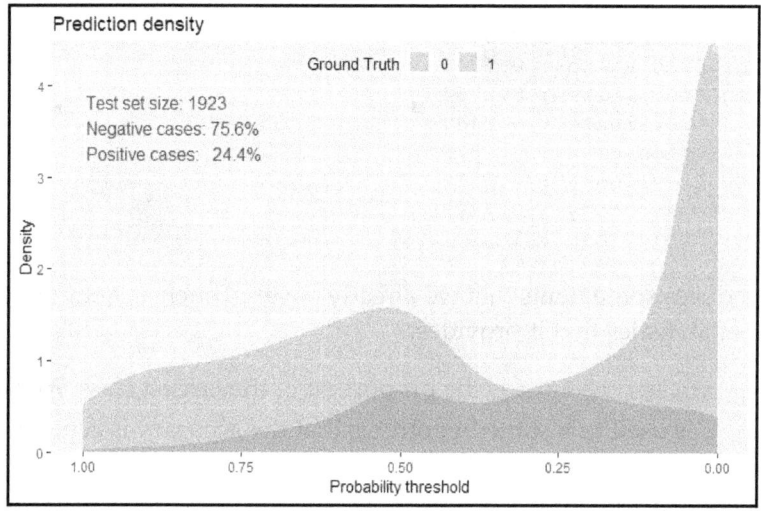

Given the different skews in the density plots from before, it sure does look like we lost some predictive power on the test data:

```
> Metrics::auc(test_y, knn_pred_test$X1)
[1] 0.8592589
```

Indeed, our area under the curve has fallen from 0.95 to 0.86. We can drill down further into this model's performance with a confusion matrix and associated results. We'll use the `caret` package and the `confusionMatrix()` function. This version provides a considerable amount of detail, and it will produce all of the statistics that we need to evaluate and select the best model. You need to specify your predictions as a factor, not probability, and the actual values need to be structured as a factor. I recommend you specify the positive class—in other words, our events:

```
> pred_class <- as.factor(ifelse(knn_pred_test$X1 >= 0.48, "1", "0"))
> caret::confusionMatrix(data = pred_class, reference = test_y, positive =
"1")
Confusion Matrix and Statistics
          Reference
Prediction    0    1
         0 1262  178
         1  191  292
               Accuracy : 0.8081
                 95% CI : (0.7898, 0.8255)
    No Information Rate : 0.7556
    P-Value [Acc > NIR] : 0.00000002214
```

```
             Kappa : 0.4853
Mcnemar's Test P-Value : 0.5322
       Sensitivity : 0.6213
       Specificity : 0.8685
     Pos Pred Value : 0.6046
     Neg Pred Value : 0.8764
         Prevalence : 0.2444
     Detection Rate : 0.1518
Detection Prevalence : 0.2512
  Balanced Accuracy : 0.7449
   'Positive' Class : 1
```

The function produces some items that we already covered such as `Accuracy` and `Kappa`. Here are the other statistics that it provides:

- `No Information Rate` is the proportion of the largest class: 76 % of no events.
- `P-Value` is used to test the hypothesis that the accuracy is actually better than `No Information Rate`.
- We'll not concern ourselves with `Mcnemar's Test`, which is used for the analysis of matched pairs, primarily in epidemiology studies.
- `Sensitivity` is the true positive rate.
- `Specificity` is the true negative rate.
- The positive predictive value (`Pos Pred Value`) is the probability of an observation being classified as being an event and it truly is an event. The following formula is used:

$$PPV = \frac{sensitivity * prevalence}{(sensitivity * prevalence) + (1 - specificity) * (1 - prevalence)}$$

- The negative predictive value (`Neg Pred Value`) is the probability of an observation being classified as a non-event and it truly isn't an event. The formula for this is as follows:

$$NPV = \frac{specificity * (1 - prevalence)}{((1 - sensitivity) * (prevalence)) + (specificity) * (1 - prevalence)}$$

- `Prevalence` is the estimated population prevalence of events, calculated here as the total of the second column (the `1` column) divided by the total observations.
- `Detection Rate` is the rate of the true positives that have been identified.

- Detection Prevalence is the predicted prevalence rate or, in our case, the bottom row divided by the total observations.
- Balanced Accuracy is the average accuracy obtained from either class. This measure accounts for a potential bias in the classifier algorithm, thus potentially over predicting the most frequent class. This is simply: *Sensitivity + Specificity divided by 2.*

You can discern some model weakness in Sensitivity and positive predictive value. Feel free to try on your own changing different distance weighting options and see if you can improve performance. Otherwise, let's proceed to SVM and compare the performance alongside what we just completed.

Support vector machine

If you recall from a previous section, the first thing we did was perform RFE to reduce our input features. We'll repeat that step in the following. We'll redo our control function:

```
> ctrl <- caret::rfeControl(
    functions = caret::lrFuncs,
    method = "cv",
    number = 10,
    verbose = TRUE
)
```

I say we shoot for around 20 to 30 total features and set our random seed:

```
> subsets <- c(20:30)
```

```
> set.seed(54321)
```

Now, in selecting the features you can use the SVM linear or the kernel functions. Let's proceed with linear, which means our specification for the following method will be svmLinear. If, for instance, you wanted to change to a polynomial kernel, then you would specify svmPoly instead or svmRadial for the radial basis function:

```
> svmProfile <- caret::rfe(
    train_df,
    train_y,
    sizes = subsets,
    rfeControl = ctrl,
    method = "svmLinear",
    metric = "Kappa"
)
```

```
> svmProfile
Recursive feature selection
Outer resampling method: Cross-Validated (10 fold)
Resampling performance over subset size:
 Variables Accuracy Kappa  AccuracySD KappaSD Selected
       20    0.8357 0.5206    0.008253 0.02915
       21    0.8350 0.5178    0.008624 0.03091
       22    0.8359 0.5204    0.008277 0.02948
       23    0.8361 0.5220    0.009435 0.02979
       24    0.8383 0.5292    0.008560 0.02572 *
       25    0.8375 0.5261    0.008067 0.02323
       26    0.8379 0.5290    0.010193 0.02905
       27    0.8375 0.5276    0.009205 0.02667
       28    0.8372 0.5259    0.008770 0.02437
       29    0.8361 0.5231    0.008074 0.02319
       30    0.8368 0.5252    0.008069 0.02401
       39    0.8377 0.5290    0.009290 0.02711

The top 5 variables (out of 24):
    V74, V35, V22, V78, V20
```

The optimal Kappa and accuracy are with 24 features. Notice that the top five features are the same as when we ran this with KNN. Here's how to plot the Kappa score per number of features:

```
> svm_results <- svmProfile$results

> ggplot2::ggplot(svm_results, aes(Variables, Kappa)) +
    ggplot2::geom_line(color = 'steelblue', size = 2) +
    ggthemes::theme_fivethirtyeight()
```

The output of the preceding code is as follows:

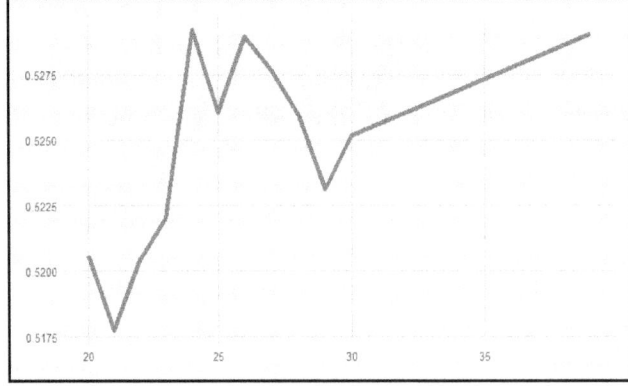

Let's select a dataframe with only the optimal features:

```
> svm_vars <- svmProfile$optVariables

> x_selected <-
    train_df[, (colnames(train_df) %in% svm_vars)]
```

With our features selected, we can train a model with cross-validation, and in the process tune the hyperparameter, C. If you recall from previously, this is the regularization parameter. We'll go forward with caret's train() function:

```
> grid <- expand.grid(.C = c(1, 2, 3))

> svm_control <- caret::trainControl(method = 'cv', number = 10)

> set.seed(1918)

> svm <- caret::train(x_selected,
    train_y,
    method = "svmLinear",
    trControl = svm_control,
    tuneGrid = grid,
    metric = "Kappa")

> svm
Support Vector Machines with Linear Kernel

4491 samples
  24 predictor
   2 classes: '0', '1'

No pre-processing
Resampling: Cross-Validated (10 fold)
Summary of sample sizes: 4041, 4042, 4042, 4041, 4042, 4043, ...
Resampling results across tuning parameters:

  C Accuracy Kappa
  1 0.8372287 0.5223355
  2 0.8367833 0.5210972
  3 0.8374514 0.5229846

Kappa was used to select the optimal model using the
 largest value.
The final value used for the model was C = 3.
```

Excellent! We have optimal `C = 3`, so let's build that model. By the way, be sure to specify we want a probability model with `prob.model = TRUE`. The linear kernel is specified with `vanilladot`:

```
> svm_fit <-
    kernlab::ksvm(
    as.matrix(x_selected),
    train_y,
    kernel = "vanilladot",
    prob.model = TRUE,
    kpar = "automatic",
    C = 3
  )
```

Do we want a dataframe of predicted probabilities on the train data? I'm glad you asked:

```
> svm_pred_train <-
    kernlab::predict(svm_fit, x_selected, type = "probabilities")

> svm_pred_train <- data.frame(svm_pred_train)
```

Our density plot in the following looks about as good as what we saw with KNN:

```
> classifierplots::density_plot(train_y, svm_pred_train$X1)
```

The output of the preceding code is as follows:

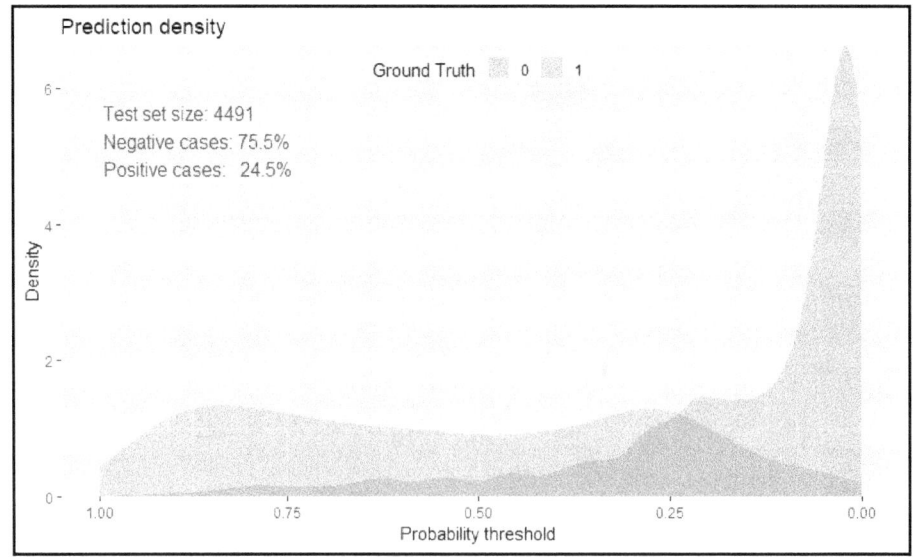

Two things before moving on to the test data, and that is AUC and the optimal score cutoff:

```
> Metrics::auc(train_y, svm_pred_train$X1)
[1] 0.8940114

> InformationValue::optimalCutoff(train_y, svm_pred_train$X1)
[1] 0.3879227
```

OK, the AUC is inferior to KNN on the training data, but the proof must be in our test data:

```
> test_svm <- test[, (colnames(test) %in% svm_vars)]

> svm_pred_test <-
    kernlab::predict(svm_fit, test_svm, type = "probabilities")

> svm_pred_test <- as.data.frame(svm_pred_test)
```

I insist we take a look at the density plot:

```
> classifierplots::density_plot(test_y, svm_pred_test$`1`)
```

The output of the preceding code is as follows:

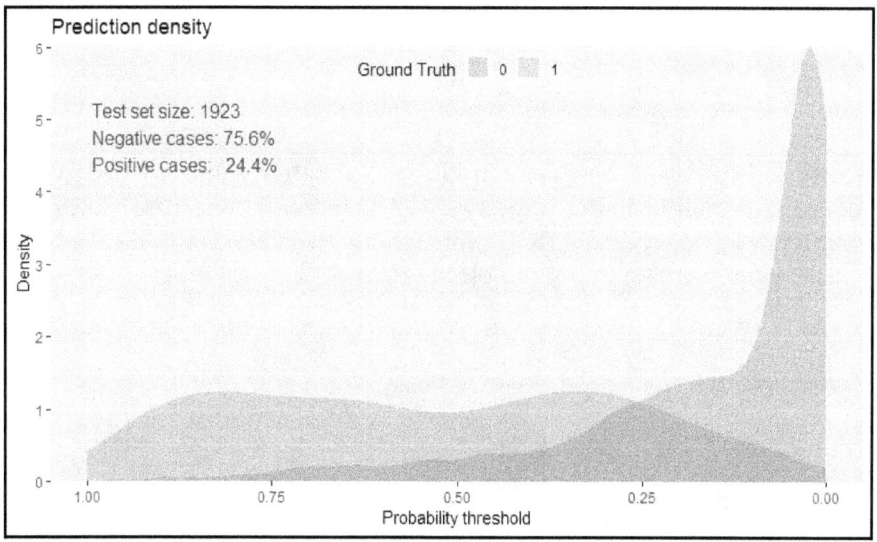

I would put forward that we have a good overall fit here:

```
> Metrics::auc(test_y, svm_pred_test$`1`)
[1] 0.8951011
```

That's more like it: excellent bias/variance tradeoff. We can start the overall comparison with KNN by moving forward with the confusion matrix and relevant stats:

```
> svm_pred_class <- as.factor(ifelse(svm_pred_test$`1` >= 0.275, "1", "0"))

> caret::confusionMatrix(data = svm_pred_class, reference = test_y,
positive = "1")
Confusion Matrix and Statistics
          Reference
Prediction    0    1
         0 1206  104
         1  247  366
               Accuracy : 0.8175
                 95% CI : (0.7995, 0.8345)
    No Information Rate : 0.7556
    P-Value [Acc > NIR] : 0.00000000004314737
                  Kappa : 0.5519
 Mcnemar's Test P-Value : 0.00000000000003472
            Sensitivity : 0.7787
            Specificity : 0.8300
         Pos Pred Value : 0.5971
         Neg Pred Value : 0.9206
             Prevalence : 0.2444
         Detection Rate : 0.1903
   Detection Prevalence : 0.3188
      Balanced Accuracy : 0.8044
       'Positive' Class : 1
```

When you compare the results across methods, we see better values for the SVM almost across the board, especially a better Kappa as well as better balanced accuracy. In the past couple of chapters, we've produced ROC plots where the various models were overlaid on the same plot. We can recreate that same plot here as well, as follows:

```
> pred.knn <- ROCR::prediction(knn_pred_test$X1, test_y)

> perf.knn <- ROCR::performance(pred.knn, "tpr", "fpr")

> ROCR::plot(perf.knn, main = "ROC", col = 1)

> pred.svm <- ROCR::prediction(svm_pred_test$`1`, test_y)

> perf.svm <- ROCR::performance(pred.svm, "tpr", "fpr")

> ROCR::plot(perf.svm, col = 2, add = TRUE)

> legend(0.6, 0.6, c("KNN", "SVM"), 1:2)
```

The output of the preceding code is as follows:

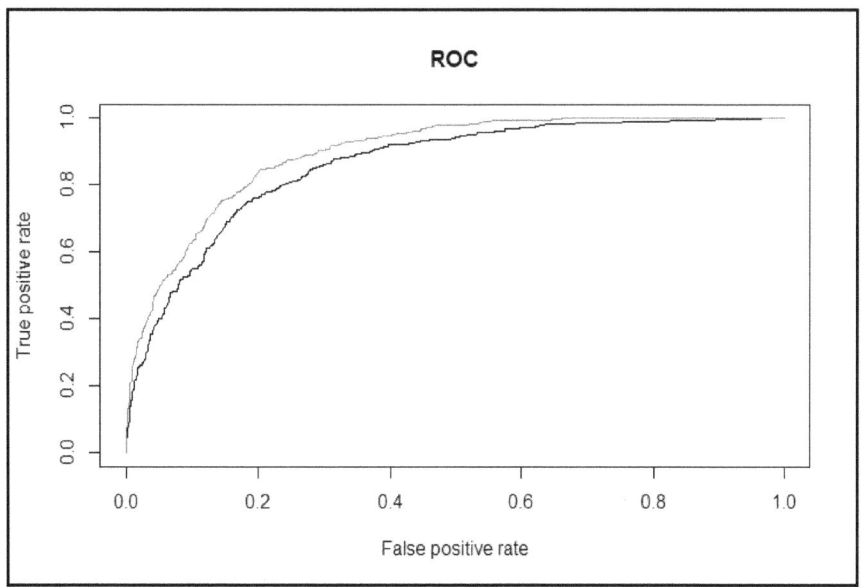

The plot shows a clear separation in the curves between the two models. Therefore, given what we've done here, the SVM algorithm performed better than KNN. Indeed, we could try a number of different methods to improve either algorithm, which could include a different feature selection and a different weighting for KNN (or kernels for SVM).

Summary

In this chapter, we reviewed two classification techniques: KNN and SVM. The goal was to discover how these techniques work and ascertain the differences between them, by building and comparing models on a common dataset. KNN involved both unweighted and weighted nearest neighbor algorithms, and for SVM, only a linear model was developed, which outperformed all other models.

We examined how to use Recursive Feature Elimination to find an optimal set of features for both methods. We used the extremely versatile `caret` package to train the models. We expanded our exploration of model performance using a confusion matrix, and the relevant statistics that one can derive from the matrix. We'll now use tree-based classifiers, which are very powerful and very popular.

6
Tree-Based Classification

"The classifiers most likely to be the best are the random forest (RF) versions, the best of which (implemented in R and accessed via caret), achieves 94.1 percent of the maximum accuracy, overcoming 90 percent in 84.3 percent of the data sets."

- Fernández-Delgado et al. (2014)

This quote from Fernández-Delgado et al. in the *Journal of Machine Learning Research* is meant to demonstrate that the techniques in this chapter are quite powerful, particularly when used for classification problems.

In previous chapters, we examined techniques used to predict label classification on three different datasets. Here, we'll apply tree-based methods with an eye to see whether we can improve our predictive power on the Santander data used in `Chapter 3`, *Logistic Regression*, and the data used in `Chapter 4`, *Advanced Feature Selection in Linear Models*.

The first item of discussion is the basic decision tree, which is simple to both build and to understand. However, the single decision tree method isn't likely to perform as well as the other methods that you've already learned, for example, **Support Vector Machines (SVMs)**, or the ones that we've yet to learn, such as neural networks. Therefore, we'll discuss the creation of multiple, sometimes hundreds, of different trees with their individual results combined, leading to a single overall prediction.

These methods, as the paper referenced at the beginning of this chapter states, perform as well as, or better than, any technique in this book. These methods are known as **random forests** and **gradient boosted trees**. Additionally, we'll work on how to use the random forest method to assist in feature elimination/selection.

Following are the topics that we'll be covering in this chapter:

- An overview of the techniques
- Datasets and modeling

An overview of the techniques

We'll now get to an overview of the techniques, covering classification trees, random forests, and gradient boosting. This will set the stage for their practical use.

Understanding a regression tree

To establish an understanding of tree-based methods, it's probably easier to start with a quantitative outcome and then move on to how it works in a classification problem. The essence of a tree is that the features are partitioned, starting with the first split that improves the RSS the most. These binary splits continue until the termination of the tree. Each subsequent split/partition isn't done on the entire dataset, but only on the portion of the prior split that it falls under. This top-down process is referred to as **recursive partitioning**. It's also a process that's **greedy**, a term you may stumble upon in reading about **machine learning** (**ML**) methods. Greedy means that during each split in the process, the algorithm looks for the greatest reduction in the RSS without any regard to how well it will perform on the later partitions. The result is that you may end up with a full tree of unnecessary branches leading to a low bias but a high variance. To control this effect, you need to appropriately prune the tree to an optimal size after building a full tree.

This diagram provides a visualization of this technique in action:

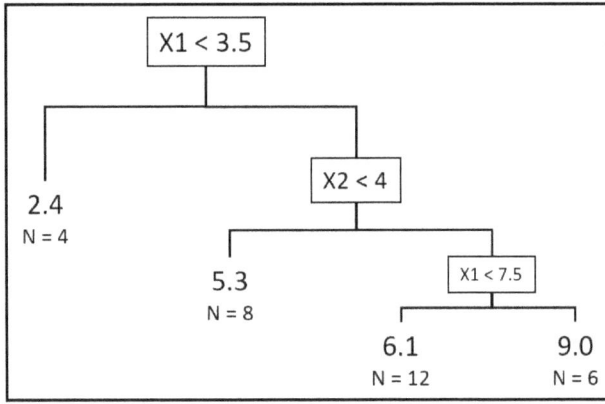

Regression tree with three splits and four terminal nodes, and the corresponding node average and number of observations

The data is hypothetical with 30 observations, a response ranging from 1 to 10, and two predictor features, both ranging in value from 0 to 10 named **X1** and **X2**. The tree has three splits leading to four terminal nodes. Each split is basically an `if...then` statement or uses the R syntax `ifelse()`. The first split is: if **X1** is less than **3.5**, then the response is split into four observations with an average value of **2.4** and the remaining 26 observations. The left branch of four observations is a terminal node as any further splits would not substantially improve the RSS. The predicted value for these four observations is that the partition of the tree becomes the average. The next split is at **X2 < 4,** and finally **X1 < 7.5.**

An advantage of this method is that it can handle highly nonlinear relationships; however, can you see a couple of potential problems? The first issue is that an observation is given the average of the terminal node under which it falls. This can hurt the overall predictive performance (high bias). Conversely, if you keep partitioning the data further and further to achieve a low bias, a high variance can become an issue. As with the other methods, you can use cross-validation to select the appropriate tree depth size.

Classification trees

Classification trees operate under the same principle as regression trees, except that the splits aren't determined by the RSS but by an error rate. The error rate used isn't what you would expect where the calculation is simply the misclassified observations divided by the total observations. As it turns out, when it comes to tree-splitting, a misclassification rate, by itself, may lead to a situation where you can gain information with a further split but not improve the misclassification rate. Let's look at an example.

Suppose we have a node, let's call it `N0`, where you have seven observations labeled `No` and three observations labeled `Yes`. We can say that the misclassified rate is 30%. With this in mind, let's calculate a common alternative error measure called the **Gini index**. The formula for a single node Gini index is as follows:

$$Gini = 1 - (probability\ of\ Class\ 1)^2 - (probability\ of\ Class\ 2)^2$$

Then, for `N0`, the Gini is $1 - (.7)^2 - (.3)^2$, which is equal to 0.42, versus the misclassification rate of 30%.

Taking this example further, we'll now create node *N1* with three observations from `Class 1` and none from `Class 2`, along with *N2*, which has four observations from `Class 1` and three from `Class 2`. Now, the overall misclassification rate for this branch of the tree is still 30%, but look at how the overall Gini index has improved:

- *Gini(N1) = 1 - (3/3)² - (0/3)² = 0*
- *Gini(N2) = 1 - (4/7)² - (3/7)² = 0.49*
- *New Gini index = (proportion of N1 x Gini(N1)) + (proportion of N2 x Gini(N2)),* which is equal to *(0.3 x 0) + (0.7 x 0.49)* or *0.343*

By doing a split on a surrogate error rate, we actually improved our model impurity, reducing it from *0.42* to *0.343*, whereas the misclassification rate didn't change. This is the methodology that's used by the `rpart()` package, which we'll be using in this chapter.

Random forest

To greatly improve our model's predictive ability, we can produce numerous trees and combine the results. The random forest technique does this by applying two different tricks in model development. The first is the use of **bootstrap aggregation**, or **bagging**, as it's called.

In bagging, an individual tree is built on a random sample of the dataset, roughly two-thirds of the total observations (note that the remaining one-third is referred to as **out-of-bag (oob)**). This is repeated dozens or hundreds of times and the results are averaged. Each of these trees is grown and not pruned based on any error measure, and this means that the variance of each of these individual trees is high. However, by averaging the results, you can reduce the variance without increasing the bias.

The next thing that random forest brings to the table is that concurrently with the random sample of the data—that is, bagging—it also takes a random sampling of the input features at each split. In the `randomForest` package, we'll use the default random number of the predictors that're sampled, which, for classification problems, is the square root of the total predictors, and for regression, is the total number of the predictors divided by three. The number of predictors the algorithm randomly chooses at each split can be changed via the model tuning process.

By doing this random sample of the features at each split and incorporating it into the methodology, you can mitigate the effect of a highly correlated predictor becoming the main driver in all of your bootstrapped trees, preventing you from reducing the variance that you hoped to achieve with bagging. The subsequent averaging of the trees that're less correlated to each other is more generalizable and robust to outliers than if you only performed bagging.

Gradient boosting

Boosting methods can become extremely complicated to learn and understand, but you should keep in mind what's fundamentally happening behind the curtain. The main idea is to build an initial model of some kind (linear, spline, tree, and so on) called the base learner, examine the residuals, and fit a model based on these residuals around the so-called **loss function**. A loss function is merely the function that measures the discrepancy between the model and desired prediction, for example, a squared error for regression or the logistic function for classification. The process continues until it reaches some specified stopping criterion. This is sort of like the student who takes a practice exam and gets 30 out of 100 questions wrong and, as a result, studies only these 30 questions that were missed. In the next practice exam, they get 10 out of those 30 wrong and so only focus on those 10 questions, and so on. If you would like to explore the theory behind this further, a great resource for you is available in *Frontiers in Neurorobotics, Gradient boosting machines, a tutorial*, Natekin A., Knoll A. (2013), at

`http://www.ncbi.nlm.nih.gov/pmc/articles/PMC3885826/.`

As just mentioned, boosting can be applied to many different base learners, but here, we'll only focus on the specifics of **tree-based learning**. Each tree iteration is small and we'll determine how small with one of the tuning parameters referred to as interaction depth. In fact, it may be as small as one split, which is referred to as a stump.

Trees are sequentially fitted to the residuals, according to the loss function, up to the number of trees that we specified (our stopping criterion).

There're a number of parameters that require tuning in the model-building process using the `Xgboost` package, which stands for **eXtreme Gradient Boosting**. This package has become quite popular for online data contests because of its winning performance. There's excellent background material on boosting trees and on `Xgboost` at the following website:

`http://xgboost.readthedocs.io/en/latest/model.html.`

In the practical examples, we'll learn how to begin to optimize the hyperparameters and produce meaningful output and predictions. These parameters can interact with each other and, if you just tinker with one without considering the other, your model may worsen the performance. The `caret` package will help us in the tuning endeavor.

Datasets and modeling

We're going to be using two of the prior datasets, the simulated data from Chapter 4, *Advanced Feature Selection in Linear Models,* and the customer satisfaction data from Chapter 3, *Logistic Regression.* We'll start by building a classification tree on the simulated data. This will help us to understand the basic principles of tree-based methods. Then, we'll move on to random forest and boosted trees applied to the customer satisfaction data. This exercise will provide an excellent comparison to the generalized linear models from before. Finally, I want to show you an interesting feature selection method using random forest, using the simulated data. By interesting, I mean it's a valuable technique to add to your feature selection arsenal, but I'll point out a couple of caveats for you to consider in practical application.

Classification tree

This exercise will be an excellent introduction to tree-based methods. I recommend applying this method to any supervised learning method because, at a minimum, you'll get a better understanding of the data and establish a good baseline of predictive performance. It may also be the only thing you need to do to solve a problem for your business partners. An example I can share was where the marketing team tasked me to try and reverse-engineer a customer segmentation done by an external vendor nearly two years in the past. We had the original survey data and the customer segment labels, but no understanding of how the data drove the segmentation.

Well, I just used the methods described in this section, and we could predict a segment with almost 100% accuracy. Plus, as you'll see, it was easy to explain why:

1. Let's get the packages installed if needed:

```
library(magrittr)
install.packages("Boruta")
install.packages("caret")
install.packages("classifierplots")
install.packages("InformationValue")
install.packages("MLmetrics")
install.packages("randomForest")
```

```
install.packages("ROCR")
install.packages("rpart")
install.packages("rpart.plot")
install.packages("tidyverse")
install.packages("xgboost")
options(scipen=999)
```

2. As for the simulated data, I discuss how I created it in Chapter 4, *Advanced Feature Selection in Linear Models*. You can find it on GitHub at this link: https://github.com/PacktPublishing/Advanced-Machine-Learning-with-R/blob/master/Data/sim_df.csv.

3. We now load it into R:

```
> sim_df <- read.csv("~/sim_df.csv", stringsAsFactors = FALSE)
```

4. The response we'll try and predict is called y. It's a numeric value of either 0 or 1 with 1 being the outcome of interest. It's slightly unbalanced, with about 30% of the responses labeled a 1. Let's confirm that and turn it into a factor, which will tell our tree function we're interested in classification:

```
> table(sim_df$y)

   0    1
7072 2928

> sim_df$y <- as.factor(sim_df$y)
```

5. Create the train/test split using the same random seed as in Chapter 4, *Advanced Feature Selection in Linear Models*:

```
> set.seed(1066)

> index <- caret::createDataPartition(sim_df$y, p = 0.7, list = F)

> train <- sim_df[index, ]

> test <- sim_df[-index, ]
```

6. To create our classification tree, we'll be using the rpart() function, using the common formula syntax:

```
> tree_fit <- rpart::rpart(y ~ ., data = train)
```

7. The next thing I like to do is look at the cptable from our model object:

```
> tree_fit$cptable
            CP nsplit rel error    xerror       xstd
```

```
1 0.20878049        0 1.0000000 1.0000000 0.01857332
2 0.19609756        1 0.7912195 0.7595122 0.01697342
3 0.01585366        2 0.5951220 0.6029268 0.01556234
4 0.01219512        6 0.5297561 0.5775610 0.01530000
5 0.01000000        8 0.5053659 0.5395122 0.01488626
```

This is an interesting table to analyze. The first column labeled CP is the cost complexity parameter. The second column, nsplit, is the number of splits in the tree. The rel error column stands for relative error. Both xerror and xstd are based on ten-fold cross-validation, with xerror being the average error and xstd the standard deviation of the cross-validation process. We can see that eight splits produced the lowest error on the full dataset and on cross-validation.

8. You can examine this using plotcp():

```
> rpart::plotcp(tree_fit)
```

The output of the preceding actions is as follows:

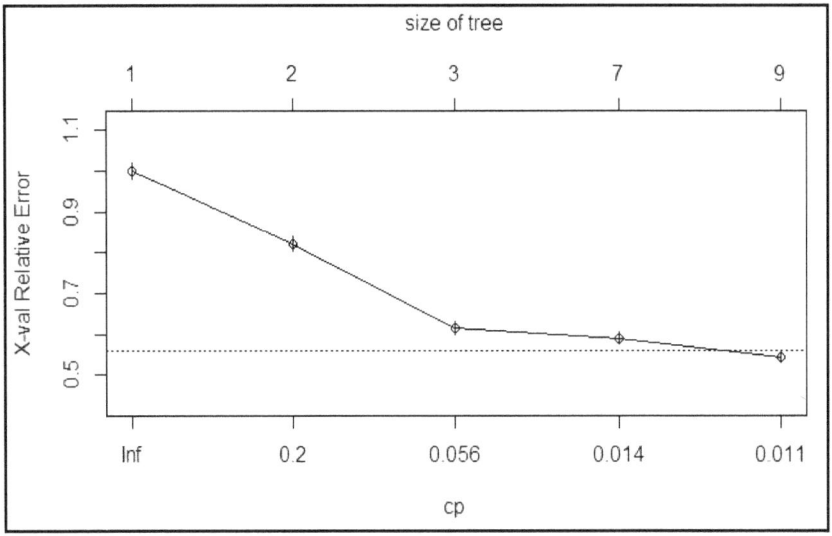

The plot shows us the cross-validated relative error by tree size with the corresponding error bars. The horizontal line on the plot is the upper limit of the lowest standard error. Selecting a different tree size, say seven, you would create an object of your desired **cp** and prune the tree simply by specifying that object in the prune() function, or you can just give the function the cp number. It would look as follows:

```
> cp = tree_fit$cptable[4, 1]
```

```
> cp
[1] 0.01219512

> cp <- min(tree_fit$cptable[, 3])
# not run
# rpart::prune(tree_fit, cp = cp)
# Or
# rpart::prune(tree_fit, cp = 0.01219512)
```

You can plot and explore the tree in a number of different ways. I prefer the version from the `rpart.plot` package. There's an excellent vignette on how to use it at the following website:

`http://www.milbo.org/rpart-plot/prp.pdf.`

Here's the first one, `type = 3` with `extra = 2` (see the vignette for more options):

```
> rpart.plot::rpart.plot(
    tree_fit,
    type = 3,
    extra = 2,
    branch = .75,
    under = TRUE
)
```

The output of the preceding command is as follows:

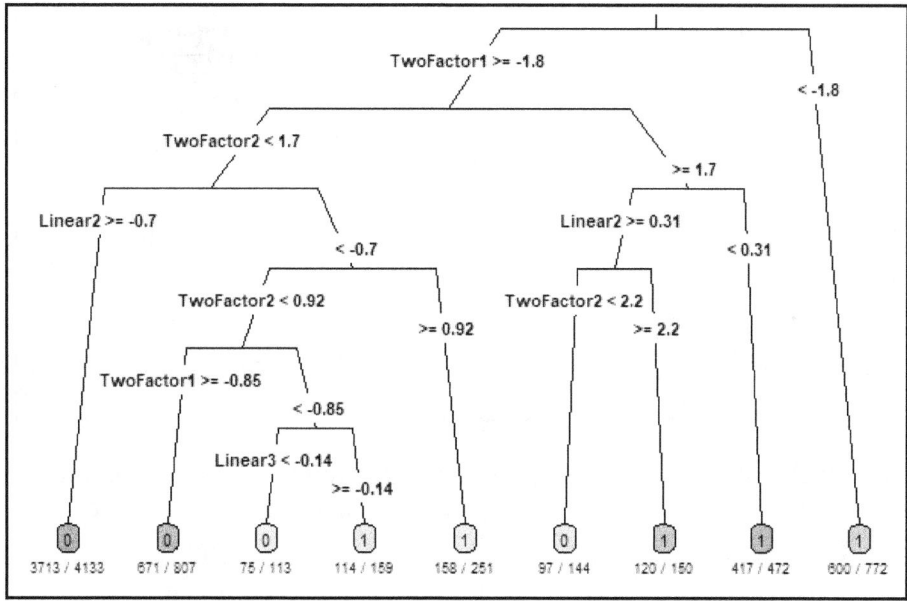

The preceding plot shows the feature at each split and the value related to that split. The first split in the tree is the feature **TwoFactor1**. If the value is less than **-1.8** then those observations end up in a terminal node. In this version of the tree, **772** observations are in that node (because the feature value is less than **-1.8**, and **600** of those observations are labeled **1**. So, you can say that the node probability is 78% (**600/772**) that an observation is a **1**. Now, if the value is equal to or greater than **-1.8**, then it goes to the next feature to split, which is **TwoFactor2**, and so forth until all observations are in a terminal node.

If you want to see all of those terminal node probabilities, a simple change to the syntax will suffice:

```
> rpart.plot::rpart.plot(
tree_fit,
type = 1,
extra = 6,
branch = .75,
under = TRUE
)
```

The output of the preceding command is as follows:

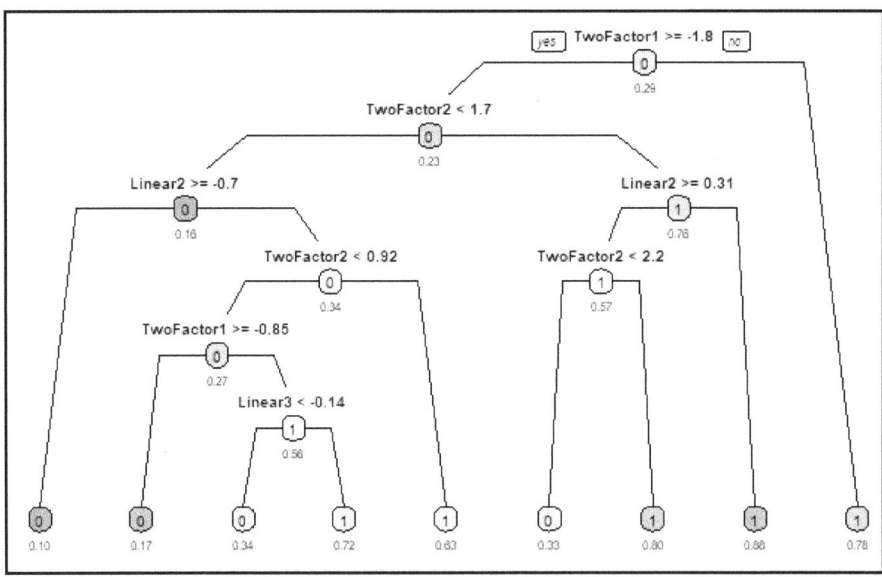

This different look shows the percentage of **1** in each terminal node and complements the preceding plot. If you want to see all of the rules leading for the nodes, you can run this:

```
> rpart.plot::rpart.rules(tree_fit)
    y
```

```
0.10 when TwoFactor1 >= -1.75 & TwoFactor2 < 1.69 & Linear2 >= -0.70
0.17 when TwoFactor1 >= -0.85 & TwoFactor2 < 0.92 & Linear2 < -0.70
0.33 when TwoFactor1 >= -1.75 & TwoFactor2 is 1.69 to 2.20 & Linear2 >=
0.31
0.34 when TwoFactor1 is -1.75 to -0.85 & TwoFactor2 < 0.92 & Linear2 <
-0.70 &
         Linear3 < -0.14
0.63 when TwoFactor1 >= -1.75 & TwoFactor2 is 0.92 to 1.69 & Linear2 <
-0.70
0.72 when TwoFactor1 is -1.75 to -0.85 & TwoFactor2 < 0.92 & Linear2 <
-0.70 &
         Linear3 >= -0.14
0.78 when TwoFactor1 < -1.75
0.80 when TwoFactor1 >= -1.75 & TwoFactor2 >= 2.20 & Linear2 >= 0.31
0.88 when TwoFactor1 >= -1.75 & TwoFactor2 >= 1.69 & Linear2 < 0.31
```

We shall now see how this simple model performs on the test set. You may recall that with elastic net, we had an **area under the curve (AUC)** of over 0.87 and a log-loss of 0.37:

```
> rparty.test <- predict(tree_fit, newdata = test)

> rparty.test <- rparty.test[, 2]

> classifierplots::density_plot(test$y, rparty.test)
```

The output of the preceding code is as follows:

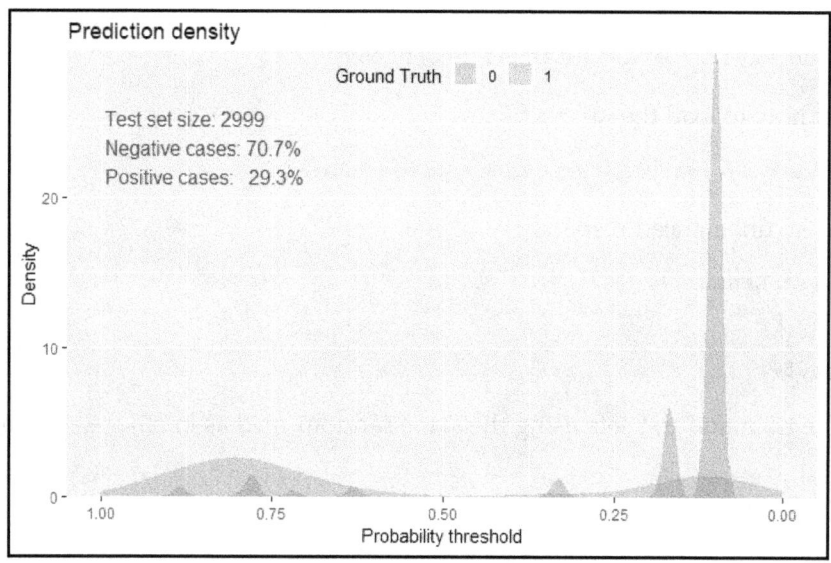

Notice the spikes in the density. The plot is capturing the probabilities from those terminal nodes. The real test will be our two favorite metrics, AUC and log-loss:

```
> ynum <- as.numeric(ifelse(test$y == "1", 1, 0))

> MLmetrics::AUC(rparty.test, ynum)
[1] 0.8201691

> MLmetrics::LogLoss(rparty.test, ynum)
[1] 0.4140015
```

OK, the performance isn't as good as using elastic net and so on, but overall I don't believe that's too bad for such a simple model that even someone in marketing can understand. We'll see if complicating things with a random forest can surpass elastic net when we look at using it for feature selection. Our next task is to use random forest and boosted trees in a classification problem.

Random forest

The customer satisfaction data was covered in Chapter 3, *Logistic Regression*. The GitHub links to the CSV and an RData file are as follows:

- https://github.com/PacktPublishing/Advanced-Machine-Learning-with-R/blob/master/Data/santander_prepd.RData
- https://github.com/PacktPublishing/Advanced-Machine-Learning-with-R/blob/master/Data/santander_prepd.csv

I'll show you how to load the RData file:

```
> santander <- readRDS("santander_prepd.RData")
```

The data has an unbalanced response:

```
> table(santander$y)

    0     1
73012  3008
```

We'll split the train and test sets using the same random seed as in Chapter 3, *Logistic Regression*:

```
> set.seed(1966)

> trainIndex <- caret::createDataPartition(santander$y, p = 0.8, list =
FALSE)
```

```
> train <- santander[trainIndex, ]

> test <- santander[-trainIndex, ]
```

With this split, we end up with one zero variance features, which we'll find and remove:

```
> train_zero <- caret::nearZeroVar(train, saveMetrics = TRUE)

> table(train_zero$zeroVar)

FALSE  TRUE
  142     1

> train <- train[, train_zero$zeroVar == 'FALSE']
```

I like to put the predictors in a matrix, and we'll need the response as a factor:

```
> x <- as.matrix(train[, -142])

> y <- as.factor(train$y)
```

We're now ready to start training a model. Recall that we have a highly unbalanced response. One of the things I highly recommend in such an instance is to structure your sample size. In fact, this can actually become a key parameter to tune. In the training data, there are only 2,405 ones alongside 58,411 zeros. I'll show an example of forcing the sample at each bagged sample in the algorithm. Again, this will take some trial and error on your part to identify the right ratio of *downsampling* the majority class to minority class. In the following example, I'm sampling 1,200 of the minority class and 3,600 of the majority class. This was some simple trial and error on my part, so see if you can do better. What this does to your predicted probabilities is skew them towards the minority class—in other words, you have a relative probability. This might not be what the business desires, so you can apply a correction to produce the corrected probability:

$$CorrectedProbability = 1/(1 + ((1/populationproportion) - 1)/((1/sampleproportion) - 1) * ((1/predictedprobability) - 1))$$

The population proportion is the actual, or the estimated proportion of the minority class, and the sample proportion is from your oversample. Predicted probability equates to the model's probability for a given observation.

The other thing I specify here is the number of trees, and 200 for starters is sufficient. In some instances, you may need a thousand or more:

```
> set.seed(1999)

> forest_fit <- randomForest::randomForest(x = x, y = y,
    ntree = 200,
    sampsize = c(3600, 1200))
```

Calling the fitted object gives us the following results:

```
> forest_fit

Call:
 randomForest(x = x, y = y, ntree = 200, sampsize = c(3600, 1200))
               Type of random forest: classification
                     Number of trees: 200
No. of variables tried at each split: 11

        OOB estimate of  error rate: 9.51%
Confusion matrix:
      0     1 class.error
0 53946 4465  0.07644108
1  1321 1084  0.54927235
```

You can notice that the out-of-bag error rate is under 10%, and it gives us a confusion matrix. My advice is to not pay that much attention to this and just make a note of it. We'll use our relative probabilities to find the best split. Besides, as we've talked about in other chapters, error/accuracy isn't the best metric to judge a model. One thing that's good to look at is the number of trees that minimized the error. That way, you can limit the number of trees in an attempt to avoid overfitting:

```
> which.min(forest_fit$err.rate[, 1])
[1] 105

> forest_fit$err.rate[105]
[1] 0.0934458
```

There you have it: only 105 trees are needed to minimize the error versus all 200. In this model, we used all 142 features. That's just computationally inefficient and prone to cause overfitting.

I'll show you what has worked quite well for me on a number of projects to reduce features. Before we go there, here's the standard feature importance plot:

```
> randomForest::varImpPlot(forest_fit)
```

The output of the preceding code is as follows:

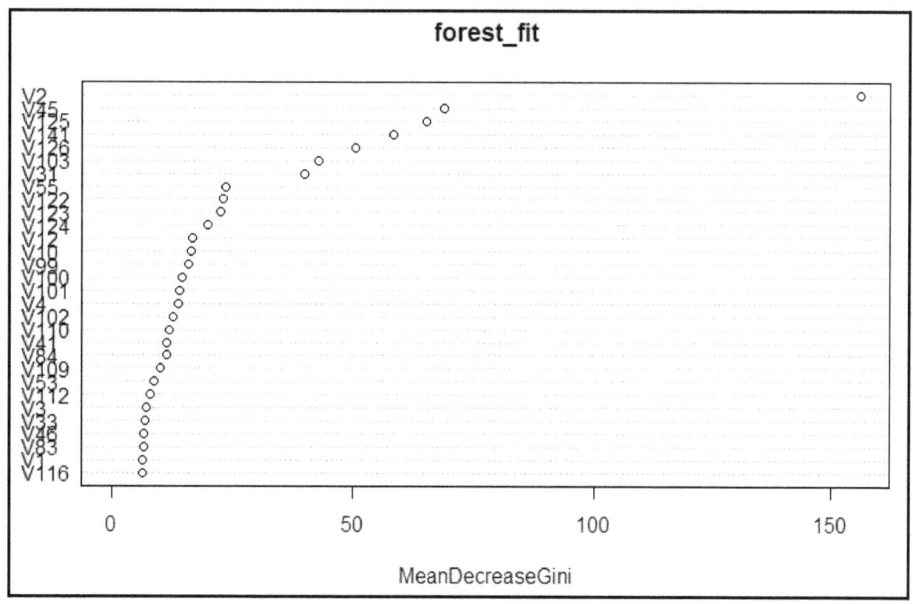

The feature importance is based on the average decrease in Gini. We can see that there're roughly a dozen or so features driving predictions, and the **V2** feature is quite suspicious. I talk about the notorious **V2** feature in `Chapter 3`, *Logistic Regression* so I won't belabor the point here.

What I'm about to present you may find controversial or unscientific. Well, I have to agree. However, it works. What I do is find the descriptive statistics for feature importance and decide, based on some experimental value or business expertise, where to filter the features. It's best to demonstrate how in our example:

```
> ff <- data.frame(unlist(forest_fit$importance))

> ff$var <- row.names(ff)

> summary(ff)
 MeanDecreaseGini              var
 Min.    :  0.00000      Length:141
 1st Qu. :  0.02172      Class :character
 Median  :  0.36412       Mode :character
 Mean    :  6.12824
 3rd Qu. :  4.02137
 Max.    :155.86878
```

In the lack of subject matter expertise or otherwise, we can cut the features based on mean Gini decrease above the third quantile:

```
> my_forest_vars <- dplyr::filter(ff, MeanDecreaseGini > 4.02)

> my_forest_vars <- my_forest_vars$var

> x_reduced <- x[, my_forest_vars]

> dim(x_reduced)
[1] 60816 36
```

That gave us just 36 input features. We could reduce it even further, but I'll let you experiment with different results. Now, build the new model with reduced features:

```
> set.seed(567)

> forest_fit2 <- randomForest::randomForest(x = x_reduced, y = y,
    ntree = 110,
    sampsize = c(3600, 1200))

> which.min(forest_fit2$err.rate[, 1])
[1] 98
```

Examine how it does on the training data first:

```
> rf_prob <- predict(forest_fit, type = "prob")

> y_prob <- rf_prob[, 2]                       .

> classifierplots::density_plot(y, y_prob)
```

The output of the preceding code is as follows:

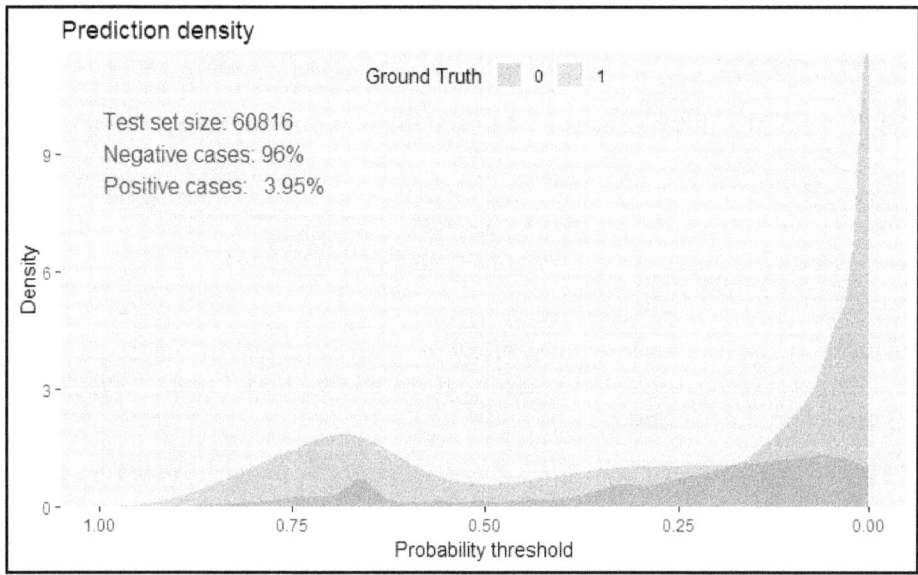

Now, pursue identifying the metrics:

```
> ynum <- as.numeric(ifelse(y == "1", 1, 0))

> MLmetrics::AUC(y_prob, ynum)
[1] 0.8154905

> MLmetrics::LogLoss(y_prob, ynum)
[1] 0.2652151
```

The AUC seems about what came about what we would expect, but the log-loss is quite a bit worse. Why? Ah, yes, our problem is the relative probabilities. We need to adjust the predicted probabilities, then recalculate log-loss. I'll make it straightforward to do this by taking the formula I discussed previously and putting it into a function:

```
> corrected_prob <- function(result, population_fraction, sample_fraction){
    value <- 1/(1+(1/population_fraction-1) /
(1/sample_fraction-1)*(1/result-1))
    return(value)
}
```

Then, we apply the function to the predicted results:

```
> yprob_corrected <- corrected_prob(result = y_prob,
    population_fraction = 0.04,
    sample_fraction = .33
```

We can see that the AUC hasn't changed, but the log-loss has improved:

```
> MLmetrics::AUC(yprob_corrected, ynum)
[1] 0.8154905

> MLmetrics::LogLoss(yprob_corrected, ynum)
[1] 0.188308
```

In fact, it's more in line now with what we saw in `Chapter 3`, *Logistic Regression*. It's worth exploring whether it can be close to the 0.14 log-loss and 0.81 AUC values we achieved with the MARS model on the test set:

```
> rf_test <- predict(forest_fit, type = "prob", newdata = test)

> rf_test <- rf_test[, 2]

> ytest <- as.numeric(ifelse(test$y == "1", 1, 0))

> MLmetrics::AUC(rf_test, ytest)
[1] 0.8149009
```

Nicely done on the AUC! Correct those probabilities and get the log-loss:

```
> rftest_corrected <- corrected_probability(result = rf_test,
    population_fraction = 0.04,
    sample_fraction = 0.33)

> MLmetrics::LogLoss(rftest_corrected, ytest)
[1] 0.1787402
```

We actually improved the log-loss versus the training data, but didn't win the battle versus MARS. What to do? Well, we're going to give **XGboost** a try next. We could go back and and tune the number of trees, oversampling fraction, or the number of features sampled per tree or even just say that, on this dataset, MARS did its job. It's been my experience that, on unbalanced labels, random forest will outperform MARS.

However, this case does demonstrate the power of MARS as your go-to baseline model. Let's do one further drill-down and plot the AUC curves of random forest versus MARS. Please note that this last step requires you to have executed the code in Chapter 3, *Logistic Regression*. If you haven't saved the results, go back and run the MARS example before proceeding with the following:

```
pred.rf <- ROCR::prediction(rftest_corrected, test$y)

perf.rf <- ROCR::performance(pred.rf, "tpr", "fpr")

ROCR::plot(perf.rf, main = "ROC", col = 1)

pred.earth <- ROCR::prediction(test_pred, test$y)

perf.earth <- ROCR::performance(pred.earth, "tpr", "fpr")

ROCR::plot(perf.earth, col = 2, add = TRUE)
legend(0.6, 0.6, c("RF", "MARS"), 1:2)
```

The output of the preceding code is as follows:

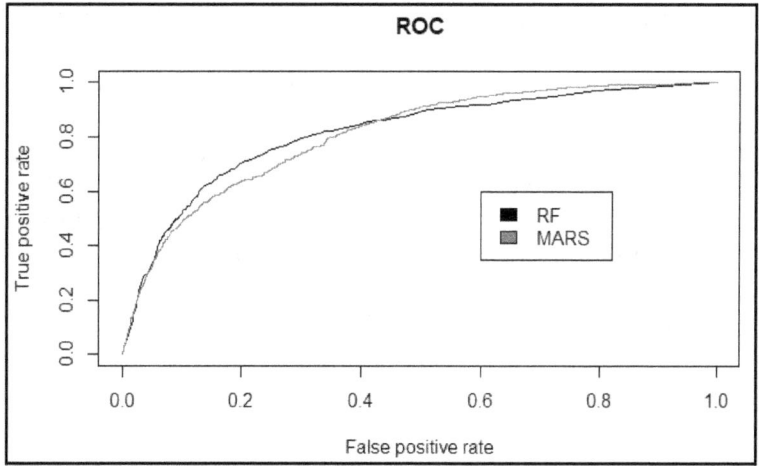

This is quite revealing. Here, we to very distinct curves where the AUC values are almost identical. Indeed, from a true positive rate of 0.4 to 0.8, random forest outperforms MARS. The key learning here is that a model performance value in and of itself isn't enough to guide model selection.

While random forest once again proved itself a capable tool for classification, let's see how gradient boosting trees can perform.

Extreme gradient boosting – classification

As mentioned previously, we'll be using the `xgboost` package in this section. Given the method's well-earned reputation, let's try it on the `santander` data.

As stated in the boosting overview, you can tune a number of parameters:

- `nrounds`: This is the maximum number of iterations (number of trees in the final model).
- `colsample_bytree`: This is the number of features, expressed as a ratio, to sample when building a tree. The default is 1 (100% of the features).
- `min_child_weight`: This is the minimum weight in the trees being boosted. The default is 1.
- `eta`: This is the learning rate, which is the contribution of each tree to the solution. The default is 0.3.
- `gamma`: This is the minimum loss reduction required to make another leaf partition in a tree.
- `subsample`: This is the ratio of data observations. The default is 1 (100%).
- `max_depth`: This is the maximum depth of the individual trees.

> Using the `expand.grid()` function, we'll build our experimental grid to run through the training process of the `caret` package. If you don't specify values for all of the preceding parameters, even if it's just a default, you'll receive an error message when you execute the function. The following values are based on a number of training iterations I've done previously. I encourage you to try your own tuning values.

Tuning this can be a daunting task computationally speaking. For our example, we'll just focus on tuning `eta` and `gamma`. Let's build the grid as follows:

```
> grid = expand.grid(
    nrounds = 100,
    colsample_bytree = 1,
    min_child_weight = 1,
    eta = c(0.1, 0.3, 0.5), #0.3 is default,
    gamma = c(0.25, 0.5),
    subsample = 1,
    max_depth = c(3)
  )
```

This creates a grid of six different models that the `caret` package will run to determine the best tuning parameters. A note of caution is in order. On a dataset of the size that we'll be working with, this process takes only a few minutes. However, in large datasets or tuning more parameters with more values per parameter, this can take hours. As such, you must apply your judgment and possibly experiment with smaller samples of the data in order to identify the tuning parameters, in case time is of the essence or you're constrained by the size of your hard drive.

Before using the `train()` function from the `caret` package, I would like to specify the `trainControl` argument by creating an object called `control`. This object will store the method that we want so as to train the tuning parameters. We'll use 5 fold cross-validation, as follows:

```
> cntrl = caret::trainControl(
+ method = "cv",
+ number = 5,
+ verboseIter = TRUE,
+ returnData = FALSE,
+ returnResamp = "final"
+ )
```

To utilize the `train.xgb()` function, just specify the formula as we did with the other models: the `train` dataset input values, labels, method, train control, metric, and experimental grid. Remember to set the random seed:

```
> set.seed(123)

> train.xgb = caret::train(
      x = x_reduced,
      y = y,
      trControl = cntrl,
      tuneGrid = grid,
      method = "xgbTree",
      metric = "Kappa"
  )
```

Since in `trControl` I set `verboseIter` to `TRUE`, you should have seen each training iteration within each k-fold.

Calling the object gives us the optimal parameters and the results of each of the parameter settings, as follows (this is abbreviated for simplicity):

```
> train.xgb
eXtreme Gradient Boosting
No pre-processing
Resampling: Cross-Validated (5 fold)
```

```
Summary of sample sizes: 48653, 48653, 48653, 48652, 48653
Resampling results across tuning parameters:

  eta gamma  Accuracy       Kappa
  0.1  0.25 0.9604545 0.001525813
  0.1  0.50 0.9604709 0.002323003
  0.3  0.25 0.9604216 0.014214973
  0.3  0.50 0.9604052 0.014215605
  0.5  0.25 0.9600434 0.015513354
  0.5  0.50 0.9599776 0.013964451


Tuning parameter 'nrounds' was held constant at a value of 100
  1
Tuning parameter 'min_child_weight' was held constant at a value of
  1
Tuning parameter 'subsample' was held constant at a value of 1
Kappa was used to select the optimal model using the largest value.
The final values used for the model were nrounds = 100, max_depth = 3, eta
  = 0.5, gamma = 0.25, colsample_bytree = 1, min_child_weight = 1
  and subsample = 1.
```

The best results are with `eta = 0.5`, and `gamma = 0.25`. Now it gets a little tricky, but this is what I've seen as best practice. First, create a list of parameters that will be used by the `xgboost` training function, `xgb.train()`. Then, turn the dataframe into a matrix of input features and a list of labeled numeric outcomes (0s and 1s). Then, turn the features and labels into the input required, as `xgb.Dmatrix`. Try this:

```
> param <- list( objective = "binary:logistic",
    booster = "gbtree",
    eval_metric = "error",
    eta = 0.5,
    max_depth = 3,
    subsample = 1,
    colsample_bytree = 1,
    gamma = 0.25
)
> train.mat <- xgboost::xgb.DMatrix(data = x_reduced, label = ynum)
```

With all of that prepared, just create the model:

```
> set.seed(1232)

> xgb.fit <- xgboost::xgb.train(params = param, data = train.mat, nrounds =
    100)
```

Before seeing how it does on the test set, let's check the variable importance and plot it. You can examine three items: **gain**, **cover**, and **frequency**. **Gain** is the improvement in accuracy that feature brings to the branches it's on. **Cover** is the relative number of total observations related to this feature. **Frequency** is the percentage of times that feature occurs in all of the trees. The following code produces the desired output:

```
> impMatrix <- xgboost::xgb.importance(feature_names = dimnames(x)[[2]],
    model = xgb.fit)

> xgboost::xgb.plot.importance(impMatrix, main = "Gain by Feature")
```

The output of the preceding command is as follows:

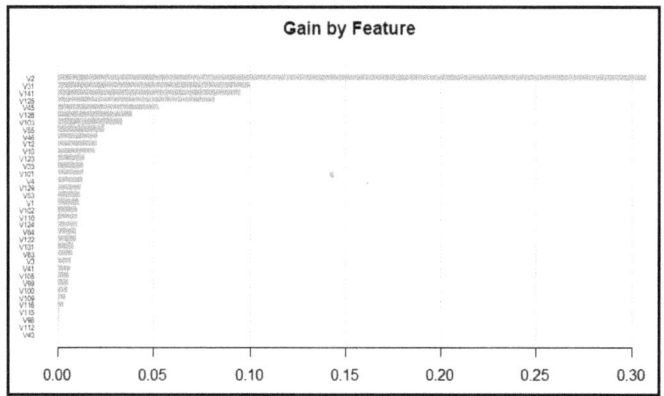

How does the feature importance compare to random forest? Feature **V2** remains the most important, and roughly the top ten are the same. Note that it does very well on the training data:

```
> pred <- predict(xgb.fit, x_reduced)

> MLmetrics::AUC(pred, y)  #.88
[1] 0.8839242

> MLmetrics::LogLoss(pred, ynum)  #.12
[1] 0.1209341
```

Impressed? Well, here is how we see it performed on the test set, which, like the training data, must be in a matrix:

```
> test_xgb <- as.matrix(test)

> test_xgb <- test_xgb[, my_forest_vars]
```

```
> xgb_test_matrix <- xgboost::xgb.DMatrix(data = test_xgb, label = ytest)

> xgb_pred <- predict(xgb.fit, xgb_test_matrix)

> Metrics::auc(ytest, xgb_pred) #.83
[1] 0.8282241

> MLmetrics::LogLoss(xgb_pred, ytest) #.138
[1] 0.1380904
```

What happened here is that the model had the lowest bias on the training data, but the performance falls off on the test data. Even so, it still has the highest AUC and lowest log-loss. Like we did with random forest, let's compare the ROC plot with `xgboost` added:

```
> ROCR::plot(perf.rf, main = "ROC", col = "black")

> ROCR::plot(perf.earth, col = "red", add = TRUE)

> pred.xgb <- ROCR::prediction(xgb_pred, test$y)

> perf.xgb <- ROCR::performance(pred.xgb, "tpr", "fpr")

> ROCR::plot(perf.xgb, col = "green", add = TRUE)

> legend(x = .75, y = .5,
    legend = c("RF", "MARS", "XGB"),
    fil = c("black", "red", "green"),
    col = c(1,2,3))
```

The output of the proceeding code is as follows:

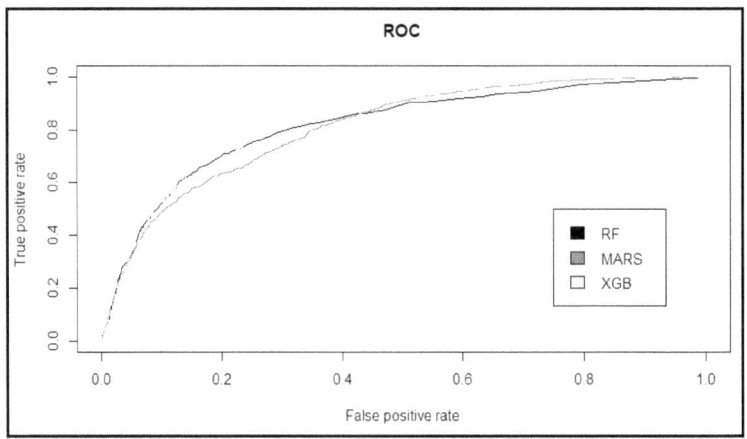

The `xgboost` model sort of combines the best of random forest and MARS in performance. All that will minimal tuning of hyperparameters. This clearly shows the power of the method and why it has become so popular.

Before we bring this chapter to a close, I want to introduce the powerful method of feature elimination using random forest techniques.

Feature selection with random forests

So far, we've looked at several feature selection techniques, such as regularization, stepwise, and recursive feature elimination. I now want to introduce an effective feature selection method for classification problems with random forests using the `Boruta` package. A paper is available that provides details on how it works in providing all the relevant features: *Kursa M., Rudnicki W. (2010), Feature Selection with the Boruta Package, Journal of Statistical Software, 36(11), 1 - 13*.

What I'll do here is provide an overview of the algorithm and then apply it to the simulated dataset. I've found it to be highly effective at eliminating unimportant features, but be advised it can be computationally intensive. However, it's usually time well spent.

At a high level, the algorithm creates **shadow attributes** by copying all of the input values and shuffling the order of their observations to decorrelate them. Then, a random forest model is built on all of the input values and a Z-score of the mean accuracy loss for each feature, including the shadow ones. Features with significantly higher Z-scores or significantly lower Z-scores than the shadow attributes are deemed **important** and **unimportant** respectively. The shadow attributes and those features with known importance are removed and the process repeats itself until all features are assigned an importance value. You can also specify the maximum number of random forest iterations. After completion of the algorithm, each of the original features will be labeled as **confirmed**, **tentative**, or **rejected**. You must decide on whether or not to include the tentative features for further modeling. Depending on your situation, you have some options:

- Change the random seed and rerun the methodology multiple (*k*) times and select only those features that are confirmed in all of the *k* runs
- Divide your data (training data) into *k* folds, run separate iterations on each fold, and select those features which are confirmed for all of the *k* folds

Note that all of this can be done with just a few lines of code. To get started, load the simulated data, `sim_df`, again. We'll create train and test sets as before:

```
> sim_df$y <- as.factor(sim_df$y)

> set.seed(1066)

> index <- caret::createDataPartition(sim_df$y, p = 0.7, list = F)

> train <- sim_df[index, ]

> test <- sim_df[-index, ]
```

To run the algorithm, you just need to call the `Boruta` package and create a formula in the `boruta()` function. Keep in mind that the labels must be a factor or the algorithm won't work. If you want to track the progress of the algorithm, specify `doTrace = 1`. But, I shall forgot that option in the following. Also, don't forget to set the random seed:

```
> set.seed(5150)

> rf_fs <- Boruta::Boruta(y ~ ., data = train)
```

As mentioned, this can be computationally intensive. Here's how long it took on my old-fashioned laptop:

```
> rf_fs$timeTaken #2.84 minutes workstation, 28.22
Time difference of 22.15982 mins
```

I ran this same thing on a high-powered workstation and it ran in two minutes.

A simple table will provide the count of the final importance decision. We see that the algorithm rejects five features and selects 11:

```
> table(rf_fs$finalDecision)

Tentative Confirmed Rejected
        0        11        5
```

Using these results, it's simple to create a new dataframe with our selected features. We start out using the `getSelectedAttributes()` function to capture the feature names. In this example, let's only select those that are confirmed. If we wanted to include confirmed and tentative, we just specify `withTentative = TRUE` in the function:

```
> fnames <- Boruta::getSelectedAttributes(rf_fs) #withTentative = TRUE

> fnames
 [1] "TwoFactor1" "TwoFactor2" "Linear2"    "Linear3"    "Linear4"
"Linear5"
 [7] "Linear6"    "Nonlinear1" "Nonlinear2" "Nonlinear3" "random1"
```

Using the feature names, we create our subset of the data:

```
> boruta_train <- train[, colnames(train) %in% fnames]

> boruta_train$y <- train$y
```

We'll go ahead now and build a random forest algorithm with the selected features and see how it performs:

```
> boruta_fit <- randomForest::randomForest(y ~ ., data = train)

> boruta_pred <- predict(boruta_fit, type = "prob", newdata = test)

> boruta_pred <- boruta_pred[, 2]

> ytest <- as.numeric(ifelse(test$y == "1", 1, 0))

> MLmetrics::AUC(boruta_pred, ytest)
[1] 0.9604841

> MLmetrics::LogLoss(boruta_pred, ytest)
[1] 0.2704204
```

This is quite an impressive performance when you compare to the results from Chapter 4, *Advanced Feature Selection in Linear Models*. I think this example serves as a good validation of the technique. Go get some computing horsepower and start using it!

Summary

In this chapter, you learned both the power of tree-based learning methods for classification problems. Single trees, while easy to build and interpret, may not have the necessary predictive power for many of the problems that we're trying to solve. To improve on the predictive ability, we have the tools of random forest and gradient-boosted trees at our disposal. With random forest, hundreds or even thousands of trees are built and the results aggregated for an overall prediction. Each tree of the random forest is built using a sample of the data called bootstrapping as well as a sample of the predictive variables. As for gradient boosting, an initial, and a relatively small, tree is produced. After this initial tree is built, subsequent trees are produced based on the residuals/misclassifications. The intended result of such a technique is to build a series of trees that can improve on the weakness of the prior tree in the process, resulting in decreased bias and variance. We also saw that, in R, we can utilize random forests as an effective feature selection/reduction method.

While these methods are extremely powerful, they aren't some sort of nostrum in the world of machine learning. Different datasets require judgment on the part of the analyst as to which techniques are applicable. The techniques to be applied to the analysis, and the selection of the tuning parameters is equally important. This fine tuning can make all of the difference between a good predictive model and a great predictive model.

In the next chapter, we'll turn our attention to using R to build neural networks and deep learning models.

Neural Networks and Deep Learning

7

"Forget artificial intelligence – in the brave new world of big data, it's artificial idiocy we should be looking out for."

– Tom Chatfield

I recall that at some meeting circa mid-2012, I was part of a group discussing the results of some analysis or other, when one of the people around the table sounded off with a hint of exasperation mixed with a tinge of fright: *this isn't one of those neural networks, is it?* I knew of his past run-ins with, and deep-seated anxiety regarding, neural networks, so I assuaged his fears, making some sarcastic comment that neural networks have basically gone the way of the dinosaur. No one disagreed! Several months later, I was gobsmacked when I attended a local meeting where the discussion focused on, of all things, neural networks and this mysterious deep learning. Machine learning pioneers, such as Ng, Hinton, Salakhutdinov, and Bengio have revived neural networks and improved their performance.

Much media hype revolves around these methods, with high-tech companies such as Facebook, Google, and Netflix investing tens, if not hundreds, of millions of dollars. These methods have yielded promising results in voice recognition, image recognition, automation, and any practical data science project. If self-driving cars ever stop running off the road and into each other, it will certainly be due to the methods we've discussed here.

In this chapter, we will discuss how the methods work, their benefits, and their inherent drawbacks so that you can become conversationally competent about them. We will start slowly by working through a simple application of a neural network, which will give you a feel for what is happening. Then, we will pursue the deep learning methodology that has burst on the scene the past couple of years, TensorFlow, using Keras as the frontend.

The following topics will be covered in this chapter:

- Introduction to neural networks
- Deep learning, a not-so-deep overview
- Creating a simple neural network
- An example of deep learning

Introduction to neural networks

Neural network is a fairly broad term that covers a number of related methods but, in our case, we will focus on a **feedforward** network that trains with **backpropagation**. I'm not going to waste our time discussing how the machine learning methodology is similar or dissimilar to how a biological brain works. We only need to start with a working definition of what a neural network is.

To know more about artificial neural networks, I think the Wikipedia entry is a good start: `https://en.wikipedia.org/wiki/Artificial_ neural_network.`

To summarize, in machine learning and cognitive science, **artificial neural networks (ANNs)** are a family of statistical learning models inspired by biological neural networks (the central nervous systems of animals, the brain) and are used to estimate or approximate functions that can depend on a large number of inputs and are generally unknown.

The motivation or benefit of ANNs is that they allow the modeling of highly complex relationships between inputs/features and response variable(s), especially if the relationships are highly nonlinear. No underlying assumptions are required to create and evaluate the model, and it can be used with qualitative and quantitative responses. If this is the yin, then the yang is the common criticism that the results are a black box, which means that there is no equation with the coefficients to examine and share with the business partners. In fact, the results are *almost* uninterpretable. The other criticisms revolve around how results can differ by just changing the initial random inputs and that training ANNs is computationally expensive and time-consuming.

The mathematics behind ANNs is not trivial by any measure. However, it is crucial to at least get a working understanding of what is happening. A good way to intuitively develop this understanding is to start with a diagram of a simplistic neural network.

The output of the preceding command is as follows:

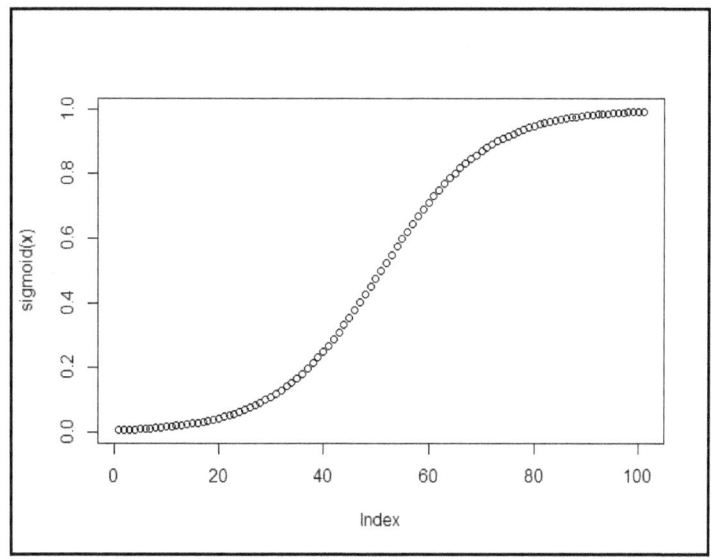

The `tanh` function (hyperbolic tangent) is a rescaling of the logistic `sigmoid` with the output between **-1** and **1**. The `tanh` function relates to `sigmoid` as follows, where *x* is the `sigmoid` function:

$$tanh(x) = 2 * sigmoid(2x) - 1$$

Let's plot the `tanh` and `sigmoid` functions for comparison purposes. Let's also use `ggplot`:

```
> install.packages("ggplot2")

> s <- sigmoid(x)

> t <- tanh(x)

> z <- data.frame(cbind(x, s, t))

> ggplot2::ggplot(z, ggplot2::aes(x)) +
    ggplot2::geom_line(ggplot2::aes(y = s, color = "sigmoid")) +
    ggplot2::geom_line(ggplot2::aes(y = t, color = "tanh"))
```

The output of the preceding command is as follows:

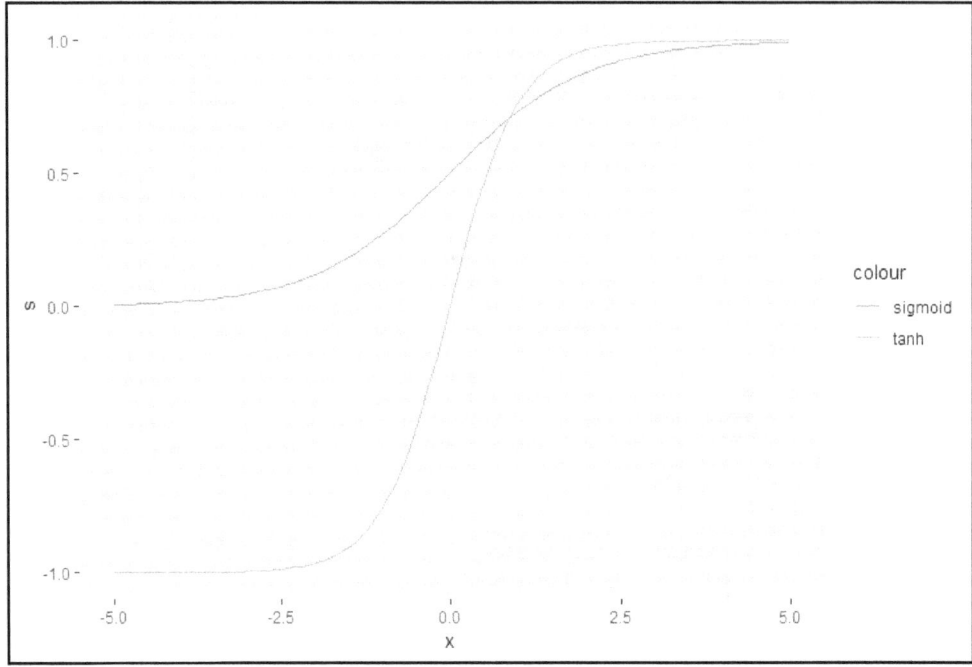

So, why use the `tanh` function versus `sigmoid`? It seems there are many opinions on the subject. In short, assuming you have scaled data with mean 0 and variance 1, the `tanh` function permits weights that are on average, close to zero (zero-centered). This helps in avoiding bias and improves convergence. Think about the implications of always having positive weights from an output neuron to an input neuron like in a `sigmoid` function activation. During backpropagation, the weights will become either all positive or all negative between layers. This may cause performance issues. Also, since the gradient at the tails of a `sigmoid` (0 and 1) are almost zero, during backpropagation, it can happen that almost no signal will flow between neurons of different layers. A full discussion of the issue is available from LeCun (1998). Keep in mind it is not a foregone conclusion that `tanh` is always better.

This all sounds fascinating, but the ANN almost went the way of disco as it just did not perform as well as advertised, especially when trying to use deep networks with many hidden layers and neurons. It seems that a slow, yet gradual revival came about with the seminal paper by Hinton and Salakhutdinov (2006) in the reformulated and, dare I say, rebranded neural network, deep learning.

Deep learning – a not-so-deep overview

So, what is this deep learning that is grabbing our attention and headlines? Let's turn to Wikipedia again to form a working definition: *Deep learning is a branch of machine learning based on a set of algorithms that attempt to model high-level abstractions in data by using model architectures, with complex structures or otherwise, composed of multiple nonlinear transformations.* That sounds as if a lawyer wrote it. The characteristics of deep learning are that it is based on ANNs where the machine learning techniques, primarily unsupervised learning, are used to create new features from the input variables. We will dig into some unsupervised learning techniques in the next couple of chapters, but you can think of it as finding structure in data where no response variable is available.

A simple way to think of it is the **periodic table of elements**, which is a classic case of finding a structure where no response is specified. Pull up this table online and you will see that it is organized based on atomic structure, with metals on one side and non-metals on the other. It was created based on latent classification/structure. This identification of latent structure/hierarchy is what separates deep learning from your run-of-the-mill ANN. Deep learning sort of addresses the question of whether there is an algorithm that better represents the outcome than just the raw inputs. In other words, can our model learn to classify pictures other than with just the raw pixels as the only input? This can be of great help in a situation where you have a small set of labeled responses but a vast amount of unlabeled input data. You could train your deep learning model using unsupervised learning and then apply this in a supervised fashion to the labeled data, iterating back and forth.

Identification of these latent structures is not trivial mathematically, but one example is the concept of regularization that we looked at in Chapter 4, *Advanced Feature Selection in Linear Models*. In deep learning, you can penalize weights with **regularization** methods such as *L1* (penalize non-zero weights), *L2* (penalize large weights), and **dropout** (randomly ignore certain inputs and zero their weight out). In standard ANNs, none of these regularization methods take place.

Another way is to reduce the dimensionality of the data. One such method is the `autoencoder`. This is a neural network where the inputs are transformed into a set of reduced dimension weights. In the following diagram, notice that **Feature A** is not connected to one of the hidden nodes:

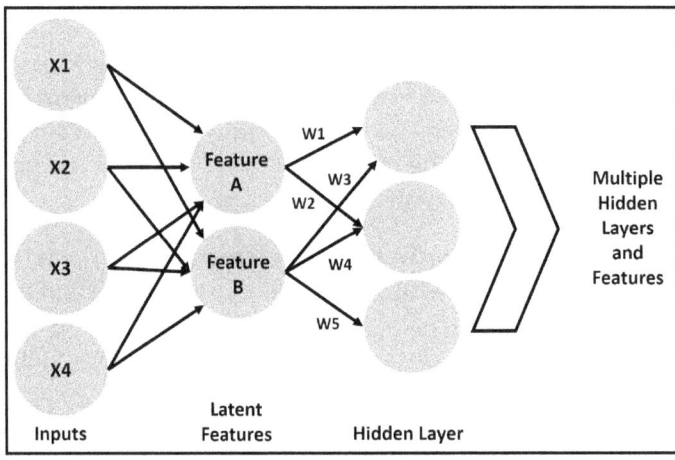

This can be applied recursively and learning can take place over many hidden layers. What you have seen happening, in this case, is that the network is developing features of features as they are stacked on each other. Deep learning will learn the weights between two layers in sequence first and then use backpropagation to fine-tune these weights. Other feature selection methods include **restricted Boltzmann machine** and **sparse coding model**.

The details of restricted Boltzmann machine and sparse coding model are beyond our scope, and many resources are available to learn about the specifics. Here are a couple of starting points: `http://www.cs.toronto.edu/~hinton/` and `http://deeplearning.net/`.

Deep learning has performed well on many classification problems, including winning a Kaggle contest or two. It still suffers from the problems of ANNs, especially the black box problem. Try explaining to the uninformed what is happening inside a neural network, regardless of the use of various in vogue methods. However, it is appropriate for problems where an explanation of *how* is not a problem and the important question is *what*. After all, do we really care why an autonomous car avoided running into a pedestrian, or do we care about the fact that it did not? Additionally, the Python community has a bit of a head start on the R community in deep learning usage and packages. As we will see in the practical exercise, the gap is closing.

While deep learning is an exciting undertaking, be aware that to achieve the full benefit of its capabilities, you will need a high degree of computational power along with taking the time to train the best model by fine-tuning the hyperparameters. Here is a list of some things that you will need to consider:

- An activation function
- Size and number of the hidden layers
- Dimensionality reduction, that is, restricted Boltzmann versus autoencoder
- The number of epochs
- The gradient descent learning rate
- The loss function
- Regularization

Deep learning resources and advanced methods

One of the more interesting visual tools you can use for both learning and explaining is the interactive widget provided by TensorFlow: `http://playground.tensorflow.org/`. This tool allows you to explore, or *tinker*, as the site calls it, the various parameters and how they impact on the response, be it a classification problem or a regression problem. I could spend – well, I have spent – hours tinkering with it.

Here is an interesting task: create your own experimental design and see how the various parameters affect your prediction.

At this point, the fastest-growing deep learning open source tool is TensorFlow. You can access TensorFlow with R, but it requires you to install Python first. What we will go through in the practical exercise is Keras, which is an API that can run on top of TensorFlow, or other backend neural networks such as Theano. The creators of Keras designed it to simplify the development and testing of deep neural networks. We will discuss TensorFlow and Keras a little more in-depth, prior to our implementation of a problem.

I also really like using MXNet, which does not require the installation of Python and is relatively easy to install and make operational. It also offers a number of trained models that allow you to start making predictions quickly. Several R tutorials are available at `http://mxnet.io/`.

I now want to take the time to enumerate some of the variations of deep neural networks along with the learning tasks where they have performed well.

Convolutional neural networks (**CNNs**) make the assumption that the inputs are images and create features from slices or small portions of the data, which are combined to create a feature map. Think of these small slices as filters or, probably more appropriately, kernels that the network learns during training. The activation function for a CNN is a rectified linear unit (ReLU). It is simply $f(x) = max(0, x)$, where x is the input to the neuron. CNNs perform well on image classification, and object detection.

Recurrent neural networks (**RNNs**) are created to make use of sequential information. In traditional neural networks, the inputs and outputs are independent of each other. With RNNs, the output is dependent on the computations of previous layers, permitting information to persist across layers. So, take an output from a neuron (y); it is calculated not only on its input (t) but on all previous layers (t-1, t-n...). It is effective at handwriting and speech detection.

Long short-term memory (**LSTM**) is a special case of an RNN. The problem with an RNN is that it does not perform well on data with long signals. Thus, LSTMs were created to capture complex patterns in data. RNNs combine information during training from previous steps in the same way, regardless of the fact that information in one step is more or less valuable than other steps. LSTMs seek to overcome this limitation by deciding what to remember at each step during training. This multiplication of a weight matrix by the data vector is referred to as a gate, which acts as an information filter. A neuron in an LSTM will have two inputs and two outputs. The input from prior outputs and the memory vector passed from the previous gate. Then, it produces the output values and output memory as inputs to the next layer. LSTMs have the limitation of requiring a healthy dose of training data and are computationally intensive. LSTMs have performed well on speech recognition problems and in complicated time series analysis.

With that, let's move on to some practical applications.

Creating a simple neural network

For this task, we will develop a neural network to answer the question of when the now-defunct Space Shuttle should use its autolanding system. The default decision is to let the crew land the craft. However, the autoland capability may be required for situations of crew incapacitation or adverse effects of gravity upon re-entry after extended orbital operations. This data is based on computer simulations, not actual flights. In reality, the autoland system went through some trials and tribulations and, for the most part, the shuttle astronauts were in charge during the landing process. Here are a couple of links for further background information:

- http://www.spaceref.com/news/viewsr.html?pid=10518
- https://waynehale.wordpress.com/2011/03/11/breaking-through/

Data understanding and preparation

To start, we will load the necessary packages and put the required ones in the environment. The data is in the MASS package:

```
> library(magrittr)

> install.packages(caret)

> install.packages(MASS)

> library(MASS)

> install.packages("neuralnet")

> install.packages("vtreat")
```

The neuralnet package will be used for building the model and caret for data preparation. Let's load the data and examine its structure:

```
> data(shuttle)

> str(shuttle)
```

The data consists of 256 observations and 7 features. Notice that all of the features are categorical and the response is use with two levels, auto and noauto, as follows:

- stability: This is stable positioning or not (stab/xstab)
- error: This is the size of the error (MM / SS / LX)
- sign: This is the sign of the error, positive or negative (pp/nn)
- wind: This is the wind sign (head / tail)
- magn: This is the wind strength (Light / Medium / Strong / Out of Range)
- vis: This is the visibility (yes / no)

Here, we will look at a table of the response/outcome:

```
> table(shuttle$use)
 auto noauto
 145    111
```

Almost 57% of the time, the decision is to use the autolander. We'll now get our training and testing data set up for modeling:

```
> set.seed(1942)

> trainIndex <-
    caret::createDataPartition(shuttle$use, p = .6, list = FALSE)

> shuttleTrain <- shuttle[trainIndex, -7]

> shuttleTest <- shuttle[-trainIndex, -7]
```

We are going to treat the data to create numeric features, and also drop the cat_P features that the function creates. We covered the idea of treating a dataframe in Chapter 1, *Preparing and Understanding Data*:

```
> treatShuttle <- vtreat::designTreatmentsZ(shuttleTrain,
colnames(shuttleTrain))

> train_treated <- vtreat::prepare(treatShuttle, shuttleTrain)

> train_treated <- train_treated[, c(-1,-2)]

> test_treated <- vtreat::prepare(treatShuttle, shuttleTest)

> test_treated <- test_treated[, c(-1, -2)]
```

The next couple portions of code I find awkward. Because `neuralnet()` requires a formula and the data in a dataframe, we have to turn the response into a numeric list and then add it to our treated train and test data:

```
> shuttle_trainY <- shuttle[trainIndex, 7]

> train_treated$y <- ifelse(shuttle_trainY == "auto", 1, 0)

> shuttle_testY <- shuttle[-trainIndex, 7]

> test_treated$y <- ifelse(shuttle_testY == "auto", 1, 0)
```

The function in `neuralnet` will call for the use of a formula as we used elsewhere, such as *y~x1+x2+x3+x4*, *data = df*. In the past, we used *y~* to specify all the other variables in the data as inputs. However, `neuralnet` does not accommodate this at the time of writing. The way around this limitation is to use the `as.formula()` function. After first creating an object of the variable names, we will use this as an input to paste the variables properly on the right-hand side of the equation:

```
> n <- names(train_treated)

> form <- as.formula(paste("y ~", paste(n[!n %in% "y"], collapse = " + ")))
```

The object `form` give us what we need to build our model.

Modeling and evaluation

In the `neuralnet` package, the function that we will use is appropriately named `neuralnet()`. Other than the formula, there are four other critical arguments that we will need to examine:

- `hidden`: This is the number of hidden neurons in each layer, which can be up to three layers; the default is 1
- `act.fct`: This is the activation function with the default logistic and `tanh` available
- `err.fct`: This is the function used to calculate the error with the default `sse`; as we are dealing with binary outcomes, we will use `ce` for cross-entropy
- `linear.output`: This is a logical argument on whether or not to ignore `act.fct` with the default `TRUE`, so for our data, this will need to be `FALSE`

You can also specify the algorithm. The default is resilient with backpropagation and we will use it along with the default of one hidden neuron for simplicity:

```
> nnfit <- neuralnet::neuralnet(form, data = train_treated, err.fct = "ce",
linear.output = FALSE)
```

Here is an abbreviated output of weights for the overall result:

```
> head(nnfit$result.matrix)
1
error                               0.024293436369
reached.threshold                   0.009929147409
steps                             181.000000000000
Intercept.to.1layhid1               0.573783967352
stability_lev_x_stab.to.1layhid1   -2.072585716776
stability_lev_x_xstab.to.1layhid1   6.859369770672
```

We can see that the error is extremely low at `0.024`. The number of steps required for the algorithm to reach the threshold, which is when the absolute partial derivatives of the error function, become smaller than this error (default = 0.1).

You can also look at what is known as generalized weights. According to the authors of the `neuralnet` package, the generalized weight is defined as the contribution of the *i*th covariate to the log-odds:

The generalized weight expresses the effect of each covariate x_i and thus has an analogous interpretation as the ith regression parameter in regression models. However, the generalized weight depends on all other covariates (Gunther and Fritsch, 2010).

TIP

The weights can be called and examined. I've abbreviated the output to the first four variables and six observations only. Note that if you sum each row, you will get the same number, which means that the weights are equal for each covariate combination. Please note that your results might be slightly different because of random weight initialization.

The results are as follows:

```
> head(fit$generalized.weights[[1]])
            [,1]            [,2]            [,3]            [,4]
1 0.0004057906237 -0.001342992917 -0.0010654093452 -0.00010947079069
2 0.0003792401307 -0.001255122173 -0.0009957006291 -0.00010230822138
3 0.0003929874040 -0.001300619751 -0.0010317943007 -0.00010601684547
4 0.0003672745975 -0.001215521390 -0.0009642849428 -0.00009908026019
5 0.0273129186450 -0.090394045943 -0.0717104759663 -0.00736825009054
6 0.0255281981170 -0.084487386479 -0.0670246655557 -0.00688678315678
```

To visualize the neural network, simply use the `plot()` function:

```
> plot(fit)
```

The following is the output of the preceding command:

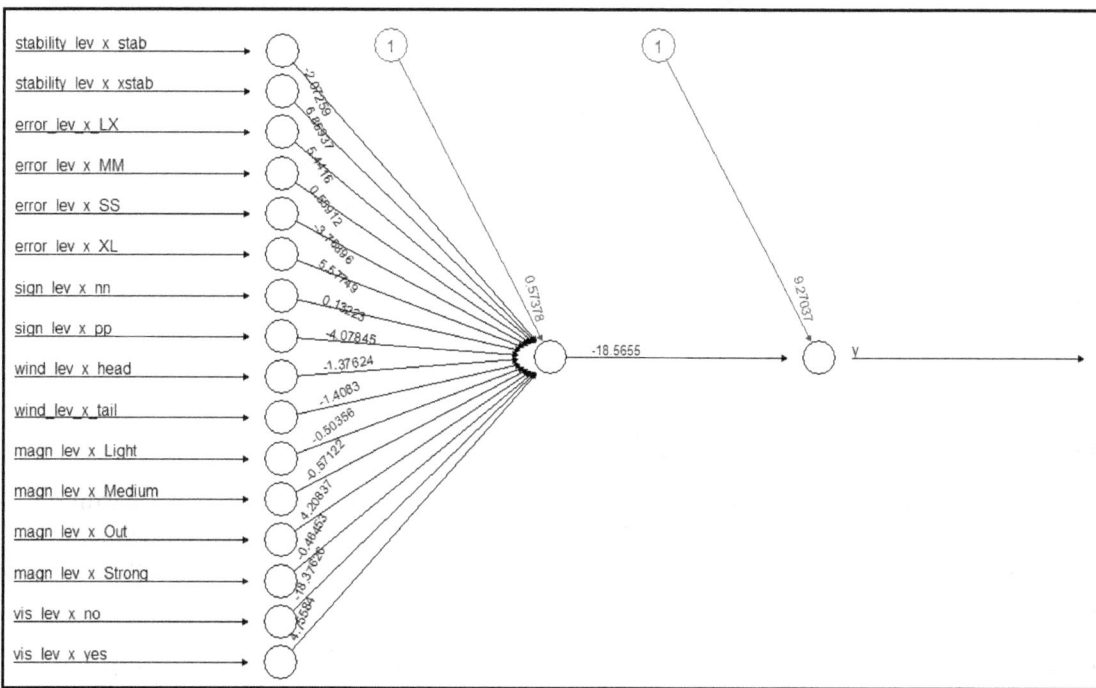

This plot shows the weights of the features and intercepts.

We now want to see how well the model performs. This is done with the `compute()` function and specifying the fit model and covariates:

```
> test_pred <- neuralnet::compute(nnfit, test_treated[, 1:16])

> test_prob <- test_pred$net.result
```

These results are in probabilities, so let's turn them into 0 or 1 and follow this up with a confusion matrix and log-loss:

```
> pred <- ifelse(test_prob >= 0.5, 1, 0)

> table(pred, test_treated$y)
pred  0   1
   0 41   0
```

```
    1   3 58
> MLmetrics::LogLoss(test_prob, test_treated$y)
[1] 0.2002453861
```

The model achieved near-perfect accuracy on the test set but had three false negatives. I'll leave it to you to see if you can build a neural network that achieves 100% accuracy!

An example of deep learning

Shifting gears away from the Space Shuttle, let's work through how to set up, train, and evaluate a deep learning model. You see these used quite a bit for image classification, NLP, and so on. However, let's look at using it for regression. You don't find too many examples of that in my opinion. As such, let's go with our Ames housing price data we used back in `Chapter 2`, *Linear Regression*. Before that, let's briefly discuss what Tensor, TensorFlow, and Keras are.

Keras and TensorFlow background

I mentioned earlier that Keras is an API, a frontend if you will, for several deep learning backends. It was originally available only for Python but has been available in R since, mid-2017. It is important to spend some time reviewing its capabilities at its documentation source: `https://keras.io/why-use-keras/`.

I must confess my colleagues brought me into Keras and using TensorFlow kicking and screaming. If *I* can get this to work, I would say that you certainly can. I must thank them, as it is very powerful, even though I have a slight bias toward MXNet. As the old saying goes, it is tough to teach old dogs new tricks!

The backend of choice, of course, is TensorFlow. We must now take a few sentences to put in plain English what a tensor is, and what TensorFlow is. A tensor is an n-dimensional array. Thus, a vector is a one-dimensional tensor, a matrix is a two-dimensional tensor and so forth. Let's say you have a multivariate time series, which would consist of a three-dimensional tensor: one dimension is the observations or length of your data, another dimension is the features, and another the timesteps or, more concretely, the lagged values. TensorFlow as a backend is an open source platform, created by Google, that uses tensors, of course, for high-performance and scalable computation. The base frontend for TensorFlow is Python. Therefore, to use Keras and R as the frontend, you must install Python, in particular the Python platform Anaconda: `https://www.anaconda.com/`.

So, if installing Anaconda becomes an issue, then the following exercise will require you to use a different backend, which is outside the scope of this discussion. Let's look at how to get this up and running. Keep in mind that I'm using a Windows-based computer:

As a caveat, it is important to inform you that I in no way guarantee that the following code will work for you as I exactly lay it out. I've installed this on several computers, and each time I encountered different problems that required me to search the internet for a specific solution. The one common factor is that you have installed Anaconda on your computer and that it is fully functional.

```
# Install reticulate package as it allows R to call python
> install.packages("reticulate")

> install.packages("keras")

> keras::install_keras() # loads the necessary python packages and may take
some time to complete

> library(keras)

> library(reticulate)
```

That was the code that worked for me on this laptop. Again, your results may vary. Also, note that I've run into a number of issues that required me to run `install_keras()` again to get it working properly.

Assuming all is well, let's get our data loaded.

Loading the data

As for this data, it is the same that we used in `Chapter 2`, *Linear Regression*. What is different is that I've prepared the data exactly as before, but saved the features and response as an RData file. You can download that from GitHub: `https://github.com/PacktPublishing/Advanced-Machine-Learning-with-R/blob/master/Data/amesDL.RData`.

Once you have that in your working directory, load it into the environment:

```
> load("amesDL.RData")
```

Notice that you now have four new objects:

- `trained`: The training data features
- `tested`: The testing data features
- `train_logy`: The log of home sales
- `test_logy`: The log of home sales

It is essential that the data is centered and scaled for a neural network (in the prior exercise, all features were either zero or one, which is acceptable). To perform this task, a function is available in the `caret` package. Let's use the training data to create the mean and standard deviation values that we will apply to both train and test data:

```
> prep <- caret::preProcess(trained, method = c("center", "scale"))

> trainT <- predict(prep, trained)
```

This gives us our transformed training data. However, Keras will not accept a dataframe as an input. It needs an array for both the features and the response. This is an easy fix with the `data.matrix()` function:

```
> train_logy <- data.matrix(train_logy)

> trainT <- data.matrix(trainT)
```

Now, you can just repeat these steps with the test data features:

```
> testT <- predict(prep, tested)

> testT <- data.matrix(testT)
```

It's about to get interesting.

Creating the model function

OK, we are going to create a model function, but not the model. The key function is `keras_model_sequential()`. There is a ton of stuff you can specify. What I'm going to show are two hidden layers with 64 neurons each. In both layers, the activation function is `relu`, which I covered earlier, and they work well for a regression problem. After the first layer, I demonstrate how to incorporate a dropout layer of 30%. Then, after the second hidden layer, I incorporate L1 regularization or LASSO, which we discussed in `Chapter 4`, *Advanced Feature Selection in Linear Models*. I thought it was important to show how to use both regularization methods, so you can use and adjust them as you deem fit.

The next function within the function is `compile()`, where I specify the loss as **mean-squared-error** (**MSE**) and the validation data metric as mean-absolute-error:

```
> model <- keras_model_sequential() %>%
    layer_dense(units = 64, activation = "relu",
                input_shape = dim(trainT)[2]
    ) %>%
    layer_dropout(0.3) %>%
    layer_dense(units = 64, activation = "relu",
                kernel_regularizer = regularizer_l1(l = 0.001)) %>%
    #layer_dropout(0.5) %>%
    layer_dense(units = 1)
  model %>% compile(
    loss = "mse",
    optimizer = optimizer_rmsprop(),
    metrics = list("mean_absolute_error")
  )
  model
}
```

Now, you can build the model and examine it. One thing of note, and something I don't see in very many vignettes out there, is to specify the seed, otherwise your results *will* vary wildly:

```
> use_session_with_seed(1800)

> model <- build_model()

> model %>% summary()
```

The output of the preceding code is as follows:

Layer (type)	Output Shape	Param #
dense_1 (Dense)	(None, 64)	7360
dropout_1 (Dropout)	(None, 64)	0
dense_2 (Dense)	(None, 64)	4160
dense_3 (Dense)	(None, 1)	65

Total params: 11,585

```
Trainable params: 11,585
Non-trainable params: 0
```

The output should be self-explanatory, which means we can finally train the model.

Model training

Training the model is quite interesting, I believe. We will pass the model to the `fit()` function, having specified the features, response, number of epochs, and validation percentage at each epoch. Here, I have gone with 100 epochs, and 20% of the training data for validation:

```
> epochs <- 100

> # Fit the model and store training stats

> history <- model %>% fit(
    trainT,
    train_logy,
    epochs = epochs,
    validation_split = 0.2,
    verbose = 0
)
```

You can examine the history object on your own, but what is very powerful is to plot the training and validation error for each epoch:

```
> plot(history, metrics = "mean_absolute_error", smooth = FALSE)
```

The output of the preceding code is as follows:

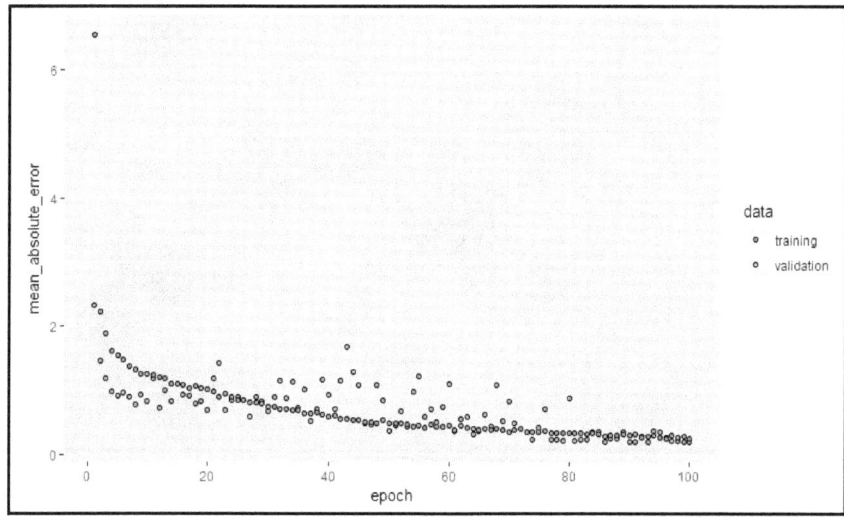

Notice how much the error differs between training and validation until we get above 80 epochs. This leads me to believe we should do well on the test data. Let's get our training baseline!

```
> min(history$metrics$mean_absolute_error)
[1] 0.248
```

To get the predicted values on the test data, just pipe the model to the `predict()` function:

```
> test_predictions <- model %>% predict(testT)
```

We now call up our metrics as we've done in other chapters. We should look at MAE obviously, but also the % error, and the R-squared:

```
> MLmetrics::MAE(test_predictions, test_logy)
[1] 0.162

> MLmetrics::MAPE(test_predictions, test_logy)
[1] 0.0133

> MLmetrics::R2_Score(test_predictions, test_logy)
[1] 0.6765795
```

Well done, I must say. To conclude evaluation, let's examine a base R plot of the predicted values versus the actuals (the log values):

```
> plot(test_predictions, test_logy)
```

The output of the preceding code is as follows:

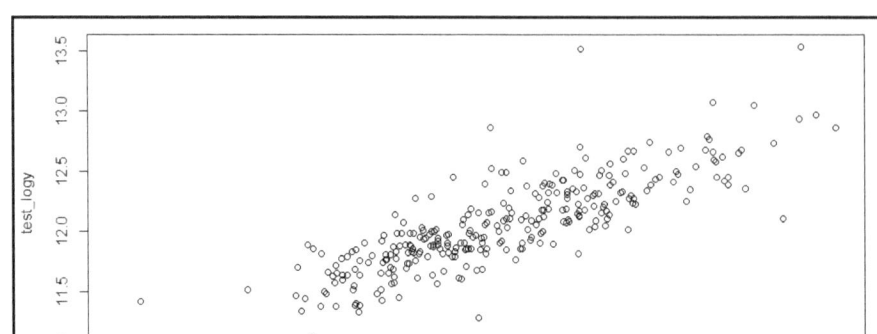

This compares similarly to what we did in `Chapter 2`, *Linear Regression*, with a number of outliers and some erratic performance on the lower- and higher-priced houses – all that with hardly any effort to adjust parameters such as the number of hidden neurons, layers, regularization, and maybe adding a linear activation unit somewhere.

In summary, using Keras with TensorFlow can challenge your sanity to code it properly to produce the results you desire, but what we've done here is establish a pipeline to make it possible for regression, and with a couple of changes, it will work for classification. All that, with very little effort around optimizing parameters, which I think is indicative of the power of the technique. Go and do likewise.

Summary

In this chapter, the goal was to get you up and running in the exciting world of neural networks and deep learning. We examined how the methods work, their benefits, and their inherent drawbacks, with applications to two different datasets. These techniques work well where complex, nonlinear relationships exist in the data. The first example was of a simple neural network on a simple dataset. The second example showed the power of using Keras with TensorFlow backend on a challenging dataset, and the performance was exemplary. I hope you will apply these methods by themselves or supplement other methods in an ensemble modeling fashion. Good luck and good hunting!

In the next chapter, we will learn about, ensembles, understand the data, and dive in deeper in modeling and evaluation.

8
Creating Ensembles and Multiclass Methods

"This is how you win ML competitions: you take other people's work and ensemble them together."

- Vitaly Kuznetsov, NIPS2014

You may have already realized that we've discussed ensemble learning. It's defined on `www.scholarpedia.org` as *the process by which multiple models, such as classifiers or experts, are strategically generated and combined to solve a particular computational intelligence problem.* In random forest and gradient boosting, we combined the *votes* of hundreds or thousands of trees to make a prediction. Hence, by definition, those models are ensembles. This methodology can be extended to any learner to create ensembles, which some refer to as meta-ensembles or meta-learners. We'll look at one of these methods referred to as **stacking**. In this methodology, we'll produce a number of classifiers and use their predicted class probabilities as input features to another classifier. This method *can* result in improved predictive accuracy. In the previous chapters, we focused on classification problems focused on binary outcomes. We'll now look at methods to predict those situations where the data consists of more than two outcomes (multiclass), a very common situation in real-world datasets.

The following are the topics that will be covered in this chapter:

- Ensembles
- Data understanding
- Modeling and evaluation

Ensembles

The quote at the beginning of this chapter mentions using ensembles to win machine learning competitions. However, they do have practical applications. I've provided a definition of what ensemble modeling is, but why does it work? To demonstrate this, I've co-opted an example from the following blog, which goes into depth at a number of ensemble methods: `http://mlwave.com/kaggle-ensembling-guide/`.

As I write this chapter, we're only a day away from the 2018 College Football Championship—the Clemson Tigers versus the Alabama Crimson Tide. Let's say we want to review our probability of winning a friendly wager where we want to take the Tide minus the points (5.5 points at the time of writing).

Assume that we've been following three expert prognosticators who said, *All have the same probability of predicting that the Patriots will cover the spread (60%)*. Now, if we favor any one of the so-called experts, it's clear that we have a 60% chance of winning. However, let's see what creating an ensemble of their predictions can do to increase our chances of profiting and humiliating friends and family.

Start by calculating the probability of each possible outcome for the experts picking Alabama, and let's assume that the probability is the same at 60%. If all three pick Alabama, we have *0.6 x 0.6 x 0.6* or a *21.6%* chance that all three are correct.

If any two of the three pick Alabama, then we have *(0.6 x 0.6 x 0.3) x 3* for a total of *43.2%*.

By using majority voting, if at least two of the three pick Alabama, then our probability of winning becomes almost *65% (21.6 + 43.2)*, which is an absolute improvement of 5%.

This is a rather simplistic example but representative nonetheless. In machine learning, it can manifest itself by incorporating the predictions from several OK or even weak learners to improve overall accuracy. The diagram that follows shows how this can be accomplished:

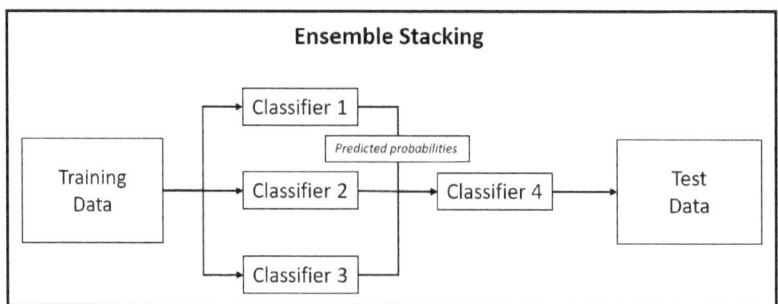

In this graphic, we build three different classifiers and use their predicted probabilities as input values to a fourth and different classifier in order to make predictions on the test data. Let's see how to apply this with R.

Data understanding

The dataset for analysis here is DNA pulled from mlbench. You don't have to install the package as I've put it in a CSV file and placed it on GitHub: https://github.com/PacktPublishing/Advanced-Machine-Learning-with-R/blob/master/Data/dna.csv.

Install the packages as needed and load the data:

```
> library(magrittr)

> install.packages("earth")

> install.packages("glmnet")

> install.packages("mlr")

> install.packages("randomForest")

> install.packages("tidyverse")

dna <- read.csv("dna.csv")
```

The data consists of 3,181 observations, 180 input features coded as binary indicators, and the Class response. The response is a factor with three labels indicating a DNA type either ei, ie, or neither—coded as n. The following is a table of the target labels:

```
> table(dna$Class)

  ei  ie   n
 767 765 1654
```

This data should be ready for analysis, but let's run some quick checks to verify, starting with missing values:

```
> na_count <-
    sapply(dna, function(y)
    sum(length(which(is.na(
    y
)))))

> table(na_count)
```

```
na_count
   0
 181
```

With no missing values, we check for zero variance features:

```
> feature_variance <- caret::nearZeroVar(dna[, -181], saveMetrics = TRUE)

> table(feature_variance$zeroVar)

FALSE
  180
```

One of the things the authors of `mlbench` did with this data is transform the nucleotide factor features (A, C, G, T) into indicator features. They also de-identified the features naming them V1 through V180.

As such, let's check feature correlation:

```
> high_corr <- caret::findCorrelation(dna[, -181], cutoff = 0.9)

> length(high_corr)
[1] 173
```

It's a highly correlated dataset. We could run our feature selection methods as we've done in previous chapters, but let's press on with all features and see what happens.

Before doing so, let's get the train and test sets created:

```
> set.seed(555)

> index <- caret::createDataPartition(y = dna$Class, p = 0.8, list = FALSE)

> train <- dna[index, ]

> test <- dna[-index, ]
```

This created an 80/20 split for us and we can move on to building an algorithm.

Modeling and evaluation

We're going to explore the use of the `mlr` package, which stand for machine learning in R. The package supports multiple classes and ensemble methods. If you're familiar with `sci-kit learn` for Python, we could say that `mlr` endeavors to provide the same functionality for R. I intend to demonstrate how to use the package on a multiclass problem, then conclude by showing how to do an ensemble on the same data, so we can compare performances.

For the multiclass problem, we'll look at how to tune a random forest and then examine how to build an ensemble using random forest in conjunction with MARS, stacking those models by calling the generalized linear model function from the `glmnet` package.

Random forest model

There are a number of approaches to learning in multiclass problems. Techniques such as random forest and discriminant analysis will deal with multiclass while some techniques and/or packages won't—for example, generalized linear models, `glm()`, in base R. The functionality built into `mlr` allows you to run a number of techniques for supervised and unsupervised learning. However, leveraging its power the first couple of times you use it can be a little confusing. If you follow the process outlined in the following, you'll be well on your way to developing powerful learning pipelines. We'll be using random forest in this demonstration.

We've created the training and testing sets, which you can do in `mlr`, but I still prefer the technique we've been doing using the `caret` package. One of the unique things about the `mlr` package is that you have to put your training data into a task structure, specifically, in this problem, a classification task. Optionally, you can place your test set in a task as well. You specify the dataset and the target containing the labels:

```
> dna_task <- mlr::makeClassifTask(data = train, target = "Class")
```

There are many ways to use `mlr` in your analysis, but I recommend creating a resample object.

In the following code block, we create a resampling object to help us in tuning the number of trees for our random forest, consisting of five subsamples. Keep in mind that you have similar flexibility in the resampling method just like the `caret` package with techniques such as cross-validation and repeated cross-validation:

```
> rdesc <- mlr::makeResampleDesc("Subsample", iters = 5)
```

The next object establishes the grid of trees for tuning with the minimum number of trees, set to `50`, and the maximum set to `200`. You can also establish multiple parameters as we did with the `caret` package. Your options can be explored by calling help for the function with `makeParamSet`:

```
> param <-
+ ParamHelpers::makeParamSet(ParamHelpers::makeDiscreteParam("ntree",
values = c(50, 75, 100, 150, 175, 200)))
```

Next, create a control object, establishing a numeric grid:

```
> ctrl <- makeTuneControlGrid()
```

With the preliminary objects created, we can now go ahead and tune the hyperparameter for the optimal number of trees in the random forest, as per our grid. Notice that we're specifying `classif.randomForest`. The previous link on the available models of `mlr` gives us all of the proper syntax you use for your desired method. One thing we should do is bring the `mlr` library into the environment, so we can use that syntax. We also use the objects we just created:

```
> library(mlr)

> tuning <-
    mlr::tuneParams(
      "classif.randomForest",
      task = dna_task,
      resampling = rdesc,
      par.set = param,
      control = ctrl)
```

Once the algorithm completes its iterations, you can call up both the optimal number of trees and the associated out-of-sample error:

```
> tuning$x
$`ntree`
[1] 175

> tuning$y
mmce.test.mean
     0.04635294
```

The optimal number of trees as per our experiment grid is `175` with a mean misclassification error of `0.046` percent. It's now a simple matter of setting this parameter for training as a wrapper around the `makeLearner()` function. Notice that I set the predicted type to `"prob"` as the default is the predicted class and not the probability:

```
> rf <-
    mlr::setHyperPars(mlr::makeLearner("classif.randomForest", predict.type
= "prob"),
    par.vals = tuning$x)
```

Now we train the model again with just `175` trees:

```
> fit_rf <- mlr::train(rf, dna_task)
```

You can see the confusion matrix on the train data:

```
> fit_rf$learner.model

          OOB estimate of error rate: 5.14%
Confusion matrix:
     ei   ie    n class.error
ei  563   26   25 0.08306189
ie   16  575   21 0.06045752
n    10   33 1281 0.03247734
```

That's better than I expected with an out-of-bag error of just over 5%. Also, there is no error for a class that's way out of balance. Additionally, it performs pretty well on the test data:

```
> mlr::calculateConfusionMatrix(pred)
        predicted
true     ei  ie    n -err.-
  ei    139   4   10     14
  ie      3 147    3      6
  n       2   3  325      5
  -err.-  5   7   13     25
```

The package has a full set of metrics available. Here, I pull up the test accuracy and log-loss:

```
> mlr::performance(pred, measures = list(acc, logloss))
      acc    logloss
0.9606918 0.2863458
```

It has an impressive 96% accuracy on the test set and a baseline log-loss of `0.286`. This leads us to the next step, where we see whether creating an ensemble by just combining the predictions of random forest and MARS can improve performance.

Creating an ensemble

Using the functionality of `mlr` again, we first need to create an object with our base learners. This is once again `classif.randomForest` and, for a MARS model, we call the `earth` package with `classif.earth`:

```
> base <- c("classif.randomForest", "classif.earth")
```

You now make a learner with those base learners, and then specify that you want the output of those learners as the predicted probability:

```
> learns <- lapply(base, makeLearner)
```

```
> learns <- lapply(learns, setPredictType, "prob")
```

The process of building the base learning object is complete. I stated earlier that the ensembling learning algorithm will be GLM from `glmnet`. For just two base learners, a CART might be more appropriate, but let's demonstrate what's possible. There are a number of methods for stacking. In the following code block, I stack with cross-validation:

```
> sl <-
    mlr::makeStackedLearner(
    base.learners = learns,
    super.learner = "classif.glmnet",
    predict.type = "prob",
    method = "stack.cv"
  )
```

Now, it gets exciting as we train our stacked model:

```
stacked_fit <- mlr::train(sl, dna_task)
```

And we establish the predicted probabilities for the test data:

```
> pred_stacked <- predict(stacked_fit, newdata = test)
```

Just for a sanity check, let's look at the confusion matrix:

```
> mlr::calculateConfusionMatrix(pred_stacked)
         predicted
true      ei   ie    n -err.-
   ei    144    4    5      9
   ie      5  146    2      7
    n      2    1  327      3
 -err.-    7    5    7     19
```

The stacked model produced six fewer classification errors. The proof is in the metrics:

```
> mlr::performance(pred_stacked, measures = list(acc, logloss))
       acc    logloss
 0.9701258 0.1101400
```

Of course, accuracy is better, but even better the log-loss improved substantially.

What have we learned? Using primarily one package, `mlr`, we built a good model with random forest, but by stacking random forest and MARS, we improved performance. Although all of that was with just a few lines of code, it's important to understand how to create and implement the pipeline.

Summary

In this chapter, we looked at very important machine learning methods for creating an ensemble model by stacking in the framework. In stacking, we used base models (learners) to create predicted probabilities that were used on input features to another model (a super learner) to make our final predictions. Indeed, the stacked method showed an improvement over the individual base model. We performed all of this using `mlr` (machine learn), which is a powerful tool for any R machine learning practitioner.

Up next, we're going to delve into the world of unsupervised learning, where we're not trying to predict a label or quantitative outcome, but rather to understand patterns in the observations or features.

9
Cluster Analysis

"Quickly bring me a beaker of wine, so that I may wet my mind and say something clever."

- Aristophanes, Athenian Playwright

In the earlier chapters, we focused on trying to learn the best algorithm in order to solve an outcome or response, for example, customer satisfaction or home prices. In all these cases, we had y, and that y is a function of x, or $y = f(x)$. In our data, we had the actual y values and we could train x accordingly. This is referred to as **supervised learning**. However, there are many situations where we try to learn something from our data, and either we do not have the y, or we actually choose to ignore it. If so, we enter the world of **unsupervised learning**. In this world, we build and select our algorithm based on how well it addresses our business needs versus how accurate it is.

Why would we try and learn without supervision? First of all, unsupervised learning can help you understand and identify patterns in your data, which may be valuable. Second, you can use it to transform your data in order to improve your supervised learning techniques.

This chapter will focus on the former and the next chapter on the latter.

So, let's begin by tackling a popular and powerful technique known as **cluster analysis**. With cluster analysis, the goal is to group the observations into a number of groups (k-groups), where the members in a group are as similar as possible while the members between groups are as different as possible. There are many examples of how this can help an organization; here are just a few:

- The creation of customer types or segments
- The detection of high-crime areas in a geography
- Image and facial recognition
- Genetic sequencing and transcription
- Petroleum and geological exploration

There are many uses of cluster analysis, but there are also many techniques. We will focus on the two most common: **hierarchical** and **k-means**. They are both effective clustering methods, but may not always be appropriate for the large and varied datasets that you may be called upon to analyze. Therefore, we will also examine **partitioning around medoids** (**PAM**) using a **Gower-based** metric dissimilarity matrix as the input. Finally, we will examine a new methodology I recently learned and applied using **random forest** to transform your data. The transformed data can then be used as an input to unsupervised learning.

A final comment before moving on: you may be asked whether these techniques are more art than science, as the learning is unsupervised. I think the clear answer is, *it depends*. In early 2016, I presented the methods here at a meeting of the Indianapolis, Indiana R-User Group. To a person, we all agreed that it is the judgment of the analysts and the business users that makes unsupervised learning meaningful and determines whether you have, say, three versus four clusters in your final algorithm. This quote sums it up nicely:

> *"The major obstacle is the difficulty in evaluating a clustering algorithm without taking into account the context: why does the user cluster his data in the first place, and what does he want to do with the clustering afterwards? We argue that clustering should not be treated as an application-independent mathematical problem, but should always be studied in the context of its end-use."*

> *- Luxburg et al. (2012)*

The following are the topics that we will be covering in this chapter:

- Hierarchical clustering
- K-means clustering
- Gower and PAM
- Random forests
- Dataset background
- Data understanding and preparation
- Modeling

Hierarchical clustering

The hierarchical clustering algorithm is based on a dissimilarity measure between observations. A common measure, and what we will use, is **Euclidean distance**. Other distance measures are also available.

Hierarchical clustering is an agglomerative or bottom-up technique. By this, we mean that all observations are their own cluster. From there, the algorithm proceeds iteratively by searching all the pairwise points and finding the two clusters that are the most similar. So, after the first iteration, there are *n-1* clusters, and after the second iteration, there are *n-2* clusters, and so forth.

As the iterations continue, it is important to understand that in addition to the distance measure, we need to specify the linkage between the groups of observations. Different types of data will demand that you use different cluster linkages. As you experiment with the linkages, you may find that some create highly unbalanced numbers of observations in one or more clusters. For example, if you have 30 observations, one technique may create a cluster of just one observation, regardless of how many total clusters that you specify. In this situation, your judgment will likely be needed to select the most appropriate linkage as it relates to the data and business case.

The following table lists the types of common linkages, but note that there are others:

Linkage	Description
Ward	This minimizes the total within-cluster variance as measured by the sum of squared errors from the cluster points to its centroid.
Complete	The distance between two clusters is the maximum distance between an observation in one cluster and an observation in the other cluster.

Single	The distance between two clusters is the minimum distance between an observation in one cluster and an observation in the other cluster.
Average	The distance between two clusters is the mean distance between an observation in one cluster and an observation in the other cluster.
Centroid	The distance between two clusters is the distance between the cluster centroids.

The output of hierarchical clustering will be a **dendrogram**, which is a tree-like diagram that shows the arrangement of the various clusters.

As we will see, it can often be difficult to identify a clear-cut breakpoint in the selection of the number of clusters. Once again, your decision should be iterative in nature and focused on the context of the business decision.

Distance calculations

As mentioned previously, Euclidean distance is commonly used to build the input for hierarchical clustering. Let's look at a simple example of how to calculate it with two observations and two variables/features.

Let's say that observation *A* costs $5.00 and weighs 3 pounds. Further, observation *B* costs $3.00 and weighs 5 pounds. We can place these values in the distance formula: *distance between A and B is equal to the square root of the sum of the squared differences*, which in our example would be as follows:

$$d(A, B) = square\ root((5 - 3)^2 + (3 - 5)^2),\ \text{which is equal to}\ 2.83$$

The value of *2.83* is not a meaningful value in and of itself, but is important in the context of the other pairwise distances. This calculation is the default in R for the `dist()` function. You can specify other distance calculations (maximum, manhattan, canberra, binary, and minkowski) in the function. We will avoid going in to detail on why or where you would choose these over Euclidean distance. This can get rather domain-specific; for example, a situation where Euclidean distance may be inadequate is where your data suffers from high-dimensionality, such as in a genomic study. It will take domain knowledge and/or trial and error on your part to determine the proper distance measure.

 One final note is to scale your data with a mean of zero and standard deviation of one, so that the distance calculations are comparable. If not, any variable with a larger scale will have a larger effect on distances.

K-means clustering

With k-means, we will need to specify the exact number of clusters that we want. The algorithm will then iterate until each observation belongs to just one of the k-clusters. The algorithm's goal is to minimize the within-cluster variation as defined by the squared Euclidean distances. So, the kth-cluster variation is the sum of the squared Euclidean distances for all the pairwise observations divided by the number of observations in the cluster.

Due to the iteration process that is involved, one k-means result can differ greatly from another result even if you specify the same number of clusters. Let's see how this algorithm plays out:

1. **Specify** the exact number of clusters you desire (k)
2. **Initialize:** k observations are randomly selected as the initial *means*
3. **Iterate:**
   - K clusters are created by assigning each observation to its closest cluster center (minimizing within-cluster sum of squares)
   - The centroid of each cluster becomes the new *mean*
   - This is repeated until convergence, that is, the cluster centroids do not change

As you can see, the final result will vary because of the initial assignment in step 1. Therefore, it is important to run multiple initial starts and let the software identify the best solution. In R, this can be a simple process, as we will see.

Gower and PAM

As you conduct clustering analysis in real life, one of the things that can quickly become apparent is the fact that neither hierarchical nor k-means is specifically designed to handle mixed datasets. By mixed data, I mean both quantitative and qualitative or, more specifically, nominal, ordinal, and interval/ratio data.

The reality of most datasets that you will use is that they will probably contain mixed data. There are a number of ways to handle this, such as doing **principal components analysis (PCA)** first in order to create latent variables, then using them as input in clustering or using different dissimilarity calculations. We will discuss PCA in the next chapter.

With the power and simplicity of R, you can use the **Gower dissimilarity coefficient** to turn mixed data to the proper feature space. In this method, you can even include factors as input variables. Additionally, instead of k-means, I recommend using the **PAM clustering algorithm**.

PAM is very similar to k-means but offers a couple of advantages. They are listed as follows:

1. First, PAM accepts a dissimilarity matrix, which allows the inclusion of mixed data
2. Second, it is more robust to outliers and skewed data because it minimizes a sum of dissimilarities, instead of a sum of squared Euclidean distances (Reynolds, 1992)

This is not to say that you must use Gower and PAM together. If you choose, you can use the Gower coefficients with hierarchical, and I've seen arguments for and against using it in the context of k-means. Additionally, PAM can accept other linkages. However, when paired, they make an effective method to handle mixed data. Let's take a quick look at both of these concepts before moving on.

Gower

The Gower coefficient compares cases pairwise and calculates a dissimilarity between them, which is essentially the weighted mean of the contributions of each variable. It is defined for two cases called *i* and *j* as follows:

$$S_{ij} = \text{sum}(W_{ijk} * S_{ijk}) / \text{sum}(W_{ijk})$$

Here, S_{ijk} is the contribution provided by the k_{th} variable, and W_{ijk} is 1 if the k_{th} variable is valid, or else *0*.

For ordinal and continuous variables, $S_{ijk} = 1 - $ *(absolute value of x_{ij} - x_{ik}) / r_k*, where r_k is the range of values for the k_{th} variable.

For nominal variables, $S_{ijk} = 1$ if $x_{ij} = x_{jk}$, or else *0*.

For binary variables, S_{ijk} is calculated based on whether an attribute is present (+) or not present (-), as shown in the following table:

Variables	Value of attribute k			
Case i	+	+	-	-
Case j	+	-	+	-
Sijk	1	0	0	0
Wijk	1	1	1	0

PAM

For **PAM**, let's first define a **medoid**.

 A medoid is an observation of a cluster that minimizes the dissimilarity (in our case, calculated using the Gower metric) between the other observations in that cluster. So, similar to k-means, if you specify five clusters, you will have five partitions of the data.

With the objective of minimizing the dissimilarity of all the observations to the nearest medoid, the PAM algorithm iterates over the following steps:

1. Randomly select k observations as the initial medoid
2. Assign each observation to the closest medoid
3. Swap each medoid and non-medoid observation, computing the dissimilarity cost
4. Select the configuration that minimizes the total dissimilarity
5. Repeat steps 2 through 4 until there is no change in the medoids

Both Gower and PAM can be called using the `cluster` package in R. For Gower, we will use the `daisy()` function in order to calculate the dissimilarity matrix and the `pam()` function for the actual partitioning. With this, let's get started with putting these methods to the test.

Random forest

Like our motivation with the use of the Gower metric in handling mixed, in fact, *messy* data, we can apply random forest in an unsupervised fashion. Selecting this method has a number of advantages:

- Robust against outliers and highly skewed variables
- No need to transform or scale the data
- Handles mixed data (numeric and factors)
- Can accommodate missing data
- Can be used on data with a large number of variables; in fact, it can be used to eliminate useless features by examining variable importance
- The dissimilarity matrix produced serves as an input to the other techniques discussed earlier (hierarchical, k-means, and PAM)

A couple of words of caution. It may take some trial and error to properly tune the random forest with respect to the number of variables sampled at each tree split (`mtry = ?` in the function) and the number of trees grown. Studies done show that the more trees grown, up to a point, provide better results, and a good starting point is to grow 2,000 trees (Shi, T. & Horvath, S., 2006).

This is how the algorithm works, given a dataset with no labels:

- The current observed data is labeled as class 1
- A second (synthetic) set of observations is created of the same size as the observed data; this is created by randomly sampling from each of the features from the observed data, so if you have 20 observed features, you will have 20 synthetic features
- The synthetic portion of the data is labeled as class 2, which facilitates using random forest as an artificial classification problem
- Create a random forest model to distinguish between the two classes
- Turn the model's proximity measures of just the observed data (the synthetic data is now discarded) into a dissimilarity matrix
- Utilize the dissimilarity matrix as the clustering input features

So what exactly are these proximity measures?

 A proximity measure is a pairwise measure between all the observations. If two observations end up in the same terminal node of a tree, their proximity score is equal to one, otherwise zero.

At the termination of the random forest run, the proximity scores for the observed data are normalized by dividing by the total number of trees. The resulting NxN matrix contains scores between zero and one, naturally with the diagonal values all being one. That's all there is to it. An effective technique that I believe is underutilized and one that I wish I had learned years ago.

Dataset background

Until a year ago, I was unaware that there were less than 300 certified Master Sommeliers in the entire world. The exam, administered by the Court of Master Sommeliers, is notorious for its demands and high failure rate.

The trials, tribulations, and rewards of several individuals pursuing the certification are detailed in the critically acclaimed documentary, *Somm*. So, for this exercise, we will try and help a hypothetical individual struggling to become a Master Sommelier find a latent structure in Italian wines.

Data understanding and preparation

Let's start with installing the R packages needed for this chapter, if you have not done so already:

```
> library(magrittr)

> install.packages("cluster")

> install.packages("dendextend")

> install.packages("ggthemes")

> install.packages("HDclassif")

> install.packages("NbClust")

> install.packages("tidyverse")

> options(scipen=999)
```

The dataset is in the `HDclassif` package. Load the data and examine the structure with the `str()` function:

```
> library(HDclassif)

> data(wine)

> str(wine)
'data.frame': 178 obs. of 14 variables:
 $ class: int 1 1 1 1 1 1 1 1 1 1 ...
 $ V1 : num 14.2 13.2 13.2 14.4 13.2 ...
 $ V2 : num 1.71 1.78 2.36 1.95 2.59 1.76 1.87 2.15 1.64 1.35 ...
 $ V3 : num 2.43 2.14 2.67 2.5 2.87 2.45 2.45 2.61 2.17 2.27 ...
 $ V4 : num 15.6 11.2 18.6 16.8 21 15.2 14.6 17.6 14 16 ...
 $ V5 : int 127 100 101 113 118 112 96 121 97 98 ...
 $ V6 : num 2.8 2.65 2.8 3.85 2.8 3.27 2.5 2.6 2.8 2.98 ...
 $ V7 : num 3.06 2.76 3.24 3.49 2.69 3.39 2.52 2.51 2.98 3.15 ...
 $ V8 : num 0.28 0.26 0.3 0.24 0.39 0.34 0.3 0.31 0.29 0.22 ...
 $ V9 : num 2.29 1.28 2.81 2.18 1.82 1.97 1.98 1.25 1.98 1.85 ...
 $ V10 : num 5.64 4.38 5.68 7.8 4.32 6.75 5.25 5.05 5.2 7.22 ...
 $ V11 : num 1.04 1.05 1.03 0.86 1.04 1.05 1.02 1.06 1.08 1.01 ...
 $ V12 : num 3.92 3.4 3.17 3.45 2.93 2.85 3.58 3.58 2.85 3.55 ...
 $ V13 : int 1065 1050 1185 1480 735 1450 1290 1295 1045 1045 ...
```

The data consists of 178 wines with 13 variables of the chemical composition and one variable, `Class`, the label for the cultivar or plant variety. We won't use this in the clustering, but as a test of model performance. The variables, `V1` through `V13`, are the measures of the chemical composition, as follows:

- `V1`: alcohol
- `V2`: malic acid
- `V3`: ash
- `V4`: alkalinity of ash
- `V5`: magnesium
- `V6`: total phenols
- `V7`: flavonoids
- `V8`: non-flavonoid phenols
- `V9`: proanthocyanidins
- `V10`: color intensity
- `V11`: hue
- `V12`: OD280/OD315
- `V13`: proline

The variables are all quantitative. We should rename them to something meaningful for our analysis. This is easily done with the `colnames()` function:

```
> colnames(wine) <- c(
    "Class",
    "Alcohol",
    "MalicAcid",
    "Ash",
    "Alk_ash",
    "magnesium",
    "T_phenols",
    "Flavanoids",
    "Non_flav",
    "Proantho",
    "C_Intensity",
    "Hue",
    "OD280_315",
    "Proline"
)
```

As the variables are not scaled, we will need to do this using the `scale()` function. This will first center the data where the column mean is subtracted from each individual in the column. Then the centered values will be divided by the corresponding column's standard deviation. We can also use this transformation to make sure that we only include columns 2 through 14, dropping class and putting it in a data frame. This can all be done with one line of code:

```
> wine_df <- as.data.frame(scale(wine[, -1]))
```

Before moving on, and out of curiosity, let's do a quick table to see the distribution of the cultivars or `Class`:

```
> table(wine$Class)

 1  2  3
59 71 48
```

We can now move on to the unsupervised learning models.

Modeling

Having created our data frame, `df`, we can begin to develop the clustering algorithms. We will start with hierarchical and then try our hand at k-means. After this, we will need to manipulate our data a little bit to demonstrate how to incorporate mixed data with Gower and random forest.

Hierarchical clustering

To build a hierarchical cluster model in R, you can utilize the `hclust()` function in the base `stats` package. The two primary inputs needed for the function are a distance matrix and the clustering method. The distance matrix is easily done with the `dist()` function. For the distance, we will use Euclidean distance. A number of clustering methods are available, and the default for `hclust()` is complete linkage.

We will try this, but I also recommend Ward's linkage method. Ward's method tends to produce clusters with a similar number of observations.

The complete linkage method results in the distance between any two clusters, that is, the maximum distance between any one observation in a cluster and any one observation in the other cluster. Ward's linkage method seeks to cluster the observations in order to minimize the within-cluster sum of squares.

It is noteworthy that the R method `ward.D2` uses the squared Euclidean distance, which is indeed Ward's linkage method. In R, `ward.D` is available but requires your distance matrix to be squared values. As we will be building a distance matrix of non-squared values, we will require `ward.D2`.

Now, the big question is how many clusters should we create? As stated in the introduction, the short, and probably not very satisfying, answer is that it depends. Even though there are cluster validity measures to help with this dilemma – which we will look at – it really requires an intimate knowledge of the business context, underlying data, and, quite frankly, trial and error. As our sommelier partner is fictional, we will have to rely on the validity measures. However, that is no panacea to selecting the numbers of clusters as there are several dozen validity measures.

As exploring the positives and negatives of the vast array of cluster validity measures is way outside the scope of this chapter, we can turn to a couple of papers and even R itself to simplify this problem for us. A paper by Miligan and Cooper, 1985, explored the performance of 30 different measures/indices on simulated data. The top five performers were CH index, Duda Index, Cindex, Gamma, and Beale Index. Another well-known method to determine the number of clusters is the **gap statistic** (Tibshirani, Walther, and Hastie, 2001). These are two good papers for you to explore if your cluster validity curiosity gets the better of you.

With R, we can use the `NbClust()` function in the `NbClust` package to pull results on 23 indices, including the top five from Miligan and Cooper and the gap statistic. You can see a list of all the available indices in the help file for the package. There are two ways to approach this process: one is to pick your favorite index or indices and call them with R; the other is to include all of them in the analysis and go with the majority rules method, which the function summarizes for you nicely. The function will also produce a couple of plots as well.

With the stage set, let's walk through the example of using the complete linkage method. When using the function, you will need to specify the minimum and maximum number of clusters, distance measures, and indices in addition to the linkage. As you can see in the following code, we will create an object called `numComplete`. The function specifications are for Euclidean distance, minimum number of clusters two, maximum number of clusters six, complete linkage, and all indices. When you run the command, the function will automatically produce an output similar to what you can see here—a discussion on both the graphical methods and majority rules conclusion:

```
> numComplete <- NbClust::NbClust(
    wine_df,
    distance = "euclidean",
    min.nc = 2,
    max.nc = 6,
    method = "complete",
    index = "all"
)
*** : The Hubert index is a graphical method of determining the number of
clusters.
 In the plot of Hubert index, we seek a significant knee that corresponds
to a
 significant increase of the value of the measure that is, the significant
peak in Hubert
 index second differences plot.

*** : The D index is a graphical method of determining the number of
clusters.
 In the plot of D index, we seek a significant knee (the significant peak
```

```
in Dindex
 second differences plot) that corresponds to a significant increase of the
value of
 the measure.
*****************************************************************************
* Among all indices:
* 1 proposed 2 as the best number of clusters
* 11 proposed 3 as the best number of clusters
* 6 proposed 5 as the best number of clusters
* 5 proposed 6 as the best number of clusters

 ***** Conclusion *****
* According to the majority rule, the best number of clusters is 3
*****************************************************************************
```

Going with the majority rules method, we would select three clusters as the optimal solution, at least for hierarchical clustering. The two plots that are produced contain two graphs each. As the preceding output states, you are looking for a significant knee in the plot (the graph on the left-hand side) and the peak of the graph on the right-hand side. This is the **Hubert Index** plot:

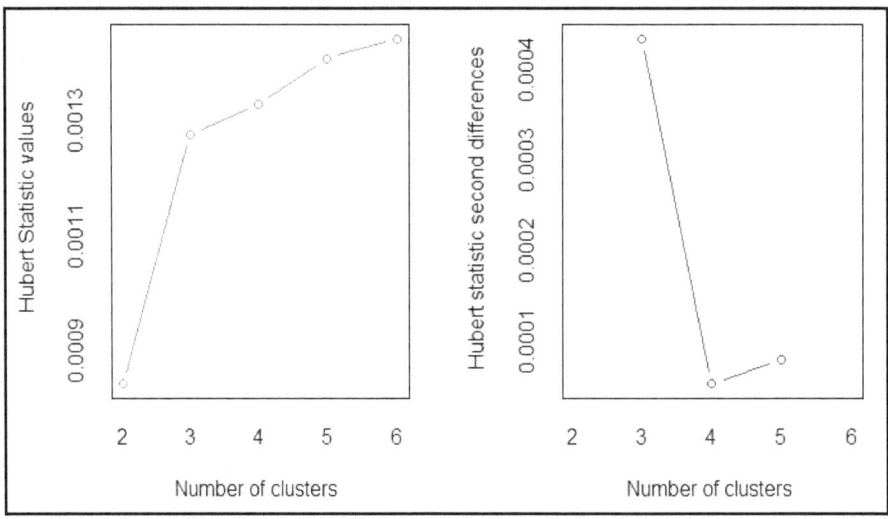

You can see that the bend or knee is at three clusters in the graph on the left-hand side. Additionally, the graph on the right-hand side has its peak at three clusters. The following **Dindex** plot provides the same information:

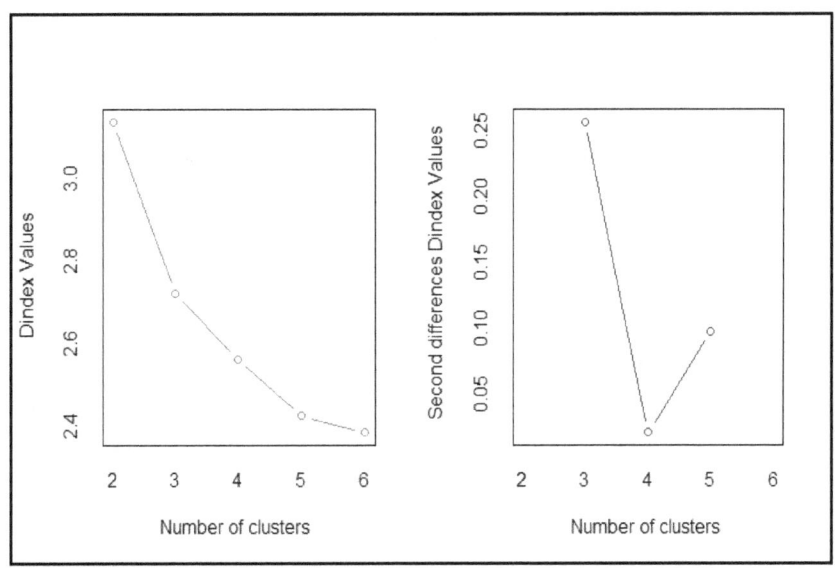

There are a number of values that you can call with the function and there is one that I would like to show. This output is the best number of clusters for each index and the index value for that corresponding number of clusters. This is done with $Best.nc. I've abbreviated the output to the first few indices:

```
> numComplete$Best.nc
                    KL       CH Hartigan    CCC    Scott
Number_clusters  5.0000  3.0000   3.0000  5.000   3.0000
Value_Index     14.2227 48.9898  27.8971  1.148 340.9634
```

You can see that the first index, KL, has the optimal number of clusters as five and the next index, CH, has it as three.

With three clusters as the recommended selection, we will now compute the distance matrix and build our hierarchical cluster object. This builds the distance matrix:

```
> euc_dist <- dist(wine_df, method = "euclidean")
```

Then, we will use this matrix as the input for the actual clustering with `hclust()`:

```
> hc_complete <- hclust(euc_dist, method = "complete")
```

The common way to visualize hierarchical clustering is to plot a **dendrogram**. We will do this with the functionality provided by the `dendextend` package:

```
> dend1 <- dendextend::color_branches(dend_complete, k = 3)

> plot(dend1, main = "Complete-Linkage")
```

The output of the preceding code is as follows:

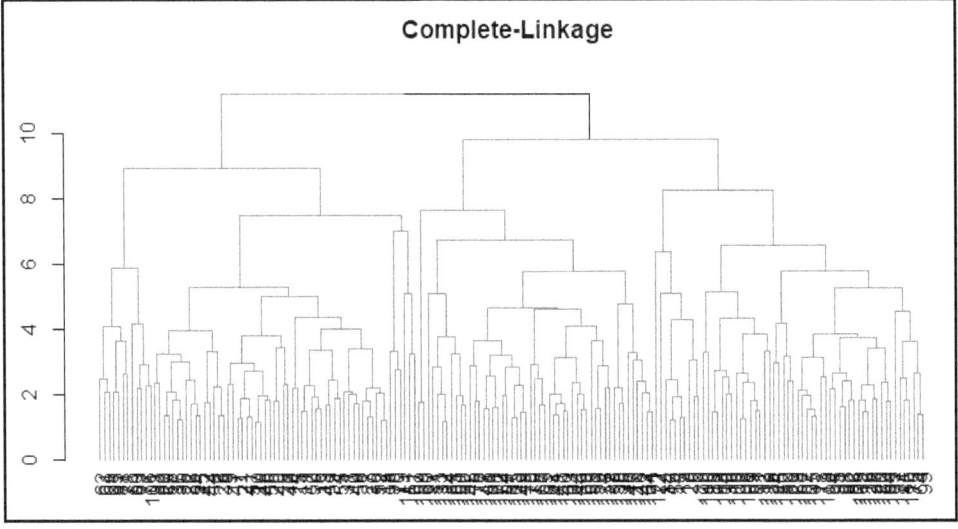

The dendrogram is a tree diagram that shows you how the individual observations are clustered together. The arrangement of the connections (branches, if you will) tells us which observations are similar. The height of the branches indicates how much the observations are similar or dissimilar to each other from the distance matrix.

Here is the table of cluster counts:

```
> complete_clusters <- cutree(hc_complete, 3)

> table(complete_clusters)
complete_clusters
 1  2  3
69 58 51
```

Out of curiosity, let's compare how this clustering algorithm compares to the **cultivar** labels:

```
> table(complete_clusters, wine$Class)
complete_clusters   1   2   3
                1  51  18   0
                2   8  50   0
                3   0   3  48
```

In this table, the rows are the clusters and columns are the cultivars. This method matched the cultivar labels at an 84 percent rate. Note that we are not trying to use the clusters to predict a cultivar, and in this example, we have no a priori reason to match clusters to the cultivars, but it is revealing nonetheless.

We will now try Ward's linkage. This is the same code as before; it first starts with trying to identify the number of clusters, which means that we will need to change the method to `Ward.D2`:

```
> numWard <- NbClust::NbClust(
    wine_df,
    distance = "euclidean",
    min.nc = 2,
    max.nc = 6,
    method = "ward.D2",
    index = "all"
)
# Output abbreviated to just show the algorithm's conclusion.
                    ***** Conclusion *****
    * According to the majority rule, the best number of clusters is 3
```

Once again, the majority rules were for a three-cluster solution. I'll let you peruse the plots on your own.

Let's move on to the actual clustering and production of the dendrogram for Ward's linkage:

```
> hc_ward <- hclust(euc_dist, method = "ward.D2")

> dend_ward <- as.dendrogram(hc_ward)

> dend2 <- dendextend::color_branches(dend_ward, k = 3)

> plot(dend2, main = "Ward Method")
```

This is the output:

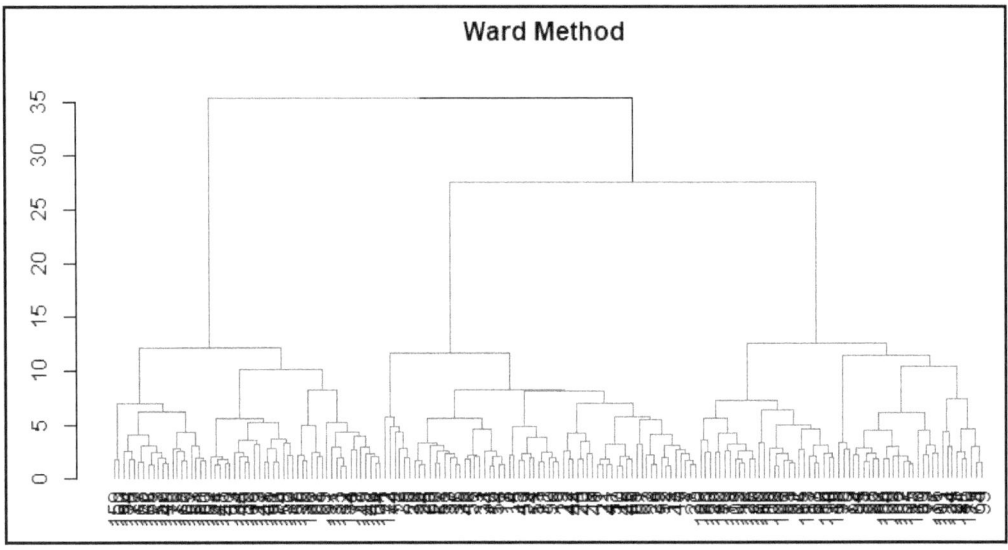

The plot shows three pretty distinct clusters that are roughly equal in size. Let's get a count of the cluster size and show it in relation to the cultivar labels:

```
> ward_clusters <- cutree(hc_ward, 3)

> table(ward_clusters, wine$Class)
ward_clusters  1   2   3
            1 59   5   0
            2  0  58   0
            3  0   8  48
```

So, cluster one has 64 observations, cluster two has 58, and cluster three has 56. This method matches the cultivar categories closer than using complete linkage.

With another table, we can compare how the two methods match observations:

```
> table(complete_clusters, ward_clusters)
                     ward_clusters
complete_clusters    1   2   3
                1   53  11   5
                2   11  47   0
                3    0   0  51
```

While cluster three for each method is exact, the other two are not. The question now is how do we identify what the differences are for the interpretation? In many examples, the datasets are very small and you can look at the labels for each cluster. In the real world, this is often impossible. I like to aggregate results by cluster and compare accordingly.

 Putting aggregated results by cluster into an interactive spreadsheet or business intelligence tool facilitates understanding by you and your business partners, helping to select the appropriate clustering method and number of clusters.

I'm going to demonstrate this by looking at the mean of the features grouped by the clusters from Ward's method. First, create a separate data frame with the scaled data (or original data, if you prefer) and the results:

```
> ward_df <- wine_df %>%
    dplyr::mutate(cluster = ward_clusters)
```

Now, do the aggregation:

```
> ward_df %>%
    dplyr::group_by(cluster) %>%
    dplyr::summarise_all(dplyr::funs(mean)) -> ward_results
```

You now can view that data frame in RStudio, or export it to your favorite BI tool. Maybe you are interested in a plot? If so, give this a try:

```
> ggplot2::ggplot(ward_results, ggplot2::aes(cluster, Alcohol)) +
    ggplot2::geom_bar(stat = "identity") +
    ggthemes::theme_stata()
```

This is the output:

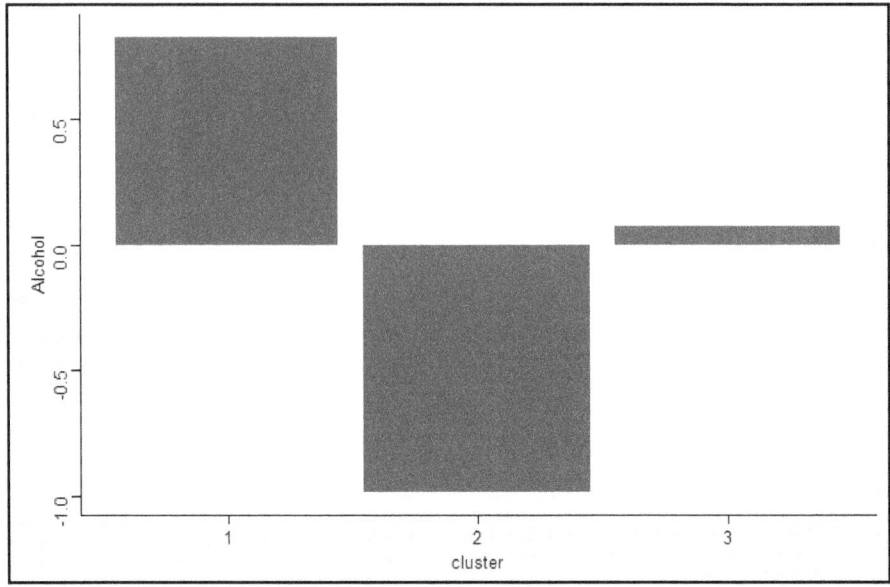

A clear separation exists between the clusters in alcohol content. With that said, let's move on to k-means.

K-means clustering

As we did with hierarchical clustering, we can also use NbClust() to determine the optimum number of clusters for k-means. All you need to do is specify kmeans as the method in the function. Let's also loosen up the maximum number of clusters to 15. I've abbreviated the following output to just the conclusion:

```
> numKMeans <- NbClust::NbClust(wine_df,
    min.nc = 2,
    max.nc = 15,
    method = "kmeans")
***** Conclusion *****

* According to the majority rule, the best number of clusters is 3
```

Once again, three clusters appears to be the optimum solution.

In R, we can use the `kmeans()` function to do this analysis. In addition to the input data, we have to specify the number of clusters we are solving for and a value for random assignments, the `nstart` argument. We will also need to specify a random seed:

```
> set.seed(1234)
> km <- kmeans(df, 3, nstart = 25)
```

Creating a table of the clusters gives us a sense of the distribution of the observations between them:

```
> table(km$cluster)

 1  2  3
62 65 51
```

The number of observations per cluster is well balanced. I have seen on a number of occasions with larger datasets and many more features that no number of k-means yields a promising and compelling result. Another way to analyze the clustering is to look at a matrix of the cluster centers for each variable in each cluster:

```
> km$centers
      Alcohol   MalicAcid        Ash    Alk_ash   magnesium    T_phenols
1   0.8328826 -0.3029551  0.3636801 -0.6084749  0.57596208  0.88274724
2  -0.9234669 -0.3929331 -0.4931257  0.1701220 -0.49032869 -0.07576891
3   0.1644436  0.8690954  0.1863726  0.5228924 -0.07526047 -0.97657548
      Flavanoids    Non_flav    Proantho C_Intensity         Hue   OD280_315
1   0.97506900 -0.56050853  0.57865427   0.1705823   0.4726504   0.7770551
2   0.02075402 -0.03343924  0.05810161  -0.8993770   0.4605046   0.2700025
3  -1.21182921  0.72402116 -0.77751312   0.9388902  -1.1615122  -1.2887761
      Proline
1   1.1220202
2  -0.7517257
3  -0.4059428
```

Note that cluster one has, on average, a higher alcohol content. Let's produce a box plot to look at the distribution of alcohol content and compare it to Ward's:

```
> par(mfrow = c(1, 2))

> boxplot(wine$Alcohol ~ km$cluster, data = wine,
    main = "Alcohol Content, K-Means")

> boxplot(wine$Alcohol ~ ward_clusters, data = wine,
    main = "Alcohol Content, Ward's")
```

This is the output:

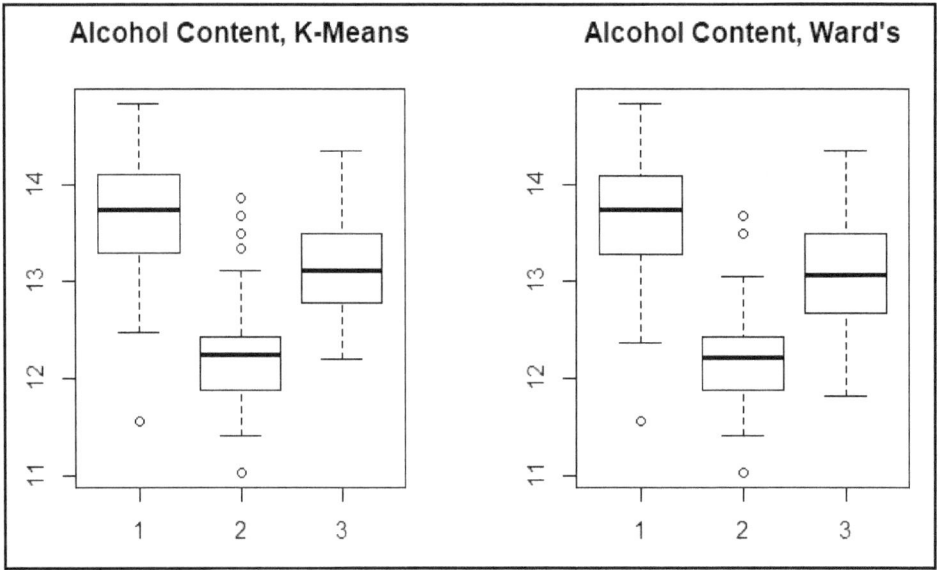

The alcohol content for each cluster is almost exactly the same. On the surface, this tells me that three clusters is the proper latent structure for the wines and there is little difference between using k-means or hierarchical clustering. Finally, let's do a comparison of the k-means clusters versus the cultivars:

```
> table(km$cluster, wine$Class)
     1   2   3
1   59   3   0
2    0  65   0
3    0   3  48
```

This is very similar to the distribution produced by Ward's method, and either one would probably be acceptable to our hypothetical sommelier.

However, to demonstrate how you can cluster on data with both numeric and non-numeric values, let's work through some more examples.

Gower and PAM

To begin this step, we will need to wrangle our data a little bit. As this method can take variables that are factors, we will convert alcohol to either high or low content. It also takes only one line of code utilizing the `ifelse()` function to change the variable to a factor. What this will accomplish is if alcohol is greater than zero, it will be `High`, otherwise, it will be `Low`:

```
> wine_df$Alcohol <- as.factor(ifelse(df$Alcohol > 0, "High", "Low"))
```

We are now ready to create the dissimilarity matrix using the `daisy()` function from the `cluster` package and specifying the method as `gower`:

```
> gower_dist <- cluster::daisy(wine[, -1], metric = "gower")
```

The creation of the cluster object is done with the `pam()` function, which is a part of the `cluster` package. We will create three clusters in this example and create a table of the cluster size:

```
> set.seed(123)

> pam_cluster <- cluster::pam(gower_dist, k = 3)

> table(pam_cluster$clustering)

 1  2  3
62 71 45
```

Now, let's see how it does compared to the cultivar labels:

```
> table(pam_cluster$clustering, wine$Class)
     1  2  3
  1 57  5  0
  2  2 64  5
  3  0  2 43
```

You can run a similar aggregation and exploration exercise with this method as described previously. Let's see how the distribution of alcohol is across the three clusters:

```
> table(pam_cluster$clustering, wine$Alcohol)
    High Low
  1   62   0
  2    1  70
  3   29  16
```

This table shows the proportion of the factor levels by the cluster. The Gower metric is very powerful for data with labels, factors, characters, missing values, and so on. I highly recommend it. One of the drawbacks with any distance matrix is that it can become a computational problem with large datasets. An effective solution is to run k-samples and compare results. Done well, you can then build a classifier to predict the cluster for your population.

Finally, we'll create a dissimilarity matrix with random forest and create three clusters with PAM.

Random forest and PAM

To perform this method in R, you can use the `randomForest()` function. After setting the random seed, simply create the model object. In the following code, I specify the number of trees as `2000` and set proximity measure to `TRUE`. You don't have to run this on scaled data:

```
> set.seed(1918)

> rf <- randomForest::randomForest(x = wine[, -1], ntree = 2000, proximity
= T)

> rf

Call:
 randomForest(x = wine[, -1], ntree = 2000, proximity = T)
               Type of random forest: unsupervised
                     Number of trees: 2000
No. of variables tried at each split: 3
```

As you can see, placing a call to `rf` did not provide any meaningful output other than the variables sampled at each split (`mtry`). Let's examine the first five rows and first five columns of the *N x N* matrix:

```
> dim(rf$proximity)
[1] 178 178


> rf$proximity[1:5, 1:5]
            1          2         3          4          5
1 1.0000000 0.27868852 0.4049296 0.36200717 0.12969283
2 0.2786885 1.00000000 0.2142857 0.12648221 0.04453441
3 0.4049296 0.21428571 1.0000000 0.26865672 0.14942529
4 0.3620072 0.12648221 0.2686567 1.00000000 0.07692308
5 0.1296928 0.04453441 0.1494253 0.07692308 1.00000000
```

One way to think of the values is that they are the percentage of times those two observations show up in the same terminal nodes! Looking at variable importance, we see that the transformed `Alcohol` input could possibly be dropped. We will keep it for simplicity:

```
> randomForest::importance(rf)
            MeanDecreaseGini
Alcohol             3.692748
MalicAcid          12.650096
Ash                10.842885
Alk_ash            11.636227
magnesium          10.672465
T_phenols          17.733783
Flavanoids         21.410838
Non_flav           11.527873
Proantho           14.494229
C_Intensity        14.795900
Hue                14.296274
OD280_315          17.815508
Proline            15.922621
```

It is now just a matter of creating the dissimilarity matrix, which transforms the proximity values (*square root(1 - proximity)*) as follows:

```
> rf_dist <- sqrt(1 - rf$proximity)

> rf_dist[1:2, 1:2]
            1         2
1 0.0000000 0.8493006
2 0.8493006 0.0000000
```

We now have our input features, so let's run a PAM clustering as we did earlier:

```
> set.seed(1776)

> pam_rf <- cluster::pam(rf_dist, k = 3)

> table(pam_rf$clustering)

 1  2  3
52 82 44

> table(pam_rf$clustering, wine$Class)
      1  2  3
  1 52  0  0
  2  7 70  5
  3  0  1 43
```

These results are comparable to the other techniques applied. Lesson learned here? If you have messy data for a clustering problem, consider using random forest to create a distance matrix, and even eliminate features from your clustering algorithm.

Summary

In this chapter, we started exploring unsupervised learning techniques. We focused on cluster analysis to both provide data reduction and data understanding of the observations.

Four methods were introduced: the traditional hierarchical and k-means clustering algorithms, along with PAM, incorporating two different inputs (Gower and random forest). We applied these four methods to find a structure in Italian wines coming from three different cultivars and examined the results.

In the next chapter, we will continue exploring unsupervised learning, but instead of finding structure among the observations, we will focus on finding structure among the variables in order to create new features that can be used in a supervised learning problem.

10
Principal Component Analysis

"The only easy day was yesterday."

- A Special Forces motivational saying

This chapter is the second one where we will focus on unsupervised learning techniques. In the previous chapter, we covered cluster analysis, which provides us with the groupings of similar observations. In this chapter, we will see how to reduce the dimensionality and improve the understanding of our data by grouping the correlated variables with **principal components analysis (PCA)**. Then, we will use the principal components in supervised learning.

In many datasets, particularly in the social sciences, you will see many variables highly correlated with each other. They may additionally suffer from high-dimensionality or, as it is better known, the **curse of dimensionality**. This is a problem because the number of samples needed to estimate a function grows exponentially with the number of input features. In such datasets, it may be the case that some variables are redundant as they end up measuring the same constructs, for example, income and poverty or depression and anxiety. The goal then is to use PCA in order to create a smaller set of variables that capture most of the information from the original set of variables, thus simplifying the dataset and often leading to hidden insights. These new variables (principal components) are highly uncorrelated with each other. In addition to supervised learning, it is also very common to use these components to perform data visualization.

From over a decade of either doing or supporting analytics using PCA, it has been my experience that it is widely used but poorly understood, especially among people who don't do the analysis but consume the results. It is intuitive to understand that you are creating a new variable from the other correlated variables. However, the technique itself is shrouded in potentially misunderstood terminology and mathematical concepts that often bewilder the layperson. The intention here is to provide a good foundation on what it is and how to use it by covering the following:

- Preparing a dataset for PCA
- Conducting PCA
- Selecting our principal components
- Building a predictive model using principal components
- Making out-of-sample predictions using the predictive model

An overview of the principal components

PCA is the process of finding the principal components. What exactly are these?

We can consider that a component is a normalized linear combination of the features (James, 2012). The first principal component in a dataset is the linear combination that captures the maximum variance in the data. A second component is created by selecting another linear combination that maximizes the variance with the constraint that its direction is perpendicular to the first component. The subsequent components (equal to the number of variables) would follow this same rule.

A couple of things here. This definition describes the **linear combination**, which is one of the key assumptions in PCA. If you ever try and apply PCA to a dataset of variables having a low correlation, you will likely end up with a meaningless analysis. Another key assumption is that the mean and variance for a variable are sufficient statistics. What this tells us is that the data should fit a normal distribution so that the covariance matrix fully describes our dataset, that is, **multivariate normality**. PCA is fairly robust to non-normally distributed data and is even used in conjunction with binary variables, so the results are still interpretable.

Now, what is this direction described here and how is the linear combination determined? The best way to grasp this subject is with visualization. Let's take a small dataset with two variables and plot it. PCA is sensitive to scale, so the data has been scaled with a mean of zero and standard deviation of one. You can see in the following diagram that this data happens to form the shape of an oval with the diamonds representing each observation:

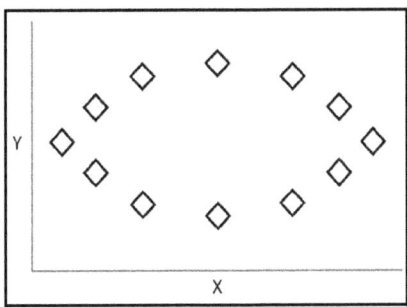

Looking at the plot, the data has the most variance along the x axis, so we can draw a dashed horizontal line to represent our **first principal component**, as shown in the following diagram. This component is the linear combination of our two variables or *PC1* = $a_{11}X_1 + a_{12}X_2$, where the coefficient weights are the variable loading on the principal component. They form the basis of the direction along which the data varies the most. This equation is constrained by *1* in order to prevent the selection of arbitrarily high values. Another way to look at this is that the dashed line minimizes the distance between itself and the data points. This distance is shown for a couple of points as arrows, as follows:

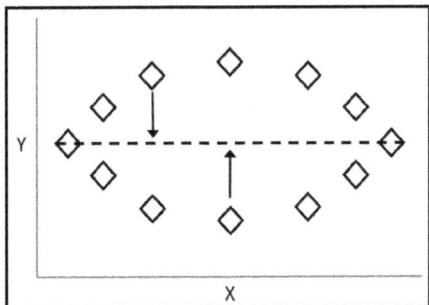

The **second principal component** is then calculated in the same way, but it is uncorrelated with the first, that is, its direction is at a right angle or orthogonal to the first principal component. The following plot shows the second principal component added as a dotted line:

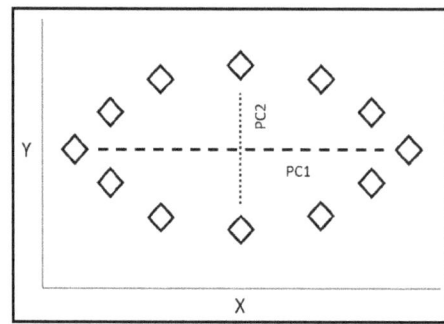

With the principal component loading calculated for each variable, the algorithm will then provide us with the principal component scores. The scores are calculated for each principal component for each observation. For **PC1** and the first observation, this would equate to the formula $Z_{11} = \alpha_{11} * (X_{11} - average\ of\ X_1) + \alpha_{12} * (X_{12} - average\ of\ X_2)$. For **PC2** and the first observation, the equation would be $Z_{12} = \alpha_{21} * (X_{11} - average\ of\ X_2) + \alpha_{22} * (X_{12} - average\ of\ X_2)$. These principal component scores are now the new feature space to be used in whatever analysis you will undertake.

Recall that the algorithm will create as many principal components as there are variables, accounting for 100 percent of the possible variance. So, how do we narrow down the components to achieve the original objective in the first place? There are some heuristics that one can use, and in the upcoming modeling process, we will look at the specifics; but a common method to select a principal component is if its **eigenvalue** is greater than one. While the algebra behind the estimation of eigenvalues and **eigenvectors** is outside the scope of this book, it is important to discuss what they are and how they are used in PCA.

The optimized linear weights are determined using linear algebra in order to create what is referred to as an eigenvector. They are optimal because no other possible combination of weights could explain variation better than they do. The eigenvalue for a principal component then is the total amount of variation that it explains in the entire dataset.

Recall that the equation for the first principal component is $PC1 = \alpha_{11}X_1 + \alpha_{12}X_2$.

As the first principal component accounts for the largest amount of variation, it will have the largest eigenvalue. The second component will have the second highest eigenvalue and so forth. So, an eigenvalue greater than one indicates that the principal component accounts for more variance than any of the original variables do by themselves. If you standardize the sum of all the eigenvalues to one, you will have the percentage of the total variance that each component explains. This will also aid you in determining a proper cut-off point.

The eigenvalue criterion is certainly not a hard-and-fast rule and must be balanced with your knowledge of the data and business problem at hand. Once you have selected the number of principal components, you can rotate them in order to simplify their interpretation.

Rotation

Should you rotate or not? As stated previously, rotation helps in the interpretation of the principal components by modifying the loading of each variable, but makes the results technically no longer a principal component. The overall variation explained by the rotated number of components will not change, but the contributions to the total variance explained by each component will change. What you will find by rotation is that the loading values will either move farther or closer to zero, theoretically aiding in identifying those variables that are important to each principal component. This is an attempt to associate a variable to only one principal component. Remember that this is unsupervised learning, so you are trying to understand your data, not test some hypothesis. In short, rotation aids you in this endeavor. I have seen both the non-rotated and rotated components used to calculate the loading. I like to use the rotated components.

The most common form of principal component rotation is known as **varimax**. There are other forms, such as **quartimax** and **equimax**, but we will focus on varimax rotation. In my experience, I've never seen the other methods provide better solutions. Trial and error on your part may be the best way to decide the issue.

 With varimax, we are maximizing the sum of the variances of the squared loading. The varimax procedure rotates the axis of the feature space and their coordinates without changing the locations of the data points.

Perhaps the best way to demonstrate this is via another simple illustration. Let's assume that we have a dataset of variables **A** through **G** and we have two principal components. Plotting this data, we will end up with the following diagram:

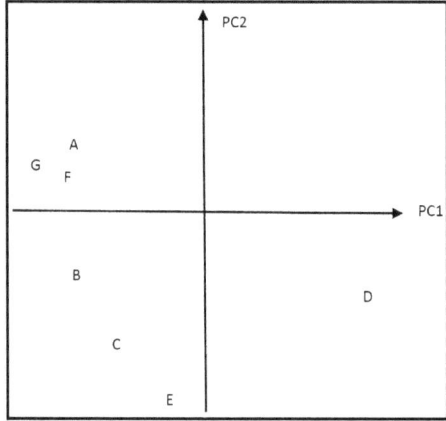

For the sake of argument, let's say that variable A's loading are -0.4 on **PC1** and 0.1 on **PC2**. Now, let's say that variable D's loading are 0.4 on **PC1** and -0.3 on **PC2**. For point E, the loading are -0.05 and -0.7, respectively. Note that the loading will follow the direction of the principal component. After running a varimax procedure, the rotated components will look as follows:

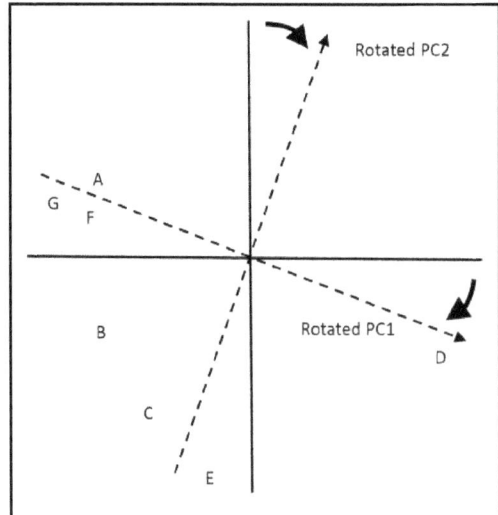

The following are the new loading on **PC1** and **PC2** after rotation:

- **Variable A**: -0.5 and 0.02
- **Variable D**: 0.5 and -0.3
- **Variable E**: 0.15 and -0.75

The loading have changed but the data points have not. With this simple illustration, we can't say that we have simplified the interpretation, but this should help you understand what is happening during the rotation of the principal components.

Data

We will be using what is referred to as the ANSUR dataset, which stands for US Army Anthropometric Survey. It consists of two separate files: one for female soldiers and one for male soldiers. I've combined the results into one dataset. You can download the data here: `https://github.com/PacktPublishing/Advanced-Machine-Learning-with-R/tree/master/Data/army_ansur.RData`.

I found this data on a data repository site called `data.world`, which allows members to share any dataset they have of interest. For example, I have a version of the Gettysburg data we used in `Chapter 1`, *Preparing and Understanding Data*, on the site. This ANSUR data consists of research done by the **Natick Soldier Research, Development and Engineering Center** (**NSRDEC**) on over 6000 Active Duty, Reserve, and National Guard soldiers for the US Army. The features are of 93 different body measurements along with assorted demographic data. The US Army and contractors use this information to order the proper quantity and size of equipment, design new equipment, and so on. As you can imagine, many of these features are highly correlated, making this data perfect for PCA.

We'll put those body measurements through the PCA process, then use that to predict body weight in pounds, using a MARS model as we learned in prior chapters. Why soldier weight? Why not? We'll lump males and females together. We could use that data as an input feature, but I won't. Use age, race, gender, or the like in a model in the banking industry subject to review, and prepare to, at a minimum, answer some tough questions. OK, enough of the introduction, let's get cracking.

Data loading and review

To begin with, load the necessary packages:

```
> library(magrittr)

> install.packages("caret")

> install.packages("DataExplorer")

> install.packages("earth")

> install.packages("ggthemes")

> install.packages("psych")

> install.packages("tidyverse")

> options(scipen = 999)
```

Now, read the data into your environment:

```
> army_ansur <- readRDS("army_ansur.RData")
```

The feature names are fairly straightforward. Here, I just put in the last few features as output:

```
> colnames(army_ansur)
  [93] "wristcircumference"     "wristheight"
  [95] "Gender"                 "Date"
  [97] "Installation"           "Component"
  [99] "Branch"                 "PrimaryMOS"
 [101] "SubjectsBirthLocation"  "SubjectNumericRace"
 [103] "Ethnicity"              "DODRace"
 [105] "Age"                    "Heightin"
 [107] "Weightlbs"              "WritingPreference"
 [109] "SubjectId"
```

I'm interested in looking at the breakdown of the "Component" and "Gender" columns:

```
> table(army_ansur$Component)

Army National Guard    Army Reserve    Regular Army
               2708             220            3140
```

```
> table(army_ansur$Gender)

Female    Male
  1986    4082
```

If we look at missing values, we can see something of interest. Here is the abbreviated output:

```
> sapply(army_ansur, function(x) sum(is.na(x)))
        PrimaryMOS    SubjectsBirthLocation    SubjectNumericRace
                 0                        0                     0
          Ethnicity                  DODRace                   Age
              4647                        0                     0
          Heightin                 Weightlbs    WritingPreference
                 0                        0                     0
         SubjectId
              4082
```

We have a bunch of missing subject IDs. Fine, let's take care of that right now:

```
> army_ansur$subjectid <- seq(1:6068)
```

Since weight is what we will predict after we build our unsupervised model, let's have a look at it:

```
> sjmisc::descr(army_ansur$Weightlbs)

## Basic descriptive statistics
 var      type label    n NA.prc  mean    sd   se  md trimmed       range
skew
  dd integer     dd 6068      0 174.8 33.69 0.43 173   173.4 321 (0-321)
0.39
```

Look at the range! We have someone who weighs zero. A plot of this data is in order, I believe:

```
> ggplot2::ggplot(army_ansur, ggplot2::aes(x = Weightlbs)) +
    ggplot2::geom_density() +
    ggthemes::theme_wsj()
```

The output of the preceding code is as follows:

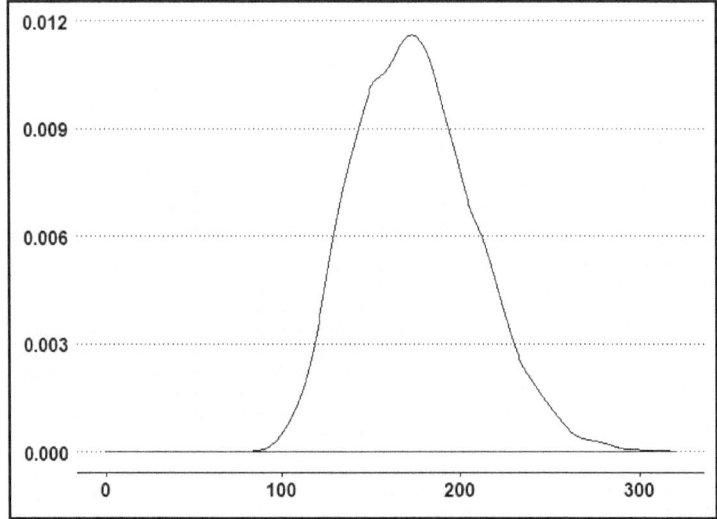

So, I would estimate we only have one or two observations of implausible weight values. Indeed, this code will confirm that assumption:

```
> dplyr::select(army_ansur, Weightlbs) %>%
    dplyr::arrange(Weightlbs)
# A tibble: 6,068 x 1
   Weightlbs
       <int>
 1         0
 2        86
 3        88
 4        90
 5        95
 6        95
 7        95
 8        96
 9        98
10       100
# ... with 6,058 more rows
```

Removing that observation is important:

```
> armyClean <- dplyr::filter(army_ansur, Weightlbs > 0)
```

We can now transition to bundling our features for PCA and creating training and testing dataframes.

Training and testing datasets

Here, we are going to put the numeric features into a dataframe along with the quantitative response. Then, we'll carve this up into train and test sets with an 80/20 split. As a closing effort, we'll scale the data, which is required for PCA.

Here, I grab those input features, including height in inches, while dropping weight in kilograms. I also include the `subjectid`:

```
> army_subset <- armyClean[, c(1:91, 93, 94, 106, 107)]
```

We've used the `dplyr` and `caret` packages to create train and test sets, and here I demonstrate the `dplyr` method:

```
> set.seed(1812)

> army_subset %>%
    dplyr::sample_frac(.8) -> train

> army_subset %>%
    dplyr::anti_join(train, by = "subjectid") -> test
```

I mentioned previously that this data had a number of high correlations. Even if you take just the first five features, that becomes clear:

```
> DataExplorer::plot_correlation(train[, 2:6])
```

The output of the preceding code is as follows:

Axilla height and acromial height are 99 percent correlated. These refer to the armpit and point of the shoulder respectively.

We need to preserve the y-values for the training data. Additionally, we have to scale the data, that is, just the input features, so drop the `subjectid` and y-values:

```
> trainY <- train$Weightlbs

> train_scale <- data.frame(scale(train[, c(-1, -95)]))
```

With that complete, we can move on to creating principal components and using them in a supervised learning example.

PCA modeling

For the modeling process, we will use the following steps:

1. Extract the components and determine the number to retain
2. Rotate the retained components
3. Interpret the rotated solution
4. Create scores from the non-rotated components
5. Use the scores as input variables for regression analysis with MARS and evaluate the performance on the test data

There are many different ways and packages used to conduct PCA in R, including what seems to be the most commonly used `prcomp()` and `princomp()` functions in base R. However, for my money, it seems that the `psych` package is the most flexible with the best options.

Component extraction

To extract the components with the `psych` package, you will use the `principal()` function. The syntax will include the data and whether or not we want to rotate the components at this time:

```
> pca <- principal(train_scale, rotate = "none")
```

You can examine the components by calling the `pca` object that we created. However, my primary intent is to determine what should be the number of components to retain. For that, a scree plot will suffice. A scree plot can aid you in assessing the components that explain the most variance in the data. It shows the `Component` number on the *x* axis and their associated `Eigenvalues` on the *y* axis. For simplicity of interpretation, I include only the first 10 components:

```
> plot(pca$values[1:10], type = "b", ylab = "Eigenvalues", xlab =
"Component")
```

The following is the output of the preceding command:

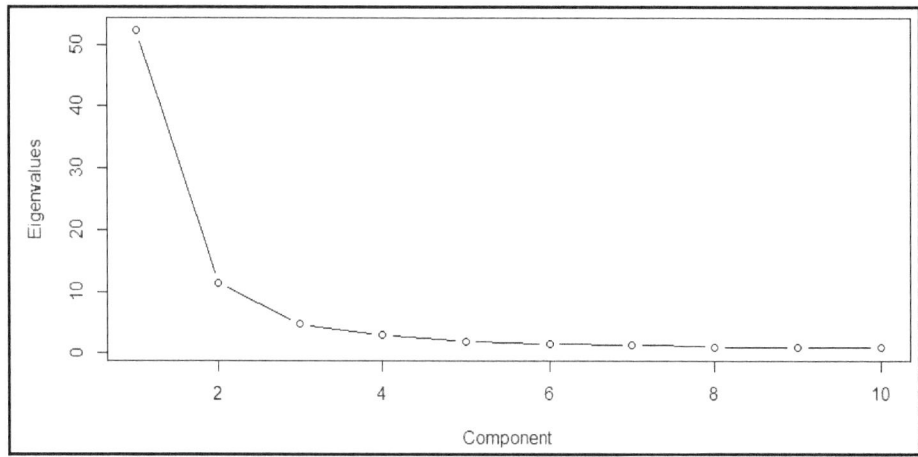

What you are looking for is a point in the scree plot where the rate of change decreases. This will be what is commonly called an elbow or bend in the plot. That elbow point in the plot captures the fact that additional variance explained by a component does not differ greatly from one component to the next. In other words, it is the breakpoint where the plot flattens out. In the plot, maybe four, five, or six components looks compelling. I think more information is needed. Here, we can see the eigenvalues of those 10 components. A rule of thumb recommends selecting all components with an eigenvalue greater than 1:

```
> head(pca$values, 10)
 [1] 52.2361 11.3294 4.7375 3.0193 1.9830 1.5153 1.2896 1.0655 1.0275
[10]  0.9185
```

Another rule I've learned over the years is that you should capture about 70 percent of the total variance, which means that the cumulative variance explained by each of the selected components accounts for 70 percent of the variance explained by all the components. That is pretty simple to do. I'm inclined to go with five components:

```
> sum(pca$values)
[1] 93

> sum(pca$values[1:5])
[1] 73.31
```

We are capturing 79 percent of the total variance with just 5 components. Let's put that together:

```
> pca_5 <- psych::principal(train_scale, nfactors = 5, rotate = "none")
```

Calling the object gives a number of results. Here are the abbreviated results for the top portion of the output:

```
> pca_5
Principal Components Analysis
Call: psych::principal(r = train_scale, nfactors = 5, rotate = "none")
Standardized loading (pattern matrix) based upon correlation matrix
                                 PC1    PC2   PC3    PC4    PC5   h2    u2 com
abdominalextensiondepthsitting 0.58   0.66 0.09 -0.08 -0.26 0.85 0.146 2.4
acromialheight                 0.92 -0.27 0.13  0.19 -0.03 0.98 0.025 1.3
acromionradialelength          0.84 -0.29 0.16 -0.04 -0.11 0.83 0.167 1.4
anklecircumference             0.67  0.34 0.00  0.02  0.34 0.69 0.314 2.0
```

Here, we see the feature loading on each of the five components. For example, `acromialheight` has the highest positive loading of the features on component 1. Here, I paste the part of the output that shows the sum of squares:

```
                       PC1    PC2   PC3  PC4  PC5
SS loading           52.24 11.33 4.74 3.02 1.98
Proportion Var        0.56  0.12 0.05 0.03 0.02
Cumulative Var        0.56  0.68 0.73 0.77 0.79
Proportion Explained  0.71  0.15 0.06 0.04 0.03
Cumulative Proportion 0.71  0.87 0.93 0.97 1.00
```

Here, the numbers are the eigenvalues for each component. When they are normalized, you will end up with the `Proportion Explained` row, which, as you may have guessed, stands for the proportion of the variance explained by each component. You can see that principal component 1 explains 56 percent of all the variance explained by the five components. Remember we previously examined the heuristic rule that your selected components should account for a minimum of 70 percent of the total variation. The `Cumulative Var` row shows the cumulative variance is 79 percent, as demonstrated previously.

Orthogonal rotation and interpretation

As we discussed previously, the point behind rotation is to maximize the loading of the variables on a specific component, which helps in simplifying the interpretation by reducing/eliminating the correlation among these components. The method to conduct orthogonal rotation is known as **varimax**. There are other non-orthogonal rotation methods that allow correlation across factors/components. The choice of the rotation methodology that you will use in your profession should be based on the pertinent literature, which exceeds the scope of this chapter. Feel free to experiment with this dataset. I think that when in doubt, the starting point for any PCA should be an orthogonal rotation.

For this process, we will simply turn back to the `principal()` function, slightly changing the syntax to account for five components and orthogonal rotation, as follows:

```
> pca_rotate <- psych::principal(train_scale, nfactors = 5, rotate =
"varimax")
```

Given the number of features, I just normally save this into a CSV file and examine it in a spreadsheet, in particular with a subject matter expert. Here, we save it and I'll come back with what are high-level summaries. When I worked in oncology market research, we always ended up with a component around the drug's efficacy, one around the drug's side effect profile, and then maybe one or two components regarding dosing, cost, or something of that ilk. The code here just removes the crazy `loading` class from the object so we can save it as a dataframe:

```
> pca_loading <- unclass(pca_rotate$loading)

> pca_loading <- data.frame(pca_loading)

> pca_loading$features <- row.names(pca_loading)

> readr::write_csv(pca_loading, "pca_loading.csv")
```

Welcome back! There is no correct answer, but my guess as to how to summarize these components would be something like this:

- **PC1**: A catchall component; 44 features have loading higher than 0.5
- **PC2**: Hips, thighs, and buttocks...with a dash of waist and chest
- **PC3**: Neck, shoulders, arms
- **PC4**: Some height measures
- **PC5**: Oddly enough, head and foot measures

This can be a fun exercise naming the components. I fondly recall the days of naming such components compassionate conservatives, pragmatic practitioners, and so on. Be that as it may, we need to create scores from these components so we can give supervised learning a go.

Creating scores from the components

We will now need to capture the component loading as the scores for each observation. These scores indicate how each observation (soldier) relates to a component. Let's do this and capture the scores in a dataframe as we will need to use it for our analysis:

```
> pca_scores <- data.frame(round(pca_5$scores, digits = 2))

> head(pca_scores)
    PC1   PC2   PC3   PC4   PC5
1 -1.37  0.29  1.06  0.09  0.29
2 -1.19 -0.45 -0.22 -1.61  0.22
3 -0.04 -1.19 -0.45 -0.69  0.05
4  1.44 -0.96  0.43 -1.87 -0.16
5  1.37  2.07  0.26  0.15  2.05
6 -0.09  0.29 -0.96 -0.07  0.17
```

We now have the scores for each component for each soldier. These are simply the features for each observation multiplied by the loading on each component and then summed. We now can bring in the response as a column in the data:

```
> pca_scores$weight <- trainY
```

With this done, I think we are compelled to examine the correlation of this data:

```
> DataExplorer::plot_correlation(pca_scores)
```

The output of the preceding code is as follows:

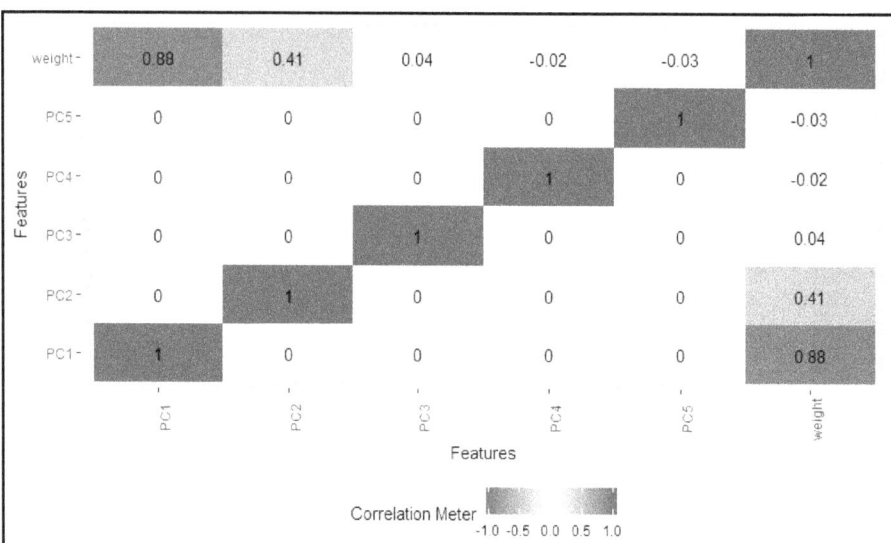

We see that components 1 and 2 are positively correlated to weight while the others seem meaningless. We must keep in mind this is univariate and our model may prove something different.

Regression with MARS

To do this part of the process, we will build a model with the `earth` package, review it on the training data, then see how it performs on the test data. We'll run a 10-fold cross-validation with the algorithm:

```
> set.seed(1492)

> earth_fit <-
    earth::earth(
    x = pca_scores[, 1:5],
    y = pca_scores[, 6],
    pmethod = 'cv',
    nfold = 10,
    degree = 1,
    minspan = -1
  )
```

Calling the summary of the model object gives us seven total terms with three of the features:

```
> summary(earth_fit)
Call: earth(x=pca_scores[,1:5], y=pca_scores[,6], pmethod="cv", degree=1,
nfold=10,
            minspan=-1)

                coefficients
(Intercept)       174.182
h(0.1-PC1)        -26.380
h(PC1-0.1)         33.806
h(0.01-PC2)       -13.181
h(PC2-0.01)        13.842
h(0.02-PC5)         1.333
h(PC5-0.02)        -0.869

Selected 7 of 7 terms, and 3 of 5 predictors using pmethod="cv"
Termination condition: RSq changed by less than 0.001 at 7 terms
Importance: PC1, PC2, PC5, PC3-unused, PC4-unused
Number of terms at each degree of interaction: 1 6 (additive model)
GRSq 0.9518 RSq 0.952 mean.oof.RSq 0.9512 (sd 0.0151)

pmethod="backward" would have selected the same model:
     7 terms 3 preds, GRSq 0.9518 RSq 0.952 mean.oof.RSq 0.9512
```

The model achieved a tremendous r-squared of 0.952 with components 1, 2, and 5. It can be a little easier to see the hinge functions at play with `plotmo`:

```
> plotmo::plotmo(earth_fit)
```

The output of the preceding code is as follows:

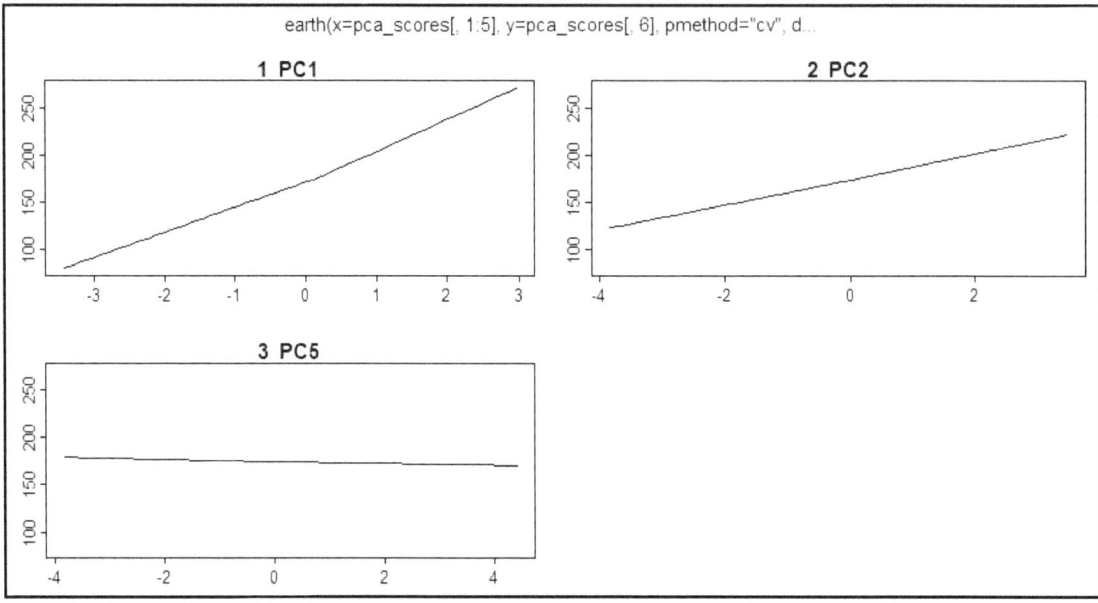

It's kind of a challenge to discern those subtle hinge functions from `plotmo`, with the exception of PC1. To see how this model really performs, save the predicted values and run some plots:

```
> ggplot2::ggplot(pca_scores, ggplot2::aes(x = earthpred, y = weight)) +
    ggplot2::geom_point() +
    ggplot2::stat_smooth(method = "lm", se = FALSE) +
    ggthemes::theme_pander()
```

The output of the preceding code is as follows:

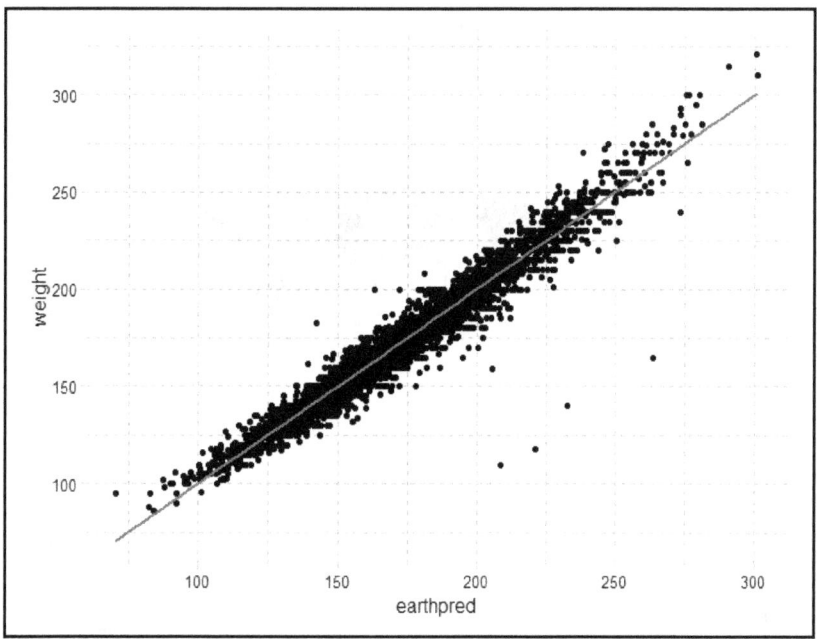

We see a nice linear relationship, but we have several outliers that make us scratch our heads. You mean our model predicts a weight of almost 225 pounds, but the soldier is less than 125 pounds? Something isn't right with those outlier predictions, perhaps measurement or data entry error; they are interesting observations nonetheless, worthy of further investigation, *time permitting*.

How about the residuals?

```
> ggplot2::ggplot(pca_scores, ggplot2::aes(x = earthpred, y = earthresid))
+
    ggplot2::geom_point() +
    ggplot2::stat_smooth(method = "loess", se = FALSE) +
    ggthemes::theme_few()
```

The output of the preceding code is as follows:

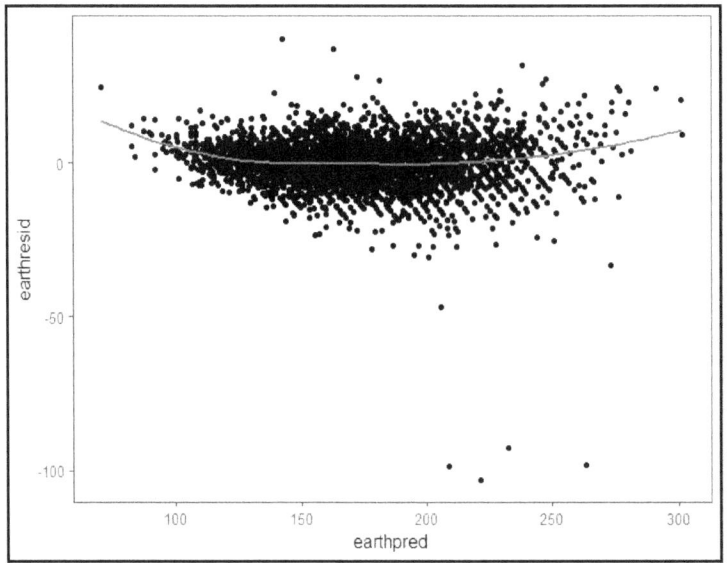

Just the slightest curvilinear relationship. We are seeing that the algorithm is underestimating, minimally, soldiers' weight at the extreme values. We already have r-squared, but RMSE and MAE are quickly callable:

```
> caret::postResample(pred = pca_scores$earthpred,
    obs = pca_scores$weight)
    RMSE Rsquared    MAE
   7.336    0.952 5.219
```

The mean absolute error is just 5 percent. Let's see if this holds on the test data.

Test data evaluation

One of the things you need to do on out-of-sample data is scale it according to the original (training) data. The predict function that comes with the `psych` package allows you to do this effortlessly. We put those scaled and scored values into a dataframe we can then use to make the out-of-sample predictions:

```
> test_reduced <- as.matrix(test[, c(-1, -95)])

> test_scores <- data.frame(predict(pca_5, test_reduced, old.data = train[,
  c(-1, -95)]))
```

Here, we just add the predicted and actual values:

```
> test_scores$testpred <- predict(earth_fit, test_scores)

> test_scores$weight <- test$Weightlbs
```

The results look good:

```
> caret::postResample(pred = test_scores$testpred,
    obs = test_scores$weight)
    RMSE Rsquared     MAE
  7.8735   0.9468  5.1937
```

The performance declined just a little bit. I think we can move forward with this model. Further exploration of the outliers is in order to see whether there is measurement error, drop them from the analysis, or truncate them. In closing, let's see the plot of actual versus predicted:

```
> ggplot2::ggplot(test_scores, ggplot2::aes(x = testpred, y = weight)) +
    ggplot2::geom_point() +
    ggplot2::stat_smooth(method = "lm", se = FALSE) +
    ggthemes::theme_excel_new()
```

The output of the preceding code is as follows:

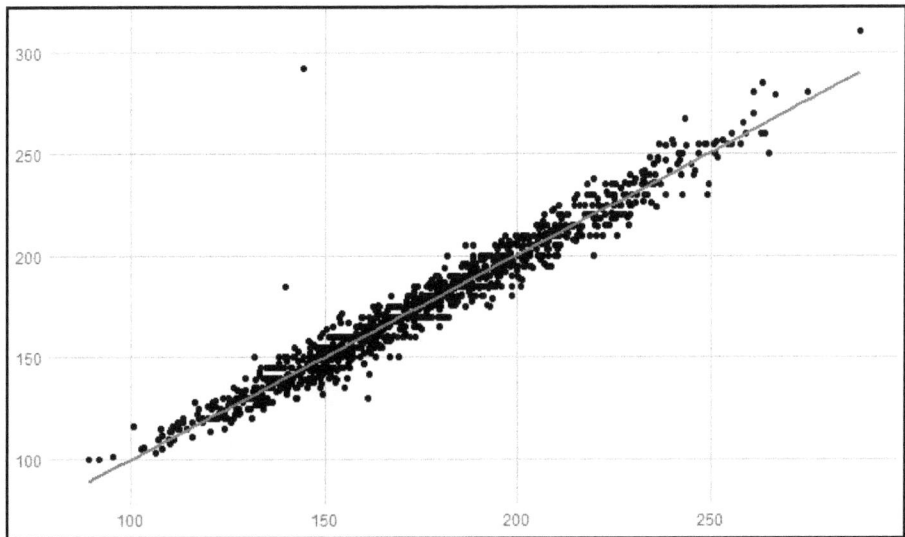

It looks similar to the training data plot. Once again, there is at least one anomaly. How can our model predict a soldier to be about 140 pounds but they are actually almost 300? We could amuse ourselves pursuing this further, but let's move on.

Summary

In this chapter, we took a second stab at unsupervised learning techniques by exploring PCA, examining what it is, and applying it in a practical fashion. We explored how it can be used to reduce the dimensionality and improve the understanding of the dataset when confronted with numerous highly correlated variables. Then, we applied it to real data of anthropometric measurements of US Army soldiers, using the resulting principal components in a regression analysis with MARS to predict a soldier's weight. Additionally, we explored ways to visualize the data and model results.

As an unsupervised learning technique, it requires some judgment along with trial and error to arrive at an optimal solution that is acceptable to business partners. Nevertheless, it is a powerful tool to extract latent insights and to support supervised learning.

In the next chapter, we will examine using unsupervised learning to look at association analysis.

11
Association Analysis

If we have data, let's look at data. If all we have are opinions, let's go with mine.

- Jim Barksdale, former Netscape CEO

You would have to live on the dark side of the Moon to not see the results of the techniques that we're about to discuss in this chapter every day. If you visit www.amazon.com, watch movies on www.netflix.com, or visit any retail website, you'll be exposed to terms such as *related products, because you watched..., customers who bought x also bought y,* and *recommended for you,* at every twist and turn. With large volumes of historical real-time or near real-time information, retailers utilize various algorithms in an attempt to increase both the quantity of buyers' purchases and the value of those purchases.

The techniques to do this can be broken down into two categories: association rules and recommendation engines. Association rule analysis is commonly referred to as market basket analysis, as it's concerned with understanding what items are purchased together. With recommendation engines, the goal is to provide a customer with other items that they'll enjoy based on how they've rated items they've viewed or purchased previously.

In this chapter, we'll focus on association analysis. It's applicable not only to making recommendations, product placement, and promotional pricing, but can be used in manufacturing, web usage, healthcare, and so on. If you're interested in how items occur together, apply what you're about to learn.

An overview of association analysis

Association analysis is a data mining technique that has the purpose of finding the optimal combination of products or services and allows marketers to exploit this knowledge to provide recommendations, optimize product placement, or develop marketing programs that take advantage of cross-selling. In short, the idea is to identify which items go well together, and profit from this.

You can think of the results of the analysis as an `if...then` statement. If a customer buys an airplane ticket, then there is a 46 % probability that they'll buy a hotel room, and if they go on to buy a hotel room, then there is a 33 % probability that they'll rent a car.

However, it isn't just for sales and marketing. It's also used in fraud detection and healthcare; for example, if a patient undergoes treatment A, then there's a 26 % probability that they'll exhibit symptom X. Before going into the details, we should have a look at some terminology, as follows:

- **Itemset**: This is a collection of one or more items in the dataset.
- **Support**: This is the proportion of the transactions in the data that contain an itemset of interest.
- **Confidence**: This is the conditional probability that, if a person purchases or does x, they'll purchase or do y; the act of doing x is referred to as the *antecedent* or **left-hand side** (**LHS**), and y is the *consequence* or **right-hand side** (**RHS**).
- **Lift**: This is the ratio of the support of x occurring together with y divided by the probability that x and y occur if they are independent. It's the **confidence** divided by the probability of x times the probability of y; for example, say that we have the probability of x and y occurring together as 10 %, and the probability of x is 20 %, and y is 30 %, then the lift would be 10 % (20 % times 30 %) or 16.67 %.

The package in R that you can use to perform a market basket analysis is **arules: Mining Association Rules and Frequent with Itemsets**. The package offers two different methods for finding rules **apriori** and **ECLAT**. There are other algorithms we can use to conduct a market basket analysis, but apriori is used most frequently, and so will be our focus.

With apriori, the principle is that, if an itemset is frequent, then all of its subsets must also be frequent. A minimum frequency (support) is determined by the analyst before executing the algorithm, and once established, the algorithm will run as follows:

- Let $k=1$ (the number of items)
- Generate itemsets of a length that is equal to or greater than the specified support
- Iterate $k + (1...n)$, pruning those that are infrequent (less than the support)
- Stop the iteration when no new frequent itemsets are identified

Once you have an ordered summary of the most frequent itemsets, you can continue the analysis process by examining the confidence and lift to offers the associations of interest.

Before we delve into the analysis, it's necessary to understand how to put your raw data into the appropriate structure, referred to as R class transactions. This can be a confusing task, so I'm going to spend some time on this before moving on to a full demonstration of association analysis.

Creating transactional data

In the world of the Internet of Things, you receive a ton of data. As you monitor devices for anomalies or failures, let's say you get some fault codes. How would you put the raw data into something meaningful for analysis in R? Well, here's a case study. We'll put together a random dataset and turn it into the proper form for use with R's `arules` package. Here's the dataframe:

```
> set.seed(270)

> faults <- data.frame(
    serialNumber = sample(1:20, 100, replace = T),
    faultCode = paste("fc", sample(1:12, 100, replace = T), sep = "")
  )
```

This gives us `20` different serial numbers, which tells us which devices being monitored have had faults. Each device has a possibility of `12` different fault codes. The limitation of association analysis as we're doing it is the fact that the transaction order isn't included. Let's assume that isn't an issue in this example and proceed. First, given the random generation of this data, we will remove the duplicates:

```
> faults <- unique(faults)
```

The structure of the dataframe before turning it into transactions is critical. The identifier column needs to be as an integer. So, if you have a customer or equipment identifier such as `123abc`, you must turn it into an integer. Then, the item of interest must be a factor. Here, we confirm that we have the proper dataframe structure:

```
> str(faults)
'data.frame': 80 obs. of 2 variables:
 $ serialNumber: int 9 8 1 18 11 20 2 16 10 20 ...
 $ faultCode : Factor w/ 12 levels "fc1","fc10","fc11",..: 2 5 1 12 1 3 6
 10 11 1 ...
```

Notice that this data is in the long format, which is usually how it's produced. As such, create a column where all values are `TRUE` and use tidyverse to reshape the data into the wide format:

```
> faults$indicator <- TRUE

> faults_wide <- tidyr::spread(faults, key = faultCode, value = indicator)
```

We now have a dataframe with the associated faults labeled as `TRUE` for each item of interest. Next, turn the data into a matrix while dropping the ID:

```
> faults_matrix <- as.matrix(faults_wide[,-1])
```

You must turn the missing `na` into something understood, so let's make them `FALSE`:

```
> faults_matrix[is.na(faults_matrix)] <- FALSE
```

Finally, we can turn this data into the `transactions` class:

```
> faults_transactions <- as(faults_matrix, "transactions")
```

To confirm it all worked, create a plot of the top 10 item frequency:

```
> arules::itemFrequencyPlot(faults_transactions, topN = 10)
```

The output of the preceding code is as follows:

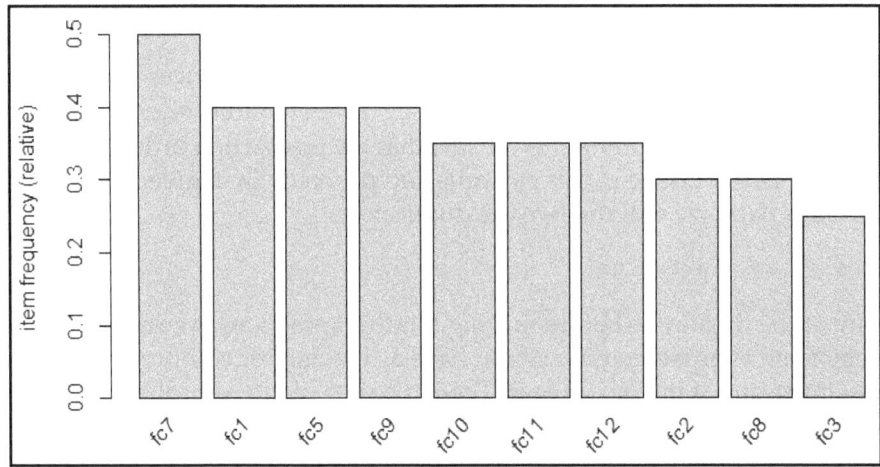

Success! Following the preceding process will get you from raw data to the appropriate structure. We'll transition to an example using data from the `arules` package itself, which you can apply to any analysis you want.

Data understanding

For our business case, we'll focus on identifying the association rules for a grocery store. The dataset will be from the `arules` package and is called `Groceries`. This dataset consists of actual transactions over 30 days from a real-world grocery store and consists of 9,835 different purchases. All of the items purchased are put into one of 169 categories, for example, bread, wine, meat, and so on.

Let's say that we want to develop an understanding of what potential customers will purchase along with beer to identify the right product placement within the store or support a cross-selling campaign.

Data preparation

For this analysis, we'll only need to load two packages, as well as the Groceries dataset:

```
> install.packages("arules")

> install.packages("arulesViz")

> library(arules)

> data(Groceries)

> str(Groceries)
    Formal class 'transactions' [package "arules"] with 3 slots
      ..@ data :Formal class 'ngCMatrix' [package "Matrix"] with 5
        slots
      .. .. ..@ i : int [1:43367] 13 60 69 78 14 29 98 24 15 29 ...
      .. .. ..@ p : int [1:9836] 0 4 7 8 12 16 21 22 27 28 ...
      .. .. ..@ Dim : int [1:2] 169 9835
      .. .. ..@ Dimnames:List of 2
      .. .. .. ..$ : NULL
      .. .. .. ..$ : NULL
      .. .. ..@ factors : list()
      ..@ itemInfo :'data.frame': 169 obs. of 3 variables:
      .. ..$ labels: chr [1:169] "frankfurter" "sausage" "liver loaf"
        "ham" ...
      .. ..$ level2: Factor w/ 55 levels "baby food","bags",..: 44 44
    44 44 44 44
    44 42 42 41 ...
      .. ..$ level1: Factor w/ 10 levels "canned food",..: 6 6 6 6 6 6
    6 6 6 6
      ...
      ..@ itemsetInfo:'data.frame': 0 obs. of 0 variables
```

This dataset is structured as a sparse matrix object, known as the `transaction` class, which we created previously.

So, once the structure is that of the class transaction, our standard exploration techniques won't work, but the `arules` package offers us other methods to explore the data. The best way to explore this data is with an item frequency plot using the `itemFrequencyPlot()` function in the `arules` package. You'll need to specify the transaction dataset, the number of items with the highest frequency to plot, and whether or not you want the relative or absolute frequency of the items. Let's first look at the absolute frequency and the top 10 items only:

```
> arules::itemFrequencyPlot(Groceries, topN = 10, type = "absolute")
```

The output of the preceding command is as follows:

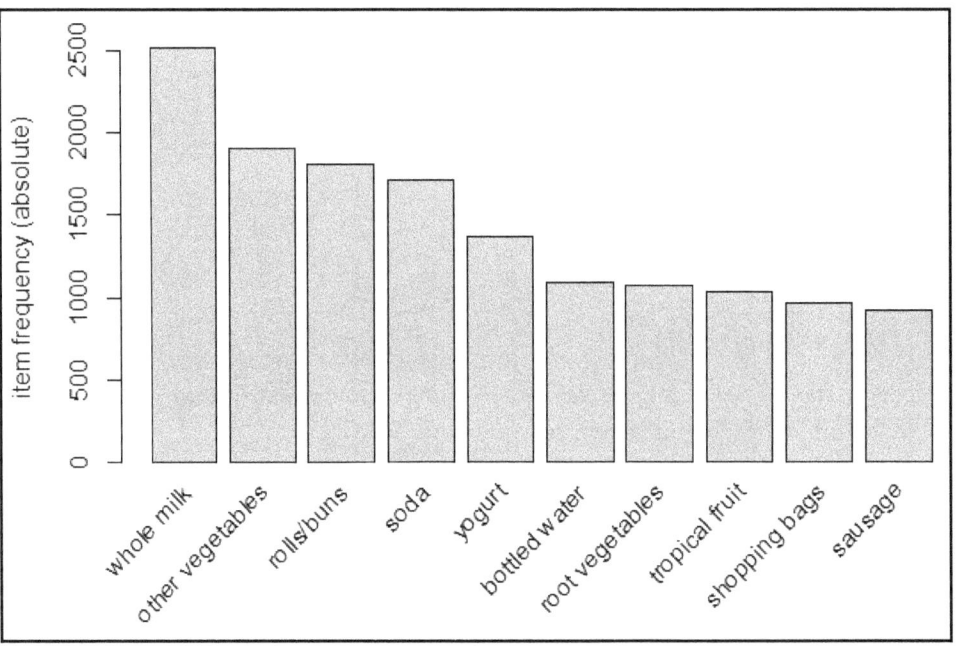

The top item purchased was **whole milk** with roughly **2,500** of the 9,836 transactions in the basket. For a relative distribution of the top 15 items, let's run the following code:

```
> arules::itemFrequencyPlot(Groceries, topN = 15)
```

The following is the output of the preceding command:

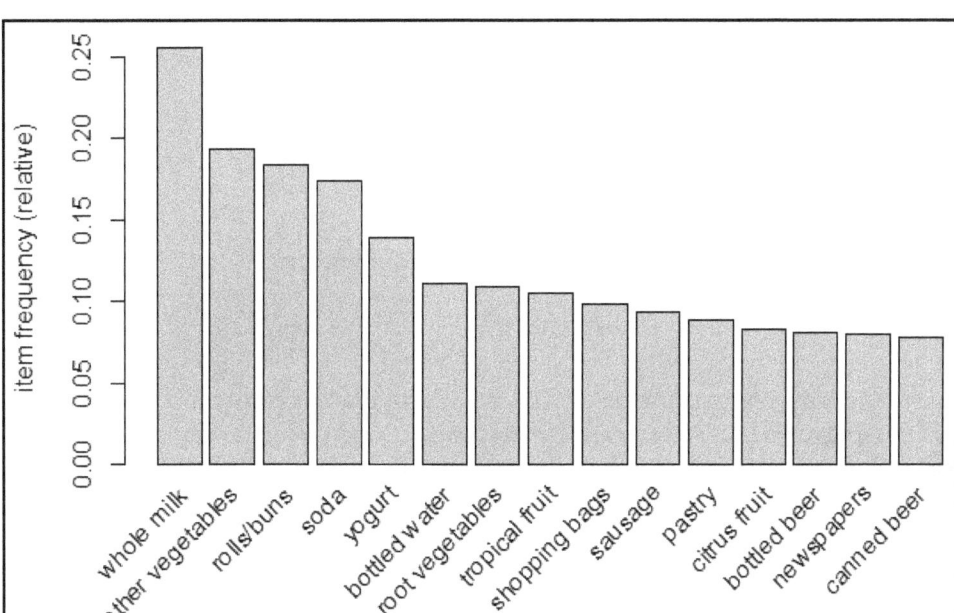

Alas, here we see that beer shows up as the 13th and 15th most purchased item at this store. Just under 10 % of the transactions related to **bottled beer** and/or **canned beer**.

For this exercise, this is all we need to do; therefore, we can move right on to the modeling and evaluation.

Modeling and evaluation

We'll start by mining the data for the overall association rules before moving on to our rules for beer specifically. Throughout the modeling process, we'll use the apriori algorithm, which is the appropriately named `apriori()` function in the `arules` package. The two main things that we'll need to specify in the function are the dataset and parameters. As for the parameters, you'll need to apply judgment when determining the minimum support, confidence, and the minimum and/or maximum length of basket items in an itemset. Using item frequency plots, along with trial and error, let's set the minimum support at 1 in 1,000 transactions and the minimum confidence at 90 %.

Additionally, let's establish the maximum number of items to be associated as 4. The following code creates the object that we'll call `rules`:

```
rules <-
  arules::apriori(Groceries, parameter = list(
    supp = 0.001,
    conf = 0.9,
    maxlen = 4
  ))
```

Calling the object shows how many rules the algorithm produced:

```
> rules
set of 67 rules
```

There are many ways to examine rules. The first thing that I recommend is setting the number of displayed digits to only two, with the `options()` function in base R. Then, sort and inspect the top five rules based on the lift that they provide, as follows:

```
> options(digits = 2)
> rules <- arules::sort(rules, by = "lift", decreasing = TRUE)
> arules::inspect(rules[1:5])
  lhs                    rhs                   support confidence lift
1 {liquor, red/blush wine}      => {bottled beer}        0.0019
   0.90 11.2
2 {root vegetables, butter, cream cheese }      => {yogurt}
   0.0010       0.91  6.5
3 {citrus fruit, root vegetables, soft cheese}=> {other vegetables}
   0.0010       1.00  5.2
4 {pip fruit, whipped/sour cream, brown bread}=> {other vegetables}
   0.0011       1.00  5.2
5 {butter,whipped/sour cream, soda}    => {other vegetables}
    0.0013       0.93  4.8
```

Lo and behold! The rule that offers the best overall lift is the purchase of `liquor` and `red wine` on the probability of purchasing `bottled beer`. I have to admit that this is pure chance and not intended on my part. As I always say, it's better to be lucky than good. Although, it's still not a very common transaction with support for only 1.9 per 1,000.

You can also sort by the support and confidence, so let's have a look at the first five rules by=`"confidence"` in descending order, as follows:

```
> rules <- arules::sort(rules, by = "confidence", decreasing = TRUE)

> arules::inspect(rules[1:5])
    lhs                    rhs                   support confidence lift
  1 {citrus fruit, root vegetables, soft cheese}=> {other vegetables}
```

```
      0.0010           1   5.2
2 {pip fruit, whipped/sour cream, brown bread}=> {other vegetables}
      0.0011           1   5.2
3 {rice, sugar}   => {whole milk}           0.0012          1   3.9
4 {canned fish, hygiene articles} => {whole milk} 0.0011    1   3.9
5 {root vegetables, butter, rice} => {whole milk} 0.0010    1   3.9
```

You can see in the table that `confidence` for these transactions is 100 %. Moving on to our specific study of beer, we can utilize a function in `arules` to develop cross-tabulations—the `crossTable()` function—and then examine whatever suits our needs. The first step is to create a table with our dataset:

```
> tab <- arules::crossTable(Groceries)
```

With `tab` created, we can now investigate joint occurrences between the items. Here, we'll look at just the first three rows and columns:

```
> tab[1:3, 1:3]
                frankfurter sausage liver loaf
    frankfurter         580      99          7
    sausage              99     924         10
    liver loaf            7      10         50
```

As you might imagine, shoppers only selected liver loaf 50 times out of the 9,835 transactions. Additionally, of the 924 times, people gravitated toward `sausage`, `ten` times they felt compelled to grab `liver loaf`. (Desperate times call for desperate measures!) If you want to look at a specific example, you can either specify the row and column number or spell that item out:

```
> tab["bottled beer","bottled beer"]
[1] 792
```

This tells us that there were 792 transactions of `bottled beer`. Let's see what the joint occurrence between `bottled beer` and `canned beer` is:

```
> tab["bottled beer","canned beer"]
[1] 26
```

I would expect this to be low as it supports my idea that people lean toward drinking beer from either a bottle or a can. I strongly prefer a bottle. It also makes a handy weapon to protect yourself from all these ruffian protesters such as *Occupy Wallstreet* and the like.

We can now move on and derive specific rules for `bottled beer`. We'll again use the `apriori()` function, but this time, we'll add a syntax around `appearance`. This means that we'll specify in the syntax that we want the left-hand side to be items that increase the probability of purchasing `bottled beer`, which will be on the right-hand side. In the following code, notice that I've adjusted the `support` and `confidence` numbers. Feel free to experiment with your settings:

```
> beer.rules <- arules::apriori(
    data = Groceries,
    parameter = list(support
    = 0.0015, confidence = 0.3),
    appearance = list(default = "lhs",
    rhs = "bottled beer"))

> beer.rules
set of 4 rules
```

We find ourselves with only 4 association rules. We've seen one of them already; now let's bring in the other three rules in descending order by lift:

```
> beer.rules <- arules::sort(beer.rules, decreasing = TRUE, by = "lift")
 > arules::inspect(beer.rules)
lhs rhs support confidence lift
1 {liquor, red/blush wine} => {bottled beer} 0.0019 0.90 11.2
2 {liquor} => {bottled beer} 0.0047 0.42 5.2
3 {soda, red/blush wine} => {bottled beer} 0.0016 0.36 4.4
4 {other vegetables, red/blush wine} => {bottled beer}0.0015 0.31
3.8
```

In all of the instances, the purchase of `bottled beer` is associated with booze, either `liquor` and/or red wine, which is no surprise to anyone. What's interesting is that `white wine` isn't in the mix here. Let's take a closer look at this and compare the joint occurrences of `bottled beer` and types of wine:

```
> tab["bottled beer", "red/blush wine"]
[1] 48
> tab["red/blush wine", "red/blush wine"]
[1] 189
> 48/189
[1] 0.25
> tab["white wine", "white wine"]
[1] 187
> tab["bottled beer", "white wine"]
[1] 22
> 22/187
[1] 0.12
```

It's interesting that 25 % of the time when someone purchased `red wine`, they also purchased `bottled beer`; but with `white wine`, a joint purchase only happened in 12 % of the instances. We certainly don't know why in this analysis, but this could potentially help us to determine how we should position our product in this grocery store. Another thing before we move on is to look at a plot of the rules. This is done with the `plot()` function in the `arulesViz` package.

There are many graphics options available. For this example, let's specify that we want `graph` showing `lift` and the rules provided and shaded by `confidence`. The following syntax will provide this accordingly:

```
> library(arulesViz)
Loading required package: grid

> plot(beer.rules,
+ method = "graph",
+ measure = "lift",
+ shading = "confidence")
```

The following is the output of the preceding command:

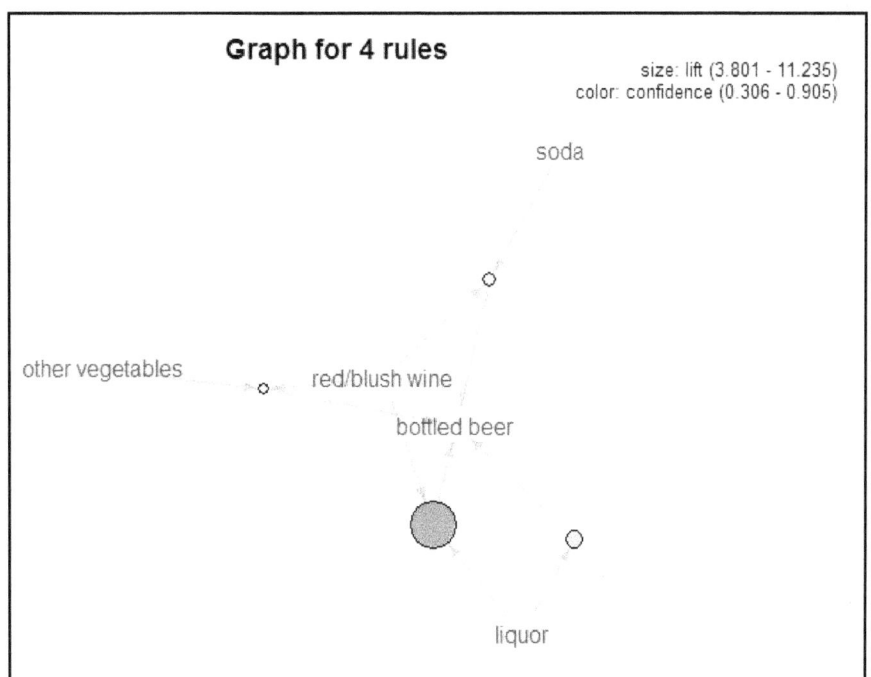

This graph shows that **liquor/red wine** provides the best **lift** and the highest level of **confidence** with both the **size** of the circle and its shading.

What we've just done in this simple exercise is to show how easy it is with R to conduct a market basket analysis. It doesn't take much imagination to figure out the analytical possibilities that we can include with this technique, for example, incorporate customer segmentation, longitudinal purchase history, and so on, as well as how to use it in advert displays, co-promotions, and so on.

Summary

In this chapter, the goal was to provide an introduction to how to use R in order to build and test association rule mining (market basket analysis). Market basket analysis tries to understand what items are purchased together or what items occur together, so you can apply the analysis to healthcare, fraud-detection, and even exploring mechanical issues. As such, we learned how to transform raw data into a transactional structure for use in the `arules` package.

We're now going to shift gears back to supervised learning. In the next chapter, we're going to cover some poorly understood but essential methods in practical machine learning, that is, analyzing time series data and determining causality.

12
Time Series and Causality

"An economist is an expert who will know tomorrow why the things he predicted yesterday didn't happen today."

- Laurence J. Peter

A univariate time series is where the measurements are collected over a standard measure of time, which could be by the minute, hour, day, week, month, and so on. What makes the time series problematic over other data is that the order of the observations matters. This dependency of order can cause standard analysis methods to produce an unnecessarily high bias or variance.

It seems that there's a paucity of literature on machine learning and time series data or it's substandard. For example, I was at a data science conference in the spring of 2018, and a highly regarded machine learning expert mentioned that vector autoregression requires the data to be stationary. We'll discuss this later. When I heard this, I almost fell over. Fake data news! I informed my colleagues trained in econometrics to their horror and dismay. This is unfortunate as so much of real-world data involves a time component. Furthermore, time series analysis can be quite complicated and tricky. I would say that if you haven't seen a time series analysis done incorrectly, you haven't been looking close enough.

Another aspect involving time series that's often neglected is causality. Yes, we don't want to confuse correlation with causation but, in time series analysis, we can apply the technique of Granger causality in order to determine whether causality, statistically speaking, exists.

In this chapter, we'll apply time series/econometric techniques to identify univariate forecast models (including ensembles), vector autoregression models, and finally, Granger causality. After completing this chapter, you may not be a complete master of the time series analysis, but you'll know enough to perform an effective analysis and understand the fundamental issues to consider when building time series models and creating predictive models (forecasts).

Following are the topics that will be covered in this chapter:

- Univariate time series analysis
- Time series data
- Modeling and evaluation

Univariate time series analysis

We'll focus on two methods to analyze and forecast a single time series: **exponential smoothing** and **Autoregressive Integrated Moving Average** (**ARIMA**) models. We'll start by looking at exponential smoothing models.

Like moving average models, exponential smoothing models use weights for past observations. But unlike moving average models, the more recent the observation, the more weight it's given relative to the later ones. There are three possible smoothing parameters to estimate: the overall smoothing parameter, a trend parameter, and the seasonal smoothing parameter. If no trend or seasonality is present, then these parameters become null.

The smoothing parameter produces a forecast with the following equation:

$$Yt + 1 = \alpha(Yt) + (1-\alpha)Yt - 1 + (1 - \alpha)2Yt - 2 + \ldots, where\ 0 < \alpha \leq 1$$

In this equation, Y_t is the value at the time, T, and alpha (α) is the smoothing parameter. Algorithms optimize the alpha (and other parameters) by minimizing the errors, **Sum of Squared Error** (**SSE**) or maximum likelihood.

The forecast equation along with trend and seasonality equations, if applicable, will be as follows:

- The forecast, where A is the preceding smoothing equation and h is the number of forecast periods: $Yt + h = A + hBt + St$

- The trend equation: $Bt = \beta(At - At - 1) + (1 - \beta)Bt - 1$
- The seasonality, where m is the number of seasonal periods:
  $St = \Omega(Yt - At - 1 - Bt - 1) + (1 - \Omega)St - m$

This equation is referred to as the **Holt-Winters method**. The forecast equation is additive in nature with the trend as linear. The method also allows the inclusion of a dampened trend and multiplicative seasonality, where the seasonality proportionally increases or decreases over time. With these models, you don't have to worry about the assumption of stationarity as in an ARIMA model. Stationarity is where the time series has a constant mean, variance, and correlation between all of the time periods. Having said this, it's still important to understand the ARIMA models as there will be situations where they have the best performance.

Starting with the autoregressive model, the value of Y at time T is a linear function of the prior values of Y. The formula for an autoregressive lag-1 model *AR(1)* is $Yt = constant + \Phi Yt - 1 + Et$. The critical assumptions for the model are as follows:

- Et denotes the errors that are identically and independently distributed with a mean zero and constant variance
- The errors are independent of Yt
- Yt, Yt-1, Yt-n... is stationary, which means that the absolute value of Φ is less than one

With a stationary time series, you can examine the **autocorrelation function (ACF)**. The ACF of a stationary series gives correlations between Yt and Yt-h for $h = 1, 2...n$. Let's use R to create an *AR(1)* series and plot it:

```
> install.packages("forecast")

> set.seed(1966)

> ar1 <- arima.sim(list(order = c(1, 0, 0), ar = 0.5), n = 200)

> forecast::autoplot(ar1, main = "AR1")
```

The following is the output of the preceding command:

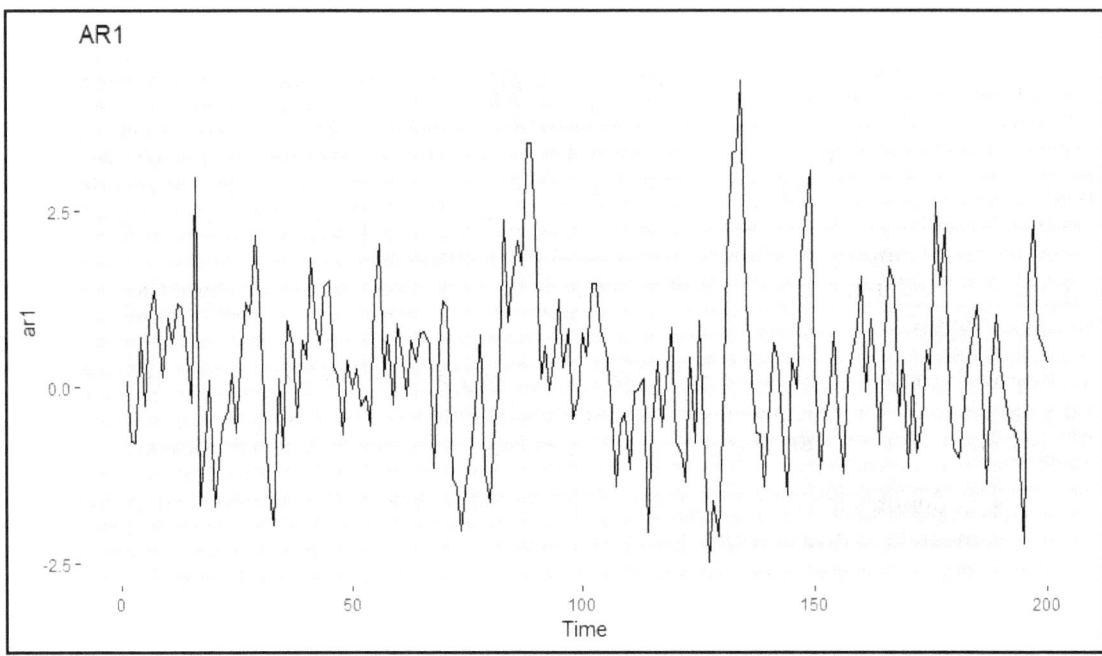

Now, let's examine ACF:

```
> forecast::autoplot(acf(ar1, plot = F), main = "ACF of simulated AR1")
```

The output of the preceding command is as follows:

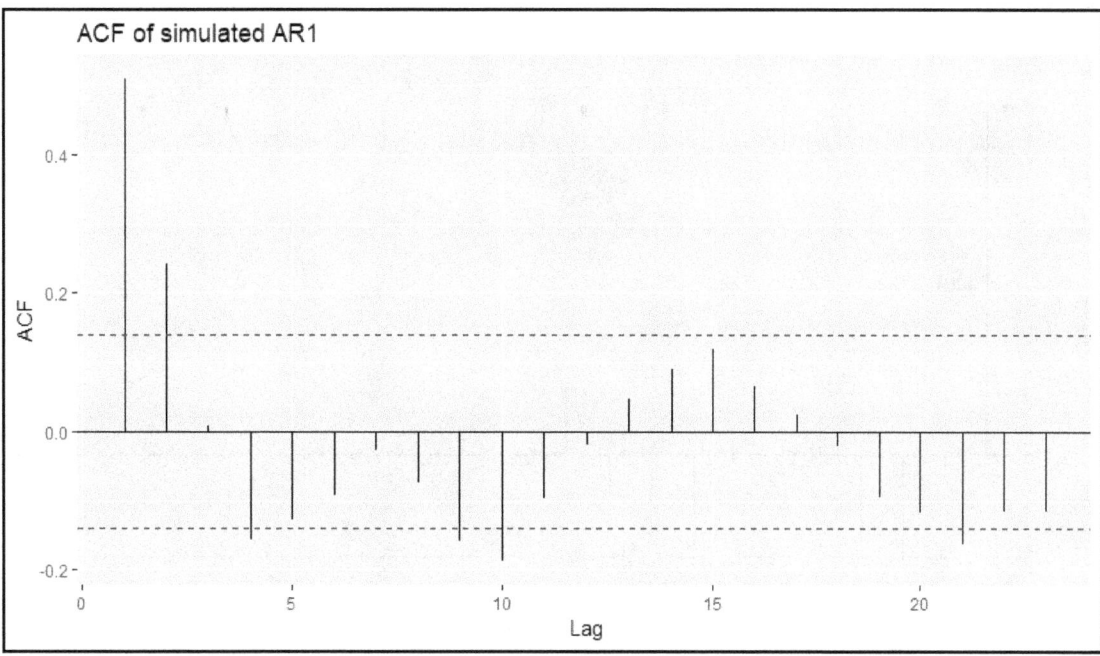

The **ACF** plot shows the correlations exponentially decreasing as the **Lag** increases. The dotted blue lines indicate the confidence bands of a significant correlation. Any line that extends above the high or below the low band is considered significant. In addition to ACF, we should also examine the **partial autocorrelation function (PACF)**. The PACF is a conditional correlation, which means that the correlation between Yt and $Yt\text{-}h$ is conditional on the observations that come between the two. One way to intuitively understand this is to think of a linear regression model and its coefficients. Let's assume that you have $Y = B0 + B1X1$ versus $Y = B0 + B1X1 + B2X2$. The relationship of X to Y in the first model is linear with a coefficient, but in the second model, the coefficient will be different because of the relationship between Y and $X2$ now being accounted for as well. Note that, in the following PACF plot, the partial autocorrelation value at lag-1 is identical to the autocorrelation value at lag-1, as this isn't a conditional correlation:

```
> forecast::autoplot(pacf(ar1, plot = F), main = "PACF of simulated AR1")
```

The following is the output of the preceding command:

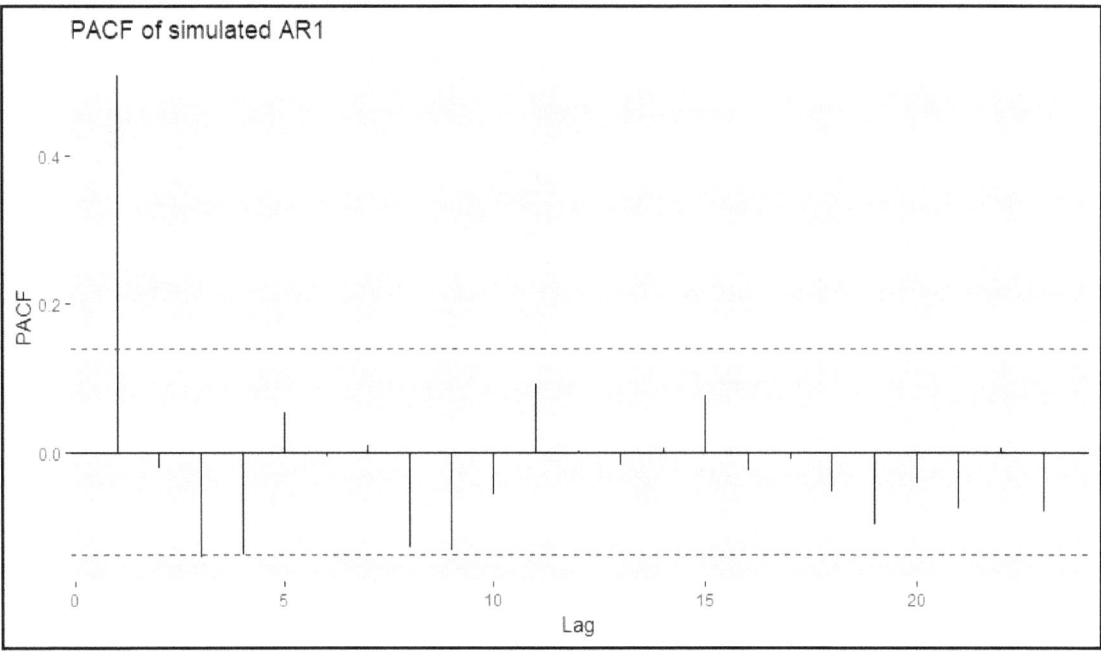

We can safely make the assumption that the series is stationary from the appearance of the preceding time series plot. We'll look at a couple of statistical tests in the practical exercise to ensure that the data is stationary but, on occasion, the eyeball test is sufficient. If the data isn't stationary, then it's possible to detrend the data by taking its differences. This is the Integrated (I) in ARIMA. After differencing, the new series becomes $\Delta Yt = Yt - Yt\text{-}1$. One should expect a first-order difference to achieve stationarity but, on some occasions, a second-order difference may be necessary. An ARIMA model with *AR(1)* and *I(1)* would be annotated as (1,1,0).

The **MA** stands for **Moving Average**. This isn't the simple moving average as the 50-day moving average of a stock price, it's rather a coefficient that is applied to the errors. The errors are, of course, identically and independently distributed with a mean zero and constant variance. The formula for an *MA(1)* model is $Yt = constant + Et + \Theta Et\text{-}1$. As we did with the *AR(1)* model, we can build an *MA(1)* in R, as follows:

```
> set.seed(123)
> ma1 <- arima.sim(list(order = c(0, 0, 1), ma = -0.5), n = 200)
> forecast::autoplot(ma1, main = "MA1")
```

The following is the output of the preceding command:

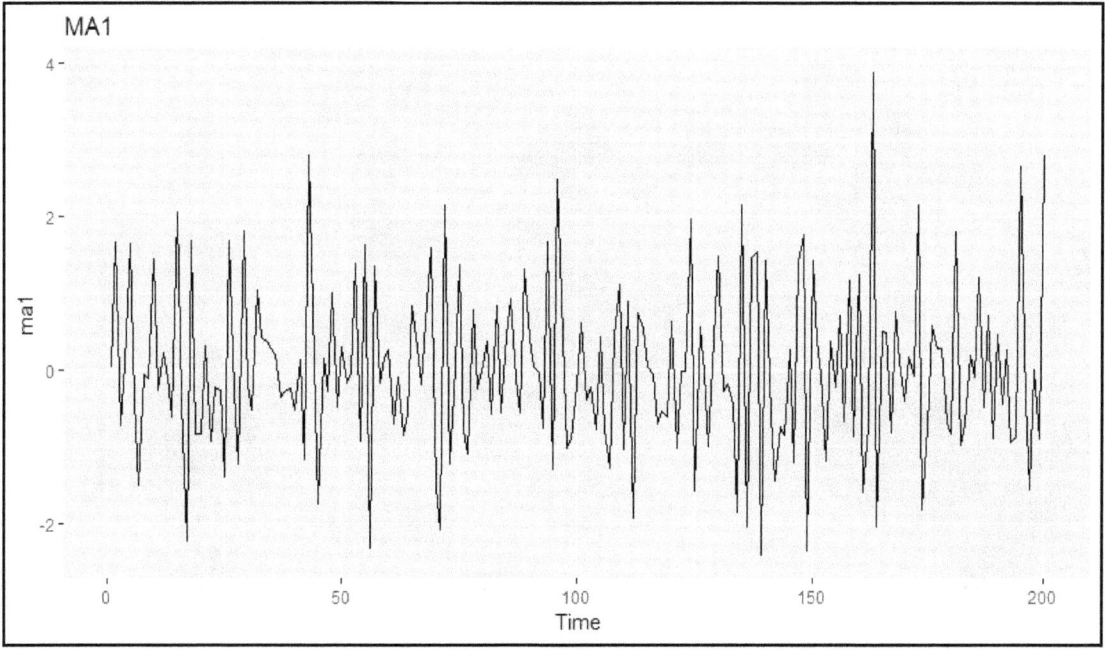

The ACF and PACF plots are a bit different from the *AR(1)* model. Note that there are some rules of thumb while looking at the plots in order to determine whether the model has AR and/or MA terms. They can be a bit subjective, so I'll leave it to you to learn these heuristics, but trust R to identify the proper model. In the following plots, we'll see a significant correlation at lag-1 and two significant partial correlations at lag-1 and lag-2:

```
> forecast::autoplot(acf(ma1, plot = F), main = "ACF of simulated MA1")
```

The output of the preceding command is as follows:

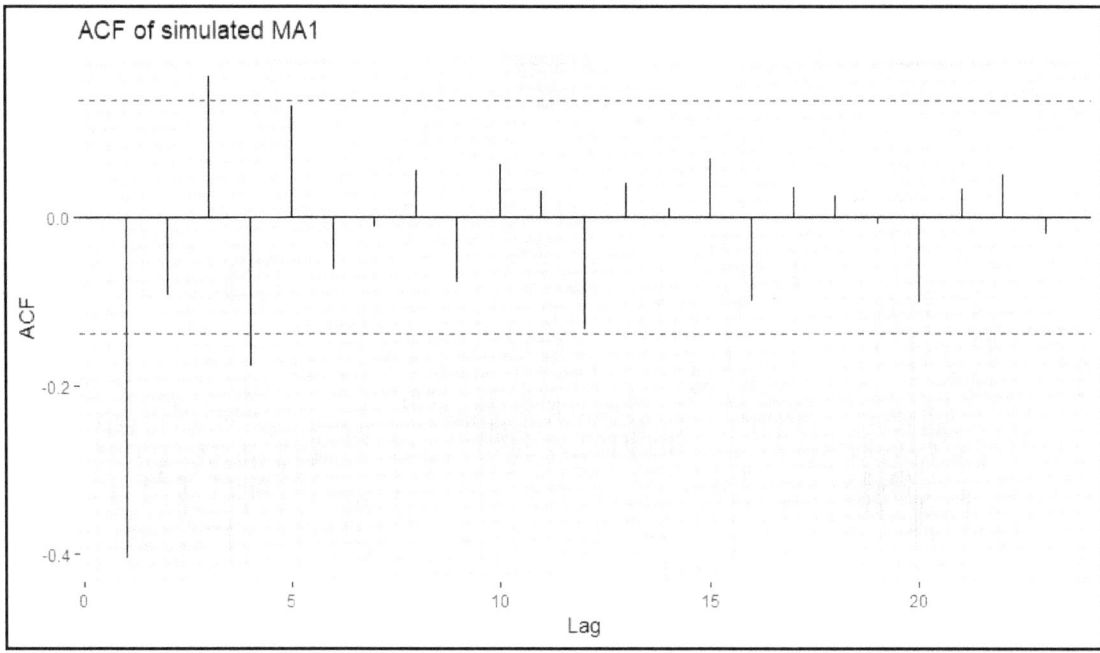

The preceding figure is the ACF plot, and now, we'll see the PACF plot:

```
> forecast::autoplot(pacf(ma1, plot = F), main = "PACF of simulated MA1")
```

The output of the preceding command is as follows:

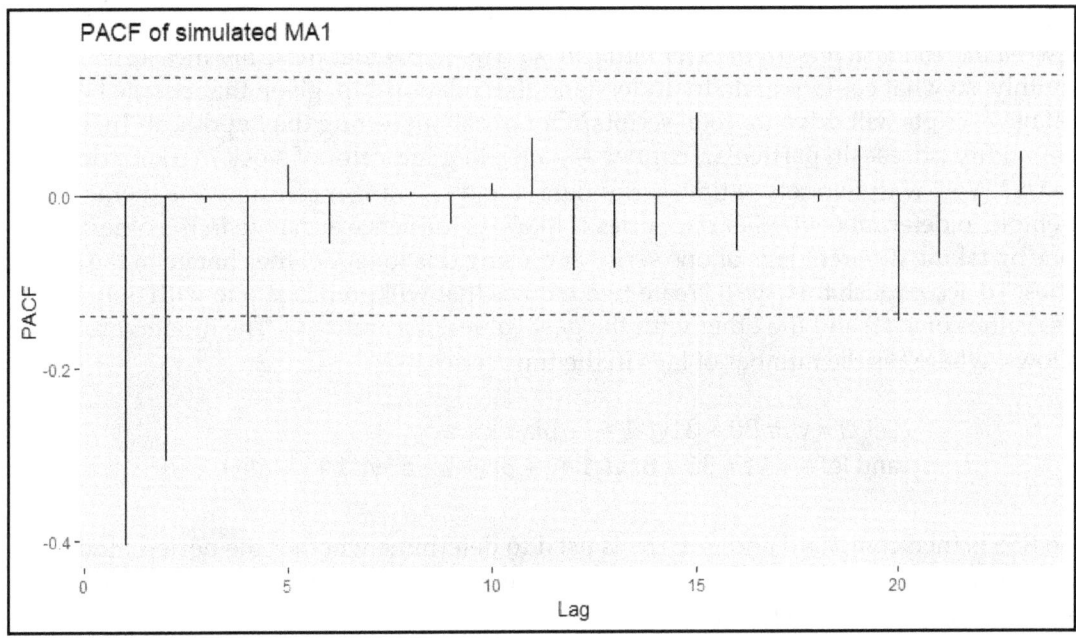

With the ARIMA models, it's possible to incorporate seasonality, including the autoregressive, integrated, and moving average terms. The non-seasonal ARIMA model notation is commonly *(p,d,q)*. With seasonal ARIMA, assume that the data is monthly, then the notation would be *(p,d,q) x (P,D,Q)12*, with the 12 in the notation taking the monthly seasonality into account. In the packages that we'll use, R can automatically identify whether the seasonality should be included; if so, the optimal terms will be included as well.

Understanding Granger causality

Imagine you're asked a question such as, *What's the relationship between the number of new prescriptions and total prescriptions for medicine X?* You know that these are measured monthly, so what could you do to understand that relationship, given that people believe that new scripts will drive up total scripts? Or how about testing the hypothesis that commodity prices—in particular, copper—is a leading indicator of stock market prices in the US? Well, with two sets of time series data, *x* and *y*, Granger causality is a method that attempts to determine whether one series is likely to influence a change in the other. This is done by taking different lags of one series and using this to model the change in the second series. To accomplish this, we'll create two models that will predict *y*, one with only the past values of *y* (Ω) and the other with the past values of *y* and *x* (π). The models are as follows, where *k* is the number of lags in the time series:

Let Ω = yt = β0 + β1yt-1 +...+ βkyt-k + ∈
and let π = yt = β0 + β1yt-1 +...+ βkyt-k + α1yt-1 +...+ αkyt-k + ∈

The RSS is then compared and `F-test` is used to determine whether the nested model (Ω) is adequate enough to explain the future values of *y* or whether the full model (π) is better. `F-test` is used to test the following null and alternative hypotheses:

- *H0*: αi = 0 for each *i* ∈[1,k], no Granger causality
- *H1*: αi ≠ 0 for at least one *i* ∈[1,k], Granger causality

Essentially, we're trying to determine whether we can say that, statistically, *x* provides more information about the future values of *y* than the past values of *y* alone. In this definition, it's clear that we aren't trying to prove actual causation, only that the two values are related by some phenomenon. Along these lines, we must also run this model in reverse in order to verify that *y* doesn't provide information about the future values of *x*. If we find that this is the case, it's likely that there's some exogenous variable, say *Z*, that needs to be controlled or would possibly be a better candidate for the Granger causation. Originally, you had to apply the method to stationary time series to avoid spurious results. This is no longer the case as I will demonstrate.

Note that research papers are available that discuss the techniques nonlinear models use, but this is outside the scope of this book. I recommend reading an excellent introductory paper on Granger causality that revolves around the age-old conundrum of the chicken and the egg (Thurman, 1988).

There are a couple of different ways to identify the proper lag structure. Naturally, we can use brute force and ignorance to test all of the reasonable lags, one at a time. We may have a rational intuition based on domain expertise or perhaps prior research that exists to guide the lag selection. If not, then you can apply **vector autoregression** (**VAR**) to identify the lag structure with the lowest information criterion, such as **Aikake's information criterion** (**AIC**) or **final prediction error** (**FPE**). For simplicity, here is the notation for the VAR models with two variables, and this incorporates only one lag for each variable. This notation can be extended for as many variables and lags as appropriate:

- $Y = constant_1 + B_{11}Y_{t-1} + B_{12}Y_{t-1} + e_1$
- $X = constant_1 + B2_1Y_{t-1} + B2_2Y_{t-1} + e2$

In R, this process is quite simple to implement as we'll see in the following practical problem.

Time series data

The planet isn't going anywhere. We are! We're goin' away.

- Philosopher and comedian, George Carlin

Climate change is happening. It always has and will, but the big question, at least from a political and economic standpoint, is the climate change man-made? I'll use this chapter to put econometric time series modeling to the test to try and learn whether carbon emissions cause, statistically speaking, climate change and, in particular, rising temperatures. Personally, I'd like to take a neutral stance on the issue, always keeping in mind the wise tenets that Mr. Carlin left for us in his teachings on the subject.

The first order of business is to find and gather the data. For temperature, I chose the **HadCRUT4** annual median temperature time series, which is probably the gold standard. This data is compiled by a cooperative effort of the Climate Research Unit of the University of East Anglia and the Hadley Centre at the UK Meteorological Office. A full discussion of how the data is compiled and modeled is available at

http://www.metoffice.gov.uk/hadobs/index.html.

The data that we'll use is provided as an annual anomaly, which is calculated as the difference of the median annual surface temperature for a given time period versus the average of the reference years (1961-1990). The annual surface temperature is an ensemble of the temperatures collected globally and blended from the **CRUTEM4** surface air temperature and **HadSST3** sea-surface datasets. Skeptics have attacked biased and unreliable: `http://www.telegraph.co.uk/comment/11561629/Top-scientists-start-to-examine-fid dled-global-warming-figures.html`. This is way outside of our scope of effort here, so we must accept and utilize this data as is, but I find it amusing nonetheless. I've pulled the data from 1919 through 2013 to match our CO2 data.

Global CO2 emission estimates can be found at the **Carbon Dioxide Information Analysis Center** (**CDIAC**) of the US Department of Energy at the following website: `http://cdiac. ornl.gov/`.

I've placed the data in a `.csv` file (`climate.csv`) for you to download and store in your working directory: `https://github.com/PacktPublishing/Advanced-Machine-Learning- with-R/blob/master/Data/climate.csv`.

Let's install libraries as needed, load the data, and examine the structure:

```
> library(magrittr)

> install.packages("tidyverse")

> install.packages("ggplot2")

> install.packages("ggthemes")

> install.packages("tseries")

> climate <- readr::read_csv("climate.csv")

> str(climate)
Classes 'tbl_df', 'tbl' and 'data.frame':   95 obs. of 3 variables:
 $ Year: int 1919 1920 1921 1922 1923 1924 1925 1926 1927 1928 ...
 $ CO2 : int 806 932 803 845 970 963 975 983 1062 1065 ...
 $ Temp: num -0.272 -0.241 -0.187 -0.301 -0.272 -0.292 -0.214 -0.105 -0.208
-0.206 ...
```

We'll put this in a time series structure, specifying the start and end years:

```
> climate_ts <- ts(climate[, 2:3],
    start = 1919,
    end = 2013)
```

With our data loaded and put in time series structures, we can now begin to understand and further prepare it for analysis.

Data exploration

Let's start out with a plot of the time series using base R:

```
> plot(climate_ts, main = "CO2 and Temperature Deviation")
```

The output of the preceding command is as follows:

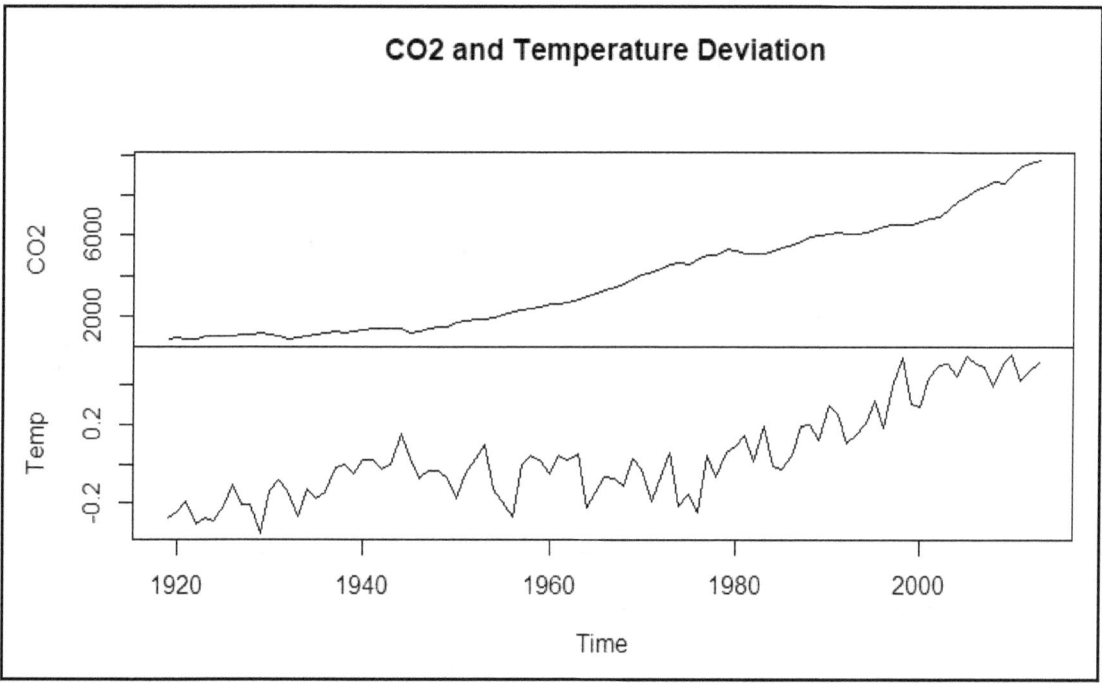

It appears that CO2 levels really started to increase after World War II and there's a rapid rise in temperature anomalies in the mid-1970s. There doesn't appear to be any obvious outliers, and variation over time appears constant. Using the standard procedure, we can see that the two series are highly correlated, as follows:

```
> cor(climate_temp)
            CO2       Temp
CO2   1.0000000 0.8404215
Temp  0.8404215 1.0000000
```

As discussed earlier, this is nothing to jump for joy about as it proves absolutely nothing. We'll look for the structure by plotting ACF and PACF for both series:

```
> forecast::autoplot(acf(climate_ts[, 2], plot = F), main="Temperature
ACF")
```

The output of the preceding code snippet is as follows:

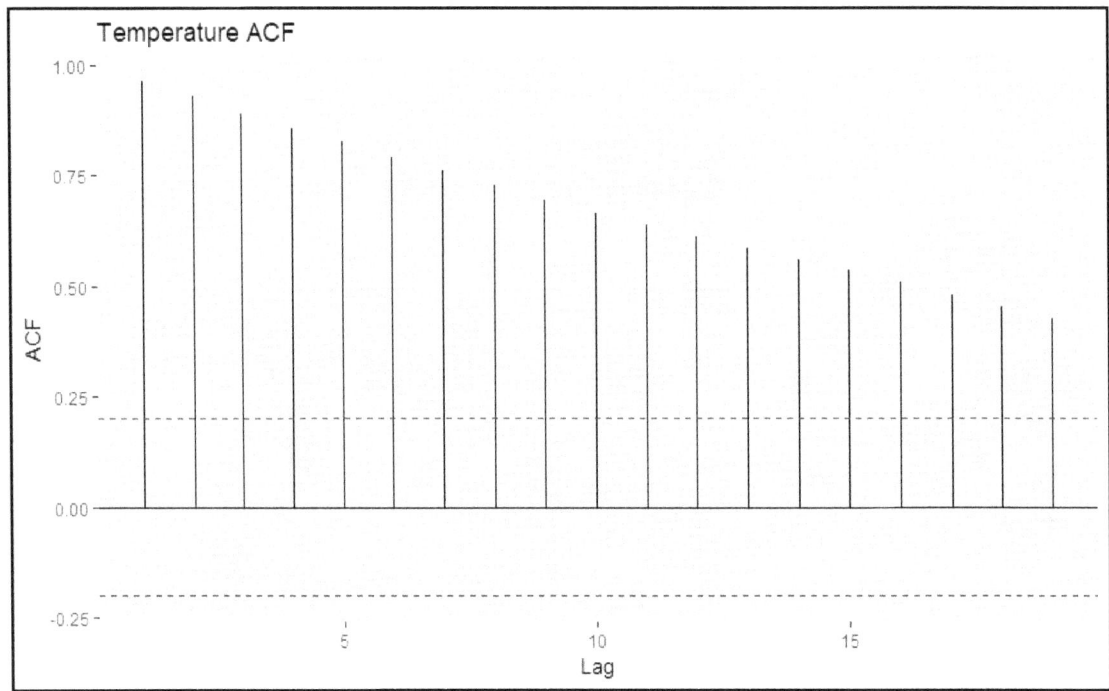

This code gives us the PACF plot for temperature:

```
> forecast::autoplot(pacf(climate_ts[, 2], plot = F), main = "Temperature
PACF")
```

The output of the preceding code snippet is as follows:

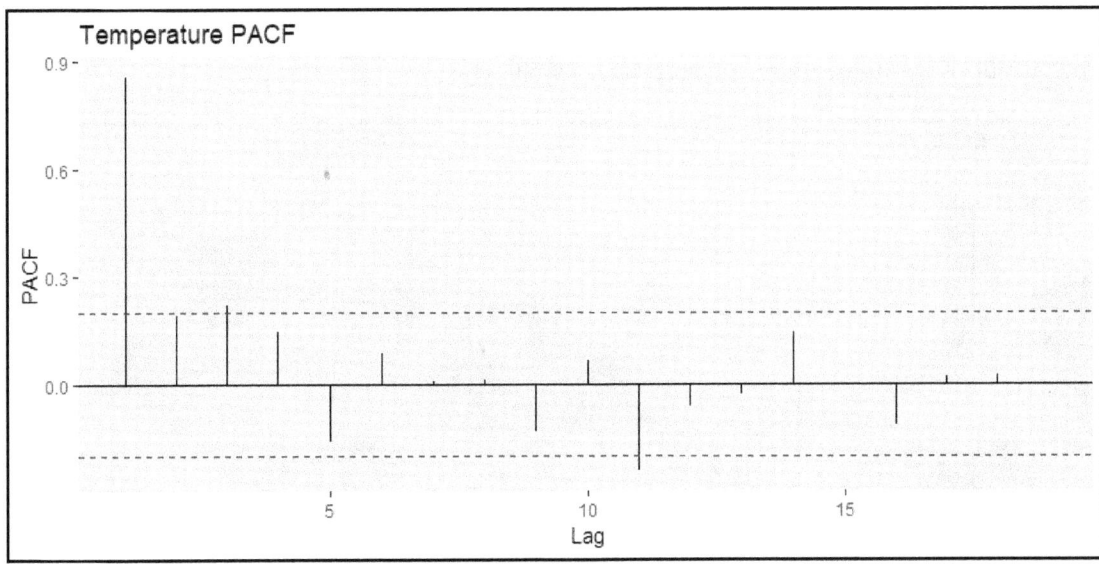

This code gives us the ACF plot for CO2:

```
> forecast::autoplot(acf(climate_ts[, 1], plot = F), main = "CO2 ACF")
```

The output of the preceding code snippet is as follows:

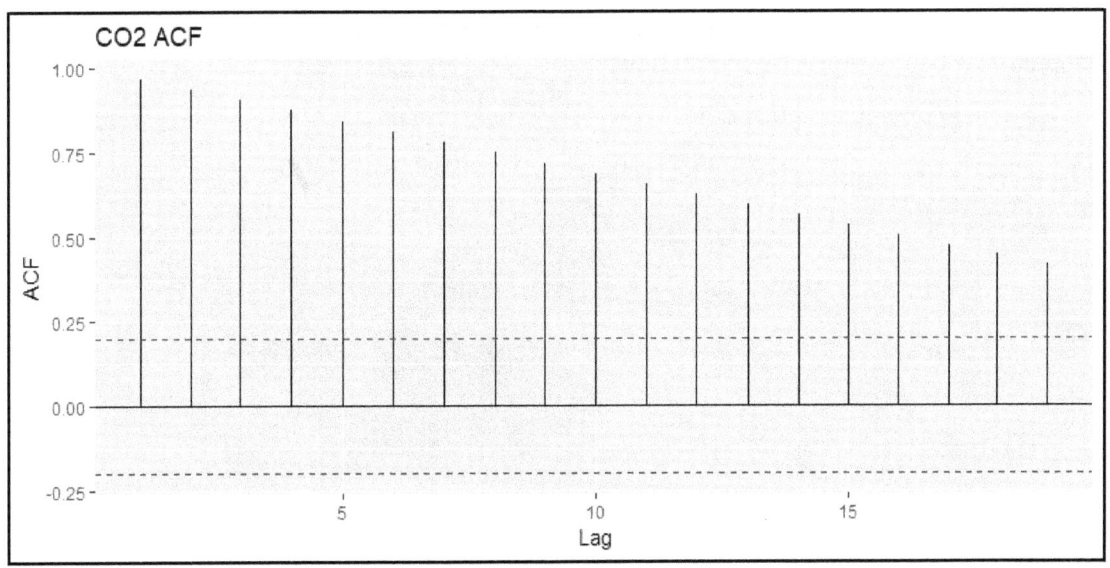

This code gives us the `PACF` plot for `CO2`:

```
> forecast::autoplot(acf(climate_ts[, 1], plot = F), main = "CO2 PACF")
```

The output of the preceding code snippet is as follows:

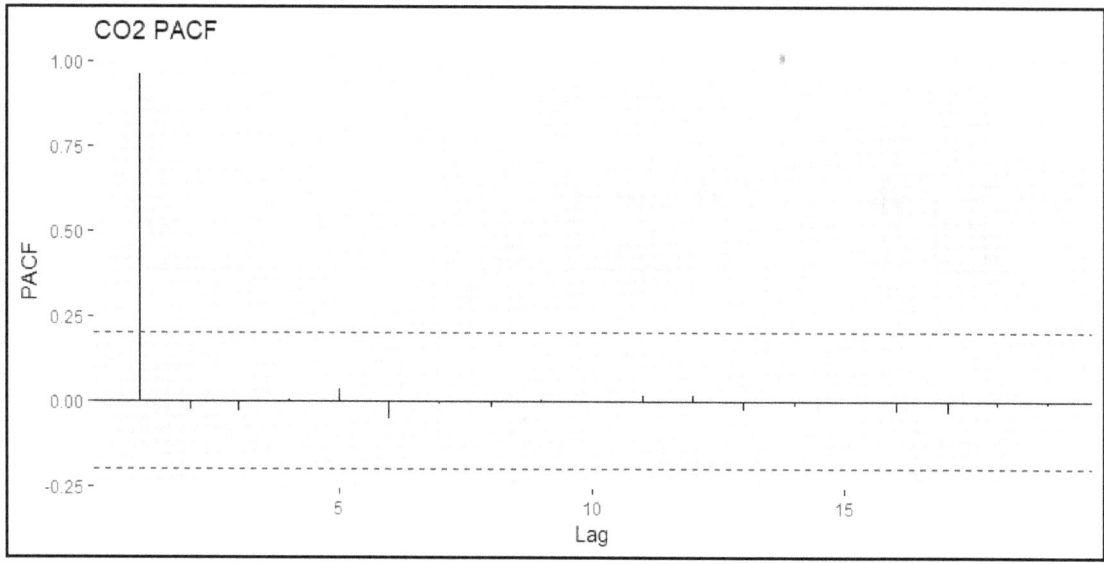

With the slowly decaying ACF patterns and rapidly decaying PACF patterns, we can assume that these series are both autoregressive, although `Temp` appears to have some significant MA terms. Next, let's have a look at the **Cross-Correlation Function (CCF)**. Note we put our *x* before our *y* in the function:

```
> forecast::autoplot(ccf(climate_ts[, 1], climate_ts[, 2], plot = F), main = "CCF")
```

The output of the preceding code is as follows:

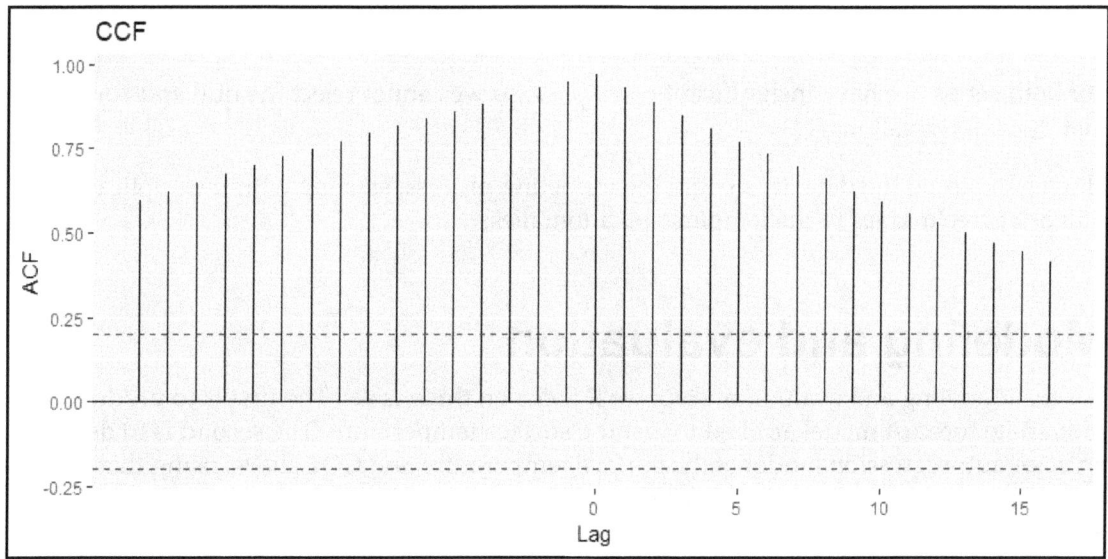

The **CCF** shows us the correlation between the temperature and lags of CO2. If the negative lags of the x variable have a high correlation, we can say that x leads y. If the positive lags of x have a high correlation, we say that x lags y. Here, we can see that CO2 is both a leading and lagging variable. For our analysis, it's encouraging that we see the former, but odd that we see the latter. We'll see during the VAR and Granger causality analysis whether this will matter or not.

Additionally, we need to test whether the data is stationary. We can prove this with the **Augmented Dickey-Fuller (ADF)** test available in the `tseries` package, using the `adf.test()` function, as follows:

```
> tseries::adf.test(climate_ts[, 1])

        Augmented Dickey-Fuller Test

data: climate_ts[, 1]
Dickey-Fuller = -1.1519, Lag order = 4, p-value =
0.9101
alternative hypothesis: stationary

> tseries::adf.test(climate_ts[, 2])

        Augmented Dickey-Fuller Test
```

```
data: climate_ts[, 2]
Dickey-Fuller = -1.8106, Lag order = 4, p-value =
0.6546
alternative hypothesis: stationary
```

For both series, we have insignificant `p-values`, so we cannot reject the null and conclude that they aren't stationary.

Having explored the data, let's begin the modeling process, starting with the application of univariate techniques to the temperature anomalies.

Modeling and evaluation

For the modeling and evaluation step, we'll focus on three tasks. The first is to produce a univariate forecast model applied to just the surface temperature. The second is to develop a vector autoregression model of the surface temperature and CO2 levels, using that output to inform our work on whether CO2 levels Granger-cause the surface temperature anomalies.

Univariate time series forecasting

With this task, the objective is to produce a univariate forecast for the surface temperature, focusing on choosing either an exponential smoothing model, an ARIMA model, or an ensemble of methods, including a neural net. We'll train the models and determine their predictive accuracy on an out-of-time test set, just like we've done in other learning endeavors. The following code creates the train and test sets:

```
> temp_ts <- ts(climate$Temp, start = 1919, frequency = 1)

> train <- window(temp_ts, end = 2007)

> test <- window(temp_ts, start = 2008)
```

To build our exponential smoothing model, we'll use the `ets()` function found in the `forecast` package. The function will find the best model with the lowest AIC:

```
> fit.ets <- forecast::ets(train)

> fit.ets
ETS(A,A,N)

Call:
 forecast::ets(y = train)

  Smoothing parameters:
    alpha = 0.3429
    beta = 1e-04

  Initial states:
    l = -0.2817
    b = 0.0095

  sigma: 0.1025

        AIC AICc BIC
-0.1516906 0.5712010 12.2914912
```

The model object returns a number of parameters of interest. The first thing to check is what does `(A,A,N)` mean. It represents that the model selected is a simple exponential smoothing with additive errors. The first letter denotes the error type, the second letter the trend, and the third letter seasonality. The possible letters are as follows:

- *A = additive*
- *M = multiplicative*
- *N = none*

We also see the parameter estimates with alpha, the smoothing parameter, for error correction (the level), and beta for slope. Initial state values were used to initiate model selection; sigma is the variation of the residuals and model criteria values are provided. You can plot how the estimates change over time:

```
> forecast::autoplot(fit.ets)
```

The output of the preceding code is as follows:

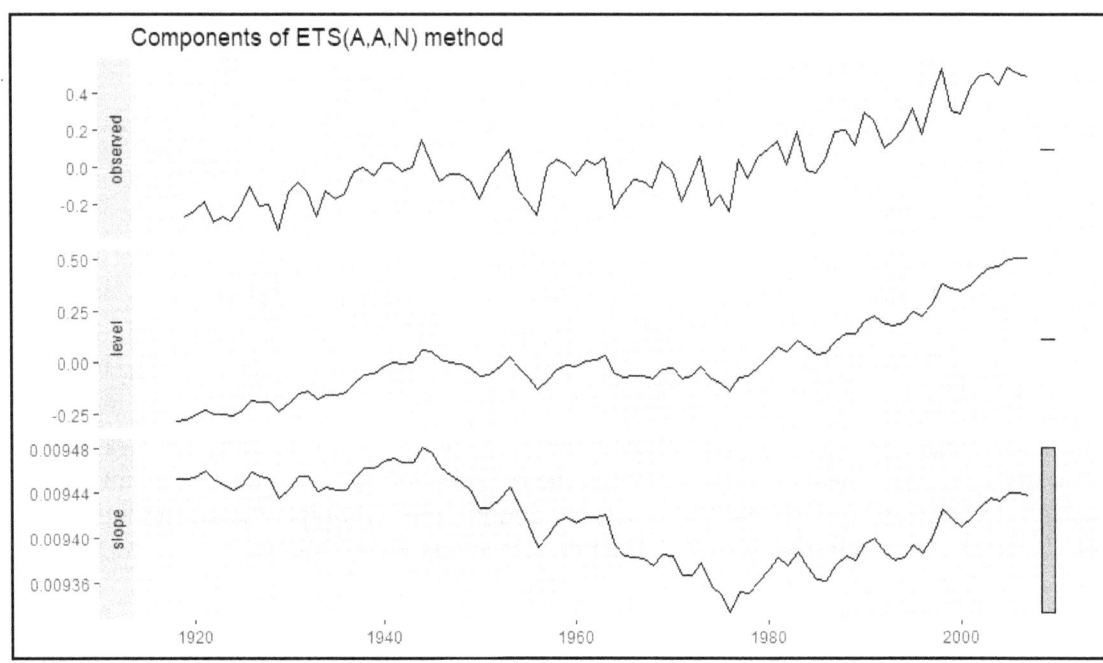

We'll now plot `forecast` and see how well it performed visually on the test data:

```
> plot(forecast::forecast(fit.ets, h = 6))
```

```
> lines(test, type = "o")
```

The output of the preceding code is as follows:

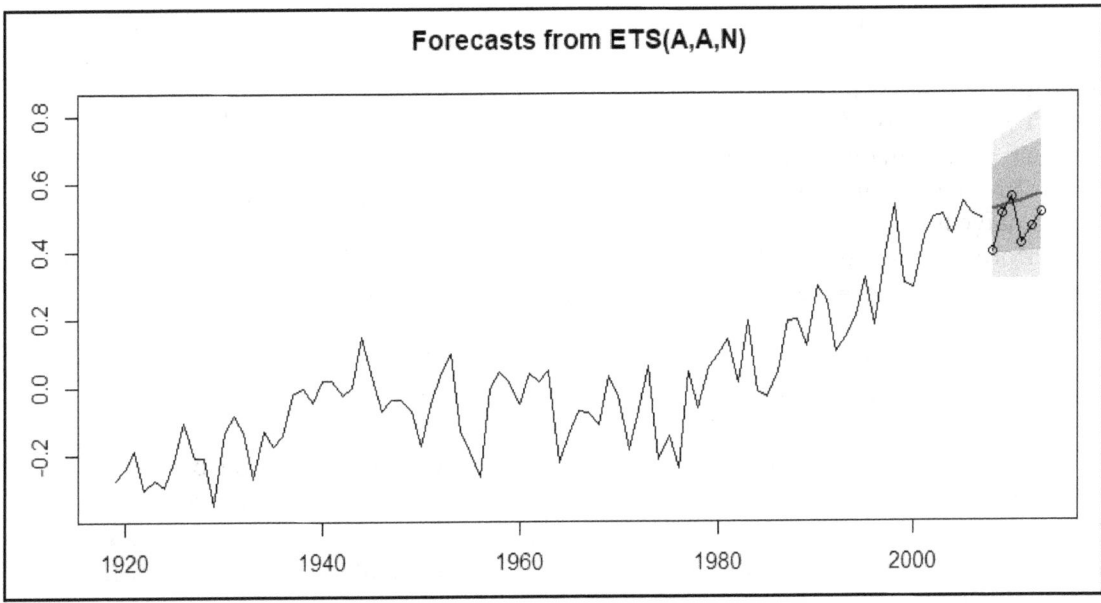

Looking at the plot, it seems that this forecast is showing a slight linear uptrend and is overestimating versus the actual values. We'll now look at the accuracy measures for the model:

```
> fit.ets %>% forecast::forecast(h = 6) %>%
    forecast::accuracy(temp_ts)
                      ME        RMSE        MAE        MPE      MAPE       MASE
Training set -0.00160570  0.10012357  0.08052241       -Inf        Inf  0.8752436
Test set     -0.06410776  0.08303044  0.07086704  -14.90784  16.12354  0.7702939
                  ACF1    Theil's U
Training set  0.1058923          NA
Test set     -0.1743445   0.7940449
```

There are eight measures for error. The one I believe we should focus on is Theil's U (actually U2 as the original Theil's U had some flaws), which is available only on the test data. Theil's U is an interesting statistic as it isn't dependent on scale, so you can compare multiple models. For instance, if in one model you transform the time series using a logarithmic scale, you can compare the statistic with a model that doesn't transform the data. You can think of it as the ratio that the forecast improves predictability over a naive forecast, or we can describe it at the **root mean square error** (**RMSE**) of the model divided by the RMSE of a naive model. Therefore, Theil's U statistics greater than 1 perform worse than a naive forecast, a value of 1 equals naive, and less than 1 indicates the model outperforms naive. Further discussion and how the statistic is derived is available at this link: http://www.forecastingprinciples.com/data/definitions/theil's%20u.html.

The smoothing model provided a statistic of 0.7940449. That isn't very impressive even though it's below one. We should strive for values at or below 0.5, in my opinion.

We'll now develop an ARIMA model, using auto.arima(), which is also from the forecast package. There are many options that you can specify in the function, or you can just include your time series data and it will find the best ARIMA fit. I recommend using the function with caution, as it can often return a model that violates assumptions for the residuals, as we shall see:

```
> fit.arima <- forecast::auto.arima(train)

> summary(fit.arima)
Series: train
ARIMA(1,1,1) with drift

Coefficients:
         ar1     ma1   drift
      0.2089 -0.7627 0.0087
s.e.  0.1372  0.0798 0.0033

sigma^2 estimated as 0.01021: log likelihood=78.09
AIC=-148.18 AICc=-147.7 BIC=-138.28

Training set error measures:
                      ME        RMSE        MAE MPE MAPE      MASE
Training set -8.396214e-05 0.09874311 0.07917484 Inf  Inf 0.8605961
                   ACF1
Training set 0.02010508
```

The abbreviated output shows that the model selected is an AR = 1, I = 1, and MA = 1, I = 1, or ARIMA(1,1,1) with drift (equivalent to an intercept term on differenced data and a slope term in undifferenced data). We can examine the plot of its performance on the `test` data in the same fashion as before:

```
> plot(forecast::forecast(fit.arima, h = 6))

> lines(test, type = "o")
```

The output of the preceding code is as follows:

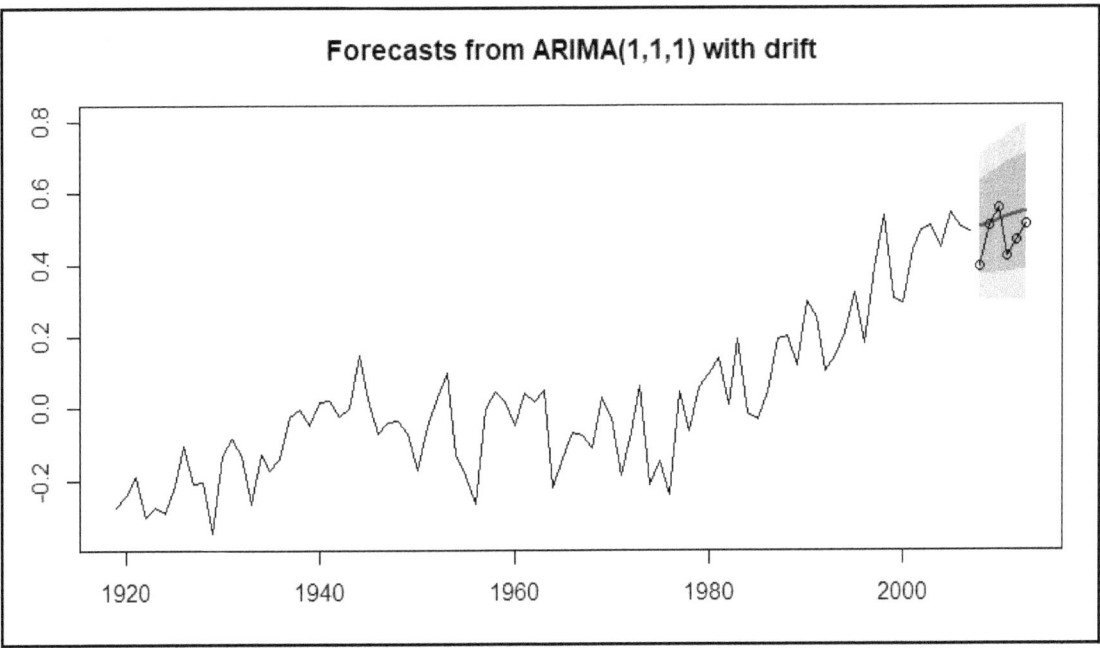

This is very similar to the prior method. Let's check those accuracy statistics, of course with a focus on Theil's U:

```
> fit.arima %>% forecast::forecast(h = 6) %>%
    forecast::accuracy(temperature)
                          ME         RMSE         MAE        MPE      MAPE
MASE
Training set -8.396214e-05 0.09874311 0.07917484        Inf       Inf
0.8605961
Test set     -4.971043e-02 0.07242892 0.06110011 -11.84965  13.89815
0.6641316
                   ACF1 Theil's U
```

```
Training set  0.02010508        NA
Test set     -0.18336583 0.6729521
```

The forecast error is slightly better with the ARIMA model. You should always review the residuals with your models and especially ARIMA, which relies on the assumption of no serial correlation in said residuals:

```
> forecast::checkresiduals(fit.arima)

  Ljung-Box test

data: Residuals from ARIMA(1,1,1) with drift
Q* = 18.071, df = 7, p-value = 0.01165

Model df: 3. Total lags used: 10
```

The output of the following code is as follows:

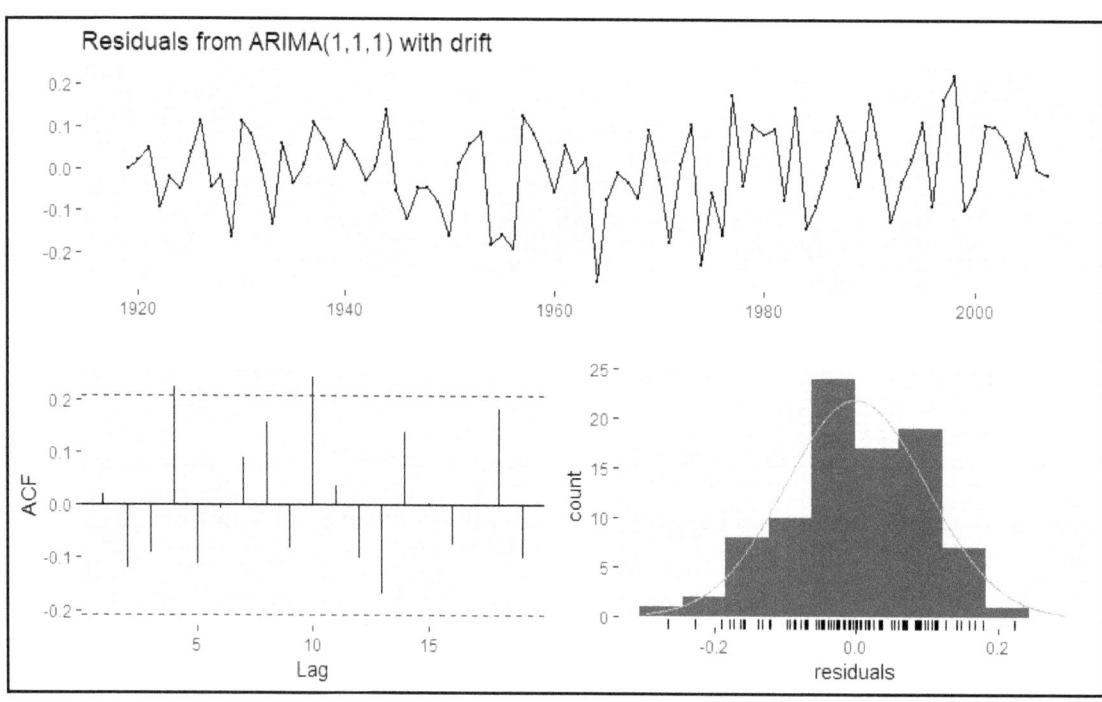

First of all, take a look at the Ljung-Box Q test. The null hypothesis is that the correlations in the residuals are zero, and the alternative is that the residuals exhibit serial correlation. We see a significant p-value so we can reject the null. This is confirmed visually in the ACF plot of the residuals where significant correlation exists at lag 4 and lag 10. With serial correlation present, the model coefficients are unbiased, but the standard errors and any statistics that rely on them are wrong. This fact may require you to manually select an appropriate ARIMA model manually through trial and error. To explain how to do that would require a separate chapter, so it's not in scope for this book.

With a couple of relatively weak models, we can try other methods, but let's look at creating an ensemble similar to what we produced in `Chapter 8`, *Creating Ensembles and Multiclass Methods*. We'll put together the two models just created and add a forward-feed neural network from the `nnetar()` function available in the `forecast` package. We won't stack the models, but simply take the average of the three models for comparison on the test data.

The first step in this process is to develop the forecasts for each of the models. This is straightforward:

```
> ETS <- forecast::forecast(forecast::ets(train), h = 6)

> ARIMA <- forecast::forecast(forecast::auto.arima(train), h = 6)

> NN <- forecast::forecast(forecast::nnetar(train), h = 6)
```

The next step is to create the ensemble values, which again is just a simple average:

```
> ensemble.fit <-
    (ETS[["mean"]] + ARIMA[["mean"]] + NN[["mean"]]) / 3
```

The comparison step is kind of an open canvas for you to produce the statistics you desire. Notice that I'm pulling the accuracy for only the test data and Theil's U. You can pull the necessary stats, such as RMSE or MAPE, should you so desire:

```
> c(ets = forecast::accuracy(ETS, temperature)["Test set", c("Theil's U")],
    arima = forecast::accuracy(ARIMA, temperature)["Test set", c("Theil's
U")],
    nn = forecast::accuracy(NN, temperature)["Test set", c("Theil's U")],
    ef = forecast::accuracy(ensemble.fit, temperature)["Test set",
c("Theil's U")])
      ets     arima        nn        ef
0.7940449 0.6729521 0.6794704 0.7104893
```

This is interesting, I think, as the exponential smoothing is dragging the ensemble performance down, and ARIMA and neural net are almost equal. Just for visual comparison, let's plot the neural network:

```
> plot(NN)

> lines(test, type = "o")
```

The output of the preceding code is as follows:

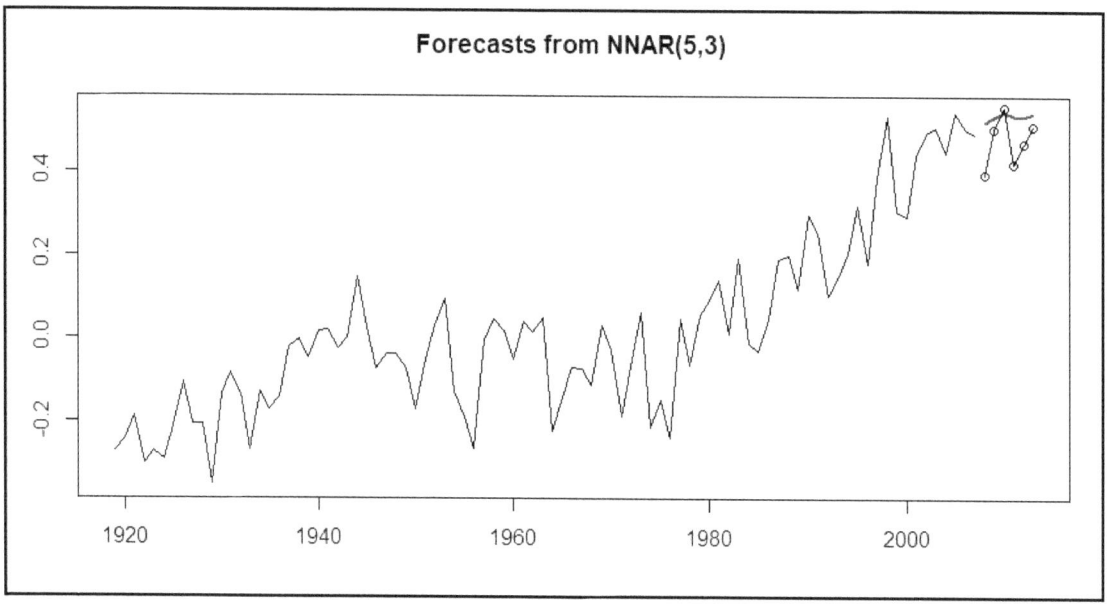

What are we to do with all of this? Here are a couple of thoughts. If you look at the time series pattern, you notice that it goes through what we could call different structural changes. There are a number of R packages to examine this structure and determine a point where it makes more sense to start the time series for forecasting. For example, there seems to be a discernible change in the slope of the time series in the mid-1960s. When you do this with your data, you're throwing away what may be valuable data points, so judgment comes into play. The implication is that if you want to totally automate your time series models, you'll need to take this into consideration.

You might try and transform the entire time series with log values (this doesn't work too well with negative values) or Box-Cox. In the `forecast` package, you can set `lambda = "auto"`, in your model function. I did this and the performance didn't improve. For the sake of example, let's try and detect structural changes and build an ARIMA model on a selected starting point. I'll demonstrate structural change with the `strucchange` package, which computationally determines changes in linear regression relationships. You can find a full discussion and vignette on the package at this link: `https://cran.r-project.org/web/packages/strucchange/vignettes/strucchange-intro.pdf`.

I find this method useful in discussions with stakeholders as it helps them to understand when and even why the underlying data generating process changed. Here goes:

```
> temp_struc <- strucchange::breakpoints(temp_ts ~ 1)

> summary(temp_struc)

	Optimal (m+1)-segment partition:

Call:
breakpoints.formula(formula = temp_ts ~ 1)

Breakpoints at observation number:
m = 1  68
m = 2  60  78
m = 3  18  60  78
m = 4  18  45  60  78
m = 5  17  31  45  60  78

Corresponding to breakdates:
m = 1  1986
m = 2  1978  1996
m = 3  1936  1978  1996
m = 4  1936  1963  1978  1996
m = 5  1935  1949  1963  1978  1996
```

The algorithm gave us five potential breakpoints in the time series, returning the information as an observation number and a year. Sure enough, 1963 indicates a structural change, but it tells us that `1978` and `1996` qualify also. Let's pursue the 1963 break as the start of our time series for an ARIMA model:

```
> train_bp <- window(temp_ts, start = 1963, end = 2007)

> fit.arima2 <- forecast::auto.arima(train_bp)

> fit.arima2 %>% forecast::forecast(h = 6) %>%
    forecast::accuracy(temperature)
```

```
                    ME          RMSE         MAE          MPE       MAPE
Training set -0.007696066 0.1034046 0.08505900   53.68130 99.93869
Test set      -0.086625082 0.1017767 0.08676477 -19.61829 19.64341
                  MASE          ACF1 Theil's U
Training set 0.7951128   0.09310454           NA
Test set      0.8110579 -0.08291170   1.057287
```

There you have it: much to my surprise performance, it's even worse than a naive forecast, but at least we've covered how to implement that methodology.

With this, we've completed the building of a univariate forecast model for the surface temperature anomalies, and now we'll move on to the next task of seeing whether CO2 levels cause these anomalies.

Examining the causality

For this chapter, this is where I think the rubber meets the road and we'll separate causality from mere correlation—well, statistically speaking, anyway. This isn't the first time that this technique has been applied to the problem. Triacca (2005) found no evidence to suggest that atmospheric CO2 Granger caused the surface temperature anomalies. On the other hand, Kodra (2010) concluded that there's a causal relationship, but put forth the caveat that their data wasn't stationary even after a second-order differencing. While this effort won't settle the debate, it'll hopefully inspire you to apply the methodology in your personal endeavors. The topic at hand certainly provides an effective training ground to demonstrate the Granger causality.

Our plan here is to first demonstrate spurious linear regression where the residuals suffer from autocorrelation, also known as serial correlation. Then, we'll examine two different approaches to Granger causality. The first will be the traditional methods, where both series are stationary. Then, we'll look at the method demonstrated by Toda and Yamamoto (1995), which applies the methodology to the raw data or, as it's sometimes called, the **levels**.

Linear regression

Let's get started with the spurious regression then, which I have seen implemented in the real world far too often. Here we simply build a linear model and examine the results:

```
> fit.lm <- lm(Temp ~ CO2, data = climate)

> summary(fit.lm)

Call:
lm(formula = Temp ~ CO2, data = climate)

Residuals:
     Min       1Q   Median       3Q      Max
-0.36411 -0.08986  0.00011  0.09475  0.28763

Coefficients:
              Estimate  Std. Error  t value   Pr(>|t|)
(Intercept) -2.430e-01   2.357e-02   -10.31   <2e-16 ***
CO2          7.548e-05   5.047e-06    14.96   <2e-16 ***
---
Signif. codes:
0 '***' 0.001 '**' 0.01 '*' 0.05 '.' 0.1 ' ' 1

Residual standard error: 0.1299 on 93 degrees of freedom
Multiple R-squared: 0.7063,  Adjusted R-squared: 0.7032
F-statistic: 223.7 on 1 and 93 DF,  p-value: < 2.2e-16
```

Notice how everything is significant, and we have an adjusted R-squared of 0.7. OK, they're highly correlated but this is all meaningless as discussed by Granger and Newbold (1974). Again, I've seen results like these presented in meetings with many people with advanced degrees, and I had to be the bad guy and challenge the results.

We can plot the serial correlation, starting with a time series plot of the residuals, which produce a clear pattern:

```
> forecast::checkresiduals(fit.lm)

    Breusch-Godfrey test for serial correlation of order up to 10

data: Residuals
LM test = 46.193, df = 10, p-value = 1.323e-06
```

The output of the preceding code is as follows:

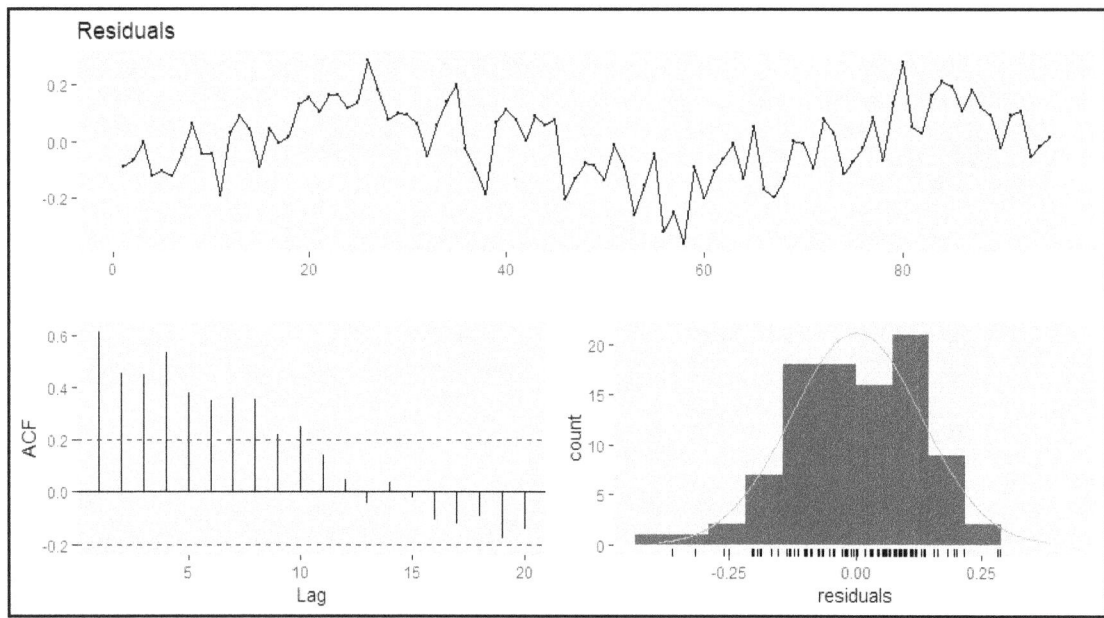

From examining the plots and the Breusch-Godfrey test, it comes as no surprise that we can safely reject the null hypothesis of no autocorrelation. The simple way to deal with autocorrelation is to incorporate lagged variables of the dependent time series and/or to make all of the data stationary. We'll do that next using vector autoregression to identify the appropriate lag structure to incorporate in our causality efforts. One of the structural change points was 1949, so we'll start there.

Vector autoregression

We've seen in the preceding section that temperature and CO2 require a first order difference. Another simple way to show this is with the `forecast` package's `ndiffs()` function. It provides an output that spells out the minimum number of differences needed to make the data stationary. In the function, you can specify which test out of the three available ones you would like to use: **Kwiatkowski, Philips, Schmidt & Shin (KPSS)**, **Augmented Dickey-Fuller (ADF)**, or **Philips-Peron (PP)**. I'll use ADF in the following code, which has a null hypothesis that the data isn't stationary:

```
> climate49 <- window(climate_ts, start = 1949)

> forecast::ndiffs(climate49[, 1], test = "adf")
```

```
   [1] 1

> forecast::ndiffs(climate49[, 2], test = "adf")
   [1] 1
```

We see that both require a first-order difference to become stationary. To get started, we'll create a difference. Then, we'll complete the traditional approach, where both series are stationary:

```
> climate_diff <- diff(climate49)
```

It's now a matter of determining the optimal lag structure based on the information criteria using vector autoregression. This is done with the VARselect function in the vars package. You only need to specify the data and number of lags in the model using lag.max = x in the function. Let's use a maximum of 12 lags:

```
> lag.select <- vars::VARselect(climate_diff, lag.max = 12)

> lag.select$selection
    AIC(n)  HQ(n)  SC(n)  FPE(n)
         5      1      1       5
```

We called the information criteria using lag$selection. Four different criteria are provided, including **AIC**, **Hannan-Quinn Criterion (HQ)**, **Schwarz-Bayes Criterion (SC)**, and **FPE**. Note that AIC and SC are covered in Chapter 2, *Linear Regression*, so I won't go over the criterion formulas or differences here. If you want to see the actual results for each lag, you can use lag$criteria. We can see that AIC and FPE have selected lag 5 and HQ and SC lag 1 as the optimal structure to a VAR model. It seems to make sense that the five-year lag is the one to use. We'll create that model using the var() function. I'll let you try it with lag 1:

```
> fit1 <- vars::VAR(climate_diff, p = 5)
```

The summary results are quite lengthy as it builds two separate models and would take up probably two whole pages. What I provide is the abbreviated output showing the results with temperature as the prediction:

```
> summary(fit1)
Residual standard error: 0.09877 on 48 degrees of freedom
Multiple R-Squared: 0.4692,  Adjusted R-squared: 0.3586
F-statistic: 4.243 on 10 and 48 DF,  p-value: 0.0002996
```

The model is significant with a resulting adjusted R-square of 0.36.

As we did in the previous section, we should check for serial correlation. Here, the VAR package provides the `serial.test()` function for multivariate autocorrelation. It offers several different tests, but let's focus on the `Portmanteau Test`, and please note that the popular Durbin-Watson test is for univariate series only. The null hypothesis is that autocorrelations are zero and the alternative is that they aren't zero:

```
> vars::serial.test(fit1, type = "PT.asymptotic")

  Portmanteau Test (asymptotic)

data: Residuals of VAR object fit1
Chi-squared = 33.332, df = 44, p-value = 0.8794
```

With `p-value` at 0.8794, we don't have evidence to reject the null and can say that the residuals aren't autocorrelated. What does the test say with 1 lag?

To do the Granger causality tests in R, you can use either the `lmtest` package and the `Grangertest()` function or the `causality()` function in the `vars` package. I'll demonstrate the technique using `causality()`. It's very easy as you just need to create two objects, one for x causing y and one for y causing x, utilizing the `fit1` object previously created:

```
> x2y <- vars::causality(fit1, cause = "CO2")

> y2x <- vars::causality(fit1, cause = "Temp")
```

It's now just a simple matter to call the Granger test results:

```
> x2y$Granger

  Granger causality H0: CO2 don't Granger-cause Temp

data: VAR object fit1
F-Test = 2.7907, df1 = 5, df2 = 96, p-value = 0.02133

> y2x$Granger

  Granger causality H0: Temp don't Granger-cause CO2

data: VAR object fit1
F-Test = 0.71623, df1 = 5, df2 = 96, p-value = 0.6128
```

The `p-value` value for CO2 differences of Granger causing temperature is 0.02133 and isn't significant in the other direction. So what does all of this mean? The first thing we can say is that Y doesn't cause X. As for X causing Y, we can reject the null at the 0.05 significance level and therefore conclude that X does Granger cause Y. However, is that the relevant conclusion here? Remember, the p-value evaluates how likely the effect is if the null hypothesis is true. Also, remember that the test was never designed to be some binary yea or nay. Since this study is based on observational data, I believe we can say that it's highly probable that *CO2 emissions Granger cause surface temperature anomalies*. But there's a lot of room for criticism on that conclusion. I mentioned upfront the controversy around the quality of the data.

However, we still need to model the original CO2 levels using the alternative Granger causality technique. The process to find the correct number of lags is the same as before, except we don't need to make the data stationary:

```
> level.select <- vars::VARselect(climate49, lag.max = 12)

> level.select$selection
AIC(n) HQ(n)  SC(n)  FPE(n)
    10     1      1       6
```

Let's try the lag 6 structure and see whether we can achieve significance, remembering to add one extra lag to account for the integrated series. A discussion on the technique and why it needs to be done is available at http://davegiles.blogspot.de/2011/04/testing-for-granger-causality.html:

```
> fit2 <- vars::VAR(climate49, p = 7)

> vars::serial.test(fit2, type = "PT.asymptotic")

   Portmanteau Test (asymptotic)

data: Residuals of VAR object fit2
Chi-squared = 32.693, df = 36, p-value = 0.6267
```

Now, to determine Granger causality for X causing Y, you conduct a Wald test, where the coefficients of X and only X are 0 in the equation to predict Y, remembering not to include the extra coefficients that account for integration in the test.

The Wald test in R is available in the `aod` package we've already loaded. We need to specify the coefficients of the full model, its variance-covariance matrix, and the coefficients of the causative variable.

 The coefficients for `Temp` that we need to test in the VAR object consist of a range of even numbers from 2 to 12, while the coefficients for CO2 are odd from 1 to 11. Instead of using c(2, 4, 6, and so on) in our function, let's create an object with base R's seq() function.

First, let's see how CO2 does Granger causing temperature:

```
> CO2terms <- seq(1, 11, 2)

> Tempterms <- seq(2, 12, 2)
```

We're now ready to run the `wald` test, described in the following code and abbreviated output:

```
> aod::wald.test(
    b = coef(fit2$varresult$Temp),
    Sigma = vcov(fit2$varresult$Temp),
    Terms = c(CO2terms)
  )

$result$`chi2`
       chi2            df           P
13.48661591 6.00000000 0.03592734
```

How about that? We have a significant p-value so let's test the other direction causality with the following code:

```
> aod::wald.test(
    b = coef(fit2$varresult$CO2),
    Sigma = vcov(fit2$varresult$CO2),
    Terms = c(Tempterms)
  )

$result$`chi2`
      chi2           df          P
4.7709016 6.0000000 0.5735146
```

Conversely, we can say that temperature doesn't Granger cause CO2. The last thing to show here is how to use a vector autoregression to produce a forecast. A `predict` function is available and we'll plot the forecast for 24 years:

```
> plot(predict(fit2, n.ahead = 24, ci = 0.95))
```

The output of the preceding code is as follows:

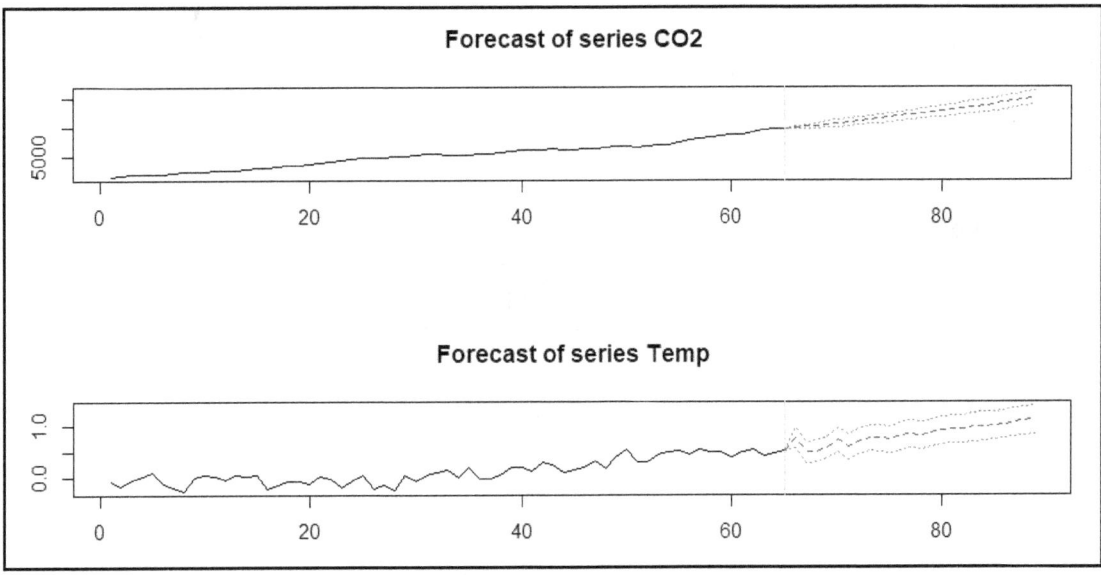

Looking out a couple of decades hence, we see temperature anomalies getting close to 1 degree. If nothing else, I hope this has stimulated your thinking on how to apply the technique to your own real-world problems or maybe even to examine the climate change data in more detail. There should be a high bar when it comes to demonstrating causality, and Granger causality is a great tool for assisting in that endeavor.

Summary

In this chapter, the goal was to discuss how important the element of time is in the field of machine learning and analytics, to identify the common traps when analyzing the time series, and to demonstrate the techniques and methods to work around these traps. We explored both the univariate and bivariate time series analysis for global temperature anomalies and human carbon dioxide emissions. Additionally, we looked at Granger causality to determine whether we can say, statistically speaking, that atmospheric CO_2 levels cause surface temperature anomalies. We discovered that the p-values are higher than 0.05 but less than 0.10 for Granger causality from CO_2 to temperature. It does show that Granger causality is an effective tool in investigating causality in machine learning problems. In the next chapter, we'll shift gears and take a look at how to apply learning methods to textual data.

Additionally, keep in mind that in time series analysis, we just skimmed the surface. I encourage you to explore other techniques around change point detection, decomposition of time series, nonlinear forecasting, and many others. Although not usually considered part of the machine learning toolbox, I believe you'll find it an invaluable addition to yours.

13
Text Mining

"What then is, generally speaking, the truth of history? A fable agreed upon. As it has been very ingeniously remarked"

- Napoleon Bonaparte

The world is awash with textual data. If you Google, Bing, or Yahoo! how much of that data is unstructured, that is, in a textual format, estimates would range from 80 to 90 percent. The real number doesn't matter. It matters that a large proportion of the data is in text format. The implication is that anyone seeking to find insights in that data must develop the capability to process and analyze text.

When I first started out as a market researcher, I used to manually pore through page after page of moderator-led focus group and interview transcripts with the hope of capturing some qualitative insight, an *aha moment* if you will, and then haggle with fellow team members over whether they had the same insight or not. Then, you would always have that one individual in a project who would swoop in and listen to two interviews—out of the 30 or 40 on the schedule—and, alas, they had their mind made up on what was really happening in the world. Contrast that with the techniques being used now, where an analyst can quickly distill data into meaningful quantitative results, support qualitative understanding, and maybe even sway the swooper.

Over the last few years, I've applied the techniques discussed here to mine physician-patient interactions, understand FDA fears on prescription drug advertising, capture patient concerns about rare cancer, and capture customer maintenance problems, to name just a few. Using R and the methods in this chapter, you too can extract the powerful information in textual data.

The following topics will be covered in this chapter:

- Text mining framework and methods
- Data overview
- Word frequency
- Sentiment analysis
- N-grams
- Topic models
- Classifying text
- Additional quantitative analysis

Text mining framework and methods

There are many different methods to use in text mining. The goal here is to provide a basic framework to apply to such an endeavor. This framework is not inclusive of all the possible methods, but will cover those that are probably the most important for the vast majority of projects that you will work on. Additionally, I will discuss the modeling methods in as succinct and clear a manner as possible, because they can get quite complicated. Gathering and compiling text data is a topic that could take up several chapters. One of the things I prefer and will put forward here is the use of the **tidy** framework. It will allow us to use **tibbles** and data frames for most of the steps, and the `tidytext` functions allow an easy transition to other types of text mining structures, such as a corpus.

The first task is to put the text files into a data frame. With that created, the data preparation can begin with the text transformation.

The following list is composed of probably some of the most common and useful transformations for text files:

- Change capital letters to lowercase
- Remove numbers
- Remove punctuation
- Remove stop words
- Remove excess whitespace characters
- Word stemming
- Word replacement

With these transformations, you are creating a more compact dataset and simplify the structure in order to facilitate relationships between the words, thereby leading to increased understanding. However, keep in mind that not all of these transformations are necessary all the time and judgment must be applied, or you can iterate to find the transformations that make the most sense.

By changing words to lowercase, you can prevent the improper counting of words. Say that you have a count for *hockey* three times and *Hockey* once, where it is the first word in a sentence. R will not give you a count of *hockey=4*, but *hockey=3* and *Hockey=1*.

Removing punctuation also achieves the same purpose, but in some cases, punctuation is important, especially if you want to tokenize your documents by sentences.

In removing stop words, you are getting rid of the common words that have no value; in fact, they are detrimental to the analysis, as their frequency masks important words. Examples of stop words are *and, is, the, not,* and *to*.

Removing whitespace makes data more compact by getting rid of things such as tabs, paragraph breaks, double-spacing, and so on.

The stemming of words can get tricky and might add to your confusion because it deletes word suffixes, creating the base word, or what is known as the **radical**. I personally am not a big fan of stemming and the analysts I've worked with agree with that sentiment. Recall that R would count this as two separate words. By running a stemming algorithm, the stemmed word for the two instances would become *famili*. This would prevent the incorrect count, but in some cases it can be odd to interpret and is not very visually appealing in a word cloud for presentation purposes. In some cases, it may make sense to run your analysis with both stemmed and unstemmed words in order to see which one facilitates understanding.

Probably the most optional of the transformations is to replace the words. The goal of replacement is to combine words with a similar meaning, for example, *management* and *leadership*. You can also use it in lieu of stemming. I once examined the outcome of stemmed and unstemmed words and concluded that I could achieve a more meaningful result by replacing about a dozen words instead of stemming. It can be important when you have manual data entry and different operators input data differently. For example, tech support person one types in the system *turbocharger*, while tech support person two types in *turbo charger* half the time, and *turbo-charger* the other half. All three versions are the same, so applying a replacement function such as `gsub()` or `grepl()` will solve the problem.

With transformations completed, one structure to create for topic modeling or classification is either a **document-term matrix (DTM)** or **term-document matrix (TDM)**. What either of these matrices does is create a matrix of word counts for each individual document in the matrix. A DTM would have the documents as rows and the words as columns, while in a TDM, the reverse is true. We will be using a DTM for our example.

Topic models

Topic models are a powerful method to group documents by their main topics. Topic models allow probabilistic modeling of term frequency occurrence in documents. The fitted model can be used to estimate the similarity between documents, as well as between a set of specified keywords using an additional layer of latent variables, which are referred to as topics (Grun and Hornik, 2011). In essence, a document is assigned to a topic based on the distribution of the words in that document, and the other documents in that topic will have roughly the same frequency of words.

The algorithm that we will focus on is **Latent Dirichlet Allocation (LDA)** with Gibbs sampling, which is probably the most commonly used sampling algorithm. In building topic models, the number of topics must be determined before running the algorithm (k-dimensions). If no a priori reason for the number of topics exists, then you can build several and apply judgment and knowledge to the final selection. LDA with Gibbs sampling is quite complicated mathematically, but my intent is to provide an introduction so that you are at least able to describe how the algorithm learns to assign a document to a topic in layperson terms. If you are interested in mastering the math associated with the method, block out a couple of hours on your calendar and have a go at it. Excellent background material is available at `http://www.cs.columbia.edu/~blei/papers/Blei2012.pdf`.

LDA is a generative process, and so the following will iterate to a steady state:

1. For each document (j), there are *1* to j documents. We will randomly assign a multinomial distribution (**Dirichlet distribution**) to the topics (k) with *1* to k topics, for example, document *A* is 25 percent topic one, 25 percent topic two, and 50 percent topic three.
2. Probabilistically, for each word (i), there are *1* to i words to a topic (k); for example, the word *mean* has a probability of 0.25 for the topic statistics.
3. For each word (i) in document (j) and topic (k), calculate the proportion of words in that document assigned to that topic; note it as the probability of topic (k) with document (j), $p(k|j)$, and the proportion of word (i) in topic (k) from all the documents containing the word. Note it as the probability of word (i) with topic (k), $p(i|k)$.

4. Resample, that is, assign w a new t based on the probability that t contains w, which is based on $p(k|j)$ times $p(i|k)$.

5. Rinse and repeat; over numerous iterations, the algorithm finally converges and a document is assigned a topic based on the proportion of words assigned to a topic in that document.

The LDA that we will be doing assumes that the order of words and documents does not matter. There has been work done to relax these assumptions in order to build models of language generation and sequence models over time (known as **dynamic topic modeling**).

Other quantitative analysis

We will now shift gears to analyze text semantically based on sentences and the tagging of words based on the parts of speech, such as noun, verb, pronoun, adjective, adverb, preposition, singular, plural, and so on. Often, just examining the frequency and latent topics in the text will suffice for your analysis. However, you may find occasions when a deeper understanding of the style is required in order to compare the speakers or writers.

There are many methods to accomplish this task, but we will focus on the following five:

- Polarity (sentiment analysis)
- Automated readability index (complexity)
- Formality
- Diversity
- Dispersion

Polarity is often referred to as sentiment analysis, which tells you how positive or negative the text is. By analyzing polarity in R, it will assign a score to each word and you can analyze the average and standard deviation of polarity by groups such as different authors, text, or topics. Different polarity dictionaries are available and we will explore them in more detail later. You can alter or change a dictionary according to your requirements.

The algorithm works by first tagging the words with a positive, negative, or neutral sentiment based on the dictionary. The tagged words are then clustered based on the four words prior and two words after a tagged word, and these clusters are tagged with what are known as **valence shifters** (neutral, negator, amplifier, and de-amplifier). A series of weights based on their number and position are applied to both the words and clusters. This is then summed and divided by the square root of the number of words in that sentence.

The automated readability index is a measure of the text complexity and a reader's ability to understand. A specific formula is used to calculate this index: *4.71(# of characters / #of words) + 0.5(# of words / # of sentences) - 21.43.*

The index produces a number, which is a rough estimate of a student's grade level to fully comprehend. If the number is 9, then a high school freshman, aged 13 to 15, should be able to grasp the meaning of the text.

The formality measure provides an understanding of how a text relates to the reader or speech relates to a listener. I like to think of it as a way to understand how comfortable the person producing the text is with the audience, or an understanding of the setting where this communication takes place. If you want to experience formal text, attend a medical conference or read a legal document. The informal text is said to be contextual in nature.

The formality measure is called **F-Measure**. This measure is calculated as follows:

- Formal words (*f*) are nouns, adjectives, prepositions, and articles
- Contextual words (*c*) are pronouns, verbs, adverbs, and interjections
- *N = sum of (f + c + conjunctions)*
- *Formality Index = 50((sum of f - sum of c / N) + 1)*

Diversity, as it relates to text mining, refers to the number of different words used in relation to the total number of words used. This can also mean the expanse of the text producer's vocabulary or lexicon richness. The `qdap` package provides five—that's right, five—different measures of diversity: `simpson`, `shannon`, `collision`, `bergen_parker`, and `brillouin`. I won't cover these five in detail but will only say that the algorithms are used not only for communication and information science retrieval but also for biodiversity in nature.

Finally, dispersion, or lexical dispersion, is a useful tool in order to understand how words are spread throughout a document and serve as an excellent way to explore text and identify patterns. The analysis is conducted by calling the specific word or words of interest, which are then produced in a plot showing when the word or words occurred in the text over time. As we will see, the `qdap` package has a built-in plotting function to analyze the text dispersion.

We have covered a framework on text mining about how to prepare the text, count words, and create topic models and, finally, dived deep into other lexical measures. Now, let's apply all this and do some real-world text mining.

Data overview

For this case study, we will take a look at the full text of State of the Union addresses. The State of the Union is an annual message that the President provides to Congress. The purpose is to provide an economic and diplomatic overview, as well as outline the legislative agenda. I would characterize it as your typical political feel-good propaganda, sprinkled with false hope and enthusiasm. I'm too old and too wise to consider it anything else.

The data is in an R package `sotu`. It consists of the text and metadata for 236 addresses, both oral and written.

 The data is technically not correct about State of the Union addresses. The proper definition for a first-term President's address in their first year in office is *address to a joint session*.

The learning goals for us are to explore work frequency, Abraham Lincoln's addresses, the sentiment of the addresses around the time of the US Civil War, topic models for the speeches from the time of the escalation of the Vietnam War to the present, political party classification modeling, and finally some of the advanced speech methods applied to two different Presidents.

Data frame creation

As per an old joke and bit of wisdom:

> *"How can you tell when a politician is lying? Their lips are moving!"*

If not already done, please install the following packages, and call the `magrittr` and `sotu` libraries:

```
> install.packages("ggplot2")

> install.packages("ggraph")

> install.packages("igraph")

> install.packages("quanteda")

> install.packages("qdap")

> install.packages("tidytext")
```

```
> install.packages("tidyverse")

> install.packages("sotu")

> install.packages("topicmodels")

> library(magrittr)

> library(sotu)
```

Since the data is located within the `sotu` package, we needed to call it to create the objects of the data like this:

```
> data(sotu_text)

> data(sotu_meta)
```

It is easy to turn this into a data frame with everything we need by adding the raw text to the metadata:

```
> sotu_meta$text <- sotu_text
```

Here are the column names. I recommend you spend a few minutes exploring this data on your own as well:

```
> colnames(sotu_meta)
[1] "president" "year" "years_active" "party" "sotu_type"
[6] "text"
```

The `text` column has the data of interest in a character string. Before we start analyzing the data, we need to tokenize the text and link it to each President. What does that mean? It means we put one token per row per document. A token can be a character, a word, an n-gram combination of words, or a sentence. This will set us up for applying tidy format procedures:

```
> sotu_meta %>%
    tidytext::unnest_tokens(word, text) -> sotu_unnest
```

All we did was just tell the `unnest_tokens()` function to take the column text and turn it into a column called `word`. The function we shall see accommodates n-grams but defaults to words. It also automatically removes all capitalization. When we tackle n-grams, we'll set that to false. Here is what the new `tibble` created looks like:

```
> sotu_unnest
# A tibble: 1,965,212 x 6
   president        year  years_active party      sotu_type word
   <chr>           <int> <chr>        <chr>      <chr>     <chr>
```

```
 1 George Washington 1790   1789-1793   Nonpartisan speech   fellow
 2 George Washington 1790   1789-1793   Nonpartisan speech   citizens
 3 George Washington 1790   1789-1793   Nonpartisan speech   of
 4 George Washington 1790   1789-1793   Nonpartisan speech   the
 5 George Washington 1790   1789-1793   Nonpartisan speech   senate
 6 George Washington 1790   1789-1793   Nonpartisan speech   and
 7 George Washington 1790   1789-1793   Nonpartisan speech   house
 8 George Washington 1790   1789-1793   Nonpartisan speech   of
 9 George Washington 1790   1789-1793   Nonpartisan speech
representatives
10 George Washington 1790   1789-1793   Nonpartisan speech   i
# ... with 1,965,202 more rows
```

With our data ready, let's get started.

Word frequency

With word frequency analysis, we want to clean this data by removing the stop words, which would just clutter our interpretation. We'll explore the top overall word frequencies, then take a look at President Lincoln's work.

Word frequency in all addresses

To get rid of stop words in a tidy format, you can use the `stop_words` data frame provided in the `tidytext` package. You call that `tibble` into the environment, then do an anti-join by word:

```
> library(tidytext)

> data(stop_words)

> sotu_tidy <- sotu_unnest %>%
    dplyr::anti_join(stop_words, by = "word")
```

Notice that the length of the data went from 1.97 million observations down to 778,161. Now, you can go ahead and see the top words. I don't do it in the following, but you can put this into a data frame if you so choose:

```
> sotu_tidy %>%
    dplyr::count(word, sort = TRUE)
# A tibble: 29,558 x 2
   word         n
   <chr>      <int>
```

```
 1 government  7573
 2 congress    5759
 3 united      5102
 4 people      4219
 5 country     3564
 6 public      3413
 7 time        3138
 8 war         2961
 9 american    2853
10 world       2581
# ... with 29,548 more rows
```

We can pass this data to `ggplot2`, in this case, words that occur more than 2,500 times:

```
> sotu_tidy %>%
    dplyr::count(word, sort = TRUE) %>%
    dplyr::filter(n > 2500) %>%
    dplyr::mutate(word = reorder(word, n)) %>%
    ggplot2::ggplot(ggplot2::aes(word, n)) +
    ggplot2::geom_col() +
    ggplot2::xlab(NULL) +
    ggplot2::coord_flip() +
    ggthemes::theme_igray()
```

The output of the preceding code is as follows:

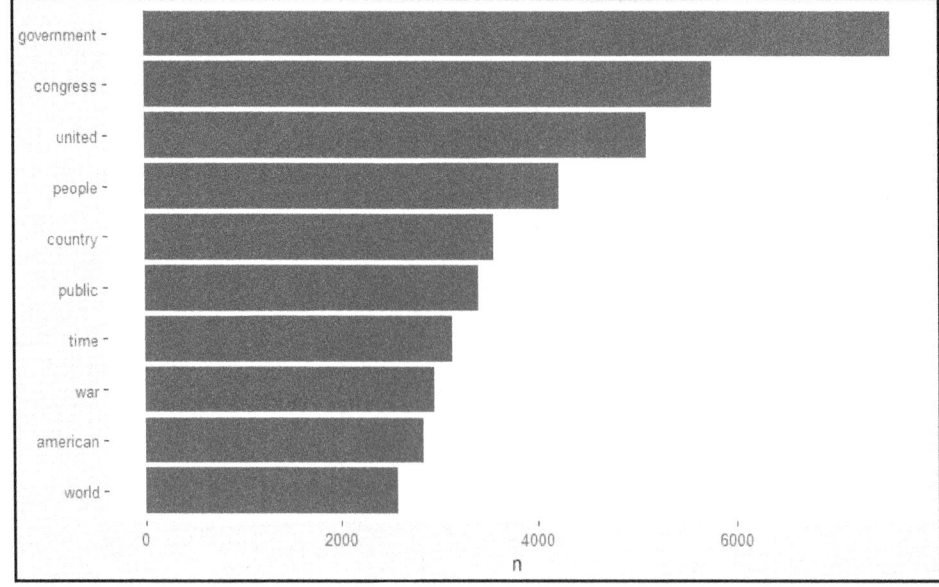

We can look at the addresses that contain the most total words:

```
> sotu_tidy %>%
    dplyr::group_by(year) %>%
    dplyr::summarise(totalWords = length(word)) %>%
    dplyr::arrange(desc(totalWords))
# A tibble: 225 x 2
    year totalWords
   <int>      <int>
 1 1981      18402
 2 1980      17553
 3 1946      12614
 4 1974      11813
 5 1979      11730
 6 1910      11178
 7 1907      10230
 8 1912      10215
 9 1911       9598
10 1899       9504
# ... with 215 more rows
```

How about that? The two longest speeches were given by Ronald Reagan, often called *The Great Communicator*. Moving on, we'll take a look at Lincoln's top word frequency, then create a word cloud for each of the separate addresses.

Lincoln's word frequency

In the same fashion as previously, we'll see the top 10 words Lincoln used. The filter to apply for Abe's addresses is 1861 through 1864:

```
> sotu_tidy %>%
    dplyr::filter(year > 1860 & year < 1865) %>%
    dplyr::count(word, sort = TRUE)
# A tibble: 3,562 x 2
   word            n
   <chr>       <int>
 1 congress       81
 2 united         81
 3 government     75
 4 people         70
 5 war            65
 6 country        62
 7 time           51
```

```
 8 union          50
 9 national       49
10 public         48
# ... with 3,552 more rows
```

No surprise that *war* is high on the list with the Civil War during that time period. One way to visualize how the addresses changed and stayed the same is to produce a word cloud for each address. A convenient way to do that is with the `qdap` package. We first need to filter out Lincoln's speeches from the tokenized data frame. Then, we produce a separate word cloud for each year. Notice that I specify a minimum frequency of seven words per year and specify no stemming. This produces the following four different plots:

```
> sotu_cloud <- sotu_tidy %>%
    dplyr::filter(year > 1860 & year < 1865)

> qdap::trans_cloud(
    text.var = sotu_cloud$word,
    grouping.var = sotu_cloud$year,
    stem = FALSE,
    min.freq = 7
  )
```

The output of the preceding code is as follows:

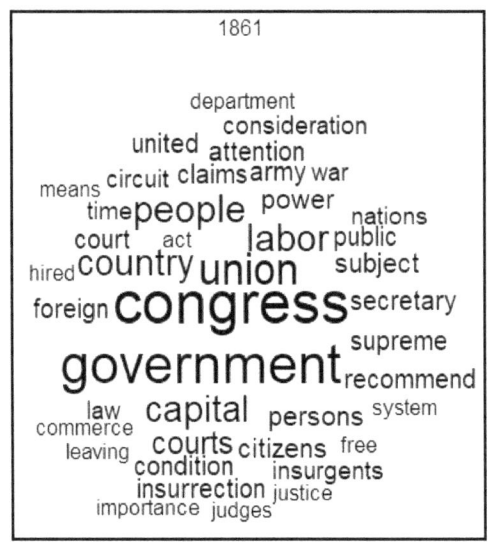

Output Frame 2:

Output Frame 3:

Output Frame 4:

Very similar themes throughout, but notice you have a clear focus on emancipation and slavery in 1862 and 1863. An interesting analytical method is to drill down on a term and put it in context, or what we can call keywords in context. However, to do that we need to transform our data. The `quanteda` package has a keyword in context function `kwic()`, but it requires the data be in a corpus, which demands that the text be back in one cell per document, and not one token per row per document. The implication to us is that we need to unnest the tidy data frame. This accomplishes that and just selects the year 1862:

```
> nested_1862 <- sotu_tidy %>%
    dplyr::filter(year == 1862) %>%
    dplyr::select(year, word) %>%
    tidyr::nest(word) %>%
    dplyr::mutate(
    text = purrr::map(data, unlist),
    text = purrr::map_chr(text, paste, collapse = " ")
  )
```

This gives us the text with stop words removed and back in one cell. To put this in a corpus structure, the `tm` package is useful:

```
> myCorpus <- tm::Corpus(tm::VectorSource(nested_1862$text))
```

For this example of keywords in context, we should look at where Lincoln discusses emancipation. An important specification in the function is how many words to the left and right of our keyword we want to see as the context of interest. Here is the abbreviated content:

```
> quanteda::kwic(x = myCorpus$content, pattern = "emancipation", window =
6)
 [text1, 1462] paper respectfully recall attention called compensated |
 [text1, 2076] plan mutual concessions plan adopted assumed |
 [text1, 2873] recommendation congress provide law compensating adopt |
 [text1, 2939] slave concurrence obtained assurance severally adopting |
 emancipation | nation consist territory people laws territory
 emancipation | follow article main emancipation length time
 emancipation | plan acted earnestly renewed advance plan
 emancipation | distant day constitutional terms assurance struggle
```

The output can be awkward to interpret at first. However, what it produces is the document number of the corpus the text is from, so with just one text cell, all output is `text1`. Then, it shows what character number our keyword starts with (`1462`). What we have left is the six words prior to our keyword and the six words after it. The first line of text would read like this: *paper respectfully recall attention called compensated emancipation nation consist territory people laws territory*. That might seem confusing, but the item of interest is the concept of compensating regions for emancipation. The full output, and including more context words, can help get a sense of Lincoln's problems and solutions for emancipation. As historical background, Lincoln delivered the address on December 1, 1862, and the political opposition in the Union was in an uproar over the Emancipation Proclamation he issued two and a half months before. Lincoln had to dance a political jig, in essence, moderating his stance by claiming that emancipation would be gradual and done with compensation. In short, looking at keywords in context can help in deriving an understanding for yourself and with your customers about how to interpret textual data.

We'll now take a look at implementing sentiment analysis in a `tidyverse` fashion.

Sentiment analysis

"We shall nobly save, or meanly lose, the last, best hope of earth."

– *Abraham Lincoln*

In this section, we'll take a look at the various sentiment options available in `tidytext`. Then, we'll apply that to a subset of the data before, during, and after the Civil War. To get started, let's explore the sentiments dataset that comes with `tidytext`:

```
> table(sentiments$lexicon)

   AFINN bing loughran    nrc
   2476 6788     4149  13901
```

The four sentiment options and researchers associated with them are as follows:

- `AFINN`: Finn, Arup, and Nielsen
- `bing`: Bing, Liu et al.
- `loughran`: Loughran and McDonald
- `nrc`: Mohammad and Turney

The `AFINN` sentiment categorizes words on a negative to positive scale from -5 to +5. The `bing` version has a simple binary negative or positive ranking; `loughran` provides six different categories including `negative`, `positive`, and such things as `superfluous`. With `nrc`, you get five categories such as `anger` or `trust`. Here is a glance at a few words and associated sentiment classification with `nrc`:

```
> get_sentiments("nrc")
# A tibble: 13,901 x 2
   word       sentiment
   <chr>      <chr>
 1 abacus     trust
 2 abandon    fear
 3 abandon    negative
 4 abandon    sadness
 5 abandoned  anger
 6 abandoned  fear
 7 abandoned  negative
 8 abandoned  sadness
 9 abandonment anger
10 abandonment fear
```

You see that a word can have multiple sentiment categories. Let's see whether Lincoln expressed `anger` in his 1862 attempt to mollify his political opponents:

```
> nrc_anger <- tidytext::get_sentiments("nrc") %>%
    dplyr::filter(sentiment == "anger")

> sotu_tidy %>%
    dplyr::filter(year == 1862) %>%
```

```
        dplyr::inner_join(nrc_anger) %>%
        dplyr::count(word, sort = TRUE)
Joining, by = "word"
# A tibble: 62 x 2
   word n
   <chr>       <int>
 1 slavery        13
 2 slave          12
 3 demand          5
 4 force           5
 5 money           5
 6 abolish         4
 7 rebellion       4
 8 cash            3
 9 deportation     3
10 fugitive        3
# ... with 52 more rows
```

OK, that is interesting and might be an indication of the challenge of taking qualitative
sentiment rankings developed recently and applying them to historical documents. We'll
expand the analysis now by looking at addresses from 1853 to 1872 using the `bing`
sentiment technique. We will build a data frame of the total `positive` and `negative`
sentiment, using that to calculate an overall sentiment score for each year:

```
> sentiment <- sotu_tidy %>%
    dplyr::inner_join(tidytext::get_sentiments("bing")) %>%
    dplyr::filter(year > 1852 & year <1873) %>%
    dplyr::count(president, year, sentiment) %>%
    tidyr::spread(sentiment, n, fill = 0) %>%
    dplyr::mutate(sentiment = positive - negative) %>%
    dplyr::arrange(year)
Joining, by = "word"
```

You can explore that on your own, but in the meantime, here is a plot of sentiment by
`president` and `year`:

```
> ggplot2::ggplot(sentiment, ggplot2::aes(year, sentiment, fill =
president)) +
    ggplot2::geom_col(show.legend = FALSE) +
    ggplot2::facet_wrap(~ president, ncol = 2, scales = "free_x") +
    ggthemes::theme_pander()
```

The output of the preceding code is as follows:

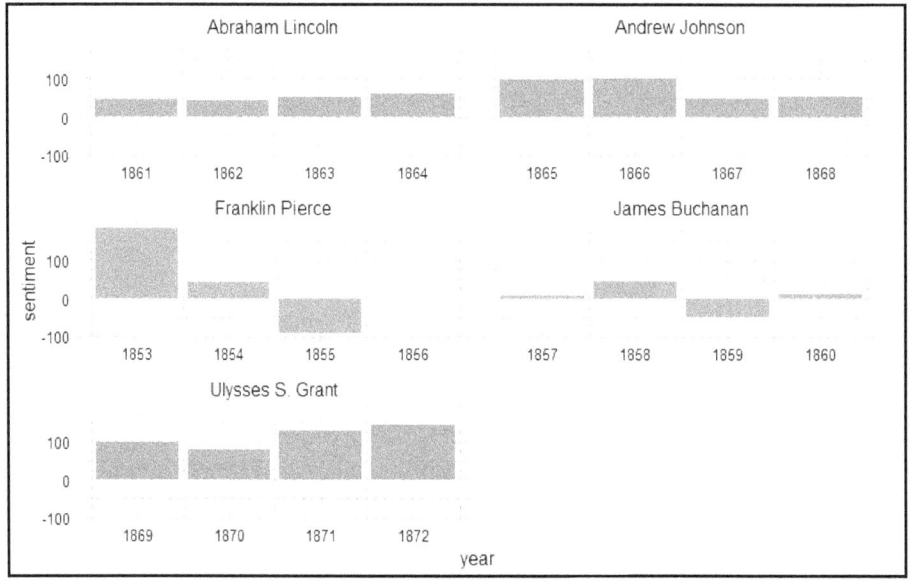

The pre-war Presidents had negative sentiment, I guess as things fell apart. Arguably, Buchanan was the worst President ever. Not even Jimmy Carter was as bad. It is interesting how positive Grant is, given, the difficulties of reconstruction, having to fight a near-guerrilla war in the south. He is as underrated a President as there is. Enough of my historical ruminations. It is an easy task to find and portray sentiment in text data using `tidytext`. Indeed, here is an example of most what words are driving `positive` or `negative` sentiment:

```
> sotu_tidy %>%
    dplyr::inner_join(tidytext::get_sentiments("bing")) %>%
    dplyr::count(word, sentiment, sort = TRUE) %>%
    dplyr::ungroup()
Joining, by = "word"
# A tibble: 3,592 x 3
   word sentiment n
        <chr> <chr>    <int>
1      peace positive 2021
2       free positive 1306
3   progress positive 1157
4    support positive  961
5 protection positive  864
6     proper positive  840
7  recommend positive  836
```

```
 8        debt negative  795
 9     freedom positive  744
10      secure positive  724
# ... with 3,582 more rows
```

Peace is the number one positive word, despite its elusiveness, and the number one negative word is *debt*. Oh well, good luck with that!

One of the things to consider in processing text is what resolutions of it help facilitate learning. We've done just words up to this point, let's shift gears to word combinations or n-grams.

N-grams

Looking at combinations of words in, say, bigrams or trigrams can help you understand relationships between words. Using tidy methods again, we'll create bigrams and learn about those relationships to extract insights from the text. I will continue with the subject of President Lincoln as that will allow you to compare what you gain with n-grams versus just words. Getting started is easy, as you just specify the number of words to join. Notice in the following code that I maintain word capitalization:

```
> sotu_bigrams <- sotu_meta %>%
    dplyr::filter(year > 1860 & year < 1865) %>%
    tidytext::unnest_tokens(bigram, text, token = "ngrams", n = 2,
    to_lower =   FALSE)
```

Let's take a look at this:

```
> sotu_bigrams %>%
    dplyr::count(bigram, sort = TRUE)
# A tibble: 17,687 x 2
   bigram n
   <chr>         <int>
 1 of the          509
 2 to the          180
 3 in the          146
 4 by the           97
 5 for the          94
 6 have been        82
 7 United States    79
 8 and the          76
 9 has been         76
10 the United       73
# ... with 17,677 more rows
```

Those pesky stop words! Fear not, as we can deal with them in short order:

```
> bigrams_separated <- sotu_bigrams %>%
    tidyr::separate(bigram, c("word1", "word2"), sep = " ")

> bigrams_filtered <- bigrams_separated %>%
    dplyr::filter(!word1 %in% stop_words$word) %>%
    dplyr::filter(!word2 %in% stop_words$word)
```

Now, it makes sense to look at Lincoln's bigrams:

```
> bigram_counts <- bigrams_filtered %>%
    dplyr::count(word1, word2, sort = TRUE)

> bigram_counts
# A tibble: 3,488 x 3
   word1    word2         n
   <chr>    <chr>     <int>
 1 United   States       79
 2 public   debt         11
 3 public   lands        10
 4 Great    Britain       9
 5 civil    war           8
 6 I        recommend     8
 7 naval    service       8
 8 annual   message       7
 9 foreign  nations       7
10 free     colored       7
# ... with 3,478 more rows
```

This is interesting, I believe. I found it surprising that *Great Britain* was there nine times, but on reflection realized they were a political thorn in the Union's side. I'll spare you the details. You can create a visual representation of these word relationships via a network graph:

```
> bigram_graph <- bigram_counts %>%
dplyr::filter(n > 4) %>%
igraph::graph_from_data_frame()

> set.seed(1861) #

> ggraph::ggraph(bigram_graph, layout = "fr") +
ggraph::geom_edge_link() +
ggraph::geom_node_point() +
ggraph::geom_node_text(ggplot2::aes(label = name), vjust = 1, hjust = 1)
```

The output of the preceding code is as follows:

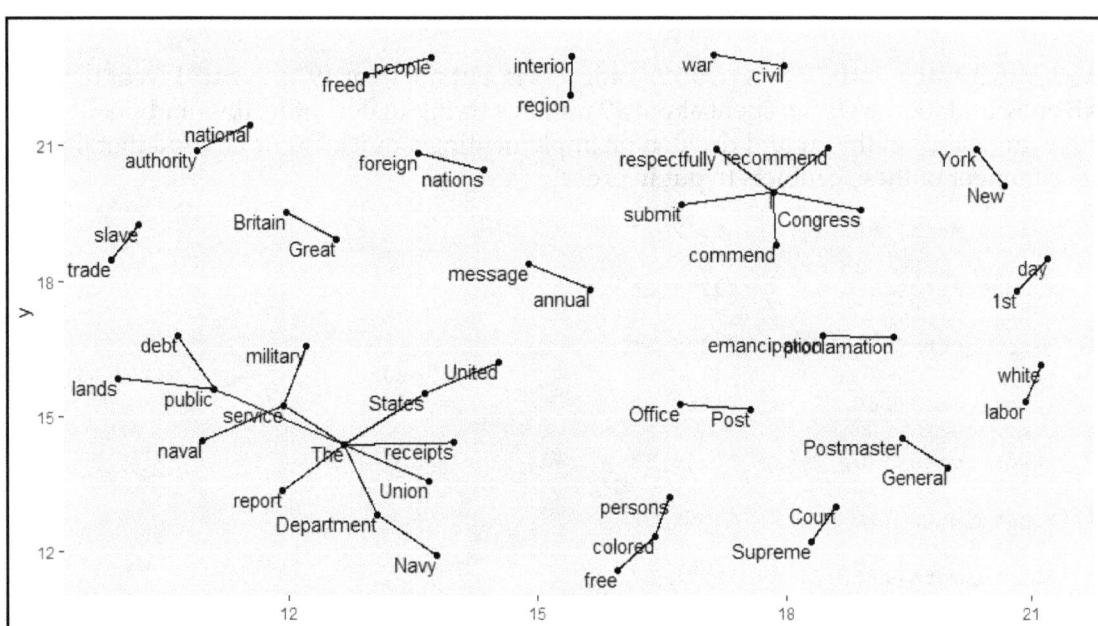

I think it is safe to say that the use of n-grams can help you learn from text. In combination with analysis by tokenizing words, we can start to see some patterns and themes. However, we can take our understanding to the next level by building topic models.

Topic models

We will leave behind the 19th century and look at these recent times of trial and tribulation (1965 through 2016). In looking at this data, I found something interesting and troubling. Let's take a look at the 1970s:

```
> sotu_meta[185:191, 1:4]
# A tibble: 7 x 4
  president         year  years_active party
  <chr>             <int> <chr>        <chr>
1 Richard M. Nixon  1970  1969-1973    Republican
2 Richard M. Nixon  1971  1969-1973    Republican
3 Richard M. Nixon  1972  1969-1973    Republican
4 Richard M. Nixon  1972  1969-1973    Republican
```

```
5 Richard M. Nixon 1974   1973-1974    Republican
6 Richard M. Nixon 1974   1973-1974    Republican
7 Gerald R.   Ford 1975   1974-1977    Republican
```

We see there are two 1972 and two 1974 addresses, but none for 1973. What? I went to the Nixon Foundation website, spent about 10 minutes trying to deconflict this, and finally threw my hands in the air and decided on implementing a quick fix. Be advised that there are a number of these conflicts to put in order:

```
> sotu_meta[188, 2] <- "1972_2"

> sotu_meta[190, 2] <- "1974_2"

> sotu_meta[157, 2] <- "1945_2"

> sotu_meta[166, 2] <- "1953_2"

> sotu_meta[170, 2] <- "1956_2"

> sotu_meta[176, 2] <- "1961_2"

> sotu_meta[195, 2] <- "1978_2"

> sotu_meta[197, 2] <- "1979_2"

> sotu_meta[199, 2] <- "1980_2"

> sotu_meta[201, 2] <- "1981_2"
```

An email to the author of this package is in order. I won't bother with that, but feel free to solve the issue yourself.

With this tragedy behind us, we'll go through tokenizing and removing stop words again for our relevant time frame:

```
> sotu_meta_recent <- sotu_meta %>%
    dplyr::filter(year > 1964)

> sotu_meta_recent %>%
    tidytext::unnest_tokens(word, text) -> sotu_unnest_recent

> sotu_recent <- sotu_unnest_recent %>%
    dplyr::anti_join(stop_words, by = "word")
```

As discussed previously, we need to put the data into a DTM before building a model. This is done by creating a word count grouped by year, then passing that to the cast_dtm() function:

```
> sotu_recent %>%
    dplyr::group_by(year) %>%
    dplyr::count(word) -> lda_words

> sotu_dtm <- tidytext::cast_dtm(lda_words, year, word, n)
```

Let's get our model built. I'm going to create six different topics using the Gibbs method, and I specified verbose. It should run 2,000 iterations:

```
> sotu_lda <-
 topicmodels::LDA(
 sotu_dtm,
 k = 6,
 method = "Gibbs",
 control = list(seed = 1965, verbose = 1)
 )

> sotu_lda
A LDA_Gibbs topic model with 6 topics.
```

The algorithm gives each topic a number. We can see what year is mapped to what topic. I abbreviate the output since 2002:

```
> topicmodels::topics(sotu_lda)
2002 2003 2004 2005 2006 2007 2008 2009 2010 2011 2012 2013 2014 2015 2016
   2    2    2    2    2    2    2    4    4    4    4    4    4    4    4
```

We see a clear transition between Bush and Obama from topic 2 to topic 4. Here is a table of the count of topics:

```
> table(topicmodels::topics(sotu_lda))

 1 2 3  4  5 6
 8 7 5 18 14 5
```

Topic 4 is the most prevalent, which is associated with Clinton's term also. This output gives us the top five words associated with each topic:

```
> topicmodels::terms(sotu_lda, 5)
      Topic 1       Topic 2     Topic 3
[1,] "future"      "america"   "administration"
[2,] "tax"         "security"  "congress"
[3,] "spending"    "country"   "economic"
[4,] "government"  "world"     "legislation"
[5,] "economic"    "iraq"      "energy"

      Topic 4       Topic 5     Topic 6
[1,] "people"      "world"     "federal"
[2,] "american"    "people"    "programs"
[3,] "jobs"        "american"  "government"
[4,] "america"     "congress"  "program"
[5,] "children"    "peace"     "act"
```

This all makes good sense, and topic 2 is spot on for the time. If you drill down further to, say, 10, 15, or 20 words, it is even more revealing, but I won't bore you further. What about an application in the tidy ecosystem and a visualization? Certainly! We'll turn the model object into a data frame first and in the process capture the per-topic-per-word probabilities called `beta`:

```
> lda_topics <- tidytext::tidy(sotu_lda, matrix = "beta")

> ap_top_terms <- lda_topics %>%
    dplyr::group_by(topic) %>%
    dplyr::top_n(10, beta) %>%
    dplyr::ungroup() %>%
    dplyr::arrange(topic, -beta)
```

We can explore that data further or just plot it as follows:

```
> ap_top_terms %>%
    dplyr::mutate(term = reorder(term, beta)) %>%
    ggplot2::ggplot(ggplot2::aes(term, beta, fill = factor(topic))) +
    ggplot2::geom_col(show.legend = FALSE) +
    ggplot2::facet_wrap(~ topic, scales = "free") +
    ggplot2::coord_flip() +
    ggthemes::theme_economist_white()
```

The output of the preceding code is as follows:

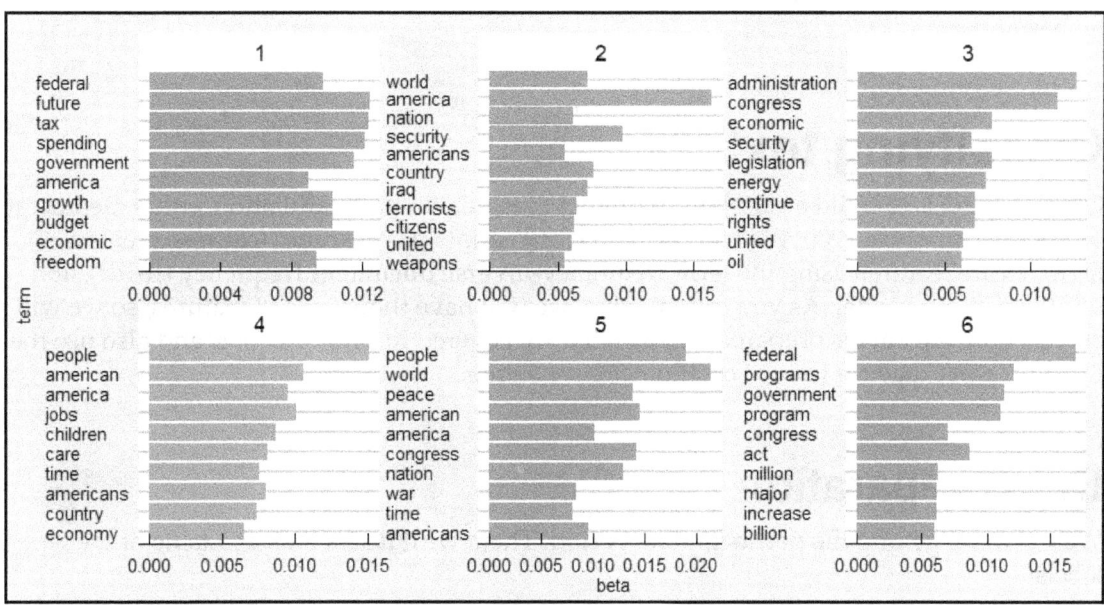

This is the top 10 words per topic based on the `beta` probability. Another thing we can do is look at the probability an address is related to a topic. This is referred to as `gamma` in the model and we can pull those in just like the `beta`:

```
> ap_documents <- tidytext::tidy(sotu_lda, matrix = "gamma")
```

We now have the probabilities of an address per topic. Let's look at the 1981 Ronald Reagan values:

```
> dplyr::filter(ap_documents, document == "1981")
# A tibble: 6 x 3
  document topic gamma
  <chr>    <int> <dbl>
1 1981         1 0.286
2 1981         2 0.0163
3 1981         3 0.0923
4 1981         4 0.118
5 1981         5 0.0777
6 1981         6 0.411
```

Topic 1 is a close second in the topic race. If you think about it, this means that more than six topics would help to create better separation in the probabilities. However, I like just six topics for this chapter for the purpose of demonstration.

Our next endeavor will consist of turning the DTM into input features for a simple classification model on predicting the political party, because partying is what politicians do best.

Classifying text

Our goal here is to build a classifier to predict Presidential party affiliation, either Democrat or Republican, since 1900. We will turn the word counts per year into features, create a DTM, create features using the **term frequency-inverse document frequency** (**tf-idf**), and use them in our model. As you can imagine, we will have thousands of features, so we will change how the data is prepared versus what we covered in prior sections, and also use the `text2vec` package for feature creation and modeling.

Data preparation

We'll start by getting the pertinent data period. Then, we'll take a look at a table of the labels:

```
> sotu_party <- sotu_meta %>%
    dplyr::filter(year > 1899)

> table(sotu_party$party)

Democratic Republican
        61         64
```

The class is well balanced.

A few things can help in the modeling process. It is a good idea here to remove numbers, remove capitalization, remove stop words, stem the words, and remove punctuation. The built-in functions from the `tm` package are handy for this, and we can apply it to a column in the data frame:

```
> sotu_tidy_party$word <- tm::removeNumbers(sotu_tidy_party$word)

> sotu_tidy_party$word <- tm::removePunctuation(sotu_tidy_party$word)

> sotu_party$text <- tolower(sotu_party$text)

> sotu_tidy_party$word <- tm::stemDocument(sotu_tidy_party$word)

> sotu_party$text <- tm::removeWords(sotu_party$text, tm::stopwords("en"))
```

Now we can go ahead and create train and test datasets using `caret` as before:

```
> set.seed(222)

> index <- caret::createDataPartition(sotu_party$party, p = 0.8, list = F)

> train <- sotu_party[index, ]

> test <- sotu_party[-index, ]
```

The objective now is to create a word-based `tokenizer` function for the training data. It is also important to specify a document ID, which will be the column values for a year. We will apply this function to our test data as well:

```
> tok_fun = word_tokenizer

> it_train = text2vec::itoken(
    train$text,
    tokenizer = tok_fun,
    ids = train$year,
    progressbar = FALSE
  )
```

Now the `create_vocabulary()` function will create a data frame of the word, its total count, and the number of documents in which it appears:

```
> vocab = text2vec::create_vocabulary(it_train)
```

This produces data with 13,541 words. A consideration is to what extent you want to remove sparse words, even before doing anything else. In this example, if we remove any word that occurs less than four times, the number of words is reduced to 5,321:

```
> pruned <- text2vec::prune_vocabulary(vocab, term_count_min = 4)
```

Before creating the DTM, you must create an object of how to map the text to the indices. This is done with the `vocab_vectorizer()` function:

```
> vectorizer = text2vec::vocab_vectorizer(pruned)
```

We now create the DTM with the structure of a sparse matrix:

```
> dtm_train = text2vec::create_dtm(it_train, vectorizer)

> dim(dtm_train)
[1] 101 5321
```

You can see that the matrix has 101 observations corresponding to each year in training data and a column for each word. The final transformation prior to modeling is to turn the raw counts in the matrix to tf-idf values. This acts as a type of data normalization by identifying how important a word is in a specific document relative to its overall frequency in all documents. The calculation is to divide the frequency of a word in a document by the total number of words in that document (tf). Then this is multiplied by the log(number of documents/number of documents containing word), which is the idf. Said another way, it adjusts the frequency of a term in a document based on how rarely it is used overall.

We do this by defining the tf-idf model to use and apply that to the training data:

```
> tfidf = text2vec::TfIdf$new()

> dtm_train_tfidf = text2vec::fit_transform(dtm_train, tfidf)
```

You can apply this process to the test data in a similar fashion:

```
> it_test = text2vec::itoken(
test$text,
tokenizer = tok_fun,
ids = test$year,
progressbar = FALSE
)

> dtm_test_tfidf = text2vec::create_dtm(it_test, vectorizer)

> dtm_test_tfidf = transform(dtm_test_tfidf, tfidf)
```

We now have our feature space created to begin classification modeling.

LASSO model

I'm going to provide limited commentary during this portion as we've done this before in `Chapter 4`, *Advanced Feature Selection in Linear Models*. We will create our model using LASSO and check the performance on the test data. Let's specify our x and y for the `cv.glmnet()` function:

```
> x <- dtm_train_tfidf

> y <- as.factor(train$party)
```

The minimum number of folds in cross-validation with `glmnet` is three, which we will use given the small number of observations:

```
> set.seed(123)
```

```
> lasso <- glmnet::cv.glmnet(
  x,
  y,
  nfolds = 3,
  type.measure = "class",
  alpha = 1,
  family = "binomial"
  )

> plot(lasso)
```

The output of the preceding code is as follows:

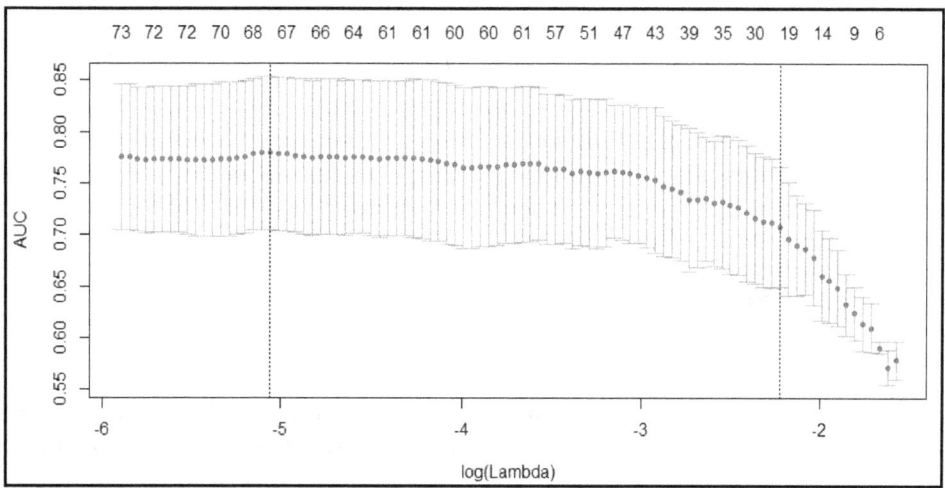

Wow! All those input features and just a handful are relevant, and the **area under the curve (AUC)** is around 0.75. Can that hold during validation?

```
> lasso_test <-
  data.frame(predict(lasso, newx = dtm_test_tfidf,
  type = 'response'), s = "lambda.1se")
> testY <- as.numeric(ifelse(test$party == "Republican", 1, 0))

> Metrics::auc(testY, lasso_test$X1)
[1] 0.8958333
```

It is a small dataset, observation-wise, but performance is OK. How could we improve this? Well, you may say we could add observations from the 19th century, but the party affiliation and political debate in that era were very different than today. You could possibly add principal components, or try ensembles. Those are just a few ideas. We'll transition now to looking at some other quantitative methods of interest.

Additional quantitative analysis

This portion of the analysis will focus on the power of the `qdap` package. It allows you to compare multiple documents over a wide array of measures. Our effort will be on comparing Teddy Roosevelt's 1908 written address and Ronald Reagan's 1982 speech. For starters, we will need to turn the text into data frames, perform sentence splitting, and then combine them to one data frame with a variable created that specifies the President. We will use this as our grouping variable in the analysis. Dealing with text data, even in R, can be tricky. The code that follows seemed to work the best, in this case, to get the data loaded and ready for analysis. I've created two text files of the addresses that I scraped off the internet. Help yourself to the files on GitHub at `https://github.com/PacktPublishing/Advanced-Machine-Learning-with-R/blob/master/Data`.

The files are called `tr.txt` and `reagan.txt`.

We will use the `readLines()` function from base R, collapsing the results to eliminate unnecessary whitespace. I also recommend putting your text encoding to ASCII, otherwise you may run into some bizarre text that will mess up your analysis. That is done with the `iconv()` function:

```
> tr <- paste(readLines("~/corpus/tr.txt"), collapse=" ")

> tr <- iconv(tr, "latin1", "ASCII", "")
```

The warning message is not an issue, as it is just telling us that the final line of text is not the same length as the other lines in the `.txt` file. We now apply the `qprep()` function from `qdap`.

This function is a wrapper for a number of other replacement functions and using it will speed up preprocessing, but it should be used with caution if more detailed analysis is required. The functions it passes through are as follows:

- `bracketX()`: Applies bracket removal
- `replace_abbreviation()`: Replaces abbreviations
- `replace_number()`: Converts numbers to words, for example, *100* becomes *one hundred*
- `replace_symbol()`: Symbols become words, for example, @ becomes *at*

```
> prep_tr <- qdap::qprep(tr)
```

The other preprocessing we should do is to replace contractions (*can't* to *cannot*); remove stop words, in our case the top 100, and remove unwanted characters, with the exception of periods and question marks. They will come in handy shortly:

```
> prep_tr <- qdap::replace_contraction(prep_tr)

> prep_tr <- qdap::rm_stopwords(prep_tr, Top100Words, separate = F)

> prep_tr <- qdap::strip(prep_tr, char.keep = c("?", ".", "!"))
```

Critical to this analysis is to now split it into sentences and add what will be the grouping variable, the year of the speech. This also creates the tot variable, which stands for *turn of talk*, serving as an indicator of sentence order. This is especially helpful in a situation where you are analyzing dialogue, say in a debate or question and answer session:

```
> address_tr <- data.frame(speech = prep_tr)

> address_tr <- qdap::sentSplit(address_tr, "speech")

> address_tr$pres <- "TR"
```

Repeat the steps for the Ronald Reagan speech:

```
> reagan <-
paste(readLines("C:/Users/cory/Desktop/data/corpus/reagan.txt"), collapse="
")

> reagan <- iconv(reagan, "latin1", "ASCII", "")

> prep_reagan <- qdap::qprep(reagan)

> prep_reagan <- qdap::replace_contraction(prep_reagan)

> prep_reagan <- qdap::rm_stopwords(prep_reagan, Top100Words, separate = F)

> prep_reagan <- qdap::strip(prep_reagan, char.keep = c("?", ".", "!"))

> address_reagan <- data.frame(speech = prep_reagan)

> address_reagan <- qdap::sentSplit(address_reagan, "speech")

> address_reagan$pres <- "reagan"
```

Concatenate the separate years into one data frame:

```
> sentences <- dplyr::bind_rows(address_tr, address_reagan)
```

One of the great things about the qdap package is that it facilitates basic text exploration, as we did before. Let's see a plot of frequent terms:

```
> plot(qdap::freq_terms(sentences$speech))
```

The output of the preceding command is as follows:

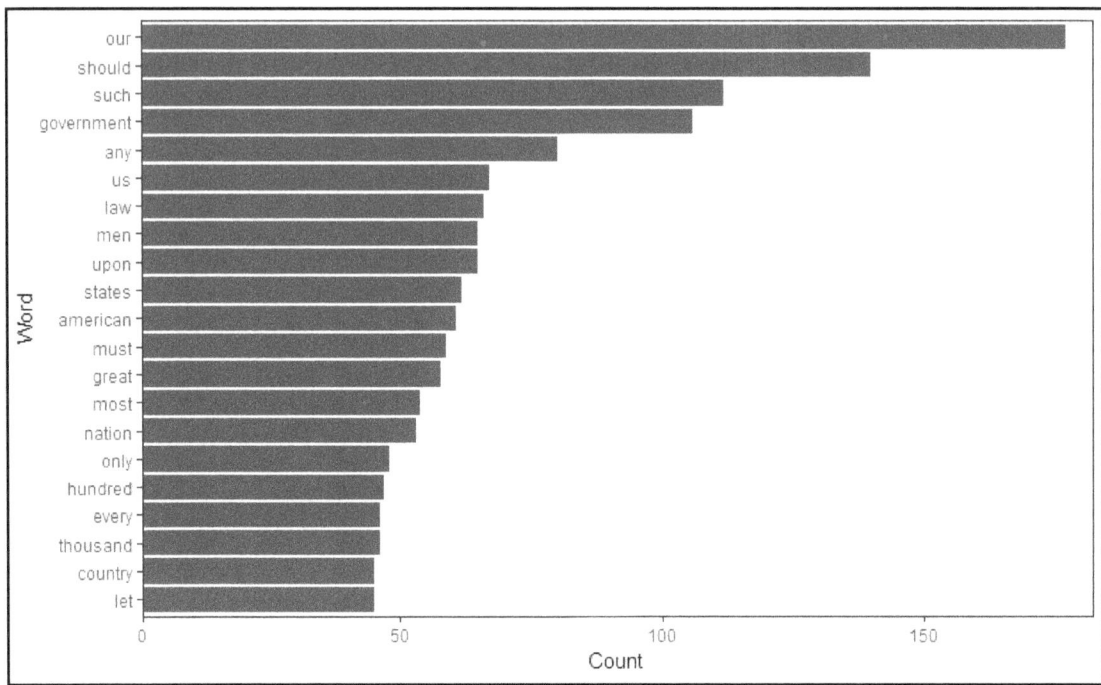

You can create a word frequency matrix that provides the counts for each word by speech:

```
> wordMat <- qdap::wfm(sentences$speech, sentences$pres)

> head(wordMat[order(wordMat[, 1], wordMat[, 2],decreasing = TRUE),])
           reagan  TR
our            69 107
us             44  17
let            33  12
government     18  77
years          17  20
america        17   7
```

This can also be converted into a DTM with the `as.dtm()` function, should you so desire.

Comprehensive word statistics are available. Here are tables of the statistics available in the package. A complete explanation of the statistics is available under `word_stats`:

```
> ws <- qdap::word_stats(sentences$speech, sentences$pres, rm.incomplete =
T)

> ws$word.elem
       pres   n.sent   n.words n.char n.syl n.poly      wps      cps
1        TR      667     12071  80780 25862   3786   18.097  121.109
2    reagan      222      2732  16935  5421    704   12.306   76.284
                 sps      psps    cpw   spw   pspw n.hapax    n.dis
1        TR   38.774     5.676  6.692 2.142  0.314    1829      639
2    reagan   24.419     3.171  6.199 1.984  0.258     815      191
            grow.rate prop.dis
1        TR     0.152    0.053
2    reagan     0.298    0.070

> ws$sent.elem
    n.state n.quest p.state p.quest
1       667       0   1.000   0.000
2       217       5   0.977   0.023
```

Notice that Reagan's speech was much shorter than Roosevelt's written address, with a third of the total sentences. Also, he made use of asking questions five times as a rhetorical device while TR did not (`n.quest` 5 versus `n.quest` 0).

To compare the polarity (sentiment scores), use the `polarity()` function, specifying the text and grouping variables:

```
> pol = qdap::polarity(sentences$speech, sentences$pres)

> pol
     pres total.sentences total.words ave.polarity sd.polarity
stan.mean.polarity
1 reagan             222        2732        0.185       0.407
0.456
2 TR                 667       12071        0.028       0.501
0.056
```

The `stan.mean.polarity` value represents the standardized mean polarity, which is the average polarity divided by the standard deviation. We see that Reagan has slightly higher sentiment than TR. This seems expected as the address has evolved from a written document to Congress, to a televised speech. You can also plot the data. The plot produces two charts. The first shows the polarity by sentences over time and the second shows the distribution of the polarity:

```
> plot(pol)
```

The output of the preceding command is as follows:

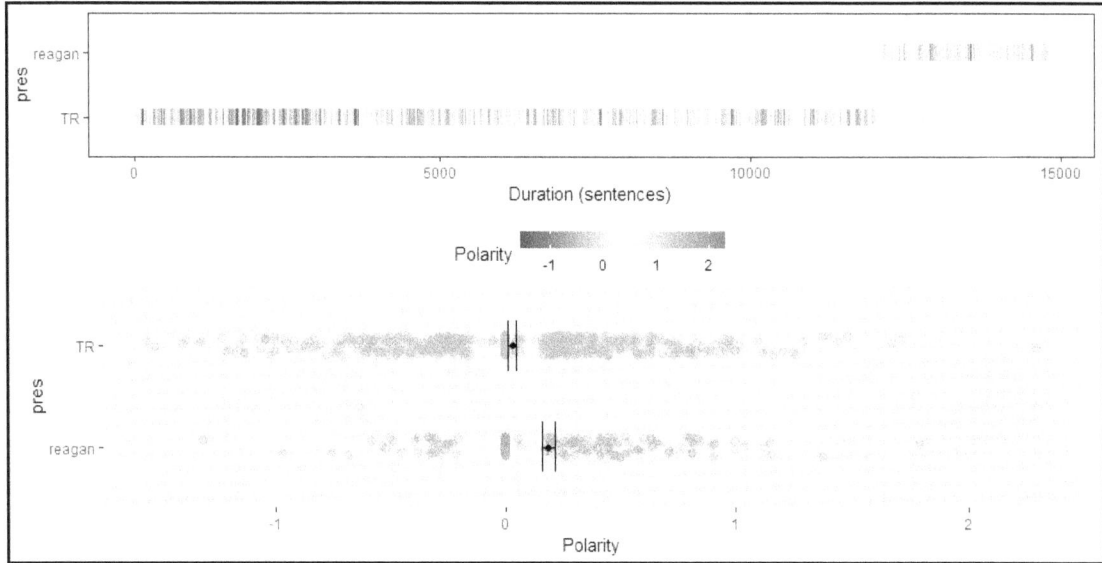

We can identify the most negative sentiment sentence by creating a data frame of the `pol` object, finding the sentence number, and producing it:

```
> pol.df <- pol$all

> which.min(pol.df$polarity)
[1] 86

> pol.df$text.var[86]
[1] "mobs frequently avenge commission crime themselves torturing death man
committing thus avenging bestial fashion bestial deed reducing themselves
level criminal."
```

Now that is negative sentiment! TR was actually quoting the Governor of Alabama about the horror of lynching. We will look at the readability index next:

```
> ari$Readability
     pres word.count sentence.count character.count
1 reagan       2732            222            16935
2     TR      12071            667            80780
  Automated_Readability_Index
1                    13.91929
2                    19.13838
```

Roosevelt's **Automated Readability Index (ARI)** is much higher than Reagan's ARI, a vestige of the language of his era. TR's sentences average 18 words. Formality analysis is next. This takes a couple of minutes to run in R, and you can overwhelm your memory if running it on a laptop or desktop computer. Therefore, we'll take a portion of TR's address, run it separately, then run it for Reagan:

```
> tr_sentences <- dplyr::filter(sentences, pres == "TR")

> tr_sentences <- tr_sentences[1:300, ]

> qdap::formality(tr_sentences$speech)
  all word.count formality
1 all       5726     72.08

> reagan_sentences <- dplyr::filter(sentences, pres == "reagan")

> formality(reagan_sentences$speech)
  all word.count formality
1 all       2732     67.15
```

TR is slightly more formal than Reagan.

Now, we will look at diversity measures. For most of the measures, TR is using a more diverse and richer lexicon than Reagan:

```
> diversity(sentences$speech, sentences$pres)
    pres    wc simpson shannon collision berger_parker brillouin
1 reagan  2732   0.998   6.653     5.896         0.025     6.104
2     TR 12071   0.999   7.491     6.659         0.011     7.101
```

One of my favorite plots is the dispersion plot. This shows the dispersion of a word throughout the text. Let's examine the dispersion of "peace", "government", and "marksmanship":

```
> dispersion_plot(
    sentences$speech,
    rm.vars = sentences$pres,
    c("peace", "government", "marksmanship"),
    color = "black",
    bg.color = "white"
)
```

The output of the preceding command is as follows:

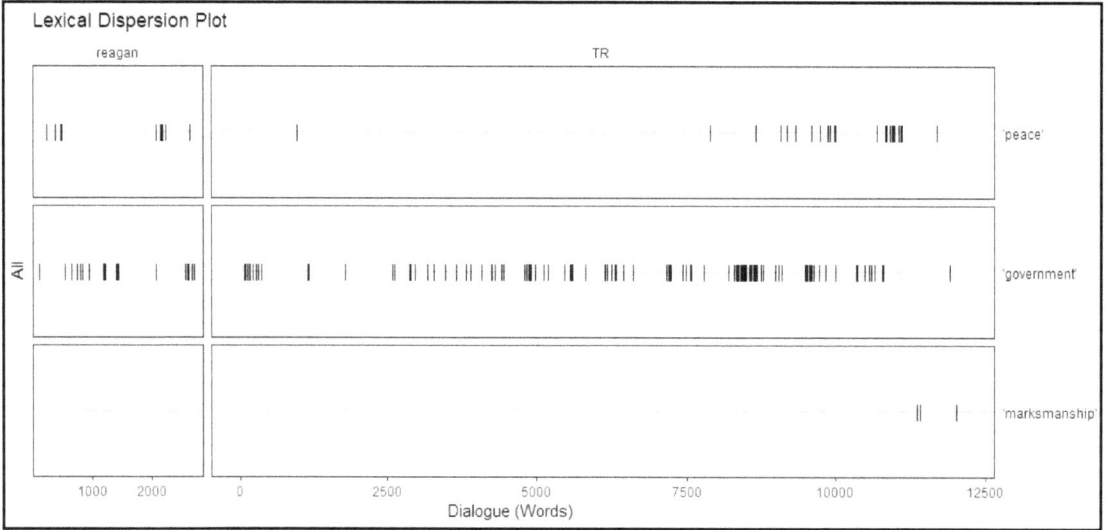

This is quite interesting as you can visualize how much longer TR's address is, as well as how he structured it to discuss foreign affairs later in the text. We can gain some insight into TR's mind with his discussion on marksmanship as he was looking at Switzerland as a shining example of how a populace could be armed and trained. You can see and understand how text analysis can provide insight into what someone is thinking, what their priorities are, and how they go about communicating them.

This completes our analysis of the two speeches. It provided some insight on to how the topics and speech formats have changed over time to accommodate political necessity. Keep in mind that this code can be adapted to text for dozens, if not hundreds, of documents and with multiple speakers, for example, screenplays, legal proceedings, interviews, social media, and so on. Indeed, text mining can bring quantitative order to what has been qualitative chaos.

Summary

In this chapter, we looked at how to address the massive volume of textual data that exists through text mining methods. We looked at a useful framework for text mining, including preparation, word frequency counts and visualization, and topic models using multiple packages in the `tidyverse`. Included in this framework were other quantitative techniques, such as polarity and formality, in order to provide a deeper lexical understanding, or what one could call style, with the `qdap` package. We applied the framework to the State of the Union addresses. Despite it not being practical to cover every possible text mining technique, those discussed in this chapter should be adequate for most problems that one might face.

14

Exploring the Machine Learning Landscape

Machine learning (**ML**) is an amazing subfield of **Artificial Intelligence** (**AI**) that tries to mimic the learning behavior of humans. Similar to the way a baby learns by observing the examples it encounters, an ML algorithm learns the outcome or response to a future incident by observing the data points that are provided as input to it.

In this chapter, we will cover the following topics:

- ML versus software engineering
- Types of ML methods
- ML terminology—a quick review
- ML project pipeline
- Learning paradigm
- Datasets

ML versus software engineering

With most people transitioning from traditional software engineering practice to ML, it is important to understand the underlying difference between both areas. Superficially, both of these areas seem to generate some sort of code to perform a particular task. An interesting fact to observe is that, unlike software engineering where a programmer explicitly writes a program with various responses based on several conditions, the ML algorithm infers the rules of the game by observing the input examples. The rules that are learned are further used for better decision making when new input data is fed to the system.

As you can observe in the following diagram, automatically inferring the actions from data without manual intervention is the key differentiator between ML and traditional programming:

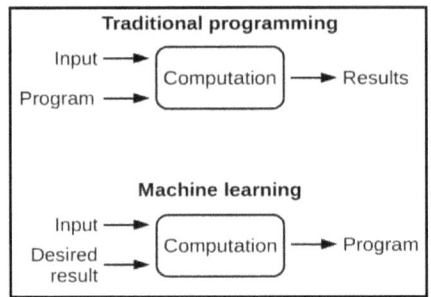

Another key differentiator of ML from traditional programming is that the knowledge acquired through ML is able to generalize beyond the training samples by successfully interpreting data that the algorithm has never seen before, while a program coded in traditional programming can only perform the responses that were included as part of the code.

Yet another differentiator is that in software engineering, there are certain specific ways to solve a problem at hand. Given an algorithm developed based on certain assumptions of inputs and the conditions incorporated, you will be able to guarantee the output that will be obtained given an input. In the ML world, it is not possible to provide such assurances on the output obtained from the algorithms. It is also very difficult in the ML world to confirm if a particular technique is better than another without actually trying both the techniques on the dataset for the problem at hand.

 ML and software engineering are not the same! ML projects may involve some software engineering in them, but ML cannot be considered to be the same as software engineering.

While there is more than one formal definition that exists for ML, the following mentioned are a few key definitions encountered often:

> *"Machine learning is the science of getting computers to act without being explicitly programmed."*
>
> *—Stanford*

> *"Machine learning is based on algorithms that can learn from data without relying on rules-based programming."*
>
> *—McKinsey and Co.*

With the rise of data as the fuel of the future, the terms AI, ML, data mining, data science, and data analytics are used interchangeably by industry practitioners. It is important to understand the key differences between these terms to avoid confusion.

> The terms AI, ML, data mining, data science, and data analytics, though used interchangeably, are not the same!

Let's take a look at the following terms:

- **AI**: AI is a paradigm where machines are able to perform tasks in a smart way. It may be observed that in the definition of AI, it is not specified whether the smartness of machines may be achieved manually or automatically. Therefore, it is safe to assume that even a program written with several `if...else` or `switch...case` statements that has then been infused with a machine to carry out tasks may be considered to be AI.
- **ML**: ML, on the other hand, is a way for the machine to achieve smartness by learning from the data that is provided as input and, thereby, we have a smart machine performing a task. It may be observed that ML achieves the same objective of AI except that the smartness is achieved automatically. Therefore, it can be concluded that ML is simply a way to achieve AI.
- **Data mining**: Data mining is a specific field that focuses on discovering the unknown properties of the datasets. The primary objective of data mining is to extract rules from large amounts of data provided as input, whereas in ML, an algorithm not only infers rules from the data input, but also uses the rules to perform predictions on any new, incoming data.
- **Data analytics**: Data analytics is a field that encompasses performing fundamental descriptive statistics, data visualization, and data points communication for conclusions. Data analytics may be considered to be a basic level within data science. It is normal for practitioners to perform data analytics on the input data provided for data mining or ML exercises. Such analysis on data is generally termed as **exploratory data analysis (EDA)**.

- **Data science**: Data science is an umbrella term that includes data analytics, data mining, ML, and any specific domain expertise pertaining to the field of work. Data science is a concept that includes several aspects of handling the data such as acquiring the data from one or more sources, data cleansing, data preparation, and creating new data points based on existing data. It includes performing data analytics. It also encompasses using one or more data mining or ML techniques on the data to infer knowledge to create an algorithm that performs a task on unseen data. This concept also includes deploying the algorithm in a way that it is useful to perform the designated tasks in the future.

The following is a Venn diagram which demonstrates the skills required by a professional working in the data science ambit. It has three circles, each of which defines a specific skill that a data science professional should have:

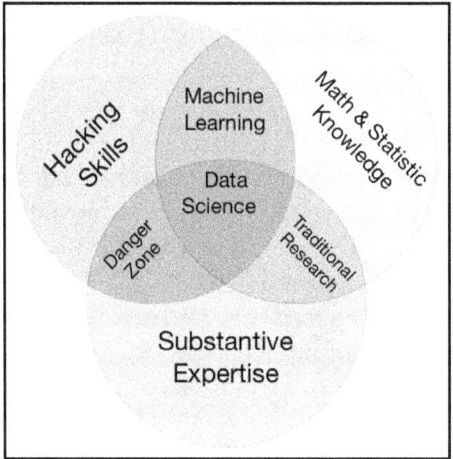

Let's explore the following skills mentioned in the preceding diagram:

- **Math & Statistic Knowledge**: This skill is required to analyze the statistical properties of the data.
- **Hacking Skills**: Programming skills play a key role in order to process the data in a quick manner. The ML algorithm is applied to create an output that will perform the prediction on unseen data.
- **Substantive Expertise**: This skill refers to the domain expertise in the field of the problem at hand. It helps the professional to be able to provide proper inputs to the system from which it can learn and to assess the appropriateness of the inputs and results obtained.

 To be a successful data science professional you need to have math, programming skills, as well as knowledge of the business domain.

As we can see, AI, data science, data analytics, data mining, and ML are all interlinked. All of these areas are the most in-demand domains in the industry right now. The right skill sets in combination with real-world experience will lead to a strong career in these areas which are currently trending. As ML forms the core of the leading space, the next section explores the various types of ML methods that may be applied to several real-world problems.

ML is everywhere! Most of the time, we may be using something that is ML-based but don't realize its existence or the influence that it has on our lives! Let's explore together some very popular devices or applications that we experience on a daily basis, which are powered by ML:

- **Virtual personal assistants** (**VPAs**) such as **Google Allo**, **Alexa**, **Google Now**, **Google Home**, **Siri**, and so on
- Smart maps that show you traffic predictions, given your source and destination
- Demand-based price surging in Uber or similar transportation services
- Automated video surveillance in airports, railway stations, and other public places
- Face recognition of individuals in pictures posted on social media sites such as Facebook
- Personalized news feeds served to you on Facebook
- Advertisements served to you on YouTube
- **People you may know** suggestions on Facebook and other similar sites
- Job recommendations on LinkedIn, based on your profile
- Automated responses on Google Mail
- Chatbots that you converse with in online customer support forums
- Search engine results filtering
- Email spam filtering

Of course, the list does not end here. The preceding applications mentioned are just a few of the basic ones that illustrate the influence that ML has on our lives today. It is not astonishing to quote that there is no subject area that ML has not touched!

The topics in this section are by no means an exhaustive description of ML, but just a quick touch point to get us started on a journey of exploration. Now that we have a basic understanding of what ML is and where it can be applied, let's delve deeper into other ML-related topics in the next section.

Types of ML methods

Several types of tasks that aim at solving real-world problems can be achieved thanks to ML. An ML method generally means a group of specific types of algorithms that are suitable for solving a particular kind of problem and the method addresses any constraints that the problem brings along with it. For example, a constraint of a particular problem could be the availability of labeled data that can be provided as input to the learning algorithm.

Essentially, the popular ML methods are supervised learning, unsupervised learning, semi-supervised learning, reinforcement learning, and transfer learning. The rest of this section details each of these methods.

Supervised learning

A supervised learning algorithm is applied when one is very clear about the result that needs to be achieved from a problem, however one is unsure about the relationships between the data that affects the output. We would like the ML algorithm that we apply on the data to perceive these relationships between different data elements so as to achieve the desired output.

The concept can be better explained with an example—at a bank, prior to extending a loan, they would like to predict if a loan applicant would pay the loan back. In this case, the problem is very clear. If a loan is extended to a prospective customer X, there are two possibilities: that X would successfully repay the loan or X would not repay the loan. The bank would like to use ML to identify the category into which customer X falls; that is, a successful repayer of the loan or a repayment defaulter.

While the problem definition that is to be solved is clear, please note that the features of a customer that will contribute to successful loan repayment or non-repayment are not clear and this is something we would like the ML algorithm to learn by observing the patterns in the data.

The major challenge here is that we need to provide input data that represents both customers that repaid their loans successfully and also customers that failed to repay. The bank can simply look at the historical data to get the records of customers in both categories and then label each record as paid or unpaid categories as appropriate.

The records, thus labeled, now become input to a supervised learning algorithm so that it can learn the patterns of both categories of customers. The process of learning from the labeled data is called **training** and the output obtained (algorithm) from the learning process is called a **model**. Ideally, the bank would keep some part of the labeled data aside from training data so as to be able to test the model created, and this data is termed as **test data**. It should be no surprise that the labeled data that is used for training the model is called **training data**.

Once the model has been built, measurements are obtained by testing the model with test data to ensure the model yields a satisfactory level of performance, otherwise model-building iterations are carried out until the desired model performance is obtained. The model that achieved the desired performance on test data can be used by the bank to infer if any new loan applicant will be a future defaulter at all and, if so, make a better decision in terms of extending a loan to that applicant.

In a nutshell, supervised ML algorithms are employed when the objective is very clear and labeled data is available as input for the algorithm to learn the patterns from. The following diagram summarizes the supervised learning process:

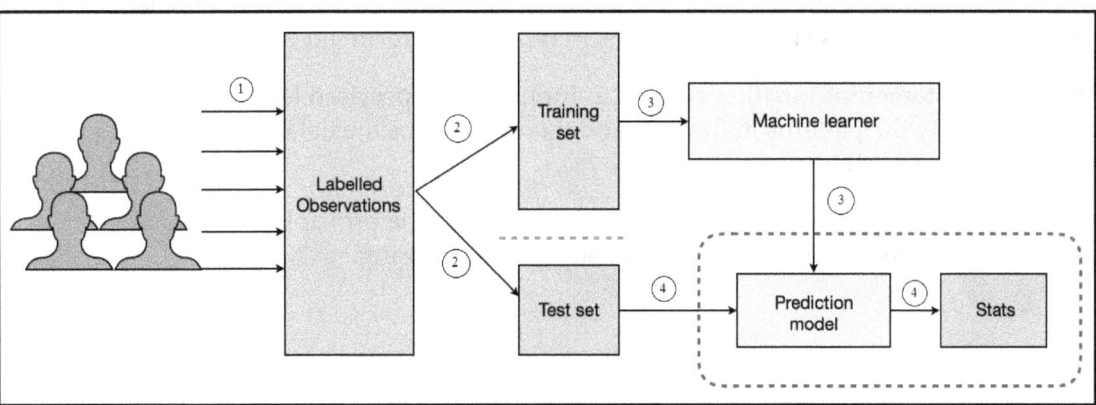

Supervised learning can be further divided into two categories, namely **classification** and **regression**. The prediction of a bank loan defaulter explained in this section is an example of classification and it aims to predict a label of a nominal type such as yes or no. On the other hand, it is also possible to predict numeric values (continuous values) and this type of prediction is called regression. An example of regression is predicting the monthly rental of a home in a prime location of a city based on features such as the demand for houses in the area, the number of bedrooms, the dimensions of the house, and accessibility to public transportation.

Several supervised learning algorithms exist, and a few popularly known algorithms in this area include **classification and regression trees** (**CART**), logistic regression, linear regression, Naive Bayes, neural networks, **k-nearest neighbors** (**KNN**), and **support vector machine** (**SVM**).

Unsupervised learning

The availability of labeled data is not very common and manually labeling data is also not cheap. This is the situation where unsupervised learning comes into play.

For example, one small boutique firm wants to roll out a promotion to its customers, who are registered on their Facebook page. While the business objective is clear—that a promotion needs to be rolled out to customers—it is unclear as to which customer falls under which group. Unlike the supervised learning method where prior knowledge existed in terms of bad debtors and good debtors, in this case there are no such clues.

When the customer information is given as input to unsupervised learning algorithms, it tries to identify the patterns in the data and thereby groups the data of the customers with similar kinds of attributes.

Birds of the same feather flock together is the principle followed in customer grouping with unsupervised learning.

The reasoning behind the formation of these organic groups from the grouping exercise may not be very intuitive. It may take some research to identify the factors that contributed to the gathering of a set of customers in a group. Most of the time, this research is manual and the data points in each group need verifying. This research may form the basis to determine the groups to which the particular promotion at hand needs to be rolled out. This application of unsupervised learning is called **clustering**. The following diagram shows the application of unsupervised ML to cluster the data points:

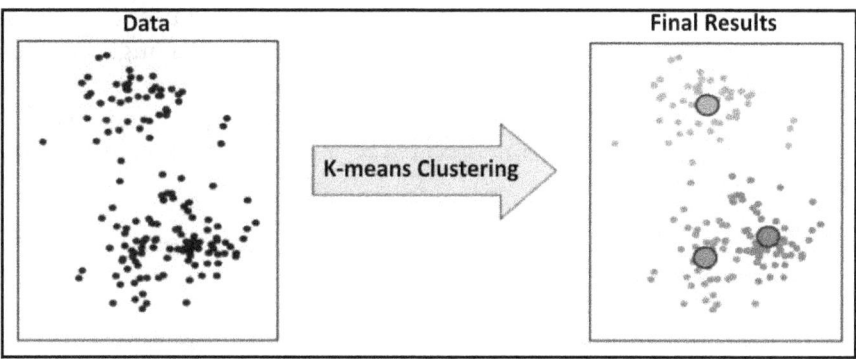

There are a number of clustering algorithms. However, the most popular ones are namely, k-means clustering, k-modes clustering, hierarchical clustering, fuzzy clustering, and so on.

Other forms of unsupervised learning do exist. For example, in retail industry, an unsupervised learning method called **association rule mining** is applied on customer purchases to identify the goods that are purchased together. In this case, unlike supervised learning, there is no need for labels at all. The task involved only requires the ML algorithm to identify the latent associations between the products that are billed together by customers. Having the information from association rule mining helps retailers place the products that are bought together in proximity. The idea is that customers can be intuitively encouraged to buy the extra products.

A priori, **equivalence class transformation** (Eclat), and **frequency pattern growth** (FPG) are popular among the several algorithms that exist to perform association rule mining.

Yet another form of unsupervised learning is anomaly detection or outlier detection. The goal of the exercise is to identify data points that do not belong to the rest of the elements that are given as input to the unsupervised learning algorithm. Similar to association rule mining, due to the nature of the problem at hand, there is no requirement for labels to be made use of by the algorithm to achieve the goal.

Fraud detection is an important application of anomaly detection in the credit cards industry. Credit card transactions are monitored in real time and any spurious transaction patterns are flagged immediately to avoid losses to the credit card user as well as the credit card provider. The unusual pattern that is monitored for could be a huge transaction in a foreign currency rather than that of a normal currency in which the particular customer generally transacts. It could be transactions in physical stores located in two different continents on the same day. The general idea is to be able to flag up a pattern that is a deviation from the norm.

K-means clustering and one-class SVM are two well-known unsupervised ML algorithms that are used to observe abnormalities in the population.

Overall, it may be understood that unsupervised learning is unarguably a very important method, given that labeled data used for training is a scarce resource.

Semi-supervised learning

Semi-supervised learning is a hybrid of both supervised and unsupervised methods. ML requires large amounts of data for training. Most of the time, a directly proportional relationship is observed between the amount of data used for model training and the performance of the model.

In niche domains such as medical imagining, a large amount of image data (MRIs, x-rays, CT scans) is available. However, the time and availability of qualified radiologists to label these images is scarce. In this situation, we might end up getting only a few images labeled by radiologists.

Semi-supervised learning takes advantage of the few labeled images by building an initial model that is used to label the large amount of unlabeled data that exists in the domain. Once the large amount of labeled data is available, a supervised ML algorithm may be used to train and create a final model that is used for prediction tasks on the unseen data. The following diagram illustrates the steps involved in semi-supervised learning:

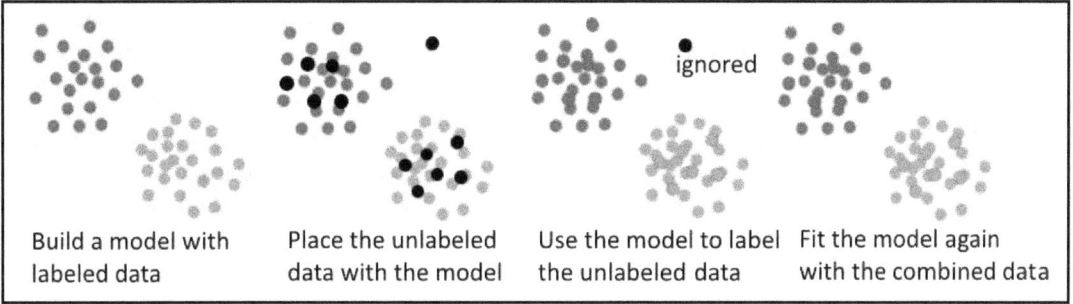

| Build a model with labeled data | Place the unlabeled data with the model | Use the model to label the unlabeled data | Fit the model again with the combined data |

Speech analysis, protein synthesis, and web content classifications are certain areas where large amounts of unlabeled data and fewer amounts of labeled data are available. Semi-supervised learning is applied in these areas with successful results.

Generative adversarial networks (GANs), **semi-supervised support vector machines (S3VMs)**, graph-based methods, and **Markov** chain methods are well-known methods among others in the semi-supervised ML area.

Reinforcement learning

Reinforcement learning (RL) is an ML method that is neither supervised learning nor unsupervised learning. In this method, a reward definition is provided as input to this kind of a learning algorithm at the start. As the algorithm is not provided with labeled data for training, this type of learning algorithm cannot be categorized as supervised learning. On the other hand, it is not categorized as unsupervised learning, as the algorithm is fed with information on reward definition that guides the algorithm through taking the steps to solve the problem at hand.

Reinforcement learning aims to improve the strategies used to solve any problem continuously by relying on the feedback received. The goal is to maximize the rewards while taking steps to solve the problem. The rewards obtained are computed by the algorithm itself going by the rewards and penalty definitions. The idea is to achieve optimal steps that maximize the rewards to solve the problem at hand.

The following diagram is an illustration depicting a robot automatically determining the ideal behavior through a reinforcement learning method within the specific context of fire:

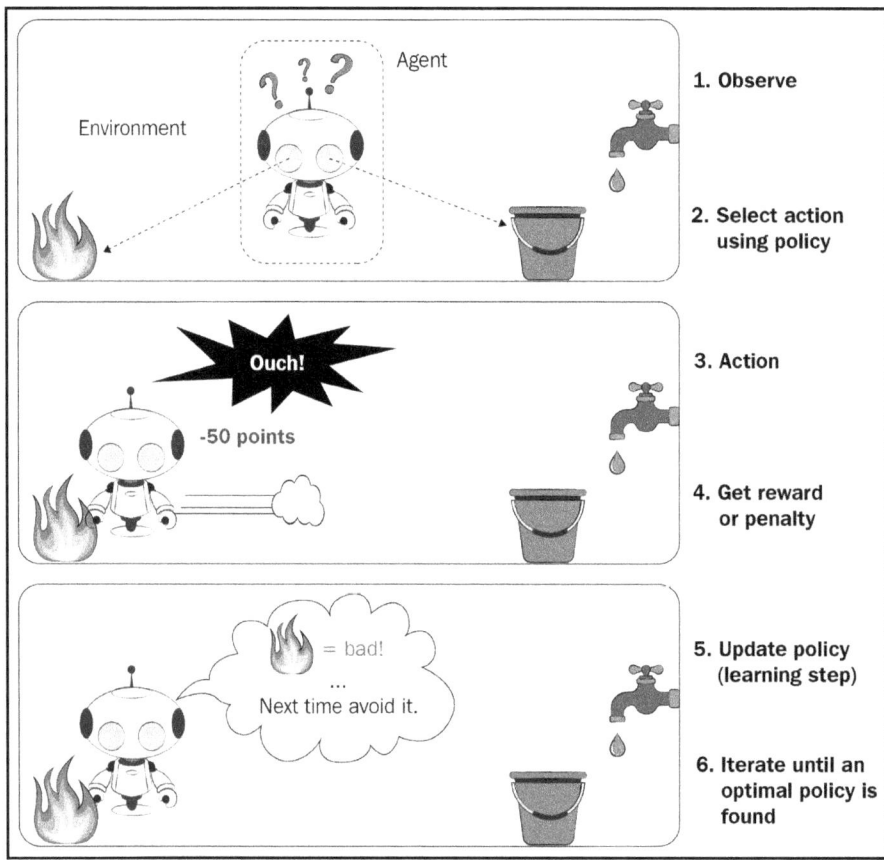

A machine outplaying humans in an Atari video game is termed as one of the foremost success stories of reinforcement learning. To achieve this feat, a large number of example games played by humans are fed as input to the algorithm that learned the steps to take to maximize the reward. The reward in this case is the final score. The algorithm, post learning from the example inputs, just simulated the pattern at each step of the game that eventually maximized the score obtained.

Though it might appear that reinforcement learning can be applied to game scenarios only, there are numerous use cases for this method in industry as well. The following examples mentioned are three such use cases:

- Dynamic pricing of goods and services based on spontaneous supply and demand targeted at achieving profit maximization is achieved through a variant of reinforcement learning called **Q-learning**.
- Effective use of space in warehouses is a key challenge faced by inventory management professionals. Market demand fluctuations, the large availability of inventory stocks, and delays in refilling the inventory are the key constraints that affect space utilization. Reinforcement learning algorithms are used to optimize the time to procure inventory as well as to reduce the time to retrieve the goods from warehouses, thereby directly impacting the space management issue referred to as a problem in the inventory management area.
- Prolonged treatments and differential drug administration is required in medical science to treat diseases such as cancer. The treatments are highly personalized, based on the characteristics of the patient. Treatment often involves variations of the treatment strategy at various stages. This kind of treatment plan is typically referred to as a **dynamic treatment regime** (DTR). Reinforcement learning helps with processing the clinical trials data to come up with the appropriate personalized DTR for the patient, based on the characteristics of the patient that are fed in as inputs to the reinforcement learning algorithm.

There are four very popular reinforcement learning algorithms, namely Q-learning, **state-action-reward-state-action** (**SARSA**), **deep Q network** (**DQN**), and **deep deterministic policy gradient** (**DDPG**).

Transfer learning

The reusability of code is one of the fundamental concepts of **object-oriented programming** (**OOP**) and it is pretty popular in the software-engineering world. Similarly, transfer learning involves reusing a model built to achieve a specific task to solve another related task.

It is understandable that to achieve better performance measurements, ML models need to be trained on large amounts of labeled data. The availability of fewer amounts of data means less training and the result is a model with suboptimal performance.

Transfer learning attempts to solve the problems arising from the availability of fewer amounts of data by reusing the knowledge obtained by a different related model. Having fewer data points available to train a model should not impede building a better model, which is the core concept behind transfer learning. The following diagram is an illustration showing the purpose of transfer learning in an image recognition task that classifies dog and cat images:

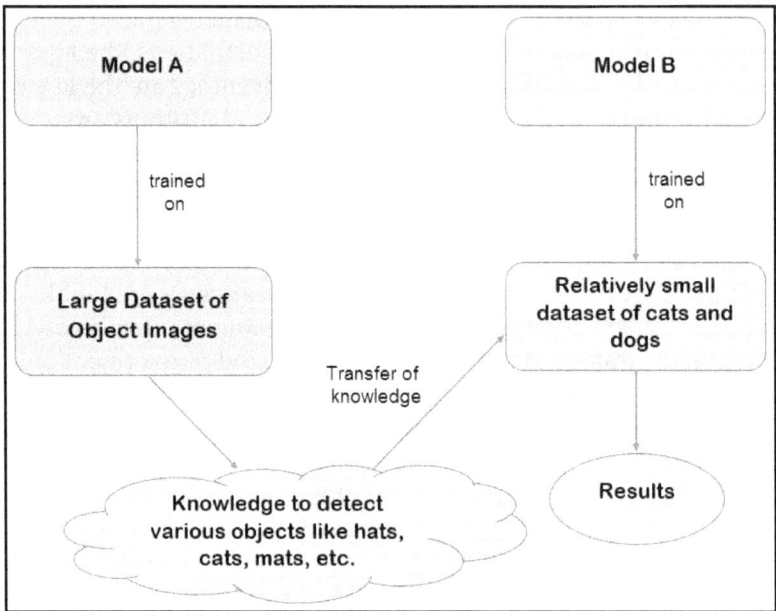

In this task, a neural network model is involved with detecting the edges, color blob detection, and so on in the first few layers. Only at the progressive layers (maybe in the last few layers) does the model attempt to identify the facial features of dogs or cats in order to classify them as one of the targets (a dog or a cat).

It may be observed that the tasks of identifying edges and color blobs are not specific to cats' and dogs' images. The knowledge to infer edges or color blobs may be generally inferred even if a model is trained on non-dog or non-cat images. Eventually, if this knowledge is clubbed with knowledge derived from inferring cat faces versus dog faces, even if they are small in number, we will have a better model than the suboptimal model obtained by training on fewer images.

In the case of a dogs-cats classifier, first, a model is trained on a large set of images that are not confined to cats' and dogs' images. The model is then taken and the last few layers are retrained on the dogs' and cats' faces. The model, thus obtained, is then tested and used post evidencing performance measurements that are satisfactory.

The concept of transfer learning is used not just for image-related tasks. Another example of it being used is in **natural language processing (NLP)** where it can perform sentiment analysis on text data.

Assume a company that launched a new product has a concept that never existed before (say, for now, a flying car). The task is to analyze the tweets related to the new product and identify each of them as being of positive, negative, or neural sentiment. It may be observed that prior, labeled tweets are unavailable in the flying car's domain. In such cases, we can take a model built based on the labeled data of generic product reviews for several products and domains. We can reuse the model by supplementing it with flying-car-domain-specific terminology to avail a new model. This new model will be finally used for testing and deploying to analyze sentiment on the tweets obtained about the newly launched flying cars.

It is possible to achieve transfer learning through the following two ways:

- By reusing one's own model
- By reusing a pretrained model

Pretrained models are models built by various organizations or individuals as part of their research work or as part of a competition. These models are generally very complex and are trained on large amounts of data. They are also optimized to perform their tasks with high precision. These models may take days or weeks to train on modern hardware. Organizations or individuals often release these models under permissive license for reuse. Such pretrained models can be downloaded and reused through the transfer-learning paradigm. This will effectively make use of the vast existing knowledge that the pretrained models possess, which would otherwise be hard to attain for an individual with limited hardware resources and amounts of data to train.

There are several pretrained models made available by various parties. The following described are some of the popular pretrained models:

- **Inception-V3 model**: This model has been trained on ImageNet as part of a large visual recognition challenge. The competition required the participants to classify a given image into one of 1,000 classes. Some of the classes include the names of animals and object names.

- **MobileNet**: This pretrained model has been built by Google and it is meant to perform object detection using the ImageNet database. The architecture is designed for mobiles.
- **VCG Face**: This is a pretrained model built for face recognition.
- **VCG 16**: This is a pretrained model trained on the **MS COCO** dataset. This one accomplishes image captioning; that is, given an input image, it generates a caption describing the image's contents.
- **Google's Word2Vec model and Stanford's GloVe model**: These pretrained models take text as input and produce word vectors as output. Distributed word vectors offer one form of representing documents for NLP or ML applications.

Now that we have a basic understanding of various possible ML methods, in the next section, we focus on quickly reviewing the key terminology used in ML.

ML terminology – a quick review

In this section, we take the popular ML terms and review them. This non-exhaustive review will helps us as a quick refresher and enable us to follow the projects covered by this book without any hiccups.

Deep learning

This is a revolutionary trend and has become a super-hot topic in recent times in the ML world. It is a category of ML algorithms that use **artificial neural networks (ANNs)** with multiple hidden layers of neurons to address problems.

Superior results are obtained by applying deep learning to several real-world problems. **Convolutional neural networks (CNNs)**, **recurrent neural networks (RNNs)** **autoencoders (AEs)**, **generative adversarial networks (GANs)**, and **deep belief networks (DBNs)** are some of the popular deep learning methods.

Big data

The term refers to large volumes of data that combine both structured data types (rows and columns similar to a table) and unstructured data types (text documents, voice recordings, image data, and so on). Due to the volume of data, it does not fit into the main memory of the hardware where ML algorithms need to be executed. Separate strategies are needed to work on these large volumes of data. Distributed processing of the data and combining the results (typically called **MapReduce**) is one strategy. It is also possible to process just enough data sequentially that can fit in a main memory each time and store the results somewhere on a hard drive; we need to repeat this process until the entirety of the data is processed completely. After the data processing, the results need to be combined to avail the final results of all the data that has been processed.

Special technologies such as Hadoop and Spark are required to perform ML on big data. Needless to say, you will need to hone specialized skills in order to apply ML algorithms successfully using these technologies on big data.

Natural language processing

This is an application area of ML that aims for computers to comprehend human languages such as English, French, and Mandarin. NLP applications enable users to interact with computers using spoken languages.

Chatbot, speech synthesis, machine translation, text classification and clustering, text generation, and text summarization are some of the popular applications of NLP.

Computer vision

This field of ML tries to mimic human vision. The aim is to enable computers to see, process, and determine the objects in images or videos. Deep learning and the availability of powerful hardware has led to the rise of very powerful applications in this area of ML.

Autonomous vehicles such as self-driving cars, object recognition, object tracking, motion analysis, and the restoration of images are some of the applications of computer vision.

Cost function

Cost function, loss function, or error function are used interchangeably by practitioners. Each is used to define and measure the error of a model. The objective for the ML algorithm is to minimize the loss from the dataset.

Some of the examples of cost function are square loss that is used in linear regression, hinge loss that is used in support vector machines and 0/1 loss used to measure accuracy in classification algorithms.

Model accuracy

Accuracy is one of the popular metrics used to measure the performance of ML models. The measurement is easy to understand and helps the practitioner to communicate the goodness of a model very easily to its business users.

Generally, this metric is used for classification problems. Accuracy is measured as the number of correct predictions divided by the total number of predictions.

Confusion matrix

This is a table that describes the classification model's performance. It is an n rows, n columns matrix where n represents the number of classes that are predicted by the classification model. It is formed by noting down the number of correct and incorrect predictions by the model when compared to the actual label.

Confusion matrices are better explained with an example—assume that there are 100 images in a dataset where there are 50 dog images and 50 cat images. A model that is built to classify images as cat images or dog images is given this dataset. The output from the model showed that 40 dog images are classified correctly and 20 cat images are predicted correctly. The following table is the confusion matrix construction from the prediction output of the model:

Model predicted labels	Actual labels		
		cats	dogs
	cats	20	30
	dogs	10	40

Predictor variables

These variables are otherwise called **independent variables** or **x-values**. These are the input variables that help to predict the dependent or target or response variable.

In a house rent prediction use case, the size of the house in square feet, the number of bedrooms, the number of houses available unoccupied in the region, the proximity to public transport, the accessibility to facilities such as hospitals and schools are all some examples of predictor variables that determine the rental cost of the house.

Response variable

Dependent variables or target or y-values are all interchangeably used by practitioners as alternatives for the term **response variable**. This is the variable the model predicts as output based on the independent variables that are provided as input to the model.

In the house rent prediction use case, the rent predicted is the response variable.

Dimensionality reduction

Feature reduction (or feature selection) or dimensionality reduction is the process of reducing the input set of independent variables to obtain a lesser number of variables that are really required by the model to predict the target.

In certain cases, it is possible to represent multiple dependent variables by combining them together without losing much information. For example, instead of having two independent variables such as the length of a rectangle and the breath of a rectangle, the dimensions can be represented by only one variable called the area that represents both the length and breadth of the rectangle.

The following mentioned are the multiple reasons we need to perform a dimensionality reduction on a given input dataset:

- To aid data compression, therefore accommodate the data in a smaller amount of disk space.
- The time to process the data is reduced as fewer dimensions are used to represent the data.
- It removes redundant features from datasets. Redundant features are typically known as **multicollinearity** in data.

- Reducing the data to fewer dimensions helps visualize the data through graphs and charts.
- Dimensionality reduction removes noisy features from the dataset which, in turn, improves the model performance.

There are many ways by which dimensionality reduction can be attained in a dataset. The use of filters, such as information gain filters, and symmetric attribute evaluation filters, is one way. Genetic-algorithm-based selection and **principal component analysis** (**PCA**) are other popular techniques used to achieve dimensionality reduction. Hybrid methods do exist to attain feature selection.

Class imbalance problem

Let's assume that one needs to build a classifier that identifies cat and dog images. The problem has two classes namely cat and dog. If one were to train a classification model, training data is required. The training data in this case is based on images of dogs and cats given as input so a supervised learning model can learn the features of dogs versus cats.

It may so happen that if there are 100 images available for training in the dataset and 95 of them are dog pictures, five of them are cat pictures. This kind of unequal representation of different classes in a training dataset is termed as a class imbalance problem.

Most ML techniques work best when the number of examples in each class are roughly equal. One can employ certain techniques to counter class imbalance problems in data. One technique is to reduce the majority class (images of dogs) samples and make them equal to the minority class (images of cats). In this case, there is information loss as a lot of the dog images go unused. Another option is to generate synthetic data similar to the data for the minority class (images of cats) so as to make the number of data samples equal to the majority class. **Synthetic minority over-sampling technique** (**SMOTE**) is a very popular technique for generating synthetic data.

It may be noted that accuracy is not a good metric for evaluating the performance of models where the training dataset experiences class imbalance problems. Assume a model built based on a class-imbalanced dataset that predicts a majority class for any test sample that it is asked to predict on. In this case, one gets 95% accuracy as roughly 95% of the images are dog images in the test dataset. But this performance can only be termed as a hoax as the model does not have any discriminative power—it just predicts dog as the class for any image it needs to predict about. In this case, it just happened that every image is predicted as a dog, but still the model got away with a very high accuracy indicating that it is a great model, whether it is in reality or not!

There are several other performance metrics available to use in a situation where a class imbalance is a problem, F1 score and the **area under the curve of the receiver operating characteristic (AUCROC)** are some of the popular ones.

Model bias and variance

While several ML algorithms are available to build models, model selection can be done on the basis of the bias and variance errors that the models produce.

Bias error occurs when the model has a limited capability to learn the true signals from a dataset provided as input to it. Having a highly biased model essentially means the model is consistent but inaccurate on average.

Variance errors occur when the models are too sensitive to the training datasets with which they are trained. Having high variance in a model essentially means that the trained model will produce high accuracies on any test dataset on average, but their predictions are inconsistent.

Underfitting and overfitting

Underfitting and overfitting are the concepts closely associated with bias and variance. These two are the biggest causes for the poor performance of the models, therefore a practitioner has to pay very close attention to these issues while building ML models.

A situation where the model does not perform well with both training data as well as test data is termed as underfitting. This situation can be detected by observing high training errors and test errors. Having an underfitting problem means that the ML algorithm chosen to fit the model is not suitable to model the features of the training data. Therefore, the only remedy is to try other kinds of ML algorithms to model the data.

Overfitting is a situation where the model learned the features of the training data so well that it fails to generalize on other unseen data. In an overfitting model, noise or random fluctuations in the training data are considered as true signals by the model and it looks for these patterns in unseen data as well, therefore impacting the poor model performance.

Overfitting is more prevalent in non-parametric and non-linear models such as decision trees, and neural networks. Pruning the trees is one remedy to overcome the problem. Another remedial measure is a technique called **dropout** where some of the features learned from the model are dropped randomly from the model therefore making the model more generalizable to unseen data. Regularization is yet another technique to resolve overfitting problems. This is attained by penalizing the coefficients of the model so that the model generalizes better. L1 penalty and L2 penalty are the types of penalties through which regularization can be performed in regression scenarios.

The goal for a practitioner is to ensure that the model neither overfits nor underfits. To achieve this, it is essential to learn when to stop training the ML data. One could plot the training error and validation error (an error that is measured on a small portion of the training dataset that is kept aside) on a chart and identify the point where the training data keeps decreasing, however the validation error starts to rise.

At times, obtaining performance measurement on training data and expecting a similar measurement to be obtained on unseen data may not work. A more realistic training and test performance estimate is to be obtained from a model by adopting a data-resampling technique called k-fold cross validation. The k in k-fold cross validation refers to a number; examples include 3-fold cross validation, 5-fold cross validation, and 10-fold cross validation. The **k-fold cross validation** technique involves dividing the training data into k parts and running the training process $k + 1$ times. In each iteration, the training is performed on k - 1 partitions of the data and the kth partition is used exclusively for testing. It may be noted that the kth partition for testing and k - 1 partitions for training are shuffled in each iteration, therefore the training data and testing data do not stay constant in each iteration. This approach enables getting a pessimistic measurement of performance that can be expected from the model on the unseen data in the future.

10-fold cross validation with 10 runs to obtain model performance is considered to be a gold standard estimate for a model's performance among practitioners. Estimating the model's performance in this way is always recommended in industrial setups and for critical ML applications.

Data preprocessing

This is essentially a step that is adopted in the early stages of an ML project pipeline. Data preprocessing involves transforming the raw data in a format that is acceptable as input by ML algorithms.

Feature hashing, missing values imputation, transforming variables from numeric to nominal, and vice versa, are a few data preprocessing steps among the numerous things that can be done to data during preprocessing.

Raw text documents' transformation into word vectors is an example of data preprocessing. The word vectors thus obtained can be fed to an ML algorithm to achieve documents classification or documents clustering.

Holdout sample

While working on a training dataset, a small portion of the data is kept aside for testing the performance of the models. The small portion of data is unseen data (not used in training), therefore one can rely on the measurements obtained for this data. The measurements obtained can be used to tune the parameters of the model or just to report out the performance of the model so as to set expectations in terms of what level of performance can be expected from the model.

It may be noted that the performance measurement reported out on the basis of a holdout sample is not as robust an estimate as that of a k-fold cross validation estimate. This is because there could be some unknown biases that could have crept in during the random split of the holdout set from the original dataset. Also, there are also no guarantees that the holdout dataset has a representation of all the classes involved in the training dataset. If we need representation of all classes in the holdout dataset, then a special technique called a **stratified holdout sample** needs to be applied. This ensures that there is representation for all classes in the holdout dataset. It is obvious that a performance measurement obtained from a stratified holdout sample is a better estimate of performance than that of the estimate of performance obtained from a nonstratified holdout sample.

70%-30%, 80%-20%, and 90%-10% are generally the sets of training data-holdout data splits observed in ML projects.

Hyperparameter tuning

ML or deep learning algorithms take hyperparameters as input prior to training the model. Each algorithm comes with its own set of hyperparameters and some algorithms may have zero hyperparameters.

Hyperparameter tuning is an important step in model building. Each of the ML algorithms comes with some default hyperparameter values that are generally used to build an initial model, unless the practitioner manually overrides the hyperparameters. Setting the right combination of hyperparameters and the right hyperparameter values for the model greatly improves the performance of the model in most cases. Hence, it is strongly recommended that one does hyperparameter tuning as part of ML model building. Searching through the possible universe of hyperparameter values is a very time-consuming task.

The *k* in k-means clustering and k-nearest neighbors classification, the number of tress and the depth of tress in random forest, and *eta* in XGBoost are all examples of hyperparameters.

Grid search and **Bayesian** optimization-based hyperparameter tuning are two popular methods of hyperparameter tuning among practitioners.

Performance metrics

A model needs to be evaluated on unseen data to assess its goodness. The term goodness may be expressed in several ways and these ways are termed as model performance metrics.

Several metrics exist to report the performance of models. Accuracy, precision, recall, F-score, sensitivity, specificity, AUROC curve, **root mean squared error** (**RMSE**), Hamming loss, and **mean squared error** (**MSE**) are some of the popular model performance metrics among others.

Feature engineering

Feature engineering is the art of creating new features either from existing data in the dataset or by procuring additional data from an external data source. It is done with the intent that adding additional features improves the model performance. Feature engineering generally requires domain expertise and in-depth business problem understanding.

Let's take a look at an example of feature engineering—for a bank that is working on a loan defaulter prediction project, sourcing and supplementing the training dataset with information on the unemployment trends of the region for the past few months might improve the performance of the model.

Model interpretability

Often, in a business environment when ML models are built, just reporting the performance measurements obtained to confirm the goodness of the model may not be enough. The stakeholders generally are inquisitive to understand the *whys* of the model, that is, what are the factors contributing to the model's performance? In other words, the stakeholders want to understand the causes of the effects. Essentially, the expectation from the stakeholders is to understand the importance of various features in the model and the direction in which each of the variables impacts the model.

For example, does a feature of *time spent on exercising every day* in the dataset for a cancer prediction model have any impact on the model predictions at all? If so, *does time spent on exercising every day* push the prediction in a negative direction or positive direction?

While the example might sound simple to generate an answer for, in real-world ML projects, model interpretability is not so very simple due to the complex relationships between variables. It is seldom that one feature, in its isolation, impacts the prediction in any one direction. It is indeed a **combination** of features that impact the prediction outcome. Thus, it is even more difficult to explain to what extent the feature is impacting the prediction.

Linear models are generally easier to explain even to business users. This is because we obtain weights for various features as a result of model training with linear algorithms. These weights are direct indicators of how a feature is contributing to model prediction. After all, in a linear model, a prediction is the linear combination of model weights and features passed through a function. It should be noted that interaction between variables in the real world are not essentially linear. So, a linear model trying to model the underlying data that has non-linear relationships may not have good predictive power. So, while linear models' interpretability is great, it comes at the cost of model performance.

On the contrary, non-linear and non-parametric models tend to be very difficult to interpret. In most cases, it may not be apparent even to the person building the models as to what exactly are the factors driving the prediction and in which direction. This is simply because the prediction outcome is a complex non-linear combination of variables. It is also known that non-linear models in general are better performing models when compared to linear models. Therefore, there is a trade-off needed between model interpretability and model performance.

While the goal of model interpretability is difficult to achieve, there is some merit in accomplishing this goal. It helps with the retrospection of a model that is deemed as being a good performing model and confirming that no noise inadvertently existed in the data that is used for model building and testing. It is obvious that models with noise as features fail to generalize on unseen data. Model interpretability helps with making sure that no noise crept into the models as features. Also, it helps build trust with business users that are eventually consumers of the model output. After all, there is no point in building a model whose output is not going to be consumed!

Non-parametric, non-linear models are difficult to interpret, if not impossible. Specialized ML methods are now available to aid black box models interpretability. **Partial dependency plot (PDP)**, **Locally interpretable model-agnostic explanations (LIME)**, and **Shapley additive explanations (SHAP)** also known as Sharpley's are some of the popular methods used by practitioners to decipher the internals of a black box model.

Now that there is a good understanding of the various fundamental terms of ML, our next journey is to explore the details of the ML project pipeline. This journey discussed in the next section helps us understand the process of building an ML project, deploying it, and obtaining predictions to use in a business.

ML project pipeline

Most of the content available on ML projects, either through books, blogs, or tutorials, explains the mechanics of machine learning in such a way that the dataset available is split into training, validation, and test datasets. Models are built using training datasets, and model improvements through hyperparameter tuning are done iteratively through validation data. Once a model is built and improved upon to a point that is acceptable, it is tested for goodness with unseen test data and the results of testing are reported out. Most of the public content available, ends at this point.

In reality, the ML projects in a business situation go beyond this step. We may observe that if one stops at testing and reporting a built model performance, there is no real use of the model in terms of predicting about data that is coming up in future. We also need to realize that the idea of building a model is to be able to deploy the model in production and have the predictions based on new data so that businesses can take appropriate action.

In a nutshell, the model needs to be saved and reused. This also means that any new data on which predictions need to be made needs to be preprocessed in the same way as training data. This ensures that, the new data has the same number of columns and also the same types of columns as training data. This part of productionalization of the models built in the lab is totally ignored when being taught. This section covers an end-to-end pipeline for the models, right from data preprocessing to building the models in the lab to productionalization of the models.

ML pipelines describe the entire process from raw data acquisition to obtaining post processing of the prediction results on unseen data so as to make it available for some kind of action by business. It is possible that a pipeline may be depicted at a generalized level or described at a very granular level. This current section focuses on describing a generic pipeline that may be applied to any ML project. Figure 1.8 shows the various components of the ML project pipeline otherwise known as the **cross-industry standard process for data mining (CRISP-DM)**.

Business understanding

Once the problem description that is to be solved using ML is clearly articulated, the first step in the ML pipeline is to be able to ascertain if the problem is of relevance to business and if the goals of the project are laid out without any ambiguities. It may also be wise to check if the problem at hand is feasible to be solved as an ML problem. These are the various aspects typically covered during the business understanding step.

Understanding and sourcing the data

The next step is to identify all the sources of data that are relevant to the business problem at hand. Organizations will have one or more systems, such as HR management systems, accounting systems, and inventory management systems. Depending on the nature of the problem at hand, we may need to fetch the data from multiple sources. Also, data that is obtained through the data acquisition step need not always be structured as tabular data; it could be unstructured data, such as emails, recorded voice files, and images.

In corporate organizations of reasonable size, it may not be possible for an ML professional to work all alone on the task of fetching the data from the diverse range of systems. Tight collaboration with other professionals in the organization may be required to complete this step of the pipeline successfully:

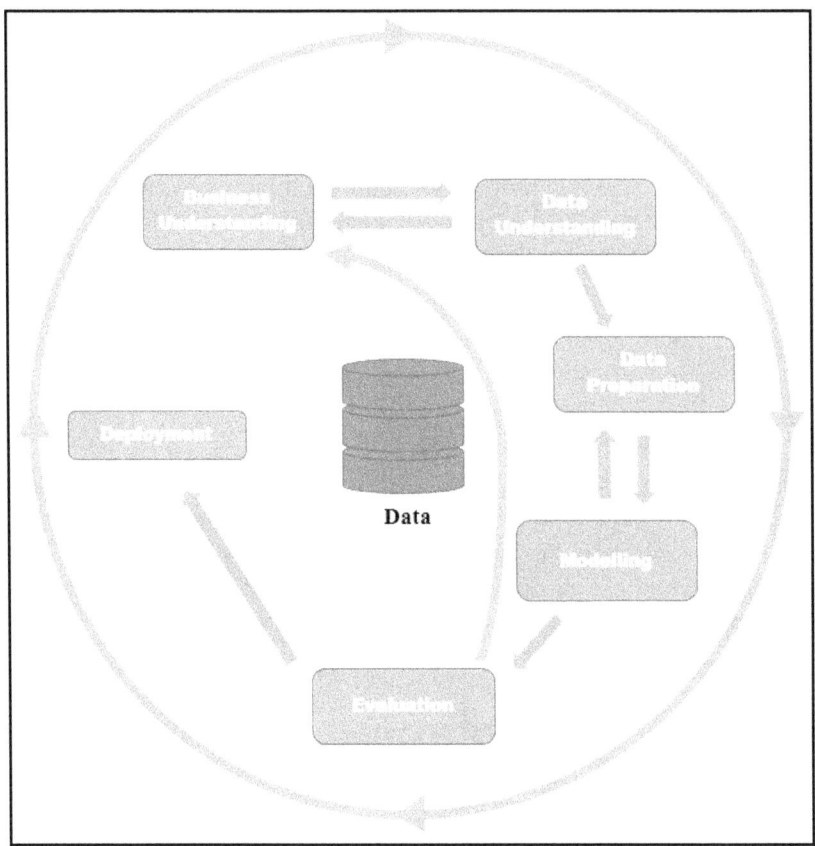

Preparing the data

Data preparation enables the creation of input data for ML algorithms to consume. Raw data that we get from data sources is often not very clean. Sometimes, the data cannot be readily fused into an ML algorithm to create a model. We need to ensure that the raw data is cleaned up and it is prepared in a format that is acceptable for the ML algorithm to take as input.

EDA is a substep in the process of creating the input data. It is a process of using visual and quantitative aids to understand the data without getting prejudice about the contents of the data. EDA gives us deeper insights into the data available at hand. It helps us to understand the required data preparation steps. Some of the insights that we could obtain during EDA are the existence of outliers in the data, missing values existence in the data, and the duplication of data. All of these problems are addressed during data cleansing which is another substep in data preparation. Several techniques may be adopted during data cleansing and the following mentioned are some of the popular techniques:

- Deleting records that are outliers
- Deleting redundant columns and irrelevant columns in data
- Missing values imputation—filling missing values with special value NA or a blank or median or mean or mode or with a regressed value
- Scaling the data
- Removing stop words such as *a*, *and*, and *how*, from unstructured text data
- Normalizing words in unstructured text documents with techniques such as stemming, and lemmatization
- Eliminating non-dictionary words in text data
- Spelling corrections on misspelled words in text documents
- Replacing non-recognizable domain-specific acronyms in the text with actual word descriptions
- Rotation, scaling, and translation of image data

Representing the unstructured data as vectors, providing labels for the records if the problem at hand needs to be dealt with by supervised learning, handling class imbalance problems in the data, feature engineering, transforming the data through transformation functions such as log transform, min-max transform, square root transform, and cube transform, are all part of the data preparation process.

The output of the data preparation step is tabular data that can be fit readily into an ML algorithm as input in order to create models.

An additional substep that is typically done in data preparation is to divide the dataset into training data, validation data, and test data. These various datasets are used for specific purposes in the model-building step.

Model building and evaluation

Once the data is ready and prior to the creation of the model, we need to pick and select the features from the list of features available. This can be accomplished through several off-the-shelf feature selection techniques. Some ML algorithms (for example, XGBoost) have feature selection inbuilt within the algorithm, therefore we need not explicitly perform feature selection prior to carrying out the modeling activity.

A suite of ML algorithms is available to try and create models on the data. Additionally, models may be created through ensembling techniques as well. One needs to pick the algorithm(s) and create models using training datasets, then tune the hyperparameters of the model using validation datasets. Finally, the model that is created can be tested using the test dataset. Issues, such as selecting the right metric to evaluate model performance, overfitting, underfitting, and acceptable performance thresholds all need to be taken care of in the model-building step itself. It may be noted that if we do not obtain acceptable performance on the model, it is required to go back to previous steps in order to get more data or to create additional features and then repeat the model-building step once again to check if the model performance improves. This may be done as many times as required until the desired level of performance is achieved by the model.

At the end of the modeling step, we might end up with a suite of models each having its own performance measurement on the unseen test data. The model that has the best performance can be selected for use in production.

Model deployment

The next step is to save the final model that can be used for the future. There are several ways to save the model as an object. Once saved, the model can be reloaded any time and it can be used for scoring the new data. Saving the model as an object is a trivial task and a number of libraries are available in Python and R to achieve it. As a result of saving the model, the model object gets persisted to the disk as a `.sav` file or a `.pkl` file or a `.pmml` object depending on the library used. The object can then be loaded into the memory to perform scoring on unseen data.

The final model that is selected for use in production can be deployed to score unseen data in the following two modes:

- **Batch mode**: Batch mode scoring is when one accumulates the unseen data to be scored in a file, then run a batch job (just another executable script) at a predetermined time to perform scoring. The job loads the model object from disk to the memory and runs on each of the records in the file that needs to be scored. The output is written to another file at a specified location as directed in the batch job script. It may be noted that the records to be scored should have the same number of columns as in the training data and the type of columns should also comply with the training data. It should be ensured that the number of levels in factors columns (nominal type data) should also match with that of the training data.

- **Real-time mode**: There are times where the business needs model scoring to happen on the fly. In this case, unlike the batch mode, data is not accumulated and we do not wait until the batch job runs for scoring. The expectation is that each record of the data, as and when it is available for scoring should be scored by the model. The result of the scoring is to be available to business users almost instantaneously. In this case, a model needs to be deployed as a web service that can serve any requests that come in. The record to be scored can be passed to the web service through a simple API call which, in turn, returns the scored result that can be consumed by the downstream applications. Again, the unscored data record that is passed in the API call should comply with the format of the training data records.

Yet another way of achieving near real-time results is by running the model job on micro batches of data several times a day and at very frequent intervals. The data gets accumulated between the intervals until a point where the model job kicks off. The model job scores and outputs the results for the data that is accumulated similar to batch mode. The business user gets to see the scored results as soon as the micro batch job finishes execution. The only difference between the micro batches processing versus the batch is that unlike the batch mode, business users need not wait until the next business day to get the scored results.

Though, the model building pipeline ends with successfully deploying the ML model and making it available for scoring, in real-world business situations, the job does not end here. Of course, the success parties flow in but there is a need to look again at the models post a certain point in time (maybe in a few months post the deployment). A model that is not maintained at regular intervals does not get very well used by businesses.

To avoid the models from perishing and not being used by business users, it is important to collect feedback on the performance of the model over a period of time and capture if any improvements need to be incorporated in the models. The unseen data does not come with labels, therefore comparing the model output with that of the desired output by business is a manual exercise. Collaborating with business users is a strong requirement to get feedback in this situation.

If there is a continued business need for the model and if the performance is not up to the mark on the unseen data that is scored with existing model, it needs to be investigated to identify the root cause(s). It may so happen that several things have changed in the data that is scored over a period of time when compared to the data on which model was initially trained. In which case, there is a strong need to recalibrate the model and it is essentially a jolly good idea to start once again!

Now that the book has covered all the essentials of ML and the project pipeline, the next topic to be covered is the learning paradigm, which will help us learn several ML algorithms.

Learning paradigm

Most learning paradigms that are followed in other books or content about ML follow a bottom-up approach. This approach starts from the bottom and works its way up. The approach first covers the theoretical elements, such as mathematical introductions to the algorithm, the evolution of the algorithm, variations, and parameters that the algorithm takes, and then delves into the application of the ML algorithm specific to a dataset. This may be a good approach; however, it takes longer really to see the results produced by the algorithm. It needs a lot of perseverance on the part of the learner to be patient and wait until the practical application of the algorithm is covered. In most cases, practitioners and certain classes of industry professionals working on ML are really interested in the practical aspects and they want to experience the power of the algorithm. For these people, the focus is not the theoretical foundations of the algorithm, but it is the practical application. The bottom-up approach works counterproductively in this case.

The learning paradigm followed in this book to teach several ML algorithms is opposite to the bottom-up approach. It rather follows a very practical top-down approach. The focus of this approach is **learning by coding**.

Each chapter of the book will focus on learning a particular class of ML algorithm. To start with, the chapter focuses on how to use the algorithm in various situations and how to obtain results from the algorithm in practice. Once the practical application of the algorithm is demonstrated using code and a dataset, gradually, the rest of the chapter unveils the theoretical details/concepts of the algorithms experienced in the chapter thus far. All theoretical details will be ensured to be covered only in as much detail as is required to understand the code and to apply the algorithm on any new datasets. This ensures that we get to learn the focused application areas of the algorithms rather than unwanted theoretical aspects that are of less importance applied in the ML world.

Datasets

Each chapter of the book describes an ML project that solves a business problem using an ML algorithm or a set of algorithms that we attempt to learn in that specific chapter. The projects considered are from different domains ranging from health care, to banking and finance, and to robots. The business problems solved in the chapters that follow are carefully selected to demonstrate solving a close-to-real-world business use case. The datasets used for the problems are popular open datasets. This will help us not only to explore the solutions covered in this book but also to examine other solutions that are developed for the problem. The problem solved in each of the chapters enriches our experience by applying ML algorithms in various domains and helps us get an understanding of how to solve the business problems in various domains successfully.

Summary

Well! We have learned so much together so far, and now we have reached the end of this chapter. In this chapter, we covered all that deals with ML, including the terminologies and the project pipeline. We also talked about the learning paradigm, the datasets, and all the topics and projects that will be covered in each chapter.

In the next chapter, we will start to work on ML ensembles to predict employee attrition.

15
Predicting Employee Attrition Using Ensemble Models

If you reviewed the recent machine learning competitions, one key observation I am sure you would make is that the recipes of all three winning entries in most of the competitions include very good feature engineering, along with well-tuned ensemble models. One conclusion I derive from this observation is that good feature engineering and building well-performing models are two areas that should be given equal emphasis in order to deliver successful machine learning solutions.

While feature engineering most times is something that is dependent on the creativity and domain expertise of the person building the model, building a well-performing model is something that can be achieved through a philosophy called **ensembling**. Machine learning practitioners often use ensembling techniques to beat the performance benchmarks yielded by even the best performing individual ML algorithm. In this chapter, we will learn about the following topics of this exciting area of ML:

- Philosophy behind ensembling
- Understanding the attrition problem and the dataset
- K-nearest neighbors model for benchmarking the performance
- Bagging
- Randomization with random forests
- Boosting
- Stacking

Philosophy behind ensembling

Ensembling, which is super-famous among ML practitioners, can be well-understood through a simple real-world, non-ML example.

Assume that you have applied for a job in a very reputable corporate organization and you have been called for an interview. It is unlikely you will be selected for a job just based on one interview with an interviewer. In most cases, you will go through multiple rounds of interviews with several interviewers or with a panel of interviewers. The expectation from the organization is that each of the interviewers is an expert on a particular area and that the interviewer has evaluated your fitness for the job based on your experience in the interviewers' area of expertise. Your selection for the job, of course, depends on consolidated feedback from all of the interviewers that talked to you. The organization deems that you will be more successful in the job as your selection is based on a consolidated decision made by multiple experts and not just based on one expert's decision, which may be prone to certain biases.

Now, when we talk about the consolidation of feedback from all the interviewers, the consolidation can happen through several methods:

- **Averaging**: Assume that your candidature for the job is based on you clearing a cut-off score in the interviews. Assume that you have met ten interviewers and each one of them have rated you on a maximum score of 10 which represents your experience as perceived by interviewers in his area of expertise. Now, your consolidated score is made by simply averaging all your scores given by all the interviewers.

- **Majority vote**: In this case, there is no actual score out of 10 which is provided by each of the interviewers. However, of the 10 interviewers, eight of them confirmed that you are a good fit for the position. Two interviewers said no to your candidature. You are selected for the job as the majority of the interviewers are happy with your interview performance.

- **Weighted average**: Let's consider that four of the interviewers are experts in some minor skills that are good to have for the job you applied for. These are not mandatory skills needed for the position. You are interviewed by all 10 interviewers and each one of them have given you a score out of 10. Similar to the averaging method, in the weighted averaging method as well, your interviews final score is obtained by averaging the scores given by all interviewers.

However, not all scores are treated equally to compute the final score. Each interview score is multiplied with a weight and a product is obtained. All the products thus obtained thereby are summed to obtain the final score. The weight for each interview is a function of the importance of the skill it tested in the candidate and the importance of that skill to do the job. It is obvious that a *good to have* skill for the job carries a lower weight when compared to a *must have* skill. The final score now inherently represents the proportion of mandatory skills that the candidate possesses and this has more influence on your selection.

Similar to the interviews analogy, ensembling in ML also produces models based on consolidated learning. The term **consolidated learning** essentially represents learning obtained through applying several ML algorithms or it is learning obtained from several data subsets that are part of a large dataset. Analogous to interviews, multiple models are learned from the application of ensembling technique. However, a final consolidation is arrived at regarding the prediction by means of applying one of the averaging, majority voting, or weighted averaging techniques on individual predictions made by each of the individual models. The models created from the application of an ensembling technique along with the prediction consolidation technique is typically termed as an **ensemble**.

Each ML algorithm is special and has a unique way to model the underlying training data. For example, a k-nearest neighbors algorithm learns by computing distances between the elements in a dataset; naive Bayes learns by computing the probabilities of each attribute in the data belonging to a particular class. Multiple models may be created using different ML algorithms and predictions can be done by combining predictions of several ML algorithms. Similarly, when a dataset is partitioned to create subsets and if multiple models are trained using an algorithm each focusing on one dataset, each model is very focused and it is specialized in learning the characteristics of the subset of data it is trained on. In both cases, with models based on multiple algorithms and multiple subsets of data, when we combine the predictions of multiple models through consolidation, we get better predictions as we leverage multiple strengths that each model in an ensemble carry. This, otherwise, is not obtained when using a single model for predictions.

The crux of ensembling is that better predictions are obtained when we combine the predictions of multiple models than just relying on one model for prediction. This is no different from the management philosophy that together we do better, which is otherwise termed as **synergy**!

Now that we understand the core philosophy behind ensembling, we are now ready to explore the different types of ensembling techniques. However, we will learn the ensembling techniques by implementing them in a project to predict the attrition of employees. As we already know, prior to building any ML project, it is very important to have a deep understanding of the problem and the data. Therefore, in the next section, we first focus on understanding the attrition problem at hand, then we study the dataset associated with the problem, and lastly, we understand the properties of the dataset through exploratory data analysis (EDA). The key insights we obtain in this section come from a one-time exercise and will hold good for all the ensembling techniques we will apply in the later sections.

Getting started

To get started with this section, you will have to download the `WA_Fn-UseC_-HR-Employee-Attrition.csv` dataset from this GitHub link `https://github.com/PacktPublishing/Advanced-Machine-Learning-with-R/blob/master/Chapter15/WA_Fn-UseC_-HR-Employee-Attrition.csv`, for the code in this chapter.

Understanding the attrition problem and the dataset

HR analytics helps with interpreting organizational data. It finds out the people-related trends in the data and helps the HR department take the appropriate steps to keep the organization running smoothly and profitably. Attrition in a corporate setup is one of the complex challenges that the people managers and HR personnel have to deal with. Interestingly, machine learning models can be deployed to predict potential attrition cases, thereby helping the appropriate HR personnel or people managers take the necessary steps to retain the employee.

In this chapter, we are going to build ML ensembles that will predict such potential cases of attrition. The job attrition dataset used for the project is a fictional dataset created by data scientists at IBM. The `rsample` library incorporates this dataset and we can make use of this dataset directly from the library.

It is a small dataset that has 1,470 records of 31 attributes. The description of the dataset can be obtained with the following code:

```
setwd("~/Desktop/chapter 15")
library(rsample)
data(attrition)
str(attrition)
mydata<-attrition
```

This will result in the following output:

```
'data.frame':1470 obs. of  31 variables:
 $ Age                     : int   41 49 37 33 27 32 59 30 38 36 ...
 $ Attrition               : Factor w/ 2 levels "No","Yes": 2 1 2 1 1 1 1 1
1 1 ....
 $ BusinessTravel          : Factor w/ 3 levels "Non-
Travel","Travel_Frequently",..: 3 2 3 2 3 2 3 3 2 3 ...
 $ DailyRate               : int   1102 279 1373 1392 591 1005 1324 1358 216
1299 ...
 $ Department              : Factor w/ 3 levels "Human_Resources",..: 3 2 2
2 2 2 2 2 2 2 ...
 $ DistanceFromHome        : int   1 8 2 3 2 2 3 24 23 27 ...
 $ Education               : Ord.factor w/ 5 levels "Below_College"<..: 2 1
2 4 1 2 3 1 3 3 ...
 $ EducationField          : Factor w/ 6 levels "Human_Resources",..: 2 2 5
2 4 2 4 2 2 4 ...
 $ EnvironmentSatisfaction : Ord.factor w/ 4 levels "Low"<"Medium"<..: 2 3
4 4 1 4 3 4 4 3 ...
 $ Gender                  : Factor w/ 2 levels "Female","Male": 1 2 2 1 2
2 1 2 2 2 ...
 $ HourlyRate              : int   94 61 92 56 40 79 81 67 44 94 ...
 $ JobInvolvement          : Ord.factor w/ 4 levels "Low"<"Medium"<..: 3 2
2 3 3 3 4 3 2 3 ...
 $ JobLevel                : int   2 2 1 1 1 1 1 1 3 2 ...
 $ JobRole                 : Factor w/ 9 levels
"Healthcare_Representative",..: 8 7 3 7 3 3 3 3 5 1 ...
 $ JobSatisfaction         : Ord.factor w/ 4 levels "Low"<"Medium"<..: 4 2
3 3 2 4 1 3 3 3 ...
 $ MaritalStatus           : Factor w/ 3 levels "Divorced","Married",..: 3
2 3 2 2 3 2 1 3 2 ...
 $ MonthlyIncome           : int   5993 5130 2090 2909 3468 3068 2670 2693
9526 5237 ...
 $ MonthlyRate             : int   19479 24907 2396 23159 16632 11864 9964
13335 8787 16577 ...
 $ NumCompaniesWorked      : int   8 1 6 1 9 0 4 1 0 6 ...
 $ OverTime                : Factor w/ 2 levels "No","Yes": 2 1 2 2 1 1 2 1
1 1 ...
 $ PercentSalaryHike       : int   11 23 15 11 12 13 20 22 21 13 ...
```

```
 $ PerformanceRating     : Ord.factor w/ 4 levels
"Low"<"Good"<"Excellent"<..: 3 4 3 3 3 3 4 4 4 3 ...
 $ RelationshipSatisfaction: Ord.factor w/ 4 levels "Low"<"Medium"<..: 1 4
2 3 4 3 1 2 2 2 ...
 $ StockOptionLevel       : int  0 1 0 0 1 0 3 1 0 2 ...
 $ TotalWorkingYears      : int  8 10 7 8 6 8 12 1 10 17 ...
 $ TrainingTimesLastYear  : int  0 3 3 3 3 2 3 2 2 3 ...
 $ WorkLifeBalance        : Ord.factor w/ 4 levels
"Bad"<"Good"<"Better"<..: 1 3 3 3 3 2 2 3 3 2 ...
 $ YearsAtCompany         : int  6 10 0 8 2 7 1 1 9 7 ...
 $ YearsInCurrentRole     : int  4 7 0 7 2 7 0 0 7 7 ...
 $ YearsSinceLastPromotion : int  0 1 0 3 2 3 0 0 1 7 ...
 $ YearsWithCurrManager   : int  5 7 0 0 2 6 0 0 8 7 ...
```

To view the `Attrition` target variable in the dataset run the following code:

```
table(mydata$Attrition)
```

This will result in the following output:

```
  No   Yes
1233   237
```

Out of the 1,470 observations in the dataset, we have 1,233 samples (83.87%) that are non-attrition cases and 237 attrition cases (16.12%). Clearly, we are dealing with a *class imbalance* dataset.

We will now visualize the highly correlated variables in the data through the `corrplot` library using the following code:

```
# considering only the numeric variables in the dataset
numeric_mydata <-
mydata[,c(1,4,6,7,10,11,13,14,15,17,19,20,21,24,25,26,28:35)]
# converting the target variable "yes" or "no" values into numeric
# it defaults to 1 and 2 however converting it into 0 and 1 to be
consistent
numeric_Attrition = as.numeric(mydata$Attrition)- 1
# create a new data frame with numeric columns and numeric target
numeric_mydata = cbind(numeric_mydata, numeric_Attrition)
# loading the required library
library(corrplot)
# creating correlation plot
M <- cor(numeric_mydata)
corrplot(M, method="circle")
```

This will result in the following output:

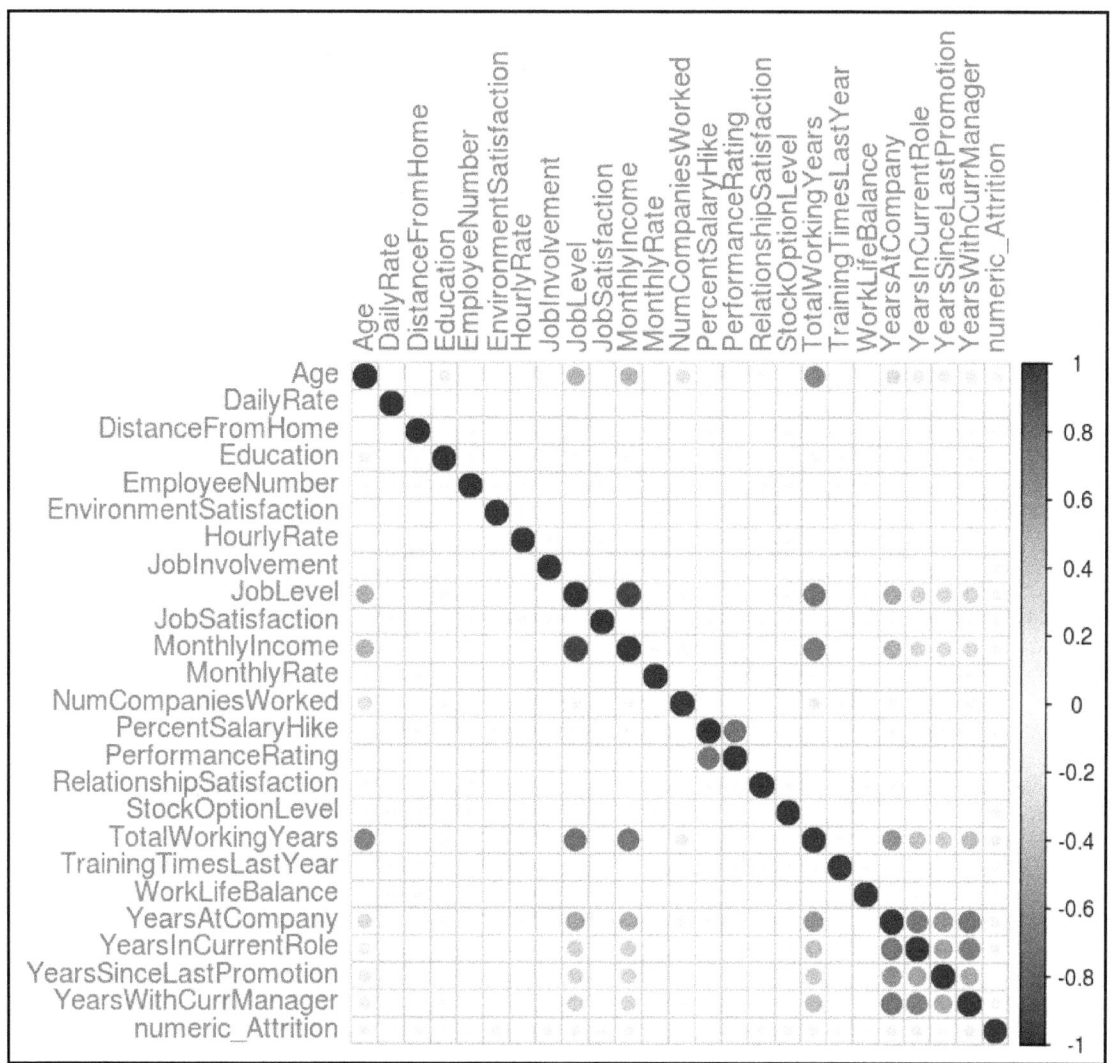

In the preceding screenshot, it may be observed that darker and larger blues dot in the cells indicate the existence of a strong correlation between the variables in the corresponding rows and columns that form the cell. High correlation between the independent variables indicates the existence of redundant features in the data. The problem of the existence of highly correlated features in the data is termed as **multicollinearity**. If we were to fit a regression model, then it is required that we treat the highly correlated variables from the data through some techniques such as removing the redundant features or by applying principal component analysis or partial least squares regression, which intuitively cuts down the redundant features.

We infer from the output that the following variables are highly correlated and the person building the model needs to take care of these variables if we are to build a regression-based model:

```
JobLevel-MonthlyIncome; JobLevel-TotalWorkingYears; MonthlyIncome-
TotalWorkingYears; PercentSalaryHike-PerformanceRating; YearsAtCompany-
YearsInCurrentRole; YearsAtCompany-
YearsWithCurrManager; YearsWithCurrManager-YearsInCurrentRole
```

Now, plot the various independent variables with the dependent `Attrition` variable in order to understand the influence of the independent variable on the target:

```
### Overtime vs Attiriton
l <- ggplot(mydata, aes(OverTime, fill = Attrition))
l <- l + geom_histogram(stat="count")

tapply(as.numeric(mydata$Attrition) - 1 ,mydata$OverTime,mean)

No Yes
0.104364326375712 0.305288461538462
```

Let's run the following command to get a graph view:

```
print(l)
```

The preceding command generates the following output:

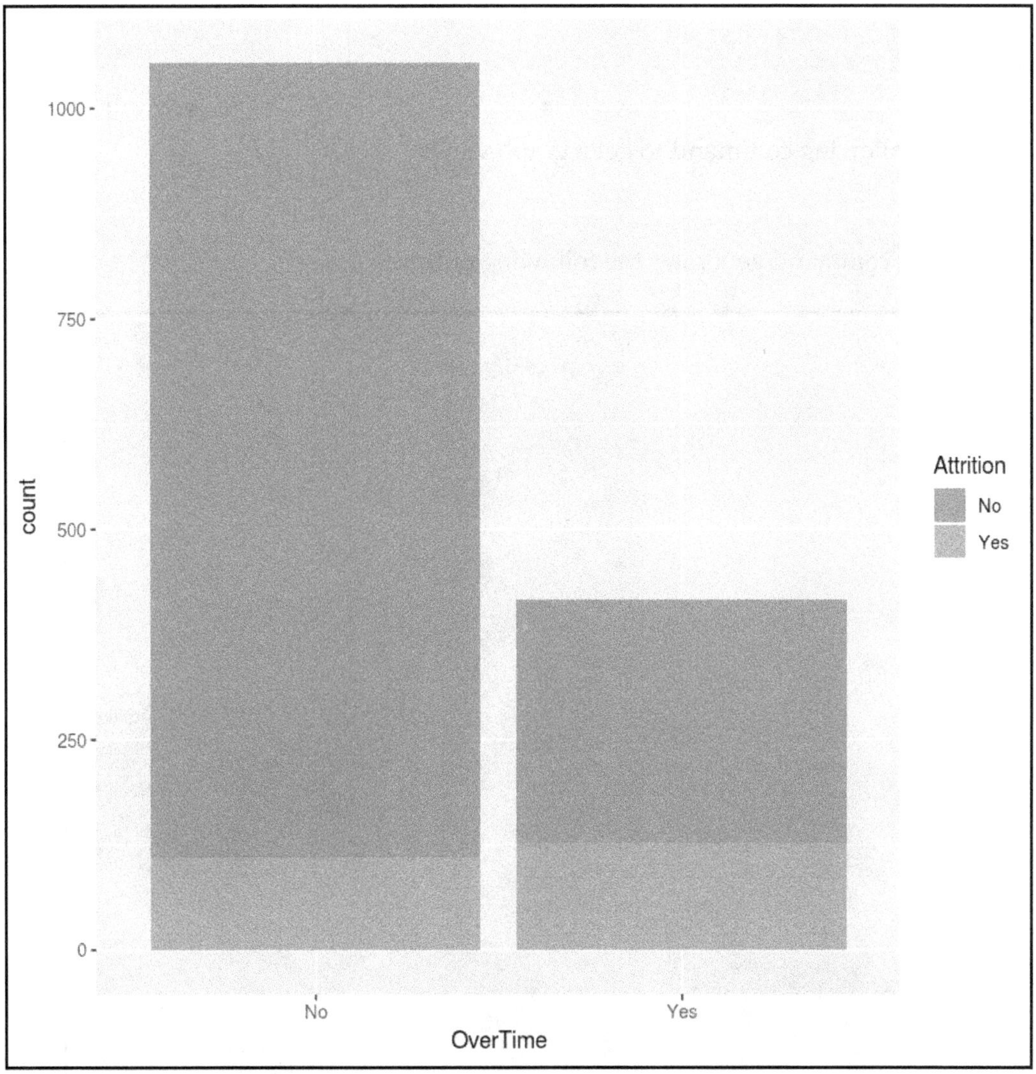

In the preceding output, it can be observed that employees that work overtime are more prone to attrition when compared to the ones that do not work overtime:

Let's calculate the attrition of the employees by executing the following commands:

```
### MaritalStatus vs Attiriton
l <- ggplot(mydata, aes(MaritalStatus,fill = Attrition))
```

```
l <- l + geom_histogram(stat="count")

tapply(as.numeric(mydata$Attrition) - 1 ,mydata$MaritalStatus,mean)
Divorced 0.100917431192661
Married 0.12481426448737
Single 0.25531914893617
```

Let's run the following command to get a graph view:

```
print(l)
```

The preceding command generates the following output:

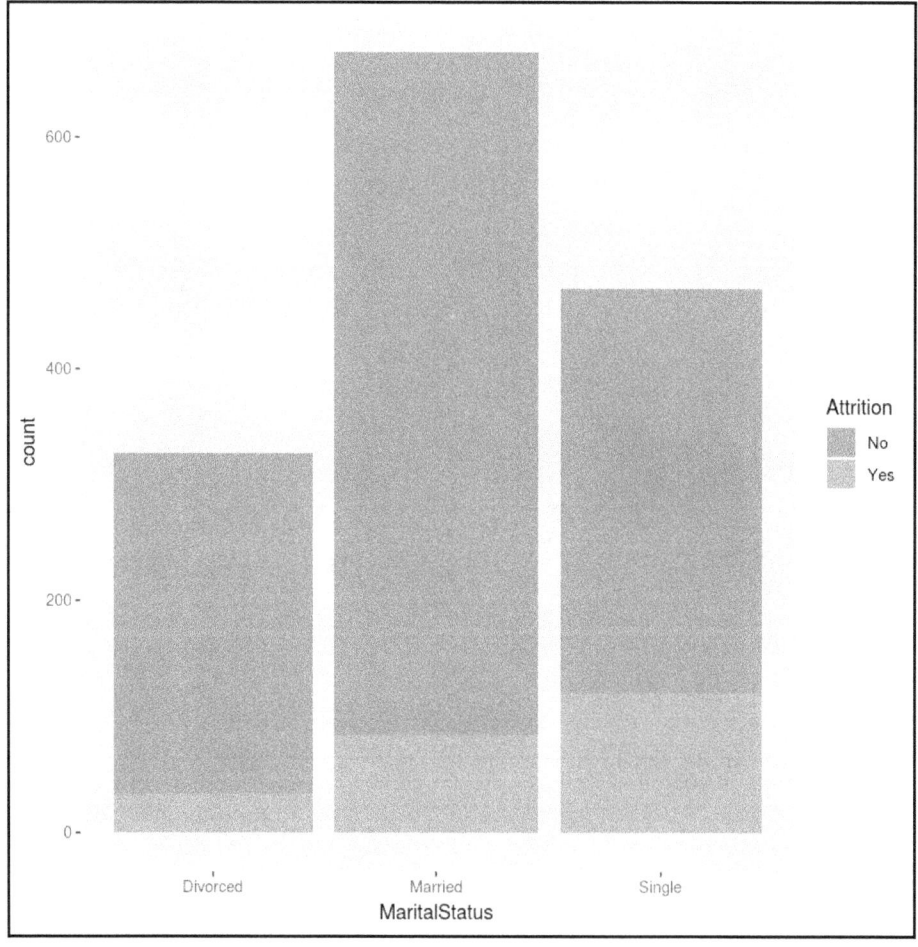

In the preceding output, it can be observed that employees that are single have more attrition:

```
###JobRole vs Attrition
l <- ggplot(mydata, aes(JobRole,fill = Attrition))
l <- l + geom_histogram(stat="count")

tapply(as.numeric(mydata$Attrition) - 1 ,mydata$JobRole,mean)

Healthcare Representative      Human Resources
              0.06870229      0.23076923
     Laboratory Technician     Manager
              0.23938224      0.04901961
     Manufacturing Director    Research Director
              0.06896552      0.02500000
         Research Scientist    Sales Executive
              0.16095890      0.17484663
       Sales Representative
              0.39759036
mean(as.numeric(mydata$Attrition) - 1)
[1] 0.161224489795918
```

Execute the following command to get a graphical representation for the same:

```
print(l)
```

Take a look at the following output generated by running the preceding command:

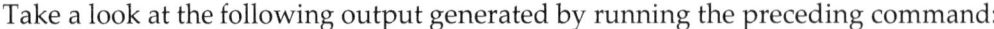

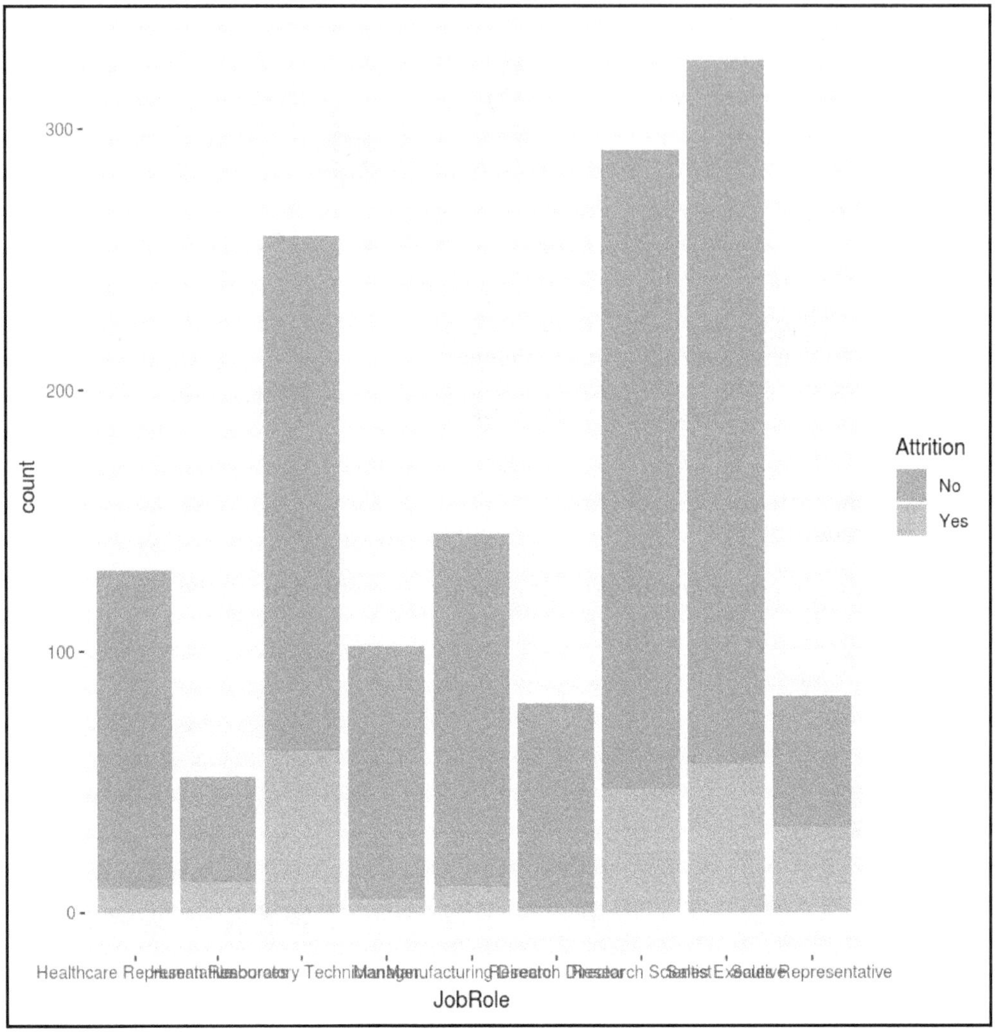

In the preceding output, it can be observed that the lab technicians, sales representatives, and employees working in human resources job roles have more attrition than other organizational roles.

Let's execute the following commands to check with the impact of the gender of an employee over attribution:

```
###Gender vs Attrition
l <- ggplot(mydata, aes(Gender,fill = Attrition))
```

```
l <- l + geom_histogram(stat="count")

tapply(as.numeric(mydata$Attrition) - 1 ,mydata$Gender,mean)

Female 0.147959183673469
Male 0.170068027210884
```

Run the following command to get a graphical representation for the same:

```
print(l)
```

This will result in the following output:

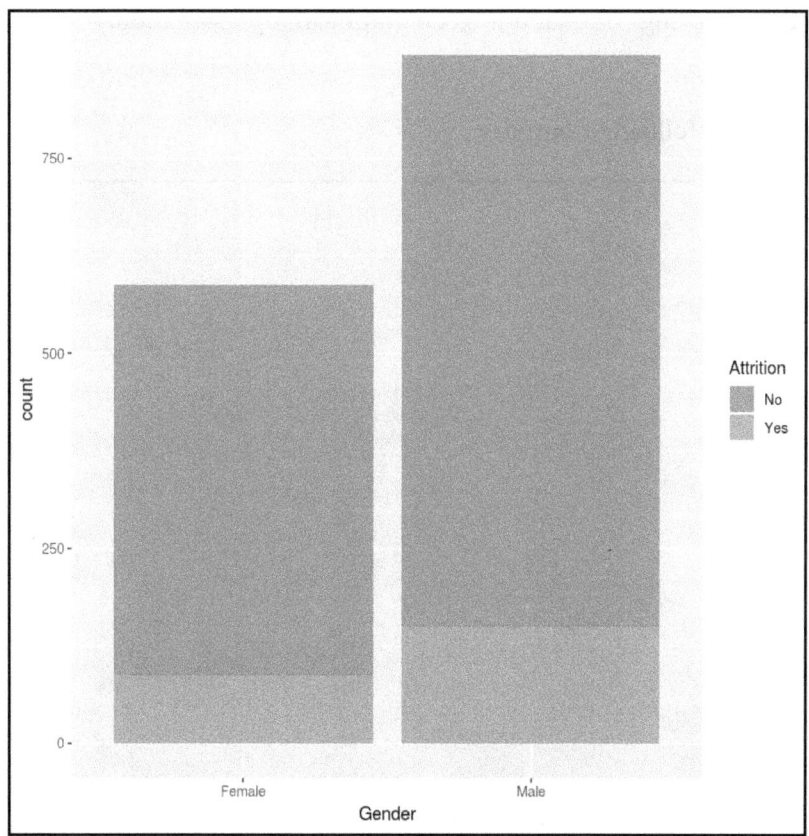

In the preceding output, you can see that the gender of an employee does not have any impact on attrition, in other words attrition is observed to be the same across all genders.

Let's calculate the attribute of the employees from various fields by executing the following:

```
###EducationField vs Attrition el <- ggplot(mydata, aes(EducationField,fill
= Attrition))
l <- l + geom_histogram(stat="count")

tapply(as.numeric(mydata$Attrition) - 1 ,mydata$EducationField,mean)

Human Resources     Life Sciences     Marketing
      0.2592593       0.1468647        0.2201258
         Medical   Other Technical   Degree
      0.1357759       0.1341463        0.2424242
```

Let's execute the following command to get a graphical representation:

```
print(l)
```

This will result in the following output:

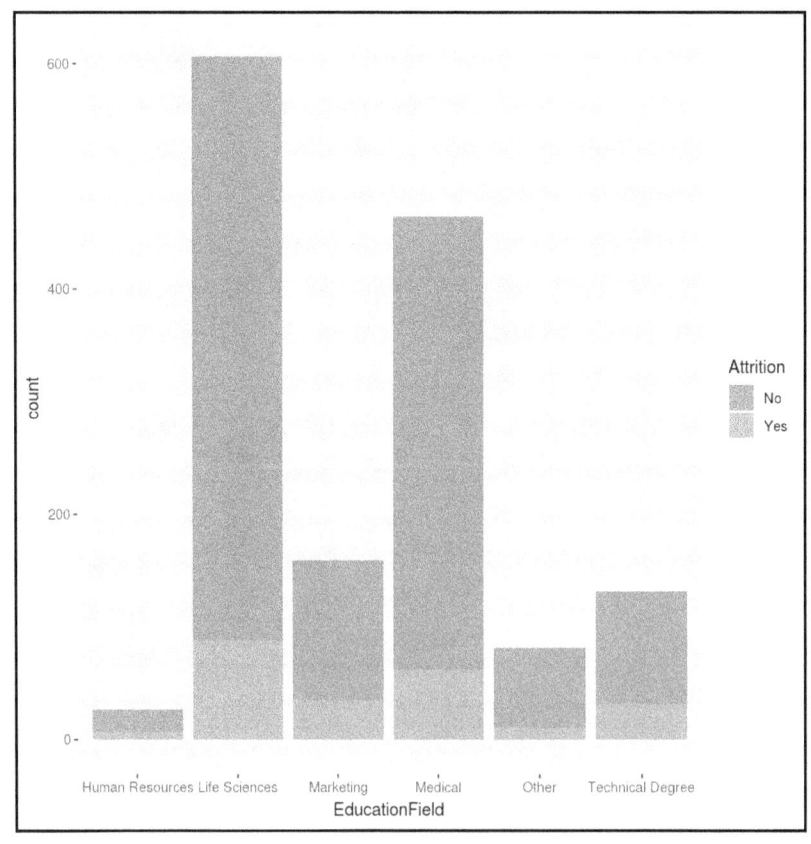

Looking at the preceding graph, we can conclude that employees with a technical degree or a degree in human resources are observed to have more attrition. Take a look at the following code:

```
###Department vs Attrition
l <- ggplot(mydata, aes(Department,fill = Attrition))
l <- l + geom_histogram(stat="count")

tapply(as.numeric(mydata$Attrition) - 1 ,mydata$Department,mean)
Human Resources   Research & Development   Sales
    0.1904762         0.1383975          0.2062780
```

Let's execute the following command to check with the attribution of various departments:

```
print(l)
```

This will result in the following output:

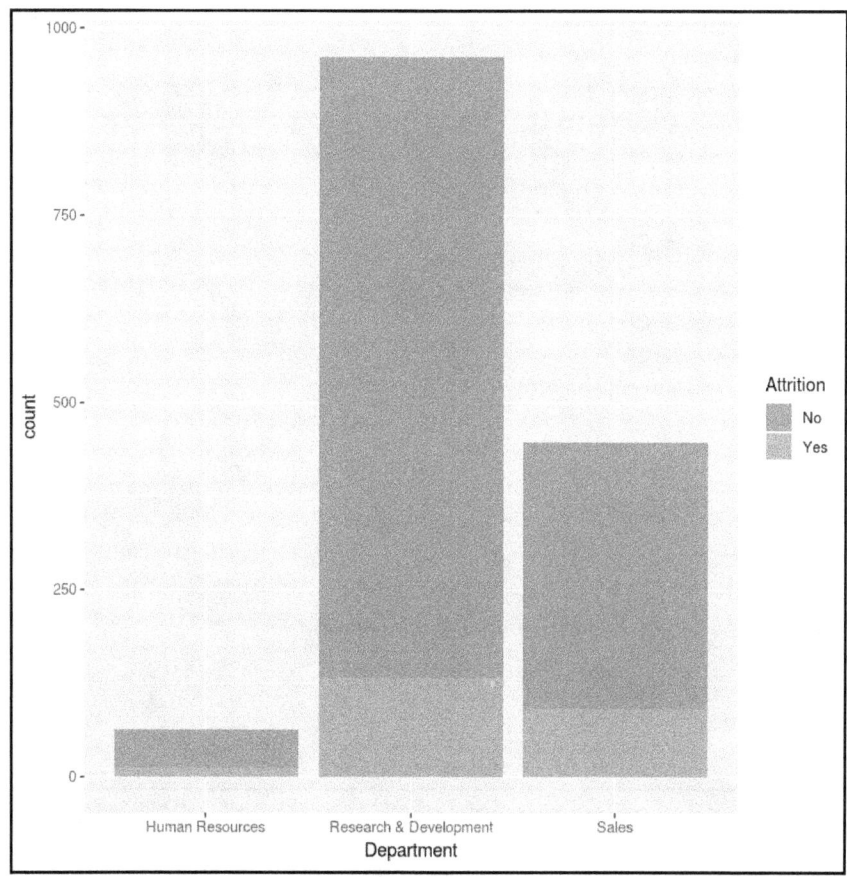

Looking at the preceding graph, we can conclude that the R and D department has less attrition compared to the sales and HR departments. Take a look at the following code:

```
###BusinessTravel vs Attrition
l <- ggplot(mydata, aes(BusinessTravel,fill = Attrition))
l <- l + geom_histogram(stat="count")

tapply(as.numeric(mydata$Attrition) - 1 ,mydata$BusinessTravel,mean)
  Non-Travel    Travel_Frequently    Travel_Rarely
   0.0800000       0.2490975          0.1495686
```

Execute the following command to get a graphical representation for the same:

```
print(l)
```

This will result in the following output:

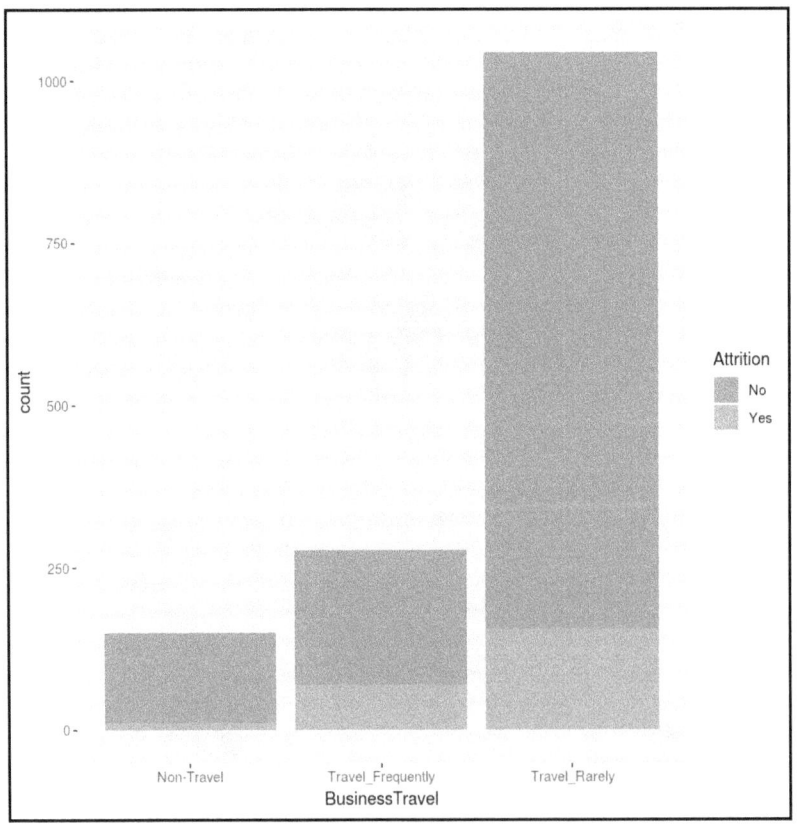

Looking at the preceding graph, we can conclude that employees with frequent travels are prone to more attrition compared to employees with a non-travel status or the ones that rarely travel.

Let's calculate the overtime of the employees by executing the following commands:

```
### x=Overtime, y= Age, z = MaritalStatus , t = Attrition
ggplot(mydata, aes(OverTime, Age)) +
  facet_grid(.~MaritalStatus) +
  geom_jitter(aes(color = Attrition),alpha = 0.4) +
  ggtitle("x=Overtime, y= Age, z = MaritalStatus , t = Attrition") +
  theme_light()
```

This will result in the following output:

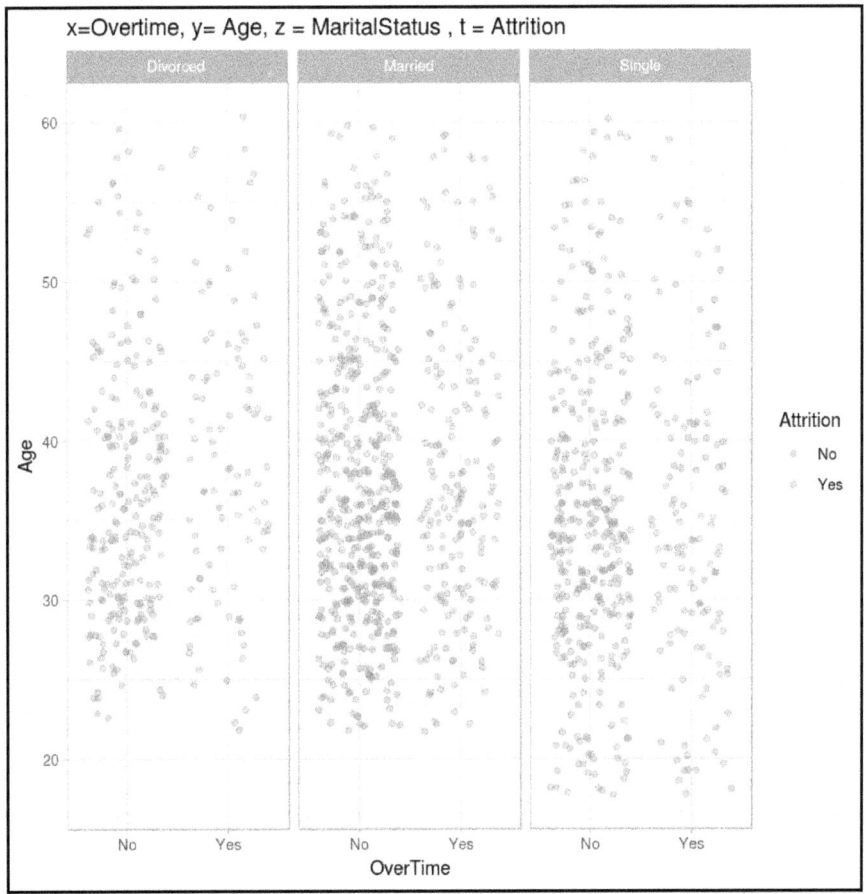

Looking at the preceding graph, we can conclude that it can be observed that employees that are young (age < 35) and are single, but work overtime, are more prone to attrition:

```
### MonthlyIncome vs. Age, by  color = Attrition
ggplot(mydata, aes(MonthlyIncome, Age, color = Attrition)) +
  geom_jitter() +
  ggtitle("MonthlyIncome vs. Age, by  color = Attrition ") +
  theme_light()
```

This will result in the following output:

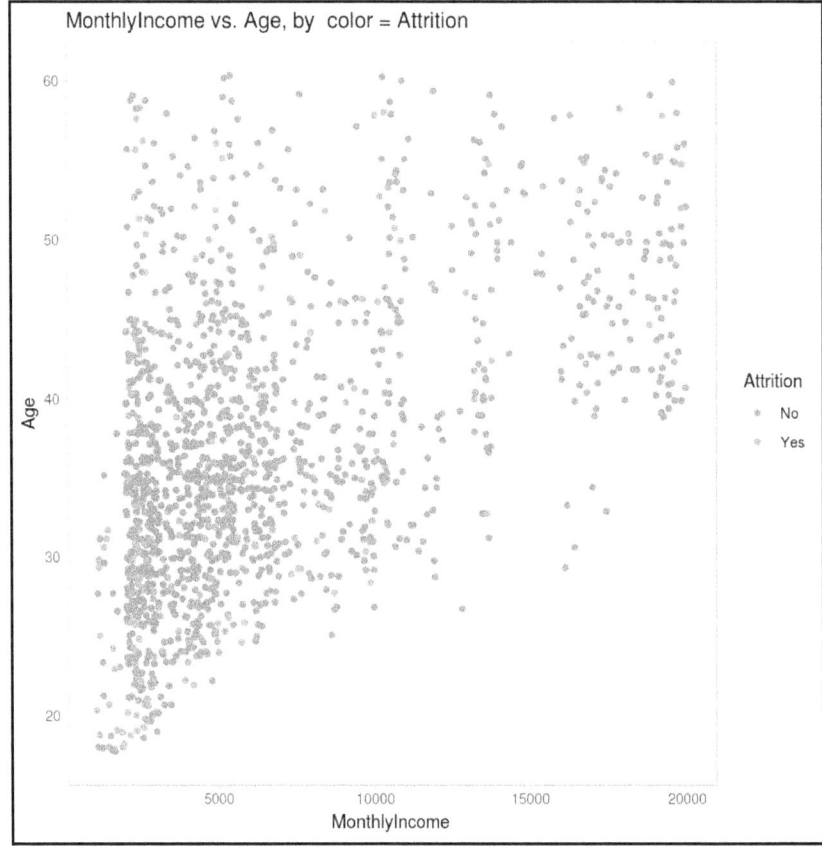

Looking at the preceding graph, we can conclude that attrition is higher in employees that are young (age < 30) and most attrition is observed with employees that earn less than $7,500.

Although we have learned a number of important details about the data at hand, there is actually so much more to explore and learn. However, so as to move to the next step, we stop here at this EDA step. It should be noted that, in a real-world situation, data would not be so very clean as we see in this attrition dataset. For example, we would have missing values in the data; in which case, we would do missing values imputation. Fortunately, we have an impeccable dataset that is ready for us to create models without having to do any data cleansing or additional preprocessing.

K-nearest neighbors model for benchmarking the performance

In this section, we will implement the **k-nearest neighbors** (**KNN**) algorithm to build a model on our IBM attrition dataset. Of course, we are already aware from EDA that we have a class imbalance problem in the dataset at hand. However, we will not be treating the dataset for class imbalance for now as this is an entire area on its own and several techniques are available in this area and therefore out of scope for the ML ensembling topic covered in this chapter. We will, for now, consider the dataset as is and build ML models. Also, for class imbalance datasets, Kappa or precision and recall or the area under the curve of the receiver operating characteristic (AUROC) are the appropriate metrics to use. However, for simplicity, we will use *accuracy* as a performance metric. We will adapt 10-fold cross validation repeated 10 times to avail the model performance measurement. Let's now build our attrition prediction model with the KNN algorithm as follows:

```
# Load the necessary libraries
# doMC is a library that enables R to use multiple cores available on the
sysem thereby supporting multiprocessing.
library(doMC)
# registerDoMC command instructs R to use the specified number of cores to
execute the code. In this case, we ask R to use 4 cores available on the
system
registerDoMC(cores=4)
# caret library has the ml algorithms and other routines such as cross
validation etc.
library(caret)
# Setting the working directory where the dataset is located
setwd("~/Desktop/chapter 15")
# Reading the csv file into R variable called mydata
mydata <- read.csv("WA_Fn-UseC_-HR-Employee-Attrition.csv")
#Removing the non-discriminatory features (as identified during EDA) from
the dataset
mydata$EmployeeNumber=mydata$Over18=mydata$EmployeeCount=mydata$StandardHou
rs = NULL
```

```
# setting the seed prior to model building ensures reproducibility of the
results obtained
set.seed(10000)
# setting the train control parameters specifying gold standard 10 fold
cross validation  repeated 10 times
fitControl = trainControl(method="repeatedcv", number=10,repeats=10)
###creating a model on the data. Observe that we specified Attrition as the
target and that model should learn from rest of the variables. We specified
mydata as the dataset to learn. We pass the train control parameters and
specify that knn algorithm need to be used to build the model. K can be of
any length - we specified 20 as parameter which means the train command
will search through 20 different random k values and finally retains the
model that produces the best performance measurements. The final model is
stored as caretmodel
caretmodel = train(Attrition~., data=mydata, trControl=fitControl, method =
"knn", tuneLength = 20)
# We output the model object to the console
caretmodel
```

This will result in the following output:

```
k-Nearest Neighbors
1470 samples
  30 predictors
   2 classes: 'No', 'Yes'
No pre-processing
Resampling: Cross-Validated (10 fold, repeated 10 times)
Summary of sample sizes: 1323, 1323, 1324, 1323, 1324, 1322, ...
Resampling results across tuning parameters:
  k    Accuracy   Kappa
   5   0.8216447  0.0902934591
   7   0.8349033  0.0929511324
   9   0.8374198  0.0752842114
  11   0.8410920  0.0687849122
  13   0.8406861  0.0459679081
  15   0.8406875  0.0337742424
  17   0.8400748  0.0315670261
  19   0.8402770  0.0245499585
  21   0.8398721  0.0143638854
  23   0.8393945  0.0084393721
  25   0.8391891  0.0063246624
  27   0.8389174  0.0013913143
  29   0.8388503  0.0007113939
  31   0.8387818  0.0000000000
  33   0.8387818  0.0000000000
  35   0.8387818  0.0000000000
  37   0.8387818  0.0000000000
  39   0.8387818  0.0000000000
```

```
41   0.8387818   0.0000000000
43   0.8387818   0.0000000000
Accuracy was used to select the optimal model using the largest value.
The final value used for the model was k = 11.
```

We can see from the model output that the best performing model is when k = 11 and we obtained an accuracy of 84% with this k value. In the rest of the chapter, while experimenting with several ensembling techniques, we will check if this 84% accuracy obtained from KNN will get beaten at all.

In a realistic project-building situation, just identifying the best hyperparameters is not enough. A model needs to be trained on a full dataset with the best hyperparameters and the model needs to be saved for future use. We will review these steps in the rest of this section.

In this case, the caretmodel object already has the trained model with k = 11, therefore we do not attempt to retrain the model with the best hyperparameter. To check the final model, you can query the model object with the code:

```
caretmodel$finalModel
```

This will result in the following output:

```
11-nearest neighbor model
Training set outcome distribution:
  No  Yes
1233  237
```

The next step is to save your best models to a file so that we can load them up later and make predictions on unseen data. A model can be saved to a local directory using the saveRDS R command:

```
# save the model to disk
saveRDS(caretmodel, "production_model.rds")
```

In this case, the caretmodel is saved as production_model.rds in the working directory. The model is now serialized as a file that can be loaded anytime and it can be used to score unseen data. Loading and scoring can be achieved through the following R code:

```
# Set the working directory to the directory where the saved .rds file is
located
setwd("~/Desktop/chapter 15")
#Load the model
loaded_model <- readRDS("production_model.rds")
```

```
#Using the loaded model to make predictions on unseen data
final_predictions <- predict(loaded_model, unseen_data)
```

 Please note that `unseen_data` needs to be read prior to scoring through the `predict` command.

The part of the code where the final model is trained on the entire dataset, saving the model, reloading it from the file whenever required and scoring the unseen data collectively, is termed as building an ML productionalization pipeline. This pipeline remains the same for all ML models irrespective of the fact that the model is built using one single algorithm or using an ensembling technique. Therefore, in the later sections when we implement the various ensembling techniques, we will not cover the productionalization pipeline but just stop at obtaining the performance measurement through 10-fold cross validation repeated 10 times.

Bagging

Bootstrap aggregation or **bagging** is the earliest ensemble technique adopted widely by the ML-practicing community. Bagging involves creating multiple different models from a single dataset. It is important to understand an important statistical technique called bootstrapping in order to get an understanding of bagging.

Bootstrapping involves multiple random subsets of a dataset being created. It is possible that the same data sample gets picked up in multiple subsets and this is termed as **bootstrapping with replacement**. The advantage with this approach is that the standard error in estimating a quantity that occurs due to the use of whole dataset. This technique can be better explained with an example.

Assume you have a small dataset of 1,000 samples. Based on the samples, you are asked to compute the average of the population that the sample represents. Now, a direct way of doing it is through the following formula:

$$Average = sum(all\ 1000\ samples)/1000$$

As this is a small sample, we may have an error in estimating the population average. This error can be reduced by adapting bootstrap sampling with replacement. In the technique, we create 10 subsets of the dataset where each dataset has 100 items in it. A data item may be randomly represented multiple times in a subset and there is no restriction on the number of times an item can be represented within a data subset as well as across the subsets. Now, we take the average of samples in each data subset, therefore, we end up with 10 different averages. Using all these collected averages, we estimate the average of the population with the following formula:

$$Average = sum(averages\ obtained\ from\ each\ of\ the\ 10\ sub\ datasets)/10$$

Now, we have a better estimate of the average as we have extrapolated the small sample to randomly generate multiple samples that are representative of the original population.

In bagging, the actual training dataset is split into multiple bags through bootstrap sampling with replacement. Assuming that we ended up with n bags, when an ML algorithm is applied on each of these bags, we obtain n different models. Each model is focused on one bag. When it comes to making predictions on new unseen data, each of these n models makes independent predictions on the data. A final prediction for an observation is arrived at by combining the predictions of the observation of all the n models. In case of classification, voting is adopted and the majority is considered as the final prediction. For regression, the average of predictions from all models is considered as the final prediction.

Decision-tree-based algorithms, such as **classification and regression trees** (**CART**), are unstable learners. The reason is that a small change in the training dataset heavily impacts the model created. Model change essentially means that the predictions also change. Bagging is a very effective technique to handle the high sensitivity to data changes. As we can build multiple decision tree models on subsets of a dataset and then arrive at a final prediction based on predictions from each of the models, the effect of changes in data gets nullified or not experienced very significantly.

One intuitive problem experienced with building multiple models on subsets of data is **overfitting**. However, this is overcome by growing deep trees without applying any pruning on the nodes.

A downside with bagging is that it takes longer to build the models when compared to building a model with a stand-alone ML algorithm. This is obvious because multiple models gets built in bagging, as opposed to one single model, and it takes time to build these multiple models.

Now, let's implement the R code to achieve a bagging ensemble and compare the performance obtained with that of the performance obtained from KNN. We will then explore the working mechanics of bagging methodology.

The `caret` library provides a framework to implement bagging with any stand-alone ML algorithm. `ldaBag`, `plsBag`, `nbBag`, `treeBag`, `ctreeBag`, `svmBag`, and `nnetBag` are some of the example methods provided in caret. In this section, we will implement bagging with three different `caret` methods such as `treebag`, `svmbag`, and `nbbag`.

Bagged classification and regression trees (treeBag) implementation

To begin, load the essential libraries and register the number of cores for parallel processing:

```
library(doMC)
registerDoMC(cores = 4)
library(caret)
#setting the random seed for replication
set.seed(1234)
# setting the working directory where the data is located
setwd("~/Desktop/chapter 15")
# reading the data
mydata <- read.csv("WA_Fn-UseC_-HR-Employee-Attrition.csv")
#removing the non-discriminatory features identified during EDA
mydata$EmployeeNumber=mydata$Over18=mydata$EmployeeCount=mydata$StandardHou
rs = NULL
#setting up cross-validation
cvcontrol <- trainControl(method="repeatedcv", repeats=10, number = 10,
allowParallel=TRUE)
# model creation with treebag , observe that the number of bags is set as
10
train.bagg <- train(Attrition ~ ., data=mydata, method="treebag",B=10,
trControl=cvcontrol, importance=TRUE)
train.bagg
```

This will result in the following output:

```
Bagged CART
1470 samples
  30 predictors
   2 classes: 'No', 'Yes'
No pre-processing
Resampling: Cross-Validated (10 fold, repeated 10 times)
```

```
Summary of sample sizes: 1324, 1323, 1323, 1322, 1323, 1322, ...
Resampling results:
  Accuracy  Kappa
  0.854478  0.2971994
```

We can see that we achieved a better accuracy of 85.4% compared to 84% accuracy that was obtained with the KNN algorithm.

Support vector machine bagging (SVMBag) implementation

The steps of loading the libraries, registering multiprocessing, setting a working directory, reading data from a working directory, removing nondiscriminatory features from data, and setting up cross-validation parameters remain the same in the SVMBag and NBBag implementations as well. So, we do not repeat these steps in the SVMBag or NBBag code. Rather, we will focus on discussing the SVMBag or NBBag specific code:

```
# Setting up SVM predict function as the default svmBag$pred function has
some code issue
svm.predict <- function (object, x)
{
 if (is.character(lev(object))) {
    out <- predict(object, as.matrix(x), type = "probabilities")
    colnames(out) <- lev(object)
    rownames(out) <- NULL
  }
  else out <- predict(object, as.matrix(x))[, 1]
  out
}
# setting up parameters to build svm bagging model
bagctrl <- bagControl(fit = svmBag$fit,
                      predict = svm.predict ,
                      aggregate = svmBag$aggregate)
# fit the bagged svm model
set.seed(300)
svmbag <- train(Attrition ~ ., data = mydata, method="bag",trControl =
cvcontrol, bagControl = bagctrl,allowParallel = TRUE)
# printing the model results
svmbag
```

This will result in the following output:

```
Bagged Model

1470 samples
  30 predictors
   2 classes: 'No', 'Yes'

No pre-processing
Resampling: Cross-Validated (10 fold, repeated 10 times)
Summary of sample sizes: 1324, 1324, 1323, 1323, 1323, 1323, ...
Resampling results:
  Accuracy   Kappa
  0.8777721  0.4749657

Tuning parameter 'vars' was held constant at a value of 44
```

You will see that we achieved an accuracy of 87.7%, which is much higher than the KNN model's 84% accuracy.

Naive Bayes (nbBag) bagging implementation

We will now do the `nbBag` implementation by executing the following code:

```
# setting up parameters to build svm bagging model
bagctrl <- bagControl(fit = nbBag$fit,
                      predict = nbBag$pred ,
                      aggregate = nbBag$aggregate)
# fit the bagged nb model
set.seed(300)
nbbag <- train(Attrition ~ ., data = mydata, method="bag", trControl =
cvcontrol, bagControl = bagctrl)
# printing the model results
nbbag
```

This will result in the following output:

```
Bagged Model

1470 samples
  30 predictors
   2 classes: 'No', 'Yes'

No pre-processing
Resampling: Cross-Validated (10 fold, repeated 10 times)
Summary of sample sizes: 1324, 1324, 1323, 1323, 1323, 1323, ...
```

```
Resampling results:

  Accuracy   Kappa
  0.8389878  0.00206872

Tuning parameter 'vars' was held constant at a value of 44
```

We see that in this case, we achieved only 83.89% accuracy, which is slightly inferior to the KNN model's performance of 84%.

Although we have shown only three examples of the `caret` methods for bagging, the code remains the same to implement the other methods. The only change that is needed in the code is to replace the `fit`, `predict`, and `aggregate` parameters in `bagControl`. For example, to implement bagging with a neural network algorithm, we need to define `bagControl` as follows:

```
bagControl(fit = nnetBag$fit, predict = nnetBag$pred , aggregate =
nnetBag$aggregate)
```

It may be noted that an appropriate library needs to be available in R for `caret` to run the methods, otherwise it results in error. For example, `nbBag` requires the `klaR` library to be installed on the system prior to executing the code. Similarly, the `ctreebag` function needs the `party` package to be installed. Users need to check the availability of an appropriate library on the system prior to including it for use with the `caret` bagging.

We now have an understanding of implementing a project through bagging technique. The next subsection covers the underlying working mechanism of bagging. This will help get clarity in terms of what bagging did internally with our dataset so as to produce better performance measurements than that of stand-alone model performance.

Randomization with random forests

As we've seen in bagging, we create a number of bags on which each model is trained. Each of the bags consists of subsets of the actual dataset, however the number of features or variables remain the same in each of the bags. In other words, what we performed in bagging is subsetting the dataset rows.

In random forests, while we create bags from the dataset through subsetting the rows, we also subset the features (columns) that need to be included in each of the bags.

Assume that you have 1,000 observations with 20 features in your dataset. We can create 20 bags where each one of the bags has 100 observations (this is possible because of bootstrapping with replacement) and five features. Now 20 models are trained where each model gets to see only the bag it is assigned with. The final prediction is arrived at by voting or averaging based on the fact of whether the problem is a regression problem or a classification problem.

Another key difference between bagging and random forests is the ML algorithm that is used to build the model. In bagging, any ML algorithm may be used to create a model however random forest models are built specifically using CART.

Random forest modeling is yet another very popular machine learning algorithm. It is one of the algorithms that has proved itself multiple times as the best performing of algorithms, despite applying it on noisy datasets. For a person that has understood bootstrapping, understanding random forests is a cakewalk.

Implementing an attrition prediction model with random forests

Let's get our attrition model through random forest modeling by executing the following code:

```
# loading required libraries and registering multiple cores to enable
parallel processing
library(doMC)
library(caret)
registerDoMC(cores=4)
# setting the working directory and reading the dataset
setwd("~/Desktop/chapter 15")
mydata <- read.csv("WA_Fn-UseC_-HR-Employee-Attrition.csv")
# removing the non-discriminatory features from the dataset as identified
during EDA step
mydata$EmployeeNumber=mydata$Over18=mydata$EmployeeCount=mydata$StandardHou
rs = NULL
# setting the seed for reproducibility
set.seed(10000)
# setting the cross validation parameters
fitControl = trainControl(method="repeatedcv", number=10,repeats=10)
# creating the caret model with random forest algorithm
caretmodel = train(Attrition~., data=mydata, method="rf",
trControl=fitControl, verbose=F)
# printing the model summary
caretmodel
```

This will result in the following output:

```
Random Forest

1470 samples
  30 predictors
   2 classes: 'No', 'Yes'

No pre-processing
Resampling: Cross-Validated (10 fold, repeated 10 times)
Summary of sample sizes: 1323, 1323, 1324, 1323, 1324, 1322, ...
Resampling results across tuning parameters:

  mtry  Accuracy   Kappa
   2    0.8485765  0.1014859
  23    0.8608271  0.2876406
  44    0.8572929  0.2923997

Accuracy was used to select the optimal model using the largest value.
The final value used for the model was mtry = 23.
```

We see the best random forest model achieved a better accuracy of 86% compared to KNN's 84%.

Boosting

A weak learner is an algorithm that performs relatively poorly—generally, the accuracy obtained with the weak learners is just above chance. It is often, if not always, observed that weak learners are computationally simple. Decision stumps or 1R algorithms are some examples of weak learners. Boosting converts weak learners into strong learners. This essentially means that boosting is not an algorithm that does the predictions, but it works with an underlying weak ML algorithm to get better performance.

A boosting model is a sequence of models learned on subsets of data similar to that of the bagging ensembling technique. The difference is in the creation of the subsets of data. Unlike bagging, all the subsets of data used for model training are not created prior to the start of the training. Rather, boosting builds a first model with an ML algorithm that does predictions on the entire dataset. Now, there are some misclassified instances that are subsets and used by the second model. The second model only learns from this misclassified set of data curated from the first model's output.

The second model's misclassified instances become input to the third model. The process of building models is repeated until the stopping criteria is met. The final prediction for an observation in the unseen dataset is arrived by averaging or voting the predictions from all the models for that specific, unseen observation.

There are subtle differences between the various and numerous algorithms in the boosting algorithms family, however we are not going to discuss them in detail as the intent of this chapter is to get a generalized understanding of ML ensembles and not to gain in-depth knowledge of various boosting algorithms.

While obtaining better performance, measurement is the biggest advantage with the boosting ensemble; difficulty with model interpretability, higher computational times, and model overfitting are some of the issues encountered with boosting. Of course, these problems can be overruled through the use of specialized techniques.

Boosting algorithms are undoubtedly super-popular and are observed to be used by winners in many Kaggle and similar competitions. There are a number of boosting algorithms available such as **gradient boosting machines** (**GBMs**), **adaptive boosting** (**AdaBoost**) , gradient tree boosting, **extreme gradient boosting** (**XGBoost**), and **light gradient boosting machine** (**LightGBM**). In this section, we will learn the theory and implementation of two of the most popular boosting algorithms such as GBMs and XGBoost. Prior to learning the theoretical concept of boosting and its pros and cons, let's first start focusing on implementing the attrition prediction models with GBMs and XGBoost.

The GBM implementation

Let's implement the attrition prediction model with GBMs:

```
# loading the essential libraries and registering the cores for
multiprocessing
library(doMC)
library(mlbench)
library(gbm)
library(caret)
registerDoMC(cores=4)
# setting the working directory and reading the dataset
setwd("~/Desktop/chapter 15")
mydata <- read.csv("WA_Fn-UseC_-HR-Employee-Attrition.csv")
# removing the non-discriminatory features as identified by EDA step
mydata$EmployeeNumber=mydata$Over18=mydata$EmployeeCount=mydata$StandardHou
rs = NULL
# converting the target attrition feild to numeric as gbm model expects all
```

```
numeric feilds in the dataset
mydata$Attrition = as.numeric(mydata$Attrition)
# forcing the attrition column values to be 0 and 1 instead of 1 and 2
mydata = transform(mydata, Attrition=Attrition-1)
# running the gbm model with 10 fold cross validation to identify the
number of trees to build - hyper parameter tuning
gbm.model = gbm(Attrition~., data=mydata, shrinkage=0.01, distribution =
'bernoulli', cv.folds=10, n.trees=3000, verbose=F)
# identifying and printing the value of hyper parameter identified through
the tuning above
best.iter = gbm.perf(gbm.model, method="cv")
print(best.iter)
# setting the seed for reproducibility
set.seed(123)
# creating a copy of the dataset
mydata1=mydata
# converting target to a factor
mydata1$Attrition=as.factor(mydata1$Attrition)
# setting up cross validation controls
fitControl = trainControl(method="repeatedcv", number=10,repeats=10)
# runing the gbm model in tandem with caret
caretmodel = train(Attrition~., data=mydata1, method="gbm",
distribution="bernoulli",  trControl=fitControl, verbose=F,
tuneGrid=data.frame(.n.trees=best.iter, .shrinkage=0.01,
.interaction.depth=1, .n.minobsinnode=1))
# printing the model summary
print(caretmodel)
```

This will result in the following output:

```
2623
Stochastic Gradient Boosting

1470 samples
  30 predictors
   2 classes: '0', '1'

No pre-processing
Resampling: Cross-Validated (10 fold, repeated 10 times)
Summary of sample sizes: 1323, 1323, 1323, 1322, 1323, 1323, ...
Resampling results:
  Accuracy    Kappa
  0.8771472   0.4094991
Tuning parameter 'n.trees' was held constant at a value of 2623
Tuning parameter 'shrinkage' was held constant at a value of 0.01
Tuning parameter 'n.minobsinnode' was held constant at a value of 1
```

You will see that with the GBM model, we have achieved accuracy above 87%, which is better accuracy compared to the 84% achieved with KNN.

Building attrition prediction model with XGBoost

Now, let's implement the attrition prediction model with XGBoost:

```
# loading the required libraries and registering the cores for
multiprocessing
library(doMC)
library(xgboost)
library(caret)
registerDoMC(cores=4)
# setting the working directory and loading the dataset
setwd("~/Desktop/chapter 15")
mydata <- read.csv("WA_Fn-UseC_-HR-Employee-Attrition.csv")
# removing the non-discriminatory features from the dataset as identified
in EDA step
mydata$EmployeeNumber=mydata$Over18=mydata$EmployeeCount=mydata$StandardHou
rs = NULL
# setting up cross validation parameters
ControlParamteres <- trainControl(method = "repeatedcv",number = 10,
repeats=10, savePredictions = TRUE, classProbs = TRUE)
# setting up hyper parameters grid to tune
parametersGrid <-  expand.grid(eta = 0.1, colsample_bytree=c(0.5,0.7),
max_depth=c(3,6),nrounds=100, gamma=1, min_child_weight=2,subsample=0.5)
# printing the parameters grid to get an intuition
print(parametersGrid)
# xgboost model building
modelxgboost <- train(Attrition~., data = mydata, method = "xgbTree",
trControl = ControlParamteres, tuneGrid=parametersGrid)
# printing the model summary
print(modelxgboost)
```

This will result in the following output:

eta	colsample_bytree	max_depth	nrounds	gamma	min_child_weight	subsample
0.1	0.5	3	100	1	2	0.5
0.1	0.7	3	100	1	2	0.5
0.1	0.5	6	100	1	2	0.5
0.1	0.7	6	100	1	2	0.5

```
eXtreme Gradient Boosting
1470 samples
```

```
   30 predictors
    2 classes: 'No', 'Yes'

No pre-processing
Resampling: Cross-Validated (10 fold, repeated 10 times)
Summary of sample sizes: 1323, 1323, 1322, 1323, 1323, 1322, ...
Resampling results across tuning parameters:

   max_depth  colsample_bytree  Accuracy   Kappa
   3          0.5               0.8737458  0.3802840
   3          0.7               0.8734728  0.3845053
   6          0.5               0.8730674  0.3840938
   6          0.7               0.8732589  0.3920721
```

Tuning parameter 'nrounds' was held constant at a value of 100
Tuning parameter 'min_child_weight' was held constant at a value of 2
Tuning parameter 'subsample' was held constant at a value of 0.5
Accuracy was used to select the optimal model using the largest value.
The final values used for the model were nrounds = 100, max_depth = 3, eta
= 0.1, gamma = 1, colsample_bytree = 0.5, min_child_weight = 2 and
subsample = 0.5.

Again, we observed that with XGBoost model, we have achieved an accuracy above 87%, which is a better accuracy compared to the 84% achieved with KNN.

Stacking

In all the ensembles we have learned about so far, we have manipulated the dataset in certain ways and exposed subsets of the data for model building. However, in stacking, we are not going to do anything with the dataset; instead we are going to apply a different technique that involves using multiple ML algorithms instead. In stacking, we build multiple models with various ML algorithms. Each algorithm possesses a unique way of learning the characteristics of data and the final stacked model indirectly incorporates all those unique ways of learning. Stacking gets the combined power of several ML algorithms through getting the final prediction by means of voting or averaging as we do in other types of ensembles.

Building attrition prediction model with stacking

Let's build an attrition prediction model with stacking:

```
# loading the required libraries and registering the cpu cores for
multiprocessing
library(doMC)
library(caret)
library(caretEnsemble)
registerDoMC(cores=4)
# setting the working directory and loading the dataset
setwd("~/Desktop/chapter 15")
mydata <- read.csv("WA_Fn-UseC_-HR-Employee-Attrition.csv")
# removing the non-discriminatory features from the dataset as identified
in EDA step
mydata$EmployeeNumber=mydata$Over18=mydata$EmployeeCount=mydata$StandardHou
rs = NULL
# setting up control paramaters for cross validation
control <- trainControl(method="repeatedcv", number=10, repeats=10,
savePredictions=TRUE, classProbs=TRUE)
# declaring the ML algorithms to use in stacking
algorithmList <- c('C5.0', 'nb', 'glm', 'knn', 'svmRadial')
# setting the seed to ensure reproducibility of the results
set.seed(10000)
# creating the stacking model
models <- caretList(Attrition~., data=mydata, trControl=control,
methodList=algorithmList)
# obtaining the stacking model results and printing them
results <- resamples(models)
summary(results)
```

This will result in the following output:

```
summary.resamples(object = results)

Models: C5.0, nb, glm, knn, svmRadial
Number of resamples: 100

Accuracy
              Min.    1st Qu.    Median      Mean    3rd Qu.       Max. NA's
C5.0      0.8082192 0.8493151 0.8639456 0.8625833 0.8775510 0.9054054      0
nb        0.8367347 0.8367347 0.8378378 0.8387821 0.8424658 0.8435374      0
glm       0.8299320 0.8639456 0.8775510 0.8790444 0.8911565 0.9387755      0
knn       0.8027211 0.8299320 0.8367347 0.8370763 0.8438017 0.8630137      0
svmRadial 0.8287671 0.8648649 0.8775510 0.8790467 0.8911565 0.9319728      0

Kappa   Min.         1st Qu.    Median      Mean    3rd Qu.       Max. NA's
C5.0    0.03992485 0.29828006 0.37227344 0.3678459 0.4495049 0.6112590      0
```

```
nb         0.00000000 0.00000000 0.00000000 0.0000000 0.0000000 0.0000000     0
glm        0.26690604 0.39925723 0.47859218 0.4673756 0.5218094 0.7455280     0
knn       -0.05965697 0.02599388 0.06782465 0.0756081 0.1320451 0.2431312     0
svmRadial  0.24565 0.38667527 0.44195662 0.4497538 0.5192393 0.7423764        0


# Identifying the correlation between results
modelCor(results)
```

This will result in the following output:

	C5.0	nb	glm	knn	svmRadial
C5.0	1.00000000	0.06912034	0.4728593	0.19511949	0.45963498
nb	0.06912034	1.00000000	0.1128155	0.07580389	0.06687541
glm	0.47285929	0.11281554	1.0000000	0.15578044	0.53965278
knn	0.19511949	0.07580389	0.1557804	1.00000000	0.23502484
svmRadial	0.45963498	0.06687541	0.5396528	0.23502484	1.00000000

We can see from the correlation table results that none of the individual ML algorithm predictions are highly correlated. Very highly correlated results mean that the algorithms have produced very similar predictions. Combining the very similar predictions may not really yield significant benefit compared with what one would avail from accepting the individual predictions. In this specific case, we can observe that none of the algorithm predictions are highly correlated so we can straightforwardly move to the next step of stacking the predictions:

```
# Setting up the cross validation control parameters for stacking the
predictions from individual ML algorithms
stackControl <- trainControl(method="repeatedcv", number=10, repeats=10,
savePredictions=TRUE, classProbs=TRUE)
# stacking the predictions of individual ML algorithms using generalized
linear model
stack.glm <- caretStack(models, method="glm", trControl=stackControl)
# printing the stacked final results
print(stack.glm)
```

This will result in the following output:

```
A glm ensemble of 2 base models: C5.0, nb, glm, knn, svmRadial
Ensemble results:
Generalized Linear Model
14700 samples
    5 predictors
    2 classes: 'No', 'Yes'
No pre-processing
```

```
Resampling: Cross-Validated (10 fold, repeated 10 times)
Summary of sample sizes: 13230, 13230, 13230, 13230, 13230, 13230, ...
Resampling results:
  Accuracy    Kappa
  0.8844966   0.4869556
```

With GLM-based stacking, we have 88% accuracy. Let's now examine the effect of using random forest modeling instead of GLM to stack the individual predictions from each of the five ML algorithms on the observations:

```
# stacking the predictions of individual ML algorithms using random forest
stack.rf <- caretStack(models, method="rf", trControl=stackControl)
# printing the summary of rf based stacking
print(stack.rf)
```

This will result in the following output:

```
A rf ensemble of 2 base models: C5.0, nb, glm, knn, svmRadial
Ensemble results:
Random Forest
14700 samples
    5 predictors
    2 classes: 'No', 'Yes'
No pre-processing
Resampling: Cross-Validated (10 fold, repeated 10 times)
Summary of sample sizes: 13230, 13230, 13230, 13230, 13230, 13230, ...
Resampling results across tuning parameters:
  mtry  Accuracy    Kappa
  2     0.9122041   0.6268108
  3     0.9133605   0.6334885
  5     0.9132925   0.6342740
Accuracy was used to select the optimal model using the largest value.
The final value used for the model was mtry = 3.
```

We see that without much effort, we were able to achieve an accuracy of 91% by stacking the predictions. Now, let's explore the working principle of stacking.

At last, we have discovered the various ensembling techniques that can provide us with better performing models. However, before ending the chapter, there are a couple of things we need to take a note of.

 There is not just one way to implement ML models in R. For example, bagging can be implemented using functions available in the `ipred` library and not by using `caret` as we did in this chapter. We should be aware that hyperparameter tuning forms an important part of model building to avail the best performing model. The number of hyperparameters and the acceptable values for those hyperparameters vary depending on the library that we intend to use. This is the reason why we paid less attention to hyperparameter tuning in the models we built in this chapter. Nevertheless, it is very important to read up the library documentation to understand the hyperparameters that can be tuned with a library function. In most cases, incorporating hyperparameter tuning in models significantly improves the model's performance.

Summary

To recollect, we were using a class-imbalanced dataset to build the attrition model. Using techniques to resolve the class imbalance prior to model building is another key aspect of getting better model performance measurements. We used bagging, randomization, boosting, and stacking to implement and predict the attrition model. We were able to accomplish 91% accuracy just by using the features that were readily available in the models. Feature engineering is a crucial aspect whose role cannot be ignored in ML models. This may be one other path to explore to improve model performance further.

In the next chapter, we will explore the secret recipe of recommending products or content through building a personalized recommendation engines. I am all set to implement a project to recommend jokes. Turn to the next chapter to continue the journey of learning.

16
Implementing a Jokes Recommendation Engine

I am sure this is something you have experienced as well: while shopping for a cellphone on Amazon, you are also shown some product recommendations of mobile accessories, such as screen guards and phone cases. Not very surprisingly, most of us end up buying one or more of these recommendations! The primary purpose of a recommendation engine in an e-commerce site is to lure buyers into purchasing more from vendors. Of course, this is no different from a salesperson trying to up-sell or cross-sell to customers in a physical store.

You may recollect the **Customers Who Bought This Item Also Bought This** heading on Amazon (or any e-commerce site) where recommendations are shown. The aim of these recommendations is to get you to buy not just one product but a product combo, therefore pushing the sales revenues in an upward direction. Recommendations on Amazon are so successful that McKinsey estimated that a whopping 35% of the overall sales made on Amazon is due to their recommendations!

In this chapter, we will learn about the theory and implementation of a recommendation engine to suggest jokes to users. To do this, we use the Jester's jokes dataset that is available in the `recommenderlab` library of R. We will cover the following major topics:

- Fundamental aspects of recommendation engines
- Understanding the Jokes recommendation problem and the dataset
- Recommendation system using an item-based collaborative filtering technique
- Recommendation system using a user-based collaborative filtering technique
- Recommendation system using an association-rule mining technique
- Content-based recommendation engine
- Hybrid recommendation system for Jokes recommendation

Fundamental aspects of recommendation engines

While the basic intent of showing recommendations is to push sales, they actually serve just beyond the better sales concept. Highly personalized content is something recommendation engines are able to deliver. This essentially means that recommendation engines on a retail platform such as Amazon are able to offer the right content to the right customer at the right time through the right channel. It makes sense to provide personalized content; after all, there is no point in showing an irrelevant product to a customer. Also, with the lower attention spans of customers, businesses want to be able to maximize their selling opportunities by showing the right products and encouraging them to buy the right products. At a very high level, personalized content recommendation is achieved in AI in several ways:

- **Mapping similar products that were bought together**: Let's take an example of an online shopper who searched for school bags on a shopping website. Very likely, the shopper would be interested in buying additional school-related items when buying a school bag. Therefore, displaying school bags along with notebooks, pencils, pens, and pencil cases ensures a higher probability of additional sales.

- **Recommendations based on customer demographics**: Showing high-end phones and stylish phone accessories as recommended products to conservative middle class customers, who generally look for steal deals, may not fetch a big upswing in sales of the recommended products. Instead, such customers might find these irrelevant recommendations to be annoying, therefore impacting their loyalty.

- **Recommendations based on similarities between customers**: Product recommendations to a customer are based on the products purchased or liked by other, similar customers. For example, recommending a newly-arrived cosmetic product to young women living in urban locations. The recommendation in this case is not just because of the attributes of the customer but because other customers of a similar type have bought this product. As the item grows in popularity among similar individuals, the product is chosen as the one to be recommended.

- **Recommendations based on product similarities**: If you search for a laptop backpack of a particular brand, along with the results of the searched item, you are also shown other brand laptop backpacks as recommendations. This recommendation is purely based on the similarity between the products.

- **Recommendations based on the historical purchase profile of customers**: If a customer has always purchased a particular brand of jeans, they are shown recommendations of newer varieties of jeans of the particular brand they tend to purchase. These recommendations are purely based on the historical purchases of the customer.
- **Hybrid recommendations**: It is possible that one or more recommendation approaches can be combined to arrive at the best recommendations for a customer. For example, a recommendation list can be arrived by using customer preferences inferred from the historical data as well as from the demographics information of the customer.

Repurchase campaigns, newsletter recommendations, rebinding the sales from abandoned carts, customized discounts and offers, and smoothened browsing experience of e-commerce sites are some of the applications of recommendation systems in the online retail industry.

Due to several prevalent use cases, it might appear that recommender systems are used in only in the e-commerce industry. However, this is not true. The following are some of the use cases of recommender systems in non e-commerce domains:

- In the pharmaceutical industry, recommender systems are applied to identify drugs patients with certain characteristics that they will respond better to
- Stocks recommendation are done based on the stock picks of a successful group of people
- YouTube and online media use a recommendation engine to serve content that is similar to the content currently being watched by the user
- Tourism recommendations are based on tourist spots that the user or similar users have visited
- Identifying skills and personality traits of future employees in various roles
- In the culinary sciences, dishes that go pair together can be explored through the application of recommender systems

The list can grow to an enormous size, given that use cases for recommendation systems exist in almost every domain.

Now that we have a basic understanding of the concept of recommendation systems and the value it offers to business, we can now move to our next section, where we attempt to understand the Jester's Jokes recommendation dataset and the problems that could be solved by building a recommendation engine.

Recommendation engine categories

Prior to implementing our first recommender system, let's explore the types of recommender systems in detail. The following diagram shows the broad categories of recommender systems:

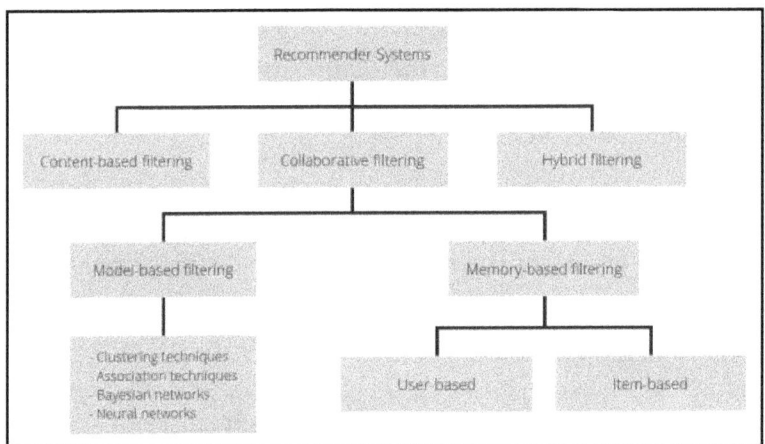

Recommender system categories

Each of the techniques shown in the diagram may be used to build a recommender system model that is capable of suggesting jokes to the users. Let's briefly explore the various recommendation engine categories.

Content-based filtering

Cognitive filtering, or content-based filtering, recommends items by comparing product attributes and customer profile attributes. The attributes of each product is represented as a set of tags or terms—typically the words that occur in a product description document. The customer profile is represented with the same terms and built by analyzing the content of products that have been seen or rated by the customer.

Collaborative filtering

Social filtering, or collaborative filtering, filters information by using the recommendations of other people. The principle behind collaborative filtering is that the customers who have appreciated the same items in the past have a high probability of displaying similar interests in the future as well.

We generally ask for reviews and recommendation from friends prior to watching a movie. A recommendation from a friend is more accepted than recommendations from others as we share some interests with our friends. This is the same principle on which collaborative filtering works.

Collaborative filtering can be further classified into memory-based and model-based as follows:

- **Memory-based**: In this method, user rating information is used to compute the likeness between users or items. This computed likeness is then used to come up with recommendations.
- **Model based**: Data mining methods are applied to recognize patterns in the data, and the learned patterns are then used to generate recommendations.

Hybrid filtering

In this class of recommendation systems, we combine more than one type of recommendation system to come up with final recommendations.

Getting started

To get started, you will have to download the supporting files from this GitHub link: `https://github.com/PacktPublishing/Advanced-Machine-Learning-with-R/tree/master/Chapter16`.

Understanding the Jokes recommendation problem and the dataset

Dr. Ken Goldberg and his colleagues, Theresa Roeder, Dhruv Gupta, and Chris Perkins, introduced a dataset to the world through their paper *Eigentaste: A Constant Time Collaborative Filtering Algorithm*, which is pretty popular in the recommender-systems domain. The dataset is named the Jester's jokes dataset. To create it, a number of users are presented with several jokes and they are asked to rate them. The ratings provided by the users for the various jokes formed the dataset. The data in this dataset is collected between April 1999 and May 2003. The following are the attributes of the dataset:

- Over 11,000,000 ratings of 150 jokes from 79,681 users
- Each row is a user (Row 1 = User #1)

- Each column is a joke (Column 1 = Joke #1)
- Ratings are given as real values from -10.00 to +10.00; -10 being the lowest possible rating and 10 being the highest
- 99 corresponds to a null rating

The `recommenderlab` package in R provides a subset of this original dataset provided by Dr. Ken Goldberg's group. We will make use of this subset for our projects covered in this chapter.

The `Jester5k` dataset provided in the `recommenderlab` library contains a 5,000 x 100 rating matrix (5,000 users and 100 jokes) with ratings between -10.00 and +10.00. All selected users have rated 36 or more jokes. The dataset is in the `realRatingMatrix` format. This is a special matrix format that the `recommenderlab` expects the data to be in, to apply the various functions that are packaged in the library.

As we are already aware, **exploratory data analysis (EDA)** is the first step for any data science project. Going by this principle, let's begin by reading the data, and then proceed with the EDA step on the dataset:

```
# including the required libraries
library(data.table)
library(recommenderlab)
# setting the seed so as to reproduce the results
set.seed(54)
# reading the data to a variable
library(recommenderlab)
data(Jester5k)
str(Jester5k)
```

This will result in the following output:

```
Formal class 'realRatingMatrix' [package "recommenderlab"] with 2 slots
  ..@ data      :Formal class 'dgCMatrix' [package "Matrix"] with 6 slots
  .. .. ..@ i       : int [1:362106] 0 1 2 3 4 5 6 7 8 9 ...
  .. .. ..@ p       : int [1:101] 0 3314 6962 10300 13442 18440 22513 27512
32512 35685 ...
  .. .. ..@ Dim     : int [1:2] 5000 100
  .. .. ..@ Dimnames:List of 2
  .. .. .. ..$ : chr [1:5000] "u2841" "u15547" "u15221" "u15573" ...
  .. .. .. ..$ : chr [1:100] "j1" "j2" "j3" "j4" ...
  .. .. ..@ x       : num [1:362106] 7.91 -3.2 -1.7 -7.38 0.1 0.83 2.91
-2.77 -3.35 -1.99 ...
  .. .. ..@ factors : list()
  ..@ normalize: NULL
```

The data structure output is pretty self explanatory and we see it provides empirical evidence for the details we have discussed already. Let's continue our EDA further:

```
# Viewing the first 5 records in the dataset
head(getRatingMatrix(Jester5k),5)
```

This will result in the following output:

```
2.5 x 100 sparse Matrix of class "dgCMatrix"
   [[ suppressing 100 column names 'j1', 'j2', 'j3' ... ]]
u2841    7.91  9.17  5.34  8.16 -8.74  7.14  8.88 -8.25  5.87  6.21  7.72
6.12 -0.73  7.77 -5.83 -8.88  8.98
u15547 -3.20 -3.50 -9.56 -8.74 -6.36 -3.30  0.78  2.18 -8.40 -8.79 -7.04
-6.02  3.35 -4.61  3.64 -6.41 -4.13
u15221 -1.70  1.21  1.55  2.77  5.58  3.06  2.72 -4.66  4.51 -3.06  2.33
3.93  0.05  2.38 -3.64 -7.72  0.97
u15573 -7.38 -8.93 -3.88 -7.23 -4.90  4.13  2.57  3.83  4.37  3.16 -4.90
-5.78 -5.83  2.52 -5.24  4.51  4.37
u21505  0.10  4.17  4.90  1.55  5.53  1.50 -3.79  1.94  3.59  4.81 -0.68
-0.97 -6.46 -0.34 -2.14 -2.04 -2.57
u2841   -9.32 -9.08 -9.13 7.77  8.59  5.29  8.25  6.02  5.24  7.82  7.96
-8.88  8.25  3.64 -0.73  8.25  5.34 -7.77
u15547 -0.15 -1.84 -1.84 1.84 -1.21 -8.59 -5.19 -2.18  0.19  2.57 -5.78
1.07 -8.79  3.01  2.67 -9.22 -9.32  3.69
u15221  2.04  1.94  4.42 1.17  0.10 -5.10 -3.25  3.35  3.30 -1.70  3.16
-0.29  1.36  3.54  6.17 -2.72  3.11  4.81
u15573  4.95  5.49 -0.49 3.40 -2.14  5.29 -3.11 -4.56 -5.44 -6.89 -0.24
-5.15 -3.59 -8.20  2.18  0.39 -1.21 -2.62
u21505 -0.15  2.43  3.16 1.50  4.37 -0.10 -2.14  3.98  2.38  6.84 -0.68
0.87  3.30  6.21  5.78 -6.21 -0.78 -1.36
## number of ratings
print(nratings(Jester5k))
```

This will result in the following output:

```
362106## number of ratings per user
```

We will print the summary of the dataset using the following command:

```
print(summary(rowCounts(Jester5k)))
```

This will result in the following output:

```
   Min. 1st Qu.  Median    Mean 3rd Qu.    Max.
  36.00   53.00   72.00   72.42  100.00  100.00
```

We will now plot the histogram:

```
## rating distribution
hist(getRatings(Jester5k), main="Distribution of ratings")
```

This will result in the following output:

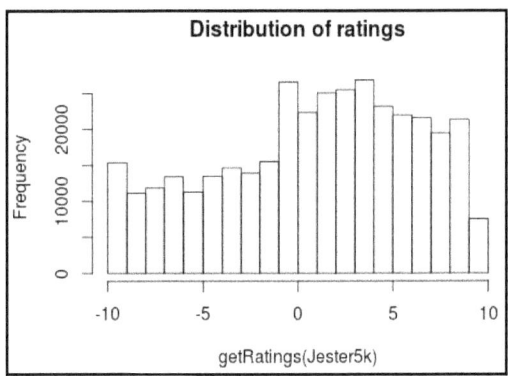

From the output, we see a somewhat normal distribution. It can also be seen that the positive ratings outnumber the negative ratings.

The `Jester5K` dataset also provides a character vector called `JesterJokes`. The vector is of length 100. These are the actual 100 jokes among others that were shown to the users to get the ratings. We could examine the jokes with the following command:

```
head(JesterJokes, 5)
```

This will result in the following output:

```
j1 "A man visits the doctor. The doctor says \"I have bad news for you.You
have cancer and Alzheimer's disease\". The man replies \"Well,thank God I
don't have cancer!\""
j2 "This couple had an excellent relationship going until one day he came
home from work to find his girlfriend packing. He asked her why she was
leaving him and she told him that she had heard awful things about him.
\"What could they possibly have said to make you move out?\" \"They told me
that you were a pedophile.\" He replied, \"That's an awfully big word for a
ten year old.\""
j3  "Q. What's 200 feet long and has 4 teeth? A. The front row at a Willie
Nelson Concert."
j4 "Q. What's the difference between a man and a toilet? A. A toilet
doesn't follow you around after you use it."
j5 "Q. What's O. J. Simpson's Internet address? A. Slash, slash, backslash,
slash, slash, escape."
```

Based on the 5,000 user ratings we have, we could perform additional EDA to identify the joke that is rated as best by the users. This can be done through the following code:

```
## 'best' joke with highest average rating
best <- which.max(colMeans(Jester5k))
cat(JesterJokes[best])
```

This will result in the following output:

```
A guy goes into confession and says to the priest, "Father, I'm 80 years
old, widower, with 11 grandchildren. Last night I met two beautiful flight
attendants. They took me home and I made love to both of them. Twice." The
priest said: "Well, my son, when was the last time you were in confession?"
"Never Father, I'm Jewish." "So then, why are you telling me?" "I'm telling
everybody."
```

We could perform additional EDA to visualize the univariate and multivariate analysis. This exploration will help us understand each of the variables in detail as well as the relationship between them. While we do not delve deep into each of these aspects, here are some thoughts that can be explored:

- Exploring the users who always provide high ratings to most jokes
- Correlation between the ratings provided to jokes
- Identification of users that are very critical
- Exploring the most popular jokes or least popular jokes
- Identifying the jokes with the fewest ratings and identifying the associations between them

Converting the DataFrame

We are going to use functions from an R library called `recommenderlab` to build recommendation engine projects in this chapter. Irrespective of the category of recommendation system we implement, there are some prerequisites that the dataset needs to satisfy to be able to apply the `recommenderlab` functions. The prebuilt `recommenderlab` functions for collaborative filtering expects `realRatingMatrix` to be supplied as input. In our case, the `Jester5k` dataset is already in this format, therefore, we could directly use this matrix to apply the `recommenderlab` functions.

In case, we were to have our data as a R DataFrame and if we intend to convert into `realRatingMatrix`, the following steps may be performed:

1. Convert the DataFrame into an R matrix as follows:

    ```
    # convert the df dataframe to a matrix
    r_mat <- as.matrix(df)
    ```

2. Convert the resultant matrix into `realRatingMatrix` with the help of the `as()` function as follows:

    ```
    # convert r_mat matrix to a recommenderlab realRatingMatrix
    r_real_mat <- as(r_mat,"realRatingMatrix")
    ```

Here, we assume that the name of the DataFrame is `df`, the code will convert it into a `realRatingMatrix` that can be used as input to the `recommenderlab` functions.

Dividing the DataFrame

Another prerequisite is to divide the dataset into train and test subsets. These subsets will be used in later sections to implement our recommendation systems and to measure the performance. The `evaluationScheme()` function from the `recommenderlab` library can be used to split the dataset into training and testing subsets. A number of user-specified parameters can be passed to this function. In the following code, `realRatingMatrix` is split according to an 80/20 training/testing split, with up to 20 items recommended for each user. Furthermore, we specify that any rating greater than `0` is to be considered a positive rating, in conformance with the predefined `[-10, 10]` rating scale. The `Jester5k` dataset can be divided into the train and test datasets with the following code:

```
# split the data into the training and the test set
Jester5k_es <- evaluationScheme(Jester5k, method="split", train=0.8,
given=20, goodRating=0)
# verifying if the train - test was done successfully
print(Jester5k_es)
```

This will result in the following output:

```
Evaluation scheme with 20 items given
Method: 'split' with 1 run(s).
Training set proportion: 0.800
Good ratings: >=0.000000
Data set: 5000 x 100 rating matrix of class 'realRatingMatrix' with 362106
ratings.
```

From the output of the `evaluationScheme()` function, we can observe that the function yielded a single R object containing both the training and test subsets. This object will be used to define and evaluate a variety of recommender models.

Building a recommendation system with an item-based collaborative filtering technique

The `recommenderlab` package of R offers the **item-based collaborative filtering** (**ITCF**) option to build a recommendation system. This is a very straightforward approach that just needs us to call the function and supply it with the necessary parameters. The parameters, in general, will have a lot of influence on the performance of the model; therefore, testing each parameter combination is the key to obtaining the best model for recommendations. The following are the parameters that can be passed to the `Recommender` function:

- **Data normalization**: Normalizing the ratings matrix is a key step in preparing the data for the recommendation engine. The process of normalization processes the ratings in the matrix by removing the rating bias. The possible values for this parameter are `NULL`, `Center`, and `Z-Score`.
- **Distance**: This represents the type of similarity metric to be used within the model. The possible values for this parameter are Cosine similarity, Euclidean distance, and Pearson's correlation.

With these parameter combinations, we could build and test 3 x 3 ITCF models. The basic intuition behind ITCF is that if a person likes item A, there is a good probability that they like item B as well, as long as items A and B are similar. It may be understood that the term *similar* does not indicate similarity between the items based on the item's attributes, but, a similarity in user preferences, for example, a group of people that liked items A also liked item B. The following diagram shows the working principle of ITCF:

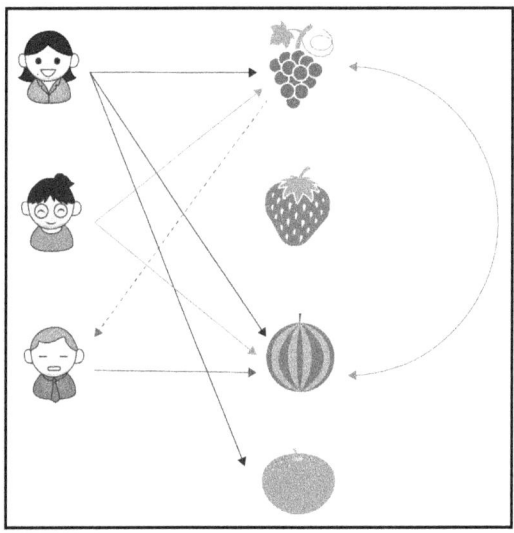

Example showing the working of item based collaborative filtering

Let's explore the diagram in a little more detail. In ITCF, the watermelon and grapes will form the similar-items neighborhood, which means that irrespective of users, different items that are equivalent will form a neighborhood. So when user X likes watermelon, the other item from the same neighborhood, which is grapes, will be recommended by the recommender system based on item-based collaborative filter.

ITCF involves the following three steps:

1. **Computing the item-based similarities through a distance measure**: This involves computing the distance between the items. The distance may be computed with one of the many distance measures, such as Cosine similarity, Euclidean distance, Manhattan distance, or Jaccard index. The output of this step is to obtain a similarity matrix where each cell corresponds to the similarity of the item specified on the row of the cell and the item specified on the column of the cell.

2. **Predicting the targeted item rating for a specific user**: The rating is arrived at by computing the weighted sum of ratings made to the item very similar to the target item.

3. **Recommending the top N items**: Once all the items are predicted, we recommend the top *N* items.

Now, let's build each one of the ITCF models and measure the performance against the test dataset. The following code trains the ITCF models with several parameter combinations:

```
type = "IBCF"
##train ITCF cosine similarity models
# non-normalized
ITCF_N_C <- Recommender(getData(Jester5k_es, "train"), type,
                    param=list(normalize = NULL, method="Cosine"))
# centered
ITCF_C_C <- Recommender(getData(Jester5k_es, "train"), type,
                    param=list(normalize = "center",method="Cosine"))
# Z-score normalization
ITCF_Z_C <- Recommender(getData(Jester5k_es, "train"), type,
                    param=list(normalize = "Z-score",method="Cosine"))
##train ITCF Euclidean Distance models
# non-normalized
ITCF_N_E <- Recommender(getData(Jester5k_es, "train"), type,
                    param=list(normalize = NULL, method="Euclidean"))
# centered
ITCF_C_E <- Recommender(getData(Jester5k_es, "train"), type,
                    param=list(normalize =
"center",method="Euclidean"))
# Z-score normalization
ITCF_Z_E <- Recommender(getData(Jester5k_es, "train"), type,
                    param=list(normalize = "Z-
score",method="Euclidean"))
#train ITCF pearson correlation models
# non-normalized
ITCF_N_P <- Recommender(getData(Jester5k_es, "train"), type,
                    param=list(normalize = NULL, method="pearson"))
# centered
ITCF_C_P <- Recommender(getData(Jester5k_es, "train"), type,
                    param=list(normalize = "center",method="pearson"))
# Z-score normalization
ITCF_Z_P <- Recommender(getData(Jester5k_es, "train"), type,
                    param=list(normalize = "Z-score",method="pearson"))
```

We now have the ITCF models, so let's get to computing the performance on the test data with each of the models we have created. The objective is to identify the best-performing ITCF model for this dataset. The following code gets the performance measurements with all the nine models on the test dataset:

```
# compute predicted ratings from each of the 9 models on the test dataset
pred1 <- predict(ITCF_N_C, getData(Jester5k_es, "known"), type="ratings")
pred2 <- predict(ITCF_C_C, getData(Jester5k_es, "known"), type="ratings")
pred3 <- predict(ITCF_Z_C, getData(Jester5k_es, "known"), type="ratings")
pred4 <- predict(ITCF_N_E, getData(Jester5k_es, "known"), type="ratings")
pred5 <- predict(ITCF_C_E, getData(Jester5k_es, "known"), type="ratings")
pred6 <- predict(ITCF_Z_E, getData(Jester5k_es, "known"), type="ratings")
pred7 <- predict(ITCF_N_P, getData(Jester5k_es, "known"), type="ratings")
pred8 <- predict(ITCF_C_P, getData(Jester5k_es, "known"), type="ratings")
pred9 <- predict(ITCF_Z_P, getData(Jester5k_es, "known"), type="ratings")
# set all predictions that fall outside the valid range to the boundary
values
pred1@data@x[pred1@data@x[] < -10] <- -10
pred1@data@x[pred1@data@x[] > 10] <- 10
pred2@data@x[pred2@data@x[] < -10] <- -10
pred2@data@x[pred2@data@x[] > 10] <- 10
pred3@data@x[pred3@data@x[] < -10] <- -10
pred3@data@x[pred3@data@x[] > 10] <- 10
pred4@data@x[pred4@data@x[] < -10] <- -10
pred4@data@x[pred4@data@x[] > 10] <- 10
pred5@data@x[pred5@data@x[] < -10] <- -10
pred5@data@x[pred5@data@x[] > 10] <- 10
pred6@data@x[pred6@data@x[] < -10] <- -10
pred6@data@x[pred6@data@x[] > 10] <- 10
pred7@data@x[pred7@data@x[] < -10] <- -10
pred7@data@x[pred7@data@x[] > 10] <- 10
pred8@data@x[pred8@data@x[] < -10] <- -10
pred8@data@x[pred8@data@x[] > 10] <- 10
pred9@data@x[pred9@data@x[] < -10] <- -10
pred9@data@x[pred9@data@x[] > 10] <- 10
# aggregate the performance measurements obtained from all the models
error_ITCF <- rbind(
  ITCF_N_C = calcPredictionAccuracy(pred1, getData(Jester5k_es,
"unknown")),
  ITCF_C_C = calcPredictionAccuracy(pred2, getData(Jester5k_es,
"unknown")),
  ITCF_Z_C = calcPredictionAccuracy(pred3, getData(Jester5k_es,
"unknown")),
  ITCF_N_E = calcPredictionAccuracy(pred4, getData(Jester5k_es,
"unknown")),
  ITCF_C_E = calcPredictionAccuracy(pred5, getData(Jester5k_es,
"unknown")),
  ITCF_Z_E = calcPredictionAccuracy(pred6, getData(Jester5k_es,
```

```
"unknown")),
  ITCF_N_P = calcPredictionAccuracy(pred7, getData(Jester5k_es,
"unknown")),
  ITCF_C_P = calcPredictionAccuracy(pred8, getData(Jester5k_es,
"unknown")),
  ITCF_Z_P = calcPredictionAccuracy(pred9, getData(Jester5k_es, "unknown"))
)
library(knitr)
kable(error_ITCF)
```

This will result in the following output:

```
|          |     RMSE|      MSE|      MAE|
|:---------|--------:|--------:|--------:|
|ITCF_N_C  | 4.533455| 20.55221| 3.460860|
|ITCF_C_C  | 5.082643| 25.83326| 4.012391|
|ITCF_Z_C  | 5.089552| 25.90354| 4.021435|
|ITCF_N_E  | 4.520893| 20.43848| 3.462490|
|ITCF_C_E  | 4.519783| 20.42844| 3.462271|
|ITCF_Z_E  | 4.527953| 20.50236| 3.472080|
|ITCF_N_P  | 4.582121| 20.99583| 3.522113|
|ITCF_C_P  | 4.545966| 20.66581| 3.510830|
|ITCF_Z_P  | 4.569294| 20.87845| 3.536400|
```

We see the output that the ITCF recommendation application on data with the Euclidean distance yielded the best performance measurement.

Building a recommendation system with a user-based collaborative filtering technique

The Jokes recommendation system we built earlier, with item-based filtering, uses the powerful `recommenderlab` library available in R. In this implementation of the **user-based collaborative filtering (UBCF)** approach, we make use of the same library.

The following diagram shows the working principle of UBCF:

Example depicting working principle of user based collaborative filter

To understand the concept better, let's discuss the preceding diagram in detail. Let's assume that there are three users: X,Y, and Z. In UBCF, users X and Z are very similar as both of them like strawberries and watermelons. User X also likes grapes and oranges. So a user-based collaborative filter recommends grapes and oranges to user Z. The idea is that similar people tend to like similar things.

The primary difference between a user-based collaborative filter and an item-based collaborative filter is demonstrated by the following recommendation captions often seen in online retail sites:

- **ITCF**: Customers who bought this item also bought
- **UBCF**: Customers similar to you bought

A user-based collaborative filter is built upon the following three key steps:

1. Find the **k-nearest neighbors** (**KNN**) to the user x, using a similarity function, w, to measure the distance between each pair of users:

$$similarity(x, i) = w(x, i), \ i \ is \ a \ member \ of \ k$$

2. Predict the rating that user *x* will provide to all items the KNN has rated, but *x* has not.

3. The *N* recommended items to user *x* is the top *N* items that have the best predicted ratings.

In short, a user-item matrix is constructed during the UBCF process and based on similar users, the ratings of the unseen items of a user are predicted. The items that get the highest ratings among the predictions form the final list of recommendations.

The implementation of this project is very similar to ITCF as we are using the same library. The only change required in the code is to change the IBCF method to use UBCF. The following code block is the full code of the project implementation with UBCF:

```
library(recommenderlab)
data(Jester5k)
# split the data into the training and the test set
Jester5k_es <- evaluationScheme(Jester5k, method="split", train=0.8,
given=20, goodRating=0)
print(Jester5k_es)
type = "UBCF"
#train UBCF cosine similarity models
# non-normalized
UBCF_N_C <- Recommender(getData(Jester5k_es, "train"), type,
                        param=list(normalize = NULL, method="Cosine"))
# centered
UBCF_C_C <- Recommender(getData(Jester5k_es, "train"), type,
                        param=list(normalize = "center",method="Cosine"))
# Z-score normalization
UBCF_Z_C <- Recommender(getData(Jester5k_es, "train"), type,
                        param=list(normalize = "Z-score",method="Cosine"))
#train UBCF Euclidean Distance models
# non-normalized
UBCF_N_E <- Recommender(getData(Jester5k_es, "train"), type,
                        param=list(normalize = NULL, method="Euclidean"))
# centered
UBCF_C_E <- Recommender(getData(Jester5k_es, "train"), type,
                        param=list(normalize =
"center",method="Euclidean"))
# Z-score normalization
UBCF_Z_E <- Recommender(getData(Jester5k_es, "train"), type,
                        param=list(normalize = "Z-
score",method="Euclidean"))
#train UBCF pearson correlation models
# non-normalized
UBCF_N_P <- Recommender(getData(Jester5k_es, "train"), type,
                        param=list(normalize = NULL, method="pearson"))
# centered
```

```
UBCF_C_P <- Recommender(getData(Jester5k_es, "train"), type,
                        param=list(normalize = "center",method="pearson"))
# Z-score normalization
UBCF_Z_P <- Recommender(getData(Jester5k_es, "train"), type,
                        param=list(normalize = "Z-score",method="pearson"))
# compute predicted ratings from each of the 9 models on the test dataset
pred1 <- predict(UBCF_N_C, getData(Jester5k_es, "known"), type="ratings")
pred2 <- predict(UBCF_C_C, getData(Jester5k_es, "known"), type="ratings")
pred3 <- predict(UBCF_Z_C, getData(Jester5k_es, "known"), type="ratings")
pred4 <- predict(UBCF_N_E, getData(Jester5k_es, "known"), type="ratings")
pred5 <- predict(UBCF_C_E, getData(Jester5k_es, "known"), type="ratings")
pred6 <- predict(UBCF_Z_E, getData(Jester5k_es, "known"), type="ratings")
pred7 <- predict(UBCF_N_P, getData(Jester5k_es, "known"), type="ratings")
pred8 <- predict(UBCF_C_P, getData(Jester5k_es, "known"), type="ratings")
pred9 <- predict(UBCF_Z_P, getData(Jester5k_es, "known"), type="ratings")
# set all predictions that fall outside the valid range to the boundary
values
pred1@data@x[pred1@data@x[] < -10] <- -10
pred1@data@x[pred1@data@x[] > 10] <- 10
pred2@data@x[pred2@data@x[] < -10] <- -10
pred2@data@x[pred2@data@x[] > 10] <- 10
pred3@data@x[pred3@data@x[] < -10] <- -10
pred3@data@x[pred3@data@x[] > 10] <- 10
pred4@data@x[pred4@data@x[] < -10] <- -10
pred4@data@x[pred4@data@x[] > 10] <- 10
pred5@data@x[pred5@data@x[] < -10] <- -10
pred5@data@x[pred5@data@x[] > 10] <- 10
pred6@data@x[pred6@data@x[] < -10] <- -10
pred6@data@x[pred6@data@x[] > 10] <- 10
pred7@data@x[pred7@data@x[] < -10] <- -10
pred7@data@x[pred7@data@x[] > 10] <- 10
pred8@data@x[pred8@data@x[] < -10] <- -10
pred8@data@x[pred8@data@x[] > 10] <- 10
pred9@data@x[pred9@data@x[] < -10] <- -10
pred9@data@x[pred9@data@x[] > 10] <- 10
# aggregate the performance statistics
error_UBCF <- rbind(
  UBCF_N_C = calcPredictionAccuracy(pred1, getData(Jester5k_es,
"unknown")),
  UBCF_C_C = calcPredictionAccuracy(pred2, getData(Jester5k_es,
"unknown")),
  UBCF_Z_C = calcPredictionAccuracy(pred3, getData(Jester5k_es,
"unknown")),
  UBCF_N_E = calcPredictionAccuracy(pred4, getData(Jester5k_es,
"unknown")),
  UBCF_C_E = calcPredictionAccuracy(pred5, getData(Jester5k_es,
"unknown")),
  UBCF_Z_E = calcPredictionAccuracy(pred6, getData(Jester5k_es,
```

```
"unknown")),
  UBCF_N_P = calcPredictionAccuracy(pred7, getData(Jester5k_es,
"unknown")),
  UBCF_C_P = calcPredictionAccuracy(pred8, getData(Jester5k_es,
"unknown")),
  UBCF_Z_P = calcPredictionAccuracy(pred9, getData(Jester5k_es, "unknown"))
)
library(knitr)
print(kable(error_UBCF))
```

This will result in the following output:

```
|         |     RMSE|      MSE|      MAE|
|:--------|--------:|--------:|--------:|
|UBCF_N_C | 4.877935| 23.79425| 3.986170|
|UBCF_C_C | 4.518210| 20.41422| 3.578551|
|UBCF_Z_C | 4.517669| 20.40933| 3.552120|
|UBCF_N_E | 4.644877| 21.57488| 3.778046|
|UBCF_C_E | 4.489157| 20.15253| 3.552543|
|UBCF_Z_E | 4.496185| 20.21568| 3.528534|
|UBCF_N_P | 4.927442| 24.27968| 4.074879|
|UBCF_C_P | 4.487073| 20.13382| 3.553429|
|UBCF_Z_P | 4.484986| 20.11510| 3.525356|
```

Based on the UBCF output, we observe that the Z-score normalized data with Pearson's correlation as the distance has yielded the best performance measurement. Furthermore, if we want, the UBCF and ITCF results may be compared (testing needs to be done on the same test dataset) to arrive at a conclusion of accepting the best model among the 18 models that are built for the final recommendation engine deployment.

 The key point to observe in the code is the UBCF value that is passed to the method parameter. In the previous project, we built an item-based collaborative filter; all that is needed is for us to replace the value passed to the method parameter with IBCF.

Building a recommendation system based on an association-rule mining technique

Association-rule mining, or market-basket analysis, is a very popular data mining technique used in the retail industry to identify the products that need to be kept together so as to encourage cross sales. An interesting aspect behind this algorithm is that historical invoices are mined to identify the products that are bought together.

There are several off-the-shelf algorithms available to perform market-basket analysis. Some of them are Apriori, **equivalence class transformation** (**ECLAT**), and **frequent pattern growth** (**FP-growth**). We will learn to solve our problem of recommending jokes to users through applying the Apriori algorithm on the Jester jokes dataset. We will now learn the theoretical aspects that underpin the Apriori algorithm.

The Apriori algorithm

The building blocks of the algorithm are the items that are found in any given transaction. Each transaction could have one or more items in it. The items that form a transaction are called an itemset. An example of a transaction is an invoice.

Given the transactions dataset, the objective is to find the items in data that are associated with each other. Association is measured as frequency of the occurrence of the items in the same context. For example, purchasing one product when another product is purchased represents an association rule. The association rule detects the common usage of items.

More formally, we can define association-rule mining as, given a set of items I = {I1,I2,..Im} and database of transactions D = {t1,t,2..tn}, where ti= { Ii1,Ii2..Iim} where Iik is element of, an association is an implication of X->Y where X,Y subset of I are set of items and X intersection Y is φ. In short, associations express an implication from X-> Y, where X and Y are itemsets.

The algorithm can be better understood by an example. So, let's consider the following table, which shows a representative list of sample transactions in a supermarket:

Transaction	Items
1	Milk, curd, chocolate
2	Bread, butter
3	Coke, jam
4	Bread, milk, butter, Coke
5	Bread, milk, butter, jam

Sample transactions in a super market

Let's try to explore some fundamental concepts that will help us understand how the Apriori algorithm works:

- **Item**: An item is any individual product that is part of each of the transactions. For example, milk, Coke, and butter are all termed as items.
- **Itemset**: Collection of one or more items. For example, *{butter, milk, coke}, {butter, milk}*.

- **Support count**: Frequency of occurrence of an itemset. For example, support count or σ *{butter, bread, milk} = 2*.

- **Support**: A fraction of transactions that contain an itemset. For example, *s = {butter, bread, milk} = 2/5*.

- **Frequent itemset**: An itemset whose support is greater than the minimum threshold.

- **Support for an itemset in a context**: Fraction of contexts that contain both *X* and *Y*:

$$s = Support\_count(X \bigcup Y)/N$$

So, *s* for *{milk, butter} -> {bread} will be s = σ {milk, butter, bread}/N = 2/5 = 0.4*

- **Confidence**: Measures the strength of the rule, whereas support measures how often it should occur in the database. It computes how often items in *Y* occur in containing *X* through the following formula:

$$c = Support\_count(X \bigcup Y)/Support\_count(X)$$

For example: For {bread} -> {butter}

c or α = σ {butter, bread} / σ {bread} = 3/3 = 1

Let's consider another example confidence for *{curd} -> {bread}*:

c or α = σ {curd,bread} / σ {bread} = 0/3 = 0

The Apriori algorithm intends to generate all possible combinations of the itemsets from the list of the items and then prunes the itemsets that have met the predefined support and confidence parameter values that were passed to the algorithm. So, it may be understood that the Apriori algorithm is a two-step algorithm:

1. Generating itemsets from the items
2. Evaluating and pruning the itemsets based on predefined support and confidence

Let's discuss step 1 in detail. Assume there are *n* items in the collection. The number of itemsets one could create is 2^n, and all these need to be evaluated in the second step in order to come up with the final results. Even considering just 100 different items, the number of itemsets generated is 1.27e+30! The huge number of itemsets poses a severe computational challenge.

The Apriori algorithm overcomes this challenge by preempting the itemsets that are generally rare or less important. The Apriori principle states that *if an itemset is frequent, all of its subsets must also be frequent*. This means that if an item does not meet the predefined support threshold, then such item does not participate in the creation of itemsets. The Apriori algorithm thus comes up with restricted number of itemsets that are viable to be evaluated without encountering a computational challenge.

The first step of the algorithm is iterative in nature. In the first iteration, it considers all itemsets of length 1, that is, each itemset contains only one item in it. Then each item is evaluated to eliminate the itemsets that are found to not meet the preset support threshold. The output of the first iteration is all itemsets of length 1 that meet the required support. This becomes the input for iteration 2, and now itemsets of length 2 are formed using only the final itemsets that are output in first iteration. Each of the itemsets formed during step 2 is checked again for the support threshold; if it is not met, such itemsets are eliminated. The iterations continue until no new itemsets can be created. The process of itemsets is illustrated in the following diagram:

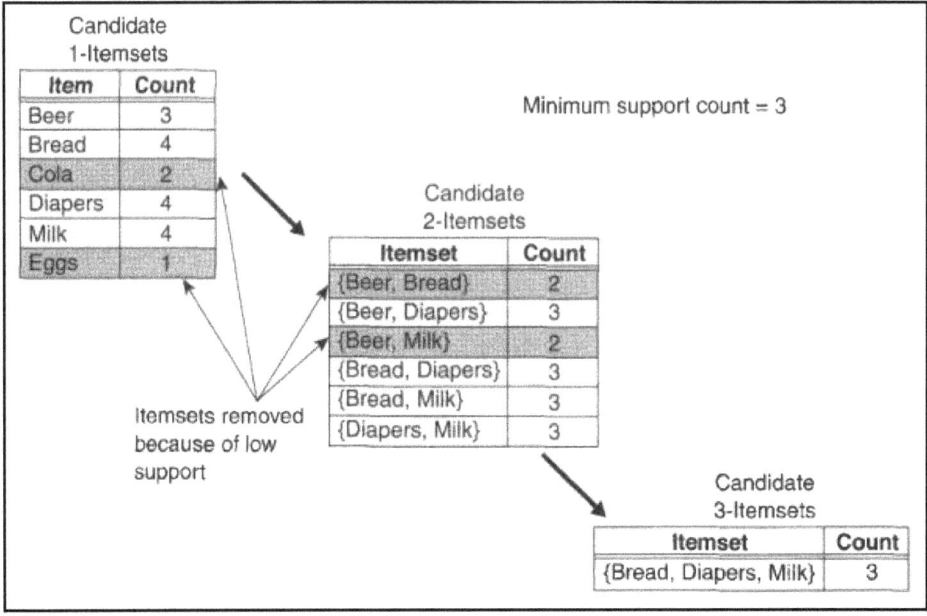

Illustration showing the itemsets creation in Apriori algorithm

Once we have all itemsets post all the step 1 iterations of the algorithm, step 2 kicks in. Each of the itemsets generated is tested to check whether it meets the predefined confidence value. If it does not meet the threshold, such itemsets are eliminated from the final output.

At a stage where all iterations are complete and the final rules are the output from Apriori, we make use of a metric called lift to consume the relevant rules from the final output. Lift defines how much more likely one item or itemset is purchased relative to its typical rate of purchase, given that we know another item or itemset has been purchased. For each itemset, we get the lift measurement using the following formula:

$$Lift(X->Y) = Confidence(X->Y)/Support(Y)$$

Let's delve a little deeper into understanding the lift metric. Assume that in a supermarket, milk and bread are bought together by chance. In such a case, a large number of transactions are expected to cover the milk and bread purchased. A lift (milk -> bread) of more than 1 implies that these items are found together more often than these items are purchased together by chance. We generally would look for lift values greater than 1 when evaluating the rules for their usefulness in business. A lift value higher than 1 indicates that the itemset generated is very strong, and therefore worth considering for implementation.

Now, let's implement the recommendation system using the Apriori algorithm:

```
# load the required libraries
library(data.table)
library(arules)
library(recommenderlab)
# set the seed so that the results are replicable
set.seed(42)
# reading the Jester5k data
data(Jester5k)
class(Jester5k)
```

This will result in the following output:

```
[1] "realRatingMatrix"
attr(,"package")
[1] "recommenderlab"
```

We can see from the output that the `Jester5k` data in the `recommenderlab` library is in the `realRatingsMatrix` format. We are also aware that the cells in this matrix contain the ratings provided by the users for various jokes and we are aware that the ratings range between -10 to +10.

Applying the Apriori algorithm on the `Jester5k` dataset give us an opportunity to understand the association between the jokes. However, prior to applying the Apriori algorithm, we will need to transform the dataset to binary values where 1 represents a positive rating and 0 represents a negative rating or no rating. The `recommenderlab` library comes up with the `binarize()` function, which can perform the required operation for us. The following code binarizes the ratings matrix:

```
# binarizing the Jester ratings
Jester5k_bin <- binarize(Jester5k, minRating=1)
# let us verify the binarized object
class(Jester5k_bin)
```

This will result in the following output:

```
[1] "binaryRatingMatrix"
attr(,"package")
[1] "recommenderlab"
```

We can observe from the output that `realRatingsMatrix` is successfully converted into `binaryRatingMatrix`. The Apriori algorithm that mines the associations expects a matrix to be passed as input rather than `binaryRatingMatrix`. We can very easily convert the `Jester5k_bin` object to the matrix format with the following code:

```
# converting the binaryratingsmatrix to matrix format
Jester5k_bin_mat <- as(Jester5k_bin,"matrix")
# visualizing the matrix object
View(Jester5k_bin_mat)
```

This will result in the following output:

	j1	j2	j3	j4	j5	j6	j7	j8	j9	j10	j11	j12	j13	j14	j15	j16	j17
u2841	TRUE	TRUE	TRUE	TRUE	FALSE	TRUE	TRUE	FALSE	TRUE	TRUE	TRUE	TRUE	FALSE	TRUE	FALSE	FALSE	TR
u15547	FALSE	FALSE	FALSE	FALSE	FALSE	FALSE	FALSE	TRUE	FALSE	FALSE	FALSE	FALSE	TRUE	FALSE	TRUE	FALSE	FA
u15221	FALSE	TRUE	TRUE	TRUE	TRUE	TRUE	TRUE	FALSE	TRUE	FALSE	TRUE	TRUE	FALSE	TRUE	FALSE	FALSE	FA
u15573	FALSE	FALSE	FALSE	FALSE	FALSE	TRUE	TRUE	TRUE	TRUE	TRUE	FALSE	FALSE	FALSE	TRUE	FALSE	TRUE	TR
u21505	FALSE	TRUE	TRUE	TRUE	TRUE	TRUE	FALSE	TRUE	TRUE	TRUE	FALSE	FALSE	FALSE	FALSE	FALSE	FALSE	FA
u15994	FALSE	FALSE	FALSE	FALSE	FALSE	FALSE	FALSE	TRUE	FALSE	TRUE	FALSE	FALSE	FALSE	FALSE	FALSE	FALSE	FA
u238	TRUE	TRUE	FALSE	FALSE	FALSE	FALSE	FALSE	TRUE	FALSE	FALSE	FALSE	FALSE	FALSE	FALSE	FALSE	FALSE	FA
u5809	FALSE	FALSE	TRUE	FALSE	FALSE	TRUE	TRUE	FALSE	FALSE	FALSE	FALSE	TRUE	FALSE	TRUE	FALSE	FALSE	FA
u16636	FALSE	FALSE	FALSE	FALSE	TRUE	FALSE	TRUE	FALSE	TRUE	FALSE	FALSE	TRUE	FALSE	TRUE	FALSE	FALSE	FA

Showing 1 to 10 of 5,000 entries

We see from the output that all the cells of the matrix are represented as TRUE and FALSE, but Apriori expects the cells to be numeric. Let's now convert the cells into 1 and 0 for TRUE and FALSE, respectively, with the following code:

```
# converting the cell values to 1 and 0
Jester5k_bin_mat_num <- 1*Jester5k_bin_mat
# viewing the matrix
View(Jester5k_bin_mat_num)
```

This will result in the following output:

	j1	j2	j3	j4	j5	j6	j7	j8	j9	j10	j11	j12	j13	j14	j15	j16	j17
u2841	1	1	1	1	0	1	1	0	1	1	1	1	0	1	0	0	
u15547	0	0	0	0	0	0	0	1	0	0	0	0	1	0	1	0	
u15221	0	1	1	1	1	1	1	0	1	0	1	1	0	1	0	0	
u15573	0	0	0	0	0	1	1	1	1	1	0	0	0	1	0	1	
u21505	0	1	1	1	1	1	0	1	1	1	0	0	0	0	0	0	
u15994	0	0	0	0	0	0	0	1	0	1	0	0	0	0	0	0	
u238	1	1	0	0	0	0	0	1	0	0	0	0	0	0	0	0	
u5809	0	0	1	0	0	1	1	0	0	0	0	1	0	1	0	0	
u16636	0	0	0	0	1	0	1	0	1	0	0	1	0	1	0	0	

Showing 1 to 10 of 5,000 entries

Now we are all set to apply the Apriori algorithm on the dataset. There are two parameters, support and confidence, that we need to pass to the algorithm. The algorithm mines the dataset based on these two parameter values. We pass 0.5 as the value for support and 0.8 as the value for confidence. The following line of code extracts the joke associations that exist in our Jester jokes dataset:

```
rules <- apriori(data = Jester5k_bin_mat_num, parameter = list(supp =
0.005, conf = 0.8))
```

This will result in the following output:

```
Apriori
Parameter specification:
 confidence minval smax arem  aval originalSupport maxtime support minlen
maxlen target   ext
       0.8    0.1    1 none FALSE            TRUE       5     0.5       1
10   rules FALSE
Algorithmic control:
 filter tree heap memopt load sort verbose
    0.1 TRUE TRUE   FALSE TRUE    2    TRUE
Absolute minimum support count: 2500
set item appearances ...[0 item(s)] done [0.00s].
```

```
set transactions ...[100 item(s), 5000 transaction(s)] done [0.02s].
sorting and recoding items ... [29 item(s)] done [0.00s].
creating transaction tree ... done [0.00s].
checking subsets of size 1 2 3 done [0.01s].
writing ... [78 rule(s)] done [0.00s].
creating S4 object  ... done [0.00s].
```

The `rules` object that was created from the execution of the Apriori algorithm now has all the joke associations that were extracted and mined from the dataset. As we can see from the output, there are `78` jokes associations that were extracted in total. We can examine the rules with the following line of code:

```
inspect(rules)
```

This will result in the following output:

```
      lhs          rhs     support confidence lift      count
[1]   {j48}    => {j50} 0.5068  0.8376860  1.084523 2534
[2]   {j56}    => {j36} 0.5036  0.8310231  1.105672 2518
[3]   {j56}    => {j50} 0.5246  0.8656766  1.120762 2623
[4]   {j42}    => {j50} 0.5150  0.8475971  1.097355 2575
[5]   {j31}    => {j27} 0.5196  0.8255481  1.146276 2598
```

The output shown is just five rules out of the overall 78 rules that are in the list. The way to read each rule is that the joke shown on the left column (`lhs`) leads to the joke on the right column (`rhs`); that is, a user that liked the joke on `lhs` of the rule generally tends to like the joke shown on `rhs`. For example, in the first rule, if a user has liked joke `j48`, it is likely that they will also like `j50`, therefore it is worth recommending joke `j50` to the user that has only read joke `j48`.

While there are several rules generated by the Apriori algorithm, the strength of each rule is specified by a metric, called `lift`. This is a metric that describes the worthiness of a rule in a business context. Note that for a rule to be considered general, it has to have a lift that is less than or equal to 1. A lift value greater than 1 signifies a better rule for implementing in business. The aim of the following lines of code is to get such strong rules to the top of the list:

```
# converting the rules object into a dataframe
rulesdf <- as(rules, "data.frame")
# employing quick sort on the rules dataframe. lift and confidence are
# used as keys to sort the dataframe. - in the command indicates that we
# want lift and confidence to be sorted in descending order
rulesdf[order(-rulesdf$lift, -rulesdf$confidence), ]
```

This will result in the following output:

```
                 rules support confidence      lift count
59 {j29,j50} => {j35}  0.5024  0.8348288 1.167266  2512
60 {j35,j50} => {j29}  0.5024  0.8301388 1.160709  2512
71 {j50,j53} => {j32}  0.5070  0.8385710 1.154420  2535
24      {j68} => {j62}  0.5478  0.8096364 1.149725  2739
72 {j32,j50} => {j53}  0.5070  0.8278903 1.149528  2535
5       {j31} => {j27}  0.5196  0.8255481 1.146276  2598
36      {j49} => {j62}  0.5578  0.8030521 1.140375  2789
78 {j36,j50} => {j32}  0.5220  0.8277831 1.139569  2610
68 {j27,j50} => {j36}  0.5128  0.8563794 1.139408  2564
66 {j36,j50} => {j35}  0.5132  0.8138281 1.137903  2566
58 {j29,j35} => {j50}  0.5024  0.8770950 1.135545  2512
32      {j69} => {j53}  0.5550  0.8171378 1.134598  2775
77 {j32,j50} => {j36}  0.5220  0.8523841 1.134093  2610
76 {j32,j36} => {j50}  0.5220  0.8755451 1.133538  2610
73 {j36,j53} => {j50}  0.5112  0.8747433 1.132500  2556
70 {j32,j53} => {j50}  0.5070  0.8747412 1.132498  2535
64 {j35,j36} => {j50}  0.5132  0.8745740 1.132281  2566
69 {j36,j50} => {j27}  0.5128  0.8131938 1.129122  2564
```

It may be observed that the output shown is only a subset of the rules output. The first rule indicates that j35 is a joke that can be recommended to a user that has already read jokes j29 and j50.

Likewise, we could just write a script to search all the jokes that a user has already read and match it with the left side of the rule; if a match is found, the corresponding right side of the rule can be recommended as the joke for the user.

Content-based recommendation engine

A recommendation engine that is solely based on the explicit or implicit feedback received from customers is termed as **content-based recommendation system**. Explicit feedback is the customer's expression of the interest through filling in a survey about preferences or rating jokes of interest or opting for newsletters related to the joke or adding the joke on the watchlist, and so on. Implicit feedback is more of a mellowed-out approach where a customer visits a page, clicks on a joke link, or just spends time reading a joke review on an e-commerce page. Based on the feedback received, similar jokes are recommended to the customers. It may be noted that content-based recommendations do not take into consideration the preferences and feedback of other customers in the system; instead, it is purely based on the personalized feedback from the specific customer.

In the recommendation process, the system identifies the products that are already positively rated by the customer with the products that the customer has not rated and looks for equivalents. Products that are similar to the positively-rated ones are recommended to the customers. In this model, the customer's preferences and behavior play a major role in incrementally fine-tuning the recommendations—that is, with each recommendation and based on whether the customer responded to the recommendation, the system learns incrementally to recommend differently. The following diagram is an illustration of how a content-based recommendation system works:

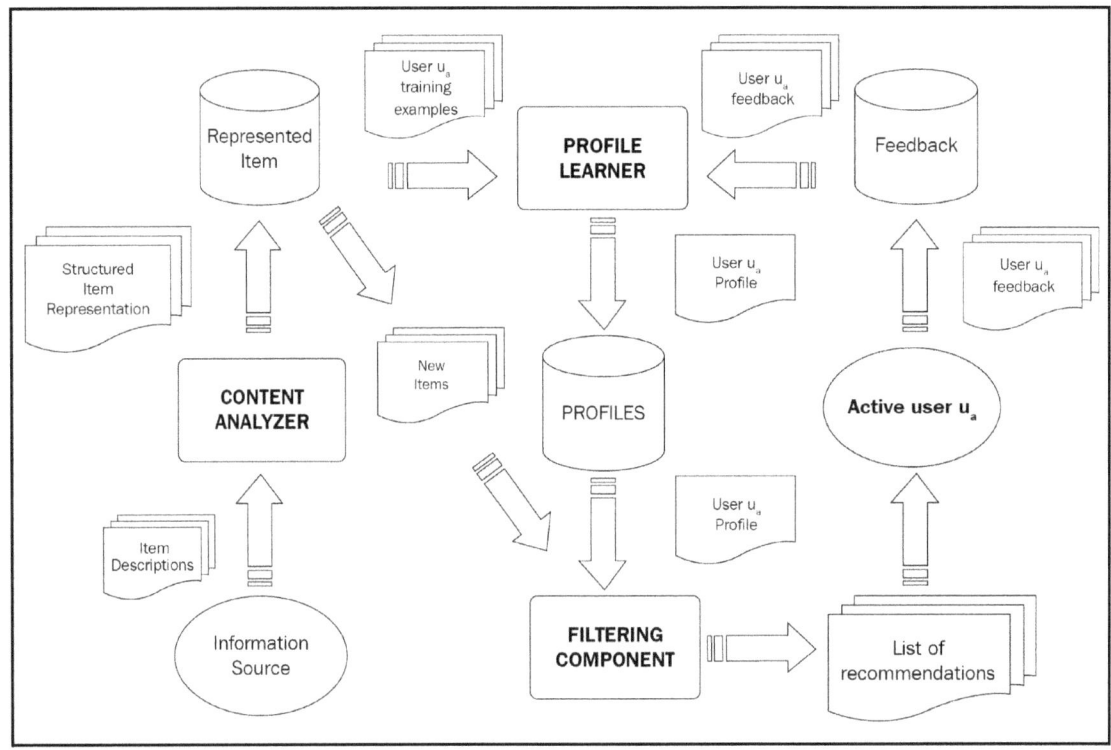

Working of a content based recommendation system

In our Jester jokes dataset, we have ratings given by users for various jokes as well as the content of the jokes themselves. Remember that the `JesterJokes` character vector incorporates the text present in the jokes themselves. Similarities between the texts present in the jokes can be used as one method to recommend jokes to users. The assumption is that if a person liked the content in a joke, and if there is another joke whose content is very similar, recommending the latter joke is probably going to be liked by the user.

Additional metadata related to jokes is not given in the Jester jokes dataset, however such metadata may be created from the content of the jokes. For example, the length of the joke, number of nouns, number of funny terms present in the joke, and central theme in the joke. Processing the text is not purely a recommendation area but it involves using NLP techniques as well. As we will be covering NLP in a different chapter, we will not cover it here.

Differentiating between ITCF and content-based recommendations

It might appear that item-based collaborative and content-based recommendations are the same. In reality, they are not the same. Let's touch upon the differences.

ITCF is totally based on user-item rankings. When we compute the similarity between items, we do not include the item attributes and just compute the similarity of items based on all customers' ratings. So the similarity between items is computed based on the ratings instead of the metadata of item itself.

In content-based recommendations, we make use of the content of both the user and the item. Generally, we construct a user profile and item profile using the content of a shared attribute space. For example, for a movie, we represent it with the actors in it and the genre (using binary coding, for example). For a user profile, we can do the same thing based on the user, such as some actors/genres. Then the similarity of user and item can be computed using cosine similarity, for example. This cosine measure leads to the recommendations.

Content-based filtering identifies products that are similar based on the tags assigned to each product. Each product is assigned weights on the basis of term frequency and inverse document frequency of each tag. After this, the user's probability of liking a product is calculated in order to arrive at the final recommendation list.

While content-based recommendation systems are highly efficient and personalized, there is an inherent problem with this model. Let's understand the over-specialization problem of content-based recommendations with an example.

Assume there are the following five movie genres:

- Comedy
- Thriller
- Science fiction
- Action
- Romance

There is this customer, Jake, who generally watches thriller and science fiction movies. Based on this preference, the content-based recommendation engine will only recommend movies related to these genres and it is never going to recommend movies from other categories. This problem arises as content-based recommendation engine solely relies on the user's past behavior and preferences to determine the recommendation.

Unlike content-recommendation systems, in ITCF recommendations, similar products build neighborhoods based on positive preferences of customers. Therefore, the system generates recommendations with products in the neighborhood that a customer might prefer. ITCF does this by making use of the correlation between the items based on the ratings given them by different users, while collaborative filtering relies on past preferences or rating correlation between users and it is able to generate recommendations for similar products even from customer's interest domain. This technique can lead to bad predictions if the product is unpopular and very few users have given feedback about it.

Building a hybrid recommendation system for Jokes recommendations

We see that both content-based filtering and collaborative filtering have their strengths and weaknesses. To overcome the issues, organizations build recommender systems that combine two or more technique and they are termed hybrid recommendation models. An example of this is a combination of content-based, IBCF, UBCF, and model-based recommender engine. This takes into account all the possible aspects that contribute to making the most relevant recommendation to the user. The following diagram shows an example approach followed in hybrid recommendation engines:

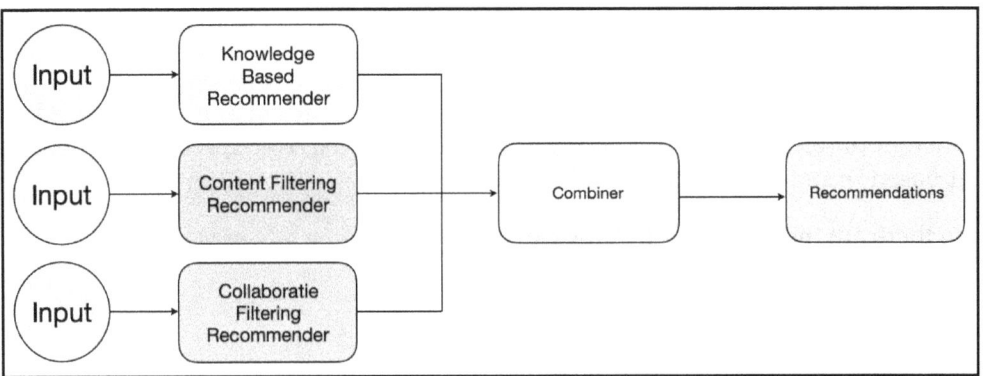

Sample approach to hybrid recommendation engine

We need to note that there is no standard approach to achieving a hybrid recommendation engine. In order to combine recommendations, here are some suggested strategies:

- **Voting**: Apply voting among the recommendation output obtained from individual recommender systems.
- **Rules-based selection**: We could devise rules that suggest weighting the output recommendations obtained from individual recommender systems. In this case, the output from recommender systems that got higher weights will be dominant and have more influence on the final recommendation outcome.
- **Combination**: Recommendations from all the recommender engines are presented together. A final list of recommendations is just the union of all recommendation output obtained from individual recommender systems.
- **Attribute integration**: Taking metadata from all recommender system to infuse it as input to another recommender.

Again, what works for a problem may not work for another, therefore these strategies need to be tested individually prior to coming up with final recommendation strategy.

The `recommenderlab` library offers the `HybridRecommender` function which allows users to train multiple recommender engines on the same set of data in one go and combine the predictions. The function has a weights parameter that offers a way to specify the weight of each of the models that will be used to combine individual predictions to arrive at the final recommendation predictions on unseen data. Implementing a hybrid recommendation-engine-based project is super straightforward and not too different from the code we learned in item-based collaborative filtering or user-based collaborative filtering projects. Anyway, let's write the code and build a hybrid recommendation engine for the `Jester5k` dataset:

```
# including the required libraries
library(recommenderlab)
# accessing the Jester5k dataset that is a part of recommenderlab library
data(Jester5k)
# split the data into the training and the test set
Jester5k_es <- evaluationScheme(Jester5k, method="split", train=0.8,
given=20, goodRating=0)
```

The preceding code is what trains a hybrid recommender. This is where it differs from the ITCF or UBCF recommenders we've built. We can observe from the code that we have used four different recommender methods that will constitute the hybrid recommender. Let's discuss each of these methods:

- The popular recommendation method simply recommends the popular jokes (determined by the number of ratings received) to users.
- The second recommender method we have used is item-based collaborative filtering method with non-normalized data but with distance being computed between items through cosine similarity.
- User-based collaborative filtering on Z-score normalized data with Euclidean distance being computed between users in the data.
- A random recommendation method that provides a random recommendation to the users.

By no means, we finalize that the combination of these four recommender methods is the best hybrid for this problem. The intention of this project is to demonstrate the implementation of the hybrid recommender. The choice of the methods involved is purely arbitrary. In reality, we may need to try multiple combinations to identify the best hybrid. The hybrid classifier is built using the following code:

```
#train a hybrid recommender model
hybrid_recom <- HybridRecommender(
  Recommender(getData(Jester5k_es, "train"), method = "POPULAR"),
  Recommender(getData(Jester5k_es, "train"), method="IBCF",
              param=list(normalize = NULL, method="Cosine")),
  Recommender(getData(Jester5k_es, "train"), method="UBCF",
                        param=list(normalize = "Z-
score",method="Euclidean")),
  Recommender(getData(Jester5k_es, "train"), method = "RANDOM"),
  weights = c(.2, .3, .3,.2)
)
# Observe the model that is built
print (getModel(hybrid_recom)
```

This will result in the following output:

```
$recommender
$recommender[[1]]
Recommender of type 'POPULAR' for 'realRatingMatrix'
learned using 4000 users.
$recommender[[2]]
Recommender of type 'IBCF' for 'realRatingMatrix'
learned using 4000 users.
$recommender[[3]]
```

```
Recommender of type 'UBCF' for 'realRatingMatrix'
learned using 4000 users.
$recommender[[4]]
Recommender of type 'RANDOM' for 'realRatingMatrix'
learned using 4000 users.
$weights
[1] 0.2 0.3 0.3 0.2
```

Observe the weights assignment in the hybrid model. We see that the popular and random recommenders are assigned 20% weight each, whereas the ITCF and UBCF methods involved in the preceding hybrid are assigned 30% weight each. It is not mandatory to set the weights while building a hybrid recommender, in which case, equal weights are assigned to each of the methods involved in the hybrid recommender. Now that our model is ready, let's make predictions and evaluate the performance with the following code:

```
# making predictions
pred <- predict(hybrid_recom, getData(Jester5k_es, "known"),
type="ratings")
# # set the predictions that fall outside the valid range to the boundary
values
pred@data@x[pred@data@x[] < -10] <- -10
pred@data@x[pred@data@x[] > 10] <- 10
# calculating performance measurements
hybrid_recom_pred = calcPredictionAccuracy(pred, getData(Jester5k_es,
"unknown"))
# printing the performance measurements
library(knitr)
print(kable(hybrid_recom_pred))
```

This will result in the following output:

```
|     |           x|
|:----|----------:|
|RMSE |   4.468849|
|MSE  |  19.970611|
|MAE  |   3.493577|
```

Summary

In this chapter, we used the recommenderlab library extensively to build the various types of joke-recommendation engines based on the Jester jokes dataset. We also learned about the theoretical concepts behind the methods.

Recommender systems is an individual ML area on its own. This subject is so vast that it cannot be covered in just one chapter. Several types of recommendation systems exists and they may be applied to datasets in specific scenarios. Matrix factorization, singular-value decomposition approximation, most popular items, and SlopeOne are some techniques that may be employed to build recommendation systems. These techniques are outside the scope of this chapter as these are rarely used in business situations to build recommendation systems, and the aim of the chapter is provide exposure to more popular techniques. Further learning on recommendation engines could be in the direction of exploring and studying these rarely-used techniques and applying them to real-world problems.

The next chapter is focused on NLP techniques. We are going to implement a sentiment-analysis engine on Amazon product reviews using several popular techniques. We'll explore semantic and syntactic approaches to analyzing text and then apply them on the Amazon review corpus. I am all geared up to turn this page and move on to the next chapter. How about you?!

References

While the `recommenderlab` library is super popular in the R community, this is not the only choice for building a recommendation system. Here are some other popular libraries you may rely on to implement recommendation engines:

- `rrecsys`: There are several popular recommendation systems, such as Global/Item/User-Average baselines, Item-Based KNN, FunkSVD, BPR, and weighted ALS for rapid prototyping. Refer to `https://cran.r-project.org/web/packages/rrecsys/index.htmlImplementations` for more information.
- `recosystem`: The R wrapper of the `libmf` library (`http://www.csie.ntu.edu.tw/~cjlin/libmf/`) for recommender system using matrix factorization. It is typically used to approximate an incomplete matrix using the product of two matrices in a latent space. Other common names for this task include collaborative filtering, matrix completion, and matrix recovery. High-performance multicore parallel computing is supported in this package.
- `rectools`: An advanced package for recommender systems to incorporate user and item covariate information, including item category preferences with parallel computation, novel variations on statistical latent factor model, focus group finder, NMF, ANOVA, and cosine models.

17
Sentiment Analysis of Amazon Reviews with NLP

Every day, we generate data from emails, online posts such as blogs, social media comments, and more. It is not surprising to say that unstructured text data is much larger in size than the tabular data that exists in the databases of any organization. It is important for organizations to acquire useful insights from the text data pertaining to the organization. Due to the different nature of the text data when compared to data in databases, the methods that need to be employed to understand the text data are different. In this chapter, we will learn a number of key techniques in **natural language processing (NLP)** that help us to work on text data.

The common definition of NLP is as follows: an area of computer science and artificial intelligence that deals with the interactions between computers and human (natural) languages; in particular, how to program computers to fruitfully process large amounts of natural language data.

In general terms, NLP deals with understanding human speech as it is spoken. It helps machines read and understand "text".

Human languages are highly complex and several ambiguities need to be resolved in order to correctly comprehend the spoken language or written text. In the area of NLP, several techniques are applied in order to deal with these ambiguities, including the **Part-of-Speech (POS)** tagger, term disambiguation, entity extraction, relations' extraction, key term recognition, and more.

For natural language systems to work successfully, a consistent knowledge base, such as a detailed thesaurus, a lexicon of words, a dataset for linguistic and grammatical rules, an ontology, and up-to-date entities, are prerequisites.

It may be noted that NLP is concerned with understanding the text from not just the syntactic perspective, but also from a semantic perspective. Similar to humans, the idea is for the machines to be able to perceive underlying messages behind the spoken words and not just the structure of words in sentences. There are numerous application areas of NLP, and the following are just a few of these:

- Speech recognition systems
- Question answering systems
- Machine translation
- Text summarization
- Virtual agents or chatbots
- Text classification
- Topic segmentation

As the NLP subject area in itself is very vast, it is not practical to cover all the areas in just one chapter. Therefore, we will be focusing on "text classification" in this chapter. We do this by implementing a project that performs sentiment analysis in the reviews expressed by Amazon.com customers. Sentiment analysis is a type of text classification task where we classify each of the documents (reviews) into one of the possible categories. The possible categories could be positive, negative, or neutral, or it could be positive, negative, or a rating on a scale of 1 to 10.

Text documents that need to be classified cannot be input directly to a machine learning algorithm. Each of the documents needs to be represented in a certain format that is acceptable for the ML algorithm as input to work on. In this chapter, we explore, implement, and understand the **Bag of Words** (**BoW**) word embedding approaches. These are approaches in which text can be represented.

As we progress with the chapter, we will cover the following topics:

- The sentiment analysis problem
- Understanding the Amazon reviews dataset
- Building a text sentiment classifier with the BoW approach
- Understanding word embedding approaches
- Building a text sentiment classifier with pretrained Word2vec word embedding based on Reuters news corpus
- Building a text sentiment classifier with GloVe word embedding
- Building a text sentiment classifier with fastText

The sentiment analysis problem

Sentiment analysis is one of the most general text classification applications. The purpose of it is to analyze messages such as user reviews, and feedback from employees, in order to identify whether the underlying sentiment is positive, negative, or neutral.

Analyzing and reporting sentiment in texts allows businesses to quickly get a consolidated high-level insight without having to read each one of the comments received.

While it is possible to generate holistic sentiment based on the overall comments received, there is also an extended area called **aspect-based sentiment analysis**. It is focused on deriving sentiment based on each area of the service. For example, a customer that visited a restaurant when writing a review would generally cover areas such as ambience, food quality, service quality, and price. Though the feedback about each of the areas may not be quoted under a specific heading, the sentences in the review comments would naturally cover the customer's opinion of one or more of these areas. Aspect-based sentiment analysis attempts to identify the sentences in the reviews in each of the areas and then identify whether the sentiment is positive, negative, or neutral. Providing sentiment by each area helps businesses quickly identify their weak areas.

In this chapter, we will discuss and implement methods that are aimed at identifying the overall sentiment from the review texts. The task can be achieved in several ways, ranging from a simple lexicon method to a complex word embedding method.

A **lexicon** method is not really a machine learning method. It is more a rule based method that is based on a predefined positive and negative words dictionary. The method involves looking up the number of positive words and negative words in each review. If the count of positive words in the review is more than the count of negative words, then the review is marked as positive, otherwise it is marked as negative. If there are an equal number of positive and negative words, then the review is marked as neutral. As implementing this method is straightforward, and as it comes with a requirement for a predefined dictionary, we will not cover the implementation of the lexicon method in this chapter.

While it is possible to consider the sentiment analysis problem as an unsupervised clustering problem, in this chapter we consider it as a supervised classification problem. This is because, we have the Amazon reviews labeled dataset available. We can make use of these labels to build classification models, and therefore, the supervised algorithm.

Getting started

The dataset is available for download and use at the following URL:

```
https://drive.google.com/drive/u/0/folders/0Bz8a_
Dbh9Qhbfll6bVpmNUtUcFdjYmF2SEpmZUZUcVNiMUw1TWN6RDV3a0JHT3kxLVhVR2M.
```

Understanding the Amazon reviews dataset

We use the Amazon product reviews polarity dataset for the various projects in this chapter. It is an open dataset constructed and made available by Xiang Zhang. It is used as a text classification benchmark in the paper: *Character-level Convolutional Networks for Text Classification* and *Advances in Neural Information Processing Systems* 28, *Xiang Zhang, Junbo Zhao, Yann LeCun, (NIPS 2015)*.

The Amazon reviews polarity dataset is constructed by taking review score 1 and 2 as negative, 4 and 5 as positive. Samples of score 3 are ignored. In the dataset, class 1 is the negative and class 2 is the positive. The dataset has 1,800,000 training samples and 200,000 testing samples.

The `train.csv` and `test.csv` files contains all the samples as comma-separated values. There are three columns in them, corresponding to class index (1 or 2), review title, and review text. The review title and text are escaped using double quotes ("), and any internal double quote is escaped by 2 double quotes (""). New lines are escaped by a backslash followed with an "n" character that is "\n".

To ensure that we are able to run our projects, even with minimal infrastructure, let's restrict the number of records to be considered in our dataset to 1,000 records only. Of course, the code that we use in the projects can be extended to any number of records, as long as the hardware infrastructure support is available. Let's first read the data and visualize the records with the following code:

```
# reading first 1000 reviews
reviews_text<-readLines('/home/sunil/Desktop/sentiment_analysis/amazon
_reviews_polarity.csv', n = 1000)
# converting the reviews_text character vector to a dataframe
reviews_text<-data.frame(reviews_text)
# visualizing the dataframe
View(reviews_text)
```

This will result in the following output:

▲	reviews_text
1	"2","Stuning even for the non-gamer","This sound tr...
2	"2","The best soundtrack ever to anything.","I'm rea...
3	"2","Amazing!","This soundtrack is my favorite musi...
4	"2","Excellent Soundtrack","I truly like this soundtra...
5	"2","Remember, Pull Your Jaw Off The Floor After He...
6	"2","an absolute masterpiece","I am quite sure any ...
7	"1","Buyer beware","This is a self-published book, a...

Showing 1 to 8 of 1,000 entries

Post reading the file, we can see that there is only one column in the dataset and this column had both the review text and the sentiment components in it. We will slightly modify the format of the dataset for the purpose of using it with sentiment analysis projects in this chapter involving the BoW, Word2vec, and GloVe approaches. Let's modify the format of the dataset with the following code:

```
# separating the sentiment and the review text
# post separation the first column will have the first 4 characters
# second column will have the rest of the characters
# first column should be named "Sentiment"
# second column to be named "SentimentText"
library(tidyr)
reviews_text<-separate(data = reviews_text, col = reviews_text, into =
c("Sentiment", "SentimentText"), sep = 4)
# viewing the dataset post the column split
View(reviews_text)
```

This will result in the following output:

	Sentiment	SentimentText
1	"2",	"Stuning even for the non-gamer","This sound track...
2	"2",	"The best soundtrack ever to anything.","I'm readin...
3	"2",	"Amazing!","This soundtrack is my favorite music of...
4	"2",	"Excellent Soundtrack","I truly like this soundtrack a...
5	"2",	"Remember, Pull Your Jaw Off The Floor After Hearin...
6	"2",	"an absolute masterpiece","I am quite sure any of y...
7	"1",	"Buyer beware","This is a self-published book, and if...

Showing 1 to 8 of 1,000 entries

Now we have two columns in our dataset. However, there is unnecessary punctuation that exists in both the columns that may cause problems with processing the dataset further. Let's attempt to remove the punctuation with the following code:

```
# Retaining only alphanumeric values in the sentiment column
reviews_text$Sentiment<-gsub("[^[:alnum:] ]","",reviews_text$Sentiment)
# Retaining only alphanumeric values in the sentiment text
reviews_text$SentimentText<-gsub("[^[:alnum:] ]","
",reviews_text$SentimentText)
# Replacing multiple spaces in the text with single space
reviews_text$SentimentText<-gsub("(?<=[\\s])\\s*|^\\s+|\\s+$", "",
reviews_text$SentimentText, perl=TRUE)
# Viewing the dataset
View(reviews_text)
# Writing the output to a file that can be consumed in other projects
write.table(reviews_text,file =
"/home/sunil/Desktop/sentiment_analysis/Sentiment Analysis
Dataset.csv",row.names = F,col.names = T,sep=',')
```

This will result in the following output:

	Sentiment	SentimentText
1	2	Stuning even for the non gamer This sound track w...
2	2	The best soundtrack ever to anything I m reading a ...
3	2	Amazing This soundtrack is my favorite music of all ...
4	2	Excellent Soundtrack I truly like this soundtrack and...
5	2	Remember Pull Your Jaw Off The Floor After Hearing ...
6	2	an absolute masterpiece I am quite sure any of you ...
7	1	Buyer beware This is a self published book and if yo...

Showing 1 to 8 of 1,000 entries

From the preceding output, we see that we have a clean dataset that is ready for use. Also, we have written the output to a file. When we build the sentiment analyzer, we can start directly reading the dataset from the `Sentiment Analysis Dataset.csv` file.

The fastText algorithm expects the dataset to be in a different format. The data input to fastText should comply the following format:

```
__label__<X>   <Text>
```

In this example, `X` is the class name. Text is the actual review text that led to the rating specified under the class. Both the rating and text should be placed on one line with no quotes. The classes are `__label__1` and `__label__2`, and there should be only one class per row. Let's accomplish the `fastText` library required format with the following code block:

```
# reading the first 1000 reviews from the dataset
reviews_text<-readLines('/home/sunil/Desktop/sentiment_analysis/amazon
_reviews_polarity.csv', n = 1000)
# basic EDA to confirm that the data is read correctly
print(class(reviews_text))
print(length(reviews_text))
print(head(reviews_text,2))
# replacing the positive sentiment value 2 with __label__2
reviews_text<-gsub("\\\"2\\\",","__label__2 ",reviews_text)
# replacing the negative sentiment value 1 with __label__1
reviews_text<-gsub("\\\"1\\\",","__label__1 ",reviews_text)
# removing the unnecessary \" characters
reviews_text<-gsub("\\\"","  ",reviews_text)
# replacing multiple spaces in the text with single space
reviews_text<-gsub("(?<=[\\s])\\s*|^\\s+|\\s+$", "", reviews_text,
```

```
perl=TRUE)
# Basic EDA post the required processing to confirm input is as desired
print("EDA POST PROCESSING")
print(class(reviews_text))
print(length(reviews_text))
print(head(reviews_text,2))
# writing the revamped file to the directory so we could use it with
# fastText sentiment analyzer project
fileConn<-file("/home/sunil/Desktop/sentiment_analysis/Sentiment Analysis
Dataset_ft.txt")
writeLines(reviews_text, fileConn)
close(fileConn)
```

This will result in the following output:

```
[1] "EDA PRIOR TO PROCESSING"
[1] "character"
[1] 1000
[1] "\"2\",\"Stuning even for the non-gamer\",\"This sound track was
beautiful! It paints the senery in your mind so well I would recomend it
even to people who hate vid. game music! I have played the game Chrono
Cross but out of all of the games I have ever played it has the best music!
It backs away from crude keyboarding and takes a fresher step with grate
guitars and soulful orchestras. It would impress anyone who cares to
listen! ^_^\""
[2] "\"2\",\"The best soundtrack ever to anything.\",\"I'm reading a lot of
reviews saying that this is the best 'game soundtrack' and I figured that
I'd write a review to disagree a bit. This in my opinino is Yasunori
Mitsuda's ultimate masterpiece. The music is timeless and I'm been
listening to it for years now and its beauty simply refuses to fade.The
price tag on this is pretty staggering I must say, but if you are going to
buy any cd for this much money, this is the only one that I feel would be
worth every penny.\""
[1] "EDA POST PROCESSING"
[1] "character"
[1] 1000\
[1] "__label__2 Stuning even for the non-gamer , This sound track was
beautiful! It paints the senery in your mind so well I would recommend it
even to people who hate vid. game music! I have played the game Chrono
Cross but out of all of the games I have ever played it has the best music!
It backs away from crude keyboarding and takes a fresher step with grate
guitars and soulful orchestras. It would impress anyone who cares to
listen! ^_^"
[2] "__label__2 The best soundtrack ever to anything. , I'm reading a lot
of reviews saying that this is the best 'game soundtrack' and I figured
that I'd write a review to disagree a bit. This in my opinino is Yasunori
Mitsuda's ultimate masterpiece. The music is timeless and I'm been
listening to it for years now and its beauty simply refuses to fade. The
```

```
price tag on this is pretty staggering I must say, but if you are going to
buy any cd for this much money, this is the only one that I feel would be
worth every penny."
```

From the output of basic EDA code, we can see that the dataset is in the required format, therefore we can proceed to our next section of implementing the sentiment analysis engine using the BoW approach. Along side the implementation, we will delve into learning the concept behind the approach, and explore the sub-techniques that can be leveraged in the approach to obtain better results.

Building a text sentiment classifier with the BoW approach

The intent of the BoW approach is to convert the review text provided into a matrix form. It represents documents as a set of distinct words by ignoring the order and meaning of the words. Each row of the matrix represents each review (otherwise called a document in NLP), and the columns represent the universal set of words present in all the reviews. For each document, and across each word, the existence of the word, or the frequency of the word occurrence, in that specific document is recorded. Finally, the matrix created from word frequency vectors represents the documents set. This methodology is used to create input datasets that are required to train the models, and also to prepare the test dataset that need to be used by the trained models to perform text classification. Now that we understand the BoW motivation, let's jump into implementing the steps to build a sentiment analysis classifier based on this approach, as shown in the following code block:

```
# including the required libraries
library(SnowballC)
library(tm)
# setting the working directory where the text reviews dataset is located
# recollect that we pre-processed and transformed the raw dataset format
setwd('/home/sunil/Desktop/sentiment_analysis/')
# reading the transformed file as a dataframe
text <- read.table(file='Sentiment Analysis Dataset.csv', sep=',',header =
TRUE)
# checking the dataframe to confirm everything is in tact
print(dim(text))
View(text)
```

This will result in the following output:

```
> print(dim(text))
[1] 1000 2
> View(text)
```

	Sentiment	SentimentText
1	2	Stuning even for the non gamer This sound track w...
2	2	The best soundtrack ever to anything I m reading a ...
3	2	Amazing This soundtrack is my favorite music of all ...
4	2	Excellent Soundtrack I truly like this soundtrack and...
5	2	Remember Pull Your Jaw Off The Floor After Hearing ...
6	2	an absolute masterpiece I am quite sure any of you ...
7	1	Buyer beware This is a self published book and if yo...

Showing 1 to 8 of 1,000 entries

The first step in processing text data involves creating a *corpus*, which is a collection of text documents. The VCorpus function in the tm package enables conversion of the reviews comments column in the data frame into a volatile corpus. This can be achieved through the following code:

```
# transforming the text into volatile corpus
train_corp = VCorpus(VectorSource(text$SentimentText))
print(train_corp)
```

This will result in the following output:

```
> print(train_corp)
<<VCorpus>>
Metadata:  corpus specific: 0, document level (indexed): 0
Content:  documents: 1000
```

From the volatile corpus, we create a **Document Term Matrix (DTM)**. A DTM is a sparse matrix that is created using the tm library's DocumentTermMatrix function. The rows of the matrix indicate documents and the columns indicate features, that is, words. The matrix is sparse because all unique unigram sets of the dataset become columns in DTM and, as each review comment does not have all elements of the unigram set, most cells will have a 0, indicating the absence of the unigram.

While it is possible to extract n-grams (unigrams, bigrams, trigrams, and so on) as part of the BoW approach, the tokenize parameter can be set and passed as part of the control list in the `DocumentTermMatrix` function to accomplish n-grams in DTM. It must be noted that using n-grams as part of the DTM creates a very high number of columns in the DTM. This is one of the demerits of the BoW approach, and, in some cases, it could stall the execution of the project due to limited memory. As our specific case is also limited by hardware infrastructure, we restrict ourselves by including only the unigrams in DTM in this project. Apart from just generating unigrams, we also perform some additional processing on the reviews text document by passing parameters to the control list in the `tm` library's `DocumentTermMatrix` function. The processing we do on the review text documents during the creation of the DTM is given here:

1. Change the case of the text to lowercase.
2. Remove any numbers.
3. Remove stop words using the English language stop word list from the Snowball stemmer project. Stop words are common words, such as a, an, in, and the, that do not add value in deciding sentiment based on review comments.
4. Remove punctuation.
5. Perform stemming, which aims at resolving a word into the base form of the word, that is, strip the plural *s* from nouns, the *ing* from verbs, or other affixes. A stem is a natural group of words with equal or very similar meaning. After the stemming process, every word is represented by its stem. The `SnowballC` library provides the capability to obtain the root for each of the words in the review comments.

Let's now create a DTM from the volatile corpus and do the text preprocessing with the following code block:

```
# creating document term matrix
dtm_train <- DocumentTermMatrix(train_corp, control = list(
  tolower = TRUE, removeNumbers = TRUE,
  stopwords = TRUE,
  removePunctuation = TRUE,
  stemming = TRUE
))
# Basic EDA on dtm
inspect(dtm_train)
```

This will result in the following output:

```
> inspect(dtm_train)
<<DocumentTermMatrix (documents: 1000, terms: 5794)>>
Non-/sparse entries: 34494/5759506
```

```
Sparsity            : 99%
Maximal term length: 21
Weighting           : term frequency (tf)
Sample              :
      Terms
Docs  book can get great just like love one read time
  111    0   3   2     0    0    0    2   1    0    2
  162    4   1   0     0    0    1    0   0    1    0
  190    0   0   0     0    0    0    0   0    0    0
  230    0   1   1     0    0    0    1   0    0    0
  304    0   0   0     0    0    3    0   2    0    0
  399    0   0   0     0    0    0    0   0    0    0
  431    9   1   0     0    0    1    2   0    0    1
  456    1   0   0     0    0    0    0   1    2    0
  618    0   2   3     1    4    1    3   1    0    1
  72     0   0   1     0    2    0    0   1    0    1
```

We see from the output that there are 1,000 documents that were processed and form rows in the matrix. There are 5,794 columns representing unique unigrams from the reviews following the additional text processing. We also see that the DTM is 99% sparse and consists of non-zero entries only in 34,494 cells. The non-zero cells represent the frequency of occurrence of the word on the column in the document represent on the row of the DTM. The weighting is done through the default 'term frequency' weighting, as we did not specify any weighting parameter in the control list supplied to the `DocumentTermMatrix` function. Other forms of weighting, such as **term frequency-inverse document frequency (TFIDF)**, are also possible just by passing the appropriate weight parameter in the control list to the `DocumentTermMatrix` function. For now, we will stick to weighting based on term frequency, which is the default. We also see from the `inspect` function that several sample documents were output along with the term frequencies in these documents.

The DTM tends to get very big, even for normal sized datasets. Removing sparse terms, that is, terms occurring only in very few documents, is the technique that can be tried to reduce the size of the matrix without losing significant relations inherent to the matrix. Let's remove sparse columns from the matrix. We will attempt to remove those terms that have at least a 99% of sparse elements with the following line of code:

```
# Removing sparse terms
dtm_train= removeSparseTerms(dtm_train, 0.99)
inspect(dtm_train)
```

This will result in the following output:

```
> inspect(dtm_train)
<<DocumentTermMatrix (documents: 1000, terms: 686)>>
Non-/sparse entries: 23204/662796
Sparsity            : 97%
```

```
Maximal term length: 10
Weighting             : term frequency (tf)
Sample                :
       Terms
Docs  book can get great just like love one read time
  174    0   0   1     1    1    2    0   2    0    1
  304    0   0   0     0    0    3    0   2    0    0
  355    3   0   0     0    1    1    2   3    1    0
  380    4   1   0     0    1    0    0   1    0    2
  465    5   0   1     1    0    0    0   2    6    0
  618    0   2   3     1    4    1    3   1    0    1
   72    0   0   1     0    2    0    0   1    0    1
  836    1   0   0     0    0    3    0   0    5    1
  866    8   0   1     0    0    1    0   0    4    0
  959    0   0   2     1    1    0    0   2    0    1
```

We now see from the output of the `inspect` function that the sparsity of the matrix is reduced to 97%, and the number of unigrams (columns of the matrix) is reduced to 686. We are now ready with the DTM that can be used for training with any machine learning classification algorithm. In the next few lines of code, let's attempt to divide our DTM into training and test dataset:

```
# splitting the train and test DTM
dtm_train_train <- dtm_train[1:800, ]
dtm_train_test <- dtm_train[801:1000, ]
dtm_train_train_labels <- as.factor(as.character(text[1:800, ]$Sentiment))
dtm_train_test_labels <- as.factor(as.character(text[801:1000,
]$Sentiment))
```

We will be using a machine learning algorithm called **Naive Bayes** to create a model. Naive Bayes is generally trained on data with nominal features. We can observe that the cells in our DTM are numeric and therefore need to be converted to nominal prior to feeding the dataset as input for creating the model with Naive Bayes. As each cell indicates the word frequency in the review, and as the number of times a word used in the review does not impact sentiment, let's write a function to convert the cell values with a non-zero value to Y, and in case of a zero, let's convert it to N, with the following code:

```
cellconvert<- function(x) {
x <- ifelse(x > 0, "Y", "N")
}
```

Now, let's apply the function on all rows of the training dataset, and test dataset we have previously created in this project with the following code:

```
# applying the function to rows in training and test datasets
dtm_train_train <- apply(dtm_train_train, MARGIN = 2,cellconvert)
```

```
dtm_train_test <- apply(dtm_train_test, MARGIN = 2,cellconvert)
# inspecting the train dtm to confirm all is in tact
View(dtm_train_train)
```

This will result in the following output:

	abl	absolut	act	action	actual	adam	add	adult	adventur	advertis	age	ago	agre
1	N	N	N	N	N	N	N	N	N	N	N	N	N
2	N	N	N	N	N	N	N	N	N	N	N	N	N
3	N	Y	N	N	N	N	N	N	N	N	N	N	N
4	N	N	N	N	N	N	N	N	N	N	N	N	N
5	N	N	N	N	N	N	N	N	N	N	N	N	N
6	N	Y	N	N	Y	N	N	N	N	N	N	N	N
7	N	N	N	N	N	N	N	N	N	N	N	N	N

Showing 1 to 8 of 800 entries

We can see from the output that all the cells in the training and test DTMs are now converted to nominal values. Thus, let's proceed to build a text sentiment analysis classifier using the Naive Bayes algorithm from the `e1071` library, as follows:

```
# training the naive bayes classifier on the training dtm
library(e1071)
nb_senti_classifier=naiveBayes(dtm_train_train,dtm_train_train_labels)
# printing the summary of the model created
summary(nb_senti_classifier)
```

This will result in the following output:

```
> summary(nb_senti_classifier)
        Length Class  Mode
apriori   2    table  numeric
tables  686    -none- list
levels    2    -none- character
call      3    -none- call
```

The preceding summary output shows that the `nb_senti_classifier` object is successfully created from the training DTM. Let's now use the model object to predict sentiment on the test data DTM. In the following code block, we are instructing that the predictions should be classes and not prediction probabilities:

```
# making predictions on the test data dtm
nb_predicts<-predict(nb_senti_classifier, dtm_train_test,type="class")
# printing the predictions from the model
print(nb_predicts)
```

This will result in the following output:

```
[1] 1 1 2 1 1 1 1 1 1 2 2 1 2 2 2 2 1 2 1 1 2 1 2 1 1 1 2 2 1 2 2 2 2 1 2 1
1 1 1 2 2 2 2 1 2 1 1 1 1 1 1 1 1 1 1 1 1 2 1 1 1 2 1 1 1 1 1 1 1 2 1 1 2 2
1 2 2 2 2 1 2 2 1 1 1 1 1 2 1 1 2 1 1 1 1 1 2 2 2 2 2 1 2 2 1 2 1 1 1 1 1 2
2 2 2 2 1 1 1 2 2 2 1 1 1 1 1 2 1 2 1 1 1 1 1 1 1 1 2 1 1 1 1 1 1 2 1 1 1 1
1 1 2 1 1 1 1 1 1 2 2 2 2 2 1 2 2 1 2 2 1 1 2 2 1 1 2 2 2 2 2 2 2 2 2 2 2 1
1 2 1 2 1 2 2 1 1 1 1 2
Levels: 1 2
```

With the following code, let us now compute the accuracy of the model using the `mmetric` function in the `rminer` library:

```
# computing accuracy of the model
library(rminer)
print(mmetric(nb_predicts, dtm_train_test_labels, c("ACC")))
```

This will result in the following output:

```
[1] 79
```

We achieved a 79% accuracy just with a very quick and basic BoW model. The model can be further improved by means of techniques such as parameter tuning, lemmatization, new features creation, and so on.

Pros and cons of the BoW approach

Now that we have an understanding of both the theory and implementation of the BoW approach, let's examine the pros and cons of the approach. When it comes to pros, the BoW approach is very simple to understand and implement and therefore offers a lot of flexibility for customization on any text dataset. It may be observed that the BoW approach does not retain the order of words specifically when only unigrams are considered. This problem is generally overcome by retaining n-grams in the DTM. However, it comes at the cost as larger infrastructure is needed to process the text and build a classifier. Another severe drawback of the approach is that it does not respect the semantics of the word. For example, the words "car" and "automobile" are often used in the same context. A model built based on BoW treats the sentences "buy used cars" and "purchase old automobiles" as very different sentences. While these sentences are the same, BoW models do not classify these sentences as the same, as the words in these sentences are not matching. It is possible to consider the semantics of words in sentences using an approach called word embedding. This is something we will explore in our next section.

Understanding word embedding

The BoW models that we discussed in our earlier section suffer from a problem that they do not capture information about a word's meaning or context. This means that potential relationships, such as contextual closeness, are not captured across collections of words. For example, the approach cannot capture simple relationships, such as determining that the words "cars" and "buses" both refer to vehicles that are often discussed in the context of transportation. This problem that we experience with the BoW approach will be overcome by word embedding, which is an improved approach to mapping semantically similar words.

Word vectors represent words as multidimensional continuous floating point numbers, where semantically similar words are mapped to proximate points in geometric space. For example, the words *fruit* and *leaves* would have a similar word vector, *tree*. This is due to the similarity of their meanings, whereas the word *television* would be quite distant in the geometrical space. In other words, words that are used in a similar context will be mapped to a proximate vector space.

The word vectors can be of *n* dimensions, and *n* can take any number as input from the user creating it (for example 10, 70, 500). The dimensions are latent in the sense that it may not be apparent to humans what each of these dimensions means in reality. There are methods such as **Continuous Bag of Words** (**CBOW**) and **Skip-Gram** that enable conceiving the word vectors from the text provided as training input to word embedding algorithms. Also, the individual numbers in the word vector represent the word's distributed weight across dimensions. In a general sense, each dimension represents a latent meaning, and the word's numerical weight on that dimension captures the closeness of its association with and to that meaning. Thus, the semantics of the word are embedded across the dimensions of the vector.

Though the word vectors are multidimensional and cannot be visualized directly, it is possible to visualize the vectors learned, by projecting them down to two dimensions using techniques such as the t-SNE dimensionality reduction technique. The following diagram displays learned word vectors in two dimensional spaces for country capitals, verb tenses, and gender relationships:

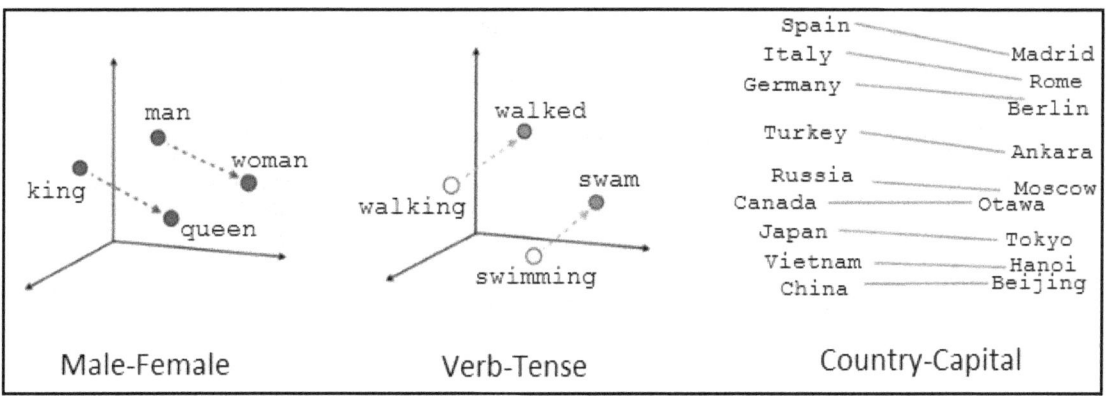

Visualization of word embeddings in a two dimensional space

When we observe the word embedding visualization, we can perceive that the vectors captured some general, and in fact quite useful, semantic information about words and their relationships to one another. With this, each word in the text now can be represented as a row in the matrix similar to that of the BoW approach, but, unlike the BoW approach, it captures the relationships between the words.

The advantage of representing words as vectors is that they lend themselves to mathematical operators. For example, we can add and subtract vectors. The canonical example here is showing that by using word vectors we can determine the following:

$$king - man + woman = queen$$

In the given example, we subtracted the gender (man) from the word vector for king and added another gender (woman), and we obtained a new word vector from the operation (*king - man + woman*) that maps most closely to the word vector for queen.

A few more amazing examples of mathematical operations that can be achieved on word vectors are shown as follows:

- Given two words, we can establish the degree of similarity between them:

```
model.similarity('woman','man')
```

And the output is as follows:

```
0.73723527
```

- Finding the odd one out from the set of words given as input:

```
model.doesnt_match('breakfast cereal dinner lunch';.split())
```

The odd one is given as the following output:

```
'cereal'
```

- Derive analogies, for example:

```
model.most_similar(positive=['woman','king'],negative=['man'],topn=
1)
```

The output is as follows:

```
queen: 0.508
```

Now, what it all means for us is that machines are able to identify semantically similar words given in a sentence. The following diagram is a gag related to word embedding that made me laugh, but the gag does convey the power of word embedding application, which otherwise would not be possible with the BoW kind of text representations:

A gag demonstrating the power of word embeddings application

There are several techniques that can be used to learn word embedding from text data. Word2vec, GloVe, and fastText are some of the popular techniques. Each of these techniques allows us to either train our own word embedding from the text data we have, or use the readily available pretrained vectors.

This approach of learning our own word embedding requires a lot of training data and can be slow, but this option will learn an embedding both targeted to the specific text data and the NLP task at hand.

Pretrained word embedding vectors are vectors that are trained on large amounts of text data (usually billions of words) available on sources such as Wikipedia. These are generally high-quality word embedding vectors made available by companies such as Google or Facebook. We can download these pretrained vector files and consume them to obtain word vectors for the words in the text that we would like to classify or cluster.

Building a text sentiment classifier with pretrained word2vec word embedding based on Reuters news corpus

Word2vec was developed by Tomas Mikolov, et al. at Google in 2013 as a response to making the neural-network-based training of the embedding more efficient, and since then it has become the de facto standard for developing pretrained word embedding.

Word2vec introduced the following two different learning models to learn the word embedding:

- **CBOW**: Learns the embedding by predicting the current word based on its context.
- **Continuous Skip-Gram**: The continuous Skip-Gram model learns by predicting the surrounding words given a current word.

Both CBOW and Skip-Gram methods of learning are focused on learning the words given their local usage context, where the context of the word itself is defined by a window of neighboring words. This window is a configurable parameter of the model.

The `softmaxreg` library in R offers pretrained `word2vec` word embedding that can be used for building our sentiment analysis engine for the Amazon reviews data. The pretrained vector is built using the `word2vec` model, and it is based on the `Reuter_50_50` dataset, UCI Machine Learning Repository (`https://archive.ics.uci.edu/ml/datasets/Reuter_50_50`).

Without any delay, let's get into the code and also review the approach followed in this code:

```
# including the required library
library(softmaxreg)
# importing the word2vec pretrained vector into memory
data(word2vec)
```

Let's examine the `word2vec` pretrained emdeddings. It is just another data frame, and therefore can be reviewed through the regular `dim` and `View` commands as follows:

```
View(word2vec)
```

This will result in the following output:

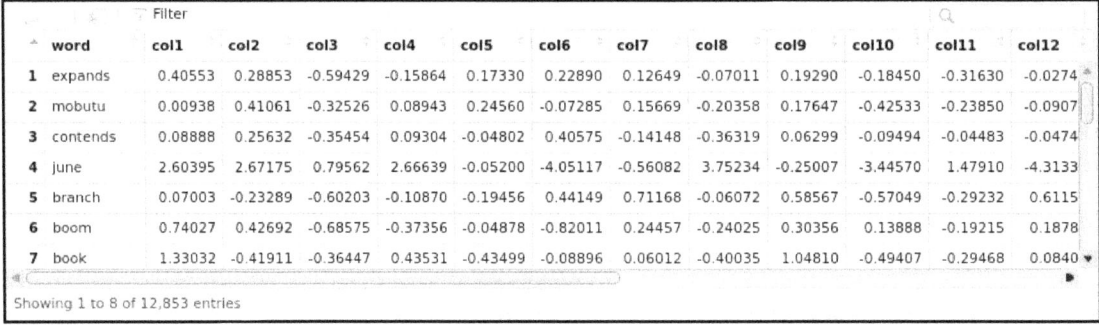

	word	col1	col2	col3	col4	col5	col6	col7	col8	col9	col10	col11	col12
1	expands	0.40553	0.28853	-0.59429	-0.15864	0.17330	0.22890	0.12649	-0.07011	0.19290	-0.18450	-0.31630	-0.0274
2	mobutu	0.00938	0.41061	-0.32526	0.08943	0.24560	-0.07285	0.15669	-0.20358	0.17647	-0.42533	-0.23850	-0.0907
3	contends	0.08888	0.25632	-0.35454	0.09304	-0.04802	0.40575	-0.14148	-0.36319	0.06299	-0.09494	-0.04483	-0.0474
4	june	2.60395	2.67175	0.79562	2.66639	-0.05200	-4.05117	-0.56082	3.75234	-0.25007	-3.44570	1.47910	-4.3133
5	branch	0.07003	-0.23289	-0.60203	-0.10870	-0.19456	0.44149	0.71168	-0.06072	0.58567	-0.57049	-0.29232	0.6115
6	boom	0.74027	0.42692	-0.68575	-0.37356	-0.04878	-0.82011	0.24457	-0.24025	0.30356	0.13888	-0.19215	0.1878
7	book	1.33032	-0.41911	-0.36447	0.43531	-0.43499	-0.08896	0.06012	-0.40035	1.04810	-0.49407	-0.29468	0.0840

Showing 1 to 8 of 12,853 entries

Here, let's use the following `dim` command:

```
dim(word2vec)
```

This will result in the following output:

```
[1] 12853 21
```

From the preceding output, we can observe that there are `12853` words that have got word vectors in the pretrained vector. Each of the words is defined using 20 dimensions, and these dimensions define the context of the words. In the next step, we can look up the word vector for each of the words in the review comments. As there are only 12,853 words in the pretrained word embedding, there is a possibility that we encounter a word that does not exist in the pretrained embedding. In such a case, the unidentified word is represented with a 20 dimension vector that is filled with zeros.

We also need to understand that the word vectors are available only at a word level, and therefore in order to decode the entire review, we take the mean of all the word vectors of the words that made up the review. Let's review the concept of getting the word vector for a sentence from individual word vectors with an example.

Assume the sentence we want to get the word vector for is, *it is very bright and sunny this morning*. Individual words that comprise the sentence are *it*, *is*, *very*, *bright*, *and*, *sunny*, *this*, and *morning*.

Now, we can look up each of these words in the pretrained vector and get the corresponding word vectors as shown in the following table:

Word	dim1	dim2	dim3	.....	....	dim19	dim20
it	-2.25	0.75	1.75	-1.25	-0.25	-3.25	-2.25
is	0.75	1.75	1.75	-2.25	-2.25	0.75	-0.25
very	-2.25	2.75	1.75	-0.25	0.75	0.75	-2.25
bright	-3.25	-3.25	-2.25	-1.25	0.75	1.75	-0.25
and	-0.25	-1.25	-2.25	2.75	-3.25	-0.25	1.75
sunny	0	0	0	0	0	0	0
this	-2.25	-3.25	2.75	0.75	-0.25	-0.25	-0.25
morning	-0.25	-3.25	-2.25	1.75	0.75	2.75	2.75

Now, we have word vectors that comprise the sentence. Please note that these are not actual word vector values but just are made up to demonstrate the approach. Also, observe that the word `sunny` is represented with zeros across the dimensions to symbolize that the word is not found in the pretrained word embedding. In order to get the word vector for the sentence, we just compute the mean of each dimension. The resulting vector is a 1 x 20 vector representing the sentence, as follows:

Sentence	-1.21875	-0.71875	0.15625	0.03125	-0.46875	0.28125	-0.09375

The `softmaxreg` library offers the `wordEmbed` function where we could pass a sentence and ask it to compute the `mean` word vector for the sentence. The following code is a custom function that was created to apply the `wordEmbed` function on each of the Amazon reviews we have in hand. At the end of applying this function to the reviews dataset, we expect to have a *n* x 20 matrix that is the word vector representation of our reviews. The *n* in the *n* x 20 represents the number of rows and 20 is the number of dimensions through which each review is represented, as seen in the following code:

```
# function to get word vector for each review
docVectors = function(x)
{
  wordEmbed(x, word2vec, meanVec = TRUE)
}
# setting the working directory and reading the reviews dataset
setwd('/home/sunil/Desktop/sentiment_analysis/')
text = read.csv(file='Sentiment Analysis Dataset.csv', header = TRUE)
# applying the docVector function on each of the reviews
# storing the matrix of word vectors as temp
temp=t(sapply(text$SentimentText, docVectors))
# visualizing the word vectors output
View(temp)
```

This will result in the following output:

1	0.9001672	0.0141028750	-1.0616862	-0.04416625	-0.3533675	-0.6738171	0.0729040000	-0.8279434	-0.45585687	0.3550463
2	1.1277574	-0.1360358824	-1.2177180	-0.15301882	-0.9068942	-1.1244064	-0.3733900980	-0.9224640	-0.18435745	0.3772624
3	0.8885871	-0.0856260294	-1.1432905	-0.01933257	-0.7176180	-0.7664569	0.0773944853	-0.6180129	-0.17120868	0.2428186
4	0.5495152	-0.2092989344	-1.1647043	-0.35540713	-0.5236916	-0.3633348	0.3810807377	-0.3947897	-0.05829189	0.0426281
5	1.0133256	-0.0268535556	-1.1575648	0.03562800	-0.3391036	-0.6837794	-0.0377413333	-0.5346906	-0.43420989	-0.1457108
6	0.8082624	-0.2846747297	-1.2788924	-0.15989108	-0.7584445	-0.6270216	0.0809281757	-0.5134580	-0.17634953	0.0652181
7	0.8902767	0.0157431081	-1.2022697	-0.14477669	-0.9319141	-0.7504433	-0.1275757432	-0.7498420	-0.38869155	0.3180145

Showing 1 to 8 of 1,000 entries

Then we review `temp` using the `dim` command, as follows:

```
dim(temp)
```

This will result in the following output:

```
1000 20
```

We can see from the output that we have word vectors created for each of the reviews in our corpus. This data frame can now be used to build classification models using an ML algorithm. The following code to achieve classification is no different from the one we did for the BoW approach:

```
# splitting the dataset into train and test
temp_train=temp[1:800,]
temp_test=temp[801:1000,]
labels_train=as.factor(as.character(text[1:800,]$Sentiment))
labels_test=as.factor(as.character(text[801:1000,]$Sentiment))
# including the random forest library
library(randomForest)
# training a model using random forest classifier with training dataset
# observe that we are using 20 trees to create the model
rf_senti_classifier=randomForest(temp_train, labels_train,ntree=20)
print(rf_senti_classifier)
```

This will result in the following output:

```
randomForest(x = temp_train, y = labels_train, ntree = 20)
              Type of random forest: classification
                    Number of trees: 20
No. of variables tried at each split: 4
        OOB estimate of  error rate: 44.25%
Confusion matrix:
      1    2 class.error
1 238 172    0.4195122
2 182 208    0.4666667
```

The preceding output shows that the Random Forest model object is successfully created. Of course, the model can be improved further; however we are not going to be doing that here as the focus is to demonstrate making use of word embeddings, rather than getting the best performing classifier.

Next, with the following code we make use of the Random Forest model to make predictions on the test data and then report out the performance:

```
# making predictions on the dataset
rf_predicts<-predict(rf_senti_classifier, temp_test)
library(rminer)
print(mmetric(rf_predicts, labels_test, c("ACC")))
```

This will result in the following output:

```
[1] 62.5
```

We see that we get a 62% accuracy from using the pretrained `word2vec` embeddings made out of the Reuters news group's dataset.

Building a text sentiment classifier with GloVe word embedding

Stanford University's Pennington, et al. developed an extension of the `word2vec` method that is called **Global Vectors for Word Representation (GloVe)** for efficiently learning word vectors.

GloVe combines the global statistics of matrix factorization techniques, such as LSA, with the local context-based learning in `word2vec`. Also, unlike `word2vec`, rather than using a window to define local context, GloVe constructs an explicit word context or word co-occurrence matrix using statistics across the whole text corpus. As an effect, the learning model yields generally better word embeddings.

The `text2vec` library in R has a GloVe implementation that we could use to train to obtain word embeddings from our own training corpus. Alternatively, pretrained GloVe word embeddings can be downloaded and reused, similar to the way we did in the earlier `word2vec` pretrained embedding project covered in the previous section.

The following code block demonstrates the way in which GloVe word embeddings can be created and used for sentiment analysis, or, for that matter, any text classification task. We are not going to discuss explicitly the steps involved, since the code is already heavily commented with detailed explanations of each of the steps:

```
# including the required library
library(text2vec)
# setting the working directory
setwd('/home/sunil/Desktop/sentiment_analysis/')
# reading the dataset
text = read.csv(file='Sentiment Analysis Dataset.csv', header = TRUE)
# subsetting only the review text so as to create Glove word embedding
wiki = as.character(text$SentimentText)
# Create iterator over tokens
tokens = space_tokenizer(wiki)
# Create vocabulary. Terms will be unigrams (simple words).
it = itoken(tokens, progressbar = FALSE)
```

```
vocab = create_vocabulary(it)
# consider a term in the vocabulary if and only if the term has appeared
aleast three times in the dataset
vocab = prune_vocabulary(vocab, term_count_min = 3L)
# Use the filtered vocabulary
vectorizer = vocab_vectorizer(vocab)
# use window of 5 for context words and create a term co-occurance matrix
tcm = create_tcm(it, vectorizer, skip_grams_window = 5L)
# create the glove embedding for each each in the vocab and
# the dimension of the word embedding should set to 50
# x_max is the maximum number of co-occurrences to use in the weighting
# function
# note that training the word embedding is time consuming - be patient
glove = GlobalVectors$new(word_vectors_size = 50, vocabulary = vocab, x_max
= 100)
wv_main = glove$fit_transform(tcm, n_iter = 10, convergence_tol = 0.01)
```

This will result in the following output:

```
INFO [2018-10-30 06:58:14] 2018-10-30 06:58:14 - epoch 1, expected cost
0.0231
INFO [2018-10-30 06:58:15] 2018-10-30 06:58:15 - epoch 2, expected cost
0.0139
INFO [2018-10-30 06:58:15] 2018-10-30 06:58:15 - epoch 3, expected cost
0.0114
INFO [2018-10-30 06:58:15] 2018-10-30 06:58:15 - epoch 4, expected cost
0.0100
INFO [2018-10-30 06:58:15] 2018-10-30 06:58:15 - epoch 5, expected cost
0.0091
INFO [2018-10-30 06:58:15] 2018-10-30 06:58:15 - epoch 6, expected cost
0.0084
INFO [2018-10-30 06:58:16] 2018-10-30 06:58:16 - epoch 7, expected cost
0.0079
INFO [2018-10-30 06:58:16] 2018-10-30 06:58:16 - epoch 8, expected cost
0.0074
INFO [2018-10-30 06:58:16] 2018-10-30 06:58:16 - epoch 9, expected cost
0.0071
INFO [2018-10-30 06:58:16] 2018-10-30 06:58:16 - epoch 10, expected cost
0.0068
```

The following uses the `glove` model to obtain the combined word vector:

```
# Glove model learns two sets of word vectors - main and context.
# both matrices may be added to get the combined word vector
wv_context = glove$components
word_vectors = wv_main + t(wv_context)
# converting the word_vector to a dataframe for visualization
word_vectors=data.frame(word_vectors)
```

```
# the word for each embedding is set as row name by default
# using the tibble library rownames_to_column function, the rownames is
copied as first column of the dataframe
# we also name the first column of the dataframe as words
library(tibble)
word_vectors=rownames_to_column(word_vectors, var = "words")
View(word_vectors)
```

This will result in the following output:

	words	X1	X2	X3	X4	X5	X6	X7	X8
1	proper	-0.183938861	0.535530344	-0.27412909	-0.461746097	-0.100504830	-0.06466068	0.27132151	0.022755206
2	Stone	-0.217368635	-0.619701624	0.10591805	0.089803070	-0.080577239	0.22282777	-0.08934084	0.214210983
3	practically	-0.178972661	-0.437024154	0.33109763	0.293728501	-0.078952595	0.30375123	0.02330199	-0.322362080
4	sings	-0.724405587	-0.028475652	0.49158170	-0.093503183	-0.710965484	0.18689734	0.08935627	0.252694234
5	Lit	0.062119633	0.026841171	0.47210883	0.196634409	0.005582331	0.72392994	0.24716580	-0.867472053
6	Jordan	0.904864848	-0.067597866	0.54857185	-0.549472168	-0.369129092	-0.86961806	-0.44172353	-0.154189382
7	Waist	0.568695709	-0.044349857	0.40858194	0.849112123	0.691710413	-0.78834027	-0.47516816	0.633008987
8	planet	-0.387996703	-0.714768857	0.34405428	0.011786014	0.091809094	0.16621399	-0.70615846	0.718172520
9	replacement	-0.072499663	-0.221350074	-0.55283985	0.209103354	0.317845784	-0.27957728	0.05697817	-0.054497272

Showing 1 to 10 of 3,019 entries

We make use of the `softmaxreg` library to obtain the mean word vector for each review. This is similar to what we did in `word2vec` pretrained embedding in the previous section. Observe that we are passing our own trained word embedding `word_vectors` to the `wordEmbed()` function, as follows:

```
library(softmaxreg)
docVectors = function(x)
{
   wordEmbed(x, word_vectors, meanVec = TRUE)
}
# applying the function docVectors function on the entire reviews dataset
# this will result in word embedding representation of the entire reviews #
dataset
temp=t(sapply(text$SentimentText, docVectors))
View(temp)
```

This will result in the following output:

1	-1.021674e-01	0.22374366	-0.31380372	-0.24523438	-0.2180971	-0.21172789	0.186605388	0.20956048	-0.04558712	-0.051
2	1.194950e-02	0.14968572	-0.30805228	-0.18293664	-0.2258637	-0.25498353	0.132375430	0.20017790	-0.10048077	-0.187
3	-4.014470e-02	0.21875645	-0.35748125	-0.21297610	-0.2207336	-0.22556214	0.183079215	0.16168858	-0.04248742	-0.077
4	-4.899985e-02	0.29007017	-0.32021912	-0.18001094	-0.1704606	-0.16176222	0.190220987	0.17813243	-0.05338900	0.081
5	-2.130447e-02	0.28866528	-0.37526279	-0.19773100	-0.2535055	-0.19100561	0.109212284	0.16018515	-0.07803226	0.011
6	1.814156e-02	0.24571046	-0.36655681	-0.16840549	-0.2477891	-0.14538835	0.142705234	0.19516599	-0.01567144	-0.100
7	-4.428909e-03	0.18590056	-0.30330482	-0.13953408	-0.1885616	-0.19064436	0.114466673	0.21589199	-0.07120269	-0.192
8	1.132957e-01	0.18632012	-0.37151759	-0.18653199	-0.2790091	-0.24254169	0.170006885	0.37763887	-0.11926454	-0.229
9	6.110208e-02	0.19142639	-0.30230704	-0.21159849	-0.2664249	-0.26331480	0.172434261	0.20212321	-0.08137470	-0.149
10	6.80377e-04	0.20381966	0.35296762	0.30145897	0.2980702	0.27664309	0.127662254	0.28347248	0.11008705	0.207

Showing 1 to 11 of 1,000 entries

We will now split the dataset into train and test portions, and use the `randomforest` library to build a model to train, as shown in the following lines of code:

```
# splitting the dataset into train and test portions
temp_train=temp[1:800,]
temp_test=temp[801:1000,]
labels_train=as.factor(as.character(text[1:800,]$Sentiment))
labels_test=as.factor(as.character(text[801:1000,]$Sentiment))
# using randomforest to build a model on train data
library(randomForest)
rf_senti_classifier=randomForest(temp_train, labels_train,ntree=20)
print(rf_senti_classifier)
```

This will result in the following output:

```
Call:
 randomForest(x = temp_train, y = labels_train, ntree = 20)
               Type of random forest: classification
                     Number of trees: 20
No. of variables tried at each split: 7


        OOB estimate of  error rate: 42.12%
Confusion matrix:
      1   2 class.error
1 250 160   0.3902439
2 177 213   0.4538462
```

Then, we use the Random Forest model created to predict labels, as follows:

```
# predicting labels using the randomforest model created
rf_predicts<-predict(rf_senti_classifier, temp_test)
# estimating the accuracy from the predictions
library(rminer)
print(mmetric(rf_predicts, labels_test, c("ACC")))
```

This will result in the following output:

```
[1] 66.5
```

With this method, we obtain an accuracy of 66%. This is despite the fact that the word embeddings are obtained from words in just 1,000 text samples. The model may be further improved by using a pretrained embedding. The overall framework to use the pretrained embedding remains the same as what we did in word2vec project in the previous section.

Building a text sentiment classifier with fastText

fastText is a library and is an extension of word2vec for word representation. It was created by the Facebook Research Team in 2016. While Word2vec and GloVe approaches treat words as the smallest unit to train on, fastText breaks words into several n-grams, that is, subwords. For example, the trigrams for the word apple are app, ppl, and ple. The word embedding for the word apple is sum of all the word n-grams. Due to the nature of the algorithm's embedding generation, fastText is more resource-intensive and takes additional time to train. Some of the advantages of fastText are as follows:

- It generates better word embeddings for rare words (including misspelled words).
- For out of vocabulary words, fastText can construct the vector for a word from its character n-grams, even if a word doesn't appear in training corpus. This is not a possibility for both Word2vec and GloVe.

The fastTextR library provides an interface to the fastText. Let's make use of the fastTextR library for our project to build a sentiment analysis engine on Amazon reviews. While it is possible to download pretrained fastText word embedding and make use of it for our project, let's make an attempt to train a word embedding based on the reviews dataset we have in hand. It should be noted that the approach in terms of making use of fastText pretrained word embedding is similar to the approach we followed in the word2vec based project that we dealt with earlier.

Similar to the project covered in the previous section, comments are included inline in the code. The comments explain each of the lines indicating the approach taken to build the Amazon reviews sentiment analyzer in this project. Let's look into the following code now:

```
# loading the required libary
library(fastTextR)
# setting the working directory
setwd('/home/sunil/Desktop/sentiment_analysis/')
# reading the input reviews file
# recollect that fastText needs the file in a specific format and we
created one compatiable file in
# "Understanding the Amazon Reviews Dataset" section of this chaptertext =
readLines("Sentiment Analysis Dataset_ft.txt")
# Viewing the text vector for conformation
View(text)
```

This will result in the following output:

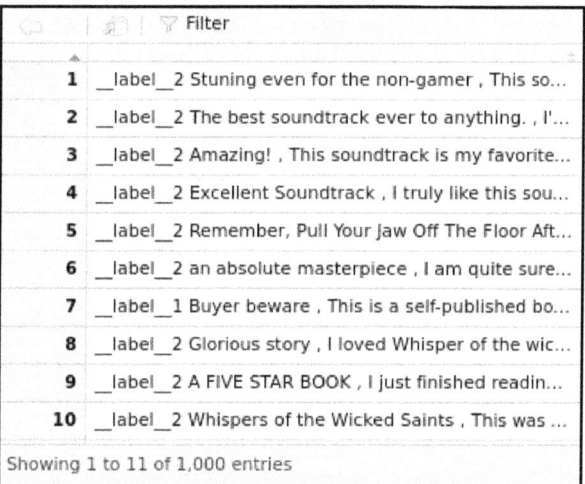

	Filter
1	__label__2 Stuning even for the non-gamer , This so...
2	__label__2 The best soundtrack ever to anything. , I'...
3	__label__2 Amazing! , This soundtrack is my favorite...
4	__label__2 Excellent Soundtrack , I truly like this sou...
5	__label__2 Remember, Pull Your Jaw Off The Floor Aft...
6	__label__2 an absolute masterpiece , I am quite sure...
7	__label__1 Buyer beware , This is a self-published bo...
8	__label__2 Glorious story , I loved Whisper of the wic...
9	__label__2 A FIVE STAR BOOK , I just finished readin...
10	__label__2 Whispers of the Wicked Saints , This was ...

Showing 1 to 11 of 1,000 entries

Now let's divide the reviews into training and test datasets, and view them using the following lines of code:

```
# dividing the reviews into training and test
temp_train=text[1:800]temp_test=text[801:1000]
# Viewing the train datasets for confirmation
View(temp_train)
```

This will give the following output:

	V1
1	__label__2 Stuning even for the non-gamer , This sound track was beautiful! It paints the senery in your mind so well I would recomend it ever
2	__label__2 The best soundtrack ever to anything , I'm reading a lot of reviews saying that this is the best 'game soundtrack' and I figured that
3	__label__2 Amazing! , This soundtrack is my favorite music of all time, hands down. The intense sadness of Prisoners of Fate (which means all
4	__label__2 Excellent Soundtrack , I truly like this soundtrack and I enjoy video game music. I have played this game and most of the music on
5	__label__2 Remember, Pull Your Jaw Off The Floor After Hearing it , If you've played the game, you know how divine the music is! Every single
6	__label__2 an absolute masterpiece , I am quite sure any of you actually taking the time to read this have played the game at least once, and h
7	__label__1 Buyer beware , This is a self-published book, and if you want to know why--read a few paragraphs! Those 5 star reviews must have
8	__label__2 Glorious story , I loved Whisper of the wicked saints. The story was amazing and I was pleasantly surprised at the changes in the bo
9	__label__2 A FIVE STAR BOOK , I just finished reading Whisper of the Wicked saints. I fell in love with the caracters. I expected an average rom
10	__label__2 Whispers of the Wicked Saints , This was a easy to read book that made me want to keep reading on and on, not easy to put down
11	__label__1 The Worst! , A complete waste of time. Typographical errors, poor grammar, and a totally pathetic plot add up to absolutely nothin
12	__label__2 Great book , This was a great book.I just could not put it down,and could not read it fast enough. Boy what a book the twist and tu
13	__label__2 Great Read , I thought this book was brilliant, but yet realistic. It showed me that to error is human. I loved the fact that this writer s
14	__label__1 Oh please , I guess you have to be a romance novel lover for this one, and not a very discerning one. All others beware! It is absolu
15	__label__1 Awful beyond belief! , I feel I have to write to keep others from wasting their money. This book seems to have been written by a 7t
16	__label__1 Don't try to fool us with fake reviews. , It's glaringly obvious that all of the glowing reviews have been written by the same person,
17	__label__2 A romantic zen baseball comedy , When you hear folks say that they don't make 'em like that anymore, they might be talking abou
18	__label__2 Fashionable Compression Stockings! , After I had a DVT my doctor required me to wear compression stockings. I wore ugly white T
19	__label__2 Jobst UltraSheer Thigh High , Excellent product. However, they are very difficult to get on for older people. I feel like I've had a full
20	__label__1 sizes recomended in the size chart are not real , sizes are much smaller than what is recomended in the chart. I tried to put it and s
21	__label__1 mens ultrasheer , This model may be ok for sedentary types, but I'm active and get around alot in my job - consistently found these
22	__label__2 Delicious cookie mix , I thought it was funny that I bought this product without knowing it was a mix. I read the header very quickly
23	__label__1 Another Abysmal Digital Copy , Rather than scratches and insect droppings, this one has random pixelations combined with muddy
24	__label__2 A fascinating insight into the life of modern Japanese teens , I thoroughly enjoyed Rising Sons and Daughters. I don't know of any
25	__label__2 i liked this album more then i thought i would , I heard a song or two and thought same o same o,but when i listened to songs like
26	__label__1 Problem with charging smaller AAAs , I have had the charger for more than two years. It charges AA batteries just fine, but has a h
27	__label__1 Works, but not as advertised , I bought one of these chargers..the instructions say the lights stay on while the battery charges...true
28	__label__1 Disappointed , I read the reviews,made my purchase and was very disappointed. The charger is convenient by charging all four bat
29	__label__1 Oh dear , I was excited to find a book ostensibly about Muslim feminism, but this volume did not live up to the expectations.One e

Use the following code to view the test dataset:

```
View(temp_test)
```

This will give the following output:

	V1
1	__label__1 I was fored to read it too , The Scarlet Letter is a good but long and discriptive book. I wouldn't tell anybody to read it unless they classic books or a Hawthorne fan. This book and also The H
2	__label__1 a tragedy , This is a tragedy in two ways. Everyone dies at the end, and if you have to or choose to read this you will experience a tragedy.I can compare this book to a lobster.People say lobs
3	__label__1 too had to read , I find the old english wording too hard to understand and too hard to read..haven't got into it too far yet but it is taking me forever to get here
4	__label__1 Simply the worse book ever. , I had to read this book for my high school English class. I hated every bit of it actually I never finished it. This book does not belong on the list of classic must re
5	__label__1 No Active Table of Contents , My rating is only for the electronic formatting of this book. I really feel like I don't have any right to complain since the book was free but -you get what you pay
6	__label__1 Should not be a requirement in high school , To me this book would turn a young person, like my self away from the key and enjoyment of reading . Being a book with extensive mistakes in i
7	__label__1 It was like a bad dream, but I couldn't wake up , This book is like a bad soap. No action. No drama. Very predictable. It is about a woman who cheated on her husband with another man. The
8	__label__1 Landscape book , I guess I should have read the last review or even the fact that the description says Landscape. I didn't think it was necessary. It's just a book right?I guess it's supposed to b
9	__label__1 THE SIMPLE CONCEPT OF SIN, TABOO , THIS BOOK IS A GREAT CLASSIC THAT EXPLOITS THE IDEA THAT A PREACHER WOULD DO THE UNTHINKABLE AND MAKE A WOMAN PREGNANT WI
10	__label__2 Excellent gift , My 12 year daughter was delighted to receive the Scarlet Letter. She has enjoyed reading it through out X-mas vacation. I had forgotten how good literature can be an exceller
11	__label__2 Great classic for the price , For a first time reading of this classic I recommend this. If you love it you may want a nicer version for the bookshelf. This is a nice quality book though. The printin
12	__label__1 Missing Custom House , My daughter needed this book for school and specifically needed an edition with the custom house. We looked inside this book on line and it shows that it includes
13	__label__2 Incredibly engrossing , I absolutely loved this book, it was so engrossing, could not put it down. Hawthorne has wonderful descriptions. it is a fascinating time in history and he brings it alive.
14	__label__1 Characterization in The Scarlet Letter , The Scarlet Letter is overloaded with many superfluous words that requires the reader to sift through them all to get to the actual story. However, the st
15	__label__2 the illiteracy of our generation , Frankly, in reading the negative reviews it is clear to me that there is a growing body of illiterates among us. It seems too, that the more a book makes one thi
16	__label__2 The Scarlet Letter e-Book , Great book, had seen the movie but the book is much more. It will hold your attention and is an easy read too.Even better, the e-book was free on Amazon!
17	__label__1 I just don't get it , I am an avid reader. I have read many so called classics . This book is just plain boring! Yawn.... I really tried to get into it. I couldn't finish it. I just kept falling asleep. This bo
18	__label__2 favorite classic , loved it in high school, love it as an adult...Great book and very informative.Book is written well with ability to keep the reader interested in the book and all it has too offer.Ch
19	__label__1 Childish Novel , It is a travesty that this novel is even classified with the classics. This is by far one of the most boring and pointless novels in existance. The plot dribbles on about sin and adul
20	__label__1 Jeff the Scorned , I hated this story. It was long. It was preachy. It was boring. Unless you're interested in catching up on battles with Puritanism, avoid this book.
21	__label__1 Ugh. , I read this book for AP English and had to do a blue-book assignment of it. The word ugh summarizes my experience.This book was written in the 19th century, and that's where it belo
22	__label__1 This book was dumb , I know that saying the book is dumb nullifies all the hard work put into it, but I just did not like it. Sure the main idea and a well written summary makes the book as a v
23	__label__1 Avg. Rating too high , I've bought this book, underlined every hint of symbolism, found all evidence of romanticism, followed every quote involving thematic oppositions, and noted every exi
24	__label__1 Received a different book , I ordered a specific ISBN No. and received a different tiny book of the same with different appearence and a different ISBN No.The picture seen online is not the o
25	__label__1 Oh my... , This novel is absolutely awful. Although it has received over 500 reviews I feel it is my duty to help bring the average star level to where it belongs, at zero. Where to begin... perhap
26	__label__1 Far too little crime and fist fights , So I heard about this from a friend at Comi-Con. He did not know much about it, but heard some people talking about it in the food court. I thought it sour
27	__label__1 Get to the point already , Too long. Re-read this and remembered how much Hawthorne's style irritates me. There is an interesting story within but he takes WAY too long to tell it.
28	__label__1 Slow moving predictable story , The story is a very simple one but the action, so to speak, doesn't really happen until the final third of the book. It was a battle to get through the dry middle!

We will now create a `.txt` file for the train and test dataset using the following code:

```
# creating txt file for train and test dataset
# the fasttext function expects files to be passed for training and testing
fileConn<-file("/home/sunil/Desktop/sentiment_analysis/train.ft.txt")
writeLines(temp_train, fileConn)
close(fileConn)
fileConn<-file("/home/sunil/Desktop/sentiment_analysis/test.ft.txt")
writeLines(temp_test, fileConn)
close(fileConn)
# creating a test file with no labels
# recollect the original test dataset has labels in it
# as the dataset is just a subset obtained from full dataset
temp_test_nolabel<- gsub("__label__1", "", temp_test, perl=TRUE)
temp_test_nolabel<- gsub("__label__2", "", temp_test_nolabel, perl=TRUE)
```

Now we will view the no labels test dataset for confirmation using the following command:

```
View(temp_test_nolabel)
```

This will result in the following output:

1	I was fored to read it too , The Scarlet Letter is a go...
2	a tragedy , This is a tragedy in two ways. Everyone ...
3	too had to read , I find the old english wording too h...
4	Simply the worse book ever. , I had to read this boo...
5	No Active Table of Contents , My rating is only for th...
6	Should not be a requirement in high school , To me t...
7	It was like a bad dream, but I couldn't wake up , Thi...
8	Landscape book , I guess I should have read the last...
9	THE SIMPLE CONCEPT OF SIN, TABOO , THIS BOOK I...
10	Excellent gift , My 12 year daughter was delighted t...

Showing 1 to 11 of 200 entries

Let's now write the no labels test dataset to a file so we can use it for testing, as follows:

```
fileConn<-
file("/home/sunil/Desktop/sentiment_analysis/test_nolabel.ft.txt")
writeLines(temp_test_nolabel, fileConn)
close(fileConn)
# training a supervised classification model with training dataset file
model<-fasttext("/home/sunil/Desktop/sentiment_analysis/train.ft.txt",
method = "supervised", control = ft.control(nthreads = 3L))
# Obtain all the words from a previously trained model=
words<-get_words(model)
# viewing the words for confirmation. These are the set of words present  #
in our training data
View(words)
```

This will result in the following output:

Now we will obtain the word vectors from a previously trained model and view the word vectors for each word in our training dataset, as follows:

```
# Obtain word vectors from a previously trained model.
word_vec<-get_word_vectors(model, words)
# Viewing the word vectors for each word in our training dataset
# observe that the word embedding dimension is 5
View(word_vec)
```

This will result in the following output:

the	0.0048942002	0.0119173910	-0.007131079	-0.0538859000	0.0631141519
I	-0.0063322317	0.0340317730	0.013798622	0.1236231849	0.1272250041
and	0.0792929615	-0.0941958507	-0.025565661	0.0298055482	0.0359003235
to	0.0081054736	-0.0231800877	0.072222504	-0.0636691093	-0.0123805664
a	0.0155201275	0.0465942640	0.082956703	-0.0899057742	-0.0420212336
of	0.0261684284	0.0131066605	-0.099206429	0.0289594168	0.0892733419
is	-0.1270621065	0.0093145892	-0.113851033	-0.0712698530	0.0564273112
it	-0.0264658609	-0.0369169824	-0.133076520	-0.1075496329	0.0285819056
this	0.0263026568	0.0273612377	-0.044421507	0.0267953683	-0.0022563544
,	0.0069336370	-0.1357625574	-0.036102463	-0.1234983876	-0.0015986823

Showing 1 to 11 of 1,466 entries

We will predict the labels for the reviews in the no labels test dataset and write it to a file for future reference. Then we will get the predictions into a data frame to compute the performance and see the estimate of the accuracy using the following lines of code:

```
# predicting the labels for the reviews in the no labels test dataset
# and writing it to a file for future reference
predict(model, newdata_file=
"/home/sunil/Desktop/sentiment_analysis/test_nolabel.ft.txt",result_file="/
home/sunil/Desktop/sentiment_analysis/fasttext_result.txt")
# getting the predictions into a dataframe so as to compute performance   #
measurementft_preds<-predict(model, newdata_file=
"/home/sunil/Desktop/sentiment_analysis/test_nolabel.ft.txt")
# reading the test file to extract the actual labels
reviewstestfile<
readLines("/home/sunil/Desktop/sentiment_analysis/test.ft.txt")
# extracting just the labels frm each line
library(stringi)
actlabels<-stri_extract_first(reviewstestfile, regex="\\w+")
# converting the actual labels and predicted labels into factors
actlabels<-as.factor(as.character(actlabels))
ft_preds<-as.factor(as.character(ft_preds))
# getting the estimate of the accuracy
library(rminer)
print(mmetric(actlabels, ft_preds, c("ACC")))
```

This will result in the following output:

```
[1] 58
```

We have a 58% accuracy with the `fastText` method on our reviews data. As a next step, we could check whether the accuracy may be further improved by making use of fastText pretrained word embedding. As we already know, implementing a project by making use of pretrained embedding is not very different from the implementation that we followed in the `word2vec` project described in the earlier section of this chapter. The difference is just that the training step to obtain word embedding needs to be discarded and the model variable in the code covered in this project code should be initiated with the pretrained word embeddings.

Summary

In this chapter, we learned various NLP techniques, namely BoW, Word2vec, GloVe, and fastText. We built projects involving these techniques to perform sentiment analysis on an Amazon reviews dataset. The projects that were built involved two approaches, making use of pretrained word embeddings and building the word embeddings from our own dataset. We tried both these approaches to represent text in a format that can be consumed by ML algorithms that resulted in models with the ability to perform sentiment analysis.

In the next chapter, we will learn about customer segmentation by making use of a wholesale dataset. We will look at customer segmentation as an unsupervised problem and build projects with various techniques that can identify inherent groups within the e-commerce company's customer base. Come, let's explore the world of building an e-commerce customer segmentation engine with ML!

18
Customer Segmentation Using Wholesale Data

In today's competitive world, the success of an organization largely depends on how much it understands its customers' behavior. Understanding each customer individually to better tailor the organizational effort to individual needs is a very expensive task. Based on the size of the organization, this task can be very challenging as well. As an alternative, organizations rely on something called **segmentation**, which attempts to categorize customers into groups based on identified similarities. This critical aspect of customer segmentation allows organizations to extend their efforts to the individual needs of various customer subsets (if not catering to individual needs), therefore reaping greater benefits.

In this chapter, we will learn about the concept and importance of customer segmentation. We'll then deep dive into learning the various **machine learning** (**ML**) methods to identify subgroups of customers based on customer characteristics. We'll implement several projects using the wholesale dataset to understand the ML techniques for segmentation. In the next section, we'll start by learning the foundations of customer segmentation and the need for ML techniques to achieve segmentation. We will cover the following topics as we progress:

- Understanding customer segmentation
- Understanding the wholesale customer dataset and the segmentation problem
- Identifying the customer segments in wholesale customer data using DIANA
- Identifying the customer segments in wholesale customer data using AGNES

Understanding customer segmentation

Customer segmentation, or market segmentation, at a basic level, is the partitioning of a broad range of potential customers in a given market into specific subgroups of customers, where each of the subgroups contains customers that share certain similarities. The following diagram depicts the formal definition of customer segmentation where customers are identified into three groups:

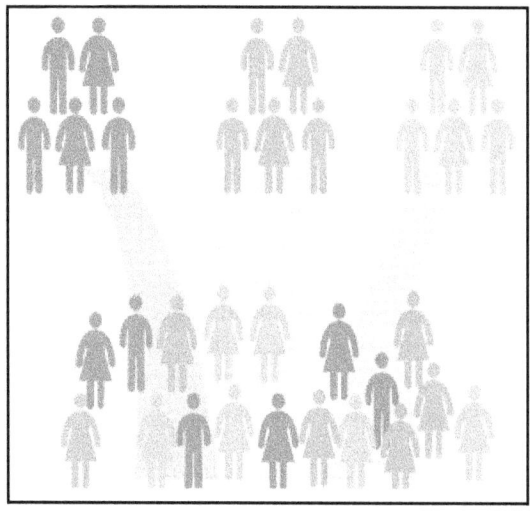

Illustration depicting customer segmentation definition

Customer segmentation needs the organizations to gather data about customers and analyze it to identify patterns that can be used to determine subgroups. The segmentation of customers could be achieved through multiple data points related to customers. The following are some of the data points:

- **Demographics**: This data point includes race, ethnicity, age, gender, religion, level of education, income, life stage, marital status, occupation
- **Psychographics**: This data point includes lifestyle, values, socioeconomic standing, personality
- **Behavioral**: This data point includes product usage, loyalties, awareness, occasions, knowledge, liking, and purchase patterns

With billions of people in the world, efficiently making use of customer segmentation will help organizations narrow down the pool and reach only the people that mean something to their business, ultimately driving conversions and revenue. The following are some of the specific objectives that organizations attempt to achieve through identifying segments in their customers:

- Identifying higher-percentage opportunities that the sales team can pursue
- Identifying customer groups that have a higher interest in the product, and customize the product according to the needs of high-interest customers
- Developing very focused marketing messages to specific customer groups so as to drive higher-quality inbound interest in the product
- Choosing the best communication channel for various segments, which might be email, social media, radio, or another approach, depending on the segment
- Concentrating on the most profitable customers
- Upselling and cross-selling other products and services
- Test pricing options
- Identifying new product or service opportunities

When an organization needs to perform segmentation, it can typically look for common characteristics, such as shared needs, common interests, similar lifestyles, or even similar demographic profiles and come up with segments in customer data. Unfortunately, creating segments is not that simple. With the availability of big data, organizations now have hundreds of characteristics of customers they can look at in order to come up with segments. It is not feasible for a person or few people in an organization to go through hundreds of types of data, find relationships between each of them, and then establish segments based on several different values possible for each data point. That's where unsupervised ML, called **clustering,** comes to rescue.

Clustering is the mechanism of using ML algorithms to identify relationships in different types of data, thereby yielding new segments based on those relationships. Simply put, clustering finds the relationship between data points so they can be segmented.

The terms **cluster analysis** and **customer segmentation** are closely related and used interchangeably by ML practitioners. However, there is an important difference between these terms.

Clustering is a tool that helps organizations put together data based on similarities and statistical connections. Clustering is very helpful in guiding the development of suitable customer segments. It also provides useful statistical measures of the potential target customers. While the objective for an organization is to identify effective customer segments from data, simply applying a clustering technique on data and grouping the data in itself may or may not offer effective customer segments. This essentially means that the output obtained from clustering, that is, the **clusters**, need to be further analyzed to get insight into the meaning of each of the clusters, and then determine which clusters can be utilized for downstream activities, such as business promotions. The following is a flow diagram that helps us to understand the role of clustering in the customer-segmentation process:

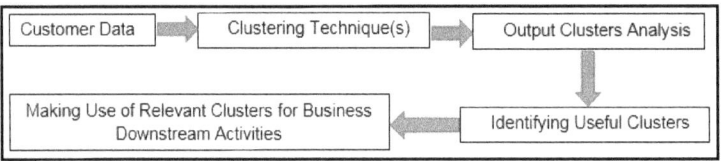

Role of clustering in customer segmentation

Now that we understand that clustering forms a stepping stone to performing customer segmentation, in the rest of the chapter, we will discuss various clustering techniques and implement projects around these techniques to create customer segments. For our projects, we make use of wholesale customer dataset. Before delving into the projects, let's learn about the dataset and perform **exploratory data analysis (EDA)** to get a better understanding of the data.

Understanding the wholesale customer dataset and the segmentation problem

The UCI Machine Learning Repository offers the wholesale customer dataset at `https://archive.ics.uci.edu/ml/datasets/wholesale+customers`. The dataset refers to clients of a wholesale distributor. It includes the annual spending in **monetary units (m.u.)** on diverse product categories. The goal of these projects is to apply clustering techniques to identify segments that are relevant for certain business activities, such as rolling out a marketing campaign. Before we actually use the clustering algorithms to get clusters, let's first read the data and perform some EDA to understand the data using the following code block:

```
# setting the working directory to a folder where dataset is located
setwd('/home/sunil/Desktop/chapter5/')
# reading the dataset to cust_data dataframe
cust_data = read.csv(file='Wholesale_customers_ data.csv', header = TRUE)
# knowing the dimensions of the dataframe
print(dim(cust_data))
Output :
440 8
# printing the data structure
print(str(cust_data))
'data.frame': 440 obs. of 8 variables:
 $ Channel : int 2 2 2 1 2 2 2 2 1 2 ...
 $ Region : int 3 3 3 3 3 3 3 3 3 3 ...
 $ Fresh : int 12669 7057 6353 13265 22615 9413 12126 7579...
 $ Milk : int 9656 9810 8808 1196 5410 8259 3199 4956...
 $ Grocery : int 7561 9568 7684 4221 7198 5126 6975 9426...
 $ Frozen : int 214 1762 2405 6404 3915 666 480 1669...
 $ Detergents_Paper: int 2674 3293 3516 507 1777 1795 3140 3321...
 $ Delicassen : int 1338 1776 7844 1788 5185 1451 545 2566...
# Viewing the data to get an intuition of the data
View(cust_data)
```

This will give the following output:

	Channel	Region	Fresh	Milk	Grocery	Frozen	Detergents_Paper	Delicassen
1	2	3	12669	9656	7561	214	2674	1338
2	2	3	7057	9810	9568	1762	3293	1776
3	2	3	6353	8808	7684	2405	3516	7844
4	1	3	13265	1196	4221	6404	507	1788
5	2	3	22615	5410	7198	3915	1777	5185
6	2	3	9413	8259	5126	666	1795	1451
7	2	3	12126	3199	6975	480	3140	545
8	2	3	7579	4956	9426	1669	3321	2566
9	1	3	5963	3648	6192	425	1716	750
10	2	3	6006	11093	18881	1159	7425	2098

Showing 1 to 10 of 440 entries

Now let's check whether there are any entries with missing fields in our dataset:

```
# checking if there are any NAs in data
print(apply(cust_data, 2, function (x) sum(is.na(x))))
Output :
Channel Region Fresh Milk
0 0 0 0
Grocery Frozen Detergents_Paper Delicassen
```

```
0  0  0  0
# printing the summary of the dataset
print(summary(cust_data))
```

This will give the following output:

```
Channel Region Fresh Milk
 Min.  :1.000 Min.  :1.000 Min.  :    3 Min.  :   55
 1st Qu.:1.000 1st Qu.:2.000 1st Qu.:  3128 1st Qu.:  1533
 Median :1.000 Median :3.000 Median :  8504 Median :  3627
 Mean  :1.323 Mean  :2.543 Mean  : 12000 Mean  :  5796
 3rd Qu.:2.000 3rd Qu.:3.000 3rd Qu.: 16934 3rd Qu.:  7190
 Max.  :2.000 Max.  :3.000 Max.  :112151 Max.  :73498
 Grocery Frozen Detergents_Paper Delicassen
 Min.  :    3.0 Min.  :    3.0 Min.  :    3 Min.  :   25.0
 1st Qu.:  256.8 1st Qu.:  408.2 1st Qu.:  2153 1st Qu.:  742.2
 Median :  816.5 Median :  965.5 Median :  4756 Median : 1526.0
 Mean  : 2881.5 Mean  : 1524.9 Mean  : 7951 Mean  : 3071.9
 3rd Qu.: 3922.0 3rd Qu.: 1820.2 3rd Qu.: 10656 3rd Qu.: 3554.2
 Max.  :40827.0 Max.  :47943.0 Max.  :92780 Max.  :60869.0
```

From the EDA, we see that there are 440 observations available in this dataset and there are eight variables. The dataset does not have any missing values. While the last six variables are goods that were brought by distributors from the wholesaler, the first two variables are factors (categorical variables) representing the location and channel of purchase. In our projects, we intend to identify the segments based on the sales into different products, therefore, the location and channel variables in the data are not very useful. Let's delete them from the dataset using the following code:

```
# excluding the non-useful columns from the dataset
cust_data<-cust_data[,c(-1,-2)]
# verifying the dataset post columns deletion
dim(cust_data)
```

This gives us the following output:

```
440 6
```

We see that only six columns are retained, confirming that the deletion of non-required columns is successful. From the summary output in the EDA code, we can also observe that the scale across all the retained columns is the same so we do not have to explicitly normalize the data.

It may be noted that most clustering algorithms involve computation of distance of some form (such as Euclidean, Manhattan, Grower). It is important that data is scaled across the columns in the dataset so as to ensure a variable does not end up as a dominating one in distance computation just because of high scale. In case of different scales observed in columns of the data, we will rely on techniques such as Z-transform or min-max transform. Applying one of these techniques on the data ensures that the columns of the dataset are scaled appropriately therefore leaving no dominating variables in the dataset to be used with clustering algorithms. Fortunately, we do not have this issue so we can continue with the dataset as it is.

Clustering algorithms impose identification of subgroups in the input dataset even if there are no clusters present. To ensure that we get meaningful clusters as output from the clustering algorithms, it is important to check whether clusters exist in the data at all. **Clustering tendency**, or the feasibility of the clustering analysis, is the process of identifying whether the clusters exist in the dataset. Given an input dataset, the process determines whether it has a non-random or non-uniform data structure distribution that will lead to meaningful clusters. The Hopkins statistic measure is used to determine cluster tendency. It takes a value between 0 and 1, and if the value of the Hopkins statistic is close to 0 (far below 0.5), it indicates the existence of valid clusters in the dataset. A Hopkins value closer to 1 indicates random structures in the dataset.

The factoextra library has a built-in get_clust_tendency() function that computes the Hopkins statistic on the input dataset. Let's apply this function on our wholesale dataset to determine whether the dataset is valid for clustering at all. The following code accomplishes the computation of the Hopkins statistic:

```
# setting the working directory to a folder where dataset is located
setwd('/home/sunil/Desktop/chapter18/')
# reading the dataset to cust_data dataframe
cust_data = read.csv(file='Wholesale_customers_ data.csv', header = TRUE)
# removing the non-required columns
cust_data<-cust_data[,c(-1,-2)]
# inlcuding the facto extra library
library(factoextra)
# computing and printing the hopikins statistic
print(get_clust_tendency(cust_data, graph=FALSE,n=50,seed = 123))
```

This will give the following output:

```
$hopkins_stat
[1] 0.06354846
```

The Hopkins statistic output for our dataset is very close to 0, so we can conclude that we have a dataset that is a good candidate for our clustering exercise.

Categories of clustering algorithms

There are numerous clustering algorithms available off the shelf in R. However, all these algorithms can be grouped into one of two categories:

- **Flat or partitioning algorithms**: These algorithms rely on an input parameter that defines the number of clusters to be identified in the dataset. The input parameter sometimes comes up as input from business directly or it can be established through certain statistical methods. For example, the **Elbow** method.

- **Hierarchical algorithms**: In these kinds of algorithms, the clusters are not identified in a single step. They involves multiple steps that run from a single cluster containing all the data points to n clusters containing single data point. Hierarchical algorithms can be further divided into the following two types:

  - **Divisive type**: A top-down clustering method where all points are initially assigned to a single cluster. In the next step, the cluster is split into two clusters which are least similar. The process of splitting the clusters is recursively done until each point has its own cluster, for example, the **DIvisive ANAlysis** (**DIANA**) clustering algorithm.

  - **Agglomerative type**: A bottom-up approach where, in the initial run, each point in the dataset is assigned n unique clusters, where n is equal to the number of observations in the dataset. In the next iteration, most similar clusters are merged (based on the distance between the clusters). The recursive process of merging the clusters continues until we are left with just one cluster, for example, **agglomerative nesting** (**AGNES**) algorithm.

As discussed earlier, there are numerous clustering algorithms available and we will focus on implementing projects using one algorithm for each type of clustering. We will implement project with k-means that is a flat or partitioning type clustering algorithm. We will then do customer segmentation with DIANA and AGNES, which are divisive and agglomerative, respectively.

Identifying the customer segments in wholesale customer data using k-means clustering

The k-means algorithm is perhaps the most popular and commonly-used clustering method from partitioning clustering type. Though we usually call the clustering algorithm k-means, multiple implementations of this algorithm exist, namely the **MacQueen, Lloyd and Forgy**, and **Hartigan-Wong** algorithms. It has been studied and found that the Hartigan-Wong algorithm performs better than the other two algorithms in most situations. K-means in R makes use of the Hartigan-Wong implementation by default.

The k-means algorithm requires the k-value to be passed as a parameter. The parameter indicates the number of clusters to be made with the input data. It is often a challenge for practitioners to determine the optimal k-value. Sometimes, we can go to a business and ask them how many clusters they would expect in the data. The answer from the business directly translates to be the k parameter value to be fed to the algorithm. In most cases though, the business is clueless as to the number of clusters. In such a case, the onus will be on the ML practitioner to determine the k-value. Fortunately, there are several methods available to determine this value. These methods can be classified into the following two categories:

- **Direct methods**: These methods rely on optimizing a criterion, such as *within cluster sums of squares* or *the average silhouette*. Examples of this method include the **V Elbow method** and the **V Silhouette method**.
- **Testing methods**: These methods consists of comparing evidence against a null hypothesis. Gap statistic is one popular example of this method.

In addition to Elbow, Silhouette, and gap statistic methods, there are more than 30 other indices and methods that have been published for identifying the optimal number of clusters. We will not delve into the theoretical details of these methods, as covering 30 methods in a single chapter is not practical. However, R offers an excellent library function, called NbClust that makes it easy for us to implement all these methods in one go. The NbClust function is so powerful that it determines the optimal clusters by varying all combinations of number of clusters, distance measures, and clustering methods and all in one go! Once the library function computes all 30 indices, the *majority rule* is applied on the output to determine the optimal number of clusters, that is, the k-value to be used as input to the algorithm. Let's implement NbClust for our wholesale dataset to determine the optimal k-value using the following code block:

```
# setting the working directory to a folder where dataset is located
setwd('/home/sunil/Desktop/chapter18/')
# reading the dataset to cust_data dataframe
cust_data = read.csv(file='Wholesale_customers_ data.csv', header = TRUE)
# removing the non-required columns
cust_data<-cust_data[,c(-1,-2)]
# including the NbClust library
library(NbClust)
# Computing the optimal number of clusters through the NbClust function
with distance as euclidean and using kmeans
NbClust(cust_data,distance="euclidean", method="kmeans")
```

This will give the following output:

```
*********************************************************************
* Among all indices:
* 1 proposed 2 as the best number of clusters
* 11 proposed 3 as the best number of clusters
* 2 proposed 4 as the best number of clusters
* 1 proposed 5 as the best number of clusters
* 4 proposed 8 as the best number of clusters
* 1 proposed 10 as the best number of clusters
* 1 proposed 12 as the best number of clusters
* 1 proposed 14 as the best number of clusters
* 1 proposed 15 as the best number of clusters
                ***** Conclusion *****
* According to the majority rule, the best number of clusters is 3
*********************************************************************
```

As per the conclusion, we see the k-value that may be used for our problem is 3. Additionally, plotting an elbow curve with the total within-groups sums of squares against the number of clusters in a k-means solution can be helpful in determining the optimal number of clusters. K-means is defined by the objective function, which tries to minimize the sum of all squared distances within a cluster (intra-cluster distance) for all clusters. In the elbow-curve plotting method, we compute the intra-cluster distance with different values of k, and the intra-cluster distance with different k's is plotted as a graph. A bend in the elbow curve suggests the k-value that is optimal for the dataset. The elbow curve can be obtained within R using the following code block:

```
# computing the the intra-cluster distance with Ks ranging from 2 to 10
library(purrr)
tot_withinss <- map_dbl(2:10, function(k){
  model <- kmeans(cust_data, centers = k, nstart = 50)
  model$tot.withinss
})
# converting the Ks and computed intra-cluster distances to a dataframe
screeplot_df <- data.frame(k = 2:10,
```

```
                                tot_withinss = tot_withinss)
# plotting the elbow curve
library(ggplot2)
print ( ggplot(screeplot_df, aes(x = k, y = tot_withinss)) +
        geom_line() +
        scale_x_continuous(breaks = 1:10) +
        labs(x = "k", y = "Within Cluster Sum of Squares") +
        ggtitle("Total Within Cluster Sum of Squares by # of Clusters
(k)") +
        geom_point(data = screeplot_df[2,], aes(x = k, y = tot_withinss),
                col = "red2", pch = 4, size = 7))
```

This will give the following output:

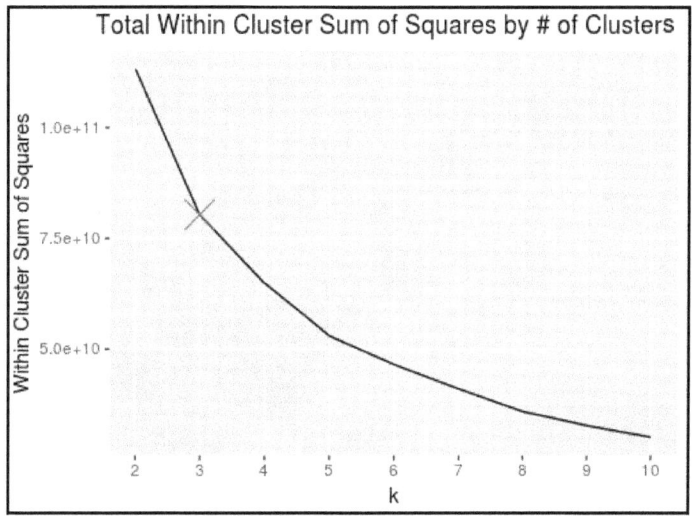

Even with the elbow curve method output, we see that the number of optimal clusters for our dataset is 3.

We see from the NbClust function that we have used the Euclidean distance as the distance. There are a number of distance types (euclidean, maximum, manhattan, canberra, binary, minkowski) that we could have used as values for this distance parameter in the NbClust function. Let's understand what this distance actually means. We are already aware that each observation in our dataset is formed by values that represent features. This essentially means each observation of our dataset can be represented as points in multidimensional space. If we have to say that two observations are similar, we would expect the distance between the two points in the multidimensional space to be lower, that is, both these points in multidimensional space are close to each other. A high distance value between the two points indicates that they are very dissimilar.

The Euclidean, Manhattan, and other types of distance measures are various ways in which distance can be measured given two points in a multidimensional space. Each of the distance measures involves a specific technique to compute the distance between the two points. The techniques involved in Manhattan and Euclidean, and the difference between their measures, are illustrated in the following screenshot:

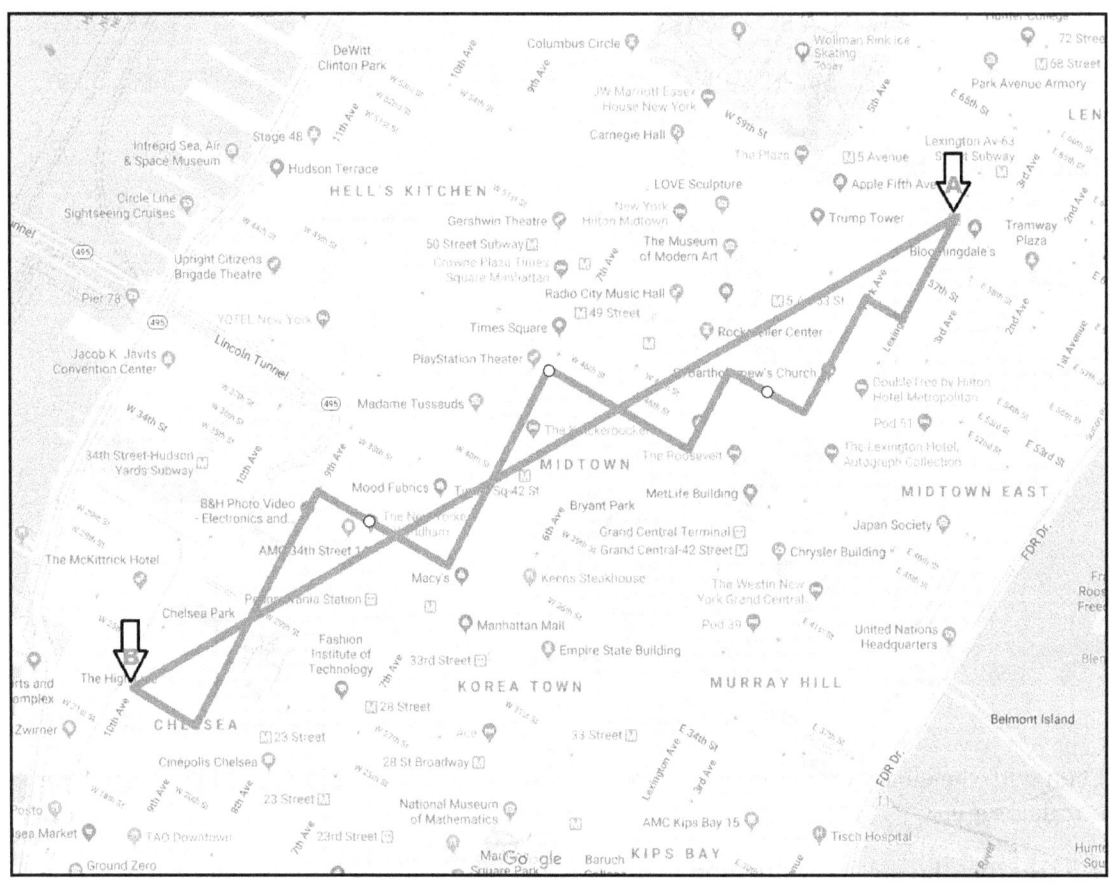

Difference between Manhattan and Euclidean distance measures

The Euclidean distance measures the shortest distance in the plane, whereas the Manhattan metric is the shortest path if one is allowed to move horizontally or vertically.

For example, if a and b are two points where a= (0,0), b = (3,4), then take a look at the following:

- `dist_euclid (a,b) = sqrt(3^2+4^2) = 5`
- `dist_manhattan(a,b) = 3+4 = 7`
- `a=(a1,...,an), b=(b1,...,bn)` (in *n* dimensions and points)
- `dist_euclid (a,b) = sqrt((a1-b1)^2 + ... + (an-bn)^2)`
- `dist_manhattan(a,b) = sum(abs(a1-b1) + ... + abs(an-bn))`

Both measure the shortest paths, but the Euclidean metric doesn't have any restrictions while the Manhattan metric only allows paths constant in all but one dimension.

Likewise, the other distance measures also involve a certain unique to measure the similarity between given points. We will not be going through each one of the techniques in detail in this chapter, but the idea to get is that a distance measure basically defines the level of similarity between given observations. It may be noted that a distance measure is not just used in `NbClust` but in multiple ML algorithms, including k-means.

Now that we've learned the various ways to identify our k-value and have implemented them to identify the optimal number of clusters for our wholesale dataset, let's implement the k-means algorithm with the following code:

```
library(cluster)
# runing kmeans in cust_data dataset to obtain 3 clusters
kmeansout <- kmeans(cust_data, centers = 3, nstart = 50)
print (kmeansout)
```

This will result in the following output:

```
> kmeansout
K-means clustering with 3 clusters of sizes 330, 50, 60
Cluster means:
      Fresh   Milk  Grocery  Frozen Detergents_Paper Delicassen
1 8253.47 3824.603 5280.455 2572.661 1773.058 1137.497
2 8000.04 18511.420 27573.900 1996.680 12407.360 2252.020
3 35941.40 6044.450 6288.617 6713.967 1039.667 3049.467
Clustering vector:
  [1] 1 1 1 1 3 1 1 1 1 2 1 1 3 1 3 1 1 1 1 1 1 3 2 3 1 1 1 2 3 1 1 1 3 1
1 3 1 2 3 3 1 1 2 1 2 2 2 1 2 1 1 3 1
 [55] 3 1 2 1 1 1 1 2 1 1 1 2 1 1 1 1 1 1 1 1 1 1 2 1 1 1 1 1 1 2 2 3 1
3 1 1 2 1 1 1 1 1 1 1 1 1 3 1 1 1 1
[109] 1 2 1 2 1 1 1 1 1 1 1 1 1 1 1 1 3 3 1 1 1 3 1 1 1 1 1 1 1 1 1 1 1 3 3
1 1 2 1 1 1 3 1 1 1 1 1 2 1 1 1 1 1 1
[163] 1 2 1 2 1 1 1 1 1 2 1 2 1 1 3 1 1 1 1 3 1 3 1 1 1 1 1 1 1 1 1 1 1 1 3
1 1 1 2 2 3 1 1 2 1 1 1 2 1 2 1 1 1 1
```

```
[217]  2 1 1 1 1 1 1 1 1 1 1 1 1 1 1 1 1 3 1 1 1 1 1 1 3 3 3 1 1 1 1 1 1 1 1 1 1
2 1 3 1 3 1 1 3 3 1 1 3 1 1 2 2 1 2 1
[271]  1 1 1 3 1 1 3 1 1 1 1 1 3 3 3 3 1 1 1 3 1 1 1 1 1 1 1 1 1 1 1 2 1 1 2
1 2 1 1 2 1 3 2 1 1 1 1 1 1 2 1 1 1 1
[325]  3 3 1 1 1 1 1 2 1 2 1 3 1 1 1 1 1 1 1 2 1 1 1 3 1 2 1 2 1 2 1 1 1 1 1
1 1 1 1 1 1 1 1 1 1 3 1 1 1 1 1 1 3
[379]  1 1 3 1 3 1 2 1 1 1 1 1 1 1 1 3 1 1 1 1 1 1 1 3 3 3 1 1 3 2 1 1 1 1 1
1 1 1 1 2 1 1 1 3 1 1 1 1 3 1 1 1 1
[433]  1 1 1 3 3 2 1 1
```

From the output k-means, we can observe and infer several things about the output clusters. Obviously, three clusters are formed and this is in line with our k parameter that was passed to the algorithm. We see that the first cluster has 330 observations in it, and the second and third clusters are small with just 50 and 60 observations. The k-means output also provides us with the cluster centroids. The **centroid** is a representative of all points in a particular cluster. As it is not feasible to study each of the individual observations assigned to a cluster and determine the business characteristics of the cluster, the cluster centroid may be used as a pseudo for the points in the cluster. The cluster centroid helps us to quickly arrive at a conclusion in terms of the definition of contents of the cluster. The k-means output also produced the cluster assignment for each observation. Each of the observations in our wholesale dataset is assigned to one of the three clusters (1,2,3).

It is possible to view the clustering results by using the `fviz_cluster()` function available in the `factoextra` library. The function provides a nice illustration of the clusters. If there are more than two dimensions (variables), `fviz_cluster` will perform **principal component analysis** (**PCA**) and plot the observations based on the first two principal components that explain the majority of the variance. The clusters visualization can be created though the following code:

```
library(factoextra)
fviz_cluster(kmout,data=cust_data)
```

This will give the following graph as output:

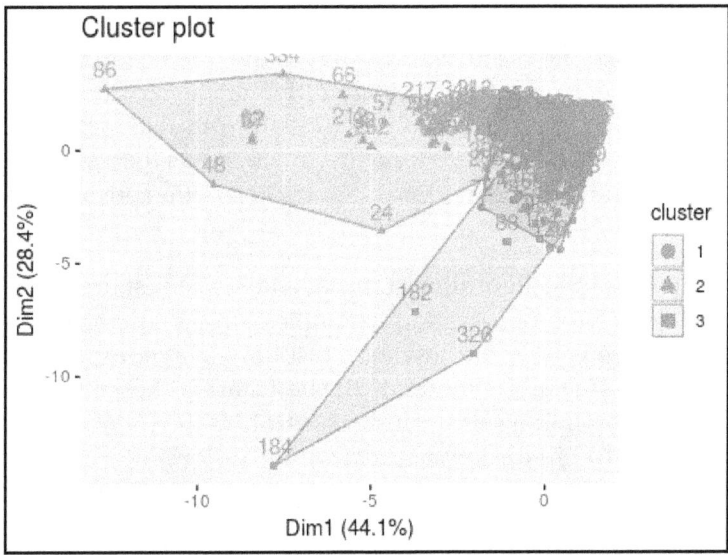

Working mechanics of the k-means algorithm

The execution of the k-means algorithm involves the following steps:

1. Randomly select k observations from the dataset as the initial cluster centroids.
2. For each observation in the dataset, perform the following:
   1. Compute the distance between the observation and each of the cluster centroids.
   2. Identify the cluster centroid that has minimum distance with the observation.
   3. Assign the observation to such closest centroid.

3. With all points assigned to one of the cluster centroids, compute new cluster centroids. This can be done by taking the mean of all the points assigned to a cluster.
4. Perform *step 2* and *step 3* repeatedly until the cluster centroids (mean) do not change or until a user-defined number of iterations is reached.

One key thing to note in k-means is that the cluster centroids in the initial step are selected randomly and the initial cluster assignments are done based on the distance between the actual observations and the randomly-picked cluster centroids. This essentially means that if we were to pick observations as cluster centroids in the initial step other than the observations that were chosen, we would obtain different clusters than the one we have obtained. In technical terms, this is called a **non-globally-optimal solution** or a **locally-optimal solution**. The `cluster` library's k-means function has the `nstart` option, which works around this problem of the non-globally-optimal solution encountered with the k-means algorithm.

The `nstart` option enables the algorithm to try several random starts (instead of just one) by drawing a number of center observations from the datasets. It then checks the cluster sum of squares and proceeds with the best start, resulting in a more stable output. In our case, we set the `nstart` value as `50`, therefore the best start is chosen by k-means post checking it with 50 random initial sets of cluster centroids. The following diagram depicts the high-level steps involved in the k-means clustering algorithm:

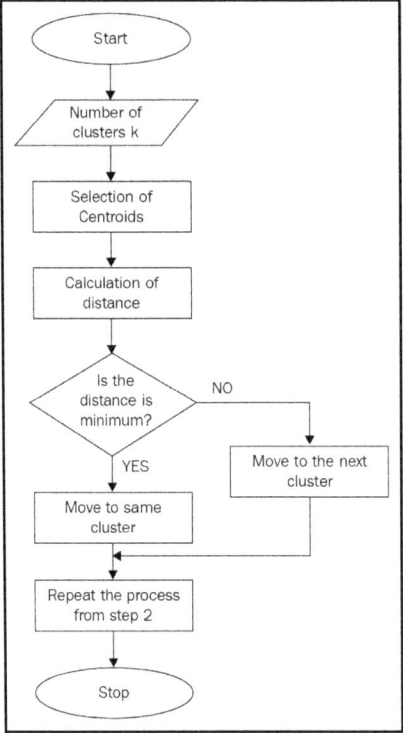

Steps in k-means clustering

In supervised ML methods, such as classification, we have ground truth, therefore, we will be able to able to compare our predictions with the ground truth and measure to report the performance of our classification. Unlike the supervised ML method, in clustering, we do not have any ground truth. Therefore, computing the performance measurement with respect to clustering is a challenge.

As an alternative to performance measurement, we use a pseudo-measure called **cluster quality**. The cluster quality is generally computed through measures known as intra-cluster distance and inter-cluster distance, which are illustrated in the following diagram:

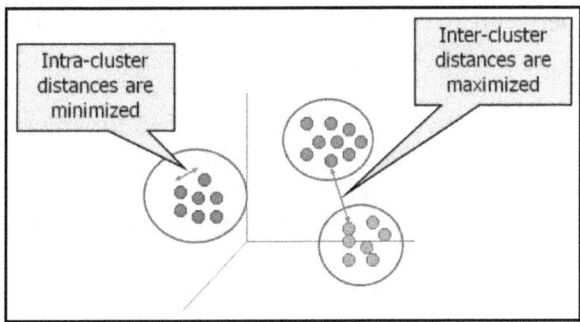

Intra-cluster distance and inter-cluster distance defined

The goal of the clustering task is to obtain good-quality clusters. Clusters are termed as **high-quality clusters** if the distance within the observations is minimum and the distance between the clusters themselves is maximum.

There are multiple ways inter-cluster and intra-cluster distances can be measured:

- **Intra-cluster**: This distance can be measured as (sum, minimum, maximum, or mean) of the (absolute/squared) distance between all pairs of points in the cluster (or) *diameter*–two farthest points (or) between the centroid and all points in the cluster.
- **Inter-cluster**: This distance is measured as sum of the (squared) distance between all pairs of clusters, where distance between two clusters itself is computed as one of the following:
    - Distance between their centroids
    - Distance between farthest pair of points
    - Distance between the closest pair of points belonging to the clusters

Unfortunately, there is no way to pinpoint the preferred inter-cluster distance and intra-cluster distance values. The **Silhouette index** is one metric that is based on inter-cluster distance and intra-cluster distance that can be readily computed and easily interpreted.

The Silhouette index is computed using the mean intra-cluster distance, *a*, and the mean nearest-cluster distance, *b*, for each of the observations participating in the clustering exercise. The Silhouette index for an observation is given by the following formula:

$$(b - a)/max(a, b)$$

Here, *b* is the distance between an observation and the nearest cluster that the observation is not a part of.

Silhouette index value ranges between [-1, 1]. A value of +1 for an observation indicates that the observation is far away from its neighboring cluster and it is very close to the cluster it is assigned to. Similarly, a value of -1 tells us that the observation is close to its neighboring cluster than to the cluster it is assigned to. A value of 0 means it's at the boundary of the distance between the two clusters. A value of +1 is ideal and -1 is the least preferred. Hence, the higher the value, the better the quality of the cluster.

The `cluster` library offers the Silhouette function, which can be readily used on our k-means clustering output to understand the quality of the clusters that were formed. The following code computes the Silhouette index for our three clusters:

```
# computing the silhouette index for the clusters
si <- silhouette(kmout$cluster, dist(cust_data, "euclidean"))
# printing the summary of the computed silhouette index
print(summary(si))
```

This will give us the following output:

```
Silhouette of 440 units in 3 clusters from silhouette.default(x =
kmout$cluster, dist = dist(cust_data, from "euclidean")) :
 Cluster sizes and average silhouette widths:
       60 50 330
0.2524346 0.1800059 0.5646307
Individual silhouette widths:
   Min. 1st Qu. Median Mean 3rd Qu. Max.
 -0.1544 0.3338 0.5320 0.4784 0.6743 0.7329
```

As we have seen, the Silhouette index can range from -1 to +1, and the latter is preferred. From the output, we see that the clusters are all good quality clusters, as the average width is a positive number closer to 1 than -1.

In fact, the Silhouette index can be used not just to measure the quality of clusters formed but also to compute the k-value. Similar to Elbow method, we can iterate through multiple values of k and then identify the k that yields the maximum Silhouette index values across the clusters. Clustering can then be performed using the k that was identified.

There are numerous cluster-quality measures described in the literature. The Silhouette index is just one measure we covered in this chapter because of its popularity in the ML community. The `clusterCrit` library offers a wide range of indices to measure the quality of clusters. We are not going to explore the other cluster-quality metrics here, but interested readers should refer to this library for further information on how to compute cluster quality.

So far, we have covered the k-means clustering algorithm to identify the clusters, but the original segmentation task we started with does not end here. Segmentation further spans to the task of understanding what each of the clusters formed from the clustering exercise mean to businesses. For example, we take our cluster centroids obtained from k-means and an attempt is made to identify what these are:

```
Fresh Milk Grocery Frozen Detergents_Paper Delicatessen
1 8253.47 3824.603 5280.455 2572.661 1773.058 1137.497
2 8000.04 18511.420 27573.900 1996.680 12407.360 2252.020
3 35941.40 6044.450 6288.617 6713.967 1039.667 3049.467
```

Here are some sample insights into each cluster:

- Cluster 1 is low spenders (average spending: 22,841.744), with the majority of spending allocated to the fresh category
- Cluster 2 is high spenders (average spending: 70,741.42), with the majority of spending in the grocery category
- Cluster 3 is medium spenders (average spending : 59,077.568), with the majority of spending in the fresh category

Now, based on the business objective, one or more clusters may be selected to target. For example, if the objective is to have high spenders spend more, promotions may be rolled out to cluster 2 individuals with spending in the `Frozen` and `Delicatessen` products less than the centroid values (that is, `Frozen: 1,996.680` and `Delicatessen: 2,252.020`).

Identifying the customer segments in the wholesale customer data using DIANA

Hierarchical clustering algorithms are a good choice when we don't necessarily have circular (or hyperspherical) clusters in the data, and we essentially don't know the number of clusters in advance. With hierarchical clustering algorithm, unlike the flat or partitioning algorithms, there is no requirement to decide and pass the number of clusters to be formed prior to applying the algorithm on the dataset.

Hierarchical clustering results in a dendogram (tree diagram) that can be visually verified to easily determine the number of clusters. Visual verification enables us to perform cuts in the dendrogram at suitable places.

The results produced by this type of clustering algorithm are reproducible as the algorithm is not sensitive to the choice of the distance metric. In other words, irrespective of the distance metric chosen, we will get the same results. This type of clustering is also suitable for datasets of a higher complexity (quadratic) and in particular for exploring the hierarchical relationships that exist between the clusters.

Divisive hierarchical clustering, also known as **DIvisive ANAlysis (DIANA)**, is a hierarchical clustering algorithm that follows a top-down approach to identify clusters in a given dataset. Here are the steps in DIANA to identify the clusters:

1. All observations of the dataset are assigned to the root, so in the initial step only a single cluster is formed.
2. In each iteration, the most heterogeneous cluster is partitioned into two.
3. **Step 2** is repeated until all the observations are in their own cluster:

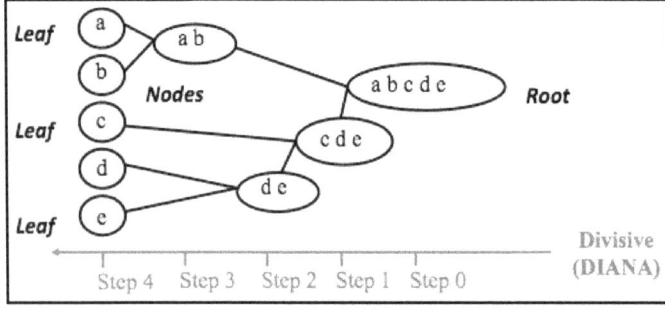

Working of divisive hierarchical clustering algorithm

One obvious question that comes up is about the technique used by the algorithm to split the cluster into two. The answer is that it is performed according to some (dis)similarity measure. The Euclidean distance is used to measure the distance between two given points. This algorithm works by splitting the data on the basis of the farthest-distance measure of all the pairwise distances between the data points. Linkage defines the specific details of fartherness of the data points. The next figure illustrates the various linkages considered by DIANA for splitting the clusters. Here are some of the distances considered to split the groups:

- **Single-link**: Nearest distance or single linkage
- **Complete-link**: Farthest distance or complete linkage
- **Average-link**: Average distance or average linkage
- **Centroid-link**: Centroid distance
- **Ward's method**: Sum of squared `euclidean` distance is minimized

Take a look at the following diagram to better understand the preceding distances:

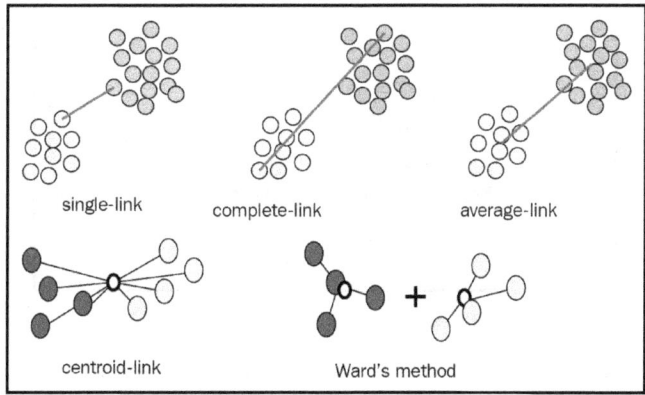

Illustration depicting various linkage types used by DIANA

Generally, the linkage type to be used is passed as a parameter to the clustering algorithm. The `cluster` library offers the `diana` function to perform clustering. Let's apply it on our wholesale dataset with the following code:

```
# setting the working directory to a folder where dataset is located
setwd('/home/sunil/Desktop/chapter18/')
# reading the dataset to cust_data dataframe
cust_data = read.csv(file='Wholesale_customers_ data.csv', header = TRUE)
# removing the non-required columns
cust_data<-cust_data[,c(-1,-2)]
# including the cluster library so as to make use of diana function
```

```
library(cluster)
# Compute diana()
cust_data_diana<-diana(cust_data, metric = "euclidean",stand = FALSE)
# plotting the dendogram from diana output
pltree(cust_data_diana, cex = 0.6, hang = -1,
        main = "Dendrogram of diana")
# Divise coefficient; amount of clustering structure found
print(cust_data_diana$dc)
```

This will give us the following output:

```
> print(cust_data_diana$dc)
[1] 0.9633628
```

Take a look at the following output:

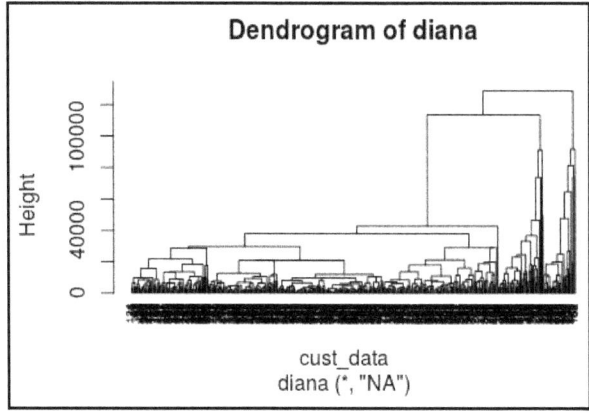

The `plot.hclust()` and `plot.dendrogram()` functions may also be used on the DIANA clustering output. `plot.dendrogram()` yields the dendogram that follows the natural structure of the splits as done by the DIANA algorithm. Use the following code to generate the dendrogram:

```
plot(as.dendrogram(cust_data_diana), cex = 0.6,horiz = TRUE)
```

This will give the following output:

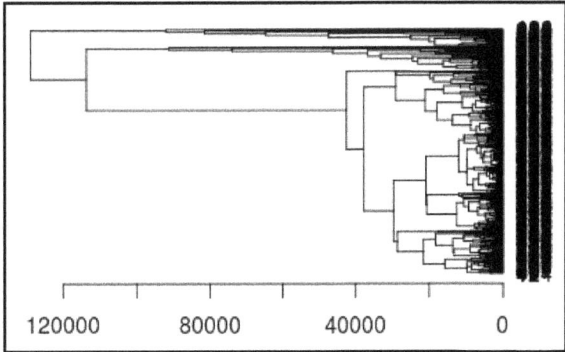

In the dendrogram output, each leaf that appears on the right relates to each observation in the dataset. As we traverse from right to left, observations that are similar to each other are grouped into one branch, which are themselves fused at a higher level.

The higher level of the fusion, provided on the horizontal axis, indicates the similarity between two observations. The higher the fusion, the more similar the observations are. It may be noted that conclusions about the proximity of two observations can be drawn only based on the level where branches containing those two observations are first fused. In order to identify clusters, we can cut the dendrogram at a certain level. The level at which the cut is made defines the number of clusters obtained.

We can make use of the `cutree()` function to obtain the cluster assignment for each of the observations in our dataset. Execute the following code to obtain the clusters and review the clustering output:

```
# obtain the clusters through cuttree
# Cut tree into 3 groups
grp <- cutree(cust_data_diana, k = 3)
# Number of members in each cluster
table(grp)
# Get the observations of cluster 1
rownames(cust_data)[grp == 1]
```

This will give the following output:

```
> table(grp)
grp
  1 2 3
364 44 32
> rownames(cust_data)[grp == 1]
  [1] "1" "2" "3" "4" "5" "6" "7" "8" "9" "11" "12" "13" "14" "15" "16"
```

```
       "17"  "18"  "19"
 [19]  "20"  "21"  "22"  "25"  "26"  "27"  "28"  "31"  "32"  "33"  "34"  "35"  "36"  "37"
 "38"  "41"  "42"  "43"
 [37]  "45"  "49"  "51"  "52"  "54"  "55"  "56"  "58"  "59"  "60"  "61"  "63"  "64"  "65"
 "67"  "68"  "69"  "70"
 [55]  "71"  "72"  "73"  "74"  "75"  "76"  "77"  "79"  "80"  "81"  "82"  "83"  "84"  "85"
 "89"  "90"  "91"  "92"
 [73]  "94"  "95"  "96"  "97"  "98"  "99"  "100" "101" "102" "103" "105" "106"
 "107" "108" "109" "111" "112" "113"
 [91]  "114" "115" "116" "117" "118" "119" "120" "121" "122" "123" "124"
 "127" "128" "129" "131" "132" "133" "134"
[109]  "135" "136" "137" "138" "139" "140" "141" "142" "144" "145" "147"
 "148" "149" "151" "152" "153" "154" "155"
[127]  "157" "158" "159" "160" "161" "162" "163" "165" "167" "168" "169"
 "170" "171" "173" "175" "176" "178" "179"
[145]  "180" "181" "183" "185" "186" "187" "188" "189" "190" "191" "192"
 "193" "194" "195" "196" "198" "199" "200"
[163]  "203" "204" "205" "207" "208" "209" "211" "213" "214" "215" "216"
 "218" "219" "220" "221" "222" "223" "224"
[181]  "225" "226" "227" "228" "229" "230" "231" "232" "233" "234" "235"
 "236" "237" "238" "239" "241" "242" "243"
[199]  "244" "245" "246" "247" "248" "249" "250" "251" "253" "254" "255"
 "257" "258" "261" "262" "263" "264" "265"
[217]  "266" "268" "269" "270" "271" "272" "273" "275" "276" "277" "278"
 "279" "280" "281" "282" "284" "287" "288"
[235]  "289" "291" "292" "293" "294" "295" "296" "297" "298" "299" "300"
 "301" "303" "304" "306" "308" "309" "311"
[253]  "312" "314" "315" "316" "317" "318" "319" "321" "322" "323" "324"
 "325" "327" "328" "329" "330" "331" "333"
[271]  "335" "336" "337" "338" "339" "340" "341" "342" "343" "345" "346"
 "347" "348" "349" "351" "353" "355" "356"
[289]  "357" "358" "359" "360" "361" "362" "363" "364" "365" "366" "367"
 "368" "369" "370" "372" "373" "374" "375"
[307]  "376" "377" "379" "380" "381" "382" "384" "385" "386" "387" "388"
 "389" "390" "391" "392" "393" "394" "395"
[325]  "396" "397" "398" "399" "400" "401" "402" "403" "404" "405" "406"
 "407" "409" "410" "411" "412" "413" "414"
[343]  "415" "416" "417" "418" "420" "421" "422" "423" "424" "425" "426"
 "427" "429" "430" "431" "432" "433" "434"
[361]  "435" "436" "439" "440"
```

We can also visualize the clustering output through the `fviz_cluster` function in the `factoextra` library. Use the following code to get the required visualization:

```
library(factoextra)
fviz_cluster(list(data = cust_data, cluster = grp))
```

This will give you the following output:

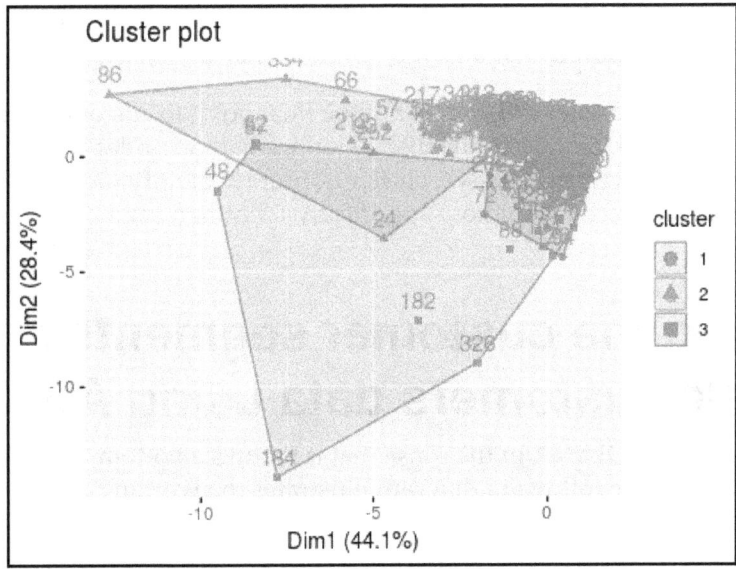

It is also possible to color-code the clusters within the dendogram itself. This can be accomplished with the following code:

```
plot(as.hclust(cust_data_diana))
rect.hclust(cust_data_diana, k = 4, border = 2:5)
```

This will give the following output:

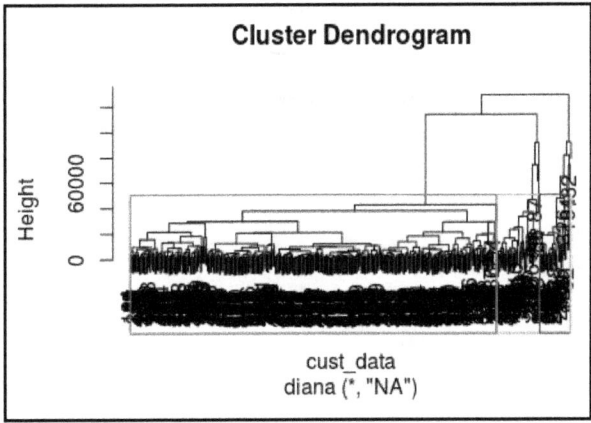

Now that the clusters are identified, the steps we discussed to evaluate the cluster quality (through the Silhouette index) apply here as well. As we have already covered this topic under the k-means clustering algorithm, we are not going to repeat the steps here. The code and interpretation of the output remains the same as what was discussed under k-means.

As discussed earlier, the cluster's output is not the final point to customer segmentation exercise we have on hand. Similar to the discussion we had on under the k-means algorithm, we could analyze the DIANA cluster output to identify meaningful segments so as to roll out business objectives to those specifically-identified segments.

Identifying the customer segments in the wholesale customers data using AGNES

AGNES is the reverse of DIANA in the sense that it follows a bottom-up approach to clustering the dataset. The following diagram illustrates the working principle of the AGNES algorithm for clustering:

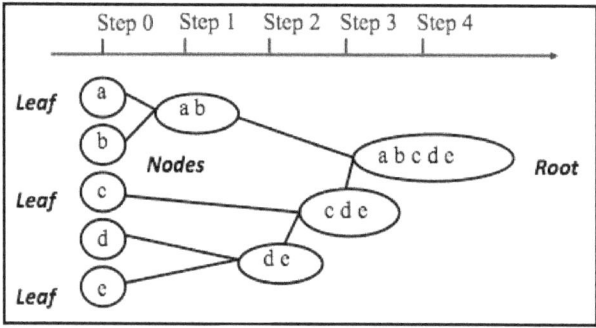

Working of agglomerative hierarchical clustering algorithm

Except for the bottom-up approach followed by AGNES, the implementation details behind the algorithm are the same as for DIANA; therefore, we won't repeat the discussion of the concepts here. The following code block clusters our wholesale dataset into three clusters with AGNES; it also creates a visualization of the clusters thus formed:

```
# setting the working directory to a folder where dataset is located
setwd('/home/sunil/Desktop/chapter18/')
# reading the dataset to cust_data dataframe
cust_data = read.csv(file='Wholesale_customers_ data.csv', header = TRUE)
# removing the non-required columns
cust_data<-cust_data[,c(-1,-2)]
# including the cluster library so as to make use of agnes function
library(cluster)
# Compute agnes()
cust_data_agnes<-agnes(cust_data, metric = "euclidean",stand = FALSE)
# plotting the dendogram from agnes output
pltree(cust_data_agnes, cex = 0.6, hang = -1,
       main = "Dendrogram of agnes")
# agglomerative coefficient; amount of clustering structure found
print(cust_data_agnes$ac)
plot(as.dendrogram(cust_data_agnes), cex = 0.6,horiz = TRUE)
# obtain the clusters through cuttree
# Cut tree into 3 groups
grp <- cutree(cust_data_agnes, k = 3)
# Number of members in each cluster
table(grp)
# Get the observations of cluster 1
rownames(cust_data)[grp == 1]
# visualization of clusters
library(factoextra)
fviz_cluster(list(data = cust_data, cluster = grp))
library(factoextra)
fviz_cluster(list(data = cust_data, cluster = grp))
plot(as.hclust(cust_data_agnes))
rect.hclust(cust_data_agnes, k = 3, border = 2:5)
```

This is the output that you will obtain:

```
[1] 0.9602911
> plot(as.dendrogram(cust_data_agnes), cex = 0.6,horiz = FALSE)
```

Take a look at the following screenshot:

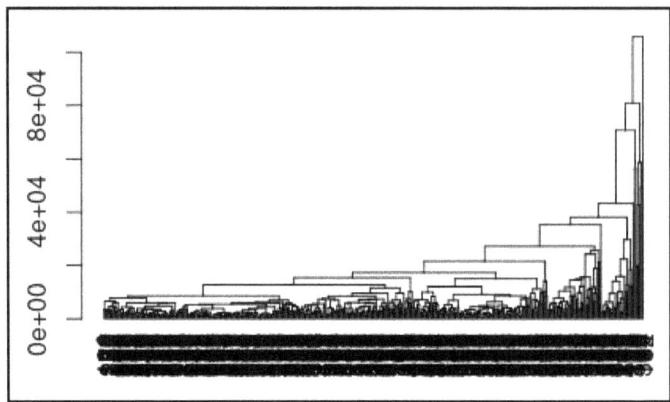

Take a look at the following code block:

```
> grp <- cutree(cust_data_agnes, k = 3)
> # Number of members in each cluster
> table(grp)
grp
  1 2 3
434 5 1
> rownames(cust_data)[grp == 1]
  [1] "1"  "2"  "3"  "4"  "5"  "6"  "7"  "8"  "9"  "10" "11" "12" "13" "14" "15"
"16" "17" "18"
 [19] "19" "20" "21" "22" "23" "24" "25" "26" "27" "28" "29" "30" "31" "32"
"33" "34" "35" "36"
 [37] "37" "38" "39" "40" "41" "42" "43" "44" "45" "46" "47" "49" "50" "51"
"52" "53" "54" "55"
 [55] "56" "57" "58" "59" "60" "61" "63" "64" "65" "66" "67" "68" "69" "70"
"71" "72" "73" "74"
 [73] "75" "76" "77" "78" "79" "80" "81" "82" "83" "84" "85" "88" "89" "90"
"91" "92" "93" "94"
 [91] "95" "96" "97" "98" "99" "100" "101" "102" "103" "104" "105" "106"
"107" "108" "109" "110" "111" "112"
[109] "113" "114" "115" "116" "117" "118" "119" "120" "121" "122" "123"
"124" "125" "126" "127" "128" "129" "130"
[127] "131" "132" "133" "134" "135" "136" "137" "138" "139" "140" "141"
"142" "143" "144" "145" "146" "147" "148"
[145] "149" "150" "151" "152" "153" "154" "155" "156" "157" "158" "159"
"160" "161" "162" "163" "164" "165" "166"
[163] "167" "168" "169" "170" "171" "172" "173" "174" "175" "176" "177"
"178" "179" "180" "181" "183" "184" "185"
[181] "186" "187" "188" "189" "190" "191" "192" "193" "194" "195" "196"
"197" "198" "199" "200" "201" "202" "203"
```

```
  [199] "204" "205" "206" "207" "208" "209" "210" "211" "212" "213" "214"
 "215" "216" "217" "218" "219" "220" "221"
  [217] "222" "223" "224" "225" "226" "227" "228" "229" "230" "231" "232"
 "233" "234" "235" "236" "237" "238" "239"
  [235] "240" "241" "242" "243" "244" "245" "246" "247" "248" "249" "250"
 "251" "252" "253" "254" "255" "256" "257"
  [253] "258" "259" "260" "261" "262" "263" "264" "265" "266" "267" "268"
 "269" "270" "271" "272" "273" "274" "275"
  [271] "276" "277" "278" "279" "280" "281" "282" "283" "284" "285" "286"
 "287" "288" "289" "290" "291" "292" "293"
  [289] "294" "295" "296" "297" "298" "299" "300" "301" "302" "303" "304"
 "305" "306" "307" "308" "309" "310" "311"
  [307] "312" "313" "314" "315" "316" "317" "318" "319" "320" "321" "322"
 "323" "324" "325" "326" "327" "328" "329"
  [325] "330" "331" "332" "333" "335" "336" "337" "338" "339" "340" "341"
 "342" "343" "344" "345" "346" "347" "348"
  [343] "349" "350" "351" "352" "353" "354" "355" "356" "357" "358" "359"
 "360" "361" "362" "363" "364" "365" "366"
  [361] "367" "368" "369" "370" "371" "372" "373" "374" "375" "376" "377"
 "378" "379" "380" "381" "382" "383" "384"
  [379] "385" "386" "387" "388" "389" "390" "391" "392" "393" "394" "395"
 "396" "397" "398" "399" "400" "401" "402"
  [397] "403" "404" "405" "406" "407" "408" "409" "410" "411" "412" "413"
 "414" "415" "416" "417" "418" "419" "420"
  [415] "421" "422" "423" "424" "425" "426" "427" "428" "429" "430" "431"
 "432" "433" "434" "435" "436" "437" "438"
  [433] "439" "440"
```

Execute the following command:

```
> fviz_cluster(list(data = cust_data, cluster = grp))
```

The preceding command generates the following output:

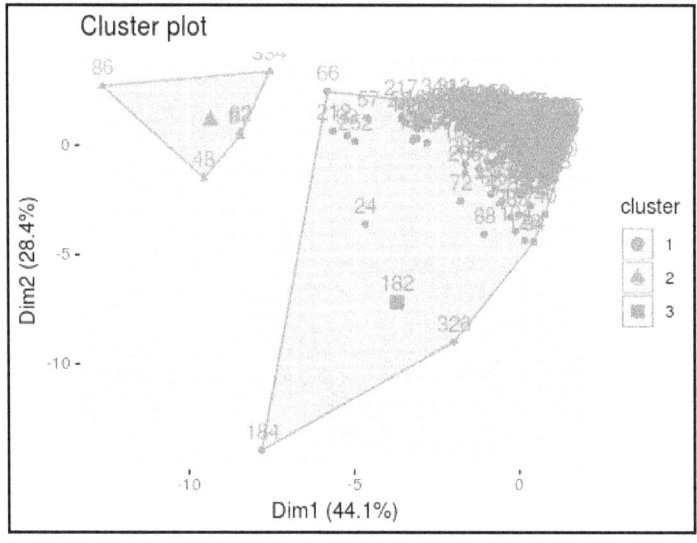

Take a look at the following commands:

```
> plot(as.hclust(cust_data_agnes))
> rect.hclust(cust_data_agnes, k = 3, border = 2:5)
```

The preceding commands generate the following output:

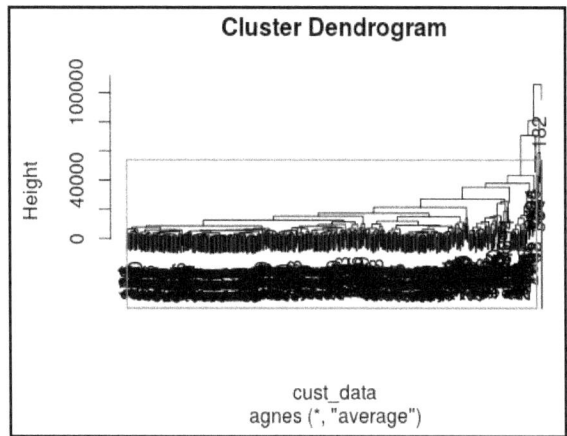

We can see from the AGNES clustering output that a large number of observations from the dataset are assigned to one cluster and very few observations were assigned to the other clusters. This is not a great output for our segmentation downstream exercise. To obtain better cluster assignments, you could try using other cluster-linkage methods aside from the default average linkage method currently used by the AGNES algorithm.

Summary

In this chapter, we learned about the concept of segmentation and its association with clustering, an ML unsupervised learning technique. We made use of the wholesale dataset available from the UCI repository and implemented clustering using the k-means, DIANA, and AGNES algorithms. During the course of this chapter, we also studied various aspects related to clustering, such as tendency to cluster, distance, linkage measures, and methods to identify the right number of clusters, and measuring the output of clustering. We also explored making use of the clustering output for customer-segmentation purposes.

Can computers see and identify objects and living creatures like humans do? Let's explore the answer to this question in the next chapter.

19
Image Recognition Using Deep Neural Networks

In 1966, Professor Seymour Papert at MIT conceptualized an ambitious summer project titled *The Summer Vision Project*. The task for the graduate student was to *plug a camera into a computer and enable it to understand what it sees*! I am sure it would have been super-difficult for the graduate student to have finished this project, as even today the task remains half complete.

A human being, when they look outside, is able to recognize the objects that they see. Without thinking, they are able to classify a cat as a cat, a dog as a dog, a plant as a plant, an animal as an animal—this is happening because the human brain draws knowledge from its extensive prelearned database. After all, as human beings, we have millions of years' worth of evolutionary context that enables us draw inferences from the thing that we see. Computer vision deals with replicating the human vision processes so as to pass them on to machines and automate them.

This chapter is all about learning the theory and implementation of computer vision through **machine learning** (**ML**). We will build a feedforward deep learning network and **LeNet** to enable handwritten digit recognition. We will also build a project that uses a pretrained Inception-BatchNorm network to identify objects in an image. We will cover the following topics as we progress in this chapter:

- Understanding computer vision
- Achieving computer vision with deep learning
- Introduction to the MNIST dataset
- Implementing a deep learning network for handwritten digit recognition
- Implementing computer vision with pretrained models

Technical requirements

For the projects covered in this chapter, we'll make use of a very popular open dataset called MNIST. We'll use **Apache MXNet**, a modern open source deep learning software framework to train and deploy the required deep neural networks.

Understanding computer vision

In today's world, we have advanced cameras that are very successful at mimicking how a human eye captures light and color; but image-capturing in the right way is just stage one in the whole image-comprehension aspect. Post image-capturing, we will need to enable technology that interprets what has been captured and build context around it. This is what the human brain does when the eyes see something. Here comes the huge challenge: we all know that computers see images as huge piles of integer values that represent intensities across a spectrum of colors, and of course, computer have no context associated with the image itself. This is where ML comes into play. ML allows us to train a context for a dataset such that it enables computers to understand what objects certain sequences of numbers actually represent.

Computer vision is one of the emerging areas where ML is applied. It can be used for several purposes in various domains, including healthcare, agriculture, insurance, and the automotive industry. The following are some of its most popular applications:

- Detecting diseases from medical images, such as CT scan/MRI scan images
- Identifying crop diseases and soil quality to support a better crop yield
- Identifying oil reserves from satellite images
- Self-driving cars
- Monitoring and managing skin condition for psoriasis patients
- Classifying and distinguishing weeds from crops
- Facial recognition
- Extracting information from personal documents, such as passports and ID cards
- Detecting terrain for drones and airplanes
- Biometrics
- Public surveillance
- Organizing personal photos
- Answering visual questions

This is just the tip of the iceberg. It's not an overstatement to say that there is no domain where we cannot find an application for computer vision. Therefore, computer vision is a key area for ML practitioners to focus on.

Achieving computer vision with deep learning

To start with, let's understand the term **deep learning**. It simply means **multilayered neural networks**. The multiple layers enable deep learning to be an enhanced and powerful form of a neural network. **Artificial neural networks** (**ANNs**) have been in existence since the 1950s. They have always been designed with two layers; however, deep learning models are built with multiple hidden layers. The following diagram shows a hypothetical deep learning model:

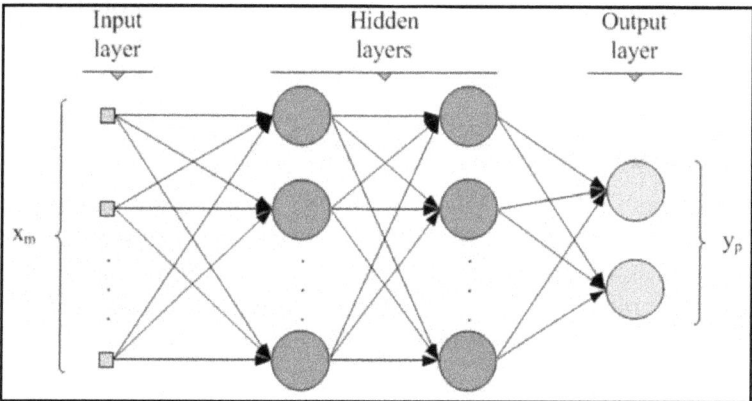

Deep learning model—High level architecture

Neural networks are heavy on computation, therefore the **central processing unit** (**CPU**) that can be enabled with a maximum of 22 cores is generally thought of as an infrastructure blocker until recently. This infrastructure limitation also limited the usage of neural networks to solve real-world problems. However, recently, the availability of a **graphical processing unit** (**GPU**) with thousands of cores enabled has exponentially powerful computation possibilities when compared to CPUs. This gave a huge push to the usage of deep learning models.

Data comes in many forms, such as tables, sounds, HTML files, TXT files, and images. Linear models do not generally learn from non-linear data. Non-linear algorithms, such as decision trees and gradient-boosting machines, also do not learn well from this kind of data. One the other hand, deep learning models that create non-linear interactions among the features give better solutions with non-linear data, so they have become the preferred models in the ML community.

A deep learning model consists of a chain of interconnected neurons that creates the neural architecture. Any deep learning model will have an input layer, two or more hidden layers (middle layers), and an output layer. The input layer consists of neurons equal to the number of input variables in the data. Users can decide on the number of neurons and the number of hidden layers that a deep learning network should have. Generally, it is something that is optimized by the user building the network through a cross-validation strategy. The choice of the number of neurons and the number of hidden layers represents the challenge of the researcher. The number of neurons in the output layer is decided based on the outcome of the problem. For example, one output neuron in case it is regression, for a classification problem the output neurons is equal to the number of classes involved in the problem on-hand.

Convolutional Neural Networks

There are multiple types of deep learning algorithms, the one we generally use in computer vision is called a **Convolutional Neural Network** (**CNN**). CNNs break down images into small groups of pixels and then run calculations on them by applying filters. The result is then compared against pixel matrices they already know about. This helps CNNs to come up with a probability for the image belonging to one of the known classes.

In the first few layers, the CNN identifies shapes, such as curves and rough edges, but after several convolutions, they are able to recognize objects such as animals, cars, and humans.

When the CNN is first built for the available data, the filter values of the network are randomly initialized and so the predictions it produce are mostly false. But then it keeps comparing its own predictions on labeled datasets to the actual ones, updating the filter values and improving performance of the CNN with each iteration.

Layers of CNNs

A CNN consists of an input and an output layer; it also has various hidden layers. The following are the various hidden layers in a CNN:

- **Convolution**: Assume that we have an image represented as pixels, a convolution is something where we have a little matrix nearly always 3 x 3 in deep learning and multiply every element of the matrix by every element of 3 x 3 section of the image and then add them all together to get the result of that convolution at one point. The following diagram illustrates the process of convolution on a pixel:

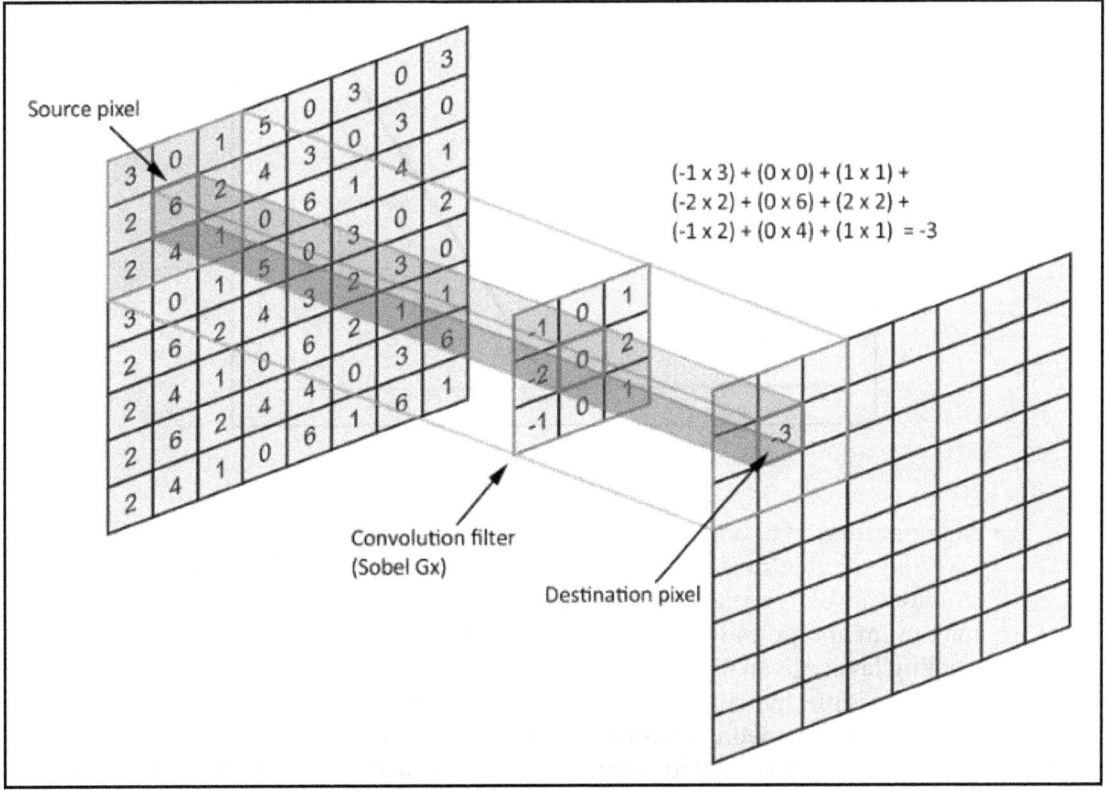

$(-1 \times 3) + (0 \times 0) + (1 \times 1) +$
$(-2 \times 2) + (0 \times 6) + (2 \times 2) +$
$(-1 \times 2) + (0 \times 4) + (1 \times 1) = -3$

Convolution application on an image

- **Rectified Linear Unit (ReLU)**: A non-linear activation that throws away the negatives in an input matrix. For example, let's assume we have a 3 x 3 matrix with negative numbers, zeros, and positive numbers as values in the cells of the matrix. Given this matrix as input to ReLU, it transforms all negative numbers in the matrix to zeros and returns the 3 x 3 matrix. ReLU is an activation function that can be defined as part of the CNN architecture. The following diagram demonstrates the function of ReLU in CNNs:

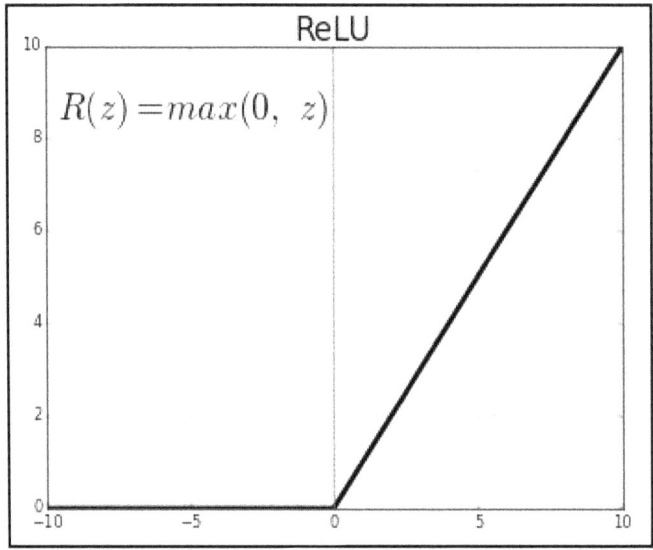

Rectified Linear Unit (ReLU) in CNNs

- **Max pooling**: Max pooling is something that can be set as a layer in the CNN architecture. It allows to identify if the specific characteristic is present in the previous level. It replaces the highest value in an input matrix with the maximum and gives the output. Let's consider an example, with a 2 x 2 max pooling layer, given a 4 x 4 matrix as input, the max pooling layer replaces each 2 x 2 in the input matrix with the highest value among the four cells. The output matrix thus obtained is non-overlapping and it's an image representation with a reduced resolution. The following diagram illustrates the functionality of max pooling in a CNN:

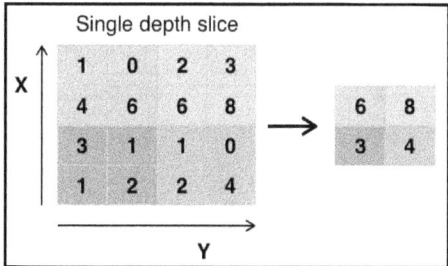

Functionality of max pooling layer in CNNs

There are various reasons to apply max pooling, such as to reduce the amount of parameters and computation load, to eliminate overfitting, and, most importantly, to force the neural network to see the larger picture, as in previous layers it was focused on seeing bits and pieces of the image.

- **Fully-connected layer**: Also known as a **dense layer**, this involves a linear operation on the layer's input vector. The layer ensures every input is connected to every output by a weight.

- **Softmax**: An activation function that is generally applied at the last layer of the deep neural network. In a multiclass classification problem, we require the fully-connected output of a deep learning network to be interpreted as a probability. The total probability of a particular observation in data (for all classes) should add up to 1, and the probability of the observation belonging to each class should range between 0 and 1. Therefore, we transform each output of the fully-connected layer as a portion of a total sum. However, instead of simply doing the standard proportion, we apply this non-linear exponential function for a very specific reason: we would like to make our highest output as close to 1 as possible and our lower output as close to 0. Softmax does this by pushing the true linear proportions closer to either 1 or 0.

The following diagram illustrates the softmax activation function:

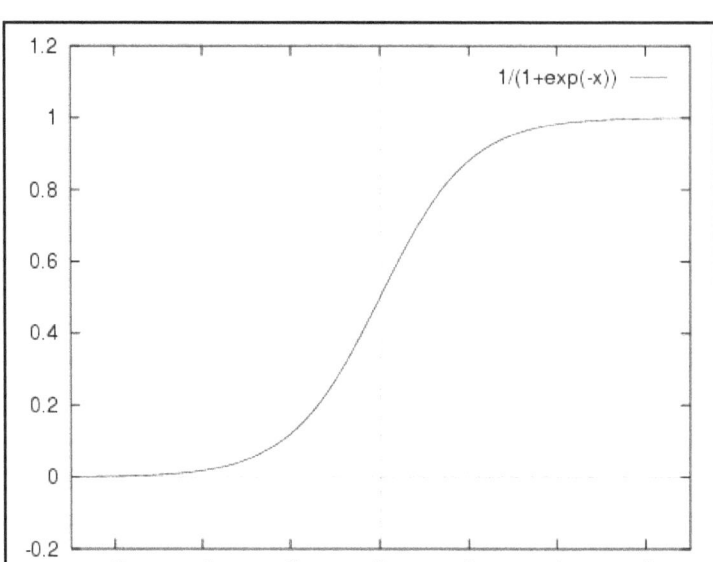

Softmax activation function

- **Sigmoid**: This is similar to softmax, except that it is applied to a binary classification, such as cats versus dogs. With this activation function, the class to which the observation belongs is assigned a higher probability compared to the other class. Unlike softmax, the probabilities do not have to add up to 1.

Introduction to the MXNet framework

MXNet is a super-powerful open source deep learning framework that is built to ease the development of deep learning algorithms. It is used to define, train, and deploy deep neural networks. MXNet is lean, flexible, and ultra-scalable, that is, it allows fast model training and supports a flexible programming model with multiple languages. The problem with existing deep learning frameworks, such as Torch7, Theano, and Caffe, is that users need to learn another system or a different programming flavor.

However, MXNet resolves this issue by supporting multiple languages, such as C++, Python, R, Julia, and Perl. This eliminates the need for users to learn a new language; therefore, they can use the framework and simplify network definitions. MXNet models are able to fit in small amounts of memory and they can be trained on CPUs, GPUs, and on multiple machines with ease. The `mxnet` package is readily available for the R language and the details of the install can be looked up in **Apache Incubator** at `https://mxnet.incubator.apache.org`.

Understanding the MNIST dataset

Modified National Institute of Standards and Technology (MNIST) is a dataset that contains images of handwritten digits. This dataset is pretty popular in the ML community for implementing and testing computer vision algorithms. The MNIST dataset is an open dataset made available by Professor Yann LeCun at `http://yann.lecun.com/exdb/mnist/`, where separate files that represent the training dataset and test dataset are available. The labels corresponding to the test and training datasets are also available as separate files. The training dataset has 60,000 samples and the test dataset has 10,000 samples.

The following diagram shows some sample images from the MNIST dataset. Each of the images also comes with a label indicating the digit shown in the following screenshot:

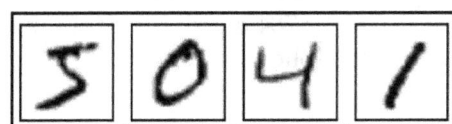

Sample images from MNIST dataset

The labels for the images shown in the preceding diagram are **5**, **0**, **4**, and **1**. Each image in the dataset is a grayscale image and is represented in 28 x 28 pixels. A sample image represented with pixels is shown in the following screenshot:

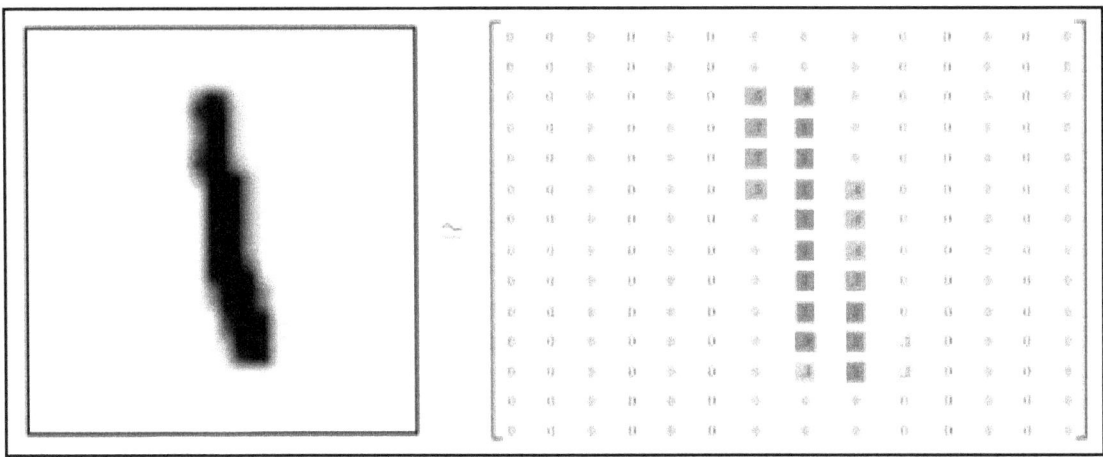

Sample image from MNIST dataset represented with 28 * 28 pixels

It is possible to flatten the 28 x 28 pixel matrix and represent it as a vector of 784 pixel values. Essentially, the training dataset is a 60,000 x 784 matrix that could be used with ML algorithms. The test dataset is a 10,000 x 784 matrix. The training and test datasets may be downloaded from the source with the following code:

```
# setting the working directory where the files need to be downloaded
setwd('/home/sunil/Desktop/book/chapter 19/MNIST')
# download the training and testing dataset from source
download.file("http://yann.lecun.com/exdb/mnist/train-images-idx3-ubyte.gz"
,"train-images-idx3-ubyte.gz")
download.file("http://yann.lecun.com/exdb/mnist/train-labels-idx1-ubyte.gz"
,"train-labels-idx1-ubyte.gz")
download.file("http://yann.lecun.com/exdb/mnist/t10k-images-idx3-ubyte.gz",
"t10k-images-idx3-ubyte.gz")
download.file("http://yann.lecun.com/exdb/mnist/t10k-labels-idx1-ubyte.gz",
"t10k-labels-idx1-ubyte.gz")
# unzip the training and test zip files that are downloaded
R.utils::gunzip("train-images-idx3-ubyte.gz")
R.utils::gunzip("train-labels-idx1-ubyte.gz")
R.utils::gunzip("t10k-images-idx3-ubyte.gz")
R.utils::gunzip("t10k-labels-idx1-ubyte.gz")
```

Once the data is downloaded and unzipped, we will see the files in our working directory. However, these files are in binary format and they cannot be directly loaded through the regular `read.csv` command. The following custom function code helps to read the training and test data from the binary files:

```
# function to load the image files
load_image_file = function(filename) {
  ret = list()
  # opening the binary file in read mode
  f = file(filename, 'rb')
  # reading the binary file into a matrix called x
  readBin(f, 'integer', n = 1, size = 4, endian = 'big')
  n = readBin(f, 'integer', n = 1, size = 4, endian = 'big')
  nrow = readBin(f, 'integer', n = 1, size = 4, endian = 'big')
  ncol = readBin(f, 'integer', n = 1, size = 4, endian = 'big')
  x = readBin(f, 'integer', n = n * nrow * ncol, size = 1, signed = FALSE)
  # closing the file
  close(f)
  # converting the matrix and returning the dataframe
  data.frame(matrix(x, ncol = nrow * ncol, byrow = TRUE))
}
# function to load label files
load_label_file = function(filename) {
  # reading the binary file in read mode
  f = file(filename, 'rb')
  # reading the labels binary file into y vector
  readBin(f, 'integer', n = 1, size = 4, endian = 'big')
  n = readBin(f, 'integer', n = 1, size = 4, endian = 'big')
  y = readBin(f, 'integer', n = n, size = 1, signed = FALSE)
  # closing the file
  close(f)
  # returning the y vector
  y
}
```

The functions may be called with the following code:

```
# load training images data through the load_image_file custom function
train = load_image_file("train-images-idx3-ubyte")
# load  test data through the load_image_file custom function
test  = load_image_file("t10k-images-idx3-ubyte")
# load the train dataset labels
train.y = load_label_file("train-labels-idx1-ubyte")
# load the test dataset labels
test.y  = load_label_file("t10k-labels-idx1-ubyte")
```

In RStudio, when we execute the code, we see `train`, `test`, `train.y`, and `test.y` displayed under the **Environment** tab. This confirms that the datasets are successfully loaded and the respective dataframes are created, as shown in the following screenshot:

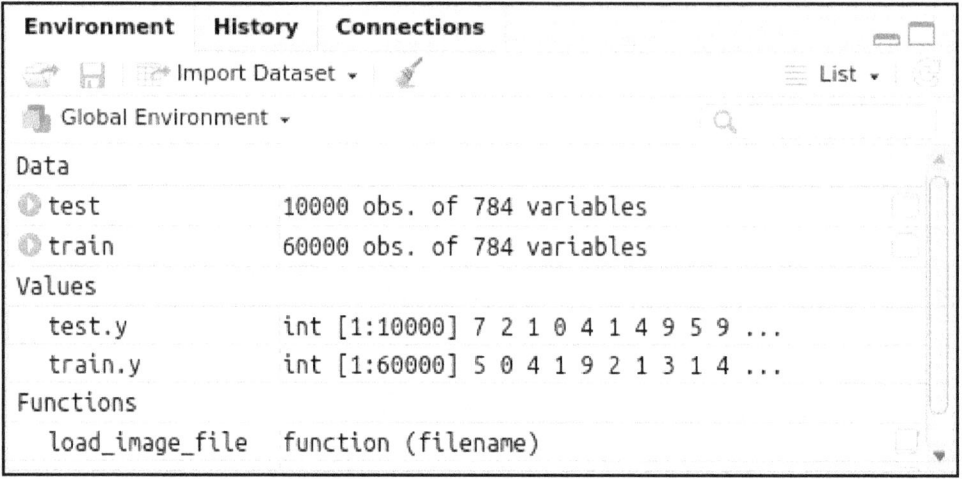

Once the image data is loaded into the dataframe, it is in the form of a series of numbers that represent the pixel values. The following is a helper function that visualizes the pixel data as an image in RStudio:

```
# helper function to visualize image given a record of pixels
show_digit = function(arr784, col = gray(12:1 / 12), ...) {
  image(matrix(as.matrix(arr784), nrow = 28)[, 28:1], col = col, ...)
}
```

The `show_digit()` function may be called like any other R function with the dataframe record number as a parameter. For example, the function in the following code block helps to visualize the 3 record in the training dataset as an image in RStudio:

```
# viewing image corresponding to record 3 in the train dataset
show_digit(train[3, ])
```

This will give the following output:

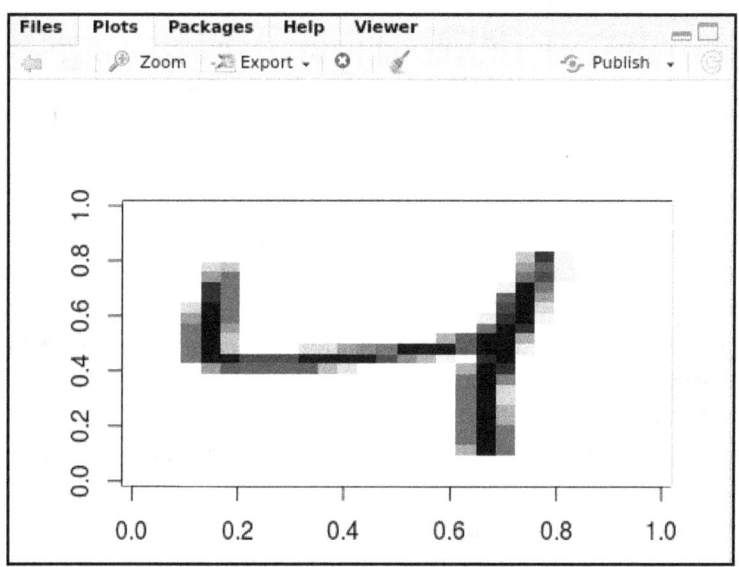

Dr. David Robinson, in his blog on *Exploring handwritten digit classification: a tidy analysis of the MNIST dataset* (`http://varianceexplained.org/r/digit-eda/`), performed a beautiful exploratory data analysis of the MNIST dataset, which will help you better understand the dataset.

Implementing a deep learning network for handwritten digit recognition

The `mxnet` library offers several functions that enable us to define the layers and activations that comprise the deep learning network. The definition of layers, the usage of activation functions, and the number of neurons to be used in each of the hidden layers is generally termed the **network architecture**. Deciding on the network architecture is more of an art than a science. Often, several iterations of experiments may be needed to decide on the right architecture for the problem. We call it an art as there are no exact rules for finding the ideal architecture. The number of layers, neurons in these layers, and the type of layers are pretty much decided through trial and error.

In this section, we'll build a simple deep learning network with three hidden layers. Here is the general architecture of our network:

1. The input layer is defined as the initial layer in the network. The `mx.symbol.Variable` MXNet function defines the input layer.

2. A fully-connected layer is defined, also called a dense layer, with 128 neurons as the first hidden layer in the network. This can be done using the `mx.symbol.FullyConnected` MXNet function.

3. A ReLU activation function is defined as part of the network. The `mx.symbol.Activation` function helps us to define the ReLU activation function as part of the network.

4. Define the second hidden layer; it is another dense layer with 64 neurons. This can be accomplished through the `mx.symbol.FullyConnected` function, similar to the first hidden layer.

5. Apply a ReLU activation function on the second hidden layer's output. This can be done through the `mx.symbol.Activation` function.

6. The final hidden layer in our network is another fully-connected layer, but with just ten outputs (equal to the number of classes). This can be done through the `mx.symbol.FullyConnected` function as well.

7. The output layer needs to be defined and this should be probabilities of prediction for each class; therefore, we apply softmax at the output layer. The `mx.symbol.SoftmaxOutput` function enables us to configure the softmax in the output.

We are not saying that this is the best network architecture possible for the problem, but this is the network we are going to build to demonstrate the implementation of a deep learning network with MXNet.

Now that we have a blueprint in place, let's delve into coding the network using the following code block:

```
# setting the working directory
setwd('/home/sunil/Desktop/book/chapter 19/MNIST')
# function to load image files
load_image_file = function(filename) {
  ret = list()
  f = file(filename, 'rb')
  readBin(f, 'integer', n = 1, size = 4, endian = 'big')
  n    = readBin(f, 'integer', n = 1, size = 4, endian = 'big')
  nrow = readBin(f, 'integer', n = 1, size = 4, endian = 'big')
  ncol = readBin(f, 'integer', n = 1, size = 4, endian = 'big')
```

```
  x = readBin(f, 'integer', n = n * nrow * ncol, size = 1, signed
= FALSE)
  close(f)
  data.frame(matrix(x, ncol = nrow * ncol, byrow = TRUE))
}
# function to load the label files
load_label_file = function(filename) {
  f = file(filename, 'rb')
  readBin(f, 'integer', n = 1, size = 4, endian = 'big')
  n = readBin(f, 'integer', n = 1, size = 4, endian = 'big')
  y = readBin(f, 'integer', n = n, size = 1, signed = FALSE)
  close(f)
  y }
# loading the image files
train = load_image_file("train-images-idx3-ubyte")
test  = load_image_file("t10k-images-idx3-ubyte")
# loading the labels
train.y = load_label_file("train-labels-idx1-ubyte")
test.y  = load_label_file("t10k-labels-idx1-ubyte")
# lineaerly transforming the grey scale image i.e. between 0 and 255 to # 0
and 1
train.x <- data.matrix(train/255)
test <- data.matrix(test/255)
# verifying the distribution of the digit labels in train dataset
print(table(train.y))
# verifying the distribution of the digit labels in test dataset
print(table(test.y))
```

This will give the following output:

```
train.y
   0    1    2    3    4    5    6    7    8    9
5923 6742 5958 6131 5842 5421 5918 6265 5851 5949

test.y
   0    1    2    3    4    5    6    7    8    9
 980 1135 1032 1010  982  892  958 1028  974 1009
```

Now, define the three layers and start training the network to obtain class probabilities and ensure the results are reproducible using the following code block:

```
# including the required mxnet library
library(mxnet)
# defining the input layer in the network architecture
data <- mx.symbol.Variable("data")
# defining the first hidden layer with 128 neurons and also naming the #
layer as fc1
# passing the input data layer as input to the fc1 layer
```

```
fc1 <- mx.symbol.FullyConnected(data, name="fc1", num_hidden=128)
# defining the ReLU activation function on the fc1 output and also # naming
the layer as ReLU1
act1 <- mx.symbol.Activation(fc1, name="ReLU1", act_type="relu")
# defining the second hidden layer with 64 neurons and also naming the #
layer as fc2
# passing the previous activation layer output as input to the
fc2 layer
fc2 <- mx.symbol.FullyConnected(act1, name="fc2", num_hidden=64)
# defining the ReLU activation function on the fc2 output and also
# naming the layer as ReLU2
act2 <- mx.symbol.Activation(fc2, name="ReLU2", act_type="relu")
# defining the third and final hidden layer in our network with 10
# neurons and also naming the layer as fc3
# passing the previous activation layer output as input to the
fc3 layer
fc3 <- mx.symbol.FullyConnected(act2, name="fc3", num_hidden=10)
# defining the output layer with softmax activation function to obtain #
class probabilities
softmax <- mx.symbol.SoftmaxOutput(fc3, name="sm")
# defining that the experiment should run on cpu
devices <- mx.cpu()
# setting the seed for the experiment so as to ensure that the results #
are reproducible
mx.set.seed(0)
# building the model with the network architecture defined above
model <- mx.model.FeedForward.create(softmax, X=train.x, y=train.y,
ctx=devices, num.round=10, array.batch.size=100,array.layout ="rowmajor",
learning.rate=0.07, momentum=0.9,  eval.metric=mx.metric.accuracy,
initializer=mx.init.uniform(0.07),
epoch.end.callback=mx.callback.log.train.metric(100))
```

This will give the following output:

```
Start training with 1 devices
[1] Train-accuracy=0.885783334343384
[2] Train-accuracy=0.963616671562195
[3] Train-accuracy=0.97510000983874
[4] Train-accuracy=0.980016676982244
[5] Train-accuracy=0.984233343303204
[6] Train-accuracy=0.986883342464765
[7] Train-accuracy=0.98848334223032
[8] Train-accuracy=0.990800007780393
[9] Train-accuracy=0.991300007204215
[10] Train-accuracy=0.991516673564911
```

To make predictions on the test dataset and get the label for each observation in the test dataset, use the following code block:

```
# making predictions on the test dataset
preds <- predict(model, test)
# verifying the predicted output
print(dim(preds))
# getting the label for each observation in test dataset; the
# predicted class is the one with highest probability
pred.label <- max.col(t(preds)) - 1
# observing the distribution of predicted labels in the test dataset
print(table(pred.label))
```

This will give the following output:

```
[1]    10 10000
pred.label
   0    1    2    3    4    5    6    7    8    9
 980 1149 1030 1021 1001  869  960 1001  964 1025
```

Let's check the performance of the model using the following code:

```
# obtaining the performance of the model
print(accuracy(pred.label,test.y))
```

This will give the following output:

```
Accuracy (PCC): 97.73%
Cohen's Kappa: 0.9748
Users accuracy:
   0    1    2    3    4    5    6    7    8    9
98.8 99.6 98.0 97.7 98.3 96.1 97.9 96.3 96.6 97.7
Producers accuracy:
   0    1    2    3    4    5    6    7    8    9
98.8 98.3 98.2 96.7 96.4 98.6 97.7 98.9 97.6 96.2
Confusion matrix
   y
x      0    1    2    3    4    5    6    7    8    9
  0  968    0    1    1    1    2    3    1    2    1
  1    1 1130    3    0    0    1    3    8    1    2
  2    0    1 1011    2    2    0    0   11    3    0
  3    1    2    6  987    0   14    2    2    4    3
  4    1    0    2    1  965    2   10    3    6   11
  5    1    0    0    4    0  857    2    0    3    2
  6    5    2    3    0    4    5  938    0    3    0
  7    0    0    2    2    1    1    0  990    3    2
  8    1    0    4    8    0    5    0    3  941    2
  9    2    0    0    5    9    5    0   10    8  986
```

To visualize the network architecture, use the following code:

```
# Visualizing the network architecture
graph.viz(model$symbol)
```

This will give the following output:

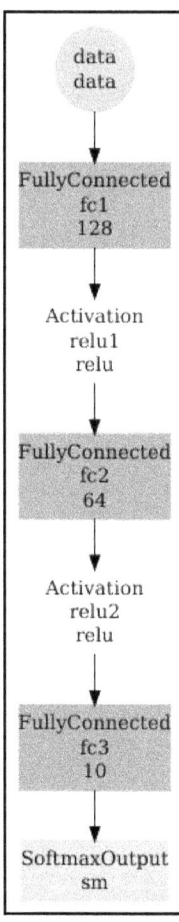

With the simple architecture running for a few minutes on a CPU-based laptop and with minimal effort, we were able to achieve an accuracy of 97.7% on the test dataset. The deep learning network was able to learn to interpret the digits by seeing the images it was given as input. The accuracy of the system can be further improved by altering the architecture or by increasing the number of iterations. It may be noted that, in the earlier experiment, we ran it for 10 iterations.

The number of iterations can simply be amended when model-building through the num.round parameter. There is no hard-and-fast rule in terms of the optimal number of rounds, so this is something to be determined by trial and error. Let's build the model with 50 iterations and observe its impact on performance. The code will remain the same as the earlier project, except with the following amendment to the model-building code:

```
model <- mx.model.FeedForward.create(softmax, X=train.x, y=train.y,
ctx=devices, num.round=50, array.batch.size=100,array.layout ="rowmajor",
learning.rate=0.07, momentum=0.9,   eval.metric=mx.metric.accuracy,
initializer=mx.init.uniform(0.07),
epoch.end.callback=mx.callback.log.train.metric(100))
```

 Observe that the num.round parameter is now set to 50, instead of the earlier value of 10.

This will give the following output:

```
[35]  Train-accuracy=0.999933333396912
[36]  Train-accuracy=1
[37]  Train-accuracy=1
[38]  Train-accuracy=1
[39]  Train-accuracy=1
[40]  Train-accuracy=1
[41]  Train-accuracy=1
[42]  Train-accuracy=1
[43]  Train-accuracy=1
[44]  Train-accuracy=1
[45]  Train-accuracy=1
[46]  Train-accuracy=1
[47]  Train-accuracy=1
[48]  Train-accuracy=1
[49]  Train-accuracy=1
[50]  Train-accuracy=1
[1]     10 10000
pred.label
     0    1    2    3    4    5    6    7    8    9
   992 1139 1029 1017  983  877  953 1021  972 1017
Accuracy (PCC): 98.21%
Cohen's Kappa: 0.9801
Users accuracy:
     0    1    2    3    4    5    6    7    8    9
  99.3 99.5 98.2 98.2 98.1 97.1 98.0 97.7 98.0 97.8
Producers accuracy:
     0    1    2    3    4    5    6    7    8    9
  98.1 99.1 98.4 97.5 98.0 98.7 98.5 98.3 98.3 97.1
```

```
Confusion matrix
   y
x       0     1     2     3     4     5     6     7     8     9
  0   973     0     2     2     1     3     5     1     3     2
  1     1  1129     0     0     1     1     3     2     0     2
  2     1     0  1013     1     3     0     0     9     2     0
  3     0     1     5   992     0    10     1     1     3     4
  4     0     0     2     0   963     2     7     1     1     7
  5     0     0     0     4     1   866     2     0     2     2
  6     2     2     1     0     3     5   939     0     1     0
  7     0     1     6     3     1     1     0  1004     2     3
  8     1     1     3     4     0     2     1     3   955     2
  9     2     1     0     4     9     2     0     7     5   987
```

We can observe from the output that 100% accuracy was obtained with the training dataset. However, with the test dataset, we observe the accuracy as 98%. Essentially, our model is expected to perform the same with both the training and test dataset for it to be called a good model. Unfortunately, in this case, we have encountered a situation known as **overfitting,** which means that the model we created did not generalize well. In other words, the model has trained itself with too many parameters or it got trained for too long and has become super-specialized with data in the training dataset alone; as an effect, it is not doing a good job with new data. Model generalization is something we should specifically aim for. There is a technique, known as **dropout**, that can help us to overcome the overfitting issue.

Implementing dropout to avoid overfitting

Dropout is defined in the network architecture after the activation layers, and it randomly sets activations to zero. In other words, dropout randomly deletes parts of the neural network, which allows us to prevent overfitting. We can't overfit exactly to our training data when we're consistently throwing away information learned along the way. This allows our neural network to learn to generalize better.

In MXNet, dropout can be easily defined as part of network architecture using the `mx.symbol.Dropout` function. For example, the following code defines dropouts post the first ReLU activation (`act1`) and second ReLU activation (`act2`):

```
dropout1 <- mx.symbol.Dropout(data = act1, p = 0.5)
dropout2 <- mx.symbol.Dropout(data = act2, p = 0.3)
```

The `data` parameter specifies the input that the dropout takes and the value of `p` specifies the amount of dropout to be done. In case of `dropout1`, we are specifying that 50% of weights are to be dropped. Again, there is no hard-and-fast rule in terms of how much dropout should be included and at what layers. This is something to be determined through trial and error. The code with dropouts almost remains identical to the earlier project except that it now includes the dropouts after the activations:

```
# code to read the dataset and transform it to train.x and train.y remains
# same as earlier project, therefore that code is not shown here
# including the required mxnet library
library(mxnet)
# defining the input layer in the network architecture
data <- mx.symbol.Variable("data")
# defining the first hidden layer with 128 neurons and also naming the #
layer as fc1
# passing the input data layer as input to the fc1 layer
fc1 <- mx.symbol.FullyConnected(data, name="fc1", num_hidden=128)
# defining the ReLU activation function on the fc1 output and also naming
the layer as ReLU1
act1 <- mx.symbol.Activation(fc1, name="ReLU1", act_type="relu")
# defining a 50% dropout of weights learnt
dropout1 <- mx.symbol.Dropout(data = act1, p = 0.5)
# defining the second hidden layer with 64 neurons and also naming the
layer as fc2
# passing the previous dropout output as input to the fc2 layer
fc2 <- mx.symbol.FullyConnected(dropout1, name="fc2", num_hidden=64)
# defining the ReLU activation function on the fc2 output and also naming
the layer as ReLU2
act2 <- mx.symbol.Activation(fc2, name="ReLU2", act_type="relu")
# defining a dropout with 30% weight drop
dropout2 <- mx.symbol.Dropout(data = act2, p = 0.3)
# defining the third and final hidden layer in our network with 10 neurons
and also naming the layer as fc3
# passing the previous dropout output as input to the fc3 layer
fc3 <- mx.symbol.FullyConnected(dropout2, name="fc3", num_hidden=10)
# defining the output layer with softmax activation function to
obtain class probabilities
softmax <- mx.symbol.SoftmaxOutput(fc3, name="sm")
# defining that the experiment should run on cpu
devices <- mx.cpu()
# setting the seed for the experiment so as to ensure that the results are
reproducible
mx.set.seed(0)
# building the model with the network architecture defined above
model <- mx.model.FeedForward.create(softmax, X=train.x, y=train.y,
ctx=devices, num.round=50, array.batch.size=100,array.layout = "rowmajor",
learning.rate=0.07, momentum=0.9,  eval.metric=mx.metric.accuracy,
```

```
initializer=mx.init.uniform(0.07),
epoch.end.callback=mx.callback.log.train.metric(100))
# making predictions on the test dataset
preds <- predict(model, test)
# verifying the predicted output
print(dim(preds))
# getting the label for each observation in test dataset; the predicted
class is the one with highest probability
pred.label <- max.col(t(preds)) - 1
# observing the distribution of predicted labels in the test
dataset
print(table(pred.label))
# including the rfUtilities library so as to use accuracy function
library(rfUtilities)
# obtaining the performance of the model
print(accuracy(pred.label,test.y))
# printing the network architecture
graph.viz(model$symbol)
```

This will give the following output and the visual network architecture:

```
[35] Train-accuracy=0.958950003186862
[36] Train-accuracy=0.958983335793018
[37] Train-accuracy=0.958083337446054
[38] Train-accuracy=0.959683336317539
[39] Train-accuracy=0.95990000406901
[40] Train-accuracy=0.959433337251345
[41] Train-accuracy=0.959066670437654
[42] Train-accuracy=0.960250004529953
[43] Train-accuracy=0.959983337720235
[44] Train-accuracy=0.960450003842513
[45] Train-accuracy=0.960150004227956
[46] Train-accuracy=0.960533337096373
[47] Train-accuracy=0.962033336758614
[48] Train-accuracy=0.96005000303189
[49] Train-accuracy=0.961366670827071
[50] Train-accuracy=0.961350003282229
[1]    10 10000
pred.label
   0    1    2    3    4    5    6    7    8    9
 984 1143 1042 1022  996  902  954 1042  936  979
Accuracy (PCC): 97.3%
Cohen's Kappa: 0.97
Users accuracy:
   0    1    2    3    4    5    6    7    8    9
98.7 98.9 98.1 97.6 98.2 97.3 97.6 97.4 94.3 94.7
Producers accuracy:
   0    1    2    3    4    5    6    7    8    9
```

```
98.3 98.3 97.1 96.5 96.8 96.2 98.0 96.1 98.1 97.7
Confusion matrix
     y
x        0     1     2     3     4     5     6     7     8     9
  0    967     0     0     0     0     2     5     1     6     3
  1      0  1123     3     0     1     1     3     5     2     5
  2      1     2  1012     4     3     0     0    14     4     2
  3      2     1     4   986     0     6     1     3    12     7
  4      0     0     3     0   964     2     5     0     5    17
  5      2     3     0     9     0   868     7     0     9     4
  6      3     2     0     0     5     3   935     0     6     0
  7      4     1     9     4     3     3     0  1001     6    11
  8      1     3     1     2     1     3     2     1   918     4
  9      0     0     0     5     5     4     0     3     6   956
```

Take a look at the following diagram:

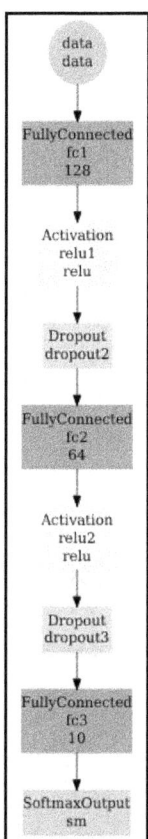

We can see from the output that dropout is now included as part of the network architecture. We also observe that this network architecture yields a lower accuracy on the test dataset when compared with our initial project. One reason could be that the dropout percentages (50% and 30%) we included are too high. We could play with these percentages and rebuild the model to determine whether the accuracy gets better. The idea, however, is to demonstrate the use of dropout as a regularization technique so as to avoid overfitting in deep neural networks.

Apart from dropout, there are other techniques you could employ to avoid an overfitting situation:

- **Addition of data**: Adding more training data.
- **Data augmentation**: Creating additional data synthetically by applying techniques such as flipping, distorting, adding random noise, and rotation. The following screenshot shows sample images created after applying data augmentation:

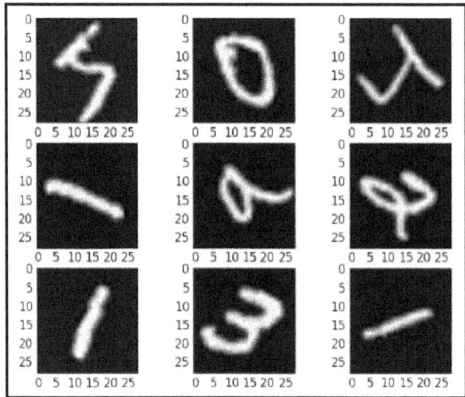

Sample images from applying data augmentation

- **Reducing complexity of the network architecture**: Fewer layers, fewer epochs, and so on.
- **Batch normalization**: A process of ensuring that the weights generated in the network do not push very high or very low. This is generally achieved by subtracting the mean and dividing by the standard deviation of all weights at a layer from each weight in a layer. It shields against overfitting, performs regularization, and significantly improves the training speed. The `mx.sym.batchnorm()` function enables us to define batch normalization after the activation.

We will not focus on developing another project with batch normalization as using this function in the project is very similar to the other functions we used in our earlier projects. So far, we have focused on increasing the epochs to improve the performance of the model, another option is to try a different architecture and evaluate whether that improves the accuracy on the test dataset. On that note, let's explore LeNet, which is specifically designed for optical character recognition in documents.

Implementing the LeNet architecture with the MXNet library

In their 1998 paper, *Gradient-Based Learning Applied to Document Recognition*, LeCun et al. introduced the LeNet architecture.

The LeNet architecture consists of two sets of convolutional, activation, and pooling layers, followed by a fully-connected layer, activation, another fully-connected layer, and finally a softmax classifier. The following diagram illustrates the LeNet architecture:

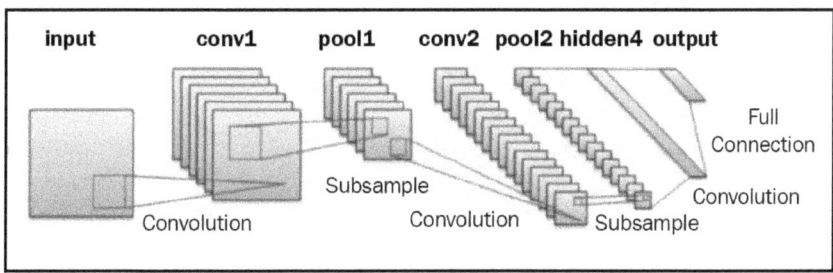

LeNet architecture

Now, let's implement the LeNet architecture with the mxnet library in our project using the following code block:

```
## setting the working directory
setwd('/home/sunil/Desktop/book/chapter 19/MNIST')
# function to load image files
load_image_file = function(filename) {
  ret = list()
  f = file(filename, 'rb')
  readBin(f, 'integer', n = 1, size = 4, endian = 'big')
  n    = readBin(f, 'integer', n = 1, size = 4, endian = 'big')
  nrow = readBin(f, 'integer', n = 1, size = 4, endian = 'big')
  ncol = readBin(f, 'integer', n = 1, size = 4, endian = 'big')
  x = readBin(f, 'integer', n = n * nrow * ncol, size = 1, signed
```

```
= FALSE)
  close(f)
  data.frame(matrix(x, ncol = nrow * ncol, byrow = TRUE))
}
# function to load label files
load_label_file = function(filename) {
  f = file(filename, 'rb')
  readBin(f, 'integer', n = 1, size = 4, endian = 'big')
  n = readBin(f, 'integer', n = 1, size = 4, endian = 'big')
  y = readBin(f, 'integer', n = n, size = 1, signed = FALSE)
  close(f)
  y
}
# load images
train = load_image_file("train-images-idx3-ubyte")
test  = load_image_file("t10k-images-idx3-ubyte")
# converting the train and test data into a format as required by LeNet
train.x <- t(data.matrix(train))
test <- t(data.matrix(test))
# loading the labels
train.y = load_label_file("train-labels-idx1-ubyte")
test.y  = load_label_file("t10k-labels-idx1-ubyte")
# linearly transforming the grey scale image i.e. between 0 and 255 to # 0
and 1
train.x <- train.x/255
test <- test/255
# including the required mxnet library
library(mxnet)
# input
data <- mx.symbol.Variable('data')
# first convolution layer
conv1 <- mx.symbol.Convolution(data=data, kernel=c(5,5), num_filter=20)
# applying the tanh activation function
tanh1 <- mx.symbol.Activation(data=conv1, act_type="tanh")
# applying max pooling
pool1 <- mx.symbol.Pooling(data=tanh1, pool_type="max", kernel=c(2,2),
stride=c(2,2))
# second conv
conv2 <- mx.symbol.Convolution(data=pool1, kernel=c(5,5), num_filter=50)
# applying the tanh activation function again
tanh2 <- mx.symbol.Activation(data=conv2, act_type="tanh")
#performing max pooling again
pool2 <- mx.symbol.Pooling(data=tanh2, pool_type="max",
                           kernel=c(2,2), stride=c(2,2))
# flattening the data
flatten <- mx.symbol.Flatten(data=pool2)
# first fullconnected later
fc1 <- mx.symbol.FullyConnected(data=flatten, num_hidden=500)
```

```
# applying the tanh activation function
tanh3 <- mx.symbol.Activation(data=fc1, act_type="tanh")
# second fullconnected layer
fc2 <- mx.symbol.FullyConnected(data=tanh3, num_hidden=10)
# defining the output layer with softmax activation function to obtain #
class probabilities
lenet <- mx.symbol.SoftmaxOutput(data=fc2)
# transforming the train and test dataset into a format required by
# MxNet functions
train.array <- train.x
dim(train.array) <- c(28, 28, 1, ncol(train.x))
test.array <- test
dim(test.array) <- c(28, 28, 1, ncol(test))
# setting the seed for the experiment so as to ensure that the
# results are reproducible
mx.set.seed(0)
# defining that the experiment should run on cpu
devices <- mx.cpu()
# building the model with the network architecture defined above
model <- mx.model.FeedForward.create(lenet, X=train.array, y=train.y,
ctx=devices, num.round=3, array.batch.size=100, learning.rate=0.05,
momentum=0.9, wd=0.00001, eval.metric=mx.metric.accuracy,
            epoch.end.callback=mx.callback.log.train.metric(100))
# making predictions on the test dataset
preds <- predict(model, test.array)
# getting the label for each observation in test dataset; the
# predicted class is the one with highest probability
pred.label <- max.col(t(preds)) - 1
# including the rfUtilities library so as to use accuracy
function
library(rfUtilities)
# obtaining the performance of the model
print(accuracy(pred.label,test.y))
# printing the network architecture
graph.viz(model$symbol,direction="LR")
```

This will give the following output and the visual network architecture:

```
Start training with 1 devices
[1] Train-accuracy=0.678916669438283
[2] Train-accuracy=0.978666676680247
[3] Train-accuracy=0.98676667680343
Accuracy (PCC): 98.54%
Cohen's Kappa: 0.9838
Users accuracy:
     0     1     2     3     4     5     6     7     8     9
 99.8 100.0  97.0  98.4  98.9  98.2  98.2  98.7  98.2  97.8
Producers accuracy:
```

```
     0    1    2    3    4    5    6    7    8    9
   98.0 96.9 99.1 99.3 99.0 99.3 99.6 97.7 98.7 98.3
   Confusion matrix
      y
   x      0    1    2    3    4    5    6    7    8    9
      0  978    0    2    2    1    3    7    0    4    1
      1    0 1135   15    2    1    0    5    7    1    5
      2    0    0 1001    2    1    1    0    3    2    0
      3    0    0    0  994    0    5    0    1    1    0
      4    0    0    1    0  971    0    1    0    0    8
      5    0    0    0    3    0  876    2    0    1    0
      6    0    0    0    0    2    1  941    0    1    0
      7    1    0    7    1    3    1    0 1015    3    8
      8    1    0    6    1    1    1    2    1  956    0
      9    0    0    0    5    2    4    0    1    5  987
```

Take a look at the following diagram:

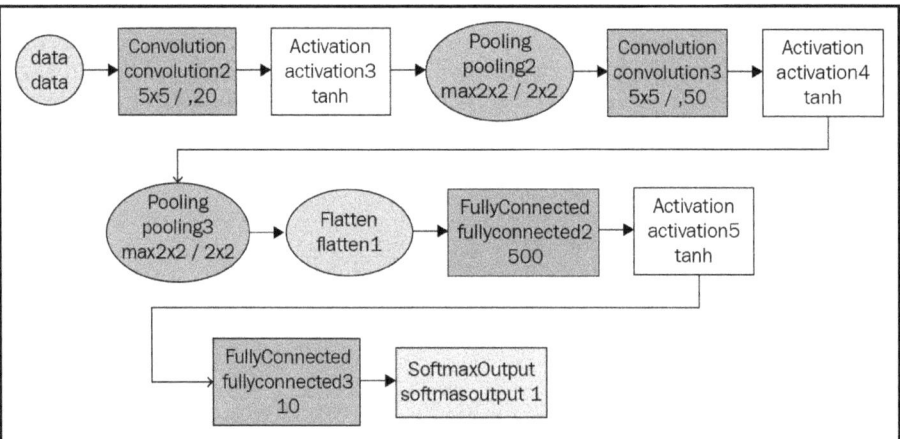

The code ran for less than 5 minutes on my 4-core CPU box, but still got us a 98% accuracy on the test dataset with just three epochs. We can also see that we obtained 98% accuracy with both the training and test datasets, confirming that there is no overfitting.

We see `tanh` is used as the activation function; let's experiment and see whether it has any impact if we change it to ReLU. The code for the project will be identical except that we need to find and replace `tanh` with ReLU. We will not repeat the code as the only lines that have changed from the earlier project are as follows:

```
ReLU1 <- mx.symbol.Activation(data=conv1, act_type="relu")
pool1 <- mx.symbol.Pooling(data=ReLU1, pool_type="max",
                           kernel=c(2,2), stride=c(2,2))
```

```
ReLU2 <- mx.symbol.Activation(data=conv1, act_type="relu")
pool2 <- mx.symbol.Pooling(data=ReLU2, pool_type="max",
                            kernel=c(2,2), stride=c(2,2))
ReLU3 <- mx.symbol.Activation(data=conv1, act_type="relu")
fc2 <- mx.symbol.FullyConnected(data=ReLU3, num_hidden=10)
```

You will get the following output on running the code with ReLU as the activation function:

```
Start training with 1 devices
[1] Train-accuracy=0.627283334874858
[2] Train-accuracy=0.979916676084201
[3] Train-accuracy=0.987366676231225
Accuracy (PCC): 98.36%
Cohen's Kappa: 0.9818
Users accuracy:
     0    1    2    3    4    5    6    7    8    9
  99.8 99.7 97.9 99.4 98.6 96.5 97.7 98.2 97.4 97.9
Producers accuracy:
     0    1    2    3    4    5    6    7    8    9
  97.5 97.2 99.6 95.6 99.7 99.2 99.7 98.0 99.6 98.2
Confusion matrix
     y
x       0     1     2     3     4     5     6     7     8     9
  0   978     0     3     1     1     2    12     0     5     1
  1     1  1132     6     0     2     1     5    11     1     6
  2     0     0  1010     1     0     0     0     1     2     0
  3     0     2     4  1004     0    23     1     3     9     4
  4     0     0     1     0   968     0     1     0     0     1
  5     0     1     0     1     0   861     2     0     3     0
  6     0     0     0     0     0     3   936     0     0     0
  7     1     0     6     3     0     1     0  1010     1     9
  8     0     0     2     0     1     0     1     0   949     0
  9     0     0     0     0    10     1     0     3     4   988
```

With ReLU being used as the activation function, we do not see a significant improvement in the accuracy. It stayed at 98%, which is the same as obtained with the `tanh` activation function.

As a next step, we could try to rebuild the model with additional epochs to see whether the accuracy improves. Alternatively, we could try tweaking the number of filters and filter sizes per convolutional layer to see what happens! Further experiments could also include adding more layers of several kinds. We don't know what the result is going to be unless we experiment!

Implementing computer vision with pretrained models

In `Chapter 14`, *Exploring the Machine Learning Landscape,* we touched upon a concept called **transfer learning**. The idea is to take the knowledge learned in a model and apply it to another related task. Transfer learning is used on almost all computer vision tasks nowadays. It's rare to train models from scratch unless there is a huge labeled dataset available for training.

Generally, in computer vision, CNNs try to detect edges in the earlier layers, shapes in the middle layer, and some task-specific features in the later layers. Irrespective of the image to be detected by the CNNs, the function of the earlier and middle layers remains the same, which makes it possible to exploit the knowledge gained by a pretrained model. With transfer learning, we can reuse the early and middle layers and only retrain the later layers. It helps us to leverage the labeled data of the task it was initially trained on.

Transfer learning offers two main advantages: it saves us training time and ensures that we have a good model even if we have a lot less labelled training data.

`Xception`, `VGG16`, `VGG19`, `ResNet50`, `InceptionV3`, `InceptionResNetV2`, `MobileNet`, `DenseNet`, `NASNet`, `MobileNetV2`, `QuocNet`, `AlexNet`, `Inception` (GoogLeNet), and `BN-Inception-v2` are some widely-used pretrained models. While we won't delve into the details of each of these pretrained models, the idea of this section is to implement a project to detect the contents of images (input) by making use of a pretrained model through MXNet.

In the code presented in this section, we make use of the pretrained Inception-BatchNorm network to predict the class of an image. The pretrained model needs to be downloaded to the working directory prior to running the code. The model can be downloaded from `http://data.mxnet.io/mxnet/data/Inception.zip`. Let's explore the following code to label a few test images using the `inception_bn` pretrained model:

```
# loading the required libraries
library(mxnet)
library(imager)
# loading the inception_bn model to memory
model = mx.model.load("/home/sunil/Desktop/book/chapter
19/Inception/Inception_BN", iteration=39)
# loading the mean image
mean.img = as.array(mx.nd.load("/home/sunil/Desktop/book/chapter
19/Inception/mean_224.nd")[["mean_img"]])
# loading the image that need to be classified
im <- load.image("/home/sunil/Desktop/book/chapter 19/image1.jpeg")
```

```
# displaying the image
plot(im)
```

This will result in the following output:

To process the images and predict the image IDs that have the highest probability of using the pretrained model, we use the following code:

```
# function to pre-process the image so as to be consumed by predict
function that is using inception_bn model
preproc.image <- function(im, mean.image) {
  # crop the image
  shape <- dim(im)
  short.edge <- min(shape[1:2])
  xx <- floor((shape[1] - short.edge) / 2)
  yy <- floor((shape[2] - short.edge) / 2)
  cropped <- crop.borders(im, xx, yy)
  # resize to 224 x 224, needed by input of the model.
  resized <- resize(cropped, 224, 224)
  # convert to array (x, y, channel)
  arr <- as.array(resized) * 255
  dim(arr) <- c(224, 224, 3)
  # subtract the mean
  normed <- arr - mean.img
  # Reshape to format needed by mxnet (width, height, channel,
num)
  dim(normed) <- c(224, 224, 3, 1)
  return(normed)
}
```

```
# calling the image pre-processing function on the image to be classified
normed <- preproc.image(im, mean.img)
# predicting the probabilties of labels for the image using the pre-trained
model
prob <- predict(model, X=normed)
# sorting and filtering the top three labels with highest
probabilities
max.idx <- order(prob[,1], decreasing = TRUE)[1:3]
# printing the ids with highest probabilities
print(max.idx)
```

This will result in the following output with the IDs of the highest probabilities:

```
[1] 471 627 863
```

Let's print the labels that correspond to the top-three predicted IDs with the highest probabilities using the following code:

```
# loading the pre-trained labels from inception_bn model
synsets <- readLines("/home/sunil/Desktop/book/chapter
6/Inception/synset.txt")
# printing the english labels corresponding to the top 3 ids with highest
probabilities
print(paste0("Predicted Top-classes: ", synsets[max.idx]))
```

This will give the following output:

```
[1] "Predicted Top-classes: n02948072 candle, taper, wax light"
[2] "Predicted Top-classes: n03666591 lighter, light, igniter, ignitor"
[3] "Predicted Top-classes: n04456115 torch"
```

From the output, we see that it has correctly labelled the image that is passed as input. We can test a few more images with the following code to confirm that the classification is done correctly:

```
im2 <- load.image("/home/sunil/Desktop/book/chapter 19/image2.jpeg")
plot(im2)
normed <- preproc.image(im2, mean.img)
prob <- predict(model, X=normed)
max.idx <- order(prob[,1], decreasing = TRUE)[1:3]
print(paste0("Predicted Top-classes: ", synsets[max.idx]))
```

This will give the following output:

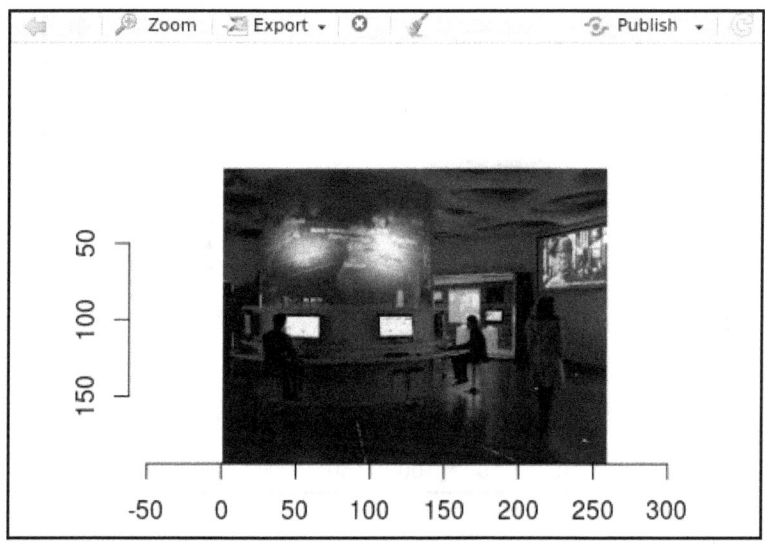

Take a look at the following code:

```
[1] "Predicted Top-classes: n03529860 home theater, home theatre"
[2] "Predicted Top-classes: n03290653 entertainment center"          [3]
"Predicted Top-classes: n04404412 television, television system"
```

Likewise, we can try for a third image using the following code:

```
# getting the labels for third image
im3 <- load.image("/home/sunil/Desktop/book/chapter 19/image3.jpeg")
plot(im3)
normed <- preproc.image(im3, mean.img)
prob <- predict(model, X=normed)
max.idx <- order(prob[,1], decreasing = TRUE)[1:3]
print(paste0("Predicted Top-classes: ", synsets[max.idx]))
```

This will give the following output:

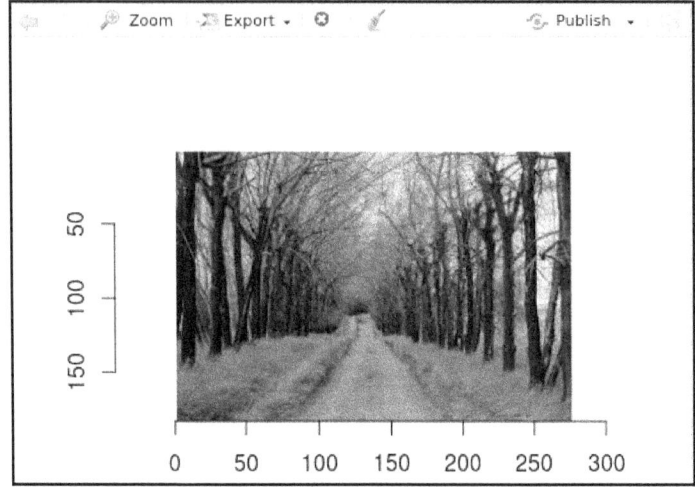

Take a look at the following output:

```
[1] "Predicted Top-classes: n04326547 stone wall"
[2] "Predicted Top-classes: n03891251 park bench"
[3] "Predicted Top-classes: n04604644 worm fence, snake fence, snake-rail
fence, Virginia fence"
```

Summary

In this chapter, we learned about computer vision and its association with deep learning. We explored a specific type of deep learning algorithm, CNNs, that is widely used in computer vision. We studied an open source deep learning framework called MXNet. After a detailed discussion of the MNIST dataset, we built models using various network architectures and successfully classified the handwritten digits in the MNIST dataset. At the end of the chapter, we delved into the concept of transfer learning and explored its association with computer vision. The last project we built in this chapter classified images using an Inception-BatchNorm pretrained model.

In the next chapter, we will explore an unsupervised learning algorithm called the autoencoder neural network. I am really excited to implement a project to capture credit card fraud using autoencoders. Are you game? Let's go!

20
Credit Card Fraud Detection Using Autoencoders

Fraud management has been known to be a very painful problem for banking and finance firms. Card-related frauds have proven to be especially difficult for firms to combat. Technologies such as chip and PIN are available and are already used by most credit card system vendors, such as Visa and MasterCard. However, the available technology is unable to curtail 100% of credit card fraud. Unfortunately, scammers come up with newer ways of phishing to obtain passwords from credit card users. Also, devices such as skimmers make stealing credit card data a cake walk!

Despite the availability of some technical abilities to combat credit card fraud, *The Nilson Report*, a leading publication covering payment systems worldwide, estimated that credit card fraud is going to soar to $32 billion in 2020 (`https://nilsonreport.com/upload/content_promo/The_Nilson_Report_10-17-2017.pdf`). To get a perspective on the estimated loss, it is more than the recent profits posted by companies such as Coca-Cola ($2 billion), Warren Buffet's Berkshire Hathaway ($24 billion), and JP Morgan Chase ($23.5 billion)!

While credit card chip technology-providing companies have been investing hugely to advance the technology to counter credit card fraud, in this chapter, we are going to examine whether and how far machine learning can help deal with the credit card fraud problem. We will cover the following topics as we progress through this chapter:

- Machine learning in credit card fraud detection
- Autoencoders and the various types
- The credit card fraud dataset
- Building AEs with the H2O library in R
- Implementation of auto encoder for credit card fraud detection

Machine learning in credit card fraud detection

The task of fraud detection often boils down to outlier detection, in which a dataset is verified to find potential anomalies in the data. Traditionally, this task was deemed a manual task, where risk experts checked all transactions manually. Even though there is a technical layer, it is purely based on a rules base that scans through each transaction, and then those shortlisted as suspicious are sent through for a manual review to make a final decision on the transaction. However, there are some major drawbacks to this system:

- Organizations need substantial fraud management budgets for manual review staff.
- Extensive training is required to train the employees working as manual review staff.
- Training the personnel to manually review transactions is time consuming and expensive.
- Even the most highly trained manual review staff carry certain biases, therefore making the whole review system inaccurate.
- Manual reviews increase the time required to fulfill a transaction. The customers might get frustrated with the long wait times required to pass a credit card transaction. This may impact the loyalty of customers.
- Manual reviews may yield false positives. A false positive not only affects the sale in the process but also lifetime value generated from the customer.

Fortunately, with the rise of **machine learning** (**ML**), **artificial intelligence** (**AI**), and deep learning, it became feasible to automate the manual credit card transaction review process to a large extent. This not only saves an intensive amount of labor but also yields better detection of credit card fraud, which otherwise is impacted due to biases that human reviewers carry.

ML-based fraud detection strategies generally can be accomplished using both supervised ML and unsupervised ML techniques.

Supervised ML models are generally used when large amounts of transaction data tagged as **genuine** or **fraud** are available. A model is trained on the labeled dataset and the resultant model is then used for classifying any new credit card transactions into one of the two possible classes.

With most organizations, the problem is that labeled data is unavailable, or very little labeled data is available. This makes supervised learning models less feasible. This is where unsupervised models come into play. They are designed to spot anomalous behavior in transactions and they do not need explicit pre-labeled data to identify the anomalous behavior. The general idea in unsupervised fraud detection is to detect behavior anomalies by identifying transactions that do not conform to the majority.

Another thing to keep in mind is that fraud events are rare, and are not as common as genuine transactions. Due to the rarity of fraud, severe class imbalance problem may be seen in datasets related to credit card fraud. In other words, one would observe that 95% or more of the data in the dataset is of genuine transactions, and less than 5% of the data belongs to fraudulent transactions. Also, even if you learn about a fraudulent transaction today, the model is likely to face an anomaly tomorrow with different features. So, the problem space of genuine transactions is well known and it is pretty much stagnant; however, the problem space for fraudulent transactions is not well known and it is not constant. Due to these reasons, it make sense to deal with the fraud detection problem with unsupervised learning rather than supervised learning.

Anomaly detection is an unsupervised learning algorithm that is also termed a **one-class classification** algorithm. It distinguishes between **normal** and **anomalous** observations. The key principle on which the algorithm is built is that anomalous observations do not conform to the expected pattern of other common observations in a dataset. It is called a one-class classification as it learns the pattern of genuine transactions, and anything that shows non-conformance to this pattern is termed as an **anomaly**, and therefore as a fraudulent **transaction**. The following figure is an illustration showing anomaly detection in a two-dimensional space:

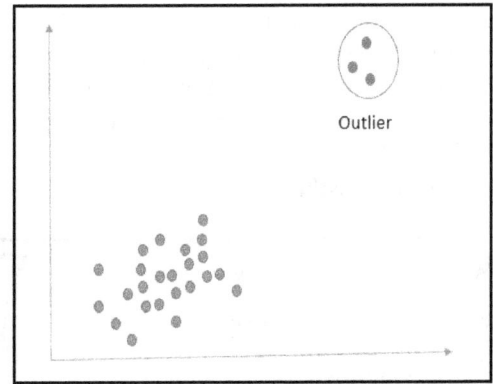

Anomaly detection illustrated in 2D space

A simple example of an anomaly is the identification of data points that are too far from the mean (standard deviation) in a time series. The following figure is an illustration displaying the data points that are identified as anomalies in a time series:

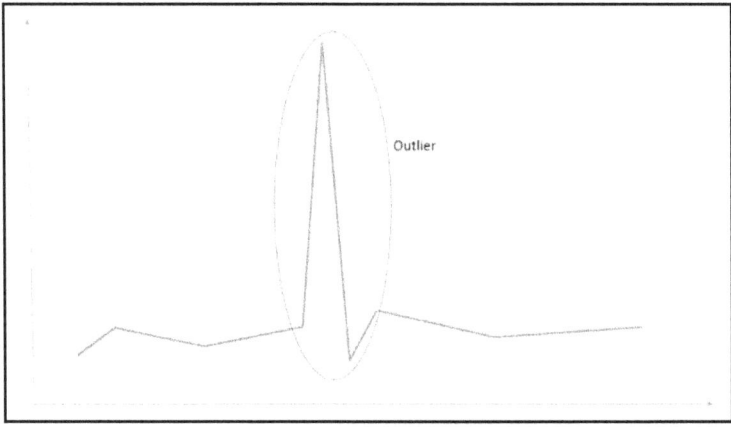

Anomaly in time series—identified through standard deviation

In this chapter, we will focus our efforts on a type of unsupervised deep learning application known as **AEs**.

Autoencoders explained

Autoencoders (**AEs**) are neural networks that are of a feedforward and non-recurrent type. They aim to copy the given inputs to the outputs. An AE works by compressing the input into a lower dimensional summary. This summary is often referred as latent space representation. An AE attempts to reconstruct the output from the latent space representation. An **Encoder**, a **Latent Space Representation**, and a **Decoder** are the three parts that make up the AEs. The following figure is an illustration showing the application of an AE on a sample picked from the MNIST dataset:

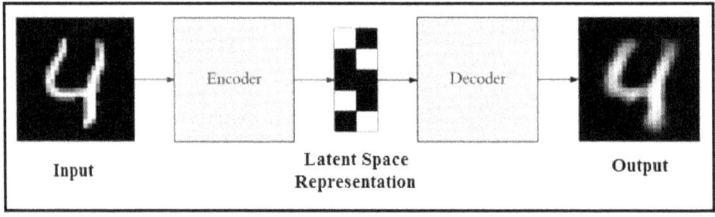

Application of AE on MNIST dataset sample

The encoder and decoder components of AEs are fully-connected feedforward networks. The number of neurons in a latent space representation is a hyperparameter that needs to be passed as part of building the AE. The number of neurons or nodes that is decided in the latent semantic space dictates the amount of compression that is attained while compressing the actual input image into a latent space representation. The general architecture of an AE is shown in the following figure:

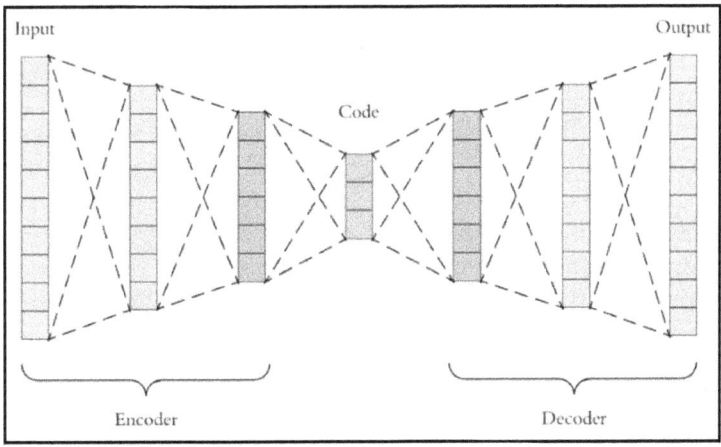

General architecture of a AE

The given input first passes through an **Encoder**, which is a fully-connected **artificial neural network** (**ANN**). The **Encoder** acts upon the **Input** and reduces its dimensions, as specified in the hyperparameter. The **Decoder** is another fully-connected ANN that picks up this reduced **Input** (latent space representation) and then reconstructs the **Output**. The goal is to get the **Output** identical to that of the **Input**. In general, the architectures of the **Encoder** and the **Decoder** are mirror images. Although there is no such requirement that mandates that the **Encoder** and **Decoder** architectures should be the same, it is generally practiced that way. In fact, the only requirement of the AE is to obtain identical output from that of the given input. Anything in between can be customized to the whims and fancies of the individual building the AE.

Mathematically, the encoder can be represented as:

$$y = h(x)$$

where x is the input and h is the function that acts on the input to represent it in a concise summary format. A decoder, on the other hand, can be represented as:

$$r = f(y) = f\big(h(x)\big)$$

While the expectation is to obtain $r = x$, this is not always the case as the reconstruction is done from a compact summary representation; therefore, there is occurrence of certain error. The error e is computed from the original input x and reconstructed output r, $e = x - r$.

The AE network then learns by reducing the **Mean Squared Error** (**MSE**), and the error is propagated back to the hidden layers for adjustment. The weights of the decoder and encoder are transposes of each other, which makes it faster to learn training parameters. The mirrored architectures of the encoder and decoder make it possible to learn the training parameters faster. In different architectures, the weights cannot be simply transposed; therefore, the computation time will increase. This is the reason for keeping the mirrored architectures for the encoder and decoder.

Types of AEs based on hidden layers

Based on the size of the hidden layer, AEs can be classified into two types, **undercomplete AEs** and **overcomplete AEs**:

- **Undercomplete AE**: If the AE simply learns to copy the input to the output, then it is not useful. The idea is to produce a concise representation as the output of the encoder, and this concise representation should consist of the most useful features of the input. The amount of conciseness achieved by the input layer is governed by the number of neurons or nodes that we use in the latent space representation. This can be set as a parameter while building the AE. If the number of neurons is set to fewer dimensions than that of the input features, then the AE is forced to learn most of the key features of the input data. The architecture where the number of neurons in latent space is less than that of input dimensions is called an undercomplete AE.
- **Overcomplete AE**: It is possible to represent the number of neurons in latent space as equal to or more than that of the input dimensions. This kind of architecture is termed an overcomplete AE. In this case, the AE does not learn anything and simply copies the input to the latent space, which in turn is propagated through to the decoder.

Apart from the number of neurons in the latent space, the following are some of the other parameters that can be used in an AE architecture:

- **Number of layers in the encoder and decoder**: The depth of the encoder and decoder can be set to any number. Generally, in a mirrored architecture of encoder and decoder, the number of layers is set as the same number. The last figure is an illustration showing the AE with two layers, excluding the input and output, in both the encoder and decoder.
- **Number of neurons per layer in encoder and decoder**: The number of neurons decreases with each layer in an encoder and it increases with each layer in a decoder. The neurons in layers of encoders and decoders are symmetric.
- **Loss function**: Loss functions such as MSE or cross-entropy are used by AEs to learn the weights during backpropagation. If the input is in the range of (0,1), then cross-entropy is used as metric, otherwise MSE is used.

Types of AEs based on restrictions

Based on the restrictions imposed on the loss, AEs can be grouped into the following types:

- **Plain Vanilla AEs**: This is the simplest AE architecture possible, with a fully-connected neural layer as the encoder and decoder.
- **Sparse AEs**: Sparse AEs are an alternative method for introducing an information bottleneck, without requiring a reduction in the number of nodes in our hidden layers. Rather than preferring an undercomplete AE, the loss function is constructed in a way that it penalizes the activations within a layer. For any given observation, the network is encouraged to learn encoding and decoding, which only relies on activating a small number of neurons.
- **Denoising AEs**: This is a type of overcomplete AE that experiences the risk of learning the **identity function** or **null function**. Essentially, the AE learns the output that is equal to the input, therefore making the AE useless. Denoising AEs avoid this problem of learning the identity function by randomly initializing some of the inputs to 0. During the computation of the loss function, the noise-induced input is not considered; therefore, the network still learns the correct weights without the risk of learning the identity function. At the same time, the AE is trained to learn to reconstruct the output, even from the corrupted input.

The following figure is a example of denoising AEs on sample images from the MNIST dataset:

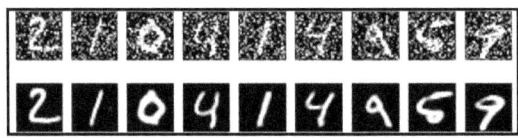

Application of denoising AEs on MNIST samples

- **Convolutional AEs**: When dealing with images as inputs, one can use convolutional layers as part of the encoder and decoder networks. Such kinds of AEs that use convolutional layers are termed **convolutional AEs**. The following figure is an illustration showing the use of convolutions in AEs:

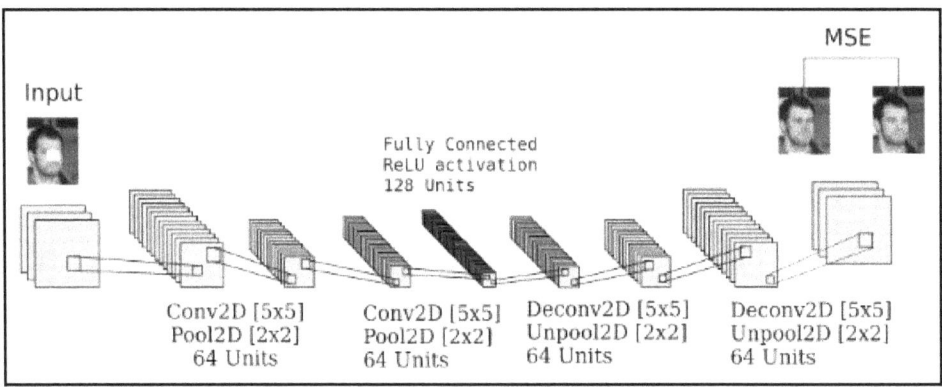

Convolutional AEs

- **Stacked AEs**: Stacked AEs are ones that have multiple layers in the encoder as well as the decoder. You can refer to the general architecture of an AE as an example illustration of a stacked AE architecture, with the encoder and decoder having two layers (excluding the input and output layers).
    - **Variational AEs**: A **variational AE** (**VAE**), rather than building an encoder that outputs a singl
- e value to describe each latent state attribute, describes a probability distribution for each latent attribute. This makes it possible to design complex generative models of data and also generate fictional celebrity images and digital artwork. The following figure is an illustration depicting the representation of data in VAEs:

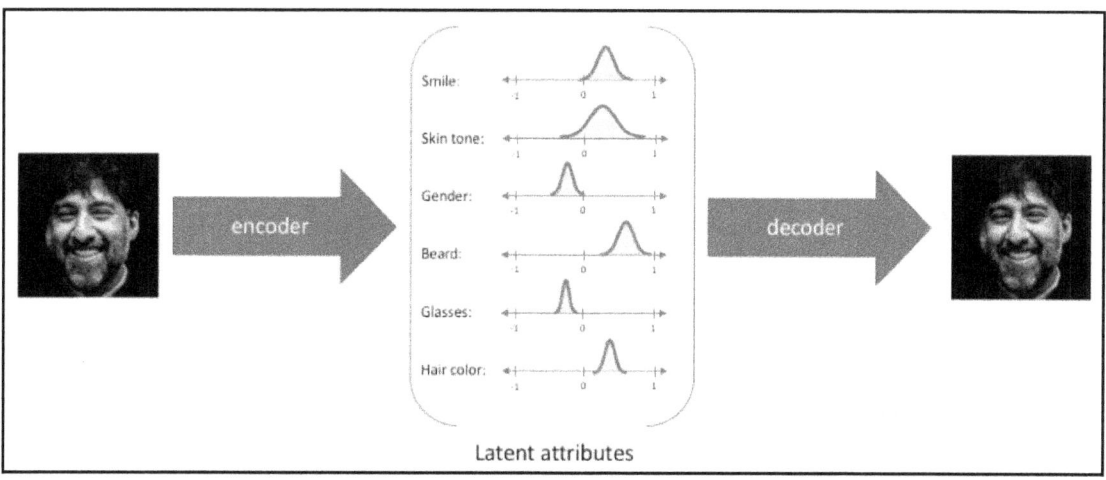

Source: https://www.jeremyjordan.me/variational-autoencoders/

In a VAE, the encoder model is sometimes referred to as the recognition model, whereas the decoder model is sometimes referred to as the generative model. The encoder outputs a range of statistical distributions for the latent features. These features are randomly sampled and used by the decoder to reconstruct the input. For any sampling of the latent distributions, the decoder is expected to be able to accurately reconstruct the input. Thus, values that are nearby to one another in latent space should correspond with very similar reconstructions.

Applications of AEs

The following are some of the practical applications where AEs may be used:

- **Image coloring**: Given a grayscale image as input, AEs can auto color the image and return the colored image as output.
- **Noise removal**: Denoising AEs are able to remove noise from images and reconstruct images without noise. Tasks such as watermark removal from videos and images can be accomplished.
- **Dimensionality reduction**: AEs represent the input data in a compressed form, but with a focus on key features alone. Therefore, things like images can be represented with reduced pixels, without much loss of information during image reconstruction.
- **Image search**: This is used to identify similar images based on a given input.

- **Information retrieval**: When retrieving information from a corpus, AEs may be used to group together all the documents that belong to a given input.
- **Topic modeling**: Variational AEs are used to approximate the posterior distribution, and it has become a promising alternative for inferring latent topic distributions of text documents.

We have covered the fundamentals that are needed for us to understand AEs and their applications. Let us understand, at a high level, the solution we are going to employ using AEs on the credit card fraud detection problem.

The credit card fraud dataset

Generally in a fraud dataset, we have sufficient data for the negative class (non-fraud/genuine transactions) and very few or no data for the positive class (fraudulent transactions). This is termed a **class imbalance problem** in the ML world. We train an AE on the non-fraud data and learn features using the encoder. The decoder is then used to compute the reconstruction error on the training set to find a threshold. This threshold will be used on the unseen data (test dataset or otherwise). We use the threshold to identify those test instances whose values are greater than the threshold as fraud instances.

For the project in this chapter, we will be using a dataset that is sourced from this URL: `https://essentials.togaware.com/data/`. This is a public dataset of credit card transactions. This dataset is originally made available through the research paper *Calibrating Probability with Undersampling for Unbalanced Classification*, A. Dal Pozzolo, O. Caelen, R. A Johnson and G. Bontempi, IEEE **Symposium Series on Computational Intelligence** (**SSCI**), Cape Town, South Africa, 2015. The dataset is also available at this URL: `http://www.ulb.ac.be/di/map/adalpozz/data/creditcard.Rdata`. The dataset was collected and analyzed during a research collaboration of Worldline and the Machine Learning Group (`http://mlg.ulb.ac.be`) of ULB (Université Libre de Bruxelles) on big data mining and fraud detection.

The following are the characteristics of the dataset:

- The paper made the dataset available as an Rdata file. There is a CSV converted version of this dataset available on Kaggle as well as other sites.
- It contains transactions made by credit cards in September 2013 by European cardholders.
- The transactions occurred on two days are recorded and is presented as the dataset.

- There are a total of 284,807 transactions in the dataset.
- The dataset suffers from a severe class imbalance problem. Only 0.172% of all transactions are fraudulent transactions (492 fraudulent transactions).
- There are a total thirty features in the dataset, namely V1, V2, ...,V28, Time, and Amount.
- The variables V1, V2, ...,V28 are the principal components obtained with PCA from the original set of variables.
- Due to confidentiality, the original set of variables that yielded the principal components are not revealed.
- The Time feature contains the seconds elapsed between each transaction and the first transaction in the dataset.
- The Amount feature is the transaction amount.
- The dependent variable is named Class. The fraudulent transactions are represented as 1 in the class and genuine transactions are represented as 0.

We will now jump into using AEs for the credit card fraud detection.

Building AEs with the H2O library in R

We will be using the AE implementation available in H2O for our project. H2O is a fully open source, distributed, in-memory ML platform with linear scalability. It offers parallelized implementations of some of the most widely used ML algorithms. It supports an easy to use, unsupervised, and non-linear AE as part of its deep learning model. The DL AE of H2O is based on the multilayer neural net architecture, where the entire network is trained together, instead of being stacked layer by layer.

The h2o package can be installed in R with the following command:

```
install.packages("h2o")
```

Additional details on the installation and dependencies of H2O in R are available at this URL: https://cran.r-project.org/web/packages/h2o/index.html.

Once the package is installed successfully, the functions offered by the h2o package, including the AE, can simply be used by including the following line in R code:

```
library(h2o)
```

This is all we need to do prior to coding our credit card fraud detection system with the AE. Without waiting any longer, let's start building our code to explore and prepare our dataset, as well as to implement the AE that captures fraudulent credit card transactions.

Autoencoder code implementation for credit card fraud detection

As usual, like all other projects, let's first load the data into an R dataframe and then perform EDA to understand the dataset better. Please note the inclusion of h2o as well as the doParallel library in the code. These inclusions enable us to use the AE that is part of the h2o library, as well as to utilize the multiple CPU cores that are present in the laptop/desktop as follows:

```
# including the required libraries
library(tidyverse)
library(h2o)
library(rio)
library(doParallel)
library(viridis)
library(RColorBrewer)
library(ggthemes)
library(knitr)
library(caret)
library(caretEnsemble)
library(plotly)
library(lime)
library(plotROC)
library(pROC)
```

Initializing the H2O cluster in localhost under the port 54321. The nthreads defines the number of thread pools to be used, this is close to the number of cpus to be used. In our case, we are saying use all CPUs, we are also specifying the maximum memory to use by H2O cluster as 8G:

```
localH2O = h2o.init(ip = 'localhost', port = 54321, nthreads =
-1,max_mem_size = "8G")
# Detecting the available number of cores
no_cores <- detectCores() - 1
# utilizing all available cores
cl<-makeCluster(no_cores)
registerDoParallel(cl)
```

You will get a similar output to that shown in the following code block:

```
H2O is not running yet, starting it now...
Note:  In case of errors look at the following log files:
    /tmp/RtmpKZvQ3m/h2o_sunil_started_from_r.out
    /tmp/RtmpKZvQ3m/h2o_sunil_started_from_r.err
java version "1.8.0_191"
Java(TM) SE Runtime Environment (build 1.8.0_191-b12)
Java HotSpot(TM) 64-Bit Server VM (build 25.191-b12, mixed mode)
Starting H2O JVM and connecting: ..... Connection successful!
R is connected to the H2O cluster:
    H2O cluster uptime:         4 seconds 583 milliseconds
    H2O cluster timezone:       Asia/Kolkata
    H2O data parsing timezone:  UTC
    H2O cluster version:        3.20.0.8
    H2O cluster version age:    2 months and 27 days
    H2O cluster name:           H2O_started_from_R_sunil_jgw200
    H2O cluster total nodes:    1
    H2O cluster total memory:   7.11 GB
    H2O cluster total cores:    4
    H2O cluster allowed cores:  4
    H2O cluster healthy:        TRUE
    H2O Connection ip:          localhost
    H2O Connection port:        54321
    H2O Connection proxy:       NA
    H2O Internal Security:      FALSE
    H2O API Extensions:         XGBoost, Algos, AutoML, Core V3, Core V4
    R Version:                  R version 3.5.1 (2018-07-02)
```

Now, to set the working directory of the data file location, load Rdata and read it into the dataframe, and view the dataframe using the following code:

```
# setting the working directory where the data file is location
setwd("/home/sunil/Desktop/book/chapter 20")
# loading the Rdata file and reading it into the dataframe called cc_fraud
cc_fraud<-get(load("creditcard.Rdata"))
# performing basic EDA on the dataset
# Viewing the dataframe to confirm successful load of the dataset
View(cc_fraud)
```

The will give the following output:

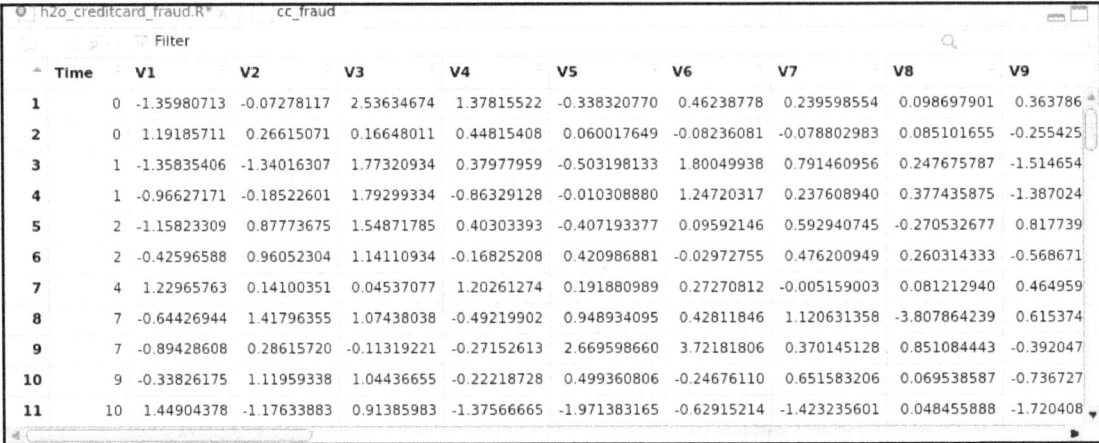

Let's now print the dataframe structure using the following code:

```
print(str(cc_fraud))
```

This will give the following output:

```
'data.frame':     284807 obs. of  31 variables:
$ Time  : num  0 0 1 1 2 2 4 7 7 9 ...
$ V1    : num  -1.36 1.192 -1.358 -0.966 -1.158 ...
$ V2    : num  -0.0728 0.2662 -1.3402 -0.1852 0.8777 ...
$ V3    : num  2.536 0.166 1.773 1.793 1.549 ...
$ V4    : num  1.378 0.448 0.38 -0.863 0.403 ...
$ V5    : num  -0.3383 0.06 -0.5032 -0.0103 -0.4072 ...
$ V6    : num  0.4624 -0.0824 1.8005 1.2472 0.0959 ...
$ V7    : num  0.2396 -0.0788 0.7915 0.2376 0.5929 ...
$ V8    : num  0.0987 0.0851 0.2477 0.3774 -0.2705 ...
$ V9    : num  0.364 -0.255 -1.515 -1.387 0.818 ...
$ V10   : num  0.0908 -0.167 0.2076 -0.055 0.7531 ...
$ V11   : num  -0.552 1.613 0.625 -0.226 -0.823 ...
$ V12   : num  -0.6178 1.0652 0.0661 0.1782 0.5382 ...
$ V13   : num  -0.991 0.489 0.717 0.508 1.346 ...
$ V14   : num  -0.311 -0.144 -0.166 -0.288 -1.12 ...
$ V15   : num  1.468 0.636 2.346 -0.631 0.175 ...
$ V16   : num  -0.47 0.464 -2.89 -1.06 -0.451 ...
$ V17   : num  0.208 -0.115 1.11 -0.684 -0.237 ...
$ V18   : num  0.0258 -0.1834 -0.1214 1.9658 -0.0382 ...
$ V19   : num  0.404 -0.146 -2.262 -1.233 0.803 ...
$ V20   : num  0.2514 -0.0691 0.525 -0.208 0.4085 ...
$ V21   : num  -0.01831 -0.22578 0.248 -0.1083 -0.00943 ...
```

```
$ V22    : num   0.27784 -0.63867 0.77168 0.00527 0.79828 ...
$ V23    : num   -0.11 0.101 0.909 -0.19 -0.137 ...
$ V24    : num   0.0669 -0.3398 -0.6893 -1.1756 0.1413 ...
$ V25    : num   0.129 0.167 -0.328 0.647 -0.206 ...
$ V26    : num   -0.189 0.126 -0.139 -0.222 0.502 ...
$ V27    : num   0.13356 -0.00898 -0.05535 0.06272 0.21942 ...
$ V28    : num   -0.0211 0.0147 -0.0598 0.0615 0.2152 ...
$ Amount: num   149.62 2.69 378.66 123.5 69.99 ...
$ Class : Factor w/ 2 levels "0","1": 1 1 1 1 1 1 1 1 1 1 ...
```

Now, to view the class distribution, use the following code:

```
print(table(cc_fraud$Class))
```

You will get the following output:

```
     0      1
284315    492
```

To view the relationship between the V1 and Class variables, use the following code:

```
# Printing the Histograms for Multivariate analysis
theme_set(theme_economist_white())
# visualization showing the relationship between variable V1 and the class
ggplot(cc_fraud,aes(x="",y=V1,fill=Class))+geom_boxplot()+labs(x="V1",y="")
```

This will give the following output:

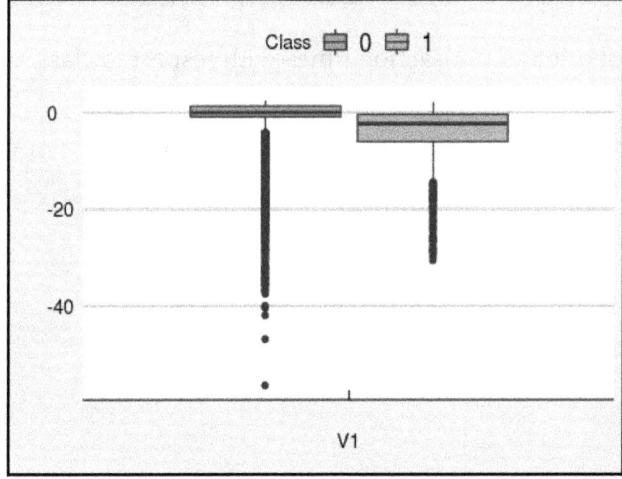

To visualize the distribution of transaction amounts with respect to class, use the following code:

```
# visualization showing the distribution of transaction amount with
# respect to the class, it may be observed that the amount are discretized
# into 50 bins for plotting purposes
ggplot(cc_fraud,aes(x = Amount)) + geom_histogram(color = "#D53E4F", fill =
"#D53E4F", bins = 50) + facet_wrap( ~ Class, scales = "free", ncol = 2)
```

This will give the following output:

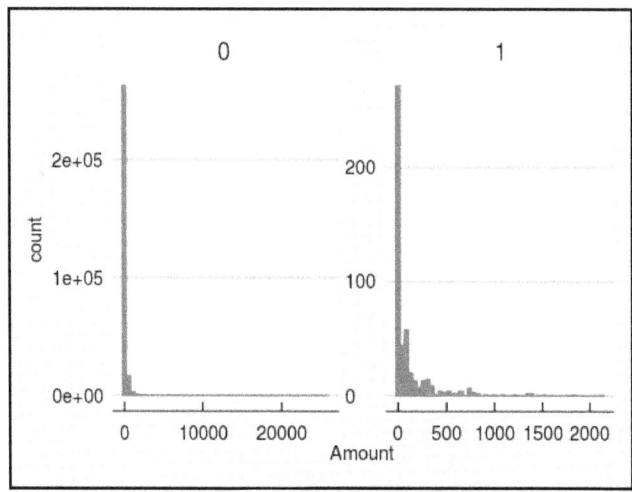

To visualize the distribution of transaction times with respect to class, use the following code:

```
ggplot(cc_fraud, aes(x =Time,fill = Class))+ geom_histogram(bins = 30)+
    facet_wrap( ~ Class, scales = "free", ncol = 2)
```

This will give the following output:

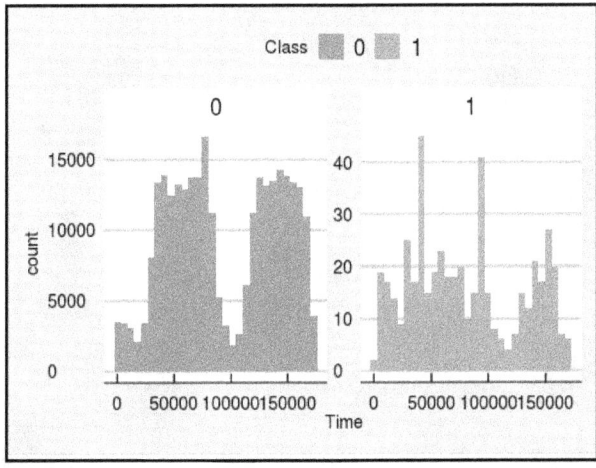

Use the following code to visualize the V2 variable with respect to `Class`:

```
ggplot(cc_fraud, aes(x =V2, fill=Class))+ geom_histogram(bins = 30)+
    facet_wrap( ~ Class, scales = "free", ncol = 2)
```

You will get the following as the output:

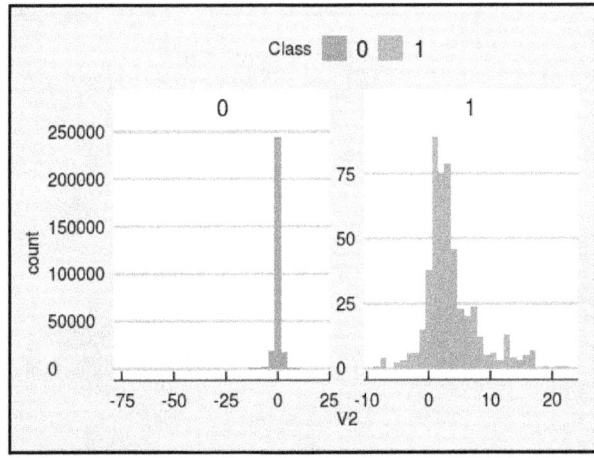

Use the following code to visualize V3 with respect to `Class`:

```
ggplot(cc_fraud, aes(x =V3, fill=Class))+ geom_histogram(bins = 30)+
    facet_wrap( ~ Class, scales = "free", ncol = 2)
```

The following graph is the resultant output:

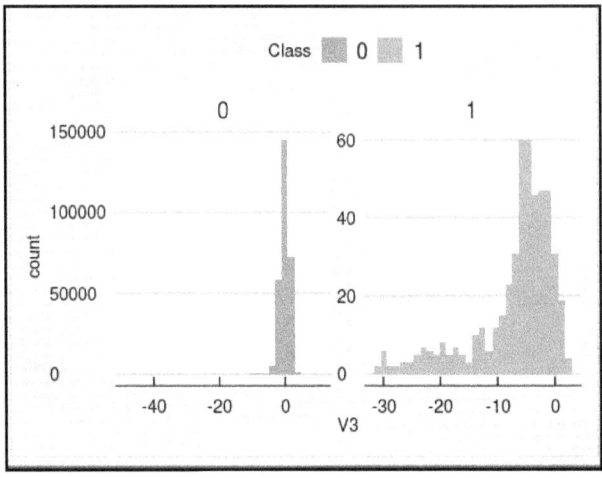

To visualize the V3 variable with respect to Class, use the following code:

```
ggplot(cc_fraud, aes(x =V4,fill=Class))+ geom_histogram(bins = 30)+
    facet_wrap( ~ Class, scales = "free", ncol = 2)
```

The following graph is the resultant output:

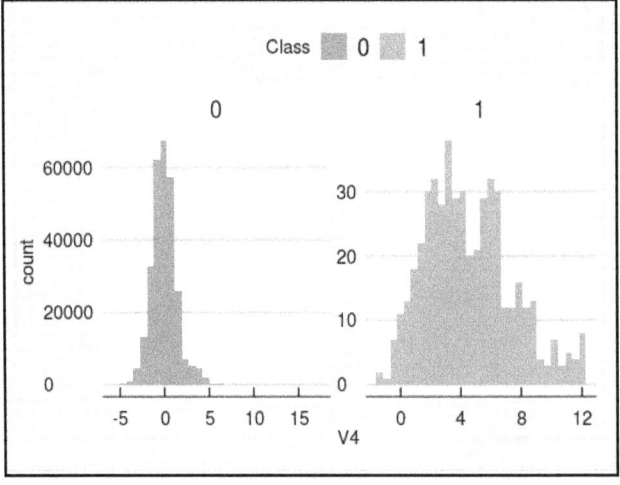

Use the following code to visualize the V6 variable with respect to Class:

```
ggplot(cc_fraud, aes(x=V6, fill=Class)) + geom_density(alpha=1/3) +
scale_fill_hue()
```

The following graph is the resultant output:

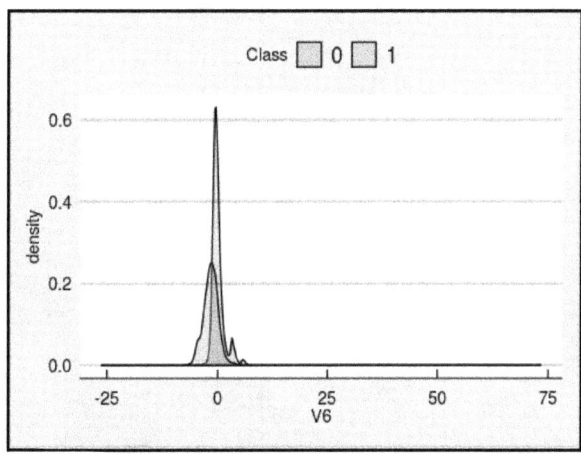

Use the following code to visualize the V7 variable with respect to Class:

```
ggplot(cc_fraud, aes(x=V7, fill=Class)) + geom_density(alpha=1/3) +
scale_fill_hue()
```

The following graph is the resultant output:

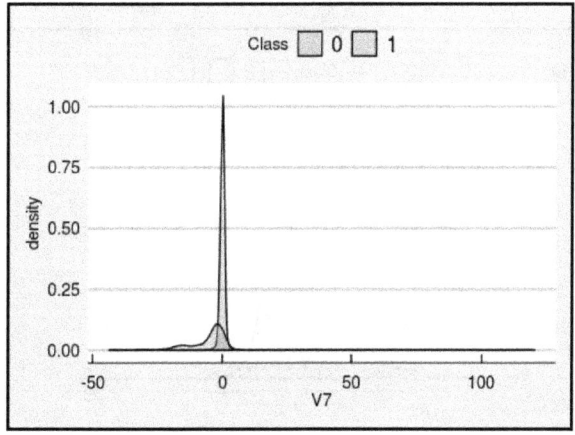

Use the following code to visualize the `V8` variable with respect to `Class`:

```
ggplot(cc_fraud, aes(x=V8, fill=Class)) + geom_density(alpha=1/3) +
scale_fill_hue()
```

The following graph is the resultant output:

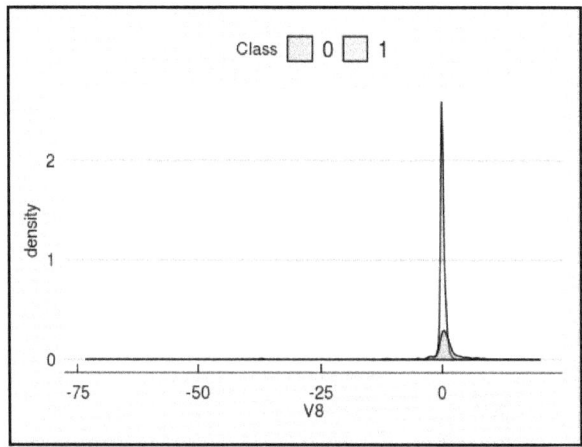

To visualize the `V9` variable with respect to `Class`, use the following code:

```
# visualizationshowing the V7 variable with respect to the class
ggplot(cc_fraud, aes(x=V9, fill=Class)) + geom_density(alpha=1/3) +
scale_fill_hue()
```

The following graph is the resultant output:

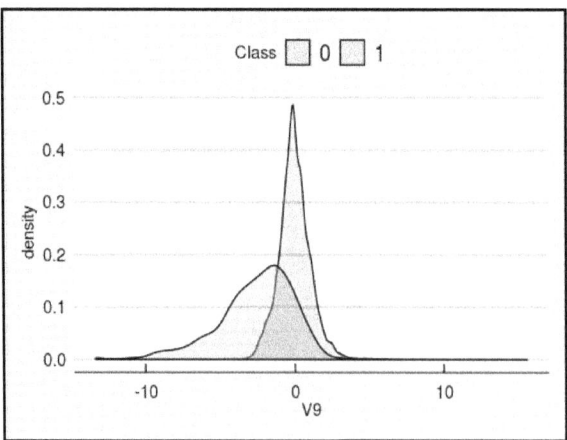

To visualize the `V10` variable with respect to `Class`, use the following code:

```
# observe we are plotting the data quantiles
ggplot(cc_fraud, aes(x ="",y=V10, fill=Class))+ geom_violin(adjust =
.5,draw_quantiles = c(0.25, 0.5, 0.75))+labs(x="V10",y="")
```

The following graph is the resultant output:

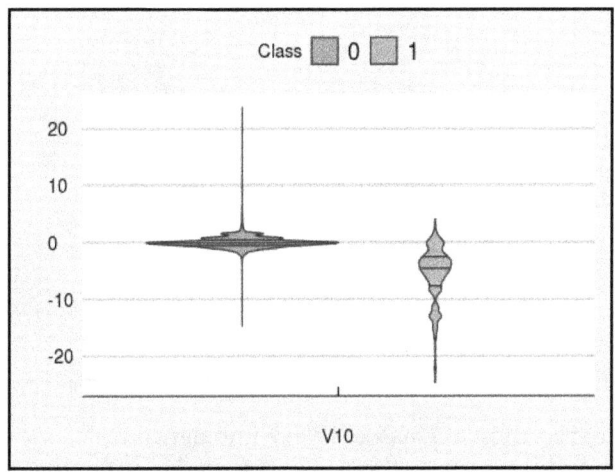

From all the visualizations related to variables with respect to class, we can infer that most of the principal components are centered on 0. Now, to plot the distribution of classes in the data, use the following code:

```
cc_fraud %>%
    ggplot(aes(x = Class)) +
    geom_bar(color = "chocolate", fill = "chocolate", width = 0.2) +
    theme_bw()
```

The following bar graph is the resultant output:

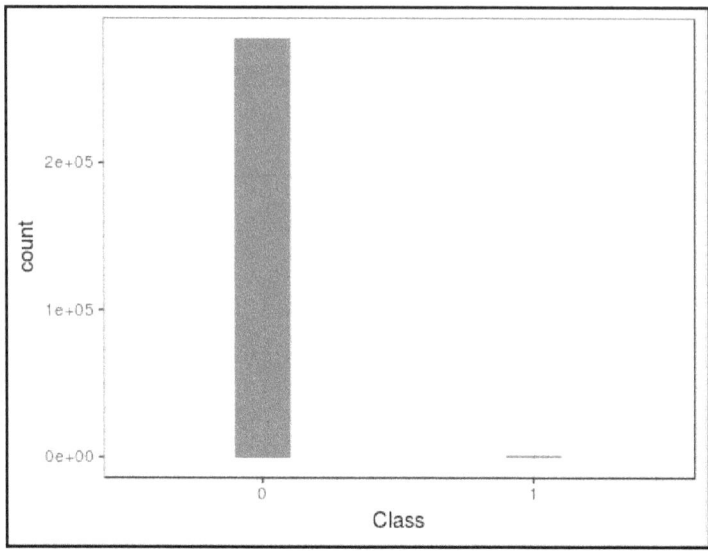

We observe that the distribution of classes is very imbalanced. The representation of the major class (non-fraudulent transactions, represented by 0) in the dataset is too heavy when compared to the minority class (fraudulent transactions: 1). In the traditional supervised ML way of dealing with this kind of problem, we would have treated the class imbalance problem with techniques such as **Synthetic Minority Over-Sampling Technique (SMORT)**. However, with AEs, we do not treat the class imbalance during data preprocessing; rather, we feed the data as is to the AE for learning. In fact, the AE is learning the thresholds and the characteristics of the data from the majority class; this is the reason we call it a one-class classification problem.

We will need to do some feature engineering prior to training our AE. Let's first focus on the Time variable in the data. Currently, it is in the seconds format, but we may better represent it as days. Run the following code to see the current form of time in the dataset:

```
print(summary(cc_fraud$Time))
```

You will get the following output:

```
Min. 1st Qu.  Median    Mean 3rd Qu.    Max.
   0   54202   84692   94814  139320  172792
```

We know that there are 86,400 seconds in a given day (60 seconds per minute * 60 minutes per hour * 24 hours per day). We will convert the `Time` variable into `Day` by considering the value in `Time` and representing it as `day1` if the number of seconds is less than or equal to 86,400, and anything over 86,400 becomes `day2`. There are only two days possible, as we can see from the summary that the maximum value represented by the time variable is `172792` seconds:

```
# creating a new variable called day based on the seconds
# represented in Time variable
 cc_fraud=cc_fraud %>% mutate(Day = case_when(.$Time > 3600 * 24 ~
"day2",.$Time < 3600 * 24 ~ "day1"))
#visualizing the dataset post creating the new variable
View(cc_fraud%>%head())
```

The following is the resultant output of the first six rows after the conversion:

21	V22	V23	V24	V25	V26	V27	V28	Amount	Class	Day
.018306778	0.277837576	-0.11047391	0.06692807	0.1285394	-0.1891148	0.133558377	-0.02105305	149.62	0	day1
.225775248	-0.638671953	0.10128802	-0.33984648	0.1671704	0.1258945	-0.008983099	0.01472417	2.69	0	day1
.247998153	0.771679402	0.90941226	-0.68928096	-0.3276418	-0.1390966	-0.055352794	-0.05975184	378.66	0	day1
.108300452	0.005273597	-0.19032052	-1.17557533	0.6473760	-0.2219288	0.062722849	0.06145763	123.50	0	day1
.009430697	0.798278495	-0.13745808	0.14126698	-0.2060096	0.5022922	0.219422230	0.21515315	69.99	0	day1
.208253515	-0.559824796	-0.02639767	-0.37142658	-0.2327938	0.1059148	0.253844225	0.08108026	3.67	0	day1

Now, use the following code to view the last six rows:

```
View(cc_fraud%>%tail())
```

The following is the resultant output of the last six rows after the conversion:

V21	V22	V23	V24	V25	V26	V27	V28	Amount	Class	Day
-0.3142046	-0.8085204	0.05034266	0.102799590	-0.4358701	0.1240789	0.217939865	0.06880333	2.69	0	day2
0.2134541	0.1118637	1.01447990	-0.509348453	1.4368069	0.2500343	0.943651172	0.82373096	0.77	0	day2
0.2142053	0.9243836	0.01246304	-1.016225669	-0.6066240	-0.3952551	0.068472470	-0.05352739	24.79	0	day2
0.2320450	0.5782290	-0.03750086	0.640133881	0.2657455	-0.0873706	0.004454772	-0.02656083	67.88	0	day2
0.2652449	0.8000487	-0.16329794	0.123205244	-0.5691589	0.5466685	0.108820735	0.10453282	10.00	0	day2
0.2610573	0.6430784	0.37677701	0.008797379	-0.4736487	-0.8182671	-0.002415309	0.01364891	217.00	0	day2

Now, let's print the distribution of transactions by the day in which the transaction falls, using the following code:

```
print(table(cc_fraud[,"Day"]))
```

You will get the following as the output:

```
  day1    day2
144786 140020
```

Let's create a new variable, `Time_day`, based on the seconds represented in the `Time` variable, and summarize the `Time_day` variable with respect to `Day` using the following code:

```
cc_fraud$Time_day <- if_else(cc_fraud$Day == "day2", cc_fraud$Time - 86400,
cc_fraud$Time)
print(tapply(cc_fraud$Time_day,cc_fraud$Day,summary,simplify = FALSE))
```

We get the following as the resultant output:

```
$day1
   Min. 1st Qu.  Median    Mean 3rd Qu.    Max.
      0   38432   54689   52948   70976   86398

$day2
   Min. 1st Qu.  Median    Mean 3rd Qu.    Max.
      1   37843   53425   51705   68182   86392
```

Use the following code the convert all character variables in the dataset to factors:

```
cc_fraud<-cc_fraud%>%mutate_if(is.character,as.factor)
```

We can further fine-tune the `Time_day` variable by converting the variable into a factor. The factors represents the time of day at which the transaction happened, for example, `morning`, `afternoon`, `evening`, and `night`. We can create a new variable called `Time_Group`, based on the various buckets of the day, using the following code:

```
cc_fraud=cc_fraud %>%
  mutate(Time_Group = case_when(.$Time_day <= 38138~ "morning" ,
                      .$Time_day <= 52327~ "afternoon",
                      .$Time_day <= 69580~"evening",
                      .$Time_day > 69580~"night"))
#Visualizing the data post creating the new variable
View(head(cc_fraud))
```

The following is the resultant output of the first six rows:

V24	V25	V26	V27	V28	Amount	Class	Day	Time_day	Time_Group
0.06692807	0.1285394	-0.1891148	0.133558377	-0.02105305	149.62	0	day1	0	morning
-0.33984648	0.1671704	0.1258945	-0.008983099	0.01472417	2.69	0	day1	0	morning
-0.68928096	-0.3276418	-0.1390966	-0.055352794	-0.05975184	378.66	0	day1	1	morning
-1.17557533	0.6473760	-0.2219288	0.062722849	0.06145763	123.50	0	day1	1	morning
0.14126698	-0.2060096	0.5022922	0.219422230	0.21515315	69.99	0	day1	2	morning
-0.37142658	-0.2327938	0.1059148	0.253844225	0.08108026	3.67	0	day1	2	morning

Use the following code to view and confirm the last six rows:

```
View(tail(cc_fraud))
```

This will give the following output, and we see that we have successfully converted the data which represent the various time of the day:

V24	V25	V26	V27	V28	Amount	Class	Day	Time_day	Time_Group
0.102799590	-0.4358701	0.1240789	0.217939865	0.06880333	2.69	0	day2	86385	night
-0.509348453	1.4368069	0.2500343	0.943651172	0.82373096	0.77	0	day2	86386	night
-1.016225669	-0.6066240	-0.3952551	0.068472470	-0.05352739	24.79	0	day2	86387	night
0.640133881	0.2657455	-0.0873706	0.004454772	-0.02656083	67.88	0	day2	86388	night
0.123205244	-0.5691589	0.5466685	0.108820735	0.10453282	10.00	0	day2	86388	night
0.008797379	-0.4736487	-0.8182671	-0.002415309	0.01364891	217.00	0	day2	86392	night

Take a look at the following code:

```
#visualizing the transaction count by day
cc_fraud %>%drop_na()%>%
  ggplot(aes(x = Day)) +
  geom_bar(fill = "chocolate",width = 0.3,color="chocolate") +
  theme_economist_white()
```

The preceding code will generate the following output:

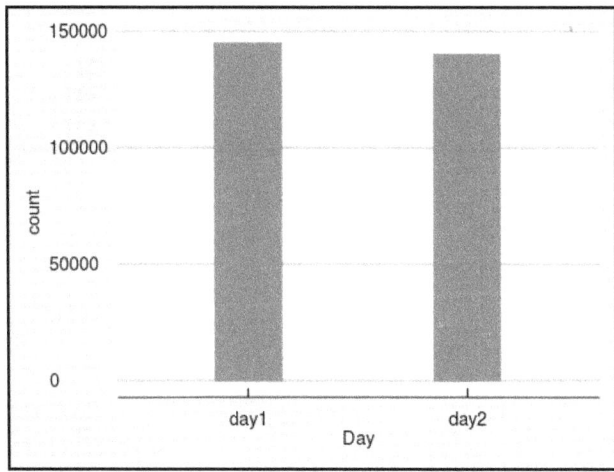

We can infer from the visualization that there is no difference in the count of transactions that happened on day 1 and day 2. Both remain close to 150,000 transactions.

Now we will convert the `Class` variable as a factor and then visualize the data by `Time_Group` variable using the following code:

```
cc_fraud$Class <- factor(cc_fraud$Class)
cc_fraud %>%drop_na()%>%
  ggplot(aes(x = Time_Group)) +
  geom_bar(color = "#238B45", fill = "#238B45") +
  theme_bw() +
  facet_wrap( ~ Class, scales = "free", ncol = 2)
```

This will generate the following output:

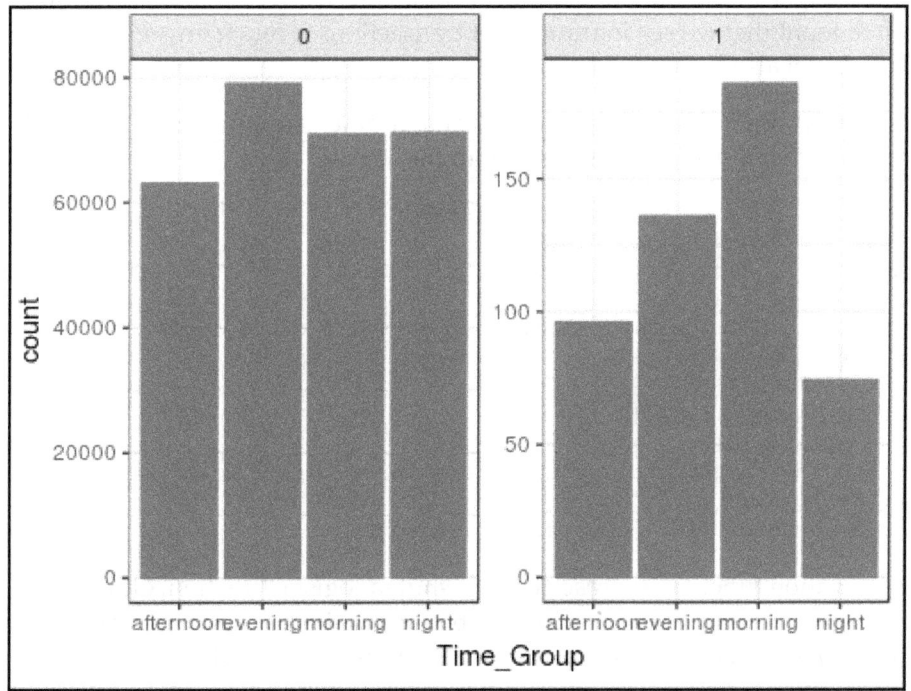

The inference obtained from this visualization is that the number of non-fraudulent transactions remains almost the same across all time periods of the day, whereas we see a huge rise in the number of fraudulent transactions during the morning `Time` group.

Let's do a last bit of exploration of the transaction amount with respect to class:

```
# getting the summary of amount with respect to the class
print(tapply(cc_fraud$Amount  ,cc_fraud$Class,summary))
```

The preceding code will generate the following output:

```
$`0`
   Min.  1st Qu.    Median      Mean  3rd Qu.       Max.
   0.00     5.65     22.00     88.29    77.05 25691.16
$`1`
   Min. 1st Qu.   Median      Mean 3rd Qu.      Max.
   0.00    1.00     9.25    122.21  105.89   2125.87
```

One interesting insight from the summary is that the mean amount in fraudulent transactions is higher compared to genuine transactions. However, the maximum transaction amount that we see in fraudulent transactions is much lower than the genuine transactions. It can also be seen that genuine transactions have a higher median amount.

Now, let's convert our R dataframe to an H2O dataframe to apply the AE to it. This is a requirement in order to use the functions from the h2o library:

```
# converting R dataframe to H2O dataframe
cc_fraud_h2o <- as.h2o(cc_fraud)
#splitting the data into 60%, 20%, 20% chunks to use them as training,
#vaidation and test datasets
splits <- h2o.splitFrame(cc_fraud_h2o,ratios = c(0.6, 0.2), seed = 148)
# creating new train, validation and test h2o dataframes
train <- splits[[1]]
validation <- splits[[2]]
test <- splits[[3]]
# getting the target and features name in vectors
target <- "Class"
features <- setdiff(colnames(train), target)
```

The tanh activation function is a rescaled and shifted logistic function. Other functions, such as ReLu and Maxout, are also provided by the h2o library and they can also be used. In the first AE model, let's use the tanh activation function. This choice is arbitrary and other activation functions may also be tried as desired.

The h2o.deeplearning function has a parameter AE and this should be set to TRUE to train a AE model. Let's build our AE model now:

```
model_one = h2o.deeplearning(x = features, training_frame = train,
                             AE = TRUE,
                             reproducible = TRUE,
                             seed = 148,
```

```
                                  hidden = c(10,10,10), epochs = 100,
    activation = "Tanh",
                                  validation_frame = test)
```

The preceding code generates the following output:

```
|========================================================================
=================================================| 100%
```

We will save the model so we do not have to retrain t again and again. Then load the model that is persisted on the disk and print the model to verify the AE learning using the following code:

```
h2o.saveModel(model_one, path="model_one", force = TRUE)
model_one<-
h2o.loadModel("/home/sunil/model_one/DeepLearning_model_R_1544970545051_1")
print(model_one)
```

This will generate the following output:

```
Model Details:
==============
H2OAutoEncoderModel: deeplearning
Model ID:  DeepLearning_model_R_1544970545051_1
Status of Neuron Layers: auto-encoder, gaussian distribution, Quadratic
loss, 944 weights/biases, 20.1 KB, 2,739,472 training samples, mini-batch
size 1
   layer units  type dropout       l1       l2 mean_rate rate_rms momentum
mean_weight weight_rms mean_bias bias_rms
1     1    34 Input  0.00 %       NA       NA        NA       NA       NA
NA          NA        NA        NA
2     2    10  Tanh  0.00 % 0.000000 0.000000  0.610547 0.305915 0.000000
-0.000347   0.309377 -0.028166 0.148318
3     3    10  Tanh  0.00 % 0.000000 0.000000  0.181705 0.103598 0.000000
0.022774    0.262611 -0.056455 0.099918
4     4    10  Tanh  0.00 % 0.000000 0.000000  0.133090 0.079663 0.000000
0.000808    0.337259  0.032588 0.101952
5     5    34  Tanh     NA 0.000000 0.000000  0.116252 0.129859 0.000000
0.006941    0.357547  0.167973 0.688510
H2OAutoEncoderMetrics: deeplearning
 Reported on training data.
 Training Set Metrics:
=====================
MSE: (Extract with `h2o.mse`) 0.0003654009
RMSE: (Extract with `h2o.rmse`) 0.01911546
H2OAutoEncoderMetrics: deeplearning
 Reported on validation data.
 Validation Set Metrics:
```

```
=======================
MSE: (Extract with `h2o.mse`) 0.0003508435
RMSE: (Extract with `h2o.rmse`) 0.01873082
```

We will now make predictions on test dataset using the AE model that is built, using the following code:

```
test_autoencoder <- h2o.predict(model_one, test)
```

This will generate the following output:

```
|=================================================================
=========================================| 100%
```

It is possible to visualize the encoder representing the data in a conscious manner in the inner layers through the `h2o.deepfeatures` function. Let's try visualizing the reduced data in a second layer:

```
train_features <- h2o.deepfeatures(model_one, train, layer = 2) %>%
  as.data.frame() %>%
  mutate(Class = as.vector(train[, 31]))
# printing the reduced data represented in layer2
print(train_features%>%head(3))
```

The preceding code will generate the following output:

```
DF.L2.C1    DF.L2.C2     DF.L2.C3     DF.L2.C4    DF.L2.C5
-0.12899115 0.1312075   0.115971952 -0.12997648 0.23081912
-0.10437942 0.1832959   0.006427409 -0.08018725 0.05575977
-0.07135827 0.1705700  -0.023808057 -0.11383244 0.10800857
DF.L2.C6    DF.L2.C7     DF.L2.C8   DF.L2.C9  DF.L2.C10  Class0.1791547
0.10325721  0.05589069 0.5607497 -0.9038150        0
0.1588236  0.11009450 -0.04071038 0.5895413 -0.8949729       0
0.1676358  0.10703990 -0.03263755 0.5762191 -0.8989759       0
```

Let us now plot the data of DF.L2.C1 with respect to DF.L2.C2 to verify if the encoder has detected the fraudulent transactions, using the following code:

```
ggplot(train_features, aes(x = DF.L2.C1, y = DF.L2.C2, color = Class)) +
  geom_point(alpha = 0.1,size=1.5)+theme_bw()+
  scale_fill_brewer(palette = "Accent")
```

This will generate the following output:

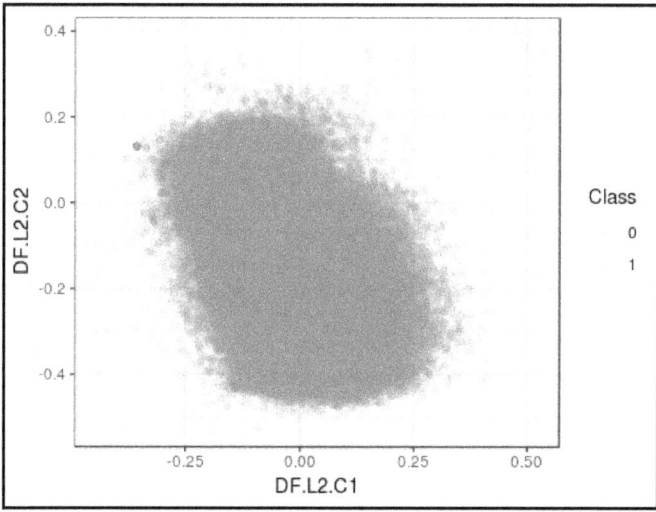

Again we plot the data of `DF.L2.C3` with respect to `DF.L2.C4` to verify the if the encoder have detected any fraud transaction, using the following code:

```
ggplot(train_features, aes(x = DF.L2.C3, y = DF.L2.C4, color = Class)) +
    geom_point(alpha = 0.1,size=1.5)+theme_bw()+
    scale_fill_brewer(palette = "Accent")
```

The preceding code will generate the following output:

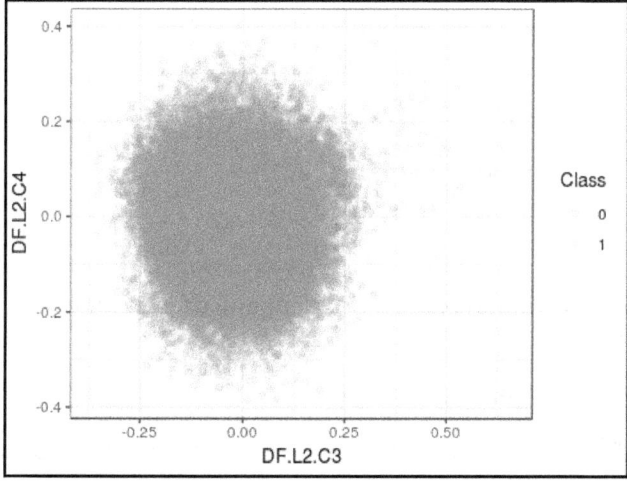

We see from the two visualizations that the fraudulent transactions are indeed detected by the dimensionality reduction approach with our AE model. Those few scattered dots (represented by 1) depicts the fraud transactions that are detected. We can also train a new model with the other hidden layers, using our first model. This results in 10 columns, since the third layer has 10 nodes. We are just attempting to slice out one layer where some level of reduction was done and use that to build a new model:

```
# let's consider the third hidden layer. This is again a random choice
# in fact we could have taken any layer among the 10 inner layers
train_features <- h2o.deepfeatures(model_one, validation, layer = 3) %>%
  as.data.frame() %>%
  mutate(Class = as.factor(as.vector(validation[, 31]))) %>%
  as.h2o()
```

The preceding code will generate the following output:

```
|=======================================================================
================================================| 100%
|=======================================================================
================================================| 100%
```

As we can see, the training models and data are successfully created. We will now go ahead and train the new model, save it and the print it. First, we will get the feature names from the sliced encoder layer:

```
features_two <- setdiff(colnames(train_features), target)
```

Then we will training a new model:

```
model_two <- h2o.deeplearning(y = target,
                              x = features_two,
                              training_frame = train_features,
                              reproducible = TRUE,
                              balance_classes = TRUE,
                              ignore_const_cols = FALSE,
                              seed = 148,
                              hidden = c(10, 5, 10),
                              epochs = 100,
                              activation = "Tanh")
```

We will then save the model to avoid retraining again, then retrieve the model and print it using the following code:

```
h2o.saveModel(model_two, path="model_two", force = TRUE)
model_two <-
h2o.loadModel("/home/sunil/model_two/DeepLearning_model_R_1544970545051_2")
print(model_two)
```

This will generate the following output:

```
Model Details:
==============
H2OBinomialModel: deeplearning
Model ID:  DeepLearning_model_R_1544970545051_2
Status of Neuron Layers: predicting Class, 2-class classification,
bernoulli distribution, CrossEntropy loss, 247 weights/biases, 8.0 KB,
2,383,962 training samples, mini-batch size 1
   layer units     type dropout        l1        l2 mean_rate rate_rms momentum
mean_weight weight_rms mean_bias bias_rms
1    1    10   Input  0.00 %        NA       NA        NA       NA       NA
NA        NA        NA        NA
2    2    10    Tanh  0.00 % 0.000000 0.000000  0.001515 0.001883 0.000000
-0.149216   0.768610 -0.038682 0.891455
3    3     5    Tanh  0.00 % 0.000000 0.000000  0.003293 0.004916 0.000000
-0.251950   0.885017 -0.307971 0.531144
4    4    10    Tanh  0.00 % 0.000000 0.000000  0.002252 0.001780 0.000000
0.073398   1.217405 -0.354956 0.887678
5    5     2 Softmax     NA 0.000000 0.000000  0.007459 0.007915 0.000000
-0.095975   3.579932  0.223286 1.172508
H2OBinomialMetrics: deeplearning
 Reported on training data.
  Metrics reported on temporary training frame with 9892 samples
 MSE:  0.1129424
 RMSE:  0.336069
LogLoss:  0.336795
Mean Per-Class Error:  0.006234916
AUC:  0.9983688
Gini:  0.9967377
Confusion Matrix (vertical: actual; across: predicted) for F1-optimal
threshold:
         0    1    Error     Rate
0     4910   62 0.012470  =62/4972
1        0 4920 0.000000   =0/4920
Totals 4910 4982 0.006268  =62/9892
Maximum Metrics: Maximum metrics at their respective thresholds
                    metric threshold    value idx
1                   max f1  0.009908 0.993739 153
2                   max f2  0.009908 0.997486 153
3              max f0point5  0.019214 0.990107 142
4              max accuracy  0.009908 0.993732 153
5             max precision  1.000000 1.000000   0
6                max recall  0.009908 1.000000 153
7           max specificity  1.000000 1.000000   0
8          max absolute_mcc  0.009908 0.987543 153
9   max min_per_class_accuracy  0.019214 0.989541 142
10 max mean_per_class_accuracy  0.009908 0.993765 153
```

```
Gains/Lift Table: Extract with `h2o.gainsLift(<model>, <data>)` or
`h2o.gainsLift(<model>, valid=<T/F>, xval=<T/F>)
```

For measuring model performance on test data, we need to convert the test data to the same reduced dimensions as the training data:

```
test_3 <- h2o.deepfeatures(model_one, test, layer = 3)
print(test_3%>%head())
```

The preceding code will generate the following output:

```
|=====================================================================
=============================================| 100%
```

We see, the data has been converted successfully. Now, to make predictions on the test dataset with `model_two`, we will use the following code:

```
test_pred=h2o.predict(model_two, test_3,type="response")%>%
  as.data.frame() %>%
  mutate(actual = as.vector(test[, 31]))
```

This will generate the following output:

```
|=====================================================================
=============================================| 100%
```

As we can see, from the output, predictions has been successfully completed and now let us visualize the predictions using the following code:

```
test_pred%>%head()
  predict         p0            p1 actual
1       0 1.0000000 1.468655e-23      0
2       0 1.0000000 2.354664e-23      0
3       0 1.0000000 5.987218e-09      0
4       0 1.0000000 2.888583e-23      0
5       0 0.9999988 1.226122e-06      0
6       0 1.0000000 2.927614e-23      0
# summarizing the predictions
print(h2o.predict(model_two, test_3) %>%
  as.data.frame() %>%
  dplyr::mutate(actual = as.vector(test[, 31])) %>%
  group_by(actual, predict) %>%
  dplyr::summarise(n = n()) %>%
  mutate(freq = n / sum(n)))
```

This will generate the following output:

```
|===========================================================================
=====================================================| 100%
# A tibble: 4 x 4
# Groups:    actual [2]
  actual predict     n    freq
  <chr>  <fct>    <int>   <dbl>
1 0      0        55811  0.986
2 0      1          817  0.0144
3 1      0           41  0.414
4 1      1           58  0.586
```

We see that our AE is able to correctly predict non-fraudulent transactions with 98% accuracy, which is good. However, it is yielding only 58% accuracy when predicting fraudulent transactions. This is definitely something to focus on. Our model needs some improvement, and this can be accomplished through the following options:

- Using other layers' latent space representations as input to build `model_two` (recollect that we currently use the layer 3 representation)
- Using ReLu or Maxout activation functions instead of `Tanh`
- Checking the misclassified instances through the `h2o.anomaly` function and increasing or decreasing the cutoff threshold MSE values, which separates the fraudulent transactions from non-fraudulent transactions
- Trying out a more complex architecture in the encoder and decoder

We are not going to be attempting these options in this chapter as they are experimental in nature. However, interested readers may try and improve the accuracy of the model by trying these options.

Finally, one best practice is to explicitly shut down the h2o cluster. This can be accomplished with the following command:

```
h2o.shutdown()
```

Summary

In this chapter, we learned about an unsupervised deep learning technique called AEs. We covered the definition, working principle, types, and applications of AEs. H2O, an open source library that enables us to create deep learning models, including AEs, was explored. We then discussed a credit card fraud open dataset and implemented a project with an AE to detect fraudulent credit card transactions.

Can deep neural networks help with creative tasks such as prose generation, story writing, caption generation for images, and poem writing? Not sure?! Let's explore RNNs, in the next chapter, a special type of deep neural network that enables us to accomplish creative tasks. Turn the page to explore the world of RNNs for prose generation.

21

Automatic Prose Generation with Recurrent Neural Networks

We have been interacting through this book for almost 200 pages, but I realized that I have not introduced myself properly to you! I guess it's time. You already know some bits about me through the author profile in this book; however, I want to tell you a bit about the city I live in. I am based in South India, in a city called Bengaluru, also know as Bangalore. The city is known for its IT talent and population diversity. I love the city, as it is filled with loads of positive energy. Each day, I get to meet people from all walks of life—people from multiple ethnicities, multiple backgrounds, people who speak multiple languages, and so on. Kannada is the official language spoken in the state of Karnataka where Bangalore is located. Though I can speak bits and pieces of Kannada, my proficiency with speaking the language is not as good as a native Kannada speaker. Of course, this is an area of improvement for me and I am working on it. Like me, many other migrants that moved to the city from other places also face problems while conversing in Kannada. Interestingly, not knowing the language does not stop any of us from interacting with locals in their own language. Guess what comes to our rescue: mobile apps such as Google translate, Google text-to-speech, and the like. These applications are built on NLP technologies called machine translation and speech recognition. These technologies in turn work on things known as **language models**. Language models is the topic we will delve into in this chapter.

The objectives of the chapter include exploring the following topics:

- The need for language modeling to address natural language processing tasks
- The working principle of language models
- Application of language models
- Relationship between language modeling and neural networks
- Recurrent neural networks

- Differences between a normal feedforward network and a recurrent neural network
- Long short-term memory networks
- A project to autogenerate text using recurrent neural networks

Understanding language models

In the English language, the character *a* appears much more often in words and sentences than the character *x*. Similarly, we can also observe that the word *is* occurs more frequently than the word *specimen*. It is possible to learn the probability distributions of characters and words by examining large volumes of text. The following screenshot is a chart showing the probability distribution of letters given a corpus (text dataset):

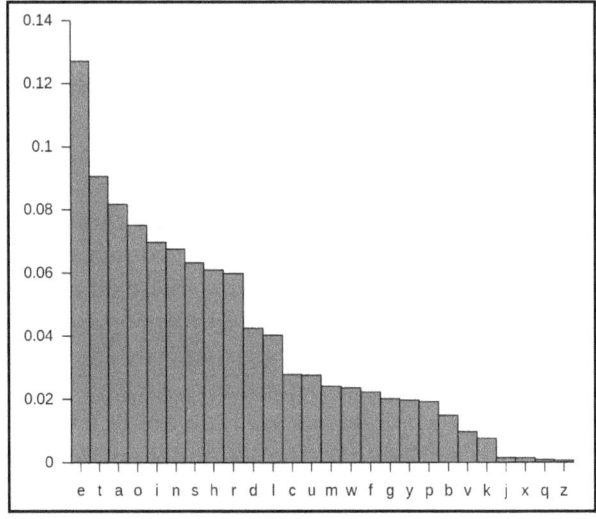

Probability distribution of letters in a corpus

We can observe that the probability distributions of characters are non-uniform. This essentially means that we can recover the characters in a word, even if they are lost due to noise. If a particular character is missing in a word, it can be reconstructed just based on the characters that are surrounding the missing character. The reconstruction of the missing character is not done randomly, but is done by picking the character that has the highest probability distribution of occurrence, given the characters that are surrounding the missing character. Technically speaking, the statistical structure of words in a sentence or characters in words follows the distance from maximal entropy.

A language model exploits the statistical structure of a language to express the following:

- Given $w\_1, w\_2, w\_3,...w\_N$ words in a sentence, a language model assigns a probability to a sentence $P(w\_1, w\_2, w\_3,.... w\_N)$.
- It then assigns probability of an upcoming word (w_4 in this case) as $P(w\_4 \mid w\_1, w\_2, w\_3)$.

Language models enable a number of applications to be developed in NLP, and some of them are listed as follows:

- **Machine translation**: P(enormous cyclone tonight) > P(gain typhoon this evening)
- **Spelling correction**: P(satellite constellation) > P(satelitte constellation)
- **Speech recognition**: P(I saw a van) > P(eyes awe of an)
- **Typing prediction**: Auto completion of in Google search, typing assistance apps

Let's now look at how the probabilities are calculated for the words. Consider a simple sentence, *Decembers are cold*. The probability of this sentence is expressed as follows:

P("Decembers are cold") = P("December") * P ("are" | "Decembers") * P("cold" | "Decembers are")

Mathematically, the probability computation of words in a sentence (or letters in a word) can be expressed as follows:

$$P(w_1, w_2, w_3, w_4, w_5, \cdots, w_n) = \prod_{i=1}^{n} P(w_1 | w_1, w_2, w_3, w_4, w_5, \cdots, w_{i-1})$$

Andrey Markov, a Russian mathematician, described a stochastic process with a property called **Markov Property** or **Markov Assumption**. This basically states that one can make predictions for the future of the process based solely on its present state, just as well as one could knowing the process's full history, hence independently from such history.

Based on Markov's assumption, we can rewrite the conditional probability of *cold* as follows:

P("cold" | "Decembers are") is congruent to P("cold" | "are")

Mathematically, Markov's assumption can be expressed as follows:

$$P(w_n | w_1, w_2, w_3, w_4, w_5, \cdots, w_{n-1}) = P(w_n | w_{n-1})$$

While this mathematical formulation represents the bigram model (two words taken into consideration at a time), it can be easily extended to an n-gram model. In the n-gram model, the conditional probability depends on just a couple more previous words.

Mathematically, an n-gram model is expressed as follows:

$$P(w_n|w_1, w_2, w_3, w_4, w_5, \cdots, w_{n-1}) = P(w_n|w_{n-k}, \cdots, w_{n-1})$$

Consider the famous poem *A Girl* by *Ezra Pound* as our corpus for building a **bigram** model. The following is the text corpus:

```
The tree has entered my hands,
The sap has ascended my arms,
The tree has grown in my breast-Downward,
The branches grow out of me, like arms.
Tree you are,
Moss you are,
You are violets with wind above them.
A child - so high - you are,
And all this is folly to the world.
```

We are already aware that in a bigram model, the conditional probability is computed just based on the previous word. So, the probability of a word can be computed as follows:

$$P(w_i|w_{i-1}) = \frac{count(w_{i-1}, w_i)}{count(w_{i-1})}$$

If we were to compute the probability of the word *arms* given the word *my* in the poem, it is computed as the number of times the words *arms* and *my* appear together in the poem, divided by the number of times the word *my* appears in the poem.

We see that the words *my arms* appeared in the poem only once (in the sentence *The sap has ascended my arms*). However, the word *my* appeared in the poem three times (in the sentences *The tree has entered my hands, The sap has ascended my arms*, and *The tree has grown in my breast-Downward*).

Therefore, the conditional probability of the word *arms* given *my* is 1/3, formally represented as follows:

P("arms" | "my") = P("arms", "my") / P("my") = 1 / 3

To calculate probability of the first and last words, the special tags <BOS> and <EOS> are added at the start and end of sentences, respectively. Similarly, the probability of a sentence or sequence of words can be calculated using the same approach by multiplying all the bigram probabilities.

As language modeling involves predicting the next word in a sequence, given the sequence of words already present, we can train a language model to create subsequent words in a sequence from a given starting sequence.

Exploring recurrent neural networks

Recurrent neural networks (RNNs) are a family of neural networks for processing sequential data. RNNs are generally used to implement language models. We, as humans, base much of our language understanding on the context. For example, let's consider the sentence *Christmas falls in the month of* --------. It is easy to fill in the blank with the word *December*. The essential idea here is that there is information about the last word encoded in the previous elements of the sentence.

The central theme behind the RNN architecture is to exploit the sequential structure of the data. As the name suggests, RNNs operate in a recurrent way. Essentially, this means that the same operation is performed for every element of a sequence or sentence, with its output depending on the current input and the previous operations.

An RNN works by looping an output of the network at time t with the input of the network at time $t+1$. These loops allow persistence of information from one time step to the next one. The following diagram is a circuit diagram representing an RNN:

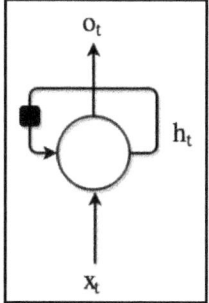

Circuit diagram representing a RNN

The diagram indicates an RNN that remembers what it knows from previous input using a simple loop. This loop takes the information from the previous timestamp and adds it to the input of the current timestamp. At a particular time step t, X_t is the input to the network, O_t is the output of the network, and h_t is the detail it remembered from previous nodes in the network. In between, there is the RNN cell, which contains neural networks just like a feedforward network.

 One key point to ponder in terms of the definition of an RNN is the timestamps. The timestamps referred to in the definition have nothing to do with past, present, and future. They simply represent a word or an item in a sequence or a sentence.

Let's consider an example sentence: *Christmas Holidays are Awesome*. In this sentence, take a look at the following timestamp:

- *Christmas* is x_0
- *Holidays* is x_1
- *are* is x_2;
- *Awesome* is x_3

If t=1, then take a look at the following:

- x_t = *Holidays* → event at current timestamp
- x_{t-1} = *Christmas* → event at previous timestamp

It can be observed from the preceding circuit diagram that the same operation is performed in the RNN repeatedly on different nodes. There is also a black square in the diagram that represents a time delay of a single time step. It may be confusing to understand the RNN with the loops, so let's unfold the computational graph. The unfolded RNN computational graph is shown in the following diagram:

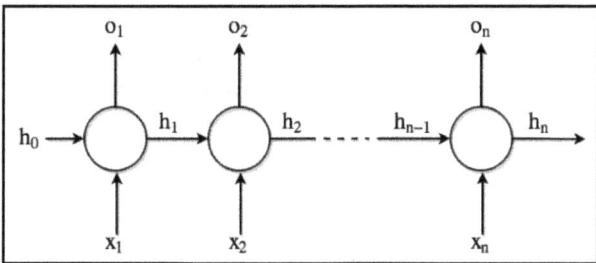

RNN—unfolded computational graph view

In the preceding diagram, each node is associated with a particular time. In the RNN architecture, each node receives different inputs at each time step x_t. It also has the capability of producing outputs at each time step o_t. The network also maintains a memory state $\mathbf{h}_t$, which contains information about what happened in the network up to the time t. As this is the same process that is run across all the nodes in the network, it is possible to represent the whole network in a simplified form, as shown in the RNN circuit diagram.

Now, we understand that we see the word **recurrent** in RNNs because it performs the same task for every element of a sequence, with the output depending on previous computations. It may be noted that, theoretically, RNNs can make use of information in arbitrarily long sequences, but in practice, they are implemented to looking back only a few steps.

Formally, an RNN can be defined in an equation as follows:

$$h_t = \phi(W X_t + U h_{t-1})$$

In the equation, h_t is the hidden state at timestamp t. An activation function such as Tanh, Sigmoid, or ReLU can be applied to compute the hidden state and it is represented in the equation as ϕ. W is the weight matrix for the input to the hidden layer at timestamp t. X_t is the input at timestamp t. U is the weight matrix for the hidden layer at time t-1 to the hidden layer at time t, and h_{t-1} is the hidden state at timestamp t.

During backpropagation, *U* and *W* weights are learned by the RNN. At each node, the contribution of the hidden state and the contribution of the current input are decided by *U* and *W*. The proportions of *U* and *W* in turn result in the generation of output at the current node. The activation functions add non-linearity in RNNs, thus enabling the simplification of gradient calculations during the backpropagation process. The following diagram illustrates the idea of backpropagation:

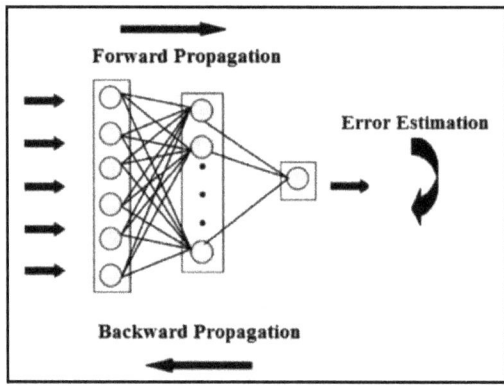

Backpropagation in neural networks

The following diagram depicts the overall working mechanism of an RNN and the way the weights *U* and *W* are learned through backpropagation. It also depicts the use of the *U* and *W* weight matrices in the network to generate the output, as shown in the following diagram:

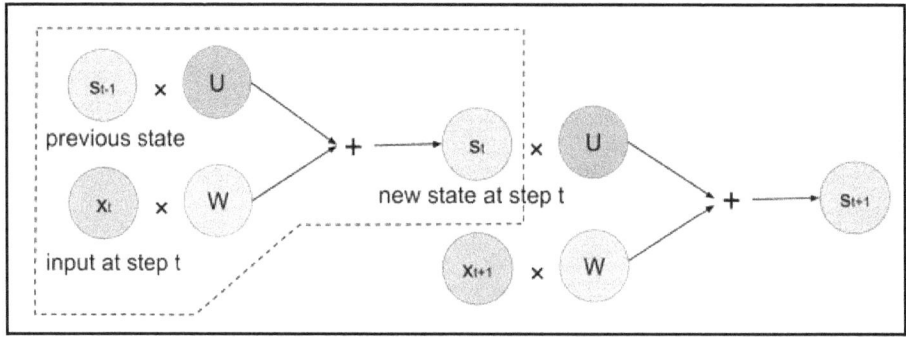

Role of weights in RNN

Comparison of feedforward neural networks and RNNs

One fundamental difference between other neural networks and RNNs is that, in all other networks, the inputs are independent of each other. However, in an RNN, all the inputs are related to each other. In an application, to predict the next word in a given sentence, the relationship between all the previous words helps to predict the current output. In other words, an RNN remembers all these relationships while training itself. This is not the case with other types of neural networks. A representation of a feedforward network is illustrated in the following diagram:

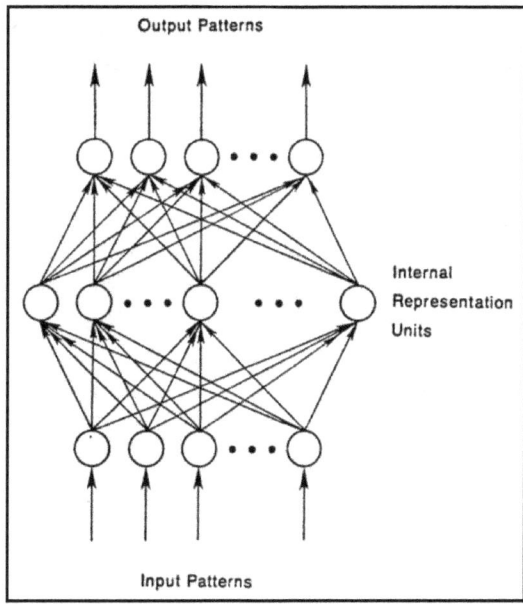

Feedforward neural network architecture

From the preceding diagram, we can see that no loops are involved in the feedforward network architecture. This is in contrast to that of the RNN architecture depicted in the diagrams of the RNN circuit diagram and the RNN unfolded computational graph. The series of mathematical operations in a feedforward network is performed at the nodes and the information is processed straight through, with no loops whatsoever.

Using supervised learning, the input that is fed to a feedforward network is transformed into output. The output in this case could be a label if it is classification, or it is a number in the case of regression. If we consider image classification, a label can be *cat* or *dog* for an image given as input.

A feedforward neural network is trained on labeled images until errors are minimized in predicting the labels. Once trained, the model is able to classify even images that it has not seen previously. A trained feedforward network can be exposed to any random collection of photographs; the categorization of the first photograph does not have any impact or influence on the second or subsequent photographs that the model needs to categorize. Let's discuss this with an example for better clarity on the concept: if the first image is seen as a *dog* by the feedforward network, it does not imply that the second image will be classified as *cat*. In other words, the predictions that the model arrives at have no notion of order in time, and the decision regarding the label is arrived at just based on the current input that is provided. To summarize, in feedforward networks no information on historical predictions is used for current predictions. This is very different from RNNs, where the previous prediction is considered in order to aid the current prediction.

Another important difference is that feedforward networks, by design, map one input to one output, whereas RNNs can take multiple forms: map one input to multiple outputs, many inputs to many outputs, or many inputs to one output. The following diagram depicts the various input-output mappings possible with RNNs:

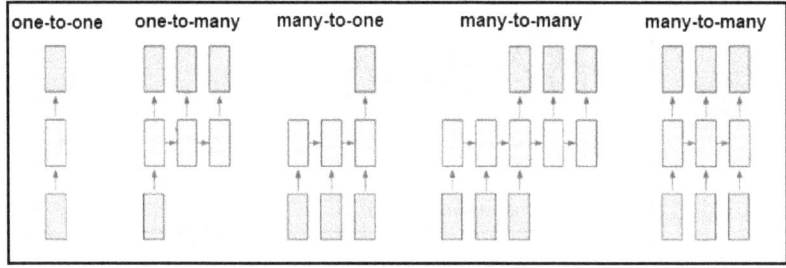

Input-output mapping possibilities with RNNs

Let's review some of the practical applications of the various input-output mappings possible with an RNN. Each rectangle in the preceding diagram is a vector and the arrows represent functions, for example, a matrix multiplication. The input vectors are the lower rectangles (colored in red), and the output vectors are the upper rectangles (colored in blue color). The middle rectangles (colored in green) are vectors that hold the RNN's state.

The following are the various forms of mapping illustrated in the diagram:

- **One input to one output**: The leftmost one is a vanilla mode of processing without RNN, from fixed-sized input to fixed-sized output; for example, image classification.
- **One input to many outputs**: Sequence output, for example, image captioning takes an image as input and it outputs a sentence of words.
- **Many inputs to one output**: Sequence input, for example, sentiment analysis where a given sentence is given as input to the RNN, and the output is a classification expressing positive or negative sentiment of the sentence.
- **Many inputs to many outputs**: Sequence input and sequence output; for example, for a machine translation task, an RNN reads a sentence in English as input and then outputs a sentence in Hindi or some other language.
- **Many inputs to many outputs**: Synced sequence input and output, for example, video classification where we wish to label each frame of the video.

Let's now review the final difference between a feedforward network and an RNN. The way backpropagation is done in order to set the weights in a feedforward neural network is different from that of what is called **backpropagation through time (BPTT)**, which is carried out in an RNN. We are already aware that the objective of the backpropagation algorithm in neural networks is to adjust the weights of a neural network to minimize the error of the network outputs compared to some expected output in response to corresponding inputs. Backpropagation itself is a supervised learning algorithm that allows the neural network to be corrected with regard to the specific errors made. The backpropagation algorithm involves the following steps:

1. Provide training input to the neural network and propagate it through the network to get the output
2. Compare the predicted output to the actual output and calculate the error
3. Calculate the derivatives of the error with respect to the learned network weights
4. Modify the weights to minimize the error
5. Repeat

In feedforward networks, it makes sense to run backpropagation at the end as the output is available only at the end. In RNNs, the output is produced at each time step and this output influences the output in the subsequent time steps. In other words, in RNNs, the error of a time step depends on the previous time step. Therefore, the normal backpropagation algorithms are not suitable for RNNs. Hence, a different algorithm known as BPTT is used to modify the weights in an RNN.

Backpropagation through time

We are already aware that RNNs are cyclical graphs, unlike feedforward networks, which are acyclic directional graphs. In feedforward networks, the error derivatives are calculated from the layer above. However, in an RNN we don't have such layering to perform error derivative calculations. A simple solution to this problem is to unroll the RNN and make it similar to a feedforward network. To enable this, the hidden units from the RNN are replicated at each time step. Each time step replication forms a layer that is similar to layers in a feedforward network. Each time step *t* layer connects to all possible layers in the time step *t+1*. Therefore, we randomly initialize the weights, unroll the network, and then use backpropagation to optimize the weights in the hidden layer. The lowest layer is initialized by passing parameters. These parameters are also optimized as a part of backpropagation. The backpropagation through time algorithm involves the following steps:

1. Provide a sequence of time steps of input and output pairs to the network
2. Unroll the network, then calculate and accumulate errors across each time step
3. Roll up the network and update weights
4. Repeat

In summary, with BPTT, the error is back propagated from the last to the first time step, while unrolling all the time steps. The error for each time step is calculated, which allows updating the weights. The following diagram is a visualization showing the backpropagation through time:

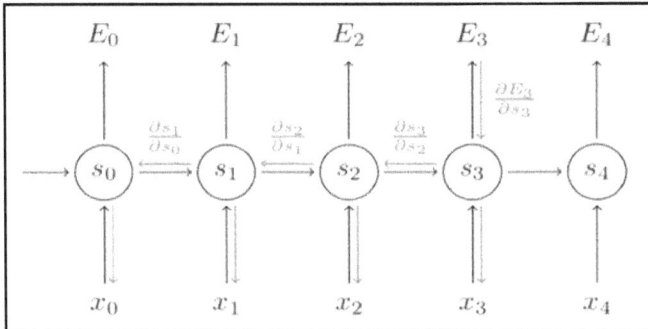

Backpropagation through time in an RNN

It should be noted that as the number of time steps increases, the BPTT algorithm can get computationally very expensive.

Problems and solutions to gradients in RNN

RNNs are not perfect, there are two main issues namely **exploding gradients** and **vanishing gradients** that they suffer from. To understand the issues, let's first understand what a gradient means. A gradient is a partial derivative with respect to its inputs. In simple layman's terms, a gradient measures how much the output of a function changes, if one were to change the inputs a little bit.

Exploding gradients

Exploding gradients relate to a situation where the BPTT algorithm assigns an insanely high importance to the weights, without a rationale. The problem results in an unstable network. In extreme situations, the values of weights can become so large that the values overflow and result in NaN values.

The exploding gradients problem can be detected through observing the following subtle signs while training the network:

- The model weights quickly become very large during training
- The model weights become NaN values during training
- The error gradient values are consistently above 1.0 for each node and layer during training

There are several ways in which one could handle the exploding gradients problem. The following are some of the popular techniques:

- This problem can be easily solved if we can truncate or squash the gradients. This is known as **gradient clipping**.
- Updating weights across fewer prior time steps during training may also reduce the exploding gradient problem. This technique of having fewer step updates is called **truncated backpropagation through time** (**TBPTT**). It is an altered version of the BPTT training algorithm where the sequence is processed one time step at a time, and periodically (*k1* time steps) the BPTT update is performed back for a fixed number of time steps (*k2* time steps). *k1* is the number of forward-pass time steps between updates. *k2* is the number of time steps to which to apply BPTT.
- Weight regularization can be done by checking the size of network weights and applying a penalty to the networks loss function for large weight values.

- By using **long short-term memory units** (**LSTMs**) or **gated recurrent units** (**GRUs**) instead of plain vanilla RNNs.
- Careful initialization of weights such as **Xavier** initialization or **He** initialization.

Vanishing gradients

We are already aware that long-term dependencies are very important for RNNs to function correctly. RNNs can become too deep because of the long-term dependencies. The vanishing gradient problem arises in cases where the gradient of the activation function is very small. During backpropagation, when the weights are multiplied with the low gradients, they tend to become very small and vanish as they go further into the network. This makes the neural network forget the long-term dependency. The following diagram is an illustration showing the cause that leads to vanishing gradients:

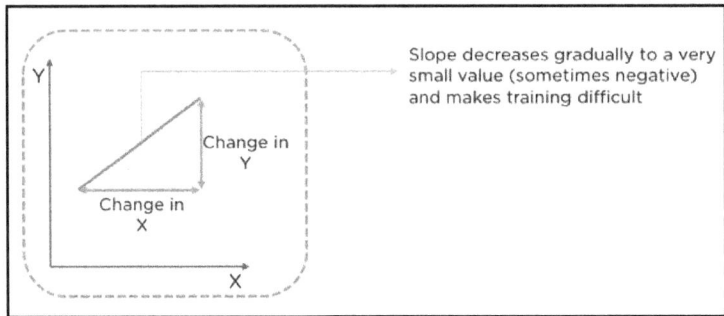

The cause of vanishing gradients

To summarize, due to the vanishing gradients problem, RNNs experience difficulty in memorizing previous words very far away in the sequence and are only able to make predictions based on the most recent words. This can impact the accuracy of RNN predictions. At times, the model may fail to predict or classify what it is supposed to do.

There are several ways in which one could handle the vanishing gradients problem. The following are some of the most popular techniques:

- Initialize network weights for the identity matrix so that the potential for a vanishing gradient is minimized.

- Setting the activation functions to ReLU instead of `sigmoid` or `tanh`. This makes the network computations stay close to the identity function. This works well because when the error derivatives are being propagated backwards through time, they remain constants of either 0 or 1, and so aren't likely to suffer from vanishing gradients.
- Using LSTMs, which are a variant of the regular recurrent network designed to make it easy to capture long-term dependencies in sequence data. The standard RNN operates in such a way that the hidden state activation is influenced by the other local activations closest to it, which corresponds to a **short-term memory**, while the network weights are influenced by the computations that take place over entire long sequences, which corresponds to a **long-term memory**. The RNN was redesigned so that it has an activation state that can also act like weights and preserve information over long distances, hence the name **long short-term memory**.

In LSTMs, rather than each hidden node being simply a node with a single activation function, each node is a memory cell in itself that can store other information. Specifically, it maintains its own cell state. Normal RNNs take in their previous hidden state and the current input, and output a new hidden state. An LSTM does the same, except it also takes in its old cell state and will output its new cell state.

Building an automated prose generator with an RNN

In this project, we will attempt to build a character-level language model using an RNN to generate prose given some initial seed characters. The main task of a character-level language model is to predict the next character given all previous characters in a sequence of data. In other words, the function of an RNN is to generate text character by character.

To start with, we feed the RNN a huge chunk of text as input and ask it to model the probability distribution of the next character in the sequence, given a sequence of previous characters. These probability distributions conceived by the RNN model will then allow us to generate new text, one character at a time.

The first requirement for building a language model is to secure a corpus of text that the model can use to compute the probability distribution of various characters. The larger the input text corpus, the better the RNN will model the probabilities.

We do not have to strive a lot to secure the big text corpus that is required to train the RNN. There are classical texts (books) such as *The Bible* that can be used as a corpus. The best part is many of the classical texts are no longer protected under copyright. Therefore, the texts can be downloaded and used freely in our models.

Project Gutenberg is the best place to get access to free books that are no longer protected by copyright. Project Gutenberg can be accessed through the URL `http://www.gutenberg.org`. There are several books such as *The Bible, Alice's Adventures in Wonderland*, and so on are available from Project Gutenberg. As of December 2018, there are 58,486 books available for download. The books are available in several formats for us to be able to download and use, not just for this project, but for any project where huge text corpus input is required. The following screenshot is of a sample book from Project Gutenberg and the various formats in which the book is available for download:

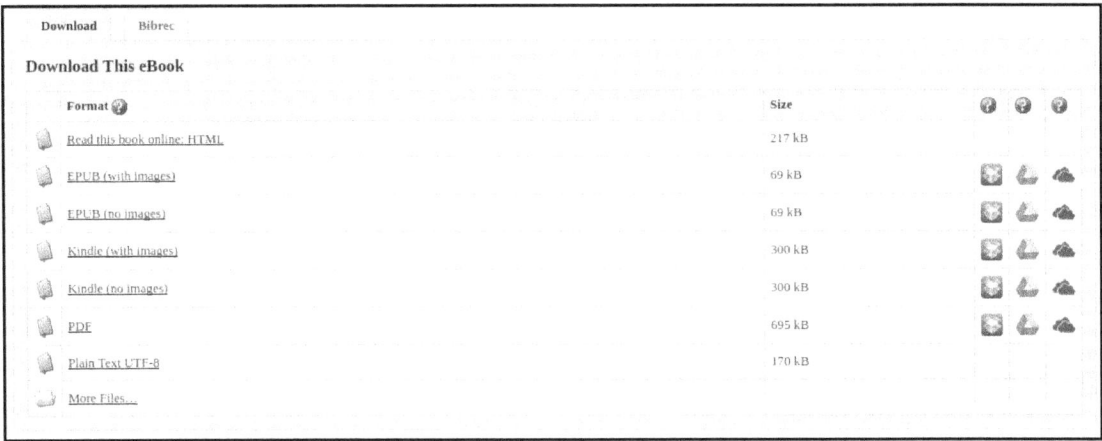

Sample book available from Project Gutenberg in various formats

Irrespective of the format of the file that is downloaded, Project Gutenberg adds standard header and footer text to the actual book text. The following is an example of the header and footer that can be seen in a book:

```
*** START OF THIS PROJECT GUTENBERG EBOOK ALICE'S ADVENTURES IN WONDERLAND
***

THE END
```

It is essential that we remove this header and footer text from the book text downloaded from Project Gutenberg website. For a text file that is downloaded, one can open the file in a text editor and delete the header and footer.

For our project in this chapter, let's use a favorite book from childhood as the text corpus: *Alice's Adventures in Wonderland* by Lewis Carroll. While we have an option to download the text format of this book from Project Gutenberg and make use of it as a text corpus, the R language's `languageR` library makes the task even more easier for us. The `languageR` library already has the *Alice's Adventures in Wonderland* book text. After installing the `languageR` library, use the following code to load the text data into the memory and print the loaded text:

```
# including the languageR library
library("languageR")
# loading the "Alice's Adventures in Wonderland" to memory
data(alice)
# printing the loaded text
print(alice)
```

You will get the following output:

```
[1] "ALICE"           "S"            "ADVENTURES"          "IN"
"WONDERLAND"
[6] "Lewis"           "Carroll"      "THE"                 "MILLENNIUM"
"FULCRUM"
  [11] "EDITION"       "3"            "0"                   "CHAPTER"
"I"
  [16] "Down"          "the"          "Rabbit-Hole"         "Alice"
"was"
  [21] "beginning"     "to"           "get"                 "very"
"tired"
  [26] "of"            "sitting"      "by"                  "her"
"sister"
  [31] "on"            "the"          "bank"                "and"
"of"
  [36] "having"        "nothing"      "to"                  "do"
"once"
  [41] "or"            "twice"        "she"                 "had"
"peeped"
  [46] "into"          "the"          "book"                "her"
"sister"
  [51] "was"           "reading"      "but"                 "it"
"had"
  [56] "no"            "pictures"     "or"            "conversations"
"in"
```

We see from the output that the book text is stored as a character vector, where each of the vector items is a word from the book text that is split by punctuation. It may also be noted that not all the punctuation is retained in the book text.

The following code reconstructs the sentences from the words in the character vector. Of course, we do not get things like sentence boundaries during the reconstruction process, as the character vector does not have as much punctuation as character vector items. Now, let's do the reconstruction of the book text from individual words:

```
alice_in_wonderland<-paste(alice,collapse=" ")
print(alice_in_wonderland)
```

You will get the following output:

```
[1] "ALICE S ADVENTURES IN WONDERLAND Lewis Carroll THE MILLENNIUM FULCRUM
EDITION 3 0 CHAPTER I Down the Rabbit-Hole Alice was beginning to get very
tired of sitting by her sister on the bank and of having nothing to do once
or twice she had peeped into the book her sister was reading but it had no
pictures or conversations in it and what is the use of a book thought Alice
without pictures or conversation So she was considering in her own mind as
well as she could for the hot day made her feel very sleepy and stupid
whether the pleasure of making a daisy-chain would be worth the trouble of
getting up and picking the daisies when suddenly a White Rabbit with pink
eyes ran close by her There was nothing so VERY remarkable in that nor did
Alice think it so VERY much out of the way to hear the Rabbit say to itself
Oh dear Oh dear I shall be late when she thought it over afterwards it
occurred to her that she ought to have wondered at this but at the time it
all seemed quite natural but when the Rabbit actually TOOK A WATCH OUT OF
ITS WAISTCOAT- POCKET and looked at it and then hurried on Alice started to
her feet for it flashed across her mind that she had never before seen a
rabbit with either a waistcoat-pocket or a watch to take out of it and
burning with curiosity she ran across the field after it and fortunately
was just in time to see it pop down a large rabbit-hole under the hedge In
another moment down went Alice after it never once considering how in the
world she was to get out again The rabbit-hole we .......
```

From the output, we see that a long string of text is constructed from the words. Now, we can move on to doing some preprocessing on this text to feed it to the RNN so that the model learns the dependencies between characters and the conditional probabilities of characters in sequences.

 One of the things to note is that, as with a character-level language model that generates the next character in a sequence, you can build a word-level language model too. However, the character-level language model has an advantage in that it can create its own unique words that are not in the vocabulary we train it on.

Let's now learn how RNN works to conceive the dependencies between characters in sequences. Assume that we only had a vocabulary of four possible letters, [a, p, l, e], and the intent is to train an RNN on the training sequence *apple*. This training sequence is in fact a source of four separate training examples:

- The probability of the letter *p* should be likely, given the context of *a, ,* in other words, the conditional probability of *p* given the letter *a* in the word *apple*
- Similar to the first point, *p* should be likely in the context of *ap*
- The *letter l* should also be likely given the context of *app*
- The *letter e* should be likely given the context of *appl*

We start to encode each character in the word *apple* into a vector using 1-of-k encoding. 1-of-k encoding represents each character in the word as all zeros, except for the single 1 at the index of the character in the vocabulary. Each character thus represented with 1-of-k encoding is then fed into the RNN one at a time with the help of a step function. The RNN takes this input and generates a four-dimensional output vectors (one dimension per character, and recollect we only have four characters in our vocabulary). This output vector can be interpreted as the confidence that the RNN currently assigns to each character coming next in the sequence. The following diagram is a visualization of the RNN learning the characters:

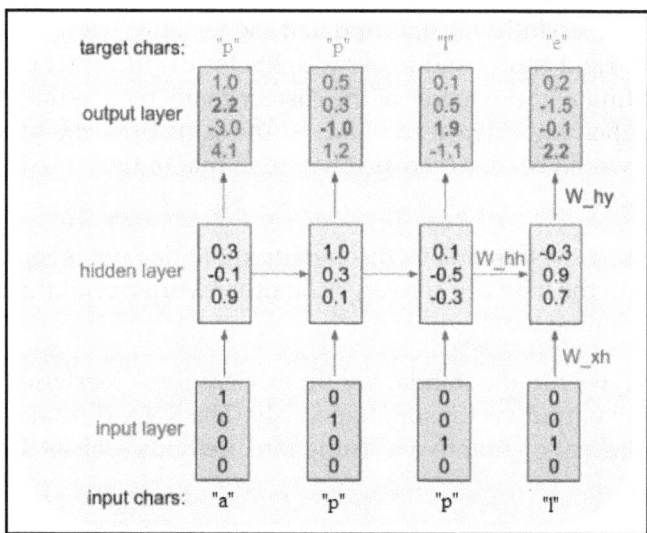

RNN learning the character language model

In the preceding diagram, we see an RNN with four-dimensional input and output layers. There is also a hidden layer with three neurons. The diagram displays the activations in the forward pass when the RNN is fed with the input of the characters *a*, *p*, *p*, and *l*. The output layer contains the confidence that the RNN assigned to each of the following characters. The expectation of the RNN is for the green numbers in the output layer to be higher than the red numbers. The high values of green numbers enable the prediction of the right characters as per the input.

We see that in the first time step, when the RNN is fed the input character *a*, it assigned a confidence of 1.0 to the next letter being *a*, 2.2 as confidence to letter *p*, -3.0 to *l*, and 4.1 to *e*. As per our training data, the sequence we considered is *apple*; therefore, the next correct character is *p* given the character *a* as input in the first time step. We would like our RNN to maximize the confidence in the first step (indicated in green) and minimize the confidence of all other letters (indicated in red). Likewise, we have a desired output character at each one of the four time steps that we would like our RNN to assign a greater confidence to.

Since the RNN consists entirely of differentiable operations, we can run the backpropagation algorithm to figure out in what direction we should adjust each one of its weights to increase the scores of the correct targets (the bold green numbers).

Based on the gradient direction, the parameters are updated and the algorithm actually alters the weight by a tiny amount in the same direction as that of the gradient. Ideally, if gradient decent has successfully run and updated the weights, we would see a slightly higher weight for the right choice and lower weights for the incorrect characters. For example, we would find that the scores of the correct character *p* in the first time step would be slightly higher, say 2.3 instead of 2.2. At the same time, the scores for the other characters *a*, *l*, and *e* would be observed as lower than that of the score that was assigned prior to gradient descent.

The process of updating the parameters through gradient descent is repeated multiple times in the RNN until the network converges, in other words, until the predictions are consistent with the training data.

Technically speaking, we run the standard softmax classifier, otherwise called the cross-entropy loss, on every output vector simultaneously. The RNN is trained with mini-batch stochastic gradient descent or adaptive learning rate methods such as RMSProp or Adam to stabilize the updates.

You may notice that the first time the character *p* is input, the output is *p*; however, the second time the same input is fed, the output is *l*. An RNN, therefore, cannot rely only on the input that is given. This is where an RNN uses its recurrent connection to keep track of the context to perform the task and make the correct predictions. Without the context, it would have been challenging for the network to predict the right output specifically, given the same input.

When we have to generate text using the trained RNN model, we provide a seed input character to the network and get the distribution over what characters are likely to come next. The distribution is then sampled and fed it right back in, to get the next letter. The process is repeated until the maximum number of characters is reached (until a specific user-defined character length), or until the model encounters an end of line character such as <EOS> or <END>.

Implementing the project

Now that we know how an RNN is able to build a character-level model, let's implement the project to generate our own words and sentences through an RNN. Generally, RNN training is computationally intensive and it is suggested that we run the code on a **graphical processing unit** (**GPU**). However, due to infrastructure limitations, we are not going to use a GPU for the project code. The mxnet library allows a character-level language model with an RNN to be executed on the CPU itself, so let's start coding our project:

```
# including the required libraries
library("readr")
library("stringr")
library("stringi")
library("mxnet")
library("languageR")
```

To use the languageR library's *ALICE'S ADVENTURES IN WONDERLAND* book text and load it into memory, use the following code:

```
data(alice)
```

Next, we transform the test into feature vectors that is fed into the RNN model. The make_data function reads the dataset, cleans it of any non-alphanumeric characters, splits it into individual characters and groups it into sequences of length seq.len. In this case, seq.len is set to 100:

```
make_data <- function(txt, seq.len = 32, dic=NULL) {
  text_vec <- as.character(txt)
```

```
  text_vec <- stri_enc_toascii(str = text_vec)
  text_vec <- str_replace_all(string = text_vec, pattern = "[^[:print:]]",
replacement = "")
  text_vec <- strsplit(text_vec, '') %>% unlist
  if (is.null(dic)) {
    char_keep <- sort(unique(text_vec))
  } else char_keep <- names(dic)[!dic == 0]
```

To remove those terms that are not part of dictionary, use the following code:

```
text_vec <- text_vec[text_vec %in% char_keep]
```

To build a dictionary and adjust it by −1 to have a 1-lag for labels, use the following code:

```
dic <- 1:length(char_keep)
 names(dic) <- char_keep
 # reversing the dictionary
 rev_dic <- names(dic)
 names(rev_dic) <- dic
 # Adjust by -1 to have a 1-lag for labels
 num.seq <- (length(text_vec) - 1) %/% seq.len
 features <- dic[text_vec[1:(seq.len * num.seq)]]
 labels <- dic[text_vec[1:(seq.len*num.seq) + 1]]
 features_array <- array(features, dim = c(seq.len, num.seq))
 labels_array <- array(labels, dim = c(seq.len, num.seq))
 return (list(features_array = features_array, labels_array = labels_array,
dic = dic, rev_dic
 = rev_dic))
 }
```

Set the sequence length as 100, then build the long sequence of text from individual words in alice data character vector. Then call the make_data() function on the alice_in_wonderland text file. Observe that seq.ln and an empty dictionary is passed as input. seq.ln dictates the context that is the number of characters that the RNN need to look back inorder to generate the next character. During the training seq.ln is utilized to get the right weights:

```
seq.len <- 100
 alice_in_wonderland<-paste(alice,collapse=" ")
 data_prep <- make_data(alice_in_wonderland, seq.len = seq.len, dic=NULL)
```

To view the prepared data, use the following code:

```
print(str(data_prep))
```

This will give the following output:

```
> print(str(data_prep))
List of 4
 $ features_array: int [1:100, 1:1351] 9 31 25 13 17 1 45 1 9 15 ...
 $ labels_array  : int [1:100, 1:1351] 31 25 13 17 1 45 1 9 15 51 ...
 $ dic           : Named int [1:59] 1 2 3 4 5 6 7 8 9 10 ...
  ..- attr(*, "names")= chr [1:59] " " " " "-" "[" "]" ...
 $ rev_dic       : Named chr [1:59] " " " " "-" "[" "]" ...
  ..- attr(*, "names")= chr [1:59] "1" "2" "3" "4" ...
```

To view the `features` array, use the following code:

```
# Viewing the feature array
View(data_prep$features_array)
```

This will give the following output:

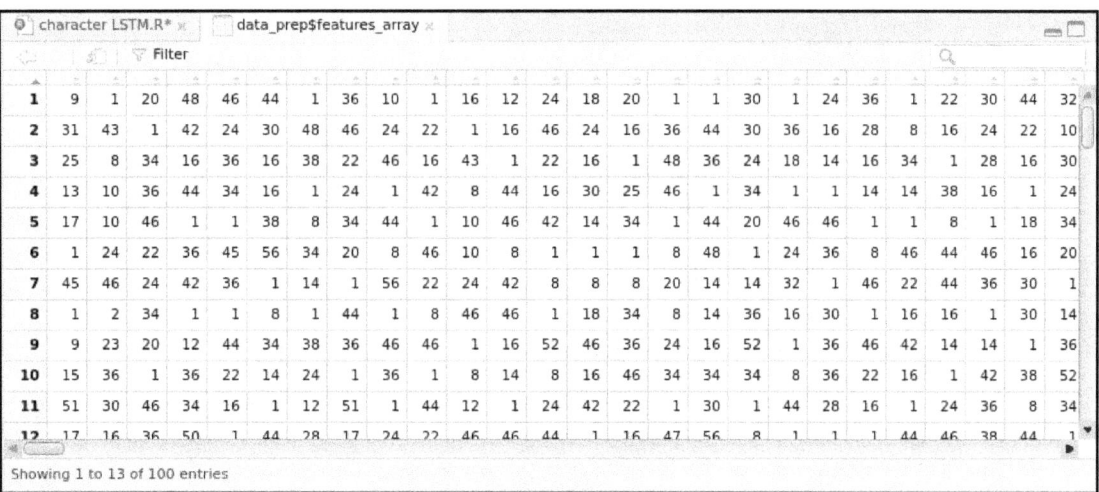

To view the `labels` array, use the following code:

```
# Viewing the labels array
View(data_prep$labels_array)
```

You will get the following output:

1	31	43	1	42	24	30	48	46	24	22	1	16	46	24	16	36	44	30	36	16	28	8	16	24	22	10
2	25	8	34	16	36	16	38	22	46	16	43	1	22	16	1	48	36	24	18	14	16	34	1	28	16	30
3	13	10	36	44	34	16	1	24	1	42	8	44	16	30	25	46	1	34	1	1	14	14	38	16	1	24
4	17	10	46	1	1	38	8	34	44	1	10	46	42	14	34	1	44	20	46	46	1	1	8	1	18	34
5	1	24	22	36	45	56	34	20	8	46	10	8	1	1	1	8	48	1	24	36	8	46	44	46	16	20
6	45	46	24	42	36	1	14	1	56	22	24	42	8	8	8	20	14	14	32	1	46	22	44	36	30	1
7	1	2	34	1	1	8	1	44	1	8	46	46	1	18	34	8	14	36	16	30	1	16	16	1	30	14
8	9	23	20	12	44	34	38	36	46	46	1	16	52	46	36	24	16	52	1	36	46	42	14	14	1	36
9	15	36	1	36	22	14	24	1	36	1	8	14	8	16	46	34	34	34	8	36	22	16	1	42	38	52
10	51	30	46	34	16	1	12	51	1	44	12	1	24	42	22	1	30	1	44	28	16	1	24	36	8	34
11	17	16	36	50	1	44	28	17	24	22	46	46	44	1	16	47	56	8	1	1	1	44	46	38	44	1
12	35	1	1	16	52	46	24	43	46	16	48	36	46	24	42	22	1	1	44	14	44	22	1	1	46	44

Showing 1 to 13 of 100 entries

Now, let's print the dictionary, which includes the unique characters, using the following code:

```
# printing the dictionary - the unique characters
print(data_prep$dic)
```

You will get the following output:

```
> print(data_prep$dic)
    -  [  ]  *  0  3  a  A  b  B  c  C  d  D  e  E  f  F  g  G  h  H  i  I
 j  J  k  K  l  L  m  M  n  N  o  O  p
 1  2  3  4  5  6  7  8  9 10 11 12 13 14 15 16 17 18 19 20 21 22 23 24 25
26 27 28 29 30 31 32 33 34 35 36 37 38
 P  q  Q  r  R  s  S  t  T  u  U  v  V  w  W  x  X  y  Y  z  Z
39 40 41 42 43 44 45 46 47 48 49 50 51 52 53 54 55 56 57 58 59
```

Use the following code to print the indexes of the characters:

```
# printing the indexes of the characters
print(data_prep$rev_dic)
```

This will give the following output:

```
   1   2   3   4   5   6   7   8   9  10  11  12  13  14  15  16  17  18  19
  20  21  22  23  24  25  26  27  28
 " " "-" "[" "]" "*" "0" "3" "a" "A" "b" "B" "c" "C" "d" "D" "e" "E" "f" "F"
 "g" "G" "h" "H" "i" "I" "j" "J" "k"
  29  30  31  32  33  34  35  36  37  38  39  40  41  42  43  44  45  46  47
```

```
48   49   50   51   52   53   54   55   56
"K"  "l"  "L"  "m"  "M"  "n"  "N"  "o"  "O"  "p"  "P"  "q"  "Q"  "r"  "R"  "s"  "S"  "t"  "T"
"u"  "U"  "v"  "V"  "w"  "W"  "x"  "X"  "y"
 57   58   59
"Y"  "z"  "Z"
```

Use the following code block to fetch the features and labels to train the model, split the data into training and evaluation in a 90:10 ratio:

```
X <- data_prep$features_array
Y <- data_prep$labels_array
dic <- data_prep$dic
rev_dic <- data_prep$rev_dic
vocab <- length(dic)
samples <- tail(dim(X), 1)
train.val.fraction <- 0.9
X.train.data <- X[, 1:as.integer(samples * train.val.fraction)]
X.val.data <- X[, -(1:as.integer(samples * train.val.fraction))]
X.train.label <- Y[, 1:as.integer(samples * train.val.fraction)]
X.val.label <- Y[, -(1:as.integer(samples * train.val.fraction))]
train_buckets <- list("100" = list(data = X.train.data, label =
X.train.label))
eval_buckets <- list("100" = list(data = X.val.data, label = X.val.label))
train_buckets <- list(buckets = train_buckets, dic = dic, rev_dic =
rev_dic)
eval_buckets <- list(buckets = eval_buckets, dic = dic, rev_dic = rev_dic)
```

Use the following code to create iterators for training and evaluation datasets:

```
vocab <- length(eval_buckets$dic)
batch.size <- 32
train.data <- mx.io.bucket.iter(buckets = train_buckets$buckets, batch.size
= batch.size, data.mask.element = 0, shuffle = TRUE)
eval.data <- mx.io.bucket.iter(buckets = eval_buckets$buckets, batch.size =
batch.size, data.mask.element = 0, shuffle = FALSE)
```

Create a multi-layer RNN model to sample from character-level language models. It has a one-to-one model configuration since, for each character, we want to predict the next one. For a sequence of length `100`, there are also `100` labels, corresponding to the same sequence of characters but offset by a position of +1. The parameter's `output_last_state` is set to `TRUE`, this is to access the state of the RNN cells when performing inference and we can see `lstm` cells are used.

```
rnn_graph_one_one <- rnn.graph(num_rnn_layer = 3,
                                num_hidden = 96,
                                input_size = vocab,
                                num_embed = 64,
```

```
                        num_decode = vocab,
                        dropout = 0.2,
                        ignore_label = 0,
                        cell_type = "lstm",
                        masking = F,
                        output_last_state = T,
                        loss_output = "softmax",
                        config = "one-to-one")
```

Use the following code to visualize the RNN model:

```
graph.viz(rnn_graph_one_one, type = "graph",
        graph.height.px = 650, shape=c(500, 500))
```

The following diagram shows the resultant output:

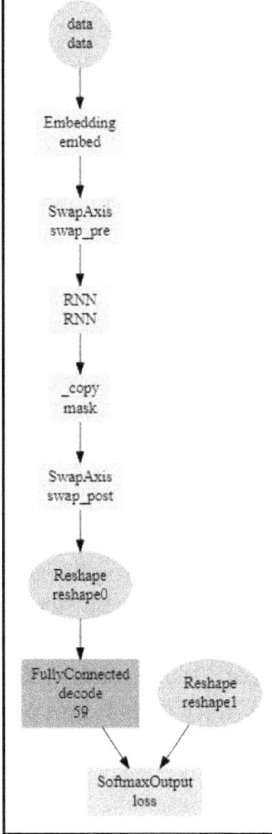

Now, use the following line of code to set the CPU as the device to execute the code:

```
devices <- mx.cpu()
```

Then, initializing the weights of the network through the Xavier initializer:

```
initializer <- mx.init.Xavier(rnd_type = "gaussian", factor_type = "avg",
magnitude = 3)
```

Use the `adadelta` optimizer to update the weights in the network through the learning process:

```
optimizer <- mx.opt.create("adadelta", rho = 0.9, eps = 1e-5, wd = 1e-8,
                           clip_gradient = 5, rescale.grad = 1/batch.size)
```

Use the following lines of code to set up logging of metrics and define a custom measurement function:

```
logger <- mx.metric.logger()
epoch.end.callback <- mx.callback.log.train.metric(period = 1, logger =
logger)
batch.end.callback <- mx.callback.log.train.metric(period = 50)
mx.metric.custom_nd <- function(name, feval) {
  init <- function() {
    c(0, 0)
  }
  update <- function(label, pred, state) {
    m <- feval(label, pred)
    state <- c(state[[1]] + 1, state[[2]] + m)
    return(state)
  }
  get <- function(state) {
    list(name=name, value = (state[[2]] / state[[1]]))
  }
  ret <- (list(init = init, update = update, get = get))
  class(ret) <- "mx.metric"
  return(ret)
}
```

Perplexity is a measure of how variable a prediction model is. If perplexity is a measure of prediction error, define a function to compute the error, using the following lines of code:

```
mx.metric.Perplexity <- mx.metric.custom_nd("Perplexity", function(label,
pred) {
  label <- mx.nd.reshape(label, shape = -1)
  label_probs <- as.array(mx.nd.choose.element.0index(pred, label))
  batch <- length(label_probs)
  NLL <- -sum(log(pmax(1e-15, as.array(label_probs)))) / batch
```

```
    Perplexity <- exp(NLL)
    return(Perplexity)
}
```

Use the following code to execute the model creation and you will see that in this project we are running it for 20 iterations:

```
model <- mx.model.buckets(symbol = rnn_graph_one_one,
                          train.data = train.data, eval.data = eval.data,
                          num.round = 20, ctx = devices, verbose = TRUE,
                          metric = mx.metric.Perplexity,
                          initializer = initializer,
      optimizer = optimizer,
                          batch.end.callback = NULL,
                          epoch.end.callback = epoch.end.callback)
```

This will give the following output:

```
Start training with 1 devices
[1] Train-Perplexity=23.490355102639
[1] Validation-Perplexity=17.6250266989171
[2] Train-Perplexity=14.4508382001841
[2] Validation-Perplexity=12.8179427398927
[3] Train-Perplexity=10.8156810097278
[3] Validation-Perplexity=9.95208184606089
[4] Train-Perplexity=8.6432934902383
[4] Validation-Perplexity=8.21806492033906
[5] Train-Perplexity=7.33073759154393
[5] Validation-Perplexity=7.03574648385079
[6] Train-Perplexity=6.32024660528852
[6] Validation-Perplexity=6.1394327776089
[7] Train-Perplexity=5.61888374338248
[7] Validation-Perplexity=5.59925324885983
[8] Train-Perplexity=5.14009899947491]
[8] Validation-Perplexity=5.29671693342219
[9] Train-Perplexity=4.77963053659987
[9] Validation-Perplexity=4.98471501141549
[10] Train-Perplexity=4.5523402301526
[10] Validation-Perplexity=4.84636357676712
[11] Train-Perplexity=4.36693337145912
[11] Validation-Perplexity=4.68806078057635
[12] Train-Perplexity=4.21294955131918
[12] Validation-Perplexity=4.53026345109037
[13] Train-Perplexity=4.08935886339982
[13] Validation-Perplexity=4.50495393289961
[14] Train-Perplexity=3.99260373800419
[14] Validation-Perplexity=4.42576079641165
[15] Train-Perplexity=3.91330125104996
```

```
[15] Validation-Perplexity=4.3941619024578
[16] Train-Perplexity=3.84730588206837
[16] Validation-Perplexity=4.33288830915229
[17] Train-Perplexity=3.78711049085869
[17] Validation-Perplexity=4.28723362252784
[18] Train-Perplexity=3.73198720637659
[18] Validation-Perplexity=4.22839393379393
[19] Train-Perplexity=3.68292148768833
[19] Validation-Perplexity=4.22187018296206
[20] Train-Perplexity=3.63728269095417
[20] Validation-Perplexity=4.17983276293299
```

Next, save the model for later use, then load the model from the disk to infer and sample the text character by character, and finally merge the predicted characters into a sentence using the following code:

```
mx.model.save(model, prefix = "one_to_one_seq_model", iteration = 20)
# the generated text is expected to be similar to the training data
set.seed(0)
model <- mx.model.load(prefix = "one_to_one_seq_model", iteration = 20)
internals <- model$symbol$get.internals()
sym_state <- internals$get.output(which(internals$outputs %in%
"RNN_state"))
sym_state_cell <- internals$get.output(which(internals$outputs %in%
"RNN_state_cell"))
sym_output <- internals$get.output(which(internals$outputs %in%
"loss_output"))
symbol <- mx.symbol.Group(sym_output, sym_state, sym_state_cell)
```

Use the following code to provide the seed character to start the text with:

```
infer_raw <- c("e")
infer_split <- dic[strsplit(infer_raw, '') %>% unlist]
infer_length <- length(infer_split)
infer.data <- mx.io.arrayiter(data = matrix(infer_split), label =
matrix(infer_split), batch.size = 1, shuffle = FALSE)
infer <- mx.infer.rnn.one(infer.data = infer.data,
                          symbol = symbol,
                          arg.params = model$arg.params,
                          aux.params = model$aux.params,
                          input.params = NULL,
                          ctx = devices)
pred_prob <- as.numeric(as.array(mx.nd.slice.axis(infer$loss_output, axis =
0, begin = infer_length-1, end = infer_length)))
pred <- sample(length(pred_prob), prob = pred_prob, size = 1) - 1
predict <- c(predict, pred)
for (i in 1:200) {
  infer.data <- mx.io.arrayiter(data = as.matrix(pred), label =
```

```
    as.matrix(pred), batch.size = 1,
    shuffle = FALSE)
      infer <- mx.infer.rnn.one(infer.data = infer.data,
                                symbol = symbol,
                                arg.params = model$arg.params,
                                aux.params = model$aux.params,
                                input.params = list(rnn.state = infer[[2]],
                                rnn.state.cell = infer[[3]]),
                                ctx = devices)
    pred_prob <- as.numeric(as.array(infer$loss_output))
    pred <- sample(length(pred_prob), prob = pred_prob, size = 1, replace =
    T) - 1
      predict <- c(predict, pred)
    }
```

Use the following lines of code to print the predicted text, after processing the predicted characters and merging them together into one sentence:

```
predict_txt <- paste0(rev_dic[as.character(predict)], collapse = "")
predict_txt_tot <- paste0(infer_raw, predict_txt, collapse = "")
# printing the predicted text
print(predict_txt_tot)
```

This will give the following output:

```
[1] "eNAHare I eat and in Heather where and fingo I ve next feeling or
fancy to livery dust a large pived as a pockethion What isual child for of
cigstening to get in a strutching voice into saying she got reaAlice glared
in a Grottle got to sea-paticular and when she heard it would heard of
having they began whrink bark of Hearnd again said feeting and there was
going to herself up it Then does so small be THESE said Alice going my dear
her before she walked at all can t make with the players and said the
Dormouse sir your mak if she said to guesss I hadn t some of the crowd and
one arches how come one mer really of a gomoice and the loots at encand
something of one eyes purried asked to leave at she had Turtle might I d
interesting tone hurry of the game the Mouse of puppled it They much put
eagerly"
```

We see from the output that our RNN is able to autogenerate text. Of course, the generated text is not very cohesive and it needs some improvement. There are several techniques we could rely upon to improve the cohesion and generate more meaningful text from an RNN. The following are some of these techniques:

- Implement a word-level language model instead of a character-level language model.
- Use a larger RNN network.

- In our project, we used LTSM cells to build our RNN. Instead of LSTM cells, we could use GRU cells, which are more advanced.
- We ran our RNN training for 20 iterations; this may be too little to get the right weights in place. We could try increasing the number of iterations and verifying the RNN yields better predictions.
- The current model used a dropout of 20%. This can be altered to check the effect on the overall predictions.
- Our corpus retained very little punctuation; therefore, our model did not have the ability to predict punctuation as characters while generating text. Including punctuation in the corpus on which an RNN gets trained may yield better sentences and word endings.
- The `seq.ln` parameter decides the number of characters that need to be looked up in the history, prior to predicting the next character. In our model, we have set this as 100. This may be altered to check whether the model produces better words and sentences.

Due to space and time constraints, we are not going to be trying these options in this chapter. One or more of these options may be experimented with by interested readers to produce better words and sentences using a character RNN.

Summary

The major theme of this chapter was generating text automatically using RNNs. We started the chapter with a discussion about language models and their applications in the real world. We then carried out an in-depth overview of recurrent neural networks and their suitability for language model tasks. The differences between traditional feedforward networks and RNNs were discussed to get a clearer understanding of RNNs. We then went on to discuss problems and solutions related to the exploding gradients and vanishing gradients experienced by RNNs. After acquiring a detailed theoretical foundation of RNNs, we went ahead with implementing a character-level language model with an RNN. We used *Alice's Adventures in Wonderland* as a text corpus input to train the RNN model and then generated a string as output. Finally, we discussed some ideas for improving our character RNN model.

How about implementing a project to win more often when playing casino slot machines? This is something we will explore in the last but one chapter of this book. Chapter 22,*Winning the Casino Slot Machine with Reinforcement Learning*. Come on, let's learn to earn free money.

22
Winning the Casino Slot Machines with Reinforcement Learning

If you have been following **machine learning** (**ML**) news, I am sure you will have encountered this kind of headline: *computers performing better than world champions in various games.* If you haven't, the following are sample news snippets from my quick Google search that are worth spending time reading to understand the situation:

- Check this out: https://www.theverge.com/2017/10/18/16495548/deepmind-ai-go-alphago-zero-self-taught/:

GOOGLE \ SCIENCE \ TECH \

DeepMind's Go-playing AI doesn't need human help to beat us anymore

The company's latest AlphaGo AI learned superhuman skills by playing itself over and over

By James Vincent | @jjvincent | Oct 18, 2017, 1:00pm EDT

- See this: https://www.makeuseof.com/tag/ais-winning-5-times-computers-beat-humans/:

4. Deepmind, the Self-Taught

Google's Deepmind may finally give nerds something to worry about because it's beating humans at **classic Atari games** — well, certain games at least. Humanity still keeps it's edge in games like Asteroid and Gravitar.

Reinforcement learning (**RL**) is a subarea of **artificial intelligence** (**AI**) that powers computer systems who are able to demonstrate better performance in games such as Atari Breakout and Go than human players.

In this chapter, we will look at the following topics:

- The concept of RL
- The multi-arm bandit problem
- Methods for solving the multi-arm bandit problem
- Real-world applications of RL
- Implementing a project using RL techniques to maximize our chances of winning at a multi-arm bandit machine

Understanding RL

RL is a very important area but is sometimes overlooked by practitioners for solving complex, real-world problems. It is unfortunate that even most ML textbooks focus only on supervised and unsupervised learning while totally ignorning RL.

RL as an area has picked up momentum in recent years; however, its origins date back to 1980. It was invented by Rich Sutton and Andrew Barto, Rich's PhD thesis advisor. It was thought of as archaic, even back in the 1980s. Rich, however, believed in RL and its promise, maintaining that it would eventually be recognized.

A quick Google search with the term RL shows that RL methods are often used in games, such as checkers and chess. Gaming problems are problems that require taking actions over time to find a long-term optimal solution to a dynamic problem. They are dynamic in the sense that the conditions are constantly changing, sometimes in response to other agents, which can be adversarial.

Although the success of RL is proven in the area of games, it is also an emerging area that is increasingly applied in other fields, such as finance, economics, and other inter-disciplinary areas. There are a number of methods in the RL area that have grown independently within the AI and operations research communities. Therefore, it is key area for a ML practitioners to learn about.

In simple terms, RL is an area that mainly focuses on creating models that learn from mistakes. Imagine that a person is put in a new environment. At first, they will make mistakes, but they will learn from them, so that when the same situation should arise in future, they will not make the same mistake again. RL uses the same technique to train the model as follows:

Environment ----------> Try and fail -----------> Learn from failures ----------> Reach goal

Historically, you couldn't use ML to get an algorithm learn how to become better than a human at performing a certain task. All that could be done was model the machine's behavior after a human's actions and, maybe, the computer would run through them faster. RL, however, makes it possible to create models that become better at performing certain tasks than humans.

Isaac Abhadu, CEO and co-founder at SYBBIO, had this wonderful explanation on Quora detailing the working of RL compared to supervised learning. He stated that an RL framework, in a nutshell, is very similar to that of supervised learning.

Suppose we're trying to get an algorithm to excel at the game of Pong. We have input frames that we will run through a model to get it to produce some random output actions, just as we would in a supervised learning setting. The difference, however, is that in the case of RL, we ourselves do not know what the target labels are, and so we don't tell the machine what's better to do in every specific situation. Instead, we apply something called a **policy gradients** method.

So, we start with a random network and feed to it an input frame so it produces a random output action to react to that frame. This action is then sent back to the game engine, which makes it produce another frame. This loop continues over and over. The only feedback it will give is the game's scoreboard. Whenever our agent does something right – that is, it produces some successful sequence – it will get a point, generally termed as a **reward**. Whenever it produces a failing sequence, it will get a point removed—this is a **penalty**.

The ultimate goal the agent is pursuing is to keep updating its policy to get as much rewards as possible. So, over time, it will figure out how to beat a human at the game.

RL is not quick. The agent is going to lose a lot at first. But we will keep feeding it frames so it keeps producing random output actions, and it will stumble upon actions that are successful. It will keep accumulating knowledge about what moves are successful and, after a while, will become invincible.

Comparison of RL with other ML algorithms

RL involves an **environment**, which is the problem set to be solved, and an **agent**, which is simply the AI algorithm. The agent will perform a certain action and the result of the action will be a change in the **state** of the agent. The change leads to the agent getting a reward, which is a positive reward, or a penalty, which is a negative reward for having performed an incorrect action. By repeating the action and reward process, the agent learns the environment. It understands the various states and the various actions that are desirable and undesirable. This process of performing actions and learning from the rewards is RL. The following diagram is an illustration showing the relationship between the agent and the environment in RL:

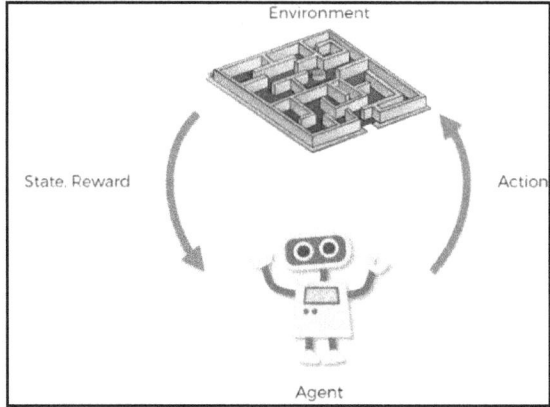

Relationship between the agent and environment in RL

RL, **deep learning** (**DL**), and ML all support automation in one way or another. All of them involve some kind of learning from the given data. However, what separates RL from the others is that RL learns the right actions by trail and error, whereas the others are focused on learning by finding patterns in the existing data. Another key difference is that for DL and ML algorithms to learn better, we will need to give them large labeled datasets, whereas this is not the case with RL.

Let's understand RL better by taking the analogy of training pets at home. Imagine we are teaching our pet dog, Santy, some new tricks. Santy, unfortunately, does not understand English; therefore, we need to find an alternative way to train him. We emulate a situation, and Santy tries to respond in many different ways. We reward Santy with a bone treat for any desirable responses. What this inculcates in the pet dog is that the next time he encounters a similar situation, he will perform the desired behavior as he knows that there is a reward. So, this is learning from positive responses; if he is treated with negative responses, such as frowning, he will be discouraged from undesirable behavior.

Terminology of RL

Let's understand the RL key terms—agent, environment, state, policy, reward, and penalty—with our pet dog training analogy:

- Our pet dog, Santy, is the agent that is exposed to the environment.
- The environment is a house or play area, depending on what we want to teach to Santy.
- Each situation encountered is called the state. For example, Santy crawling under the bed or running can be interpreted as states.
- Santy, the agent, reacts by performing actions to change from one state to another.
- After changes in states, we give the agent either a reward or a penalty, depending on the action that is performed.
- The policy refers to the strategy of choosing an action for finding better outcomes.

Now that we understand each of the RL terms, let's define the terms more formally and visualize the agent's behavior in the diagram that follows:

- **States**: The complete description of the world is known as the states. We do not abstract any information that is present in the world. States can be a position, a constant, or a dynamic. States are generally recorded in arrays, matrices, or higher order tensors.
- **Actions**: The environment generally defines the possible actions; that is, different environments lead to different actions, based on the agent. The valid actions for an agent are recorded in a space called an action space. The possible valid actions in an environment are finite in number.
- **Environment**: This is the space where the agent lives and with which the agent interacts. For different types of environments, we use different rewards and policies.
- **Reward and return**: The reward function is the one that must be kept track of at all times in RL. It plays a vital role in tuning, optimizing the algorithm, and stopping the training of the algorithm. The reward is computed based on the current state of the world, the action just taken, and the next state of the world.
- **Policies**: A policy in RL is a rule that's used by an agent for choosing the next action; the policy is also known as the agent's brain.

Take a look at the following flowchart to understand the process better:

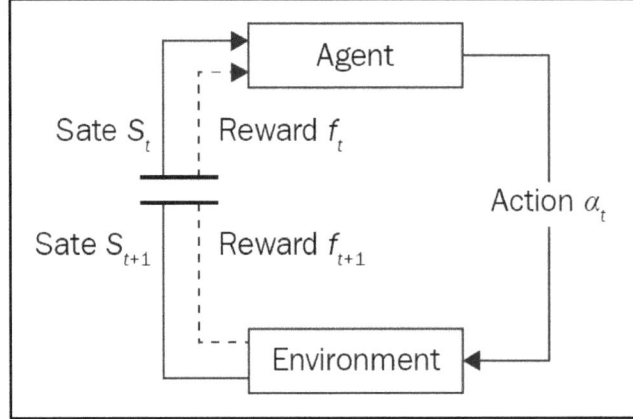

Agent behavior in RL

At each step, *t*, the agent performs the following tasks:

1. Executes action a_t
2. Receives observation s_t
3. Receives scalar reward r_t

The environment implements the following tasks:

1. Changes upon action a_t
2. Emits observation s_{t+1}
3. Emits scalar reward r_{t+1}

Time step *t* is incremented after each iteration.

The multi-arm bandit problem

Let me start with an analogy to understand this topic better. Do you like pizza? I like it a lot! My favorite restaurant in Bangalore serves delicious pizzas. I go to this place almost every time I feel like eating a pizza, and I am almost sure that I will get the best pizza. However, going to the same restaurant every time worries me that I am missing out on pizzas that are even better and served elsewhere in the town!

One alternative available is to try out restaurants one by one and sample the pizzas there, but this means that there is a very high probability that I will end up eating pizzas that aren't very nice. However, this is the one way for me to find a restaurant that serves better pizzas than the one I am currently aware of. I am aware you must be wondering why am I talking about pizzas when I am supposed to be talking about RL. Let me get to the point.

The dilemma with this task arises from incomplete information. In other words, to solve this task, it is essential to gather enough information to formulate the best overall strategy and then explore new actions. This will eventually lead to a minimization of overall bad experiences. This situation can otherwise be termed as the **exploration** versus **exploitation** dilemma:

Exploration versus exploitation dilemma

The preceding diagram aptly summarizes my best-pizza problem.

The **multi-arm bandit problem** (**MABP**) is a simplified form of the pizza analogy. It is used to represent similar kinds of problems, and finding a good strategy to solve them is already helping a lot of industries.

A **bandit** is defined as someone who steals your money! A one-armed bandit is a simple slot machine. We find this sort of machine in a casino: you insert a coin into the slot machine, pull a lever, and pray to the luck god to get an immediate reward. But the million-dollar question is why is a slot machine called a bandit? It turns out that all casinos configure the slot machines in such a way that all gamblers end up losing money!

A multi-arm bandit is a hypothetical but complicated slot machine where we have more than one slot machine lined up in a row. A gambler can pull several levers, with each lever giving a different return. The following diagram depicts the probability distribution for the corresponding reward that is different to each layer and unknown to the gambler:

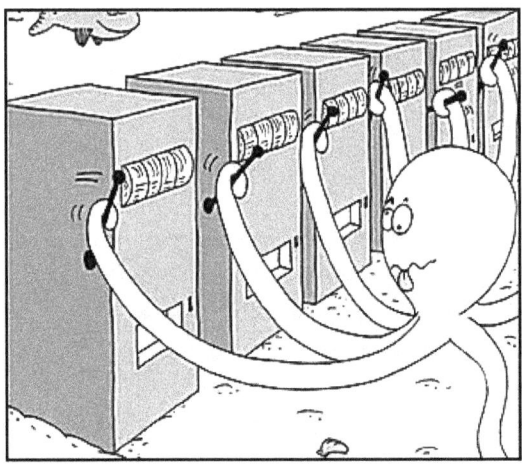

Multi-arm bandit

Given these slot machines and after a set of initial trials, the task is to identify what lever to pull to get the maximum reward. In other words, pulling any one of the arms gives us a stochastic reward of either R=+1 for success, or R=0 for failure; this is called an **immediate reward**. A multi-arm bandit that issues a reward of 1 or 0 is called a **Bernoulli**. The objective is to pull the arms one-by-one in a sequence while gathering information to maximize the total payout over the long run. Formally, a Bernoulli MABP can be described as a tuple of (A,R), where the following applies:

- We have KK machines with reward probabilities, {θ1,...,θK}.
- At each time step, t, we take an action, a, on one slot machine and receive a reward, r.
- A is a set of actions, each referring to the interaction with one slot machine. The value of action a is the expected reward, $Q(a) = E[r|a] = \theta$. If action a at time step t is on the i-th machine, then $Q(a_t) = \theta_i$. Q(a) is generally referred to as the action-value function.
- R is a reward function. In the case of the Bernoulli bandit, we observe a reward, r, in a stochastic fashion. At time step t, $r_t = R(a_t)$ may return reward 1 with a probability of $Q(a_t)$ or 0 otherwise.

We can solve the MABP with multiple strategies. We will review some of the strategies shortly in this section. To decide on the best strategy and to compare the different strategies, we need a quantitative method. One method is to directly compute the cumulative rewards after a certain predefined number of trials. Comparing the cumulative rewards from each of the strategies gives us an opportunity to identify the best strategies for the problem.

At times, we may already know the best action for the given bandit problem. In those cases, it may be interesting to look at the concept of regret.

Let's imagine that we know of the details of the best arm to pull for the given bandit problem. Assume that by repeatedly pulling this best arm, we get a maximum expected reward, which is shown as a horizontal line in the following diagram:

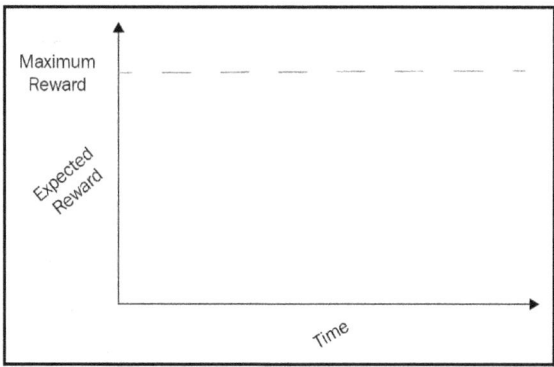

Maximum reward obtained by pulling the best arm for a MABP

As per the problem statement, we need to make repeated trials by pulling different arms of the multi-arm bandit until we are approximately sure of the arm to pull for the maximum average return at time *t*. There are a number of rounds involved while we explore and decide upon the best arm. The number of rounds, otherwise called **trials**, also incurs some loss, and this is called **regret**. In other words, we want to maximize the reward even during the learning phase. Regret can be summarized as a quantification of exactly how much we regret not picking the optimal arm.

The following diagram is an illustration showing the regret due to trials done to find the best arm:

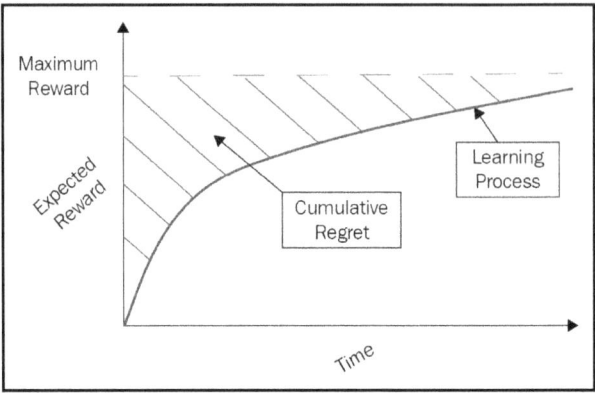

Concept of regret in MAB

Strategies for solving MABP

Based on how the exploration is done, the strategies to solve the MABP can be classified into the following types:

- No exploration
- Exploration at random
- Exploration smartly with preference to uncertainty

Let's delve into the details of some of the algorithms that fall under each of the strategy types.

Let's consider one very naive approach that involves playing just one slot machine for a long time. Here, we do no exploration at all and just randomly pick one arm to repeatedly pull to maximize the long-term rewards. You must be wondering how this works! Let's explore.

In probability theory, the law of large numbers is a theorem that describes the result of performing the same experiment a large number of times. According to this law, the average of the results obtained from a large number of trials should be close to the expected value, and will tend to become closer as more trials are performed.

We can just play with one machine for a large number of rounds so as to eventually estimate the true reward probability according to the law of large numbers.

However, there are some problems with this strategy. First and foremost, we do not know the value of a large number of rounds. Second, it is super resource intensive to play the same slot repeatedly for large number of times. And, most importantly, there is no guarantee that we will obtain the best long-term reward with this strategy.

The epsilon-greedy algorithm

The greedy algorithm in RL is a complete exploitation algorithm, which does not care for exploration. Greedy algorithms always select the action with the highest estimated action value. The action value is estimated according to past experience by averaging the rewards associated with the target action that have been observed so far.

However, use of a greedy algorithm can be a smart approach if we are able to successfully estimate the action value to the expected action value; if we know the true distribution, we can just select the best actions. An epsilon-greedy algorithm is a simple combination of the greedy and random approaches.

Epsilon helps to do this estimate. It adds exploration as part of the greedy algorithm. In order to counter the logic of always selecting the best action, as per the estimated action value, occasionally, the epsilon probability selects a random action for the sake of exploration; the rest of the time, it behaves as the original greedy algorithm and select the best known action.

The epsilon in this algorithm is an adjustable parameter that determines the probability of taking a random, rather than principled, action. It is also possible to adjust the epsilon value during training. Generally, at the start of the training process, the epsilon value is often initialized to a large probability. As the environment is unknown, the large epsilon value encourages exploration. The value is then gradually reduced to a small constant (often set to 0.1). This will increase the rate of exploitation selection.

Due to the simplicity of the algorithm, the approach has become the de facto technique for most recent RL algorithms.
Despite the common usage that the algorithm enjoys, this method is far from optimal, since it takes into account only whether actions are most rewarding or not.

Boltzmann or softmax exploration

Boltzmann exploration is also called **softmax exploration**. As opposed to either taking the optimal action all the time or taking a random action all the time, this exploration favors both through weighted probabilities. This is done through a softmax over the network's estimates of values for each action. In this case, although not guaranteed, the action that the agent estimates to be optimal is most likely to be chosen.

Boltzmann exploration has the biggest advantage over epsilon greedy. This method has information about the likely values of the other actions. In other words, let's imagine that there are five actions available to an agent. Generally, in the epsilon-greedy method, four actions are estimated as non-optimal and they are all considered equally. However, in Boltzmann exploration, the four sub-optimal choices are weighed by their relative value. This enables the agent to ignore actions that are estimated to be largely sub-optimal and give more attention to potentially promising, but not necessarily ideal, actions.

The temperature parameter (τ) controls the spread of the softmax distribution, so that all actions are considered equally at the start of training, and actions are sparsely distributed by the end of training. The parameter is annealed over time.

Decayed epsilon greedy

The value of epsilon is key in determining how well the epsilon-greedy algorithm works for a given problem. Instead of setting this value at the start and then decreasing it, we can make epsilon dependent on time. For example, epsilon can be kept equal to 1 / log(t + 0.00001). As time passes, the epsilon value will keep reducing. This method works as over the time that epsilon is reduced, we become more confident of the optimal action and less exploring is required.

The problem with the random selection of actions is that after sufficient time steps, even if we know that some arm is bad, this algorithm will keep choosing that with probability *epsilon/n*. Essentially, we are exploring a bad action, which does not sound very efficient. The approach to get around this could be to favor exploration of arms with strong potential in order to get an optimal value.

The upper confidence bound algorithm

The **upper confidence bound** (**UCB**) algorithm is the most popular and widely used solution for MABPs. This algorithm is based on the principle of optimism in the face of uncertainty. This essentially means, the less uncertain we are about an arm, the more important it becomes to explore that arm.

Assume that we have two arms that can be tried out. If we have tried out the first arm 100 times but the second arm only once, then we are probably reasonably confident about the payoff of the first arm. However, we are very uncertain about the payoff of the second arm. This gives rise to the family of UCB algorithms. This can be further explained through the following diagram:

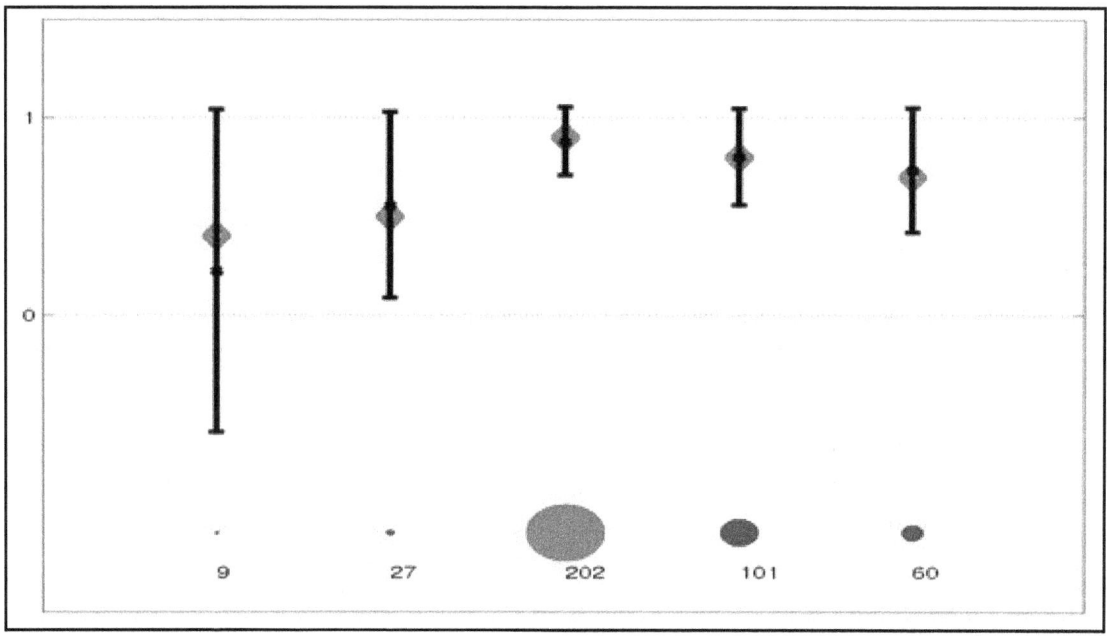

Illustration to explain upper confident bound algorithm

In the preceding diagram, each bar represents a different arm or an action. The red dot is the true expected reward and the center of the bar represents the observed average reward. The width of the bar represents the confidence interval. We are already aware that, by the law of large numbers, the more samples we have, the closer the observed average gets to the true average, and the more the bar shrinks.

The idea behind UCB algorithms is to always pick the arm or action with the highest upper bound, which is the sum of the observed average and the one-sided width of the confidence interval. This balances the exploration of arms that have not been tried many times with the exploitation of arms that have.

Thompson sampling

Thompson sampling is one of the oldest heuristics for MABPs. It is a randomized algorithm based on Bayesian ideas, and has recently generated significant interest after several studies demonstrated it to have better empirical performance compared to other methods.

 There is a beautiful explanation I found on `https://stats.stackexchange.com/questions/187059/could-anyone-explain-thompson-sampling-in-simplest-terms`. I do not think I can do better job at explaining Thompson sampling than this. You can refer to this for further reference.

Multi-arm bandit – real-world use cases

We encounter so many situations in the real world that are similar to that of the MABP we reviewed in this chapter. We could apply RL strategies to all these situations. The following are some of the real-world use cases similar to that of the MABP:

- Finding the best medicine/s among many alternatives
- Identifying the best product to launch among possible products
- Deciding the amount of traffic (users) that we need to allocate for each website
- Identifying the best marketing strategy for launching a product
- Identifying the best stocks portfolio to maximize profit
- Finding out the best stock to invest in
- Figuring out the shortest path in a given map
- Click-through rate prediction for ads and articles
- Predicting the most beneficial content to be cached at a router based upon the content of articles
- Allocation of funding for different departments of an organization
- Picking best-performing athletes out of a group of students given limited time and an arbitrary selection threshold

So far, we have covered almost all of the basic details that we need to know to progress to the practical implementation of RL to the MABP. Let's kick-start coding solutions to the MABP in our next section.

Solving the MABP with UCB and Thompson sampling algorithms

In this project, we will use upper confidence limits and Thompson sampling algorithms to solve the MABP. We will compare their performance and strategy in three different situations—standard rewards, standard but more volatile rewards, and somewhat chaotic rewards. Let's prepare the simulation data, and once the data is prepared, we will view the simulated data using the following code:

```
# loading the required packages
library(ggplot2)
library(reshape2)
# distribution of arms or actions having normally distributed
# rewards with small variance
# The data represents a standard, ideal situation i.e.
# normally distributed rewards, well seperated from each other.
mean_reward = c(5, 7.5, 10, 12.5, 15, 17.5, 20, 22.5, 25, 26)
reward_dist = c(function(n) rnorm(n = n, mean = mean_reward[1], sd = 2.5),
                function(n) rnorm(n = n, mean = mean_reward[2], sd = 2.5),
                function(n) rnorm(n = n, mean = mean_reward[3], sd = 2.5),
                function(n) rnorm(n = n, mean = mean_reward[4], sd = 2.5),
                function(n) rnorm(n = n, mean = mean_reward[5], sd = 2.5),
                function(n) rnorm(n = n, mean = mean_reward[6], sd = 2.5),
                function(n) rnorm(n = n, mean = mean_reward[7], sd = 2.5),
                function(n) rnorm(n = n, mean = mean_reward[8], sd = 2.5),
                function(n) rnorm(n = n, mean = mean_reward[9], sd = 2.5),
                function(n) rnorm(n= n, mean = mean_reward[10], sd = 2.5))
#preparing simulation data
dataset = matrix(nrow = 10000, ncol = 10)
for(i in 1:10){
  dataset[, i] = reward_dist[[i]](n = 10000)
}
# assigning column names
colnames(dataset) <- 1:10
# viewing the dataset that is just created with simulated data
View(dataset)
```

This will give the following output:

	1	2	3	4	5	6	7	8	9	10
1	4.149237778	5.888279	13.304435	15.120000	12.965377	21.153600	19.13103	24.57462	18.74083	28.06800
2	5.059478264	10.874230	11.166362	12.516016	13.943657	15.020042	19.25578	25.00683	23.76171	27.05061
3	3.467250585	7.972316	5.998070	14.808509	17.710216	20.667930	17.89901	18.89610	27.81120	22.95005
4	7.938168600	5.658568	9.931715	11.951624	14.619567	14.732171	22.87764	22.53336	25.72053	29.62265
5	0.400014843	13.337330	7.984847	10.583597	18.151797	14.914904	18.23737	21.41147	23.49669	26.56870
6	0.842827341	3.338184	10.976940	10.043226	14.410810	21.004781	21.08666	20.68848	25.37411	28.77236
7	3.215329818	10.602251	11.122269	17.754088	15.913660	14.394352	23.42259	24.89070	28.53676	27.14854
8	5.092451482	9.180472	9.360382	18.056287	18.810285	19.951591	21.50963	19.37048	29.26286	24.12532
9	5.037962926	8.654043	11.238688	11.320735	16.390107	18.304221	24.48018	24.63981	23.24713	26.00143
10	8.307128299	10.360202	7.851721	13.247117	17.318780	16.899383	13.93125	22.31321	27.18642	23.80562
11	5.077739425	9.371812	10.600990	15.584548	14.613774	15.905005	22.36483	23.28086	25.52875	22.31566
12	3.137229831	12.192822	5.635964	13.175608	13.676766	17.664532	20.84425	26.37394	26.57615	22.31213

Showing 1 to 12 of 10,000 entries

Now, create a melted dataset with an arm and reward combination, and then convert the arm column to the nominal type using the following code:

```
# creating a melted dataset with arm and reward combination
dataset_p = melt(dataset)[, 2:3]
colnames(dataset_p) <- c("Bandit", "Reward")
# converting the arms column in the dataset to nominal type
dataset_p$Bandit = as.factor(dataset_p$Bandit)
# viewing the dataset that is just melted
View(dataset_p)
```

This will give us the following output:

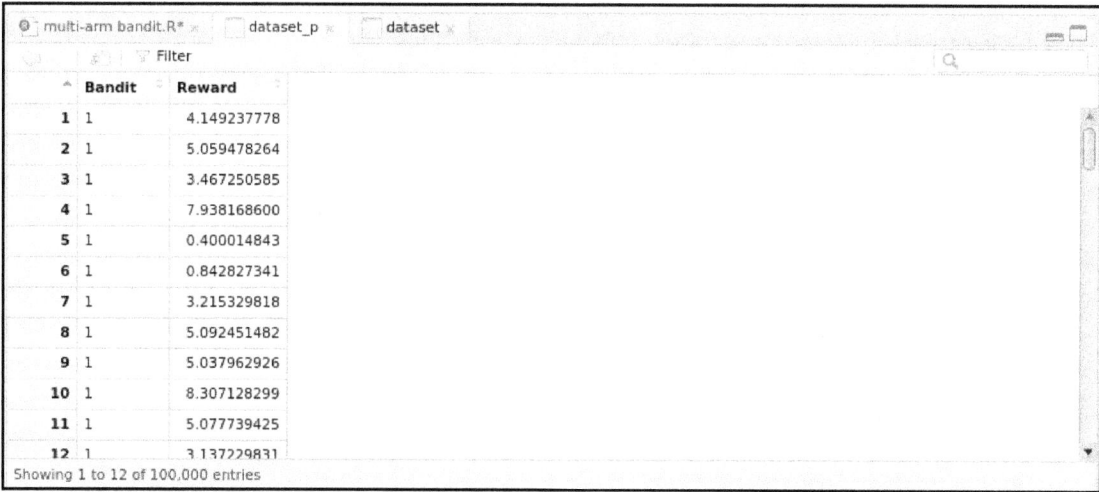

Now, plot the distributions of rewards from bandits using the following code:

```
#ploting the distributions of rewards from bandits
ggplot(dataset_p, aes(x = Reward, col = Bandit, fill = Bandit)) +
    geom_density(alpha = 0.3) +
    labs(title = "Reward from different bandits")
```

This will give us the following output:

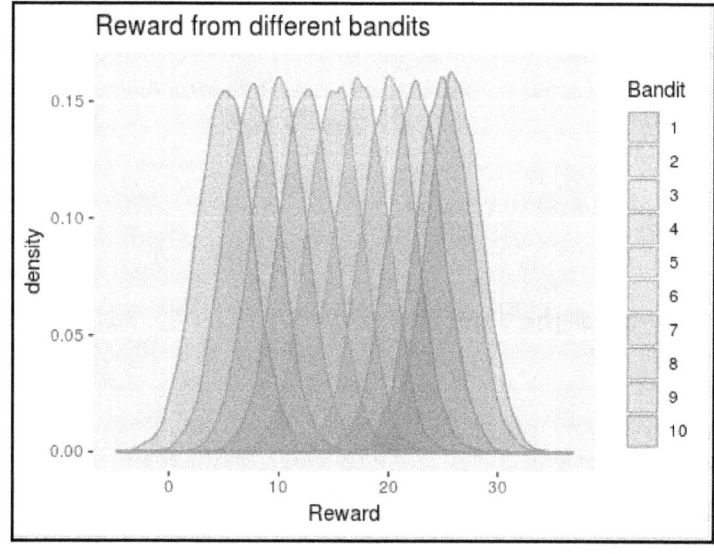

Now let's implement the UCB algorithm on the hypothesized arm with a normal distribution using the following code:

```
# implementing upper confidence bound algorithm
UCB <- function(N = 1000, reward_data){
  d = ncol(reward_data)
  bandit_selected = integer(0)
  numbers_of_selections = integer(d)
  sums_of_rewards = integer(d)
  total_reward = 0
  for (n in 1:N) {
    max_upper_bound = 0
    for (i in 1:d) {
      if (numbers_of_selections[i] > 0){
        average_reward = sums_of_rewards[i] / numbers_of_selections[i]
        delta_i = sqrt(2 * log(1 + n * log(n)^2) /
numbers_of_selections[i])
        upper_bound = average_reward + delta_i
      } else {
        upper_bound = 1e400
      }
      if (upper_bound > max_upper_bound){
        max_upper_bound = upper_bound
        bandit = i
      }
    }
    bandit_selected = append(bandit_selected, bandit)
    numbers_of_selections[bandit] = numbers_of_selections[bandit] + 1
    reward = reward_data[n, bandit]
    sums_of_rewards[bandit] = sums_of_rewards[bandit] + reward
    total_reward = total_reward + reward
  }
  return(list(total_reward = total_reward, bandit_selected bandit_selected,
numbers_of_selections = numbers_of_selections, sums_of_rewards =
sums_of_rewards))
}
# running the UCB algorithm on our
# hypothesized arms with normal distributions
UCB(N = 1000, reward_data = dataset)
```

You will get the following as the resultant output:

```
$total_reward
       1
25836.91
$numbers_of_selections
 [1]   1   1   1   1   1   1   2   1  23 968
$sums_of_rewards
```

```
[1]      4.149238     10.874230      5.998070     11.951624     18.151797
21.004781     44.266832     19.370479    563.001692
[10] 25138.139942
```

Next, we will implement the Thompson sampling algorithm using a **normal-gamma** prior and normal likelihood to estimate posterior distributions using the following code:

```
# Thompson sampling algorithm
rnormgamma <- function(n, mu, lambda, alpha, beta){
  if(length(n) > 1)
    n <- length(n)
  tau <- rgamma(n, alpha, beta)
  x <- rnorm(n, mu, 1 / (lambda * tau))
  data.frame(tau = tau, x = x)
}
T.samp <- function(N = 500, reward_data, mu0 = 0, v = 1, alpha = 2,
beta = 6){
  d = ncol(reward_data)
  bandit_selected = integer(0)
  numbers_of_selections = integer(d)
  sums_of_rewards = integer(d)
  total_reward = 0
  reward_history = vector("list", d)
  for (n in 1:N){
    max_random = -1e400
    for (i in 1:d){
      if(numbers_of_selections[i] >= 1){
        rand = rnormgamma(1,
                          (v * mu0 + numbers_of_selections[i] *
mean(reward_history[[i]])) / (v + numbers_of_selections[i]),
                          v + numbers_of_selections[i],
                          alpha + numbers_of_selections[i] / 2,
                          beta + (sum(reward_history[[i]] -
mean(reward_history[[i]])) ^ 2) / 2 + ((numbers_of_selections[i] * v) / (v
+ numbers_of_selections[i])) * (mean(reward_history[[i]]) - mu0) ^ 2 / 2)$x
      }else {
        rand = rnormgamma(1, mu0, v, alpha, beta)$x
      }
      if(rand > max_random){
        max_random = rand
        bandit = i
      }
    }
    bandit_selected = append(bandit_selected, bandit)
    numbers_of_selections[bandit] = numbers_of_selections[bandit] + 1
    reward = reward_data[n, bandit]
    sums_of_rewards[bandit] = sums_of_rewards[bandit] + reward
    total_reward = total_reward + reward
```

```
    reward_history[[bandit]] = append(reward_history[[bandit]], reward)
  }
  return(list(total_reward = total_reward, bandit_selected =
bandit_selected, numbers_of_selections = numbers_of_selections,
sums_of_rewards = sums_of_rewards))
}
# Applying Thompson sampling using normal-gamma prior and Normal likelihood
to estimate posterior distributions
T.samp(N = 1000, reward_data = dataset, mu0 = 40)
```

You will get the following as the resultant output:

```
$total_reward
      10
24434.24
$numbers_of_selections
 [1]  16  15  15  14  14  17  16  19  29 845
$sums_of_rewards
 [1]     80.22713    110.09657    141.14346    171.41301    212.86899
293.30138    311.12230    423.93256    713.54105 21976.59855
```

From the results, we can infer that the UCB algorithm quickly identified that the 10th arm yields the most reward. We also observe that Thompson sampling tried the worst arms a lot more times before finding the best one.

Now, let's simulate the data of bandits with normally distributed rewards with large variance and plot the distributions of rewards by using the following code:

```
# Distribution of bandits / actions having normally distributed rewards
with large variance
# This data represents an ideal but more unstable situation: normally
distributed rewards with much larger variance,
# thus not well separated from each other.
mean_reward = c(5, 7.5, 10, 12.5, 15, 17.5, 20, 22.5, 25, 26)
reward_dist = c(function(n) rnorm(n = n, mean = mean_reward[1], sd = 20),
                function(n) rnorm(n = n, mean = mean_reward[2], sd = 20),
                function(n) rnorm(n = n, mean = mean_reward[3], sd = 20),
                function(n) rnorm(n = n, mean = mean_reward[4], sd = 20),
                function(n) rnorm(n = n, mean = mean_reward[5], sd = 20),
                function(n) rnorm(n = n, mean = mean_reward[6], sd = 20),
                function(n) rnorm(n = n, mean = mean_reward[7], sd = 20),]
                function(n) rnorm(n = n, mean = mean_reward[8], sd = 20),
                function(n) rnorm(n = n, mean = mean_reward[9], sd = 20),
                function(n) rnorm(n = n, mean = mean_reward[10], sd = 20))
#preparing simulation data
dataset = matrix(nrow = 10000, ncol = 10)
for(i in 1:10){
  dataset[, i] = reward_dist[[i]](n = 10000)
```

```
}
colnames(dataset) <- 1:10
dataset_p = melt(dataset)[, 2:3]
colnames(dataset_p) <- c("Bandit", "Reward")
dataset_p$Bandit = as.factor(dataset_p$Bandit)
#plotting the distributions of rewards from bandits
ggplot(dataset_p, aes(x = Reward, col = Bandit, fill = Bandit)) +
  geom_density(alpha = 0.3) +
  labs(title = "Reward from different bandits")
```

You will get the following graph as the resultant output:

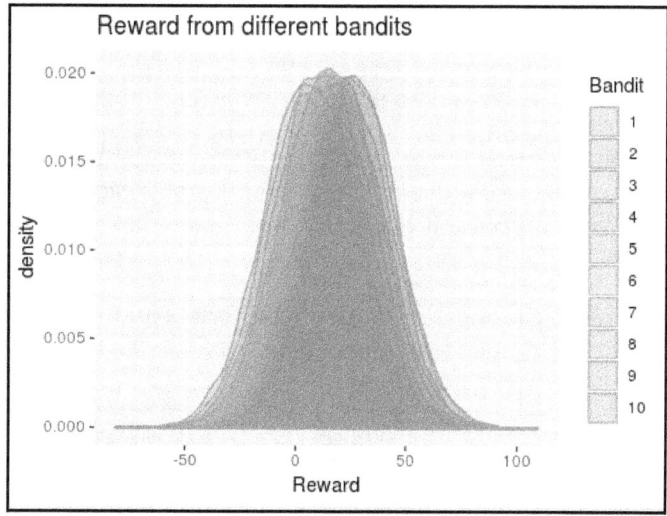

Apply UCB on rewards with higher variance using the following code:

```
# Applying UCB on rewards with higher variance
UCB(N = 1000, reward_data = dataset)
```

You will get the following output:

```
$total_reward
       1
25321.39
$numbers_of_selections
 [1]   1   1   1   3   1   1   2   6 903  81
$sums_of_rewards
 [1]     2.309649    -6.982907   -24.654597    49.186498     8.367174
-16.211632    31.243270   104.190075 23559.216706  1614.725305
```

Next, apply Thompson sampling on rewards with higher variance by using the following code:

```
# Applying Thompson sampling on rewards with higher variance
T.samp(N = 1000, reward_data = dataset, mu0 = 40)
```

You will get the following output:

```
$total_reward
       2
24120.94
$numbers_of_selections
 [1]   16   15   14   15   15   17   20   21 849   18
$sums_of_rewards
 [1]    94.27878    81.42390   212.00717   181.46489   140.43908
249.82014   368.52864   397.07629 22090.20740 305.69191
```

From the results, we can infer that when the fluctuation of rewards is greater, the UCB algorithm is more susceptible to being stuck at a suboptimal choice and never finds the optimal bandit. Thompson sampling is generally more robust and is able to find the optimal bandit in all kinds of situations.

Now let's simulate the more chaotic distribution bandit data and plot the distribution of rewards from bandits by using the following code:

```
# Distribution of bandits / actions with rewards of different distributions
# This data represents an more chaotic (possibly more realistic) situation:
# rewards with different distribution and different variance.
mean_reward = c(5, 7.5, 10, 12.5, 15, 17.5, 20, 22.5, 25, 26)
reward_dist = c(function(n) rnorm(n = n, mean = mean_reward[1], sd = 20),
                function(n) rgamma(n = n, shape = mean_reward[2] / 2, rate
                = 0.5),
                function(n) rpois(n = n, lambda = mean_reward[3]),
                function(n) runif(n = n, min = mean_reward[4] - 20, max =
mean_reward[4] + 20),
                function(n) rlnorm(n = n, meanlog = log(mean_reward[5]) -
0.25, sdlog = 0.5),
                function(n) rnorm(n = n, mean = mean_reward[6], sd = 20),
                function(n) rexp(n = n, rate = 1 / mean_reward[7]),
                function(n) rbinom(n = n, size = mean_reward[8] / 0.5, prob
= 0.5),
                function(n) rnorm(n = n, mean = mean_reward[9], sd = 20),
                function(n) rnorm(n = n, mean = mean_reward[10], sd = 20))
#preparing simulation data
dataset = matrix(nrow = 10000, ncol = 10)
for(i in 1:10){
  dataset[, i] = reward_dist[[i]](n = 10000)
}
```

```
colnames(dataset) <- 1:10
dataset_p = melt(dataset)[, 2:3]
colnames(dataset_p) <- c("Bandit", "Reward")
dataset_p$Bandit = as.factor(dataset_p$Bandit)
#plotting the distributions of rewards from bandits
ggplot(dataset_p, aes(x = Reward, col = Bandit, fill = Bandit)) +
  geom_density(alpha = 0.3) +
  labs(title = "Reward from different bandits")
```

You will get the following graph as the resultant output:

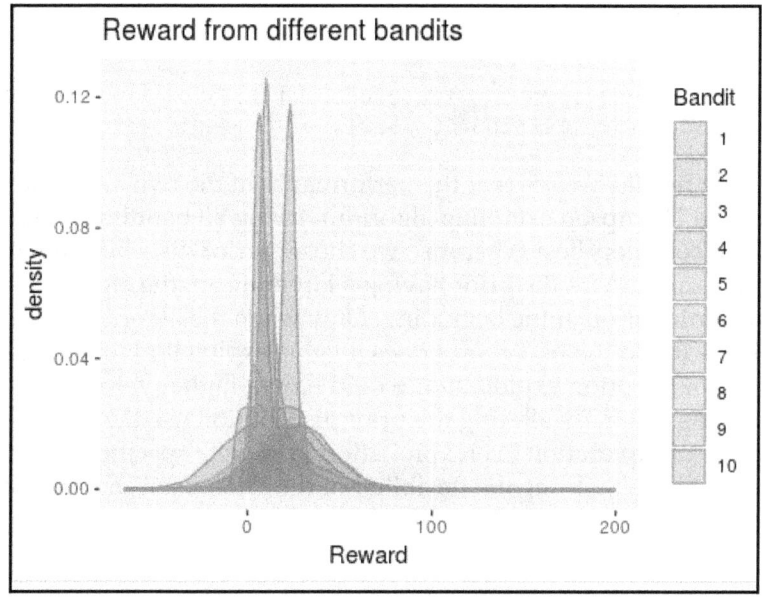

Apply UCB on rewards with different distributions by using the following code:

```
# Applying UCB on rewards with different distributions
UCB(N = 1000, reward_data = dataset)
```

You will get the following output:

```
$total_reward
       1
22254.18
$numbers_of_selections
 [1]    1   1   1   1   1   1   1 926  61   6
$sums_of_rewards
 [1]      6.810026      3.373098      8.000000     12.783859     12.858791
11.835287      1.616978 20755.000000 1324.564987   117.335467
```

Next, apply Thompson sampling on rewards with different distributions by using the following code:

```
# Applying Thompson sampling on rewards with different distributions
T.samp(N = 1000, reward_data = dataset, mu0 = 40)
```

You will get the following as the resultant output:

```
$total_reward
       2
24014.36
$numbers_of_selections
 [1]   16   14   14   14   14   15   14   51  214  634
$sums_of_rewards
 [1]    44.37095    127.57153    128.00000    142.66207    191.44695
169.10430    150.19486   1168.00000   5201.69130  16691.32118
```

From the preceding results, we see that the performance of the two algorithms is similar. A major reason for the Thompson sampling algorithm trying all bandits several times before choosing the one it considers best is because we chose a prior distribution with a relatively high mean in this project. With the prior having a larger mean, the algorithm favors **exploration overexploitation** at the beginning. Only when the algorithm becomes very confident that it has found the best choice does it value exploitation over exploration. If we decrease the mean of the prior, exploitation would have a higher value and the algorithm would stop exploring faster. By altering the prior distribution used, you can adjust the relative importance of exploration overexploitation to suit the specific problem at hand. This is more evidence highlighting the flexibility of the Thompson sampling algorithm.

Summary

In this chapter, we learned about RL. We started the chapter by defining RL and its difference when compared with other ML techniques. We then reviewed the details of the MABP and looked at the various strategies that can be used to solve this problem. Use cases that are similar to the MABP were discussed. Finally, a project was implemented with UCB and Thompson sampling algorithms to solve the MABP using three different simulated datasets.

We have almost reached the end of this book. The appendix of this book, *The Road Ahead*, as the name reflects, is a guidance chapter suggesting details on what's next from here to become a better R data scientist. I am super excited that I am at the last leg of this R projects journey. Are you with me on this as well?

Creating a Package

We are going to conclude this book by going through the process to create your own R package. If you are doing so, I recommend you start. I've put most of the functionality of data preparation from Chapter 1, *Preparing and Understanding Data*, into my own package. I'm not planning on putting it on CRAN, nor any package for that matter, with probably the exception of a package of American Civil War data like the Gettysburg file. So why bother with creating a package? If you are going to create code and put it into production, why would you not create a package with version control, examples, and other features? Plus, with RStudio, it is easy to do. So, we will use a simple example with one small function to show how easy it is.

Creating a new package

Before getting started, you will need to load two packages:

```
> install.packages("roxygen2")

> install.packages("devtools")
```

You now want to open **File** in RStudio and select **New Project**, which will put you at this point:

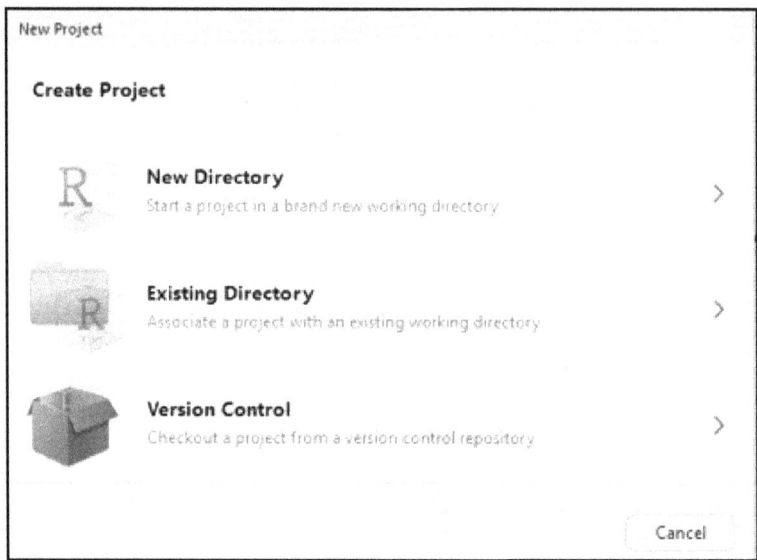

Select a new directory as desired, and specify **R Package**, as shown in the following screenshot:

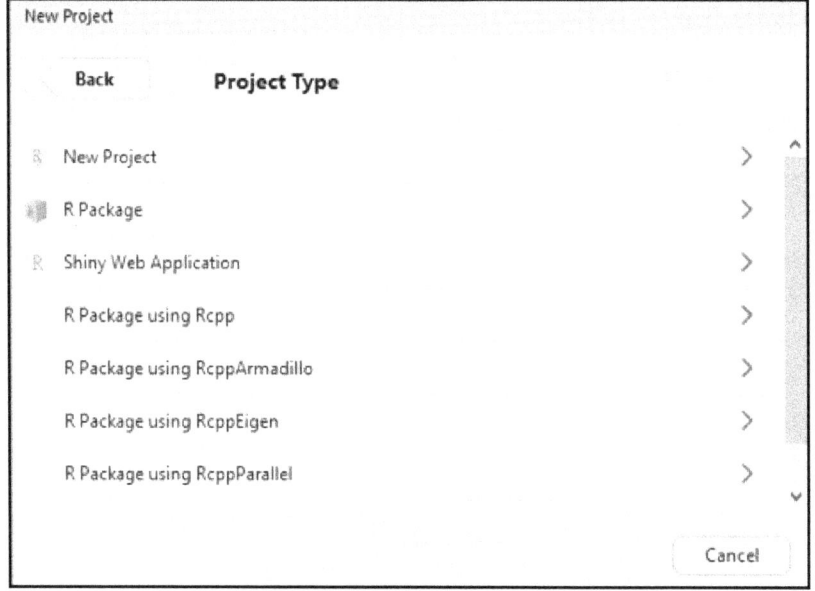

You will now name your package – I've innovatively called this one **package** – and select **Create Project**:

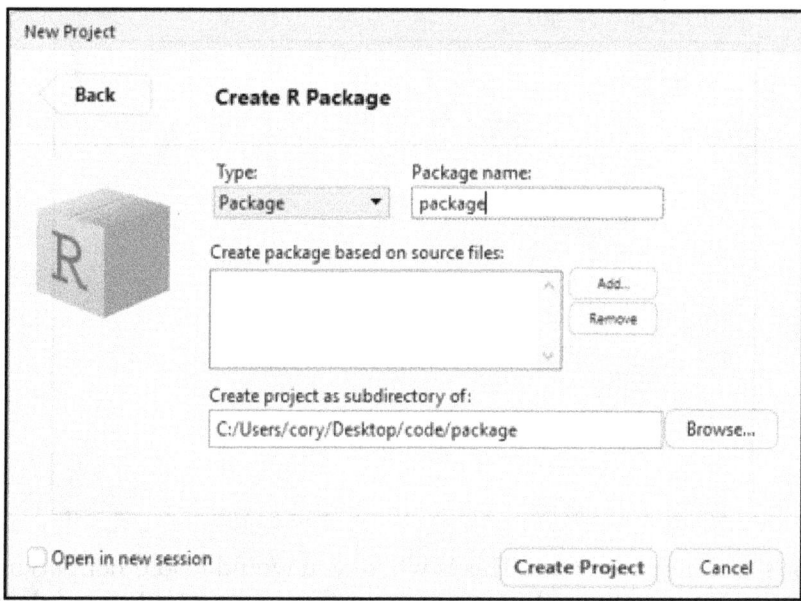

Go to your **Files** tab in RStudio and you should see several files populated like this:

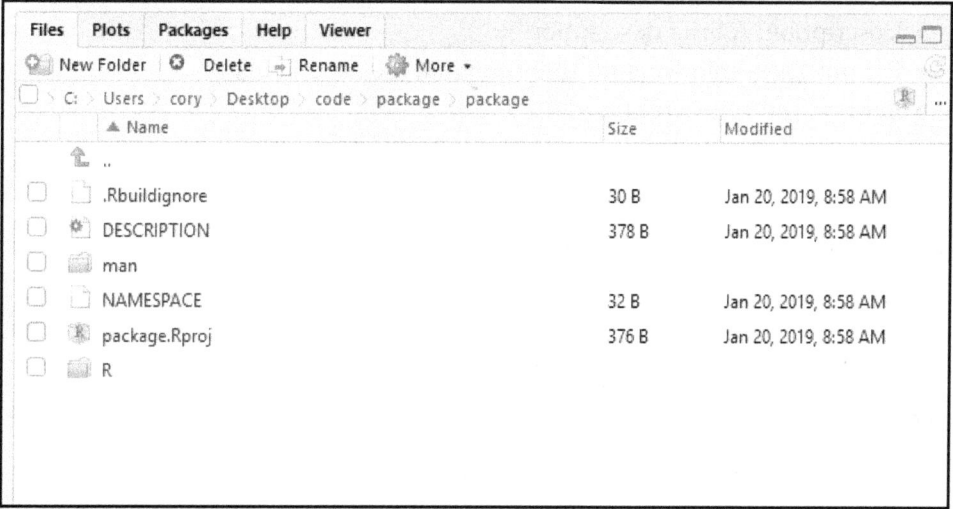

Notice the folder called R. That is where we will put the R functions for our package. But first, click on **Description** and fill it out accordingly, and save it. Here is my version, which will be a function to code all missing values in a dataframe to zero:

I've left imports and suggests blank. This is where you would load other packages, such as tidyverse or caret. Now, open up the `hello.R` function in the R folder, and delete all of it. The following format will work nicely:

- Title: Your package title of course
- Description: A brief description
- Param: The parameters for that function; the arguments
- Return: The values returned
- Examples: Provide any examples of how to use the function
- Export: Here, write the function you desire

Here is the function for our purposes, which just turns all NAs to zero:

```
#' @title package
#'
#' @description Turns NAs in a dataframe into zeroes
#'
#' @param dataframe
#'
#' @return dataframe
#'
#' @examples
#' dataset <- matrix(sample(c(NA, 1:5), 25, replace = TRUE), 5)
```

```
#' df <- as.data.frame(dataset)
#' package::na2zero(df)
#'
#' @export

na2zero <- function(dataframe)
{
 dataframe[is.na(dataframe)] <- 0
 return(dataframe)
}
```

You will now go to **Build - Configure Build Tools** and you should end up here:

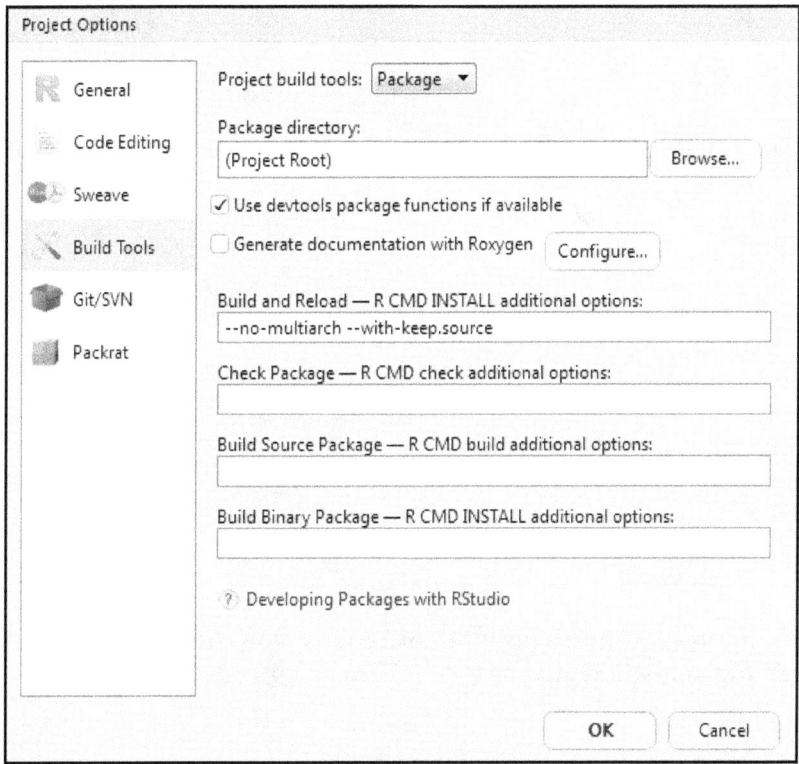

Click the checkmark for **Generate documentation with Roxygen**. Doing so will create this popup, which you can close and hit OK. You probably want to rename your function now from `hello.R` to something relevant. Now comes the moment of truth to build your package. Do this by clicking **Build - Clean and Rebuild**.

Now you can search for your package, and it should appear:

Click on it and go through the documentation:

There you have it, a useless package, but think of what you can do by packaging your own or your favorite functions, and anyone who inherits your code will thank you.

Summary

In this final chapter, we went through the process of creating an R package, which can help you and your team put your code into production. We created one user-defined function for our package, but your only limit is your imagination. That concludes the primary chapters of the book. I hope you've enjoyed it and can implement the methods in here, as well as other methods you learn over time. Thank You!

Other Books You May Enjoy

If you enjoyed this book, you may be interested in these other books by Packt:

Machine Learning with R Cookbook - Second Edition
AshishSingh Bhatia, Yu-Wei, Chiu (David Chiu), Recommended for You

ISBN: 9781787284395

- Create and inspect transaction datasets and perform association analysis with the Apriori algorithm
- Visualize patterns and associations using a range of graphs and find frequent item-sets using the Eclat algorithm
- Compare differences between each regression method to discover how they solve problems
- Detect and impute missing values in air quality data
- Predict possible churn users with the classification approach
- Plot the autocorrelation function with time series analysis
- Use the Cox proportional hazards model for survival analysis
- Implement the clustering method to segment customer data
- Compress images with the dimension reduction method
- Incorporate R and Hadoop to solve machine learning problems on big data

Machine Learning Algorithms - Second Edition
Giuseppe Bonaccorso

ISBN: 9781789347999

- Study feature selection and the feature engineering process
- Assess performance and error trade-offs for linear regression
- Build a data model and understand how it works by using different types of algorithm
- Learn to tune the parameters of Support Vector Machines (SVM)
- Explore the concept of natural language processing (NLP) and recommendation systems
- Create a machine learning architecture from scratch

R Deep Learning Essentials - Second Edition

Mark Hodnett, Joshua F. Wiley

ISBN: 9781788992893

- Build shallow neural network prediction models
- Prevent models from overfitting the data to improve generalizability
- Explore techniques for finding the best hyperparameters for deep learning models
- Create NLP models using Keras and TensorFlow in R
- Use deep learning for computer vision tasks
- Implement deep learning tasks, such as NLP, recommendation systems, and autoencoders

Leave a review - let other readers know what you think

Please share your thoughts on this book with others by leaving a review on the site that you bought it from. If you purchased the book from Amazon, please leave us an honest review on this book's Amazon page. This is vital so that other potential readers can see and use your unbiased opinion to make purchasing decisions, we can understand what our customers think about our products, and our authors can see your feedback on the title that they have worked with Packt to create. It will only take a few minutes of your time, but is valuable to other potential customers, our authors, and Packt. Thank you!

Index

A

adaptive boosting (AdaBoost) 392
agent 608
agglomerative nesting (AGNES) algorithm
  about 478
  customer segmentation, identifying in wholesale
    customers data 496, 497, 500, 501
Aikake's Information Criterion (AIC) 265
Alexa 333
Amazon reviews dataset
  about 438
  reference 438
  using 438, 439, 440, 442
Apache Incubator
  reference 511
Apache MXNet
  using 504
Apriori algorithm
  about 420, 423, 424, 425, 426, 427
  frequent itemset 421
  item 420
  itemset 420
  itemset support, in context 421
  support 421
  support count 421
area under the curve (AUC) 76, 143, 319
area under the curve of the receiver operating
  characteristic (AUROC) 349
Artificial Intelligence (AI) 329, 331, 538, 606
artificial neural network (ANN) 344, 505, 541
artificial neural networks (ANNs)
  about 162
  reference 162
aspect based sentiment analysis 437
association analysis
  about 243, 244

data 246
data, preparing 247, 249
evaluation process 249, 251, 253, 254
modeling process 249, 251, 253, 254
transactional data, creating 245, 246
association-rule mining
  about 337, 419
  Apriori algorithm 420, 421, 423, 424, 425, 426,
    427
  recommendation system, building with 419
attrition prediction model
  building, with extreme gradient boosting
    (XGBoost) 394, 395
  building, with stacking 396, 397, 398
  implementing, with gradient boosting machine
    (GBM) 392, 394
  implementing, with random forests 390, 391
attrition
  dataset 366, 368, 370, 371, 373, 374, 375,
    377, 378, 379, 380, 381
  problem 366, 368, 370, 371, 373, 374, 375,
    377, 378, 379, 380, 381
Augmented Dickey-Fuller (ADF) 271, 284
Autocorrelation Function (ACF) 257
autoencoders (AEs), based on hidden layers
  architecture 543
  over complete autoencoders 542
  under complete autoencoders 542
autoencoders (AEs), based on restrictions
  about 543
  convolutional autoencoders 544
  denoising autoencoders 543
  plain Vanilla autoencoders 543
  sparse autoencoders 543
  stacked autoencoders 544
  variational autoencoder (VAE) 544
autoencoders (AEs)

about 344, 540, 541, 542
applications 545, 546
architecture 541
building, with H2O library in R 547, 548
code implementation, for credit card fraud
detection 548, 549, 550, 551, 552, 553, 554,
555, 556, 558, 559, 560, 561, 562, 563, 565,
566, 567, 568, 570, 571
automated prose generator
building, with RNN 587, 588, 590, 591, 592,
593
project, implementing 593, 594, 595, 596, 597,
599, 601, 602, 603
Automated Readability Index (ARI) 325
Autoregressive Integrated Moving Average
(ARIMA) model 256

B

backpropagation 162
backpropagation through time (BPTT) 583, 584
Bag of Words (BoW) 436
bandit 611
batch mode 359
Bayesian optimization-based hyperparameter
tuning 352
Bernoulli 612
big data 345
Boltzmann exploration 616
boosting 391, 392
bootstrap aggregation 136
bootstrap aggregation (bagging)
about 384, 385, 386
bagged classification and regression trees
(treeBag), implementing 386, 387
naive Bayes (nbBag) bagging, implementing
388, 389
support vector machine bagging (SVMBag),
implementing 387, 388
bootstrapping with replacement 384
BoW approach
cons 449
pros 449
text sentiment classifier, building with 443, 444,
445, 447, 448, 449

C

Carbon Dioxide Information Analysis Center
(CDIAC) 266
categorical variables
exploring 15, 17
central processing unit (CPU) 505
centroid 484
class imbalance problem 348, 546
classification 336
classification and regression trees (CART) 336,
385
classification methods 62
classification model
creating 316
creating, with LASSO 318, 319
feature, creating with text2vec package 316, 318
feature, modeling with text2vec package 316,
318
classification tree
about 135
building, with simulated data 138, 140, 142, 144
cluster analysis 194, 473
cluster quality 487
clustering 337, 473
clustering algorithms
categories 478
flat or partitioning algorithms 478
hierarchical algorithms 478
clustering tendency 477
Cohen's Kappa statistic 72, 117
collaborative filtering
about 404
memory-based 405
model-based 405
computer vision
about 345, 504, 505
applications 504
implementing, with pretrained model 532, 533,
534, 535, 536
with deep learning 505, 506
confusion matrix 346
consolidated learning 365
content-based filtering 404
content-based recommendation engine
about 427, 429

versus item-based collaborative filtering (ITCF)
430
Continuous Bag of Words (CBOW) 450
convolutional autoencoders 544
Convolutional Neural Network (CNN) 344, 506
Convolutional Neural Network (CNN), layers
  about 507
  convolution 507
  fully-connected layer 509
  max pooling 508
  Rectified Linear Unit (ReLU) 508
  sigmoid 510
  softmax 509
convolutional neural networks (CNN) 170
Cook's D 38
correlation 23, 26
cost function 346
credit card fraud dataset
  about 546, 547
  characteristics 546
  reference 546
credit card fraud detection
  autoencoder code, implementation 548, 549,
    550, 551, 552, 553, 554, 555, 556, 558, 559,
    560, 561, 562, 563, 565, 566, 567, 568, 570,
    571
  with machine learning 538, 539, 540
Cross-Correlation Function (CCF) 270
cross-entropy 163
cross-industry standard process for data mining
  (CRISP-DM) 355
CRUTEM4 266
curse of dimensionality 219
customer segmentation, data points
  behavioral 472
  demographics 472
  psychographics 472
customer segmentation
  about 472, 473, 474
  identifying, in wholesale customer data with
    DIANA 490, 491, 492, 493, 495, 496
  identifying, in wholesale customer data with k-
    means clustering 479, 480, 481, 483, 484
  identifying, in wholesale customers data with
    AGNES 496, 497, 499, 500, 501

objectives 473
problem 474, 475, 476, 478
wholesale customer dataset 474, 475, 476, 478

D

data analytics 331
data cleansing
  techniques 357
data frame
  creating 297, 298
data mining 331
data preprocessing 350
data science 332
data science professional, skills
  Hacking Skills 332
  Math & Statistic Knowledge 332
  Substantive Expertise 332
data
  about 185, 186, 201
  creating 111, 113
  manipulating 111
  overview 297
  preparing 114, 116, 201
  reading 11, 13
  treating 21, 22, 23
dataset
  about 201
  creating 88, 90
datasets 361
decayed epsilon greedy 616
decoder 540
deep belief networks (DBNs) 344
deep deterministic policy gradient (DDPG) 341
deep learning model
  building 176
  data, loading 177
  functions, creating 178, 180
  learning 180, 182
deep learning network
  dropout, implementing to avoid overfitting 522,
    524, 525, 526, 527
  implementing, for handwritten digit recognition
    515, 516, 517, 519, 520, 522
  LeNet architecture, implementing with MXNet
    library 527, 529, 530, 531

deep learning
  about 167, 344, 505, 608
  Convolutional Neural Network (CNN) 506
  methods 169, 170
  resources 169, 170
  used, for computer vision 505, 506
deep Q network (DQN) 341
dense layer 509
descriptive statistics 14, 15
dimensionality reduction 347
Dirichlet distribution 294
distance calculations 196
DIvisive ANAlysis (DIANA)
  about 478, 490
  customer segmentation, identifying in wholesale
    customer data 490, 491, 492, 493, 495, 496
divisive hierarchical clustering 490
Document Term Matrix (DTM) 444
document-term matrix (DTM) 294
dropout 167, 350, 522
Duan's Smearing Estimator 56
duplicate observations
  handling 13
dynamic topic modeling 295
dynamic treatment regime (DTR) 341

E

eigenvalue 222
eigenvectors 222
elastic net
  about 88
  evaluation process 99, 101, 103, 104
  modeling process 99, 101, 103, 104
Elbow method 478
encoder 540
ensemble 365
ensembles
  about 184, 185
  creating 190, 191
ensembling
  about 363
  philosophy 364, 365, 366
environment 608
epsilon-greedy algorithm 615
equimax 223

equivalence class transformation (ECLAT) 337,
  420
Euclidean distance 107, 195
exploding gradients
  about 585
  problem, handling 585
exploitation 611
exploration
  about 611
  selecting, over exploitation 628
exploratory data analysis (EDA) 331, 357, 406,
  474
exponential smoothing 256
extreme gradient boosting (XGBoost)
  about 392
  attrition prediction model, building 394, 395
eXtreme Gradient Boosting
  about 137
  reference 137
  working 152, 153, 155, 157

F

F-Measure 296
False Positive Rate (FPR) 81
fastText
  text sentiment classifier, building 462, 463, 465,
    466, 467, 468
feature engineering 352
feedforward network 162
feedforward neural network
  versus recurrent neural networks (RNNs) 581,
    582, 583
Final Prediction Error (FPE) 265
frequency pattern growth (FPG) 337, 420
fully-connected layer 509

G

gated recurrent units (GRUs) 585
Generalized Cross Validation (GCV) 52, 79
Generalized Linear Model (GLM) 72
generalized weights 174
generative adversarial networks (GANs) 339, 344
Gini index 135
GloVe word embedding
  text sentiment classifier, building with 458, 459,

460, 461, 462
Google Allo 333
Google Home 333
Google Now 333
Gower dissimilarity coefficient 197, 198
gradient boosted trees 133
gradient boosting machine (GBM) 392
Gradient boosting
  about 137
  reference 137
gradient clipping 585
gradients
  about 585
  exploding gradients 585
  problems and solutions 585
  vanishing gradients 585
Granger causality 264, 265
graphical processing unit (GPU) 505, 593
grid search 352
Gutenberg
  about 588
  reference 588

H

H2O library
  autoencoders, building in R 547, 548
h2o package
  reference 547
HadCRUT4 265
HadSST3 266
handwritten digit recognition
  deep learning network, implementing 515, 516,
    517, 519, 520, 522
Hannan-Quinn Criterion (HQ) 285
Hartigan-Wong algorithm 479
heavy-tailed 49
heteroscedasticity 36
hierarchical algorithms
  about 478
  agglomerative type 478
  divisive type 478
hierarchical clustering
  about 194, 195, 204, 206, 208, 210, 211, 212
  distance calculations 196
high-quality clusters 487

holdout sample 351
Holt-Winters method 257
hybrid filtering 405
hybrid recommendation engine
  combination strategies 431
hybrid recommendation system
  building, for Jokes recommendation 430, 431,
    432, 433
hyperparameter tuning 351

I

identity function 543
immediate reward 612
independent variables 347
Information Value (IV) 66, 68
item-based collaborative filtering (ITCF)
  about 411
  item-based similarities, computing through
    distance measure 412
  recommendation system, building with 411, 412,
    414
  targeted item rating for specific user, predicting
    413
  top N items, recommending 413
  versus content-based recommendation engine
    429, 430
itemset 420

J

Jokes recommendation
  DataFrame, converting 409
  DataFrame, dividing 410
  dataset 405, 407, 408, 409
  hybrid recommendation system, building for 430,
    431, 432, 433
  problem 405, 407, 408, 409

K

k-fold cross validation 350
k-means clustering 194, 197, 212, 214
  customer segmentation, identifying in wholesale
    customer data 479, 480, 481, 483, 484
  execution 485, 487, 488, 489
K-Nearest Neighbors (KNN) 105, 106, 107
k-nearest neighbors (KNN)

about 336, 381, 416
performance, benchmarking 381, 383, 384
k-value, determining
with direct methods 479
with testing methods 479
Keras
about 176, 177
reference 176
kernel trick 109
KNN modeling 117, 119, 121, 123, 125
Kwiatkowski, Philips, Schmidt & Shin (KPSS) 284

L

L1-norm 87
L2-norm 87
language models
about 573, 574, 575, 576
machine translation 575
spelling correction 575
LASSO
about 87
evaluation process 96, 97, 99
modeling process 96, 97, 99
used, for creating classification model 318, 319
Latent Dirichlet Allocation (LDA) 294
latent space representation 540
lazy learning 106
learning by coding 360
learning paradigm 360
LeNet 503
LeNet architecture
about 527
implementing, with MXNet library 527, 529, 530, 531
lexicon method 437
light gradient boosting machine (LightGBM) 392
likelihood 63
Lincoln's word frequency 301, 304, 305
linear combination 220
linear regression 29, 62
linearity 23, 26
Lloyd and Forgy algorithm 479
locally-optimal solution 486
logistic regression 62, 63
logistic regression algorithm

cross-validation, used for building model 71, 73, 74, 76
Information Value (IV) 66, 68
Information Value (IV), used for selecting feature 68, 70
training 64, 66
Weight Of Evidence (WOE) 66, 68
logits 94
long short-term memory (LSTM) 170, 586, 587
long-term memory 587
loss function 137

M

machine learning (ML) 134
about 329, 331
in credit card fraud detection 538, 539, 540
versus software engineering 329, 330, 331, 332, 333
MacQueen algorithm 479
MapReduce 345
margin 108
market-basket analysis 419
Markov Assumption 575
Markov chain methods 339
Markov Property 575
max pooling 508
Mean Squared Error (MSE) 352, 542
mean-squared-error (MSE) 179
medoid 199
Mining Association Rules and Frequent Itemsets 244
missing values
handling 17, 19
ML methods, types
about 334
reinforcement learning 339, 340
semi-supervised learning 338, 339
supervised learning 334, 335, 336
transfer learning 341, 342, 343
unsupervised learning 336, 337, 338
ML project, pipeline
about 354
business understanding 355
data, preparing 356, 357
data, sourcing 355

data, understanding 355
model deployment 358, 360
model evaluation 358
model, building 358
ML terminology
big data 345
class imbalance problem 348
computer vision 345
confusion matrix 346
cost function 346
data preprocessing 350
deep learning 344
dimensionality reduction 347
feature engineering 352
holdout sample 351
hyperparameter tuning 351
model accuracy 346
model bias 349
model variance 349
model, interpretability 353, 354
natural language processing (NLP) 345
overfitting 349, 350
performance metrics 352
predictor variables 347
response variable 347
reviewing 344
underfitting 349, 350
MNIST dataset
reference 511, 515
using 511, 512, 513, 514
model 335
model accuracy 346
model assumptions, univariate linear regression
homoscedasticity 36
linearity 36
no collinearity 36
non-correlation of errors 36
presence of outliers 37
model bias 349
model variance 349
models, text mining framework
topic models 294
modes, model deployment
batch mode 359
real-time mode 359

monetary units (m.u.) 474
multi-arm bandit problem (MABP)
about 610, 611, 613
Boltzmann exploration 616
decayed epsilon greedy 616
epsilon-greedy algorithm 615
real-world use cases 618
solving, with strategies 614, 615
solving, with with UCB and Thompson sampling
algorithms 619, 620, 621, 622, 624, 625, 626,
627, 628
Thompson sampling 618
upper confidence bound (UCB) algorithm 616,
617
multicollinearity 347, 370
multilayered neural networks 505
Multivariate Adaptive Regression Splines (MARS)
about 39
evolution 77, 79, 81
training 77, 79, 81
multivariate linear regress
reverse transformation, of natural log predictions
58
multivariate linear regression
about 38
data, loading 39, 41, 42, 44, 45
data, preparing 39, 41, 42, 44, 45
MARS, evaluation process 52, 53, 55
MARS, modeling process 52, 53, 55, 56
reverse transformation, of natural log predictions
56
stepwise regression, evaluation process 46, 47,
49, 51
stepwise regression, modeling process 46, 47,
49, 51
multivariate normality 220
MXNet framework 510
MXNet library
LeNet architecture, implementing 527, 529, 530,
531

N

n-grams 309, 311
Naive Bayes 447
naive Bayes (nbBag) bagging

implementation 388, 389
Natick Soldier Research, Development and
    Engineering Center (NSRDEC) 225
natural language processing (NLP) 343, 345
natural log predictions
    reverse transformation 56, 58
near-zero variance 19, 21
network architecture 515
neural networks
    about 162, 164, 166
    creating 171
    data 171, 173
    data preparation 171, 173
    model, building 173, 175
    model, evaluation 173, 175
non-globally-optimal solution 486
normal-gamma prior 623
null function 543

O

object-oriented programming (OOP) 341
one-class classification algorithm 539
Ordinary Least Squares (OLS) 61
out-of-bag (oob) 136
outlier detection
    drawbacks 538
over complete autoencoders 542
overfitting
    about 349, 350, 385, 522
    avoiding, with dropout 522, 524, 525, 526, 527

P

PAM clustering algorithm
    about 197, 198, 199
    Gower dissimilarity coefficient 215, 216
    random forest 216, 218
Part-of-Speech (POS) tagger 435
Partial Autocorrelation Function (PACF) 259
partial dependency plot (PDP) 354
partitioning around medoids (PAM) 194
PCA modeling
    about 231
    component extraction 231, 232, 233
    interpretation 234
    orthogonal rotation 234

regression, with MARS 236, 237, 238, 239, 240
scores, creating from components 235, 236
test data evaluation 240, 241
penalty 607
performance metrics 352
personalized content recommendation
    archiving 402, 403
Philips-Peron (PP) 284
polarity 295
policy gradients method 607
predictor variables 347
pretrained models
    computer vision, implementing 532, 533, 534,
        535, 536
    Google's Word2Vec model 344
    inception-V3 model 343
    MobileNet 344
    reference 532
    Stanford's GloVe model 344
    VCG 16 344
    VCG Face 344
pretrained Word2vec word embedding
    text sentiment classifier, building with 453, 455,
        456, 457, 458
principal component analysis (PCA) 348, 484
principal components analysis (PCA)
    about 197, 219
    data, loading 226
    data, preparing 225
    data, reviewing 227, 228
    testing datasets 229, 230
    training datasets 229, 230
principal components
    overview 220, 221, 222
    rotation 223, 224

Q

Quantile-Quantile (Q-Q) 38
quantitative analysis 295, 296, 320, 322, 325,
    327
quartimax 223

R

R-squared 29
R

autoencoders, building with H2O library 547, 548

radical 293

random forest model
  evaluation process 187, 189, 190
  modeling process 187, 189, 190

random forest
  about 133, 136, 137, 200, 201
  used, for feature selection method 144, 146, 149, 151, 157, 159

random forests
  attrition prediction model, implementing 390, 391
  for randomization 389

real-time mode 359

Receiver Operating Characteristic (ROC) chart
  used, for model comparison 81, 82

recommendation engine, categories
  about 404
  collaborative filtering 404
  content-based filtering 404
  hybrid filtering 405

recommendation engine
  fundamental aspects 402, 403

recommendation system
  building, with association-rule mining 419
  building, with item-based collaborative filtering (ITCF) 411, 412, 414
  building, with user-based collaborative filtering (UBCF) 415, 416, 419

Recommender function, parameter
  data normalization 411
  distance 411

Rectified Linear Unit (ReLU) 508

recurrent neural networks (RNN) 170

recurrent neural networks (RNNs)
  about 344, 577
  automated prose generator, building 587, 588, 590, 591, 592, 593
  exploring 577, 578, 579, 580
  gradients, problems and solutions 585
  text, generating 602
  versus feedforward neural network 581, 582, 583

Recursive Feature Elimination (RFE) 117

recursive partitioning 134

regression 336

regression tree 134, 135

regret 613

regularization
  about 167
  overview 86

reinforcement learning (RL), terminology
  about 610
  action 609
  agent 609
  environment 609
  penalty 609
  policy 609
  return 609
  reward 609
  state 609

reinforcement learning (RL)
  about 339, 340, 606, 607
  comparing, with other ML algorithms 608
  multi-arm bandit problem (MABP) 610, 611, 613, 614
  use cases 341

Residual Sum of Squares (RSS) 30

response variable 347

restricted Boltzmann machine
  about 168
  reference 168

reward 607

ridge regression
  about 87
  evaluation process 91, 93, 94, 95
  modeling process 91, 93, 94, 95

Root Mean Square Error (RMSE) 47

root mean squared error (RMSE) 352

S

Schwarz-Bayes Criterion (SC) 285

segmentation 471

semi-supervised support vector machines (S3VMs) 339

sentiment analysis 306, 308
  about 437
  problem 437

serial correlation 282

Shapley additive explanations (SHAP) 354

short-term memory 587
shrinkage penalty 86
sigmoid 510
Silhouette index 488
Siri 333
Skip-Gram 450
softmax 509
softmax exploration 616
software engineering
    versus machine learning (ML) 329, 330, 331,
      332, 333
sparse coding model
    about 168
    reference 168
stacking 183
    about 395
    attrition prediction model, building with 396, 397,
      398
state 608
state-action-reward-state-action (SARSA) 341
stratified holdout sample 351
Subject Matter Experts (SMEs) 11
sum of squared error (SSE) 163, 256
supervised learning 193, 334, 335, 336
support vector 109
support vector machine (SVM) 336
support vector machine bagging (SVMBag)
    implementation 387, 388
support vector machines (SVM)
    about 105, 107, 108, 110, 133
    evolution process 125, 128, 130
    modeling process 125, 128, 130
synergy 365
synthetic minority over-sampling technique
    (SMOTE) 348

T

TensorFlow 176, 177
term frequency-inverse document frequency (tf-idf)
    316
term frequency-inverse document frequency
    (TFIDF) 446
term-document matrix (TDM) 294
test data 335
text classification 316

text mining framework
    about 292, 293
    methods 292, 293
    quantitative analysis 295, 296
text sentiment classifier
    building, with BoW approach 443, 444, 445,
      447, 448, 449
    building, with fastText 462, 463, 465, 466, 467,
      468
    building, with GloVe word embedding 458, 459,
      460, 461, 462
    building, with pretrained Word2vec word
      embedding based on Reuters news corpus
      453, 455, 456, 457, 458
text2vec package
    used, for creating feature to classification model
      316, 318
    used, for feature modeling for classification
      model 316
    used, for feature modeling to classification model
      318
The Nilson Report
    reference 537
Thompson sampling
    about 618
    MABP, solving with UCB 619, 620, 621, 622,
      624, 625, 626, 627, 628
    reference 618
tidyverse
    reference 12
time series data
    about 265
    data exploration 267, 269, 271
topic models
    about 294
    building 311, 314, 316
training 335
training data 335
transfer learning 341, 342, 343, 532
tree-based learning 137
trials 613
True Negative Rate 74
True Positive Rate (TPR) 74, 81
truncated backpropagation through time (TBPTT)
    585

U

UCI Machine Learning Repository
  reference 454
under complete autoencoders 542
underfitting 349, 350
univariate linear regression
  about 30, 31, 32
  model assumptions, reviewing 36, 38
  model, building 33, 34, 36
univariate time series analysis
  about 256, 258, 260, 263
  Granger causality 264, 265
univariate time series
  evaluation process 272
  forecasting 272, 275, 276, 279, 280, 282
  linear regression 283, 284
  model, causality 282
  model, examining 282
  modeling process 272
  vector autoregression 284, 286, 288
unsupervised learning 193, 336, 337, 338
unsupervised learning models
  about 204
  hierarchical clustering 204, 206, 208, 210, 211, 212
  k-means clustering 212, 214
upper confidence bound (UCB) algorithm
  about 616, 617
  MABP, solving with Thompson sampling 619, 620, 621, 622, 624, 625, 626, 627, 628
user-based collaborative filtering (UBCF)
  about 415

recommendation system, building 416, 419

V

V Elbow method 479
V Silhouette method 479
valence shifters 295
vanishing gradients
  about 585, 586, 587
  problem, handling 586
Variance Inflation Factor (VIF) 50
variational autoencoder (VAE) 544
varimax 223, 234
vector autoregression (VAR) 265
virtual personal assistants (VPAs) 333

W

Weight Of Evidence (WOE) 66, 68
wholesale customer dataset
  reference 474
word embedding 450, 451, 452, 453
word frequency
  about 299
  in addresses 299, 301
Word2vec
  CBOW model 453
  continuous Skip-Gram model 453

X

x-values 347

Z

zero variance 19, 21